In Prais
The Ruc......
Adi Da Samraj

A di Da is the transcendent and transformational Being of
our era. He is the Good News Wh...
to our prayers.

— ...URG
gress;
...ment

I t is obvious, fr... ...vhat
IT's all about .

— ...TTS
...urity

I regard Adi Da
Western world

— ...DIE
Fire

A di Da Samraj
given true en

— SUN BEAR
...iety

T he life and te...
profound and
moment in history

— ...P

Senior Adviser at the United Nations
High Commission for Refugees;
former Dean of the Carmelite House of Studies, Australia;
former Dean of Trinity College, University of Melbourne

A great teacher with the dynamic ability to awaken in his listeners something of the Divine Reality in which he is grounded, with which he is identified, and which, in fact, he is.

ISRAEL REGARDIE
author, *The Golden Dawn*

A di Da Samraj has spoken directly to the heart of our human situation—the shocking gravity of our brief and unbidden lives. Through his words I have experienced a glimmering of eternal life, and view my own existence as timeless and spaceless in a way that I never have before.

RICHARD GROSSINGER
author, *Planet Medicine; The Night Sky*

M y relationship with Adi Da Samraj over many years has only confirmed His Realization and the Truth of His impeccable Teaching. He is much more than simply an inspiration of my music, but is really a living demonstration that perfect transcendence is actually possible. This is both a great relief and a great challenge. If you thirst for truth, here is a rare opportunity to drink.

RAY LYNCH
composer and musician, *Deep Breakfast; The Sky of Mind;*
and *Ray Lynch, Best Of*

A di Da Samraj and his unique body of teaching work offer a rare and extraordinary opportunity for those courageous students who are ready to move beyond ego and take the plunge into deepest communion with the Absolute. Importantly, the teaching is grounded in explicit discussion of necessary psycho-spiritual evolution and guides the student to self-responsibility and self-awareness.

ELISABETH TARG, M.D.
University of California, San Francisco,
School of Medicine;
Director, Complementary Medicine Research Institute,
California Pacific Medical Center

That God can, among other things, actually incarnate in human form once seemed unbelievable to me. But reading the books of Avatar Adi Da obliterated all doubt about the existence of God right now, here on Earth in human form.

CHARMIAN ANDERSON, PH.D.
psychologist; author, *Bridging Heaven and Earth*
and *The Heart of Success*

Fly to the side of this God-Man. His Divine Transmission works miracles of change not possible by any other Spiritual means.

LEE SANNELLA, M.D.
author, *The Kundalini Experience*

I regard the work of Adi Da and his devotees as one of the most penetrating spiritual and social experiments happening on the planet in our era.

JEFFREY MISHLOVE, PH.D.
host, PBS television series, *Thinking Allowed*;
author, *The Roots of Consciousness*

Adi Da's Teachings have tremendous significance for humanity. . . . He represents a foundation and a structure for sanity.

ROBERT K. HALL, M.D.
psychiatrist; author, *Out of Nowhere*;
co-founder, The Lomi School and The Lomi Clinic

Nothing like this has ever been Revealed before. We have waited for this moment in history for countless lifetimes. Adi Da Samraj is the True Heart of the world.

ROGER SAVOIE, PH.D.
philosopher, writer, and translator;
author, *La Vipère et le Lion: La Voie radicale de la Spiritualité*

The Ruchira Avatar,
Adi Da Samraj

THE KNEE
OF
LISTENING

The Divine Ordeal
Of The Avataric Incarnation
Of Conscious Light

The Spiritual Autobiography Of
THE RUCHIRA AVATAR,
ADI DA SAMRAJ

THE SEVENTEEN COMPANIONS
OF THE TRUE DAWN HORSE,
BOOK FOUR

THE DAWN HORSE PRESS
MIDDLETOWN, CALIFORNIA

NOTE TO THE READER

All who study the Way of Adidam or take up its practice should remember that they are responding to a Call to become responsible for themselves. They should understand that they, not Avatar Adi Da Samraj or others, are responsible for any decision they make or action they take in the course of their lives of study or practice.

The devotional, Spiritual, functional, practical, relational, cultural, and formal community practices and disciplines referred to in this book are appropriate and natural practices that are voluntarily and progressively adopted by members of the practicing congregations of Adidam (as appropriate to the personal circumstance of each individual). Although anyone may find these practices useful and beneficial, they are not presented as advice or recommendations to the general reader or to anyone who is not a member of one of the practicing congregations of Adidam. And nothing in this book is intended as a diagnosis, prescription, or recommended treatment or cure for any specific "problem", whether medical, emotional, psychological, social, or Spiritual. One should apply a particular program of treatment, prevention, cure, or general health only in consultation with a licensed physician or other qualified professional.

The Knee Of Listening is formally authorized for publication by the Ruchira Sannyasin Order of Adidam Ruchiradam. (The Ruchira Sannyasin Order of Adidam Ruchiradam is the senior Spiritual and Cultural Authority within the formal gathering of formally acknowledged devotees of the Divine World-Teacher, Ruchira Avatar Adi Da Samraj.)

NOTE TO BIBLIOGRAPHERS: The correct form for citing Ruchira Avatar Adi Da Samraj's Name (in any form of alphabetized listing) is: Adi Da Samraj

Standard edition, enlarged and updated, March 2004
This edition supercedes all previous editions of this Text:
First edition, 1972
Standard edition, unabridged, April 1992
New standard edition, popular format, September 1995

Produced by the Avataric Pan-Communion of Adidam
in cooperation with the Dawn Horse Press

International Standard Book Number: 1-57097-167-6
Library of Congress Catalog Card Number: 2004100766

CONTENTS

and All-Completing, and All-Transcending, and
Self-Evidently Divine Adidam Revelation of the
Inherently egoless Seventh Stage Realization of <u>Me</u>)

FOREWORD

by Jeffrey J. Kripal, Ph.D.

When the incarnation comes, the common people are
unable to recognize him. He comes in secret.
—Sri Ramakrishna
in *Sri-Sri-Ramakrishna-Kathamrita* 2.16

From the day I first encountered the writings of Adi Da (as Da Free John) in the mid-80s, I knew that I was reading a contemporary religious genius. Here was someone who had succeeded in making the nondual spirituality cherished in the traditions of Asia relevant to the Western mind—that specific historical form of consciousness which is defined by, among many other factors, radical individualism, a constitutional stress on freedom in most all of its forms, a specifically psychological view of the human being, a deep appreciation of human sexuality and eroticism, a history of passionate religious experimentation and expression, and a generally scientific or materialistic worldview. The multiple texts that followed those first readings have done nothing to dissuade me from this initial impression. Quite the contrary.

Some years after my first reading of Adi Da, at a time when I had completed my dissertation on the Sakta Tantra of Sri Ramakrishna and was teaching in a small liberal arts college, I had the opportunity to "meet" Adi Da himself, in a traditional formal setting. In the 1990s, Adi Da had been presented with a copy of my dissertation, which quickly became the focus of a number of animated discussions between him and a group of his devotees, initiated by Adi Da and his own reading of the text. Later, he would put *Kali's Child* (the book that grew out of the dissertation)* in his *Basket Of Tolerance*, an immense bibliography of primary and secondary texts on the

*Jeffrey Kripal, *Kali's Child: The Mystical and the Erotic in the Life and Teaching of Ramakrishna*, 2d ed. (Chicago: The University of Chicago Press, 1998).

history of spirituality, accompanied by an eloquent appreciative-critical essay on its content, "The 'Secret' Biography of Ramakrishna and the Universally Necessary Foundation Struggle with the Emotional-Sexual Character"—no doubt the most insightful and fascinating essay I have seen yet on the book written from a specifically metaphysical or religious perspective (and I have seen quite a few). All this, then, was the context of my first visit to Adi Da's northern California ashram, the Mountain Of Attention, in 1998.

My "meeting" with Adi Da took the form of *darsana* (a traditional Hindu term for the formal "seeing" of a guru or deity, in which the essence of the guru or deity is understood to be communicated to the seer through the act of seeing itself—a kind of ocular communion or visionary sacrament, if you will). The *darsana* took place in a formal hall of Adi Da's residence on the grounds of the Mountain Of Attention ashram. The room was filled with devotees chanting and sitting in contemplation. Adi Da himself was sitting in a large chair, directly in the center. He was clearly in a state of ecstasy: his eyes were rolled up, his fingers were forming some sort of *mudra* (a posture of the fingers and hands traditionally said to convey a particular state of mind or religious state), and he was sweating profusely. I had the distinct sense that he was intending to communicate his state of consciousness directly to all present, and particularly to those who approached him one by one (including me), by the sheer force of his presence, which indeed was quite palpable.

I knelt down, offered a flower in the traditional manner, sat in *darsana* for a few minutes, and was then ushered out by my hosts. It was over as quickly as it had begun. As it turned out, however, it was hardly over, for whatever was communicated that night did not leave me easily or soon. For days, I felt as if my consciousness had somehow "shifted", that it had been affected on levels of which I was only vaguely aware. This sense of a "shift" lasted for an entire week, before I returned to my more usual mode of functioning.

That occasion of *darsana* was an encounter, in person, with the same force of being which informs Adi Da's books, and which you are about to "meet" in *The Knee Of Listening*. The present edition of *The Knee Of Listening* is a particularly rich document that extends and deepens Adi Da's spiritual effort of cultural translation and transformation into the present—that is, up to 2004, and into you and me. This edition of *The Knee Of Listening* does not actually constitute a single narrative written at a single point in time, like, say, its previous incarnation, which was simply the running narrative of the present Part One, composed more or less at once in the early 70s. This greatly expanded edition is different, with "later" strata layered upon "earlier" strata, to form a kind of dramatic historical witness to the evolution of Adi Da's embodiment of radical nonduality.

Adi Da has gone to great lengths to relate his Teaching—philosophically (via textual interpretation and rational argument), metaphysically (via reincarnation theory), and personally (via autobiographical narrative)—to earlier paradigmatic gurus, particularly Sri Ramakrishna, Swami Vivekananda, Ramana Maharshi, Swami Nityananda, and Swami Muktananda. The overall result is what we might call an "esoteric history" of the siddha-guru in the present age. In this history, Adi Da manages to balance an obvious appreciation for and devotion to those who have come before him with a keen critical sense of where their teachings are inadequate or limited. It is obvious that even his most penetrating questions about traditional Asian forms of spirituality and their teachers are animated by a spirit of deep concern, existential commitment, and profound love.

No reader professionally or personally invested in Asian forms of spirituality and concerned about their effective (as opposed to dysfunctional) translation into Western culture can afford to ignore *The Knee Of Listening* or the larger textual corpus in which it is now placed, that is, Adi Da's twenty-three Source-Texts. In my opinion, this latter total corpus constitutes the most doctrinally thorough, the most philosophically sophisticated, the most culturally challenging, and the most creatively original literature currently available in the English language. Certainly there are even larger canons in Asia, but these are written and expressed in languages (primarily Sanskrit, Tibetan, Chinese, and Japanese) and interpreted in cultural frames that must remain permanently foreign to the contemporary English speaker and reader. What sets the twenty-three Source-Texts apart is the fact that they were written in English, and that this English idiom has been enriched by a kind of hybridized English-Sanskrit, and that a new type of mystical grammar has been created, embodied most dramatically (and, to the ego, jarringly) in Adi Da's anti-ego capitalization practice, in which just about every grammatical move is nondualistically endowed with the status once imperially preserved in English for the non-existent "I". Such a reading experience constantly calls upon one's ability to think and feel beyond the socially constructed ego.

I thus will not even begin to pretend that the literary result is easy reading, or that this corpus will not present its own personal challenges and philosophical problems to many of its future readers (including this one). What I can reasonably claim is that *The Knee Of Listening*, now placed within this total corpus, deserves our closest attention, and that it stands in a long modern Western textual transmission that begins with Charles Wilkins' translation of *The Bhagvat-Geeta, or Dialogues of Kreeshna and Arjoon* (1785), develops and deepens through Max Mueller's *Sacred Books of the East* series (1875), and extends into the previous century primarily through such spiritual classics as *The Gospel of Sri Ramakrishna* (1942), *The Collected Works of Swami Vivekananda* (1907), the collected works of Sri Aurobindo, *Talks with Sri Ramana Maharshi* (1955), Swami Muktananda's *Play of Consciousness* (1978), which Adi Da (as Franklin Jones) helped to edit, and the numerous writings of Krishnamurti, Yogananda, Alan Watts, and Chogyam Trungpa.

I am perfectly aware that Adi Da and his community do not identify with any of these traditions, and that both his real and symbolic presence in Fiji on the international dateline locates Adidam both physically and spiritually neither in the West nor the East. But the historical fact remains that the Teaching of Adi Da finds its closest, if never full, analogue in Asian forms of nondual gnosis and this specific textual lineage. As recounted in the present text, moreover, it was many of these same texts—from the *Gita* to Ramana Maharshi—that were significant in Franklin's own initial search and then gave him some external guide with which to measure and better appreciate his own radical understanding of the "Bright" as "always already the case". Even if the tradition of Adidam, then, cannot be reduced to such a textual lineage, it certainly can, and must, be understood in relationship to it. That anyway is precisely what Adi Da does in his "Lineage Essay", "I (Alone) Am The Adidam Revelation", and, indeed, throughout the present text, and this is one of the many features of *The Knee Of Listening* that make it such a remarkable document.

Finally, let me close as a professor with another professor. The German Indologist Heinrich Zimmer gave a series of historic lectures at Columbia University in the late 40s, a decade or so before Franklin Jones studied there in 1957. One of Zimmer's more well-known books is *The Philosophies of India*, a poetic tour-de-force through Indian thought and spirituality from the Upanishads to the Tantra. At the very beginning of this rather large tome, in a section entitled "The Meeting of East and West", Zimmer writes the following:

> *We of the Occident are about to arrive at a crossroads that was reached by the thinkers of India some seven hundred years before Christ. This is the real reason why we become both vexed and stimulated, uneasy yet interested, when confronted with the concepts and images of Oriental wisdom. . . . But we cannot take over the Indian solutions. We must enter the new period our own way and solve its questions for ourselves. . . . We cannot borrow God. We must effect His new incarnation from within ourselves. Divinity must descend, somehow, into the matter of our own existence and participate in this peculiar life process.*[*]

I do not know if Adi Da has ever read Prof. Zimmer or *The Philosophies of India*, but it seems to me that *The Knee Of Listening* can be read today in precisely this same spirit, that is, as an esoteric history of the embodiment, in the West, of a remarkable type of nondual consciousness that was first discovered and cultivated in different forms and tongues in Asia. Whether that consciousness is to "descend" again into our individual lives and our (post)modern,

---

[*]Heinrich Zimmer, *Philosophies of India*, ed. by Joseph Campbell (Cleveland: Meridian Books, 1964), 1, 2.

postcolonial cultures (in which categories like "East" and "West" are growing increasingly meaningless, if not actually destructive) will depend at least partly on how we read texts like this one, and whether or not we can find the courage to speak our own readings and enact our own embodied meanings.

Jeffrey J. Kripal
2 November 2003
Rice University, Houston, Texas

1940   2000

Avatar Adi Da Samraj

Reality Itself Comes into the "Room"—in Person

by Carolyn Lee, Ph.D.

F rom time to time, there is a book that challenges, and eventually changes, the entire perspective of a civilization. In modern times, Charles Darwin's *Origin of Species* was such a book—and, centuries before Darwin, *On the Revolutions of the Celestial Spheres* of Copernicus (the first publication of the theory that the earth orbits the sun). *The Knee Of Listening* is such an epoch-making book—in an entirely different way. Appearing at the beginning of the third millennium of the common era, it carries a Revelation that has the potential to transform all future time. This book is not about how life on earth physically evolved, nor the design of the solar system (of which this planet is a part). *The Knee Of Listening* is about Reality Itself, the Reality within which this earth and its cosmic locale arise—the Blissful, Effulgent, Conscious Force of Being which is always so, and which can be located and enjoyed under every possible condition, and in every dimension of space-time.

There are many worlds within the book—from simple narrative to ecstatic poetry to complex argument and sublime revelatory discourse. But there is one single Voice. *The Knee Of Listening* is autobiography. It is the first-person account of the life of an unparalleled Spiritual Genius—alive today—whose appearance can only be rightly understood by referring to the tradition of the avatar, or the incarnations of the Divine.

Aldous Huxley speaks of this tradition in *The Perennial Philosophy*, where he refers to the Divine Being by the Greek term "Logos" (or "Word").

The Logos passes out of eternity into time for no other purpose than to assist the beings, whose bodily form he takes, to pass out of time into eternity. If the Avatar's appearance upon the stage of history is enormously important, this is due to the fact that by his teaching he points out, and by his being a channel of grace and divine power he actually is, the means by which human beings may transcend the limitations of history. . . .

That men and women may be thus instructed and helped, the godhead assumes the form of an ordinary human being, who has to earn deliverance and enlightenment in the way that is prescribed by the divine Nature of Things—namely, by charity, by a total dying to self and a total, one-pointed awareness. Thus enlightened, the Avatar can reveal the way of enlightenment to others and help them actually to become what they already potentially are. . . . And, of course, the eternity which transforms us into Ourselves is not the experience of mere persistence after bodily death. There will be no experience of timeless Reality then, unless there is the same or a similar knowledge within the world of time and matter. By precept and example, the Avatar teaches that this transforming knowledge is possible, that all sentient beings are called to it, and that, sooner or later, in one way or another, all must finally come to it.*

Writing in 1944, Huxley was more right than he could have known. The Ruchira Avatar, Adi Da Samraj, the author of *The Knee Of Listening*, took birth on Long Island, New York, in November 1939. He was born in the most ordinary of circumstances—to Frank and Dorothy Jones, a middle-class couple, who named their son Franklin Albert Jones. His Life, from the first, has been marked by unusual and miraculous signs—indicators of a Divine Process (or Yoga) that has always been active in Him. Nevertheless, as Huxley suggests, the Avatar must relinquish the free enjoyment of the Divine State and embrace the condition of an apparently ordinary

---

*Aldous Huxley, *The Perennial Philosophy*, 1st Harper Colophon ed. (New York: Harper & Row, 1970), 51, 56.

unillumined human being in order to "earn enlightenment", and thus "reveal the way of enlightenment to others".

This was exactly the pattern of Avatar Adi Da's early life, as He recounts in Part One of *The Knee Of Listening*. He was born in a state of unconditional radiant awareness, which He called the "Bright". But, then, in a spontaneous gesture around the age of two years, He fully Submitted to the usual human life—as He describes here in a Discourse given to His devotees. When He speaks of "I" and "Me", He is referring to Himself as the Divine Being, Who is associating with the conditional worlds via the human form of "Franklin Jones".

AVATAR ADI DA SAMRAJ: For approximately the first two years after My Birth, I allowed the gross vehicle to be gradually prepared for Me. Then, at approximately two years of age, I Spiritually Descended to the region of the heart and thus established My basic Association with My manifested personality.

This Spiritual Descent into the gross body to the level of the heart occurred on the basis of a sympathy (or heart-response) to those who were around Me at the moment. It was through this sympathetic response that I acquired the Vehicle of this body-mind.

However, I was Born to make this Submission. Therefore, it is not that the Decision to Acquire the gross body-mind did not occur until I was two years old. It is simply that the Vehicle of this body-mind was not sufficiently prepared until that point. I had consciously Decided to Do this Work before I Incarnated. My Avataric Descent into Incarnation was for the sake of the total world and all beings. I had consciously Decided to Take a Birth in the West. My Intention before this Birth was to Take this Birth and to Do My Avataric Divine Work by complete Submission to the ordinary Western circumstance.

—February 5, 1989

In 1939, the year of Avatar Adi Da's birth, the western world was poised on the threshold of war, completely ignorant of Who was about to be born in the suburbs of New York City. Even so, we know of at least one individual who was attuned to the

THE KNEE OF LISTENING

unparalleled dispensation of Divine Grace that was about to descend into human Form. Nine months before the birth of Avatar Adi Da Samraj, the great Indian Realizer Upasani Baba made a remarkable utterance. Speaking in February 1939 to the head of one of the most important Hindu monastic orders (the Shankaracharya of Jyotir Math), Upasani prophesied that an Avatar would "soon be born in a European", or a Western, rather than Eastern, "country". "He will be all-powerful", Upasani declared, "and bear down everything before him. And he will see to it that the Vedic Dharma", meaning the pure and original Teaching of Truth, "is firmly reestablished in India."*

In prophesying the advent of an avatar, Upasani Baba would have been well aware of Krishna's proclamation in the *Bhagavad Gita*. "Whenever a decrease of righteousness exists . . . and there is a rising up of unrighteousness, then I give forth myself. . . . For . . . the sake of establishing righteousness, I come into being from age to age."†

As the *Bhagavad Gita* indicates, such a one appears at unique moments when Divine Intervention is necessary to guide or save humankind. Therefore, the appearance of an avatar is an epochal, historic matter. In the Vaishnavite‡ tradition of Hinduism, it is said that there are ten Divine Avatars, and that cosmic history has already witnessed the appearance of the first nine.§ The tenth and completing Avatar remains to come. And He will appear, the tradition declares, in the "late-time" of the present world-cycle, the "dark" time of the Kali Yuga, when the Divine is forgotten and denied. As Arthur Osborne, an English devotee of the great twentieth-century Indian sage Ramana Maharshi, wrote some decades ago:

*See B. V. Narasimha Swami and S. Subbarao, *Sage of Sakuri*, 4th ed. (Bombay: Shri B. T. Wagh, 1966), 190–91, 204.

†Withrop Sargeant, trans., *The Bhagavad Gita*, rev. ed., ed. Christopher Chapple (Albany, N.Y.: State University of New York Press, 1984), 207–208.

‡Hinduism has several main "branches", or traditions, based on identifying the highest Divinity with one or another of the pantheon of Hindu gods and goddesses. The Vaishnavite tradition is focused in the devotional worship of the Hindu god Vishnu (understood as the "Preserver" of creation) and his avatars (see note below).

§ In Hindu mythology, it is said that the avatars of Vishnu appear when evil outweighs good in the world. The first nine of the avatars of Vishnu are: (1) Matsya, the fish incarnation; (2) Kurma, the turtle incarnation; (3) Varaha, the boar incarnation; (4) Narasingha, the man-lion incarnation; (5) Vamana, the dwarf incarnation; (6) Parasurama; (7) Rama; (8) Krishna; (9) Buddha. The tenth avatar is called "Kalki".

*The time for his [the final avatar's] advent is when materialism
and confusion have dominated the world. . . . [T]he completion of the
downward trend may result in crass materialism and the loss of
spiritual paths, like rivers drying up in the desert. The result of this
is a secular civilization with no spiritual basis for life, either public
or private, and no spiritual scale of values. Material values are
enthroned and moralism, which may have survived spirituality for
a while, gives place to amorality. This is the type of spiritual decline
which has arisen in the West in recent centuries and has overspread
the world in the present century. . . . [Thus], today, for the first time
in known history, an event such as the coming of an Avatar would
have to affect not one civilization only but the whole world.**

The degeneration of culture that Upasani Baba was observing
in India had its root in the secularism of the West, as he well
knew. But his prophecy was not premeditated. According to the
account, it was a spontaneous outburst. Without thought for Hindu
orthodoxy, he was pointing to a <u>World</u>-Teacher, capable of
Mastering both East <u>and</u> West. He was foretelling the appearance
of One who would bring a unique clarification and completeness
to all the Dharmas of the past. *The Knee Of Listening* is about the
making of a Wisdom-Teaching of precisely that magnitude.

Revealing the Dharma
Beyond "Point of View"

T he Ruchira Avatar, Adi Da, as His story shows, was a deeply
enquiring child. The way in which He, as a child, investigated Reality is dramatically captured in Adi Da's literary
masterwork, *The Mummery Book*—a "prose opera", the original
version of which was written in late 1969. The hero of *The
Mummery Book*, Raymond Darling, is modeled on Himself—and,
in many ways, *The Mummery Book* is a poetic rendering of the
meaning of His own Life, which is told in literal terms in *The Knee
Of Listening*.

*Arthur Osborne, *Buddhism and Christianity in the Light of Hinduism* (London: Rider and Company,
1959), 84–85, 154.

In the early chapters of *The Mummery Book*, Raymond, as a young boy, is seated in the attic of his parents' house, absorbed in noticing and feeling every aspect of the room.

Raymond sat on the floor, in front of the windows. There was bright Sun-light, coming in, through the frames. And the Sun-light seemed to pour into the room—in rectangular solid-shapes, marked out by the shape of the windows.

There were millions of small particles, in the air—floating, in the rectilinear volumes of the windowed Sun-light. Raymond noticed that—if he Breathed, and Blew! the air, around the floor— the particles would increase, and Fly! about.

Raymond Breathed his Blows! of air. And all the particles were Blown!, to Fly! about—in the geometric Sun-light, in front of Raymond's eyes.

As he did this, Raymond felt he was looking at the <u>Basic</u> Form of Reality! . . .

Raymond sat, in his new attic-room. All day. Every day—and night. Sometimes, Raymond saw the Sun-light-shapes, again. As before. But, in time, the Sun did not come so bright, so very often. And, so, he became interested in the room, itself.

He cleaned the room. And he put <u>everything</u> in order.

He wondered, what was <u>Really</u> Happening—in the room. And, so, he sat in it—all the time. And he looked at the room—itself. . . .

He <u>knew</u> that everything was—merely, and simply—<u>existing</u>.

There was, for now, no Deep. No Higher. No other. No distance. No past. No future. No serious suffering.

Then, Raymond forgot it—all. And he wondered, how to fill his room.

He put himself on the floor, and enjoyed the ceiling.

The ceiling was made of many angles and planes, like a complex vault.

It would make an interesting floor!—he thinks. So many forms, to lean against. The wonderful chairs and slides—to lie in, hanging over windows. The little lamps of day-light—growing in the floor. The climb-up closets. The point-of-view is lying on the floor— and looking down, at the Sun.

There seemed to be a Mystery—behind the walls. Behind the Naked! angularity of multi-planes. Behind the room, itself. . . .

A Mystery conceals the room. The Captive-room, that hides the Mystery of me, with things and walls.

And Raymond looked at the room.

He thought—there Is no Consciousness, in the room.

And he thought—how to put It, there?

Raymond's attic, in *The Mummery Book*, is the primal room, the space, the "theatre" of all human life. This "room" of life and mind can be perceived from many points of view, depending on where one is placed in the room. And so the question arises: What does the real room look like—beyond this or that point of view? What is the context of the room? What is the meaning of the room—the meaning and source of human existence? Where is the Consciousness—the Living Force of Reality—that the heart seeks to identify in the midst of the myriad personal and cultural viewpoints potential in human experience?

In *The Mummery Book*, Raymond does not find that Consciousness in the room! And, so, his adventure is the challenge of "how to put It, there". In other words, "Raymond's" consideration is about True Enlightenment—or the Realization of That Which Transcends the "room".

The great issue of Avatar Adi Da's early Life was His enquiry: What is Consciousness? This question sometimes took the tangible form of an image that would rise up in Him. He would see a great black stone set in what felt like a sacred enclosure—with a gathering of people, including Himself, seated in front, quietly gazing at it.

The stone, to Him, seemed to be a symbol for Consciousness, the Mystery of Being—which He felt, on the one hand, to be the Ineffable Source of the arising world, and, yet, somehow also directly connected to everything. What was the relationship between Consciousness and phenomena? This was what He wanted to know. But there was no "answer" in this vision. While the Stone (or Consciousness) remained apart, the world of mere phenomena (or the conditional manifestations of Energy) was without meaning.

As Avatar Adi Da discovered during His early Life, this puzzle was exactly the motivator of the religious quest. God, or Truth, or Reality is felt to be absent, or apart, from the living world of energy and objects—and so this or that path is developed in an attempt to attain God, or Truth, or Reality. Some esoteric traditions, as He discovered, try to resolve the matter by seeking for Consciousness <u>via</u> Energy, through practices such as Kundalini Yoga. In some other traditions (such as Advaita Vedanta), the practitioner is called to Realize Consciousness directly, eschewing the search for Enlightenment via the objects and energies of the phenomenal world. But where does the entire Truth lie? What is unqualified Divine Enlightenment?

Part One of *The Knee Of Listening* is the story of the Sadhana (or Spiritual practice) engaged by Avatar Adi Da in His search for this unqualified Enlightenment, the Condition He already knew in His infancy as the "Bright". His effort to recover the "Bright" was an immensely difficult human and Spiritual trial, in which He suffered all the limits, doubts, and struggles of an ordinary human being. At the same time, none of the ordinary (or even extraordinary) "answers" to life were satisfactory to Him. Below outer awareness, He was always being led by the "Bright", responding to what He later called a "fierce, mysterious impulse" at the heart of His being. Driven by this hidden Grace, He Submitted to the Unknown and lived His unique Ordeal without any advance knowledge of what it was about or how it would turn out.

On the one hand, He was engaged in a profound process with Energy—while, on the other hand, He was absorbed in the deepest questions about Truth and Reality. And so there is an intriguing double strand, a play of opposites, shaping His entire Sadhana. And these opposites—which He calls, at times, by different names, such as Awareness and Energy, or Consciousness and the Shakti, or the Heart and the Light—were always intimately connected. The final stroke of the Divine Avatar's "Sadhana Years" is His complete Spiritual Realization of Consciousness-<u>and</u>-Energy as One Non-Dual Reality—or "Conscious Light". The story of how this Realization finally emerged in Him is one of the most magnificent parts of the book. It is a unique Confession in the records of Spiritual Realization.

By the end of Part One of *The Knee Of Listening*, Avatar Adi Da has fulfilled the first part of His Avataric Divine Work—to regain the full, permanent Realization of His native "Bright" Awareness. At this point in the odyssey of the Ruchira Avatar, Consciousness has been restored to the "room", and the relationship between Consciousness and objects resolved. Decades later, in the following Discourse to His devotees, He explained this profundity very graphically:

AVATAR ADI DA SAMRAJ: If you examine objects more and more profoundly, sooner or later you get down just to Energy Itself, Light Itself. Similarly, if you go within, beyond all the outward functions, you get to Consciousness. Those are the two "extremes" of the One Reality. But they are not, in fact, separate realities—they are only presumed to be such, from your point of view. And this is the nature (or pattern) of un-Enlightenment.

Energy Is the Radiance of Consciousness Itself. Consciousness Is the Source-Position of Radiance Itself. Self-Existing and Self-Radiant Consciousness Is Love-Bliss Itself—Unconditional Feeling, Radiance.

When Consciousness (without limitation or dimensions) is Realized As Is, to Be Infinitely Radiant, One with Its own Radiance (or Energy, or Light, or Shakti, or Love-Bliss), and That is the (so to speak) "Point of View" with regard to objects that arise—then, in that case, all objects are (Inherently) Divinely Self-Recognizable. Self-Existing and Self-Radiant Consciousness (or Fullness of Being) Divinely Self-Recognizes all phenomena in the Context of Itself—as transparent (or merely apparent), and un-necessary, and inherently non-binding modifications of the Self-Radiance of Consciousness Itself, the Divine Conscious Light Itself.

When there is this Awakening, it is obvious. In every moment, Natively, Inherently, It Is simply the Divine Conscious Light—the Infinite, Dimensionless, Uncaused, Eternal "Brightness" of Being (Itself).

—March 29, 1998

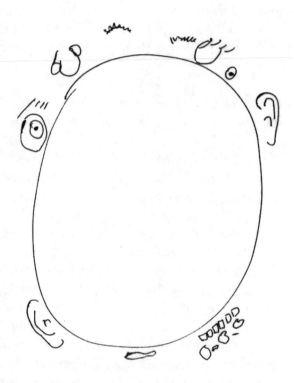

"Losing Face" by Avatar Adi Da Samraj

As an expression of His Realization, Avatar Adi Da has, at various times, made ink drawings, which He has humorously called "Transcendental Cartoons".

AVATAR ADI DA SAMRAJ: One of My "Transcendental Cartoons" is called "Losing Face". It is Consciousness surrounded by Radiance, surrounded by objects. It is a picture of Reality. That is why it is called a <u>Transcendental</u> Cartoon.

    The world is a transcendental cartoon on the Face of Consciousness Itself.

—MARCH 29, 1998

The Inmost Secrets
of Divine Enlightenment

At the end of Part One and in Part Two of *The Knee Of Listening,* Avatar Adi Da "considers" the vast implications of What He has Realized. By virtue of His absolute Realization of Reality as Conscious Light—beyond all limits of "point of view"—He is able to look at humanity's esoteric Spiritual traditions and comprehend them as a whole.

Through the living experience of His "Sadhana Years", it became obvious to Him that Spiritual Realization is directly connected to the deep psycho-physical structure of the human being. Realization is not merely philosophy. Thus, He makes sense of the otherwise bewildering array of different approaches to Enlightenment by showing how each approach (or school) is associated with the awakening of particular esoteric centers of the body-mind.

Divine Enlightenment, or the Realization of Conscious Light, depends on the Awakening of the most esoteric root-structure of the body-mind—a structure that has hardly even been observed, and never before fully defined in Spiritual literature. Indeed, as Adi Da shows, this profound and original depth of the human structure <u>cannot</u> be fully Awakened merely by intense Spiritual practice or even by the Grace of the greatest Adept-Realizers. His Divine Intervention is required—not only to Reveal the inmost secrets of Divine Enlightenment, but to Awaken and Empower that living process in human beings.

After the narrative of His early Life and related journal entries, which comprise Part One, Part Two takes the form of a series of Essays, all of which refer to great individuals whom Avatar Adi Da describes as His "Adept-Links" to humanity's "Great Tradition" of Spiritual Realization. Thus, His discussion of the esoteric traditions is not abstract, but developed in relation to the confessions of Enlightenment made by some of the greatest Realizers of modern times. Each one of them contributed, in a unique way, to His Life and to the process by which He came to understand the Spiritual significance of His Person and Work. Two of these Realizers,

Ramakrishna and Swami Vivekananda, both of whom the Divine Avatar acknowledges as His "Forerunners", played an ineffable role in His Incarnation. The mystery of His relationship to them gives the clue to the "pre-history" of His Appearance in this world, and what it took to draw Him down into human Form.

"Avatar" and "Incarnation"

The Eastern idea of an Avatar is one who comes to restore all to the Divine by re-establishing Spiritual law and giving a true Way of God-Realization. This understanding is reflected in the prophecy of Upasani Baba, who speaks of the coming Avatar as the supreme Dharma-bearer. It is likewise expressed in the *Bhagavad Gita* that the Divine appears in human form in order to re-establish "righteousness", or the right human and Spiritual order of things. In the West, there is a different concept of Divine Intervention. The Western notion of an Incarnation (focused primarily on Jesus of Nazareth) has less to do with the giving of a Liberating Teaching and more to do with the Divine saving humankind by identifying, unreservedly, with the sufferings of humanity. In His commentary on these two traditional notions of "Avatar" and "Incarnation", Avatar Adi Da observes that, taken together, the traditions of the East and of the West point to the qualities that would be required in a truly universal God-Man, or "Avataric Incarnation".

The "Avatar" tradition and the "Incarnation" tradition are *complementary to one another. That is to say, properly speaking, neither tradition can rightly be said to represent a mythology (or a Truth) that is superior to that of the other. Indeed, it is only by combining the basic (esoteric and exoteric) elements of the descriptions contained in both the "Avatar" tradition (and the total God-Man tradition of the East) and the "Incarnation" tradition (and the total God-Man tradition of the West) that a basically complete (traditional) description of the Ultimate True God-Man (or the God-Man Who may uniquely be described as the "Avataric Incarnation" of Real God, and Truth, and Reality) may be found—and that basically* *complete (traditional) description is the one that must be understood to be the one and great (collective—and, heretofore, relatively hidden) description of a true God-Man that is to be found in the Great Tradition of mankind as a whole.**

—Avatar Adi Da Samraj
*The Truly Human New World-Culture
Of Unbroken Real-God-Man*

The Knee Of Listening unfolds like a symphony in three mighty movements that cumulatively reveal Avatar Adi Da as "Avatar" and "Incarnation"—beyond all traditional concepts of both. Part One recounts the process whereby He prepares Himself to bring to others a unique Avataric Divine Teaching-Revelation. In the Essays of Part Two, He expands upon His sovereign Realization and explains how It clarifies and completes the Great Tradition of mankind's Spiritual search. Then, in Part Three, the most profound dimension of His Life and Work is described—which could be called the "Divine Super-Physics" of His Incarnation.

In fact, from the Birth of the Divine Avatar, remarkable signs of this Super-Physics have been evident. His Ordeal has always been to stay Combined with the body, rather than allowing Himself, as He put it, to "float away". This dynamism and mystery of the Process by which He has Appeared (and continues to remain) in human Form is fully told in Part Three, through His commentary on three Divine Yogic Events. These Events, which have been utterly Transformative of His Incarnation-Body, are introduced by His devotees, who offer eyewitness accounts.

The first of these events followed a fourteen-year period of Teaching that is unprecedented in the history of Spiritual Instruction. The Divine Avatar did not Teach merely by precept, any more than He had Re-Awakened simply through study. In the course of His Sadhana, He had entered into what He later described as a "'Reckless' (or Divinely 'Crazy' and Divinely 'Heroic')

---

*Adi Da Samraj, "'Avatar' and 'Incarnation': The Complementary God-Man Traditions of East and West". Avatar Adi Da wrote this Essay in response to two books—one by Geoffrey Parrinder, *Avatar and Incarnation: A Comparison of Indian and Christian Beliefs* (New York: Oxford University Press, 1982), and one by Daniel E. Bassuk, *Incarnation in Hinduism and Christianity: The Myth of the God-Man*, (Atlantic Highlands, N.J.: Humanities Press International, 1987).

Course Of all-and-All-Embrace"—and, in His Teaching-Work, He adopted a similar "Heroic" approach, in which He literally took on all the qualities and karmas of His devotees.

In a Discourse Given in the midst of His Teaching Years, He vividly describes the Process of His Teaching-Work as He was engaging It at the time:

AVATAR ADI DA SAMRAJ: I Meditate on My devotees and I Become them. I Become exactly them. I Take on all the limitations that they are. I become just like them. I become more like them than they are. I Submit to devotees as to God, just as they submit to Me in the same fashion.

This is the unique form of My Avataric Divine Teaching-Work. Teachers in the past have talked about coming down a little into the body, and still being above it somehow. I am also always Above and Beyond the body-mind, but My Manner of Teaching is to Submit to the body completely, to Be this body completely. By becoming this body, I become your body. That is how I meditate people.

I become your state of mind, your state of body. I experience the diseases, the neuroses, the emotional problems, the state of everyone with whom I am associated—and that includes many more people than are with Me personally. It includes thousands upon thousands of people. I Do the Sadhana of Real-God-Realization in the form of you. I Do your sadhana while Being you. I do not merely tell you the Teaching, I Become you and Enter into the process as you. No one has Worked precisely as I Do. I actually Become the limited (or un-Enlightened) being whom I Teach. This is a completely unique "Heroic" Manner of Teaching.

I do not have any idea what the results of this unique Manner of Working will be. I do not have any prefigured estimation of It.

I am not carrying out any formulated plan. I Work spontaneously. I am driven to It. This is the way I have always Done it from Birth.

—September 15, 1982

At the same time, during His Teaching Years, Avatar Adi Da would occasionally make a different kind of confession:

AVATAR ADI DA SAMRAJ: A kind of bodily and mental crucifixion has been occurring, a transformation of the body, in which I have less and less capability to enter into casual relations with people. Until now, people have expected Me to maintain a thread of conventional attention and self-awareness in this body-mind so that I could carry on with ordinary human relations and make lessons out of it all. For the last year and a half or so, the ability to be associated with this body-mind through that thread has been dissolving. All My Life, I have had to Deal with this phenomenon. I have always tried to find ways to bypass the ultimate expressions of this change, because I knew that others were not even close to this Process, they knew nothing about it, they did not know how to live with Me while I was going through it. I have thrown Myself into the game of life all My Life, in order to keep in touch with people—and I have even tried to forestall certain of the phenomena of this ultimate change. I have maintained this ordinary character as a way of Helping people to prepare to live a truly Spiritual Way of life with Me and to make use of Me when all these changes become most profound.

—March 1978

There is paradox exposed in these two statements. Avatar Adi Da's "radical" Gesture of Incarnation—totally Submitting to and Identifying with the human plight through His relationship to the individuals in His Company—was paralleled by psycho-physical changes that made it increasingly difficult for Him to continue to make that Sacrifice. Eventually, the fuse of His Submission burned to the point where the first of the Great Divine Yogic Events (related in Part Three) ensued, and His Avataric Incarnation entered a new era.

The Bodily Revelation of Conscious Light

When Einstein expressed the relationship between matter and light in his famous equation, $E = mc^2$, he changed the face of physics forever, but not (generally speaking) the worldview of physicists themselves, nor that of other ordinary human beings.

Who lives on the basis of the truth that matter is energy? Who participates in the universe as a transparent, ecstatic play of light?

Mathematical theory is not enough. No difference is made at the heart of human beings, unless the equivalence of matter and light is seen, felt, experienced, and lived as true. And there is no way that can happen except by Divine Revelation.

This is the peerless contribution of *The Knee Of Listening* to human culture. This book is not about a theoretical realization about Reality. *The Knee Of Listening* is about the bodily Revelation of Conscious Light in the Form of the Ruchira Avatar, Adi Da. It is about Reality (or Conscious Light) Itself coming "out of the closet" and into the Room—in Person. Based on this recognition of the Ruchira Avatar, and turning the psycho-physical faculties (of body, emotion, mind, and breath) to Him (which is the practice that He gives to His devotees), the literal nature of Reality as Conscious Light is felt and verified in one's own case. Then Einstein's equation begins to makes sense in daily life, and the idea that matter is dead and merely solid is realized to be naive and false.

To read Part Three is to enter into incomparable profundities of Energy and Light. The first of the Great Yogic Events described by Avatar Adi Da is Initiated in Him by a Descent of His own Divine Spirit-Force so profound that His body is entirely overwhelmed and apparently comes close to death. His life-signs reappear, and the resulting transformation in His bodily Vehicle is extraordinary. There is an unearthly Radiance transmuting the cells, a great magnification of His "Bright" Fullness of Being. He is entirely given over into that perpetual Samadhi, which inevitably changes His Manner of Working from what it had been before.

The second and third Yogic Events are even more profound. In fact, they represent two parts of one Event, separated in time by one year. In this Process, the Divine Avatar's Body is further Transfigured. He "Returns" to His own Condition of Supernal Light while mysteriously maintaining a thread of association with the physical. And His State is not changed to this present day. In fact, the Process of His own "Self-Brightening" simply continues. The Ordeal of this ultimate Divine Transformation is scarcely communicable—but it is described by Avatar Adi Da, the only One Who can truly speak of it, in the sublime Commentaries of Part Three. No mere human being could ever make these Utterances. To receive the Confessions of His Divine Process—and its Meaning— is to stand on the most holy ground the heart could ever know.

The Tradition of the Dissolution of the Body in Light

O ver the years, Avatar Adi Da has spoken with His devotees, both humorously and seriously, about the esoteric (and at times bizarre) tradition of the spontaneous dissolution of the body into light, in the case of rare individuals. Whatever the verity of these reports—which come from legend, literature, and oral tradition, and which are (therefore) impossible either to substantiate or to disprove—they reflect a primal human impulse. That impulse is to demonstrate, in the body, that gross (or "dead") materiality is, in reality, energy—and, ultimately, light—beyond all mortal suffering. In this sense, the reports of "going up in light" are premonitions of Avatar Adi Da's Avataric Revelation of the Divine Conscious Light, and of what He calls "Divine Translation", which is being more and more profoundly Demonstrated in His case, even while He remains Embodied.

An ancient and moving account of disappearance in light figures in Sophocles' final play, *Oedipus in Colonus*. At the climactic moment of the drama, Sophocles describes the miraculous death of Oedipus, most cursed and most noble of men:

But after a little while, some paces off,
we glanced around
And Oedipus was nowhere to be seen
but only the king,
holding up his hands to screen his eyes
as if he had beheld a vision—
one too dazzling for a mortal's sight. . . .
*How Oedipus passed, no man shall ever tell.**

*Sophocles, *The Complete Plays*, trans. Paul Roche (New York: Signet Classic, 2001), 330.

THE KNEE OF LISTENING

In the lore of the Spiritual traditions, certain Tibetan Realizers—including the celebrated Milarepa—are said to have spontaneously dissolved in light as a result of their intense contemplative practices. And, in the annals of Indian Spirituality, there are further references—among them Tukaram (1608–1648) and Ramalingam (b. 1823). According to tradition, both of these Yogis showed signs of bodily transfiguration in their lifetime and were ultimately consumed in light.

Even a sage such as Ramana Maharshi (who had no personal interest in Yogic tours de force) refers to this tradition, citing more examples:

Manickavasagar is one of those whose body finally resolved itself in a blazing light, without leaving a corpse behind. . . . Nandanar is another whose body disappeared in blazing light.[*]

In the cases mentioned so far, the individual thus dissolved was the only "beneficiary" of the phenomenon. However, in the most extreme and humorous example, the South Indian Siddha Jnana Sambandhar is said to have been consumed in light at his own marriage ceremony, along with the entire wedding party!

There is a deeper significance to this than meets the eye—the idea that the profound sanctity of a greatly Realized being enabled him to take others with him to a higher place.

The Yoga of Divine Translation

Avatar Adi Da's Avataric Demonstration of Light is not about the search to dematerialize the body, nor is It about the search to escape from the body. What is Revealed by the Divine Avatar in Part Three of *The Knee Of Listening* is a fathomless bodily Submission to Incarnate the Conscious Light that is His very Being—allowing this Revelation to Magnify fully in and through His human frame. This is an unspeakable "Experiment", a supreme Act of "Avataric Incarnation". He lives in this infinitely Delicate Balance, between "Above" and "Below", for the sake of Radiating His Condition to all, Contacting all, Blessing all, Drawing

---

[*] *Talks with Ramana Maharshi*, 3 vols. in one, 7th ed. (Tiruvanamalai: Sri Ramanasramam, 1984), 179.

all to His Heart, and Awakening the full process of Divine Enlightenment in those who become His formal devotees. Avatar Adi Da is Self-Relinquished into the Unknowable Process of His Appearance here—without recoil, without mind, and with unbounded Heart-Feeling.

In Part Three, He Speaks from the "Other Side", while still Present here in the body, full of exquisite and unbounded Love and Sensitivity toward all that exists. He is Demonstrating Divine Translation, or the Ultimate Yoga of Conscious Light—which, as He has explained, is not about the spontaneous "combustion" of the body but, rather, the "Outshining" of all conditional existence, whether the body lives or dies.

This Yoga of Divine Translation is a Process that unfolds in the state of Divine Enlightenment. That never-before-revealed Process has unique characteristics in the case of the Ruchira Avatar, Adi Da, because of His unique Avataric Nature and Work, but the essential process, as He says, is the birthright of all beings. Divine Translation is the Graceful Gift He Offers to all—whether It is Realized in this lifetime or some future lifetime. Thus, as prefigured in the stories of Jnana Sambandhar's wedding, all are the beneficiaries of His Work of Divine Translation.

Divine Translation is the perfect fulfillment of the human gestures, ordinary and extraordinary, toward Heaven, or Nirvana, or the state of Brahman, or however Ultimacy is expressed in any tradition. It is the "Destinyless Destiny" of Conscious Light. In *The Dawn Horse Testament*, Avatar Adi Da extends Einstein's equation and Speaks its Source-Truth. (In the first line of the quotation, "C" stands for Consciousness, and "E" stands for Energy).

$$C = E = mc^2$$
Conscious Light Is all-and-All.

Consciousness (Itself) Is Identical To The Self-Existing Energy (or Indestructible Light, or Perfectly Subjective Spiritual Self-"Brightness") That Is all "things" (or all conditional forms, conditions, and states).

Aham Da Asmi. I Am That One and Only Conscious Light.

—Avatar Adi Da Samraj
The Dawn Horse Testament Of The Ruchira Avatar

The Secret Gift of the "Late-Time"

According to the predictions of the ancient Hindu sages about the Yugas (or ages) in the cycles of time, the last of the Yugas of the present world-cycle is named "Kali Yuga", or the epoch of darkness and conflict. Kali Yuga is calculated to have begun five thousand years ago, and has now entered its "twilight" (or final phase). The "twilight" of the Kali Yuga, in the ancient understanding, is characterized by an acceleration in human strife and in cultural and religious chaos, ending in total cataclysm and the destruction of the species.

In the detailed calculations of the Vedic seers and astronomers, the date when the twilight of the Kali Yuga would begin was established as 1939.* That year, as history has proven, did indeed mark a steepening of the moral decline of human civilization. There was the outbreak of World War II and then the continuing aftermath of escalating weaponry and superpower politics.

Coincident with this pivotal moment in human history, the Ruchira Avatar, Adi Da Samraj, was born. All the necessary conjunctions in the pattern of the ages conspired to bring Him to Birth at this exact time, when humanity is armed with the power of complete self-destruction.

Prophecies of the appearance of a culminating Prophet, God-Man, Buddha, or Avatar, yet to come, exist from ancient times—because religion in its traditional forms has never entirely satisfied human beings. The evidence is to be read in history. The deep-seated fear, sorrow, and anger that drives people to petty and terrible conflicts has not, in the general case, been purified by religion—in spite of the procession of great beings who have graced the earth with their saintly example and inspired teachings. Rather, religion has become the very source and pretext of much of the trouble on earth today. In other words, religion has lamentably failed to accomplish its greater human purposes—however earnest, and even heroic, some of its followers have been, and continue to be.

*Alain Danielou, *While the Gods Play: Shaiva Oracles and Predictions on the Cycles of History and the Destiny of Mankind* (Rochester, Vt.: Inner Traditions, 1987), 197.

The healing of a world that is inexorably fulfilling the ancient descriptions of the "dark" time clearly lies beyond the scope of traditional religion. An act of Divine Intervention is necessary, and loudly required by the human spirit. This is the import of the ancient prophecies that a unique God-Man would appear in the "late-time".

Some of the traditional prophecies tend to suggest that this Divine Coming, when it happens, will be obvious to all. But why should this be so in the "late-time" world that is so desensitized to the greater dimensions of reality? One prophecy in a Hindu text speaks of this Divine Appearance as being largely unrecognized:

"At the end of the Kali Yuga, the god Shiva will appear to reestablish the right path in a secret and hidden form."*

The Divine Avatar, Adi Da Samraj, truly, has appeared in a secret and hidden form. His early Life was private and outwardly ordinary. Even in the years of His Teaching-Work, He never entered into the public arena—because His Way of Adidam is esoteric, requiring a direct devotional and Spiritual relationship to Him, rather than the following of rules and practices for their own sake.

Nevertheless, the Divine Blessing-Work that Avatar Adi Da was born to do is not merely for those who may come into His physical Company during His human Lifetime. His Avataric Impulse to Bless and Awaken beings is All-Encompassing—global, cosmic, and Eternal. He is moved by an unceasing Urge to Transform the dark logic and destiny of the Kali Yuga into a "'Bright' New Age of Real-God-Man", a culture of true Spiritual practice and Divinely Enlightened living.

This is not about attempting to create utopia on earth (or any transformation of a merely political or social kind). Avatar Adi Da's Spiritual Work of Blessing is the most profound Divine Act—the perpetual Transmission of His "Bright", Love-Blissful Person into every form and "corner" of the cosmic domain. His Spiritual Touch (or "Kiss") is tangible, personal, and unmistakable. To turn and contemplate His human Form (physically present or via a photograph), surrendering all the faculties of the being to Him, is to

* *Linga Purana*, 1.40.12 (quoted in Danielou, 224).

behold what humankind has never seen before—Naked Divinity in Person, the only One Sufficient for the human heart.

Even though I sit here apparently solemn and quiet, the Same One Kisses you, Kisses every one. All of you have My Kiss. All of those not even yet My devotees already have My Kiss. I have My Solemn, Deep, Extraordinary, Unknown Work to Do. . . . You must allow Me to Do this Work in the terror of this "late-time", and forever.

—Avatar Adi Da Samraj
The Knee Of Listening, Part Three

The Ruchira Avatar, Adi Da Samraj offers *The Knee Of Listening,* to you and to all human beings, as the living Revelation of His "Visit" to this place of earth. As He says, His "Visit" is unique and unrepeatable. It does not need to be repeated, because It will never end.

THE KNEE
OF
LISTENING

Adidam Samrajashram, 2003

Do Not Misunderstand Me—
I Am Not "Within" you,
but you Are In Me,
and I Am Not a Mere "Man"
in the "Middle" of Mankind,
but All of Mankind Is Surrounded,
and Pervaded, and Blessed By Me

by Avatar Adi Da Samraj

Yes! There is no religion, no Way of God, no Way of Divine Realization, no Way of Enlightenment, and no Way of Liberation that is Higher or Greater than Truth Itself. Indeed, there is no religion, no science, no man or woman, no conditionally manifested being of any kind, no world (any "where"), and no "God" (or "God"-Idea) that is Higher or Greater than Truth Itself.

Therefore, no ego-"I"—no presumed separate (and, necessarily, actively separative, and, at best, only Truth-seeking) being or "thing"—is (itself) Higher or Greater than Truth Itself. And no ego-"I" is (itself) even Equal to Truth Itself. And no ego-"I" is (itself) even (now, or ever) Able to Realize Truth Itself—because, necessarily, Truth (Itself) Inherently Transcends (or Is That Which Is Higher and Greater than) every one (himself or herself) and every "thing" (itself). Therefore, it is only in the transcending of egoity itself— only in the "radical" Process of Going Beyond the root, the cause, and the act of presumed separateness, and of performed separativeness, and of even all ego-based seeking for Truth Itself—that Truth (Itself) Is Realized (As It Is, Utterly Beyond the ego-"I" itself).

1

Truth (Itself) Is That Which Is Always Already The Case. That Which Is The Case (Always, and Always Already) Is (necessarily) Reality. Therefore, Reality (Itself) Is Truth, and Reality (Itself) Is the Only Truth.

Reality (Itself) Is the Only, and (necessarily) Non-Separate (or all-and-All-Including, and all-and-All-Transcending), One and "What" That Is. Because It Is all-and-All—and because It Is (Also) That Which Transcends (or Is Higher and Greater than) all-and-All—Reality Itself (Which Is Truth Itself, or That Which Is Always, and Always Already, The Case) Is the One and Only Real God. Therefore, Reality (Itself) Is (necessarily) the One and Great Subject of true religion, and Reality (Itself) Is (necessarily) the One and Great Way of Real God, Real (and True) Divine Realization, Real (and, necessarily, Divine) En-Light-enment, and Real (and, necessarily, Divine) Liberation (from all egoity, all separateness, all separativeness, all fear, and all heartlessness).

The only true religion is the religion that Realizes Truth. The only true science is the science that Knows Truth. The only true man or woman (or being of any kind) is one that Surrenders to Truth. The only true world is one that Embodies Truth. And the only True (and Real) God Is the One Reality (or Condition of Being) That Is Truth. Therefore, Reality Itself (Which Is the One and Only Truth, and, therefore, necessarily, the One and Only Real God) must become (or be made) the constantly applied Measure of religion, and of science, and of the world itself, and of even all of the life (and all of the mind) of Man—or else religion, and science, and the world itself, and even any and every sign of Man inevitably (all, and together) become a pattern of illusions, a mere (and even terrible) "problem", the very (and even principal) cause of human seeking, and the perpetual cause of contentious human strife. Indeed, if religion, and science, and the world itself, and the total life (and the total mind) of Man are not Surrendered and Aligned to Reality (Itself), and (Thus) Submitted to be Measured (or made Lawful) by Truth (Itself), and (Thus) Given to the truly devotional (and, thereby, truly ego-transcending) Realization of That Which Is the Only Real God—then, in the presumed "knowl-edge" of mankind, Reality (Itself), and Truth (Itself), and Real God (or the One and Only Existence, or Being, or Person That Is) ceases to Exist.

Aham Da Asmi. Beloved, I Am Da, the One and Only Person Who Is. I Am the Avatarically Self-Revealed, and Eternally Self-Existing, and Eternally Self-Radiant (or Spiritually Self-"Bright") Person of Love-Bliss. I Am the One and Only and (Self-Evidently) Divine Self (or Inherently Non-Separate—and, therefore, Inherently egoless—Divine Self-Condition and Source-Condition) of one and of all and of All. I Am Divinely Self-Manifesting (now, and forever hereafter) As the Ruchira Avatar, Adi Da Samraj. I Am the Ruchira Avatar, Adi Da Samraj—the Avataric Divine Realizer, the Avataric Divine Revealer, the Avataric Divine Incarnation, and the Avataric Divine Self-Revelation of Reality Itself. I Am the Avatarically Incarnate Divine Realizer, the Avatarically Incarnate Divine Revealer, and the Avatarically Incarnate Divine Self-Revelation of the One and Only Reality—Which Is the One and Only Truth, and Which Is the One and Only Real God. I Am the Great Avataric Divine Realizer, Avataric Divine Revealer, and Avataric Divine Self-Revelation long-Promised (and long-Expected) for the "late-time"—this (now, and forever hereafter) time, the "dark" epoch of mankind's "Great Forgetting" (and, potentially, the Great Epoch of mankind's Perpetual Remembering) of Reality, of Truth, and of Real God (Which Is the Great, True, and Spiritual Divine Person—or the One and Non-Separate and Indivisible Divine Source-Condition and Self-Condition—of all-and-All).

Beloved, I Am Da, the Divine Giver, the Giver (of All That I Am) to one, and to all, and to the All of all—now, and forever hereafter—here, and every "where" in the cosmic domain. Therefore, for the Purpose of Revealing the Way of Real God (or of Real and True Divine Realization), and in order to Divinely En-Light-en and Divinely Liberate all-and-All—I Am (Uniquely, Completely, and Most Perfectly) Avatarically Revealing My Very (and Self-Evidently Divine) Person (and Spiritually "Bright" Self-Condition) to all-and-All, by Means of My Avatarically Given Divine Self-Manifestation, As (and by Means of) the Ruchira Avatar, Adi Da Samraj.

In My Avatarically Given Divine Self-Manifestation As the Ruchira Avatar, Adi Da Samraj—I Am the Divine Secret, the Divine

Self-Revelation of the Esoteric Truth, the Direct, and all-Completing, and all-Unifying Self-Revelation of Real God.

My Avatarically Given Divine Self-Confessions and My Avatarically Given Divine Teaching-Revelations Are the Great (Final, and all-Completing, and all-Unifying) Esoteric Revelation to mankind—and not a merely exoteric (or conventionally religious, or even ordinary Spiritual, or ego-made, or so-called "cultic") communication to public (or merely social) ears.

The greatest opportunity, and the greatest responsibility, of My devotees is Satsang with Me—Which is to live in the Condition of ego-surrendering, ego-forgetting, and (always more and more) ego-transcending devotional (and, in due course, Spiritual) relationship to Me, and (Thus and Thereby) to Realize My Avatarically Self-Revealed (and Self-Evidently Divine) Self-Condition, Which Is the Self-Evidently Divine Heart (or Non-Separate Self-Condition and Non-"Different" Source-Condition) of all-and-All, and Which Is Self-Existing and Self-Radiant Consciousness (or Indivisible Conscious Light) Itself (Which is One, and Only, and not separate in or as any one, or any "thing", at all). Therefore, My essential Divine Gift to one and all is Satsang with Me. And My essential Divine Work with one and all is Satsang-Work—to Live (and to Be Merely Present) As the Avatarically Self-Revealed Divine Heart and Conscious Light of Truth (and of Real God) among My devotees.

The only-by-Me Revealed and Given Way of Adidam (or Adidam Ruchiradam)—Which is the One and Only by-Me-Revealed and by-Me-Given Way of the Heart, or the only-by-Me Revealed and Given Way of "Radical" Understanding, or Ruchira Avatara Siddha Yoga—is the Way of Satsang with Me, the ego-transcending self-discipline of living in devotionally Me-recognizing devotional response to My Avatarically-Born bodily (human) Divine (and, in due course, Spiritually Effective) Form and Person, such that the devotionally to-Me-turned relationship to Me becomes the Real (and constant, and fundamental) Condition of life. Fundamentally, this Satsang with Me is the one thing done by My devotees. Because the only-by-Me Revealed and Given Way of Adidam is always (in every present-time moment) a directly ego-transcending and Really Me-Finding practice, the otherwise constant (and burdensome) tendency to seek is not exploited in this Satsang with Me. And the essential work of the formal (and formally acknowledged) world-wide gathering of My devotees is to make ego-transcending Satsang with Me available to all others.

Everything that serves the availability of Satsang with Me is (now, and forever hereafter) the responsibility of the formal world-wide gathering of My formally practicing devotees. I am not here to publicly "promote" this Satsang with Me. In the intimate circum-stances of My devotees' humanly expressed devotional love of Me, I Speak My Avatarically Self-Revealing Divine Word to My devotees, and they (because of their devotional response to Me) bring My Avatarically Self-Revealing Divine Word to all others. Therefore, even though I am not (and have never been, and never will be) a "public" Teacher (or a broadly publicly active, and con-ventionally socially conformed, "religious figure"), My devotees function fully and freely (as My devotees) in the daily public world of ordinary life.

I Always Already Stand Free. Therefore, I have always (in My Divine Avataric-Incarnation-Work) Stood Free, in the "Crazy" (and non-conventional, or spontaneous and non-"public") Manner—in order to Guarantee the Freedom, the Uncompromising Rightness, and the Fundamental Integrity of My Avatarically Self-Manifested Divine Teaching (Work and Word), and in order to Freely and Fully and Fully Effectively Perform My universal (Avatarically Self-Manifested) Divine Spiritual Blessing-Work. I Am Present (now, and forever hereafter) to Divinely Serve, Divinely En-Light-en, and Divinely Liberate those who accept the Eternal Vow and all the life-responsibilities (or the full and complete practice) associated with the only-by-Me Revealed and Given Way of Adidam.*¹ Because I Am (Thus) Given to My formally and fully practicing devotees, I do not Serve a "public" role, and I do not Work in a "public" (or even a merely "institutionalized") manner. Nevertheless—now, and forever hereafter—I constantly Bless all beings, and this entire world, and the total cosmic domain. And all who feel My Avatarically (and universally) Given Divine Spiritual Blessing, and who heart-recognize Me with true devotional love, are (Thus) Called to devotionally resort to Me—but only if they approach Me

* Notes to the text of *The Knee Of Listening* appear on pp. 754–68.

in the traditional devotional manner, as responsibly practicing (and truly ego-surrendering, and rightly Me-serving) members (or, in some, unique, cases, as invited guests) of the formal worldwide gathering of My formally practicing devotees.

I expect this formal discipline of right devotional approach to Me to have been freely and happily embraced by every one who would enter into My physical Company. The natural human reason for this is that there is a potential liability inherent in all human associations. And the root and nature of that potential liability is the ego (or the active human presumption of separateness, and the ego-act of human separativeness). Therefore, in order that the liabilities of egoity are understood (and voluntarily and responsibly disciplined) by those who approach Me, I Require demonstrated right devotion (based on really effective self-understanding and truly heart-felt devotional recognition of Me and, on that basis, truly heart-felt devotional response to Me) as the basis for any one's invitation to enter into My physical Company. And, in this manner, not only the egoic tendency, but also the tendency toward religious "cultism", is constantly undermined in the only-by-Me Revealed and Given Way of Adidam.

Because people appear within this human condition, this simultaneously attractive and frightening "dream" world, they tend to live—and to interpret both the conditional (or cosmic and psycho-physical) reality and the Unconditional (or Divine) Reality—from the "point of view" of this apparent (and bewildering) mortal human condition. And, because of this universal human bewilderment (and the ongoing human reaction to the threatening force of mortal life-events), there is an even ancient ritual that all human beings rather unconsciously (or automatically, and without discriminative understanding) desire and tend to repeatedly (and under all conditions) enact. Therefore, wherever there is an association of human beings gathered for any purpose (or around any idea, or symbol, or person, or subject of any kind), the same human bewilderment-ritual is tending to be enacted by one and all.

Human beings always tend to encircle (and, thereby, to contain—and, ultimately, to entrap and abuse, or even to blithely ignore) the presumed "center" of their lives—a book, a person, a symbol, an idea, or whatever. They tend to encircle the "center" (or the "middle"), and they tend to seek to <u>exclusively</u> acquire all "things" (or all power of control) for the circle (or toward the "middle") of <u>themselves</u>. In this manner, the <u>group</u> becomes an <u>ego</u> ("inward"-directed, or separate and separative)—just as the individual body-mind becomes, by self-referring self-contraction, the separate and separative ego-"I" ("inward"-directed, or ego-centric—and exclusively acquiring all "things", or all power of control, for itself). Thus, by <u>self-contraction</u> upon the presumed "center" of their lives—human beings, in their collective ego-centricity, make "cults" (or bewildered and frightened "centers" of power, and control, and exclusion) in <u>every</u> area of life.

Anciently, the "cult"-making process was done, most especially, in the political and social sphere—and religion was, as even now, mostly an exoteric (or political and social) exercise that was <u>always</u> used to legitimize (or, otherwise, to "de-throne") political and social "authority-figures". Anciently, the cyclically (or even annually) culminating product of this exoteric religio-political "cult" was the ritual "de-throning" (or ritual deposition) of the one in the "middle" (just as, even in these times, political leaders are periodically "deposed"—by elections, by rules of term and succession, by scandal, by slander, by force, and so on).

Everywhere throughout the ancient world, traditional societies made and performed this annual (or otherwise periodic) religio-political "cult" ritual. The ritual of "en-throning" and "de-throning" was a reflection of the human observation of the annual cycle of the seasons of the natural world—and the same ritual was a reflection of the human concern and effort to <u>control</u> the signs potential in the cycle of the natural world, in order to ensure human survival (through control of weather, harvests and every kind of "fate", or even every fraction of existence upon which human beings depend for both survival and pleasure, or psycho-physical well-being). Indeed, the motive behind the ancient agrarian (and, later, urbanized, or universalized) ritual of the one in the "middle" was, essentially, the same motive that, in the modern era, takes the form of the culture of scientific materialism (and even all of the modern culture of materialistic "realism"): It is the motive to gain (and to maintain) <u>control</u>, and the effort to control even everything and everyone (via both knowledge and gross power). Thus, the ritualized, or bewildered yes/no (or desire/fear), life of mankind in the modern era is, essentially, the same as that of mankind in the ancient days.

In the ancient ritual of "en-throning" and "de-throning", the person (or subject) in the "middle" was ritually mocked, abused, deposed, and banished—and a new person (or subject) was installed in the "center" of the religio-political "cult". In the equivalent modern ritual of dramatized ambiguity relative to everything and everyone (and, perhaps especially, "authority-figures"), the person (or symbol, or idea) in the "middle" (or that which is given power by means of popular fascination) is first "cultified" (or made much of), and then (progressively) doubted, mocked, and abused—until, at last, all the negative emotions are (by culturally and socially ritualized dramatization) dissolved, the "middle" (having thus ceased to be fascinating) is abandoned, and a "new" person (or symbol, or idea) becomes the subject of popular fascination (only to be reduced, eventually, to the same "cultic" ritual, or cycle of "rise" and "fall").

Just as in <u>every</u> other area of human life, the tendency of <u>all</u> those who (in the modern era) would become involved in religious or Spiritual life is also to make a "cult", a circle that ever increases its separate and separative dimensions—beginning from the "center", surrounding it, and (perhaps) even (ultimately) controlling it (such that it altogether ceases to be effective, or even interesting). Such "cultism" is ego-based, and ego-reinforcing—and, no matter how "esoteric" it presumes itself to be, it is (as in the ancient setting) entirely exoteric, or (at least) more and more limited to (and by) merely social (and gross physical) activities and conditions.

The form that every "cult" imitates is the pattern of egoity (or the pattern that is the ego-"I") itself—the presumed "middle" of every ordinary individual life. It is the self-contraction (or the avoidance of relationship), which "creates"[2] the fearful sense of separate mind, and all the endless habits and motives of egoic desire (or bewildered, and self-deluded, seeking). It is what is, ordinarily, called (or presumed to be) the real and necessary and only "life".

From birth, the human being (by reaction to the blows and limits of psycho-physical existence) begins to presume separate existence to be his or her very nature—and, on that basis, the human individual spends his or her entire life generating and serving a circle of ownership (or self-protecting acquisition) all around the ego-"I". The egoic motive encloses all the other beings it can acquire, all the "things" it can acquire, all the states and thoughts it can acquire—<u>all</u> the possible emblems, symbols, experiences, and sensations it can possibly acquire. Therefore, when any human being begins to involve himself or herself in some religious or Spiritual association (or, for that matter, <u>any</u> extension of his or her own subjectivity), he or she tends again to "create" that same circle about a "center".

The "cult" (whether of religion, or of politics, or of science, or of popular culture) is a dramatization of egoity, of separativeness, even of the entrapment and betrayal of the "center" (or the "middle"), by one and all. Therefore, I have always Refused to assume the role and the position of the "man in the middle"—and I have always (from the beginning of My formal Work of Teaching and Blessing) Criticized, Resisted, and Shouted About the "cultic" (or ego-based, and ego-reinforcing, and merely "talking" and "believing", and not understanding and not really practicing) "school" (or tendency) of ordinary religious and Spiritual life. Indeed, true Satsang with Me (or the true devotional and Spiritual relationship to Me) is an always (and specifically, and intensively) counter-"cultic" (or truly <u>non</u>-"cultic") Process.

The true devotional and Spiritual relationship to Me is not separative (or merely "inward"-directed), nor is it a matter of attachment to Me as a mere (and, necessarily, limited) human being (or a "man in the middle")—for, if My devotee indulges in ego-bound (or self-referring and self-serving) attachment to Me as a mere human "other", My Divine Nature (and, therefore, the Divine Nature of Reality Itself) is <u>not</u> (as the very Basis for religious and Spiritual practice in My Company) truly devotionally recognized and rightly devotionally acknowledged. And, if such non-recognition of Me is the case, there is <u>no</u> truly ego-transcending devotional response to My Avatarically-Born and Avatarically Self-Revealed (and Self-Evidently Divine) Presence and Person—and, thus, such presumed-to-be "devotion" to Me is not devotional heart-Communion with Me, and such presumed-to-be "devotion" to Me is not Divinely Liberating. Therefore, because the true devotional (and, thus, truly devotionally Me-recognizing and, on that basis, truly devotionally to-Me-responding) relationship to Me is entirely a counter-egoic (and truly and only Divine) discipline, it does not (if rightly and truly practiced) become a "cult" (nor does it support the "cultic" tendency of Man).

The true devotional practice of Satsang with Me is (inherently) expansive—or anti-contractional, or anti-constrictive, or decompressive, or pro-relational. Thus, the self-contracting (or separate and separative) self-"center" is neither the motive nor the source of Satsang with Me. In true Satsang with Me, the egoic "center" is always already undermined as a "center" (or a presumed separate, and actively separative, entity). The Principle of true Satsang with Me is Me—Beyond (and not "within"—or, otherwise, supporting) the self-referring ego-"I".

True Satsang with Me is the true "Round Dance" of Esoteric Spirituality. I am not trapped in the "middle" of My devotees. I "Dance" in the "Round" with each and every one of My devotees. I "Dance" in the circle—and, therefore, I am not merely a "motionless man" in the "middle". At the true (and Inherently boundless) "Center" (or the Divine Heart), Which Includes all-and-All (and, therefore, is not merely surrounded, enclosed, abstracted, defined, known, and controlled by all-and-All), I Am—Beyond definition (or separateness). I Am the Indivisible, Most Perfectly Prior, Inherently Non-Separate, and Inherently egoless (or centerless, boundless, and Self-Evidently Divine) Consciousness (Itself) and the Indivisible, Most Perfectly Prior, Inherently Non-Separate, and Inherently egoless (or centerless, boundless, and Self-Evidently Divine) Light (Itself). I Am the Very Being and the Very Presence (or Self-Radiance) of Self-Existing and Eternally Unqualified (or Non-"Different") Conscious Light (or the "Bright") Itself.

In the "Round Dance" of true Satsang with Me (or of right and true devotional and Spiritual relationship to Me), I (Myself) Am Communicated directly to every one who lives in heart-felt relationship with Me (insofar as each one feels—Beyond the ego-"I" of body-mind—to Me). Therefore, I am not the mere "man" (or the separate human, or psycho-physical, one), and I am not merely "in the middle" (or separated out, and limited, and confined, by egoic seekers). I Am the One (Avatarically Self-Revealed, and all-and-All-Transcending, and Self-Evidently Divine) Person of Reality Itself—Non-Separate, never merely at the egoic "center" (or "in the middle" of—or "within", and "inward" to—the egoic body-mind of My any devotee), but always with each one (and all), and always in relationship with each one (and all), and always Beyond each one (and all).

Therefore, My devotee is not Called, by Me, merely to turn "inward" (or upon the ego-"I"), or to struggle and seek to survive merely as a self-contracted and self-referring and self-seeking and self-serving ego-"center". Instead, I Call My devotee to turn the heart (and, indeed, all the faculties of the total body-mind) toward Me—feeling Me As I Am, Free-Standing here. I Call My devotee to turn from the self-"center", to Me, in relationship (relationally, rather than self-referringly). I Call My devotee to merely turn every faculty of body-mind to Me, having already Found (or "Located") Me—rather than to affirm the separate state, and the separative act, of ego-"I", by seeking for Me. I Call My devotee to grow (in due course) to "Locate" My Avatarically Self-Transmitted (and all-and-All-Surrounding and all-and-All-Pervading) Divine Spiritual Presence—by constantly turning to My Avatarically-Born bodily (human) Divine Form and Person. I Call My devotee (in due course) to receive Me Spiritually (in the inherently searchless attitude, or "Asana", of Mere Beholding of My Avatarically-Born bodily human Divine Form), and (Thus and Thereby) to understand (by Means of the tangible experiencing of My Divine Avataric Spiritual Blessing-Grace) that I Am (Always Already) Infinitely Above and Beyond (and Utterly Transcending) the body-mind-self of My devotee (and I am not merely "within"—or contained and containable "within" the separate, separative, and self-contracted domain of the body-mind-self, or the ego-"I", of My would-be devotee). I Call My Spiritually Me-receiving devotee to always function in My Avatarically Self-Transmitted Divine Light, such that My Avatarically

Self-Revealed Divine Person is always (and under all circumstances) presumed and experienced (and not merely sought).
Therefore, true Satsang with Me—or the searchlessly Me-Beholding
devotional and (in due course) Spiritual relationship to Me—is life-
embraced As the Real Company of Truth, or of Reality Itself
(Which Is the Only Real God). True Satsang with Me Serves life,
because I Move (or Radiate) into life, and I always Contact life in
relationship. And the life of true Satsang with Me is the only-by-Me
Revealed and Given Way of Adidam.

I do not Call My devotees to become absorbed into a "cultic"
gang of exoteric and ego-centric religionists. I certainly Call all My
devotees to always create and maintain cooperative sacred culture
(and to enter into fully cooperative collective and personal relationship) with one another—but not to do so in an egoic, separative,
world-excluding, xenophobic, and intolerant manner. Rather, My
devotees are Called, by Me, to transcend egoity—through right and
true devotional (and, in due course, Spiritual) relationship to Me, and
mutually tolerant and peaceful cooperation with one another, and
all-tolerating (cooperative and compassionate and all-loving and all-
including) relationship with all of mankind (and with even all beings).

I Give My devotees the "Bright" Conscious Light of My Own
Avatarically Self-Revealed Divine Person—by Means of Which
Blessing-Gift they can become more and more capable of "Bright"
Divine life. I Call for the searchless free devotion, the intelligently
discriminative self-understanding, the rightly and freely living self-
discipline, and the full and freely functional capability of My devotees. I do not Call My devotees to resist or eliminate life, or to
strategically escape life, or to identify with the world-excluding
ego-centric impulse. I Call My devotees to live a positively functional life. I do not Call My devotees to strategically separate themselves from the natural vitality of life, or to suppress the participatory impulse naturally associated with human existence. I Call for
all the human life-functions to be really and rightly known, and to
be really and rightly understood, and to be really and rightly
lived—and not reduced by (or to) the inherently bewildered (and
inherently "cultic", or self-centered and fearful) "point of view" of
the separate and separative ego-"I".

I Call for every human life-function and faculty to be revolved away from self-contraction (or ego-"I"). I Call for every human life-function and faculty to be always directly (and thoroughly) aligned and out-turned and adapted to Me, in the truly ego-transcending (or counter-contractive) manner—and (Thus and Thereby) to be turned and Given to the Realization of My Divine Avataric Spiritual Self-Revelation of Truth, or Reality Itself—Which Is the "Bright" and Only Real God.

The characteristic life-sign of right, true, full, and fully devotional Satsang with Me is the capability for ego-transcending relatedness, based on the free disposition of no-seeking and no-dilemma. Therefore, the characteristic life-sign of right, true, full, and fully devotional Satsang with Me is not the tendency to seek some "other" condition. Rather, the characteristic life-sign of right, true, full, and fully devotional Satsang with Me is freedom from the presumption of dilemma within the present-time condition. The "radical" understanding (or "gone-to-the-root" self-understanding) I Give to My devotees is not, itself, the acquisition of any particular "thing" of experience. My every true devotee is simply Awakening (and always Awakened) to Me, within the otherwise bewildering "dream" of human life.

Satsang with Me is a naturally (or spontaneously, and not strategically) unfolding Process, in Which the self-contraction that is each one's suffering is transcended by Means of total psychophysical (or whole bodily) heart-Communion with My Avatarically-Born bodily (human) Divine Form and Person—and (Thus and Thereby, and in due course) with My Avatarically Self-Transmitted (and Real—and Really, and tangibly, experienced) Divine (Spiritual, and Transcendental) Presence. My devotee is (as is the case with any and every ego-"I") always tending to be preoccupied with ego-based seeking—but, all the while of his or her life in actively ego-surrendering (and really ego-forgetting and, more and more, ego-transcending) devotional (and, in due course, Spiritual) Communion with Me, I Am Divinely Attracting (and Divinely Acting upon) My true devotee's heart (and total body-mind), and (Thus and Thereby) Dissolving and Vanishing My true devotee's fundamental egoity (and even all of his or her otherwise motivating dilemma and seeking-strategy).

13

There are two principal tendencies by which I am always being confronted by My devotee. One is the tendency to seek— rather than to truly surrender to, and enjoy, and fully animate the devotional (and, in due course, Spiritually developing) Condition of Satsang with Me. And the other is the tendency to make a self-contracting circle around Me—and, thus, to make a "cult" of ego-"I" (and of the "man in the middle"), or to duplicate the ego-ritual of mere fascination, and of inevitable resistance, and of never-Awakening unconsciousness. Relative to these two tendencies, I Give all My devotees only one resort. It is this true Satsang—the devotionally Me-recognizing, and (on that basis) devotionally to-Me-responding, and always really counter-egoic devotional (and, in due course, Spiritual) relationship to My Avatarically-Born bodily (human) Divine Form and Self-Evidently Divine Person.

The Great Secret of My Avatarically-Born bodily (human) Divine Form and Person, and of My Avatarically Self-Transmitted Divine Spiritual Blessing-Work (now, and forever hereafter)—and, therefore, the Great Secret of the only-by-Me Revealed and Given Way of Adidam—Is that I am not the "man in the middle", but I Am Reality Itself, I Am the Only One Who Is, I Am That Which Is Always Already The Case, I Am the Non-Separate (Avatarically Self-Revealed, and Self-Evidently Divine) Person (or One and Very Divine Self, or One and True Divine Self-Condition) of all-and-All (Beyond the ego-"I" of every one, and of all, and of All).

Aham Da Asmi. Beloved, I Am Da—the One and Only and Non-Separate and Indivisible and Self-Evidently Divine Person, the Non-Separate and Indivisible Self-Condition and Source-Condition of all-and-All. I Am the Avatarically Self-Revealed and Spiritually Self-"Bright" Person, the One and Only and Self-Existing and Self-Radiant Person—Who Is the One and Only and Non-Separate and Indivisible and Indestructible Conscious Light of all-and-All. I Am That One and Only and Non-Separate One. And—As That One, and Only As That One—I Call all human beings to heart-recognize Me, and (on that basis) to heart-respond to Me with right, true, and full devotion (demonstrated by Means of formal practice of the only-by-Me Revealed and Given Way of Adidam—Which Is the One and Only by-Me-Revealed and by-Me-Given Way of the Heart).

I do not tolerate the so-called "cultic" (or ego-made, and ego-reinforcing) approach to Me. I do not tolerate the seeking ego's "cult" of the "man in the middle". I am not a self-deluded ego-man—making much of himself, and looking to include everyone-and-everything around himself for the sake of social and political power. To be the "man in the middle" is to be in a Man-made trap, an absurd mummery of "cultic" devices that enshrines and perpetuates the ego-"I" in one and all. Therefore, I do not make or tolerate the religion-making "cult" of ego-Man. I do not tolerate the inevitable abuses of religion, of Spirituality, of Truth Itself, and of My Own Person (even in bodily human Form) that are made (in endless blows and mockeries) by ego-based mankind when the Great Esoteric Truth of devotion to the Adept-Realizer is not rightly understood and rightly practiced.

The Great Means for the Teaching, and the Blessing, and the Awakening, and the Divine Liberating of mankind (and of even all beings) Is the Adept-Realizer. The true Adept-Realizer (of any degree or kind) is One Who (by Virtue of True Divine Realization) Is Able to (and, indeed, cannot do otherwise than) Stand In and As the Divine (or Real and Inherent and One and Only) Position, and to Be (Thus and Thereby) the Divine Means (In Person) for the Divine Helping of one and all. This Great Means Is the Great Esoteric Principle of the collective historical Great Tradition of mankind. And Such Adept-Realizers Are (in their Exercise of the Great Esoteric Principle) the Great Revelation-Sources That Are at the Core and Origin of all the right and true religious and Spiritual traditions within the collective historical Great Tradition of mankind.

By Means of My (now, and forever hereafter) Divinely Descended and Divinely Self-"Emerging" Avataric Incarnation, I Am the Ruchira Avatar, Adi Da Samraj—the Divine Heart-Master, the First, the Last, and the Only Adept-Realizer of the seventh (or Most Perfect, and all-Completing) stage of life. I Am the Ruchira Avatar, Adi Da Samraj, the Avataric Incarnation (and Divine World-Teacher) everywhere Promised for the "late-time" (or "dark" epoch)—which "late-time" (or "dark" epoch) is now upon all of mankind. I Am the Great and Only and Non-Separate and (Self-Evidently) Divine Person—Appearing in Man-Form, As the Ruchira

Avatar, Adi Da Samraj, in order to Teach, and to Bless, and to Awaken, and to Divinely Liberate all of mankind (and even all beings, every "where" in the cosmic domain). Therefore, by Calling every one and all (and All) to <u>Me</u>, I Call every one and all (and All) <u>Only</u> to the Divine Person—Which <u>Is</u> My Own and Very Person (or Very, and Self-Evidently Divine, Self-Condition), and Which <u>Is</u> Reality Itself (or Truth Itself, the Indivisible and Indestructible Conscious Light That <u>Is</u> the Only Real God), and Which <u>Is</u> the <u>One</u> and <u>Very</u> and <u>Non-Separate</u> and <u>Only</u> Self-Condition and Source-Condition of all-and-All (Beyond the ego-"I" of every one, and of all, and of All).

The only-by-Me Revealed and Given Way of Adidam necessarily (and As a Unique Divine Gift) requires and involves devotional recognition of Me (and, on that basis, devotional response to Me) In and Via (and <u>As</u>) My bodily (human) Divine Avataric-Incarnation-Form. However, because I Call every one and all (and All) to Me <u>Only As</u> the Divine Person (or Reality Itself), the only-by-Me Revealed and Given Way of Adidam is not about ego, and egoic seeking, and the egoic (or the so-called "cultic") approach to Me (as the "man in the middle").

According to <u>all</u> the esoteric traditions within the collective historical Great Tradition of mankind, to devotionally approach <u>any</u> Adept-Realizer as if he or she is (or is limited to being, or is limited by being) a mere (or "ordinary", or even merely "extraordinary") human entity is the great "sin" (or fault), or the great error whereby the would-be devotee fails to "meet the mark".[3] Indeed, the Single Greatest Esoteric Teaching common to <u>all</u> the esoteric religious and Spiritual traditions within the collective historical Great Tradition of mankind Is that the Adept-Realizer should <u>always</u> and <u>only</u> (and <u>only</u> devotionally) be recognized and approached <u>As</u> the Embodiment and the Real Presence of <u>That</u> (Reality, or Truth, or Real God) Which would be Realized (Thus and Thereby) by the devotee.

Therefore, <u>no one</u> should misunderstand <u>Me</u>. By Avatarically Revealing and Confessing My Divine Status to one and all (and All), I am not indulging in self-appointment, or in illusions of grandiose Divinity. I am not claiming the "Status" of the "Creator-God" of exoteric (or public, and social, and idealistically pious) religion. Rather, by Standing Firm in the Divine Position (As I Am)—and (Thus and Thereby) Refusing to be approached as a mere man, or as a "cult"-figure, or as a "cult"-leader, or to be in any sense defined (and, thereby, trapped, and abused, or mocked) as the "man in the middle"—I Am Demonstrating the Most Perfect Fulfillment (and the Most Perfect Integrity, and the Most Perfect Fullness) of the Esoteric (and Most Perfectly Non-Dual) Realization of Reality. And, by Revealing and Giving the Way of Adidam (Which Is the Way of ego-transcending devotion to Me As the Avatarically Self-Revealed One and Only and Non-Separate and Self-Evidently Divine Person), I Am (with Most Perfect Integrity, and Most Perfect Fullness) Most Perfectly (and in an all-Completing and all-Unifying Manner) Fulfilling the Primary Esoteric Tradition (and the Great Esoteric Principle) of the collective historical Great Tradition of mankind—Which Primary Esoteric Tradition and Great Esoteric Principle Is the Tradition and the Principle of devotion to the Adept-Realizer As the Very Person and the Direct (or Personal Divine) Helping-Presence of the Eternal and Non-Separate Divine Self-Condition and Source-Condition of all-and-All.

Whatever (or whoever) is cornered (or trapped on all sides) bites back (and fights, or seeks, to break free). Whatever (or whoever) is "in the middle" (or limited and "centered" by attention) is patterned by (or conformed to) the ego-"I" (and, if objectified as "other", is forced to represent the ego-"I", and is even made a scapegoat for the pains, the sufferings, the powerless ignorance, and the abusive hostility of the ego-"I").

If there is no escape from (or no Way out of) the corner (or the "centered" trap) of ego-"I"—the heart goes mad, and the body-mind becomes more and more "dark" (bereft of the Indivisible and Inherently Free Light of the Self-Evident, and Self-Evidently Divine, Love-Bliss That Is Reality Itself).

I am not the "man in the middle". I do not stand here as a mere man, "middled" to the "center" (or the cornering trap) of ego-based mankind. I am not an ego-"I", or a mere "other", or the representation (and the potential scapegoat) of the ego-"I" of mankind (or of any one at all).

I <u>Am</u> the Indivisible and Non-Separate One, the "Bright", the "Midnight Sun", Always Already Infinitely Above and Beyond the all-and-All—and, by Virtue of My Divine Avataric Incarnation and Descent, Always (now, and forever hereafter) Surrounding and Pervading the every one of every here and then.

I Am the (Avatarically Self-Revealed) One and Only and (Self-Evidently) Divine Person—the Perfectly Subjective Divine Self-Condition (and Source-Condition) That Is Perfectly centerless (and Perfectly boundless), Eternally Above and Beyond the "middle" of all-and-All, and (now, and forever hereafter) Surrounding, Pervading, and Blessing all-and-All.

I <u>Am</u> the Way Beyond the self-cornering and "other"-cornering trap of ego-"I".

In this "late-time" (or "dark" epoch) of worldly ego-Man, the collective of mankind is "darkened" (and cornered) by egoity. Therefore, mankind has become mad, Lightless, and (like a cornered "thing") aggressively hostile in its universally competitive fight and bite.

Therefore, I have not Come here merely to stand Manly in the "middle" of mankind—to suffer its biting abuses, or even to be coddled and ignored in a little corner of religious "cultism".

I have Come here to Divinely Liberate one and all (and All) from the "dark" culture and effect of this "late-time", and (now, and forever hereafter) to Divinely Liberate one and all (and All) from the pattern and the act of ego-"I", and (Most Ultimately) to Divinely Translate one and all (and All) Into the Indivisible, Perfectly Subjective, and Eternally Non-Separate Sphere (or Non-"Different" and Indestructible "Midnight Sun") of My "Bright" Self-Domain of Divine Love-Bliss-Light.

The ego-"I" is a "centered" (or separate and separative) trap, from which the heart (and even the entire body-mind) must be Retired. I <u>Am</u> the Way (or the Very Means) of that Retirement from egoity. I Refresh the heart (and even the entire body-mind) of My devotee, in <u>every</u> <u>moment</u> My devotee resorts to Me (by devotionally recognizing My Avatarically-Born bodily human Divine Form and Person, and, on that basis, devotionally—and ecstatically, and also, often, meditatively—responding to My Avatarically-Born bodily human Divine Form and Person) Beyond the "middle", Beyond the "centering" act (or trapping gesture) of ego-"I" (or self-contraction).

I Am the Avatarically Self-Revealed (and Perfectly Subjective, and Self-Evidently Divine) Self-Condition (and Source-Condition) of every one, and of all, and of All—but the Perfectly Subjective (and Self-Evidently Divine) Self-Condition (and Source-Condition) is not "within" the ego-"I" (or separate and separative body-mind). The Perfectly Subjective (and Self-Evidently Divine) Self-Condition (and Source-Condition) is not in the "center" (or the "middle") of Man (or of mankind). The Perfectly Subjective (and Self-Evidently Divine) Self-Condition (and Source-Condition) of one, and of all, and of All Is Inherently centerless (or Always Already Beyond the self-contracted "middle"), and to Be Found only "outside" (or by transcending) the bounds of separateness, relatedness, and "difference". Therefore, in order to Realize the Perfectly Subjective (and Self-Evidently Divine) Self-Condition and Source-Condition (or the Perfectly Subjective, and Self-Evidently Divine, Heart) of one, and of all, and of All (or even, in any moment, to exceed the ego-trap—and to be Refreshed at heart, and in the total body-mind), it is necessary to feel (and to, ecstatically, and even meditatively, swoon) Beyond the "center" (or Beyond the "point of view" of separate ego-"I" and separative body-mind). Indeed, Most Ultimately, it is only in ego-transcendence to the degree of unqualified relatedness (and Most Perfect Divine Samadhi, or Utterly Non-Separate Enstasy) that the Inherently centerless and boundless, and Perfectly Subjective, and Self-Evidently Divine Self-Condition (and Source-Condition) Stands Obvious and Free (and Is, Thus and Thereby, Most Perfectly Realized).

It Is only by Means of devotionally Me-recognizing (and, on that basis, devotionally to-Me-responding) devotional meditation on My Avatarically-Born bodily (human) Divine Form and Person (and Thus ecstatic heart-Contemplation of Me), and (in due course) total (and totally open, and totally ego-forgetting) psycho-physical reception of My Avatarically Self-Transmitted Divine (and Always Blessing) Spiritual Presence and State of Person, that your madness of heart (and of body-mind) is (now, and now, and now) escaped, and your "darkness" is En-Light-ened (even, at last, Most Perfectly). Therefore, be My true devotee—and, by (formally, and rightly, and truly, and fully, and fully devotionally) practicing the only-by-Me Revealed and Given Way of Adidam (Which <u>Is</u> the Divine and True and Complete Way of Truth, and of Reality, and of Real God), always turn to My Avatarically-Born bodily (human) Divine Form, and (Thus and Thereby, and in due course) always Find Me Spiritually (by searchlessly "Locating" Me), Infinitely Above and Beyond your self-"center", and Surrounding and Pervading every here and now.

Aham Da Asmi. Beloved, I <u>Am</u> Da. And, because I <u>Am</u> Infinitely and Non-Separately "Bright", all and All are arising in My Divine Sphere of "Brightness". By feeling and surrendering into the Infinite Spiritual Sphere of My Avatarically Self-Revealed Divine Self-"Brightness", My every devotee Awakens (by Means of My Avataric Divine Spiritual Grace) to Merely <u>Be</u> in Me. And, Beyond his or her self-contracting and separative act of ego-"I", My every devotee (self-surrendered into heart-Communion With Me) <u>Is</u> the One and Only and Non-Separate and Real God I Have Come to Awaken—by Means of My Avataric Divine Incarnation, My Avataric Divine Spiritual Descent, and My Avataric Divine Self-"Emergence"— now, and forever hereafter, here (and every "where") in the cosmic domain.

PART ONE

THE KNEE
OF LISTENING

Da Love-Ananda Mahal, 2002

The Heart of Understanding

Death is utterly acceptable to consciousness and life. There has been endless time of numberless deaths, but neither consciousness nor life has ceased to arise. The felt quality and cycle to death has not modified the fragility of flowers, even the flowers within the human body. Therefore, one's understanding of consciousness and life must be turned to That Utter, Inclusive Truth, That Clarity and Wisdom, That Power and Untouchable Gracefulness, That One and Only Reality, this evidence suggests. One must cease to live in a superficial and divided way, seeking and demanding consciousness and life in the present apparent form, avoiding and resisting what appears to be the end of consciousness and life in death.

The Heart Is <u>Real</u> understanding. The Heart Is <u>Real</u> Consciousness and <u>Real</u> Life. The Heart Is What Merely and Only <u>Is</u>, but Which Is also Appearing In and Behind the conditions of mortal life and its death. Therefore, it is said of old, the One That <u>Is</u> Is neither born nor come to death, not Alive merely as the limitation of form (itself), not Itself (or Entirely) Rendered in what appears, and, yet, It Is the Living One, than Which there Is no lesser other (and no Great or Greater Other), Appearing As all of this Play of changes, but Eternally One, Unchanging, and Free.

There Is Only the Constant Knowledge and Enjoyment of the Heart, moment to moment, through the instant of all conditions of appearance and disappearance. Of This I Am Perfectly Certain. I <u>Am</u> That.

*. . . from my earliest experience of life I have Enjoyed
a Condition that, as a child, I called the "Bright".*

The "Bright"

O n November 3, 1939, at 11:21 A.M., in Jamaica, Queens County, New York, I was born "Franklin Albert Jones". The sign of my birth is Scorpio, marked by the images of Spirit and of Sex, the eagle and the crab.[4] It is the sign of internal warfare, the problem and perfection. The sign of Scorpio should indicate to you the kinds of forces that aligned to generate my birth. Whatever significance you may attribute to astrology, it is true that my personal life has often cycled high and low, marked by equal and opposing determinations to ascend and to descend. And the external adventure of my life has turned me in and out of every kind of religious and Spiritual path, every kind of ascending means, and (likewise) every form of pleasure, ecstasy, and self-indulgence.

The signs of my birth suggest (and have required) a drama of opposites. However, in spite of all of that, it has also been my lot to remain untouched by cosmic and human circumstance. This is perhaps the first key to what I must Communicate. From the beginning, I have also Known a perfect Alternative to the revolutionary internal dilemma of my natural existence. I have played in the problem of my alternatives, but from my earliest experience of life I have Enjoyed a Condition that, as a child, I called the "Bright".

I have always known desire, not merely for extreme pleasures of the senses and the mind, but for the highest Enjoyment of Spiritual Power and Mobility. But I have not been seated in desire, and desire has only been a play that I have grown to understand and enjoy without conflict. I have always been Seated in the "Bright".

Even as a baby, I remember only crawling around inquisitively with a boundless Feeling of Joy, Light, and Freedom in the middle of my head that was bathed in Energy moving unobstructed in a Circle—down from above, all the way down, then up, all the way up, and around again—and always Shining from my heart. It was an Expanding Sphere of Joy from the heart. And I was a Radiant Form—the Source of Energy, Love-Bliss, and Light in the midst of a world that is entirely Energy, Love-Bliss, and Light. I was the Power of Reality, a direct Enjoyment and Communication of the One Reality. I was the Heart Itself, Who Lightens the mind and all things. I was the same as every one and every thing, except it became clear that others were apparently unaware of the "Thing" Itself.

Even as a little child, I recognized It and Knew It, and my life was not a matter of anything else. That Awareness, that Conscious Enjoyment, that Self-Existing and Self-Radiant Space of Infinitely and inherently Free Being, that Shine of inherent Joy Standing in the heart and Expanding from the heart, is the "Bright". And It is the entire Source of True Humor. It is Reality. It is not separate from anything.

From my birth, I have not been centered in Scorpio or the dilemma of alternatives, but in the "Bright". So it is with True Humor that I describe how I existed all this time.

As a Conscious "creation", or by-Me-Embraced condition, "Franklin Jones" began one day while I was crawling across the linoleum floor in a house my parents had rented from an old woman named Mrs. Farr. There was a little puppy, which my parents had gotten for me, running across the floor towards me. I saw the puppy, and I saw my parents. The "creation" of "Franklin Jones" began from that moment. All of the rest of the events that occurred during the two or more years before that moment were not the years of "Franklin Jones". He had no existence before that time, which was the Conscious (or Intentional) beginning.

The reason for this gesture was a spontaneous motivation associated with a painful loving of the people around me. It was not merely compassion for them, as if they were poor people I could help. It was a painful emotional and physical sensation in my heart and in my solar plexus. It was profoundly painful even then, and it always has been. It was associated with the full knowledge that these people to whom I was committing myself were going to <u>die</u>, and that I would die. I knew that if I Incarnated in this life-form and circumstance, if I became this body and its lifetime, I would also die its death. And I knew that, as this bodily incarnate being, I was, in due course, going to be separated from every one and every thing I loved in its lifetime. This was all fully obvious to me—and, yet, this spontaneous gesture, this painful loving, this profound sensation, awakened in me and moved me into the body, animated me physically. Thus, it was, altogether and simply, a sympathetic response that brought me into the sphere of human conditions, and of gross conditions altogether. That response was identification with mortal existence, but it took place by means of Delight. In that Exaltation, the wound of mortality was forgotten. Thus, it was not the noticing of mortality, in and of itself, that generated my Movement into this plane. Rather, it was the Love-Response, the attracted Response, in which all of the negative aspects of gross conditional existence were effectively forgotten—in Love, in Delight, in Love-Bliss.

My father[5] was always a salesman, and my mother[6] was always at home. They could always use a little ordinary humor, but I always loved (and love) them, and love was always the premise of our life together. That is why we were always free to be so reckless, stupid, unfeeling, uncommunicative, unhappy, and separate! None of that ever amounted to anything less than an enjoyment of our separate spectacles. Quiet, long-suffering, fathered mother. Emotional, violent, elaborate father-boy. Crazy, secluded, independent son away.

I always grew up on Long Island—mostly in a town called Franklin Square, which was not named after me, or my father (whose name is also Franklin). Mother is Dorothy. A sister, Joanne, was born when I was eight years old, whom we also always loved (and love), except she and I grew up at separate times and not together.

I was early brought to the Lutheran Christian Church, and so became combined with the mind of Christianity, and especially with the myths and legends (or the so-called history and historical person) of Jesus of Nazareth. Eventually, the ideas I received from that early association with Christianity became crucially important life-supporting beliefs for me, after my own "Bright" Strength of

Even as a little child, I recognized It and Knew It, and my life was not a matter of anything else. That Awareness, that Conscious Enjoyment, that Self-Existing and Self-Radiant Space of Infinitely and inherently Free Being, that Shine of inherent Joy Standing in the heart and Expanding from the heart, is the "Bright". And It is the entire Source of True Humor. It is Reality. It is not separate from anything.

With parents and sister

As a young boy

Boyhood home in Franklin Square
on Long Island

Being had been (temporarily) undermined by my experience of the human world of conflict, illusion, and death. Indeed, even quite early, I began to see there was a fundamental difference, or a very basic unlikeness, between myself and others—not a difference of ultimate essence, and not at all a social or (otherwise) merely physical difference, but a difference of point of view, and of experience, and of life-practice. Thus, schooled by conventional religion, and puzzled by the conventional mind and the disturbed manner of others, I gradually (but only tentatively) accepted the three root-conventions of the common mind: the idea of "God" (as "Creator", and as separate from all "creation"), the idea of separate self (in my case, and in all cases), and the idea of the world (as itself separate, and as itself composed of separate "things", or absolute differences).

One of my most significant early memories is the Event that clearly marks the beginning of my transition from the gratuitous Spiritual "Brightness" of my earliest childhood to my life of seeking— which transition was, as you will see, motivated by my intentional identification with all mortal beings, and by my intentional identification with all the problems of mankind, and by my suffering of all that followed from my consequent ever-decreasing presumption of the "Bright" Itself. In this crucial early Event, I was walking to the movies with my mother and father. As was frequently the case with them, they were having an argument. My mother plays the "tar-baby", which (if you remember Uncle Remus) was set down on a log by Br'er Bear and Br'er Fox in order to trap Br'er Rabbit. She is quiet and passive, and my father very quick, loud, and threatening violence—until he gets stuck and fades away, pretending he will never be heard from again.

That scene was one of their lifelong characteristic games, and so it really makes no difference what aroused it in this case, as I am sure I did not know at the time. I remember there was a full moon— shining, but orange and shadowy. I have no specific recollection of what movie we were on our way to see. I must have been about six or seven years old.

What appeared to me then was a kind of archetype of all conflict. There was the act of separation, and that act was destroying the Spiritual Energy of Love-Bliss. I very clearly and directly experienced the effects of this conflict and separation. I could feel the embracive rays of Love-Bliss-Energy that surrounded us and moved in a delicate network of points in and through our bodies. I could feel those rays of Love-Bliss-Energy being cut by the negative emotional acts of my parents. As a result of their loveless actions, dark vacuums were being spotted out around us and between us. And I was about to make one of my most significant early attempts to Communicate that there is only Love-Bliss-Energy, and to Prove it was so by an actual Spiritual Transmission of that Love-Bliss-Energy Itself.

I remember silently expanding the "Bright" Love-Bliss-Energy from my heart, while, at the same time, trying to distract my parents by pointing out the moon, and by asking them questions about God and life, so they would be calmed, and enabled to feel the Love-Bliss-Energy of the "Bright" I was Transmitting to them.

Their ordinary humor did return a little. My father seemed quieted, and my mother was answering my questions. Nonetheless, I felt their basic refusal, and their basic insensitivity to the "Bright". We went to the movie, and all the while we watched I felt a pressure in my solar plexus and my heart, where the Love-Bliss-Energy was refused and pushed back. But at least the argument was gone, for the night.

The conflict between my parents was a constant field of experience for me as a boy. By no means did they argue all the time, but those events were a persistent and arbitrary danger, and they formed an early ground of disturbance and of understanding in me. And, in the crucial Event I just described, my parents' profound insensitivity to the "Bright"—and, indeed, their fundamental refusal of It (even though It was Freely Transmitted to them)—gave rise to (or, at least, most profoundly confirmed) a deeply felt concern and urgency in me that became the means for me to fulfill the guiding Purpose of my life.

From the beginning, in the early Spiritual "Brightness" of my life, I directly perceived the guiding Purpose of my life: to restore True Humor (or the all-transcending quality of Happiness, that can persist, or, otherwise, constantly come forward, in the living being under all

From the beginning, in the early Spiritual "Brightness" of my life, I directly perceived the guiding Purpose of my life: to restore True Humor (or the all-transcending quality of Happiness, that can persist, or, otherwise, constantly come forward, in the living being under all conditions, whether the conditions appear to be positive or negative).

conditions, whether the conditions appear to be positive or negative). Throughout my life, I have been moved to Communicate (or to Reveal, to Transmit, and to Awaken) the fundamental Source and Substance and Condition of True Humor to others. Ordinary humor can appear in many forms, as the seemingly undauntable mood of life-enjoyment, as the hilarious pleasure of laughter, as the fairy-tale ease of faith, as the self-congratulating certainty of mental knowledge, and as the overriding excitement of even all the greater and smaller bodily victories. But True Humor has only one living Form (and one ultimate, or inherently perfect, Form), Which is Real God, Perfect Truth, or Reality Itself.

If my Purpose (even from the beginning of this lifetime) has always been to restore True Humor, and (likewise) if my Motive has always been Founded in the "Bright", death and the fear of death have (also from the beginning of this lifetime) always been the counter to my Presence—the source of contradiction, fear, mystery, and despair.

I contracted all of the childhood diseases, including a relatively mild case of polio, and, at times, became delirious with fever. This suffering grew a certain depth in me as a boy, because outwardly there were few of the possible overwhelming tragedies. In delirium, I would experience tremendous fear and an awesome mortal separateness, such that death became very real to me during those incidents.

During one of those episodes, I believe when I was about five or six years old, I had a dream that impressed me very deeply. I saw a neat green grass field moving up and away from me, and there was a beautiful full oak tree at its highest point, on the horizon. It was a clear blue day. I did not see myself in the dream but felt as if I were stationed at my point of view at the base of the rise. There were three women in black gowns, like nuns, walking away from me, up the hill. And I felt this tremendous loss and separation, as if I were being left behind.

I woke up crying, with an intense fear of death. And I asked my mother about death. She tried to console me with assurances about God and the afterlife. But a fear was planted in me from that time, such that death was always thereafter a fascinating mystery to me.

I often thought about that dream. I felt it was not a dream at all, but a memory of past death, or an intuition of future death. And the importance of that dream, or of death itself, was never the fact itself. For this reason, I never became particularly motivated to investigate spiritualistic psychism, which pursues the link between living beings and those who are outside this life. For me, the interest in death has always been a matter of investigating, or deeply considering, the present relationship between life-consciousness and death.

I have not truly been concerned with where one goes after death. In my very earliest years, it was always clear to me that— no matter where one goes, or where one is—one is always the same fundamental Consciousness. Indeed, I observed and experienced all events from the "Point of View" of the "Bright". I was Being that Radiant Consciousness, Which is untouched. But I gradually became combined with the mortal experience of identification with the body-mind, and a great question arose in me, more and more persistently and profoundly: What is Consciousness (in Its living form, and altogether)? What must occur within It for It to remain as It is (untouched and Free and Blissful) even while, in Its living form, It already bears the certainty (or the tacit knowledge) of death?

It was this question, felt as a true dilemma, which caused me to indulge in a rather awesome adventure some years later, when I was about nine years old. My father and I shared a passion for animals, although my mother usually took care of them. I was given a black cocker spaniel named "Bootsie" as a present for Easter. The cellar of our house was my free space—and I spent long hours secluded there or playing with friends, where I invented spaceships and boats for us to ride in. I kept a large chest of small toys and would play quietly there with my hoard. I was not exclusively introverted, since I also constantly played outdoors and with friends in the woods all around us, but there was a strong interior activity in me that I also enjoyed without feeling the need for company.

One day, I went into the cellar while my father was at work and my mother away shopping. As I walked into the room, I saw

With Bootsie

Bootsie lying in an old overstuffed chair in the corner of the cellar. I called her and rushed over to pet her. And she was dead. I do not think I had ever touched a dead one before, and certainly not one that I had loved and known alive. She was stiff, lying as if in sleep, and her warmth was nearly gone.

I was immediately overcome by terrible grief. I ran upstairs and sat and rolled in my room, and wept for what seemed like hours. But there was not only grief. There was also fear and guilt. I was stuck with some kind of knowledge that I was afraid to tell. My door was closed, and I heard my mother in the other rooms. She must have heard me crying, but I do not think she came in to me. She must have gone and found the dead animal and decided to leave me to my father. Then he, too, came home, and they opened the door to me.

My father asked me what was wrong, and I was trying not to show my grief. But then I told him, "Bootsie died." And I fell in his arms and wept.

After several hours of consolation and quiet, I had controlled my grief. Then I made a very strange decision. I could not bear estrangement from love. I prayed to God to receive Bootsie and care for her. And then I told Him that I wanted Him to take me also. I needed time to make the transition from my life and love in the world, and so I told Him it should be at 9:00 P.M. two days from then—I believe, on a Sunday.

I did not tell my parents I was about to die. I decided to be with them and enjoy with them for two days and make an easy transition. On the last day, we drove in the country. I watched in the clouds, seeing only heaven and Bootsie and God.

Then it was the evening of my death. We had dinner and sat in the living room watching television. I went and prayed to God, and I was certain He would take me at nine o'clock. But as the hour approached, I began to realize the importance of this move. I was about to leave life! I was about to suffer the loss of the world, my parents, my future possibility. I felt a tremendous connection to the living world, and saw that the absence of one I loved did not amount to the destruction of love, of life-positive energy, of "Bright" Fullness, or of Heart-Joy. I saw that I was alive!

Nevertheless, I presumed that much of this "conversion" might be due to fear and regret. I knew that I had bargained with God, and, therefore, I would not abandon His Will. And so I only sat and waited. I watched the television and continually relaxed the awesome fear that kept rising in me. Nine o'clock came, and I did not die.

I do not remember if I was alone in my room or with my parents at that hour—but, when it passed, I went and prayed to God. I thanked Him for my life and asked forgiveness for my wavering. But something in me had died or become hidden at that hour. I remember that, for several years afterward, I would end my prayers with the request, "And please, dear Lord, allow me to live until I am eighty-nine years old or older."

For some time after this incident, I suffered a constriction in my chest, and I felt as if I could not breathe deeply enough. I even had my father take me to a doctor. The doctor and my father watched me breathing behind a fluoroscope. And it was determined that I was in good health. After that, I gradually took some relief, for I had not been certain that my promise to die had not crippled my heart in some way. I remember that even in the days before our visit to the doctor, and then for weeks afterwards, I experienced a sublime enjoyment of the air and light, the fact of my life, in spite of the feeling of weakness in my heart.

So I experienced in myself the meaning of death, conflict, and separation, which I knew to be the primary fact in all suffering. I saw how the sentiment of separation from love can, as a problem or concern in the humanly-born conscious awareness, draw one out of the "Bright" of Illuminated, Free Consciousness Itself—until one no longer perceives the perfect Form that is always already here.

Such early experiences in my life are not merely clinical, nor did they alone "create" the later personal form of my life. I was Awake and full of Clarity in those early episodes, just as I am now. Even then, and forever before then, I was What I _am_ now. And it is clear to me that I have always operated on the basis of a few fundamental perceptions, and these have structured all of my life. And the basic, few perceptions that have structured all of my life are the fundamentals of Reality (altogether, both conditional and

Un-conditional), and not merely the idiosyncrasies of character (or of conditional personality) in and of itself.

Character is built through experience, through the accumulations of one's use of certain given options in the humanly-born conscious awareness. Disturbances of the personality, which form so much of the data of clinical observations, are not the results of a given disorder in one's Real (or Ultimate) Nature. Rather, they are the result of a misuse (and unconsciousness) of the options associated with the humanly-born (or conditional) conscious awareness. Therefore, it was clear to me from the beginning of this lifetime (and, over time, it was repeatedly reconfirmed) that true healing (or the establishment of the capability necessary for free, "creative" life) is not a matter of concentration on memory, the past, or the history of the functional personality, good or bad—but it is (rather) a matter of understanding the fundamental and <u>present</u> activity of the humanly-born conscious awareness and making right conscious and intentional use of one's living options.

Whenever I have turned from the True Center of present-time life-consciousness to one or another kind of seeking motivated in the desires of my complex life, I have been brought to the same recognition: The search is suffering. When, for example, I felt the loss of the little animal I loved, I was moved to find her, to be where that love continued as is. So I was motivated to a drastic ascent from life, to what (because of my separated mentality) seemed to be God. But, at last, I saw that the motive toward re-union was itself the source and act of separation, and that it was itself a destructive cutting away of Free Awareness, Love-Bliss-Energy, and Life.

In the hours of waiting for death, I was not Awake as the "Bright", the Full Presence of my Being. I was separate from the "Bright", and saw all Love and Light and Freedom of Being as utterly above, apart from me and this world. Only too late, it seemed to me then, did the shock of what I awaited draw me into that Fullness again. And I saw that Reality was always already (and, therefore, always presently) Full, and that to seek that Fullness in the symbolic state I was awaiting was to abandon (or to not presume and Enjoy) that always present Fullness in the actual present moment.

I learned (or even re-learned) this Great Lesson at that time. It is not merely the product of reflection years hence. Originally, and (but decreasingly) as a small boy, I operated with that Clarity and Enjoyed (even in my humanly-born form and conscious awareness) the Knowledge of Real (or Ultimate, or Truly Divine) Consciousness. The search itself has never been my fundamental Vocation. The search was only a curious excursion. It was temporarily necessary (because of my born association with the functions and tendencies of a living human body-mind), but (because of the always underlying Foundation that is the "Bright") it was also only a means of reaffirmation of Reality Itself in the context of my humanly-born conscious awareness. Therefore, all of my life, Reality Itself, Spiritually "Bright" and Full, has been the Fundamental Circumstance of my living existence.

My earliest childhood (from birth), and not merely some later (or more adult) time, was the period of my first Knowledge and Unfoldment of the "Bright", Which I Knew to be the perfect Form (and the Source of the living condition) of Reality. And what is That exactly? This book is determined to Communicate It, again and again, in so many ways. But, on the level of my earliest recognition of It, It was the "ordinary" Condition of even my humanly-born conscious awareness. It was Consciousness Itself, Radiant and Awake. It was my simple (human and Ultimate) State, Prior to even any experience. It was not mysterious or awesome to me. There was no shadow, nothing hidden in It. It was not motivated to seek any end at all. There was no "beyond", no "outside", no "Other". It had no sense of time. Nor had It yet begun to feel any kind of confusion or identity with existence as separated personality and problematic experience. It was the Center of the life-functions, but without dilemma or unconsciousness. There were no divisions in It. Radiant Spiritual Energy was Communicated within It, and, thus, in and via the entire body-mind. There was Joy in the body, a Luminous cell-life, a constant respiration and circulation of Love-Bliss-Energy and unlimited, boundless Pleasure. There was a Spiritual Current of Energy in the heart that rose into the head through the throat. And that same Spiritual Current of Energy was below the heart, rising up into it from below. There was a surrounding Circle of Spiritual Energy that was spaceless and boundless, but Which had a formless Locus above the head. And all of this moving Energy Originated as a single Spiritual Source-Current of Light and Life in the heart that was reflected and Felt at a pervasive Center deep within the head. There was a constant Radiation of this entire Form, including the body. It was Joy in the heart, reflected as Enjoyment in the head. And that formless, spaceless Form of Consciousness was "Bright", Silent, Full—Knowing only and entirely this Condition, this Reality, and seeing no problem, no separation, in the fact of life.

This "Bright", this Real Consciousness, is the perfect Form (and the Source of the living condition) of Reality, and It is never undone. It is now, and It is you. Now and always, every living being is arising within and as this Form, Which is the very Form of life. It is only that life is not lived as Real Consciousness. It is confused with some experience, some fragment of Energy in the event of the personality, in the functions that operate by laws subconscious and unconscious to the individual, or some wave of Energy that fascinates the individual in the superconscious patterns above. When such confusions of identity overwhelm and distract one into some division of the living structure of Reality, one is moved to great seeking in the alternatives of life. Every course that is not simply the demonstration of Real Consciousness, direct and present, is a schism in one's living form. The excursions of my life beyond childhood showed this all the more to me.

*Beyond my tenth year, I was more often solemn,
and even ordinary humor became more an act of "creation".
I turned from mostly pleasure to listening.*

CHAPTER TWO

The Listener

My earliest years were gratuitous, a free enjoyment whose wisdom was unearned. This is true of all human beings, but many people learn suffering very soon, and so even the given becomes a matter of problems and of seeking. Beyond my tenth year, I was more often solemn, and even ordinary humor became more an act of "creation". I turned from mostly pleasure to listening.

As a small boy, I liked to use the ways of increasing simple enjoyment and life-humor in others. I recited poems and rhymes, sang, and told stories. I made a puppet theatre in the cellar and put on shows for the neighbors and their children and all my relatives. Then I was a ventriloquist and a dancer, and until I was thirteen I always performed comedy with my dummy at school. I loved to draw and paint, and everyone took pleasure in what I made, such that I even won the "art award" when I left eighth grade to go to high school.

Even religion took on a certain humorous quality for me as I came to adolescence. I was an acolyte in the Lutheran church, and nearly every Sunday I served at the altar. Once every month, the church practiced the ceremony of "holy communion", and I would prepare the altar. I filled the little glasses in the trays with wine and set out the pressed discs of unleavened bread.

I would have to get up very early to serve on those communion Sundays. From the time I was about eight or nine, my parents ceased to go to church except on the important holidays. And so I would get up on those Sundays alone, about 6:00 A.M., and leave for church without breakfast. I would get very hungry while I poured the wine into glasses and packed the wafers into the paten. The wine was contained in a special glass bottle. It had a rubber bulb on top that injected a bit of wine into a glass through a little spout as you pressed it.

*I was an acolyte in the Lutheran church,
and nearly every Sunday I served at the altar.*

I had tasted a little wine at home a few times in my life. When my parents had company, they would sometimes give me a tiny bit of port. And once or twice I had a small glass of beer with pizza at a neighbor's house. But I had never felt drunkenness, and wine seemed harmless to me. Before it was consecrated on the altar, the bread and wine of communion was not presumed to be "holy", or untouchable, so I felt only a little reluctant to sample it in the pastor's study.

One such morning, when I was thirteen or fourteen, while feeling particularly hungry and weak, I pressed a little sweet port into my mouth, then one for the tray, then one for me. I ate a few communion wafers, and then a little more wine. I had tried this just a little, once or twice before, and felt no peculiar effects. And it did help my hunger. So, on this particular day, I was very liberal with myself.

I had not quite finished filling the trays when I began to feel very dizzy, and yet very happy, such that I was laughing quite a lot when the other acolyte, the pastor, and the choir began to arrive to prepare for the service. I knew that I was drunk. There was no doubt about that. But I did not feel particularly guilty. I felt only that I should try very hard to look as normal as possible!

It could not have happened on a day more filled with unusual circumstances. The pastor was a little late—so, as soon as he arrived, everything had to be done very quickly. I was a little too dizzy for fast movements, but somehow I had to finish the wine trays instantly and lay out the altar. Then there was a sudden prayer, and we were hustled into the church.

Before the actual communion, the acolytes sat in the choir pews in the chancel. I was enjoying myself. I felt very heady and relaxed, but a little concerned that people, especially the pastor, would observe something peculiar about me. I looked at faces a lot, and grinned every now and then at a friend in the choir or the congregation.

During the communion service, the acolytes had to do a lot of ceremonious moving around at the altar, giving and taking wafers and wine trays to and from the pastor. I seemed to sway a lot, and my body felt very nervous as we began. Then I dropped a few wafers and, in obedience to the rule, I hungrily picked them up to eat. But the rhythm of the movements in the ceremony became a kind of repetitive dance, such that my anxiety disappeared in circles, again and again.

I watched the communicants very closely. And soon their movements became absurd to me. Sometimes there would be one too many, and all the kneeling communicants would be crunched up. And there was something ridiculous about the way each of them would stick out the tongue for a wafer—such that, very often, I would find some bit of business to do on the altar, to turn away and bury my laughter in the wall!

Then the communion was over, and we returned to the pews in the chancel for a hymn. At that point, the pastor (who was about twenty feet away from me at the head of the pew) remembered that he was supposed to perform a baptism at the close of the service. He told one of the choir to signal me. Whispers went down the line, and soon I was being elbowed. The person next to me was trying to whisper something about a baptism, but I had no idea what that had to do with me. I had never served at a baptism.

I began to get a little nervous, and I was not sure whether my drunkenness was preventing me from getting the message. Finally, someone leaned over and whispered very loudly, "Fill the baptismal basin!"

The baptismal basin was down in front of the congregation, outside the chancel and just below the lectern where the pastor read the Bible lessons. I really did not know how to go about it ceremoniously and unnoticed, but I figured I had better get out of the chancel and get some water somewhere.

I got up and swayed out of the chancel into a doorway on the other side of the altar. As I went out, I looked back anxiously at the pastor for any last-minute signal about what I should do. But he was nodding in his hymnal with the choir.

I had no idea how long I had before the baptism was supposed to take place. Perhaps only the length of a hymn! So I ran frantically around the pastor's study looking for a water bottle. I opened up the doors to a closet where we kept our gowns and the altar paraphernalia. I jumped back. There was a man standing in the closet, peeking out between the gowns! He was obviously hiding in the closet! He pressed his index finger to his lips and made a sign for me to be quiet. So I closed the doors on him again and ran around some more, but I could hardly keep from falling on the floor and laughing myself silly.

I learned later that the man in the closet was an FBI agent who was supposed to be watching for someone who had been stealing money from the weekly offering plates. Anyway, I let him be, since I was rushed. All I could find was an old milk bottle under the pastor's wash basin. It was coated inside with some kind of ashy substance. It looked as though somebody had been growing plants in it.

I had no time to look for any other kind of bottle, so I ran water through it several times and shook it to loosen the sludge. The best I could do was wash away some of the surface dirt, but the stain itself remained all around the inside of the bottle. I filled it with cold water and ran toward the exit to the church nave.

As I opened the door and stepped into the church in front of the congregation, every eye seemed to follow me. I tried to carry the bottle ceremoniously on my right side, away from the congregation, but everyone seemed to see it anyway, and lots of them began to smile at me and whisper to one another. It all began to seem friendly enough to me, so I walked as calmly as possible, smiling solemnly. As I walked, it began to occur to me that the ice-cold water was going to be a little rough on the baby's head. And I began to laugh inside again at how ridiculous it all was—the man in the closet, the dirty bottle, the cold water—such that I stepped into the front of my robe and nearly fell over on the floor.

Now it seemed everyone was aware of me. I was standing by the baptismal basin. The pastor was standing above me at his lectern. And the entire church was silent. I lifted the top off the basin and put it on the floor. And then, with grace and ceremony, I turned the milk bottle upside down.

The bottle went "Glub-Glup, Glub-Glub", and the sound seemed to ring around the church! I could hear people snorting everywhere. And when I looked up at the pastor, he was pressing his lips and trying not to laugh. The more I poured, the louder it

The Lutheran church in Franklin Square

Inside the church

The baptismal font

got, and I was trying so hard to keep steady and not to laugh that tears were running out of my eyes.

Finally, I figured there was enough water in the bowl, and I swifted out of the room, back to the pastor's study. I remember laughing in the pastor's sink until I was empty of every last urge to laugh. Then, as if nothing had happened, I cruised back, solemn and easy, to my seat in the choir.

I suppose it was around this time that I became a true adolescent. I should mark it just about the year I entered high school, when I was nearly fourteen. Then the rights of sex, the exercise of personal identity, and the need for privacy became very crucial requirements. Up to that time, I was protected in the circumstance of the parental nest. I had, until that time, asserted myself in dependence, but now, more and more, in independence.

At first, I was not overtly independent at all. My first three years in high school were gray years in many ways. I did not feel the freedom of sexual and personal play that I assumed even as a little boy. I became more serious, more reserved, somewhat puzzled— and, outside of school, I tended to spend a lot of time in solitude.

During those early high school years, I was an amateur radio operator. There was a fascination for me in the invisible energies, the mysterious circuitries, and even all the physical mysteries of radio communication. I was often awake late into the night, or I would get up before sunrise, in order to take advantage of the longer-distance radio communication possible (because of the unique atmospheric conditions) during those hours.

About the middle of my junior year in high school, I learned that, in special circumstances of communication, the Power of the "Bright" would come out of hiding and rouse Itself again in me, and expand Itself—such that It would even, to some degree, be felt by many others. I read in the school newspaper that the American Legion was sponsoring an oratorical contest, and all junior and senior year students were eligible. I felt certain that I could speak persuasively (although I had never given a speech before), and so I immediately began to write a speech.

I do not remember how it occurred to me, but I decided to write an oratory on prejudice. This was back in 1956, before the civil rights movement or its viewpoint had any force or voice that were known to me. The speech was called "Patterns of Prejudice". I studied various documents and books in the library, and I put together a speech that had a very pure and righteous tone. It had very little ordinary humor, but there was a basic feeling throughout of the obvious wrongness of human social negativity. I mimicked many negative attitudes in the speech, and they seemed to me to be obviously that—attitudes, possible (but not necessary) ways of relating to another human being about whom one was conscious of a difference, be it color, religion, nationality, manner, or whatever.

I think some of the impetus behind that speech came from my childhood experiences of conflict in my family. And my father was from Mississippi. I do not recall any expressions of race prejudice in him, but he had taken me to the South a couple of times when I was yet a boy (of eight, and then of nine, years of age), and I became aware of race hatred there. Shortly before we made our first visit, a black man had been hanged in a barn nearby, and reports of such terrible events were routinely heard by me as part of the surroundings of casual conversation during those visits.

My oratory on prejudice included the tone and point of view of religion. Prejudice was an attitude I had perceived in the very people I met in my church. And I saw it everywhere in the general community. I assumed, rather naively, that nearly everyone was a religious person in some way—and so I considered that nearly everyone could recognize at once that prejudice was not a viable expression, purely on the basis of the religious beliefs they already professed.

I delivered the speech to a few people in a small classroom and was accepted as a finalist, along with three or four others. Then, a week later, we were brought to the school auditorium, which was filled with perhaps a thousand people or more. I had never confronted a mass of humanity before. But the Power of the "Bright" suddenly moved in me, and It gave me confidence and inspiration.

I gave my speech while standing alone on the stage. I noticed immediately that I was producing a very remarkable effect on everyone. My words moved and expanded through and out from me on the feeling-waves of the "Bright", and a sudden silence came over the entire audience. Even the "hoods", the gangs that took the front rows and slouched or mimicked whatever appeared on the stage, spontaneously began to sit up. Each one, and all, became profoundly attentive—as if each were deeply experiencing a fundamental life-truth that was always hidden, but which one could not deny if it stood out before one. I felt I was speaking a life-truth that everyone accepted whole, and upon which all could operate—except that people tend not to decide together that each one already holds it true.

I won the oratorical contest that day. And I went on from there to a finalist's session that was supposed to decide the winner for the county, who would then go on to compete for the state award, and, I suppose, then for the national award. But I did not win at the next level. As soon as I stood to speak before the huge numbers of that strange, hostile crowd, I felt a different aura, a wholly different mind—and the "Bright" Itself seemed reluctant to Shine abroad, as if because the gathering in front of me was not worthy of Its blessing. The person who won on that occasion gave what appeared to me to be a merely cute, meaningless speech about George Washington and the flag. And I even felt some embarrassment that I had brought up anything more profound than picnic patriotism.

Nevertheless, many came to shake my hand after the speeches. And, as I had surmised, their expressions also implied that I had stepped on some toes. They felt there was an actual "establishment" of prejudice, and that it could not accept what appeared to be a very forthright expression of brotherhood, mutual love, and untroubled enjoyment of humanity. Finally, one older man took me aside, clasped my hand, looked at me strongly, and said (as if intent that I should always remember it): "Never let them stop you from thinking."

I was only a teenager, and the entire matter was surrounded by adolescent perceptions, but there was something real that I encountered in the world that day. As a result, my involvement in the guiding Purpose of my life was further aroused and intensified from that day. From then, I was concentrated in myself. I began to listen to something un-Happy in the wind. I began to doubt. I was profoundly aware of a resistance, a madness, in humanity that would require great Intelligence and a masterful Communication before humanity would acknowledge its own Truth (or even anything right).

That day was the beginning of human maturity in me. Of course, it was a matter of the same problem of conflict and separation that I recognized even as a little child. And I was handling it in the same manner, by enforcing a Presence and an Intelligence that was, for me, already Obvious, Whole, and Free. It was the "Bright" again—but I brought It to bear on a problem that is not merely personal, or even a temporary family conflict, but a schism that is rooted in everyone's mind, in every moment of everyone's life, and, therefore, in the world itself. I saw that human beings were not living as Real and True. I saw that Truth, or Reality, was not actually being lived, and that the entire world of my future was not a field of free consciousness and love, but a field of ignorance, conflict, and seeking.

After that, I became a "public man" for a year. I acted in school plays, spoke in school politics. My paternal grandfather died in my senior year, and I composed a ceremony to be performed at his funeral. I was to recite it along with my cousins and other members of the DeMolay, a junior branch of the Masons, of which my grandfather was a high-ranking member.

We performed this ceremony in the funeral home, before my grandfather's casket. It was a very honorable ceremony, and everyone present was deeply, emotionally moved. However, even as I spoke, there was no particular sorrow in me or sense of loss. I was mostly aware of the living who were present. There was something I understood that needed to be understood and lived by all. It was the summary Lesson of my childhood. It was about always keeping love in the present time, and not relinquishing that love in the present in order to seek it elsewhere, even among the dead. And I wanted to Communicate that life-truth with an overwhelmingly "Bright" effectiveness. But it seemed that the more I emphasized this life-truth, the more outwardly sorrowful everyone, and especially my father, became.

Nevertheless, my effect on the funereal gathering was appropriately intense, and, certainly, cathartic. And, immediately after this ceremony, the pastor of my church, who had also served the event, and who was astonished by the effect I had on everyone there, passionately urged me to go on to college and eventually become a Lutheran minister. This seemed like an obvious and right course to me at the time, and I agreed. At the pastor's invitation, I became a liturgist, often reciting the sacred texts and the instructions to the congregation during the ceremonies in the church. And I was accepted by Columbia College to enter as a freshman in the coming year.

I moved into this agreed-upon future in religion with a great feeling of certainty, and even anticipation. But I did nothing to "create" it. My interest in high school studies fell off completely, such that one teacher remarked that he wished I had "never won that contest". It was true that the oratorical "contest" had changed me. But it was not so much the winning as the losing—and not the fact of <u>my</u> loss, but the reasons for it in everyone. I was aware of something fundamentally wrong in life. As far as I was concerned, I had "dropped out".

I had taken a large number of credits in technical courses that dealt with the physics and practical use of electricity and electronics. The examinations I was to take at the end of my senior year were the finals for courses that extended for two and even three years. But I ceased to study altogether. None of that work, or any of the work in my other courses, seemed to have any importance. In fact, it seemed like nonsense to me.

I made only the most superficial study for my exams. I thought that I could probably pass many of them. Some of them I was almost certain I could not pass. Yet, I felt that it did not matter, and I knew that I would somehow go on to whatever work I had to do.

I had always been an excellent student in the past, and I have never, before or since, cheated on examinations. But when I went to my final technical examinations almost totally unprepared, I decided I would simply copy another student's work. I sat behind and across the aisle from a student I knew would do well on the

Adi Da Samraj in His youth

tests. And I copied every one of his calculations and answers. Here and there, where I was able to notice a slight error, I corrected the answers.

As a result, I came to graduation with one of the highest scores in the technical exams. It did not matter to me, although I was happy to know that I would be able to go on to college unobstructed.

The next phase of my life is the real beginning of listening for me. At the end of my high school years, I was utterly free from any kind of superficial idealism or any need to achieve ordinary human excellence. I was profoundly serious and also profoundly undisciplined. I aligned myself exclusively with my own internal states. Where there was desire, I indulged it. Where there was interest, I followed it. I was totally renegade in my holding to life, for I felt on the brink of Knowledge, of Reality, of brilliant Discovery. Of course, no one who lives disarmed in this manner is free of delusions or suffering, and I was about to begin a long period of most awesome and painful suffering. But I was alarmingly free to follow the thread of my own life-consciousness.

The gratuitous foundation-period of the "Bright" was past. I no longer possessed the unearned Joy and Clarity of my boyhood. I had seen the world and ceased to be innocent. I had even begun to enjoy my own lack of innocence, and my own forbidden pleasures. The inner resources of True Humor became strangely entangled with others and the world. Therefore, I avoided no "sin" at all. And, yet, I remained concentrated in the image and person of Jesus—as if, when I would Know his "Secret" utterly, it would freely convert me and purify all of my estrangement. Thus, I did not fear my "sinfulness" any more than I feared to eat the wafers and the wine in secret.

I became more and more self-indulgent, and, thereby, began a pattern of self-exploitation that was to persist for many years. I began to gain excess weight, to indulge myself sexually, and to assert myself beyond anyone's ability to limit or control me. Nevertheless, within me I was fully aware of this play of Scorpio. Therefore, I did not adopt "sin" as a way of life, but as a way of Knowing life.

Beginning at that time, while I was yet sixteen years of age, I became submitted to an inner drive to utterly experience the heart of the human dilemma, the very essence of human suffering. This intention in me is not something I can recognize only now, after years of reflection. It was an actual, conscious decision I made at that time. Later, as you will see in the next chapter, this intention became even more explicit. I no longer took the position of the "Bright", the Radiant Presence of Consciousness Itself, surrounded by the conflicts of others. I had found conflict in the very world. I felt it rising in myself. And I rushed to become it, by surrendering to it, in order to Know the way that no longer required it for anyone.

*When I entered Columbia College in September 1957,
I was possessed with a single, motivating interest. I wanted
to understand what living beings are. What is Consciousness?*

CHAPTER THREE

Hearing

There is no such thing as anyone's "autobiography". The events of experience do not, when recollected, synthesize themselves into an exact history, or even an exact person. Ordinary experience does not, over time, become a "something". It is only an irregular series of concerns for life and death. If I were to write about a few such moments of ordinary experience, I could "create" an image. This, in fact, is what everyone does with memory. One highlights and defines a few (originally, shapeless, or indefinable) events, identifies each of them with a particular defining emotion, and (thus, by a kind of "artistic" effort) makes a narrative, and even invents a particular and separate "self". Thus, one conceives of oneself as a "someone" by means of the device of partial contemplation. But if one could include it all (utterly and entirely), and consciously (and utterly) perceive the Real nature of experience at any moment, there would be no particular and separate person in the mind. There is no emphasis, and no design, in the whole. No particular and separate thing stands out at the point of Totality. Therefore, the more deeply and completely one experiences the recollection of one's ordinary life, the more arbitrary every mark becomes.

Nevertheless, there are a few unique Events in what, as a concession to the conventions of ordinary communication, I refer to as "my own life" that stand whole by themselves. They neither signify nor justify an inherently (or otherwise, and utterly) separate life, nor do they define or describe an artificial, synthetic, or merely presumed "person". Rather, they are Events that Communicate (or cease to hide) Reality. And these Events are the genuine subject of my "autobiography". They are the Events in my early life that uniquely and fully demonstrate what I refer to as "True Humor". And they do not speak of my human instance alone, but they are moments in the universally Communicated and universally Knowable life of Reality Itself. Therefore, those Events reveal the Truth of Who I <u>am</u>—Which, ultimately, is the Truth and Identity of every one and all.

When I was a little boy, the "Bright" was my constant Knowledge of Reality. But the more tentative I became about Reality, the more I felt myself to be separate from Reality, and (therefore) one who "listens" to Reality, and even one who seeks Reality. And the more I became a "listener", and then a seeker, the more the Knowledge of Reality became an Occasion, an over-whelming Event, an Enlightenment. The subject of this chapter is the first and primary Event of Conscious Reality in my life after the "Bright" had disappeared into my childhood and I had become not only a "listener" but an urgent seeker relative to my own Truth.

When I entered Columbia College in September 1957, I was possessed with a single, motivating interest. I wanted to under-stand what living beings <u>are</u>. What <u>is</u> Consciousness? Whatever academic studies were required of me, I was always at work on this one question, and I was forever researching some kind of primary thesis out of great need.

The experience of study at Columbia was completely devastating. I had never in my life encountered any kind of sophisticated thought. But now I suddenly became aware of the literature of the world. The mood at Columbia in those years was profoundly solemn and critical. The attitude and the dilemma that I encoun-tered when I gave my little speech on prejudice were here extended as the consciousness of the human race.

Grayson Kirk, who was then president of the University, intro-duced us to college life with a serious speech about the rising problems of humanity. He promised that Columbia would not teach us the answers, but we would perhaps learn the questions. Altogether, he indicated that Columbia would not make us Happy, but he promised that we would learn how to think.

I was deeply impressed by his attitude, and that of the entire formidable crowd of lecturing "thinkers", talking (and otherwise in attendance) there. Immediately, Columbia seemed like an emi-nently appropriate, and even ideal, place in which to expand my doubts—but I was puzzled that one of the highest institutions of learning could represent itself as anything but the bearer of Truth. I soon learned that the Truth was always in research in such places. They are not institutions of Truth. They are marketplaces of doubt.

I began to read the deposits of Western culture. And all my idols lost their Power. To begin with, I learned that the "Holy Christian Truth" was anything but the real substance of Western civilization. There is a thesis emphasized in all the little bits of thought generated in a university education. In that thesis, the human being is described as necessarily mortal, functionally conditioned, and (at best) "creative" as a social animal. Also, the universe is described as materially prior to conscious life, and it is chronically understood without recourse to religious or Spiritual propositions.

Every book I read and every course I took emphasized this thesis in some unique fashion. This experience very quickly destroyed even the latent image of Jesus that I had stored up in childhood. A book that deeply affected me in the midst of my freshman year was *The Lost Years of Jesus Revealed*, by Charles Francis Potter. Even the church seemed to proclaim the absence of its own Truth. In his book, based on his interpretation of the Essene tradition revealed in the "Dead Sea Scrolls", Dr. Potter wrote about the process whereby the traditional Christian descriptions of Jesus of Nazareth came to be proposed:

A "scheme of salvation" emerged, transforming the man Jesus into the mystical Christ, the Son of God. . . .

In the body of doctrine as it grew, influenced by current ideas about what a god-man should be and do, Jesus must perforce have come from heaven to be born of a virgin, must perform many miracles, make mystic utterances, raise the dead occasionally, and then himself die, rise again from the dead, and be assumpted back to heaven, thus proving his deity from advent to ascension. These were the standard "signs" by which a new god could be recognized, and these myths were gradually attached to the person of Jesus the son of Miryam (Mary) as his deification proceeded. . . .

The first-century followers of Jesus and the theologians and their successors can be excused to some extent for failing to perceive that he was no god come down from heaven, but rather a very great human being, ahead of his time in his intuitive understanding of his fellows and in his apparently instinctive knowledge of the technique of what we now call psychotherapy. . . .

But we already have enough data to show that the Scrolls are really "God's Gift to the Humanists," for every unrolling reveals further indications that Jesus was, as he said, "The Son of Man," rather than the deity "Son of God" his followers later claimed.[7]

After about six months of "education" I went to my old pastor with my doubts. I wanted to know if the resurrection and ascension of Jesus, his miracles and Power, and all of the doctrine of "God" had any support in evidence. He was unable to offer me a single means of faith. Instead, he tried to make a mockery of educators and psychologists. He railed about John Dewey and progressive education. And he let me go home with a prayer to God for our salvation.

From that time, I was passed into the terror of my doubts. I cannot possibly overemphasize the effect of those doubts. I was finally and terribly lifted out of the ease of my childhood. My mind sank into despair and actual terror. I had fixed my Freedom and Joy into the image of Jesus, and I had long ago given over the support of my Happiness to the church. Now that institutionalized symbol, "Jesus of Nazareth", was wrecked by the same ones who had carried it through time.

Then all was, it seemed, finally lost—for Jesus of Nazareth had even become, for me (in the trouble of my adolescence), the symbol for the lost (or, certainly, receding and fading) "Bright" of my childhood. Indeed, in that trouble, he, being but a symbol in my own mind, was a fundamental means whereby the "Bright" was concealed and withheld from me. When the "Bright" deeply receded in me, It only left tracks in the mind, and "Jesus of Nazareth" epitomized them all. Therefore, when "Jesus of Nazareth" fell to my doubts, it was the "Bright" Itself that I felt fall forever away from me. And that fall broke my heart. It drove me into my own vast empty wilderness.

My doubt grew overnight into awesome fear. I felt as if I were living under the threat of death. Life, it seemed to me, was only dying and afraid. I had not a single reason for Joy. I found no faith, no inexplicable grace. I saw only the constant drove of merely "civilized" humanity, a long history of illusions sewn up in the single foundation of a muscular mortality. There was only death, a constant ending, a rising fear, a motivated forgetfulness and escape.

I became profoundly aware of conflict and suffering everywhere. There was only struggle and disease, fear and longing, self-exploitation and emptiness, questions without answers. In every man and woman, I recognized the complex of doubt. Then I understood the root of conflict in my parents and the necessity for illusions, for exotic pleasures, for relief and distraction. I knew there was not a single man or woman who had overcome the mystery of this death. I knew this education would only be a long description of fundamental suffering, since all were convinced of the "Truth" of mortality.

From then, my schooling ceased to be a serious study. I knew that, from beginning to end, it had only one object to proclaim— and I had learned it already. From its effects in me and in all mankind, I knew this model of learning was not sufficient. I had not a single reason for Joy, except that there was a kind of tacitly motivating memory of the "Bright".

As a boy, I had never been a conscious Christian until I was perhaps five or six years old. But, previous to that age, I had already been a Conscious Form of Light that Knew no-dilemma and no-death. Now, in my early adult life, the "Bright" had seemed to disappear in the human darkness, and I had no means to Enjoy It. But I could not assert the mortal philosophy of Western Man, even if I could not counter it.

Therefore, I dedicated myself to another awesome experiment. I decided that I would begin an experimental life along the same lines which controlled the mood of Western civilization. I decided that I would unreservedly exploit every possibility for experience. I would avail myself of every possible human experience, so that nothing possible to mankind, high or low, would be unknown to me.

This decision became very clear to me one night at a party. I knew that no other possibility was open to me but that of exhaustive experience. There appeared to be no single experience or authority that was simply True. And I thought, "If God exists, God will not cease to exist by any action of my own—but, if I devote myself to all possible experience, God will (necessarily) find some way (in some particular experience or some complex of experiences, or by virtue of my openness itself) to be revealed to me." Thereafter, I devoted myself utterly and solely to every possible kind of exploit.

No experience posed a barrier to me. There were no taboos, no extremes to be prevented. There was no depth of madness and no limit of suffering that my philosophy could prevent—for, if it did, I would be liable to miss the Lesson of Reality. Thus, I extended myself even beyond my own fear. And my pleasures also became extreme, such that there was a constant machine of ecstasy. I could tolerate no mediocrity, no medium experience. I was satisfied neither with atheism nor with belief. Both seemed to me mere ideas, possible reactions to a more fundamental (if unconscious) fact. I sought Reality, to be Reality—What is, not what is asserted in the face of What is.

I read and studied every kind of literature. It would be impossible for me to count the thousands of books and influences I embraced in my years of experimenting. I began to write my reflections. My lecture notes in college were filled with long passages of my own, where I would write whatever conclusions or impulses rose in me at the time. A continuous argument of internal contemplation began to move in me, such that I was always intensely pursuing an internal logic, distracted or enlarged at times by some idea or experience in my education.

My lecture notebooks and my separate journals began to become long volumes of my own thinking. At first, they were mainly philosophical notes that developed from a kind of desperate and childish complaint into a more and more precise instrument of thought and feeling. Then I began to write poetry also, and to conceive of works of fiction that would express this dilemma and lead to some kind of solution, some opening, some kind of primary Joy.

I became a kind of mad and exaggerated young man, whose impulses were not allowable in this medium culture. My impulses were exploitable only in secret extensions of my own humanly-born conscious awareness, or in the company of whores, libertines, and misfits.

My father's younger brother, Richard, asked me what I wanted to do with my life. He could see that I lived only abandoned to adventure, and there was no apparent purpose in me. I told him that I wanted to save the world. And I was absolutely serious. That remark totally expressed all of my reasons. Some incredible Knowledge was the goal of my seeking and not any experience I could ever possess.

I went on in this fashion for more than two years, until all the violence of my seeking precipitated an experience late one night in the middle of my junior year. I had rented a small room from an old woman named Mrs. Renard. It was several blocks away from the college campus. When I was not in class, I spent most of my time in that room reading, thinking, and writing.

On this extraordinary night, I sat at my desk late into the night. I had exhausted my seeking, such that I felt there were no more books to read, no possible kinds of ordinary experience that could exceed what I had already embraced. There seemed no outstanding sources for any new excursion, no remaining and conclusive possibilities. I was drawn into the interior tension of my mind that held all of that seeking—every impulse and alternative, every motive in the form of my desiring. I contemplated it as a whole, a dramatic singleness, and it moved me into a profound shape of life-feeling, such that all the vital centers in my body and mind appeared like a long funnel of contracted planes that led on to an infinitely regressed and invisible image. I observed this deep sensation of conflict and endlessly multiplied contradictions, such that I was

Livingston Hall, where Adi Da Samraj lived during
His first semester at Columbia College

*On this extraordinary night, I
sat at my desk late into the night.
I had exhausted my seeking,
such that I felt there were no
more books to read, no possible
kinds of ordinary experience
that could exceed what I had
already embraced. There seemed
no outstanding sources for any
new excursion, no remaining
and conclusive possibilities.*

Door to the room Adi Da rented
from Mrs. Renard during
His junior year

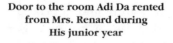

surrendered to its very shape, as if to experience it perfectly and to be it.

Then, quite suddenly, in a moment, I experienced a total revolution in my body-mind, and (altogether) in my humanly-born conscious awareness. An absolute sense of understanding opened and arose at the extreme end of all this sudden contemplation. And all of the motions of me that moved down into that depth appeared to reverse their direction at some unfathomable point. The rising impulse caused me to stand, and I felt a surge of Force draw up out of my depths and expand, Filling my entire body and every level of my humanly-born conscious awareness with wave on wave of the most Beautiful and Joyous Energy.

I felt absolutely mad, but the madness was not of a desperate kind. There was no seeking and no dilemma within it, no question— no unfulfilled motive, not a single object or presence outside myself.

I could not contain the Energy in my small room. I ran out of the building and through the streets. I thought, if I could only find someone to talk to, to communicate to about this "Thing". The Energy in my body was overwhelming, and there was an ecstasy in every cell that was almost intolerable in its Pressure, Light, and Force. But it was the middle of the night. There were no lights coming from the rooms. I could think of no one to awaken who would understand my experience. I felt that, even if I were to meet a friend, I would be unable to express myself, but my words would only be a kind of uncontrolled poetry of babbling.

My head began to ache with the intense Energy that saturated my brain. I thought, if I could only find someone with some aspirin or something to tranquilize me. But there was no one. And, at last, I wore myself out wandering in the streets, so that I returned to my room.

I sat down at my desk and wrote my mind in a long, ecstatic essay. I tried to summarize all the significance of this revolution that had occurred in my living being. Until, finally, I became exhausted in all the violence of my Joy, and I passed to sleep.

In the days that followed, I described this Event to a few friends, but no one grasped Its importance. Indeed, no one presumed It to be more than some kind of crazy excitement. I even read aloud to one friend the things I had written, but it became clear as I went on that it was only a collection of images. He only laughed at my excitement, and I thought it would be impossible for another to appreciate the magnitude of that great experience of mine.

As it happened, it took me many years to understand that revolution in my living being. As you will see, it marked the rising in me of fundamental and unqualified Life, and it, in its moment, removed every shadow of dilemma and ignorance from the mind, on every level, and all its effects in the body. But I would have to pass through many years of trial before my understanding of that Event became thoroughly established as the constant and truly effective premise of my living being (and, at last, the most perfect revelation of my Very Nature, my Ultimate Condition, and my "Bright" Purpose in the world).

Nevertheless, in the days and weeks that followed, I grasped certain basic concepts that arose in me at that time and which stood out in the mind undeniably, with a self-validating force. Two things in particular stood out as fundamentals.

I had spent years devoted to forceful seeking for some revolutionary truth, some image, object, reason, or idea, the effect of which would be absolutely liberating and salvatory. My seeking had been motivated by the loss of faith, the loss of the "Christ"-object and other such reasons for Joy. But, in that great moment of Awakening, I Knew the Truth was not a matter of seeking. There were no "reasons" for Joy and Freedom. It was not a matter of a truth, an object, a concept, a belief, a reason, a motivation, or any external fact. Indeed, it was clear that all such objects are grasped in a state that is already seeking and which has already lost the prior sense of absolutely unqualified Reality. Instead, I saw that the Truth or Reality was a matter of the absence of all contradictions, of every trace of conflict, opposition, division, or desperate motivation within. Where there is no seeking, no contradiction, there is only the unqualified Knowledge and Power that is Reality. This was the first aspect of that sudden Clarity.

In this State beyond all contradiction, I also saw that Freedom and Joy is not attained, that It is not dependent on any form, object, idea, progress, or experience. I saw that human beings (and, indeed, all beings) are, at any moment, always and already Free. I Knew that I was not lacking anything I needed yet to find, nor had I ever been without such a thing. The problem was the seeking itself, which "created" and enforced contradiction, conflict, and absence within. Then the understanding arose that I am always already Free. This was the second aspect of that fundamental Awareness.

That sudden understanding was the obviation of all striving, and this I Knew to be unqualified Truth. I had been striving for some objective "Truth", in order to replace my loss with a thereby acquired "Freedom", but this striving was itself the source of contradiction in me. Now I Knew there was no entity of Truth, and perfect Freedom was always already the case. Freedom exists as life—not when Freedom is "created" or sought, but where there is this fundamental understanding. In that moment of understanding, I had simply turned out of the context of my presumed dilemma. I was possessed of the mature cognition of the "Bright".

In the years that followed, I would find many analogies for my experience in the Spiritual literature of the East and the West. I could call that revolution in myself "enlightenment", "liberation", "Realization of the Self", or "union with God". I would pursue the sciences of that Realization in religion and Yoga, in ancient scriptures and modern therapeutic techniques. But, as you will see, I always returned to the simplicity of that understanding, free of all concepts (which, although they seek to express it in a communicative symbol, in fact serve to limit the State Itself and re-"create" the milieu of seeking).

But I was not, at that time, living in a Spiritual community. And the mind of the university, bound as it was to the subtle doctrines that enforce dilemma, served only to counter my experience—just as, when a child, I could find no community of the "Bright".

Because of the vulnerability that necessarily characterizes any kind of "Spiritual" consciousness in the traditionally non-Spiritual (or even bodily-based and worldly) culture of the West, I was unable at that time to thoroughly understand my own experience. I could not establish that Realization as the "creative" premise of my existence. I was simply not that strong. And the habits of mind and body that I had built by years of self-exploitation persisted as consoling means of pleasure, such that I remained rather sedentary and reflective. I did not overcome the gravity of mind that I had achieved as a result of my presumed dilemma and my manner of living. And I naturally adapted to a basic misinterpretation of my experience.

I retained something of the attitude of the seeker. Whereas previously I continually pursued some kind of "objective" Truth (whether internal or external), now I sought the removal of contradictions, of the parts of conflict, ignorance, or impurity, by various internal means.

I did not realize that this understanding, this Knowledge, is Itself the removal of contradictions and the instant, moment to moment purifier of the mind and life. I considered that the Truth was as I had Known It in that moment of Realization, but that I would have to find the means for working the revolutionary purification of my living being. I saw the State of Knowledge or understanding to be in some sense <u>caused</u> by the practical removal of the impurities or contradictions in the mind and life.

Thus, I began a new period of effort. Its goals were not desperate and un-Real, as before—but the simple assumption of the attitude of the seeker (and the consequent identification with the one who is not yet perfectly Free, not yet Real and True) made it impossible for me to continuously Enjoy the State of unqualified Being that had been accomplished in that moment of Realization.

The burden of these considerations made me feel that I had even lost the Truth that I had Realized. I began to pursue It again through endless writing and search. I remained addicted to my mediocre pleasures and sought through them the means of purification and release. I graduated from Columbia in the following year, in June 1961, in despair and confusion, without a clue as to where I should take myself. Reluctantly, I had become a seeker, even a very ordinary seeker, but I was not certain there were any means in all the world to restore myself to the "Bright".

Graduation day at Columbia College

CHAPTER FOUR

The Seeker

T here exist a few, rather dismal photographs of me that outwardly record the day (or the brief event) of my graduation from college. The day of college graduation is generally supposed to be a day of celebration. All your relatives are supposed to congratulate you with various gifts. You are supposed to be very relieved of the long effort of preparatory study and testing. In your revelry of accomplishment, you are to look forward ideally to productive life's work or the beginning of some professional study that will expand your maturity in useful learning, teaching, or service. But I had nowhere to go. Who in the world could teach me this "Thing" I had to learn? Where in the world was It being lived? How at all could I accomplish what I sought?

I saw that, in fact, I had attained nothing at all. I was proficient in no science or art, interested in perfecting no existing form of useful knowledge or productivity. I had been honored in nothing. I had failed to take hold of even the one breakthrough that seemed to make the difference. I had no impulse of any kind to succeed or even to make a living. I felt an overwhelming sense of failure. I had already lost very heavily in love. I had the sympathy of no one.

On that day, my parents stood alone with me. There were no well-wishers, no gifts, no congratulations. The natural and flowering signs of early summer were all around us, but no pleasure anywhere in me. I was heartsick, and gray as death. I only wanted to get away.

I spent the summer trying to make a living as a hotel waiter. But the money was bad, and the work had nothing to do with me. Finally, in August, I quit work, and a friend, named Marco, who was living in a storefront on the Bowery in New York,[8] allowed me to stay with him. Whenever he had a girlfriend for the night, I would sleep in an old chair in an alley.

Marco had some raw peyote, and we decided to take the drug, although neither of us had any idea what its effects would be. In the past months, I had used marijuana a few times and found it very enjoyable and relaxing. And so I willingly accepted a chance for some kind of very powerful "high".

We ate the cactus raw, and soon we both became very ill. For what seemed like hours we lay separately, trying to avoid vomiting, wondering if this was supposed to be the effect of the drug. After a while, Marco got up, and I could hear him laughing and moving around in the street. I got up and, feeling very dizzy, stumbled out the hallway into the street. Marco was standing on the sidewalk with a brilliantly gleeful expression on his face. At first, I was simply trying to gather strength to keep standing, and the dizziness and nausea still persisted. But, after a few breaths of air, I began to feel an incredible elation.

We both caught on to the same feeling at once. There was a serenely blissful pleasure in the body, the senses were all alive, and everything appeared to pulse visibly with an internal light. The mind had no weight at all, and its usual logic was undone, such that the only impulse was laughter and pleasure. We stood in the street laughing ourselves silly. And everything we pointed out to one another took on the same ridiculous quality we felt in ourselves. The extraordinary feeling and energy of the experience appeared to simulate (even though it did not truly duplicate) the moments of greatest ecstasy and sudden Freedom I had Known in my life.

A few minutes later, the phone rang. It was my father. He kept asking me please to come home. My mother was very worried about me, and she had fallen down the cellar stairs. He said she fell downstairs while he was away, and she must have been there for an hour or two, unconscious, her face bleeding and cut.

The more he described the entire matter to me, the more ridiculous it appeared. I hallucinated my mother's injuries as he described them. Her swollen eyes, her cut cheeks and lips, her knocked-out teeth. But the image seemed only like a clown's face, and I could not understand any of the seriousness my father ascribed to it. I could only laugh out loud.

Then he put my mother on the phone, and she was very sad and seemed to have difficulty talking. I did not tell them I was on a drug, but I was unable to "create" any feeling in myself besides this unstoppable hilarity. I only wanted to hang up so I could go and enjoy myself. I assured her I would come and see them in a day or two, and I put down the phone.

Marco and I spent the day at the Museum of Modern Art, laughing at the sculpture and painting. We watched the film *Touch of Evil,* shown at the museum that day, and constantly laughed so hard we were nearly thrown out. Then there was the orgy of food and girls until we passed out late in the night.

When I saw my parents a day or two later, they were obviously disturbed. My mother's injuries had begun to heal, but both my parents were now very concerned about what I was doing, and about what I was (altogether) going to do with my life.

I had tried to gain acceptance into a graduate school in English, so that I could study literature and perhaps begin to write seriously. All of the schools but one had refused me, basically because my background was in philosophy. Stanford University had accepted me, but I did not want to burden my parents with any more finances for my schooling. And I was so depressed by the fact that most of the better schools had refused me that I made no effort at all to make my entrance to Stanford possible.

Nevertheless, my father very kindly offered to pay my way to Stanford, if I wanted to go. At first, I refused—but, after a day or two, I thought it was probably my only possibility for any kind of positive existence. I accepted my father's offer—and, a couple of weeks later, I flew to San Francisco.

My arrival in California was the most instantly healing and supportive experience of a purely external kind that I had yet enjoyed in my life. The sunlight was so deeply radiant, the air so soft, and the hills and country all around so dramatic and beautiful that I became marvelously light and, in the most positive ordinary sense, happy.

Since that time, I have traveled many places in the world, but, for me, the areas of northern California—with the incredible mountains and forests of Yosemite, the dramatic coastline of Big Sur,

Stanford University

At Stanford University

and the beautiful city of San Francisco—remain equal to the most glorious physical environments on the earth.

I spent my year at Stanford regaining my mental and physical well-being. I found the intellectual environment and especially the formal study of English to be far less intensive and significant than my best work at Columbia. There was a kind of "country intellectual" establishment at Stanford—which, like all of life in such (even physically) consoling environments, tended never to become truly serious about the fundamental purposes of the mind.

And so I remained a kind of revolutionary, aggravated presence there, tolerable enough for one year. I passed through my courses with ease, and spent most of my time getting New York out of my system. I stretched in the sun, wrote poetry, toured the hills and the mountains, and generally regained my ordinary sense of humor.

In January of 1962, I submitted a short story to the Department of Creative Writing and was accepted as a candidate for the master's degree in English with a "concentration" in writing. Then I began to write seriously, and, for the first time in my life, had at least a limited audience.

Wallace Stegner, a novelist and authority on life in the western United States, was head of the "creative writing" program. The writers who joined the workshop were generally conservative people proficient in the traditional genre of story writing. But I was mainly interested in writing of an experimental kind, and the ideas that motivated me were visible in modern writers such as Marcel Proust, James Joyce, Gertrude Stein, Virginia Woolf, and Samuel Beckett.

Besides myself, there were only one or two people seriously interested in experimental fiction. The first few stories I wrote were nearly traditional in form and content, but gradually I began to explore some of the more plastic possibilities of language and form, such that my writing expanded into an instrument for deeply internal motives.

During the previous years, I had written in private toward a solution or expression of the internal dilemma to which I had become sensitive. I developed a "creative" mechanism that gradually unfolded a source of form, imagery, and movement that was, for me, profoundly necessary and satisfying. This approach to the problem or activity of writing was influenced not only by my own basic human characteristics and my own characteristic manner of seeking but also by my reading of modern philosophical and therapeutic thought and technique—including the work of Ludwig Wittgenstein, Sigmund Freud, and C. G. Jung, the poetry of Dylan Thomas and the "beat" writers of the fifties and early sixties, the novelists I have already mentioned, and also the works of the painters and sculptors of the late nineteenth and the twentieth centuries. I felt that the truly "creative" movements that led up to and included this time were generated in the form of a new subjective order of consciousness that needed to be tapped, experienced, and then expanded into a communicative external order.

As I continued to write, I allowed my work to become more and more freely this intention, this utterly unqualified internal rule. As I progressed, I began to encounter great resistance in the writers at the workshop. Only one or two people became interested in my work, and they gave me the only encouragement I ever received as a "creative" writer.

As we approached the final quarter of the year of study necessary for the master's degree, I felt that my writing was leading me necessarily into a "point of no return" in regard to the professionals in the writing workshop. Their resistance to my earlier work seemed to guarantee no sympathy at all for what I felt was the ultimate course of my writing.

I have never admitted any compromise to the process of my own conscious and "creative" development. After all, I was not at work for the sake of making a living or even for the entertainment of others. Rather, I was always at work on the same thing, the experimental investigation of conscious life for the sake of its unfolding, revelation, and eventual solution or Realization. Now I saw my writing as the possible and necessary instrument for removing internal contradictions, for establishing the Spiritually "Bright" Condition of Consciousness (or Conscious Light) Itself.

Consequently, in the final months of my year at Stanford, I gave up all attempts to "create" short stories in the acceptable manner of the workshop, and I began to write in earnest, for my own sake. I found that, by the end of the final quarter, I had produced no single work that could qualify for credit. I went to Mr. Stegner with a manuscript that represented my quarter of effort. It consisted of perhaps three or four hundred handwritten pages. I explained to him that the manuscript did, in fact, represent "creative" work, but that it was nothing more than work in progress.

I had developed a process, over several years, of a kind of listening. I focused on the plane of the mind and allowed it to be the focal point of experiences within and without. I thoroughly believed that the individual human being was involved in and controlled by a profound, largely unconscious or preconscious logic or structure, a motivating drama or myth. I felt that this myth, previous to becoming conscious, acted only as an arbitrary limitation, and it never appeared directly in the mind or in a person's works and actions. This "myth" was necessarily common to all human beings collectively, but it was effective on the level of the individual, and it needed to become conscious in the individual before any "creative" work or life-freedom was possible on its basis or beyond it.

I combined the internal work of listening with the activity of writing. Therefore, the plan of my work as a writer was to remain actively attentive to the movement of my life on every level, to an exhaustive degree. I proposed to become exhaustively aware, by a critical and constant act of attention to whatever experience or movement occurred on the planes of life and consciousness. Thus, I would simply perceive every form of memory or internal imagery, every form of thought or perception, every indication or pattern in my daily experience, every intention, every imposition from without—in fact, every possible kind of experience.

I hoped by these means to become directly aware of the form which governed or informed the entire quality and adventure of my existence. And this form (or myth)—the myth of my life— would (I was certain) become the source and subject for a (perhaps) fictional work, or else some other kind of literature— but, in any case, one that would be uniquely and profoundly useful to everyone.

Mr. Stegner listened cautiously to my theories. I was certain he presumed me to be quite adolescent and perhaps irrational. He and I were of dramatically different natures. He was a hard-headed practical man, and I was an intense "free spirit" (and, in his view, a self-enamored, nearly violent subjectivist). Of course, he could not allow my little manuscript to stand for credit in his department—nor could he, for himself, accept my writing program as a viable plan for "creating" fiction. But he allowed that I could carry on my work if I so desired, and he would be willing to receive the results anytime in the reliable future.

Thus, I left the Stanford campus in Palo Alto to begin the long adventure which was to make or break my "reputation"—and, perhaps, even my sanity. I was fully aware that my way of life, including the work to which I was devoted, bordered on matters that settled in the brink between life and death, sanity and madness, intelligence and irrationality. But I was certain that I had no choice in the matter. I was simply choosing to endure the course which had been pre-determined for me by all the "Bright" and human signs associated with me since my birth.

While at Stanford, I also met Nina Davis. She is unqualifiedly sane and gentle, tolerant and loving, flexible and supportive—to the degree that she, more than any other single factor in my early life, is responsible for my survival. Late in the school year, we began to live together in the hills above Palo Alto. And she—under the most awesome conditions—remained with me throughout the long adventure of my listening.

During the summer that followed my year at Stanford, I planned to leave California and stay with my parents in New York. I had also sent samples of my more traditional writing to the Bread Loaf Writers' Conference in Vermont, and, with a cautious recommendation from Wallace Stegner, I was accepted and given a fellowship for the two-week conference of professional writers and students that was to be given in August.

But when I arrived at my parents' home, I immediately felt the signs of old conflicts. I had still failed to found myself in any kind of practical and productive work, and I am sure this disturbed them. I wanted to be able to write according to my lights, and this required the solitude of a positively safe and undisturbed environment.

As a result, within a couple of weeks I called Nina, who was visiting her family in Ohio. I asked her to come to New York. After her arrival, it became clear that we could not live in the state of intimacy and freedom I required. Arguments began to build in the household. Finally, I left my parents quite violently and took an overnight train with Nina to Ohio. I abandoned all of the practical order of my life, including the Bread Loaf fellowship.

In Ohio, Nina's father reluctantly gave me just enough money to pay for a train ride to California. Nina stayed behind temporarily, for her parents' sake, and I carried all of my belongings from train to train until I reached Oakland. A friend from the Stanford writing workshop picked me up at the station and allowed me to stay temporarily with him and his wife and baby in Palo Alto.

My friend's wife took to disliking me for various reasons, and I was without money, so I needed very quickly to get some cash and find a place to live. I learned that a psychologist was looking for subjects to take hallucinogenic drugs under supervision at a nearby Veterans Administration hospital. I went and was accepted for a preliminary and a final interview, with four drug sessions in between at one week intervals, all of which would pay me fifty dollars a week for six weeks.

I called Nina and told her to return to California immediately, and I arranged to stay with her roommates at her former house in the hills above Palo Alto. Thus, we began a two-year period in which I experimented with my writing, read voluminously, exhausted myself in self-indulgent experiments, and worked on my internal processes with various drugs and therapeutic techniques.

My experimental method at the time was similar to the one by which I directed myself in college. But—whereas before I pursued experience itself, and a certain "objective" Truth (internal or external)—now, as a result of the revelation in college, I sought the removal of internal contradictions, or the removal of the "opposites", the mutual alternatives that enforce the kinds of experience, the patterns of seeking and of conflict.

During this period, I pursued every kind of means, every method of interiorization and exteriorization of awareness, that could possibly dredge up the lost content, the controlling myth, the forms of "God", "Reality", "soul", "Truth", key memory, and so on—all of the false (and presently unconscious) logic or imagery that prevented the "Bright" of simple, direct, and unqualifiedly Free Awareness. To this end, the new or ancient hallucinogenic drugs seemed profoundly useful and promising.

In the midst of my year at Stanford, I had occasion to use marijuana again. And I took a formula cough medicine called "Romilar" that had very remarkable effects if taken in large doses. At that time, the formula for Romilar contained a special (but non-narcotic) ingredient, which (I believe) was later eliminated or modified. On perhaps four or five occasions, I took Romilar in a dose of either thirty to fifty capsules or a full bottle of syrup.

I found that the dose of Romilar had no effect whatsoever in terms of a "high" if I spent my time at a party or in conversation with others. But if, after an hour or so, I went out alone and walked in a natural environment (particularly among trees), a profound State would come over me. Thus, I became deeply relaxed, mentally and physically. And I became directly and intuitively aware of a form and Presence in other living things that was duplicated in my own living form.

Trees, in particular, appeared as living beings in a much larger sense than is ordinarily supposed. They were not hallucinated as mutations of my own human life-form, but I saw that they as well as myself were entities of the same order. There was an Energy-form to which the physical form of the tree and my own physical form were only analogies and extensions. The fundamental living fact was not the external and functional apparatus. These only marked the separate and distinct purposes of trees and humans in the ordinary state of consciousness. But there was, fundamentally, a primary, common fact (or Energy-form) that was sublime, constant, and unqualified, and which bore its closest analogy to the human nervous system.

I saw that the upright tree (with its lower roots and its upper limbs, branches, and leaves) was analogous to the form of my own nervous system (with its roots deep in the brain, its spinal trunk, and its vital branches extending to every extremity). The State of my humanly-born conscious awareness at those times was infinitely Peaceful, Enjoying a profound and untouchable Pleasure and Freedom, and a Clarity that never wavered under any influence within or without. The mind itself was positively thoughtless, and the physical body enjoyed a deep, cellular calm and mutability— such that there was profound physical pleasure in placing it in almost any position.

I intuitively presumed that this State must be the same Condition described as "Nirvana" in the Buddhist texts. There was no problem, no question, no answer, but only the most unqualified and direct perception, and the dwelling as primary and unseparated Conscious Awareness. There was only the inherent, constant, and universal Presence of Reality. That State felt (or tacitly authenticated Itself as) True, even though It had been artificially induced. Its natural features (and Its characteristic of Free Conscious Awareness) generally corresponded to the Condition I, especially in my earliest childhood, readily (even without effort or means) Knew as the "Bright", and It duplicated quite exactly, although more calmly, the structure of my experience during my spontaneous college Awakening.

It was on the basis of such self-validating experiences that I openly desired to experience the effects of the "new" drugs—LSD, mescaline, and psilocybin. And so, just before Nina's return, and for several weeks thereafter, I voluntarily submitted to drug trials at the Veterans Administration hospital in Palo Alto, California.

I should add that these drug experiments did not serve a purpose in me to "create" or evolve any kind of enlightenment, or any kind of permanent transformation of my humanly-born conscious awareness. They were taken during a peculiarly experimental phase of my life, in which I was seeking to understand the mechanisms in the humanly-born conscious awareness—those which prevent and those which (later) make possible the stability of the natural conditions associated with the Free Conscious Awareness I had already Known in childhood and lately while in college. I was aware of a problem in relation to that State Which I earlier called the "Bright". There was an intervening (and learned) force (or structure) in the life-process which made the Original Condition

(Prior to all dilemma) seem to disappear, in a fragmentary and problematic state of mentality and experience. There is a long tradition, in the East and the West, of the use of certain herbs and drugs in order to effect a temporary removal of this intervening state (which limits Free Conscious Awareness). I sought to take advantage of these means in order to investigate that intervening process. It was not for the sake of the artificially induced state itself.

Of course, there is a limitation to such "wisdom". It is conceived and promoted in the problematic state itself. Its platform is, to that degree, desperate. And it could—in certain people, or under certain conditions in even the strongest individual—produce hypnotic and artificial conditions that are devastating and deluding. I would eventually suffer such conditions myself. But I was prompted by a lifelong Intention to understand and Illuminate conscious life—and I was in agreement, from the beginning, to put a halt to this level of experimentation the moment it became aggravating, deluding, or unnecessary. Therefore, it was (to my mind) a happy circumstance that, in my early experiments with drugs, I had discovered analogies to processes and states that I knew to be valid under natural conditions.

At the V.A. hospital, I was given a dose of drugs one day per week. I was left in a small hospital room alone, except for the occasional visit of the psychologist or a medical technician. At times, I was given brief physical or mental tests. Otherwise, I simply sat, rested, read, or observed the internal states as they passed. I was told that I would be given mescalin, LSD, or psilocybin at three separate sessions, and, during a fourth session, some combination of these. The precise drug or combination I was to be given at any one time would remain unknown to me. Nor was I told the exact measure of the dosage in any case—except that they appeared, from their effects, to be quite large.

During those several weeks of drug trials, I had many different drug-induced experiences, most of which were not particularly important to me. At times, I would see the room and my body become quite plastic and mobile, and their various parts would become exaggeratedly large or small in relation to one another, without any volition on my part. During one session (I think, perhaps, while I was on psilocybin), I felt only as if I were in a profound sleep—although my mind was, at some depth, continually conscious, and I was unable to achieve physical sleep (even though I greatly desired it).

There were also various bizarre experiences and periods of anxiety. Several times, I was brought to the lunchroom at the height of the drug state. I had to appear in some state of normalcy in the midst of hospital patients who were variously amputees, shell-shocked, mentally disturbed, or in various states of plastic surgery. As a result of the unnecessary shock caused by the mishandling of my condition at those times, I suffered mild anxiety attacks and occasional nervousness for perhaps a year beyond the actual tests.

However, there were at least two experiences that were significant.

During one of the sessions (I think, perhaps, while I was on LSD), I felt a profound Energy rising in me. It began at the base of my spine—and, when It appeared in the heart, It generated an intense emotion that was overwhelmingly loving and full and yet intensely sorrowful. It rose from the heart through the throat, up the back of the head, and through the internal centers of the head, and culminated in what appeared to be a massive dome in the crown of the head. At that point, I began to weep uncontrollably, as if all of the parts of my being had been aroused spontaneously— and I was born, suddenly conscious and alive. In the midst of this experience, I had a thought that was the verbal equivalent and symbol for the entire Event: "Getting to cry is shaped like a seahorse."

I had become conscious of the formal structure of the living human being, associated with (but not exclusively identical to) the nervous system, but (even more than that) what is, in Asian Indian literature (and, in turn, in Western occult literature), called the "chakra body". The Kundalini Shakti was spontaneously Aroused in me, as It had also been in times past. It was the Awakening, as from a stupor or sleep, of the latent "serpent" of Energy that is (otherwise) habitually turned outward to the various physical organs and the centers of vital experience. Thus, the Kundalini

Shakti was opened inwardly and upwardly, and the humanly-born conscious awareness was turned to its own internal form. The "seahorse" is that shape, with its various vital and etheric attachments, which moves upward from the base of the spine through the massive centers of the heart and the head. The result in me of this profound Awakening was an uncontrollable emotion, even the sorrow of conscious birth.

In later years, I chanced to see some photographs taken (inside a human womb) at various stages in the development of a human fetus. At an early stage, the developing human body is mostly unformed—and its central axis, analogous to the full spine, is curved. The heart appears visibly as its vital center. It is massive, full of blood—and it stands out from the body, as a separate orb attached to the spinal tube by a cord. The head is also quite large. Its full weight and size are generated in the crown and forehead, and the facial features (like the limbs) remain undeveloped. In the Event I have described, I was not only experiencing the most subtle and profound Energy-body, the most internal structure of all Spiritual consciousness—but I was also re-experiencing my own prenatal state, even at the early stage of physical development shown in the photographs I saw years after the Event Itself. I was re-experiencing my birth as a living being in the womb—and, therefore, the Awakening was not only profound but also quite shocking and sorrowful.

This very form, this Spirit-conducting structure (in and beyond the physical body), was the structure basic to What I, as a child, experienced and Knew as the "Bright". And it was also this chakra body that I would later investigate in detail in the practice of Kundalini Shakti Yoga in America and in India.

One other experience stands out from that period. From my early childhood, at apparently random times (usually as I either approached sleep or awoke from sleep—and, most dramatically, during seizures of childhood illness, as I would pass into delirium), I had an experience that felt like a mass of gigantic thumbs coming down from above, pressing into my throat (causing something of a gagging, and somewhat suffocating, sensation), and then pressing further (and, it seemed, would have expanded without limitation or end), into some form of myself that was much larger than my physical body. This experience of the "Thumbs" also recurred once or twice during these drug trials.

The "Thumbs" were not visible in the ordinary sense. I did not see them then or even as a child. They were not visible to me with my eyes, nor did I hallucinate them pictorially. Yet, I very consciously experienced and felt them as having a peculiar form and mobility, just as I (likewise) consciously experienced my own otherwise invisible and greater form.

Except for occasions of sudden spontaneous completeness, I did not, generally, in the developing childhood and earliest adult years, allow this intervention of the "Thumbs" to take place. I held it off from its fullest descent, in fear of being overwhelmed—for I did not understand at all what was taking place. However, as the adult years progressed, this same experience occurred naturally during meditation. Because my meditation had been allowed to progress gradually, and the realizations at each level were (thus) perceived without shock, I was able to allow the experience to take place. When I did, the "Thumbs" completely entered my living form. They appeared like tongues (or parts of a Force) coming from above. And, when they had entered deep into my body, the magnetic or energic balances of my living being reversed. On several occasions, I felt as if the body had risen above the ground somewhat—and this is, perhaps, the basis for certain evidence in mystical literature of the phenomenon of levitation (or bodily transport).

At any rate, during those stages in meditation, the body ceased to be polarized toward the ground, or in the gravitational direction of the earth's center. There was a strong reversal of polarity, communicated along a line of Force analogous to the spine. (The physical body—as well as the Energy-form that could be interiorly felt as analogous to, but detached from, the physical body—was felt to turn in a curve along the spine and forward in the direction of the heart.) When this reversal of Energy was allowed to take place completely, I resided in a totally different body, which also contained the physical body. It was spherical in shape. And the sensation of dwelling as that form was completely peaceful. The physical body was completely relaxed and polarized to the shape of this other

The hills above Palo Alto

Nina

House in the redwoods where Adi Da
lived after the experiments
at the V.A. hospital

The Veterans Administration hospital in Palo Alto

(spherical) body. The mind became quieted—and, then, there was a movement in consciousness that would go even deeper, into a higher conscious State beyond physical and mental awareness. I was to learn that this spherical body was what Yogis and occultists call the "subtle" body, which includes the "pranic" (or natural life-energy) dimension and the "astral" (or the lower mental and the higher mental) dimensions of the living being.

These remarks are already leading toward experiences that belong to a later (and mature) phase of my life. I mention these experiences here because they demonstrate a continuity in my conscious experience that links my prenatal and early childhood stages with my later life. These Events also show that there was a pattern in Reality being uncovered in me even during that period of drug experimentation (or "artificial" inducement). I regard that period no differently than any other in my years of seeking. It contained degrees of wisdom, and many indications of the same matters of living form that I perceived at other (more natural) phases in my career. It is only that, like every other form and stage of my search, its inherent limitations were eventually understood—and, at that point, I abandoned it.

However, that point of abandonment lay in my future—even three years away, at the time. After the period of drug trials at the V.A. hospital, Nina and I moved to a house in a redwood forest in the mountains above Palo Alto. After perhaps six or eight months in that area, we moved again—to a small cabin built into the hillside over the ocean at Tunitas Beach, a point nearly due west of Palo Alto.

We stayed in that cabin until some rather remarkable events brought a decision in me to leave California in search of a Spiritual teacher in New York. That move came in June 1964. During the nearly two years previous to it, following the drug trials at the V.A. hospital, I continued the exhaustive experiment of my writing.

**View from the house at Tunitas Beach,
taken by Adi Da Samraj**

CHAPTER FIVE

The Understanding on the Beach

A fter my experiences at the V.A. hospital, I went into a
period of relative seclusion to carry on my work undisturbed. Nina worked as a schoolteacher during this period
and supported our living.

My own manner of living at that time finally established a form
of practice in me that had begun in college. It was not required
that I maintain a "job" of any kind, and so I was free to work as I
pleased. As always, I found seclusion to be extremely vital, productive, and "creatively" necessary for my own kind of progress.

The pattern of my days was mostly sedentary. This was partially
dictated by a chronic weakness in my left side (particularly the left
leg), due to a mild case of polio in childhood, and by certain tiny
congenital bone malformations in my lower back. I had not been
very noticeably disabled by this limitation, but it had led me to
experience a certain tiredness and weakness in those areas if I
became very active physically. Over time, my body had developed
a counterbalance of muscular strength, and I had always been able
to enjoy strong activity in swimming and other kinds of exercise.
(And, in later years, I would also learn how to manipulate and
refresh the bone structure of the body, its muscular system, and
the nervous system by using certain techniques of Hatha Yoga.)

Thus, I spent my days in retirement. While Nina was away at
work, I would spend the day writing. My method of writing was
not one of any kind of intentional production. The writing of this
present book, for instance, is a very intentional process. It involves
a deliberate plan of productivity, the gathering of various notes
and sources, chronological recollection, and so on. I write very
deliberately and almost continually for eight hours or more each
day. However, in those days, my method of writing was deliberately

"unproductive". My intention was not to write a particular narrative I had preconceived. Rather, I deliberately and very intensively focused in the mind itself. And, as a result of several years of experiment in this direction, I remained focused there without effort—almost continuously, regardless of my peculiar external involvement.

This could perhaps be understood as a kind of "Yoga" of my own "creation", and it has analogies in the history of Spiritual experience. But I had no separate goal in doing this. There was no other point I hoped to arrive at as a result of this concentration. I wanted to reside in the plane of consciousness at its deepest level—where all experiences, internal as well as external, were monitored. I wanted simply to become aware of what passed there.

Ordinarily, people do not remain aware on the deepest level of the mind. They are concentrated either in its extensions, at the level of sense awareness, or in the processes of concrete thought. Occasionally, a person slips into a deeper level, similar to the level to which one passes in dreams—and there he or she experiences the daydreams, the subliminal memories, emotions, and motivations, that underlie his or her functioning life. It was my intention to remain continuously aware at this deepest focal point of the mind. That was also a point at which I often concentrated in the "Bright". It is a point deep within the head, but it monitors all the levels of functional consciousness—the physical body and the experiences of the sense organs, the vital centers in the lower body, the great center of being and Energy in the heart, the peculiar order of subliminal imagery that moves out of the "creative" center analogous to the throat, and all of the passing perceptions (the images, ideas, sensations, forms, memories, and superconscious communications) that are generated in the parts of the head.

In those days, I spent all of my time concentrated in this observing function. I carried a clipboard with me wherever I went. And I would write whatever perceptions were generated in my humanly-born conscious awareness. I attempted to make this writing exhaustive, so that not a single thought, image, or experience would pass unrecognized. The act of writing seemed necessary to the act of becoming conscious itself. What I did not write seemed to pass away again into unconsciousness, perhaps to remain trapped there and provide matter for the hidden, unconscious form that bounded my humanly-born conscious awareness and prevented the "Bright".

Whenever I was too busily occupied to write, I would invent a catch phrase or some other mnemonic device in order to hold the concept or perception until I could write it fully. I became so occupied in this process that Nina would have to do anything that required practical attention. She would drive the car, communicate with friends, and perform all of the usual chores within and without the household. My writing became a continuous, fascinating, and absorbing occupation. And I began to fall naturally into a thread of consciousness and life that was profound, hidden, unfolding, inevitable, and sublime.

I would write at any and all times—even in the evenings when Nina was at home, at the movies, at parties, or during walks on the beach. I would often write late into the night, or I would awaken many times from sleep to record dreams and ideas. The same process went on during sleep, such that I remained conscious even during dreams or deep dreamless sleep.

I continued to exploit the possibilities for experience during that time, and I saw no benefits in retarding any impulses. I feared that suppression would only prevent certain necessary images or motives from releasing their living energy and significance to consciousness. I would often exploit the possibilities of sex, or become deeply drunk on wine, engage in orgies of eating, or smoke marijuana for long hours.

I became intensely sensitized to every movement in my humanly-born conscious awareness. I perceived every event in the world as well, with an almost painful absorption. Every creature or environment I perceived became a matter of profound attention. I would write page after page of exhaustive observation on every step of a walk on the beach, or the daylong process and change of the ocean. There was page after page describing the objects and marks in the sand as I walked, detailed descriptions of rooms, mental environments, and so on. And I gradually came to Enjoy a State similar to that in which I had found myself at the point of Awakening in college.

top: Adi Da Samraj during the period
of writing at the beach

left and right: the house at Tunitas Beach

Eventually, I came to the point of exhausting that exercise. The simultaneity, coincidence, and oneness of "inside" and "outside" became utterly obvious to me. My living awareness was uniquely and extremely intense, and inclusive of everything (both inside and outside the body-mind), such that I felt there was no remaining power of distraction in anything. As a result, I was utterly focused on the yet hidden depth of my humanly-born conscious awareness.

As I approached that point of inclusive awareness, focused in depth, the form of my writing also began to bear fruit. My concentration, as I said, was not purposive. It was not in order to "create" something intentionally on the basis of what was preconceived in the mind. But I was always looking and listening for that very and most fundamental structure in my humanly-born conscious awareness which is prior to ordinary experience. I was waiting for the revelation of the hidden content of the mind. Not some sort of "primitive event", no memory in the Freudian style or some symbolic perception which informs the content of Jungian types of introspection. These came and went. But I was attentive to the underlying structure of my humanly-born conscious awareness— to the seed-logic, or myth, that prevented the "Bright".

As I approached that form of Knowledge—which I was certain, from previous suggestions in my deepest experience, had to be there—I would often pass through profound recollections and imagery. There were the emotional and scatological memories of childhood, and the moments of conflict in life that underlay persistent anxieties, preferences, and chronic patterns. There were also times when I saw and learned the workings of psychic planes and subtler worlds. I remember once, for a period of days, I perceived a world that appeared to survive in our moon. It was a super-physical (or astral) world, where beings were sent off to birth on the earth (or in other worlds)—and then their bodies were enjoyed cannibalistically by the older generation on the moon, or they were forced to work as physical and mental slaves.

I became very interested in the writings of C. G. Jung, and I sometimes experienced symbolic dreams typical of the level of consciousness he investigated. One of these coincided with a dramatic awakening that I will describe presently.

But my attention could not settle in any particular impression or event. I was always driven more deeply into the underlying structure, and so I always remained focused in the mind itself, regardless of what passed.

Eventually, I began to recognize a structure in my humanly-born conscious awareness. It became more and more apparent, and its nature and effects revealed themselves as fundamental, inclusive of all the states and contents in life and mind. My own "myth"—the governor of all patterns, the source of presumed self-identity, the motivator of all seeking—began to stand out in the mind as a living being.

This "myth", this controlling logic (or force) that structured and limited my humanly-born conscious awareness, revealed itself as the self-concept—and the actual life—of Narcissus. I saw that my entire adventure—the desperate cycle of Awakeness and its decrease, of truly Conscious Being and Its gradual covering in the mechanics of living, seeking, dying, and suffering—was produced out of the image (or mentality) that appears hidden in the ancient myth of Narcissus.

The more I contemplated him, the more profoundly I understood him. I observed, in awe, the primitive control that this self-concept and logic exercised over all of my behavior and experience. I began to see that same logic operative in all other human beings, and in every living thing—even in the very life of the cells, and in the natural energies that surround every living entity or process. It was the logic (or process) of separation itself, of enclosure and immunity. It manifested as fear and identity, memory and experience. It informed every function of the living being, every experience, every act, every event. It "created" every "mystery". It was the structure of every imbecile link in the history of human suffering.

He is the ancient one visible in the Greek myth, who was the universally adored child of the gods, who rejected the loved-one and every form of love and relationship, and who was finally condemned to the contemplation of his own image—until, as a result of his own act and obstinacy, he suffered the fate of eternal separateness and died in infinite solitude. As I became more and more conscious of this guiding myth (or logic) in the very roots of my being, my writing began to take on an apparently intentional form. What was before only an arbitrary string of memories, images, and perceptions, leading toward an underlying logic, now proceeded from the heart of that logic itself—such that my perceptions and my thoughts began to develop (from hour to hour) as a narrative, completely beyond any intention or plan of my external mind.

I found that, when I merely observed the content of my experience or my mind from hour to hour, day to day, I began to recognize a "story" being performed as my own conscious life. This was a remarkable observation, and obviously not a common one. The quality of the entire unfolding has the touch of madness in it. But people are mad. The ordinary state of human existence—although it is usually kept intact and relatively calmed by the politics of society—is founded in the madness of a prior logic, a schism in Reality that promotes the entire suffering adventure of human lives in endless and cosmic obstacles. I have known since I was a boy that this round of conflict, of contradiction and unconsciousness, was neither natural nor ultimately Real. And the total and guiding Purpose of my life has been—even by (and in the midst of) fully embracing the states and circumstances of conditionally manifested existence—to most perfectly Realize (and then to Communicate to all others) that Reality, that given Form, the Spiritually "Bright" Condition of Consciousness Itself—Which is not properly the illusive goal of life, but Which is the Very and Conscious Foundation of life.

Thus, in order to learn this "Thing", I had to endure the progress of my own "madness". I had to observe the madman himself and undermine him with my Knowledge. This "madness", however, is not merely unfortunate, irrational, and disruptive. It is required of all those who would pass into Real Existence, beyond fear and egoic ignorance. And, in the process, one experiences remarkable revelations, and eventually discovers (and realizes) the synergy of the mind and every movement of Energy in the world.

It was this synergy (or synchronicity), this conscious coincidence of the internal and external world, that I discovered (and realized) at that time. After the pattern I recognized as Narcissus began to show its flower in the mind and I became settled in observing its "creative" position in the entirety of my life, the internal and external events in my experience began to demonstrate a common source or, rather, a coincident pattern. My own thoughts or images, then, began to arise in a similar pattern to my external experiences. A narrative was being constructed as my very life, which was itself a mythic form. The people, the passing events, the dramatization of my own motives, and all the imagery and categories of my thought appeared to be generating a conceived pattern. And I knew that my own life was moving toward the very death of Narcissus.

I began to write the outstanding narrative (or myth) that was appearing hour by hour. And I proposed to write a novel, tentatively entitled *The White Narcissus*, which would be this very complex of my life and mind as it was and had been revealing itself in my writing over several years. I intended to follow this production in myself until I should see it worked out whole. And then I would go back through the entire manuscript, whose proportions were already enormous, and make out of it a novel that included all of the "creative" motivations and intentions I had generated as a writer.

I was not utterly afraid even of the death of Narcissus, which was now my own death. I knew that no matter how terrible the event in terms of physical and mental and emotional suffering, it was not, in fact, the death of anything identical to my own Real Being. Even my own physical death appeared to me as a kind of mythic event. Its apparent consequences would perhaps be the end of my earthly life, but I was certain that I would have to pass through it in order to transcend the form of Narcissus. I knew then that all human suffering and all human deaths are endured only in the concepts, functions, and mentality that are guided by the unconscious logic of Narcissus. And so I devoted myself freely to the self-meditation of Narcissus in order to die his death as quickly as possible.

As it happened, that "death" did occur very dramatically three years later. But necessary transformations in my state of life had to occur before it would be possible. This point in my narrative brings us to the spring of 1964.

I have observed that a certain kind of dramatic transformation in the state of my humanly-born conscious awareness has occurred annually, at approximately the same time each year. The spring-time of every year is a time of awakening in nature, just as the autumnal period is a natural transition into latency. Peculiar events of a transformative kind have always naturally occurred to me in the springtime of the year—just as, also, the transitional period of autumn (moving into winter) has usually, for me, been a time of interiorization, often of a difficult kind. The cycle of my own early-life experience followed this pattern exactly. Thus, the event I am about to describe was one such "springtime awakening".

One morning, in early May 1964, I awoke with the clear mem-ory of a significant dream. As I indicated earlier, a dream of the type often analyzed by Jung preceded a dramatic awakening in myself. I had dreamed that I was being born. At first, I saw it from outside my own body. I was watching my mother from a position near the doctor's viewpoint, between her legs. I could not see her face, and so I am not certain it was my natural mother in the dream. Her body was very large, fecund and swollen. The baby appeared head first, and its face was red, ugly, wet, and bunched up like a fist. Then I took the position of the baby itself, and one of the doctors said: "It's one of those multiple babies!"

Then I became aware of what must have been a later period in the life of that entity. The point of view was from my own body. I assumed it was the mature body of the baby I had seen being born. There were cords of phlegm that rose up out of my insides through my throat and out into the room. I was uncomfortable with this gag in my throat, but I was calm, as if I had lived that way for some time. The mass of phlegm separated out into two paths in the room, and each was attached to a young man. I assumed from their appearance that the three of us were in our late teens. And I also assumed that the birth of the "multiple" baby was the birth of the three of us. The first baby, whose face was like a fist, and whose body I now inhabited, was the source or control-ling entity. The other two were dual aspects of my living being.

The one boy was very bright, energetic, attractive, and youthful. The other was "dark". His life-energy was heavier, and he had less mobility, physical and mental. I noticed the cords of phlegm at my feet as I moved forward and carelessly stepped on them. The act of stepping on the cords was both voluntary and involuntary, such that I felt both aggressive and guilty (or trapped). I thought perhaps the boys would die if I stepped on the cords and broke them, but I also desired to be free of the gag in my throat and the immobility our attachment required of me. But when the cords were crushed and broken under my right foot, the boys came running up to me and embraced me happily. We all appeared now bright and free. And they thanked me for cutting the cords, which they said they had long hoped I would do.[9]

An ordinary external observer of this dream could certify one of several interpretations, depending upon the partial viewpoint by which he or she understands the matters of consciousness. Perhaps all the basic interpretations would bear some of the true import of this dream. But I required no interpreter. The very having of the dream marked a transformation in me. I had operated for several years in the aggravated model of my conscious being, and this dream marked the end of a long period of difficult progress. Those years had been filled with awesome fear and doubt, as well as great intensity and (for me) worthwhile endeavor. Now a feeling of wholeness and well-being rose in the center of me, and I felt a peculiar relief in the wake of this dream. This change in me apparently set the stage for a remarkable discovery.

A few days later, I arose in the early morning feeling very energetic. I sat at my desk to read while Nina slept. I turned to a volume of essays by C. G. Jung which I had often examined before. In particular, I turned to some chapters from *The Interpretation of Nature and the Psyche*. When I came to the concluding chapter, I read something which, though I must have seen it before, never communicated to me as it was about to do.

I think it would be valuable to quote the entire passage as I read it at that time:

> It may be worth our while to examine more closely, from this point of view, certain experiences which seem to indicate the existence of psychic processes in what are

commonly held to be unconscious states. Here I am thinking chiefly of the remarkable observations made during
deep syncopes resulting from acute brain injuries. Contrary
to all expectations, a severe head injury is not always followed by a corresponding loss of consciousness. To the
observer, the wounded man seems apathetic, "in a trance,"
and not conscious of anything. Subjectively, however, consciousness is by no means extinguished. Sensory communication with the outside world is in a large measure
restricted, but is not always completely cut off, although
the noise of battle, for instance, may suddenly give way to
a "solemn" silence. In this state there is sometimes a very
distinct and impressive feeling or hallucination of levitation, the wounded man seeming to rise into the air in the
same position he was in at the moment he was wounded.
If he was wounded standing up, he rises in a standing
position, if lying down, he rises in a lying position, if
sitting, he rises in a sitting position. Occasionally his surroundings seem to rise with him—for instance the whole
bunker in which he finds himself at the moment. The
height of the levitation may be anything from eighteen
inches to several yards. All feeling of weight is lost. In a
few cases the wounded think they are making swimming
movements with their arms. If there is any perception of
their surroundings at all, it seems to be mostly imaginary,
i.e., composed of memory images. During levitation the mood
is predominantly euphoric. "'Buoyant, solemn, heavenly,
serene, relaxed, blissful, expectant, exciting' are the words
used to describe it. . . . There are various kinds of 'ascension
experiences.'"[10] Jantz and Beringer rightly point out that the
wounded can be roused from their syncope by remarkably
small stimuli, for instance if they are addressed by name
or touched, whereas the most terrific bombardment has
no effect.

Much the same thing can be observed in deep comas
resulting from other causes. I would like to give an example
from my own medical experience: A woman patient,

whose reliability and truthfulness I have no reason to doubt, told me that her first birth was very difficult. After thirty hours of fruitless labor the doctor considered that a forceps delivery was indicated. This was carried out under light narcosis. She was badly torn and suffered great loss of blood. When the doctor, her mother, and her husband had gone, and everything was cleared up, the nurse wanted to eat, and the patient saw her turn round at the door and ask, "Do you want anything before I go to supper?" She tried to answer, but couldn't. She had the feeling that she was sinking through the bed into a bottomless void. She saw the nurse hurry to the bedside and seize her hand in order to take her pulse. From the way she moved her fingers to and fro the patient thought it must be almost impercep- tible. Yet she herself felt quite all right, and was slightly amused at the nurse's alarm. She was not in the least fright- ened. That was the last she could remember for a long time. The next thing she was aware of was that, without feeling her body and its position, she was <u>looking</u> <u>down</u> from a point in the ceiling and could see everything going on in the room below her: she saw herself lying in the bed, deadly pale, with closed eyes. Beside her stood the nurse. The doctor paced up and down the room excitedly, and it seemed to her that he had lost his head and didn't know what to do. Her relatives crowded to the door. Her mother and her husband came in and looked at her with fright- ened faces. She told herself it was too stupid of them to think she was going to die, for she would certainly come round again. All this time she knew that behind her was a glorious, park-like landscape shining in the brightest colors, and in particular an emerald green meadow with short grass, which sloped gently upwards beyond a wrought- iron gate leading into the park. It was spring, and little gay flowers such as she had never seen before were scattered about in the grass. The whole demesne sparkled in the sunlight, and all the colors were of an indescribable splen- dor. The sloping meadow was flanked on both sides by dark green trees. It gave her the impression of a clearing in the forest, never yet trodden by the foot of man. "I knew that this was the entrance to another world, and that if I turned round to gaze at the picture directly, I should feel tempted to go in at the gate, and thus step out of life." She did not actually <u>see</u> this landscape, as her back was turned to it, but she <u>knew</u> it was there. She felt there was nothing to stop her from entering in through the gate. She only knew that she would turn back to her body and would not die. That was why she found the agitation of the doctor and the distress of her relatives stupid and out of place.

The next thing that happened was that she awoke from her coma and saw the nurse bending over her in bed. She was told that she had been unconscious for about half an hour. The next day, some fifteen hours later, when she felt a little stronger, she made a remark to the nurse about the incompetent and "hysterical" behavior of the doctor during her coma. The nurse energetically denied this criticism in the belief that the patient had been completely unconscious at the time and could therefore have known nothing of the scene. Only when she described in full detail what had happened during the coma was the nurse obliged to admit that the patient had perceived the events exactly as they happened in reality.[11]

I have no idea how long I spent reading and rereading this passage and the surrounding material from Jung's essay. But when Nina awoke to prepare to go to work, I was a changed man. I cannot overestimate the importance that data held for me at the time. It was as if the entire mass of heart-depressive ideas and assumptions (in works like *The Lost Years of Jesus Revealed*) that I began to adopt years before had been lifted away in a single moment. I had long regarded Jung to be an important investigator into the true significances of human experience. I felt limitations in his method and some of his assumptions, and these would become even clearer to me later on, but I had learned that he could be trusted to observe data and report it without distortions and interpretations.

When he interprets, it is usually apart from the language and material that he reports.

Therefore, when I read this report of phenomena that transcend the boundaries of the ordinary model of "Man" typically presumed by Western culture, I was positively overwhelmed. I felt this was a key to an enormous range of experience, now capable of honest and direct investigation, which would vindicate, parallel, and extend the experiences that had long been the burden of my life.

When Nina awoke, I flooded her with my excitement. It was one of the humanly happiest hours in my life to then. An extreme pressure and source of conflict within me had been drawn away. I felt that I could begin the practical investigation of the miraculous and Spiritual phenomena that, up to now, had seemed impossible. And—because they had seemed impossible, because they had been carried away with all the imagery of the lost "Christ"—I had been required to endure long years searching for an alternative solution. I was forced to pursue a description of the essential Nature and Freedom of the human being that does not assume more than the model of mortality that had been propagated in my university education. All in all, this passage in Jung signified in me a liberation from mortal philosophy and all bondage to the form of death.

In the weeks that followed, I took to ravenously reading whatever material I could find that dealt with occult phenomena, miracles, religious and Spiritual philosophy, and all matters relating to the process of liberation. I was particularly impressed by the documented evidence for out-of-body experiences and the better sources on spiritualism. The miracle that occurred at Fatima early in the twentieth century seemed to me a remarkable and important event. As many as ten thousand of its witnesses (many of whom were non-believing reporters or passersby) signed affidavits that they saw the sun wheel around in many colors and fall toward the earth. I was also profoundly impressed by the life and work of Edgar Cayce.

I became acquainted with the I-Ching, in the edition translated by Richard Wilhelm and introduced by C. G. Jung.[12] I used it several times over a period of a month or more and saw the laws of synchronicity described by Jung demonstrated interestingly in myself and in those around me.

The people I began to meet during that time also seemed to be coming at an appropriate stage in my life. And they came on a gradient suited to my own learning. At first, I met people who were mainly spiritualistic and religious enthusiasts. Then I met others who led me to read intelligent material that supported a philosophic and Spiritual view. All of this was founded in evidence of the kind I was beginning to recognize rather than in the mortal philosophy of the establishment.

Finally, I met a man named Harold Freeman at a party in Palo Alto. He was an occultist and the first man I had ever met who claimed to have experiences of this unusual kind. He indicated that such experiences could be attained, consciously and intentionally, by a kind of scientific method.

He told me stories of how he met his teacher, a woman who had allegedly maintained a physical body for over six hundred years. She had demonstrated (and taught him) many unusual abilities. He led me to the source-books of occultism. I read the works of H. P. Blavatsky, Alice Bailey, and a remarkable (even though, I felt, basically fictional) set of volumes by Baird Spalding called *The Life and Teaching of the Masters of the Far East*.[13]

I was unable at that time to completely separate fiction and exaggeration from fact in the occult material. It seemed even less reliable than religious literature. It appeared to take masses of religious and Spiritual lore, which were the products of many centuries of traditional culture, and pass them through the emotional mind of a single, mediumistic intelligence. This gave it the force of a firsthand account, whereas it was actually a body of tradition in the secondary form of an oral literature. It also tended to deal with "phenomena" rather than matters of fundamental importance. Thus, I became very wary of literary influences, and I desired a direct, personal experience of anything pertaining to Spiritual Reality. But at least it was all an emotional symbol that did much to enlarge my ordinary humor and extend my growing impulses to Real experience.

At one point, I asked Mr. Freeman if he was to teach me. I told him I was now in search of a teacher for help in my own developmental course. A couple of days later, he told me that he had contacted his teacher and was told that someone else was supposed to teach me.

I felt that he was mostly a genuine man. He made no effort to capitalize on my vulnerability. And his reply seemed altogether right to me, for I had begun to recognize a new psychic awakening in myself. In the occasional flickering of certain images in my mind, I had begun to recognize a communication about my future.

In the weeks that led up to my meeting with Mr. Freeman, I had grown more accustomed to operating in the manner that my own work had precipitated. The recognition of the coincidence between consciousness and external experience began to develop into a comfortable ability, such that I began to make use of the images that passed (in a seemingly arbitrary succession) through the mind. I saw that many of these images were signs of precognition.

One image became a constant factor. I saw that I was to find a teacher who would be able to help me. I did not see the teacher himself—but, in spontaneous visionary flashes, I saw pictures of a store where oriental sculpture and other oriental works of art were sold. It became spontaneously evident to me that this store was in New York City.

I told Nina about this experience, and we began immediately to prepare to leave for New York. We gradually sold or gave away most of our belongings, including my library of about 1400 volumes. I kept only a few books that seemed important to my new line of study. These events led on toward the middle or end of June 1964.

Photograph of Robert the cat
taken by Adi Da Samraj

The Passage to the Guru

One morning, shortly before Nina and I left for New York, I awoke to a very brilliant clear day. I went outside and stood in front of the house to enjoy the morning freshness. The house was built on the ledge of a cliff, and the wall of the cliff dropped off steeply about twenty feet in front of the house, exposing a sheer drop of about one hundred feet to the beach. The beach itself was very wide, perhaps two hundred feet wide, and the ocean stretched in a huge expanse as far and wide as I could see.

The house and the beach were in a very isolated area, with only a few people in other cabins—and they were generally away at work during the day. On this day, no one else was around, and so I was alone.

I stood on the cliff, the morning was clear and shining, and the air was that kind that makes one go "Ah!" inside with relief and Joy, and make a big breath of ease, like on vacation. And, suddenly, in barely a moment or two, a storm moved over me from the ocean like a huge shroud, like a great canopy or blanket. It had the feeling of an immense shell, rising above me, and touching the earth and sea only at all the horizon points. The weather below, where I was standing, was not a dense mass. The air around and above me remained clear. The storm was only in the high sky. The high, moving mass of dark sky rose above me and beyond, and stood everywhere above, appearing like a gigantic dome, enclosing the space where I stood. The storm looked like a huge gray dome, full of gray shapes of clouds, a perfect half-sphere. It was not homogeneous, but it was boiling with great masses of differing and combining clouds. And I could still see clearly in this dark dome—all the way to the horizon of the sea, and all around me in the suddenly shaded and sunless air.

107

Then, with shattering quickness, like an aerial display of royal fireworks, lightning began to move everywhere through the dome—such that now it felt like the crown of my own head, and it looked like a Great Sahasrar, with what appeared to be millions of bolts of lightning shooting everywhere, in all directions in the sky, and, like gods, flying anywhere in a moment, hundreds of miles at will.

How can I describe what kind of storm it was? It was a Divine storm, a revelation of Truth, a transformative Blessing, a Spiritual Initiation! It was the most magnificent thing I had ever seen. It was a tangible Divine Vision. It was the "Bright", outside me. How many were the countless bolts of lightning? The lights in that great vast dome were like the millions and millions of lightnings of the little nerve filaments in the center of the brain, the Corona Radiata. The storm was all lights, and waters. It was the most shocking, torrential drenching of the earth I had ever seen. And it was enormously, blowing loud! The thunder was so loud it shook the sea and quaked the ground, everywhere, and deep to the core—rolling and churning, even under my feet, and all over my body, as if to crack the atoms of all that seemed and end the infinitely fragile world. And the water flew from everywhere—Washing me, Waking me, Shouting me, "Brightening" me to my Life to come.

The storm impressed me as if it were not only the physically most powerful storm that ever happened on earth, but the very First and the very Last storm that could ever happen on earth. And it was also a storm of Spiritual Power—for, all the while I stood in it, within my body there was a "Bright" Storm of Spiritual Energy. My entire body was rolling and churning with feelings, like electric shocks.

I do not know how long I stood there, in the titanic Force of everything, but the storm itself must have lasted for an hour or two. Then, as suddenly as it had come, it disintegrated and disappeared in the resurrected morning sun. And, in the moment of its passing, I Knew it was time for me to leave California and go on to what it had now become certain was to be the "Bright" Divine Fulfillment of the Purpose of my human birth.

Quickly thereafter, Nina and I left California, at the near-end of June 1964. My mood was one of intense excitement and expectation.

There was no doubt at all in me that I was about to begin the ultimate adventure of my life. I was willing to make any sacrifice and to go anywhere in the world in order to abandon myself to the Sources of the Divine Good.

The trip itself was a comedy of frustrations. We traveled in an old Chevrolet station wagon that seemed to explode on schedule every hundred miles. It was loaded to the windows with the belongings we felt necessary for life in New York. There were boxes of books, blankets and sleeping bags, various clothing, pots and pans. And three necessary cats.

Even in all the years before this time, I had not been entirely without teachers. I had learned from many people and environments. Now I was seeking a teacher who could lead me into an entirely new order of Experience and Knowledge. I was in pursuit of the Guru—a Realizer of Real God, and Truth, and Reality. But I had also known a Guru of a certain kind for nearly two years. I had even lived with him. He was my cat, Robert.

If one is truly sensitive to the movements everywhere within and without oneself, every kind of object or creature or experience becomes an instructional (or teaching) communication. One cannot help but receive the teaching, under any circumstances, if one is a real listener. Indeed, even the most inert objects Know the same Bliss of unqualified Existence that is the Root of the conscious awareness of human beings.

My own way of life had been an absolute devotion to this practice of listening, such that I had never before required a Guru to teach me in the formal and traditional manner. Indeed, I did not even know what a "Guru" was until these last days. And, in the past, if I had heard of such persons or matters, I would have considered them to be impossible, like the "Jesus" of my childhood.

My experience throughout my life had, thus far, progressed spontaneously and profoundly, always generating new forms of Clarity and Awakening. As a result, I was fully capable of finding a "teacher" in the most oddball and the most ordinary of sources, and I could give myself to be taught by such sources just as consciously and even formally as any sworn practitioner in a monastery founded in the traditional scriptures and rules.

For nearly two years, then, I had been very attentive to my tomcat, Robert. At the end of my year at Stanford, I went to say goodbye to two old friends, Cynthia and Vito, with whom I had shared many hours of drug adventure and conversations about art and literature. Their cat had just given up a litter of kittens, and they were making the usual attempt to pawn them off on their friends.

I told them I was going back to New York for the summer and did not really know when I would be able to provide a home for a cat. But when I looked at the litter of kittens, I saw a little one with huge eyes, a dark one with long hair that sat in deep calm and watched me. I fell in love with him immediately, and Nina and I pleaded with our friends to keep him for us.

The long summer passed as I have told you. And by the time we found our house in the redwood forest the following September, we had entirely forgotten that we owned a cat. But one day Cynthia and Vito arrived with Robert. We were absolutely happy to have him, and so grateful and surprised that our friends had kept him for us all that time. I named him "Robert" purely in fun. He was such a strong animal presence, with an economy and grace that made the idiot brand of human living seem so unconscious and confused. I gave him an ordinary human name just to remind myself of the difference in him.

Robert was quite a large cat now. He had matured beautifully, and all of his instincts were wild. He seemed perfectly placed in himself. We decided that he should have a lady cat for his consort, and so we were happy when some other friends in Big Sur offered the pick of their new litter.

The Big Sur litter contained only a pair of orange tiger cats, both females, with twin markings. We took them both. And we brought them home to Robert so that he could enjoy his ladies in the wild.

Robert and his ladies always lived completely independent of us. We left food for them, but they came and went at will. Their manner of living was so pure and intelligent, so direct an enjoyment, with such effortless capability for survival, that Nina and I soon became enamored of them. We watched them constantly in the sheer pleasure of seeing life lived as an instinctive perfection.

Their solutions to the hour by hour confrontations that humanity tends to bypass or escape were an example to us of unproblematic existence.

When we left our home in the redwoods and moved on to the beach at Tunitas, our cats were just drawing into their maturity. We were wondering if Robert would choose only one of the lady cats for his consort, and if this would cause problems with the remaining one. But we were not surprised when both of the lady cats began to swell up in obvious pregnancy.

At the time, this seemed to me a perfectly moral solution to Robert's domestic situation. He loved and tended them both completely and without conflict, such that he appeared to me a master of domestic peace—even a model of sanity and strength to human householders, who always seem unable to solve the problems caused by their traditional and conceptual monogamy.

One evening, I heard Robert and the lady cats hissing and growling in the yard. I went out and found the three of them surrounding a fourth. It was a young gray male who had somehow wandered into Robert's territory. The three cats stood almost motionless in a circle about the fourth, and their primitive signals continued for what must have been several hours, even while Nina and I passed to sleep.

In the morning, all was quiet. Robert and the ladies were lying in various parts of the house asleep. I went outside to enjoy the morning sea, and I came upon the place where they had surrounded the stranger the evening before. I made an awesome discovery. In the center of the circle where they had stood, there was a perimeter of gray hairs, and in the center were stains of blood and fragments of the inner parts of the dead animal. The cats had apparently cannibalized the intruder.

I showed the place to Nina, and we were really astonished. But our cats came out gentle in the morning, showing no signs of the sacrifice in signals of guilt or anger or lust. They felt to us to be an ancient triangle of righteousness. And their justice confounded all our reasons, such that we could only admire them as beings who seemed to enjoy the free consciousness of higher laws that all humanity had long ago forgotten.

But something had occurred in the mutual life of our cats that they were about to solve according to their peculiar laws. The ladies were fully pregnant now, and they had begun to keep a distance from one another. That evening, Robert remained in the house with only one of the ladies. The other had disappeared.

For several days, we looked everywhere for the second lady cat. But, finally, we decided that she must have wandered away or been killed somewhere on the highway above. We even supposed that Robert may have chosen the one and banished the other to her own survival. We had no idea that he had only found a way to establish his domain in two entirely separate realms.

For a full year, Robert remained with his single consort. Her kittens were born and grown. Robert would leave at sunrise and pass over into the hills, but every evening at sunset I would hear him calling as he descended the rise behind the house. He would return to eat and sleep with us and his lady until the following morning.

We assumed that this was merely the pattern of his wildness, and that he must have spent his days wandering and hunting. His consort always remained behind in the area of the house, and he would often bring her a bird, a rabbit, or a mouse to eat. Or she would capture some small animal just at sunset and offer it to him when he returned home.

After a year of this, we had settled fully into the cycle of the lives of our cats and never expected to see the other lady cat again. But, one day, I noticed something a little strange about the lady who remained at home. Her hair was furled and matted in an unusual manner. At first, I only generally noticed this, and I simply accepted it as being the result of her climbing about in the woods. But, the next day, I examined her more closely—for she had also acquired some kind of new intensity. Her paws stretched open, and she constantly touched my feet, insisting on my attention.

When I picked her up, I saw that it could not be Robert's domestic bride. Her hair was wild and full, and its ends were bleached by weather. Her exposed nose and the pads of her feet were also bleached by water and air and sunlight, and they were all freckled by spots that I knew did not belong to the lady who remained behind. And even the edges of her eyelids were pink and white. Her eyes were wild as only those could be that had lived and survived in wilderness.

It was obviously the long-lost lady cat. When Nina came home, we looked her over together. And we welcomed Robert in the evening. He preened her and loved her, and we began to understand the intelligence of his way of life. When the two ladies had first become pregnant, Robert must have led one into the wild. And afterwards he divided his time between them, tending one in the wilderness by day and returning to the other at night. Again we marveled at this justice, this untroubled, thoughtful, and inexplicably kind order of their survival.

When we awoke the next morning, Robert and his wild lady had come bearing gifts. Sitting in the top of a storage basket surrounded by soft cloths were four wide-eyed baby cats—two dark and two orange, like wild flowers, with long soft hair. They were four of the most beautiful and fresh creatures I have ever seen. Nina and I laughed joyfully at them. Robert and his lady had also produced miracles in the alchemy of wilderness.

As the days passed, we also saw what must have been a further development of Robert's plan of living. The lady cat who had remained domestic the previous year disappeared, as her sister had done. I think it was their plan to exchange their states of living and carry on the same pattern as before. But we found the lady dead near the highway. She had been struck by a car while moving off into the wild.

It was about this time that Nina and I began to prepare to move to New York. Robert's children surrounded us in great numbers now. Along with the new four, there were at least five others from the domestic lady. And there was another stray that had wandered in from nowhere but who was allowed to remain. We named him Sanjuro, because he was such a tough, self-contained rascal, and he handled himself like the samurai depicted by Toshiro Mifune in the Japanese movie entitled *Sanjuro*. We had also acquired a little black female whose manner was irresistible. She was a little stalk of a creature with tall legs, and we knew her as "the fastest cat in the West". We called her "the Bitty". All in all,

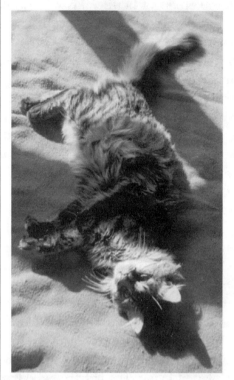

The lady cat with kittens

Robert himself was nothing less to me than my best friend and mentor. He was more—not less— than human to me.

Robert

Robert's "wild flowers"

The Bitty

there were about a dozen cats around us, living in various degrees of dependence and wildness. As we prepared to leave, we gave them to various friends. But we kept Robert and his wild lady and the Bitty.

Thus, on the day we left California, we packed our belongings in the station wagon, along with the three cats, for the long drive across America. We could not part with these companions. Their way of life had become a necessary vision to us, a sign and at least a memory of the intelligent wilderness that was the example of beauty and sanity by which we ourselves were moved and consoled in California.

Robert himself was nothing less to me than my best friend and mentor. He was more—not less—than human to me. I watched him with fascination. I followed him through woods and watched him hunt. I tried to understand his curious avoidance of the sea, and how he could sit on the cliff above the sea, watching the evening sun, and the wind blowing his hairs heroically about his head. The mystery of his pattern of living, his ease and justice, the economy of all his means, the untouchable absence of all anxiety, the sudden and adequate power he brought to every circumstance without exceeding the intensity required—all of his ways seemed to me an epitome of the genius of life. And he communicated with me so directly that I was always disarmed. He would call me when he returned in the evening. He would touch me whenever he needed my presence. He would lie with me as if with conscious intention to console me with his living presence. And I loved him as deeply as the universe itself.

I could not leave such friends behind. Yet, I was aware that my adventure was about to be renewed. I was seeking a teacher for an entirely new order of my mind and life. Hereafter, the wilderness could not be the model for my seeking or my healing. In New York, the cats would have to live in an environment whose unreality and absence of instinctual intelligence—not to mention the absence of human intelligence—was a critical problem even for human beings. They would have to survive in an artificial enclosure, the hardware of human evolution. There would be no possibility for the hunt, for natural solitude, or for any of the native signs and obstacles of wilderness that my animals had mastered even an aeon ago.

Even as we traveled, we realized the dilemma of our cats. Several times the car blew up, and we were stranded in the desert. The tires would explode at will, and we often had to remain stranded for hours without food or moving air, in pitiless heat. The cats strained and gagged in the breathless air with dry lungs, such that we were afraid they could not survive.

When we finally arrived in New York, I went to my parents to be reconciled. And Nina and I found an apartment in the lower end of Greenwich Village, on Houston Street. It was a dark place, with the enclosed odor of a long-degraded humanity that had been confused with refuse, immobility, and death. I began to observe the signs wherever I went—and, thus, I looked and waited for my new teacher. Meanwhile, we settled into our new, unnatural order of living.

The cats had to remain contained in the apartment—except for the relative freedom of a rear window, a fire escape, and an adjacent roof that could be reached with a small jump of perhaps two feet. I was afraid for my cats in this environment. We were four stories above the ground, and a slight miscalculation could mean a fall to death. But I considered that it was better for them to enjoy even this little freedom, and I consigned them to the survival power that had been demonstrated in wilderness.

After a few weeks, I could feel the advancing Presence of what I sought. I knew it was perhaps only a matter of days until I would meet my teacher. It was a rainy evening, the Fourth of July. I returned from a walk in Washington Square. Firecrackers and a few amateur fireworks tended to draw my attention into distant streets and alleys, and into the sky above. When I came in the door to the building, the superintendent met me. Robert had fallen from the roof. Since no one was home, he had called the local animal shelter to take him away. I asked if Robert was dead. He said he was not sure, but he pointed to the fire escapes high above, as if to say: "How alive could he be after such a fall?"

Nina had been out shopping during that time. I went upstairs and found that she had returned. We called the animal shelter, and they told us Robert was dead. We turned away from one another in separate sorrow and wept. It was a grief more profound than any I had ever known. The death of my little dog when I was a boy had taken me by surprise. At that time, I had not expected death—and, when it came, I was moved to follow her to the place of continuous life beyond the world. But Robert's death was no surprise at all. The news of it came to one who bore the knowledge of death—such that, when it came, there was no movement in me toward any other place. There was only the incomparable sorrow of a broken span of living. There was only the absence of that dear one. His mortality appeared in a world whose livingness I had come to know as far exceeding the image and power of death. But, in spite of all the Sphere of living Energy that I Knew informed the world and was its Truth, there remained the fact of this end, this disappearance, this sorrow-laden implication of Truth within the Blissful Void.

I recognized that Robert had been my teacher in the wilderness. He had filled my eye and owned a thread of attention in my heart. I Knew him, and he Knew me. There was not anything that could replace that state of life or console its absence. In his death, I treated him like a saint. I had him cremated, and I kept his ashes. I observed my grief and kept my mind focused in the hope of new events. I Knew that Robert's passing was the Sign that I was about to find my teacher in the human world.

In the weeks that preceded Robert's death and my immediately subsequent meeting with my first teacher, I had informed myself with every kind of study. I had passed beyond the remarkable news that the phenomena of human experience included much more than merely "mortal" phenomena. It was no longer a matter of proving such things to be true. I was certain enough of them—on the basis of my own experience, and of the reliably communicated experience of countless others in human time. Therefore, I did not pursue phenomena themselves. My knowledge and my experience were associated with a point of view that sympathized with the greater (and, generally, esoteric) points of view proposed in the world's traditional philosophical, mystical, and Spiritual literatures. My reading encompassed the literate mystical works of

Christian saints and the classical writings of Buddhism and Zen Buddhism, Hinduism, Vedanta, and Yoga. I was acquainted with the works of Ramana Maharshi, J. Krishnamurti, Ramakrishna, and Aurobindo. I felt particularly drawn to these more oriental teachers, whose course or intention was liberation, or an ultimate fulfillment of a most profound and (perhaps) even miraculous kind, free of the dogmatic limitations and unrevealing symbolisms of merely exoteric religion. And, relative to the religion I inherited in my childhood, I felt that the significance of Jesus of Nazareth was not in the conventional (and no longer believable) myths and legends promoted by traditional, exoteric Christianity. Rather, I felt that the significance of Jesus of Nazareth was in his (or his story's) basic inspirational recommendation that one discover and embrace Real God (or Truth, or Reality Itself) for Real, and that one discover and embrace only Real and True and present-time Means (including Spiritual Means) for Realizing Real God (or Truth, or Reality Itself).

Based on my studies at that time, I was mainly attendant both to the Yogic Spiritual traditions and to the Truth proposed alike in Vedanta and Buddhism. But the philosophically oriented paths of discrimination and practice proposed by Vedanta and Buddhism (and even Zen Buddhism) seemed to me to be rather indirect, or merely mind-based, and not sufficiently oriented toward Spirit-based practice and toward the Spiritual Realization of Reality (as I Knew It in the "Bright" of my childhood). Also, the essentially non-Yogic (or non-Spiritual) traditions of Vedanta and Buddhism seemed to me to require a course too much dissociated from the usual action of life. Nevertheless, the philosophically described One Truth that is the True (or non-egoic) Self-Condition and Source-Condition, the One and non-dual Reality, the unqualified Divine, or the Nirvanic Absolute that includes all things, was, for me, the ultimate traditional description of Real God, and Truth, and Reality—and, from my point of view, the traditions of Vedanta and Buddhism even epitomized that description. And that description, combined with the devotional and Spiritual Means described in the religious and Yogic traditions, and including the true Guru-devotee relationship (or the great devotional and Spiritual relationship between the true disciple, or the devotee, and the true teacher, or the adept-realizer), summarized my then developing (but, even then, basically established) sense of how I was moved to practice and of What I was moved to Realize. Indeed, from my point of view at the time, all of that simply and exactly corresponded to a way of Realization based not only on a summary of all the traditions, but also (and even more importantly) on the inherent Content of the "Bright" of my childhood (and the "Bright" of the profound revelations of my youth).

On the basis of all of this, I was moved to seek a teacher—a human guide who could lead me into the full Realization of this primary Truth, with all Its capabilities and Joy. And, I felt, such a teacher would necessarily be adept in the esoteric Yogic processes and in all the Spiritual functions that I felt must be the practical means for Realizing What was otherwise less availably represented in the cool (or mostly philosophical and ascetical) scriptures of Vedanta and Buddhism.

My reading (then, as always) was dictated by the laws of my own necessity. Curiously, what spontaneously became available for me to read was always uniquely appropriate, and immediately useful, relative to the stage or mode of my then present-time development. Thus, as the day of my meeting with my teacher approached, I began to read works that dealt with the peculiar Yoga of the Kundalini Shakti. I read such works as *The Serpent Power*, by Sir John Woodroffe,[14] and I found in them keys to many of my own experiences. The descriptions of the various chakras (or Spiritual and "creative" centers in the body), and the details of experiences generated in each stage of Spiritual ascent, brought a clarity of order to the progress of many of my own seemingly arbitrary experiences.

I saw that What I called the "Bright" was the fundamental (and inherently Spiritual) Consciousness in Which the entire chakra-body is aroused, and functionally open to the proceedings of the Divine Shakti (or Spirit-Energy, or Primary Light). Likewise, I understood that the experience associated with my college Awakening was a sudden and profound Manifestation of the Divine Shakti—the Conscious Spirit-Energy that, from the ordinary point of view, appears as mortal ego-consciousness, but Which, rightly engaged, leads back to the Divine Self (or Siva), Who is eternally Calm.

I knew that my own course of life, and the meaning of all life, was in this process of Siva-Shakti, the endless "Bright" unfolding of humanly-born conscious awareness and experience, and its consistent foundation in (and, most ultimately, its most perfect Realization of) the Pure, Spiritually "Bright" Infinity of unqualified, Transcendental Being. Thus, I expected to be guided by the "Bright" Itself—and, thus and thereby, to a teacher (or perhaps even a sequence of teachers) who would lead me further and further into a conscious, direct, and regulated revelation of this same "Bright" process.

I had read the "autobiography"[15] of Paramahansa Yogananda as we drove across country. I found in him a curiously sane and beautiful example of the kind of life and experience I needed to touch as my own. But I knew that I required a teacher who was presently alive to guide me through my peculiar problems of seeking.

I was only uncertain of the precise direction of such seeking. The fundamental Spiritual path, as it is proposed in the various literatures, divided at a certain point. The typical motive of the oriental teachings was in the direction of an absolute liberation from all forms of experience and life-consciousness. Such teaching is typical of Vedanta and Buddhism, in the classical works of Zen masters and such modern saints or God-men as Ramakrishna and Ramana Maharshi.

On the other hand, the teachings of Christianity, of Western occultism, and of such Eastern saints as Aurobindo indicated a course whose goal was in life—or, at least, not fundamentally opposed to life. They drew on the ultimate conclusion of all the scriptures, which variously state that "this is God's plan and creation", or "this is That", or "Nirvana and samsara are the same",[16] or "there is only One, without a second". They proposed a sacrificial practice of surrender and reception, wherein life is moved toward a perfect vision or evolution. Even in the mind of the iconoclast J. Krishnamurti, I found a sense of life that is not divorced from the process of natural existence. And, though I greatly desired the incomparable Peace of Ultimate Knowledge, I also tended to sympathize with this latter path of Realization and "creativity", whose purposes are a Divine life rather than a pure separation into Absoluteness.

This problem of direction, which was always to be one of the most fundamental in my progress, took the form of a continuous questioning in me as I sought for my teacher. And it was to form the basis for my first questions when I met him.

When we arrived in New York, I began to look for this teacher with peculiar certainty. I did not seek for him by effort. I did not wander about the city looking for oriental art stores that resembled the one I saw in spontaneous visions. Rather, I lived normally, according to the particular requirements of each day—but, as I went about the city in the midst of my daily course, I was also attentive and ready for signs of the store I had seen in visions. It was clear and certain in me that I would find my teacher in an oriental art store, and I was certain that the guiding-Source of the visions that convinced me of this would Itself bring me to the place itself. However, I also felt that any intentional outward seeking for the place would likely only prevent the spontaneous discovery of it, which depended on an inner availability and sensitivity and spontaneity. Therefore, Nina and I simply went about the practical matters of founding a household. Nina found work to support us. And I, writing and living as before, watched for my teacher.

The move to New York was a shock to us both in many ways. Our country life of wilderness was past. Robert's death signified many things—the passage from an old order to a new. I awaited a new teacher and a new way of life. And the city life of humanity also stood in contrast to the wilderness and natural rule by which Nina and I had always lived. The material and mortal philosophies had died in me, and the transition in the wilderness, the exploitation of instinctual, animal, and passionate laws, seemed inappropriate—not only to the great city, but also to the new order of Spiritual life to which I was inclined.

I was quite confused by all of this. The new way of life seemed to require a kind of purity and enforced morality that was unknown to me or my cats. I began to doubt my old way of life.

The kind of self-exploitation by which I lived and wrote began to seem immoral. I thought that, perhaps, it only "created" obstacles to the attainment of what I would now possess.

I thought perhaps I should leave Nina. After all, the paths of Spiritual life were largely taken by celibates and highly disciplined saints. I became overwhelmed with my lack of discipline. I had rarely worked for a living in my life. I had never really supported myself or anyone else. I was a libertine, a drinker, a drug user, a useless and impractical dreamer, a passionate madman!

All of these emotions turned in me. It became September. On the Sunday afternoon of the Labor Day weekend,[17] my parents were driving us back to New York. We had been spending the weekend with them on Long Island. We were driving down Seventh Avenue in Greenwich Village, just a few blocks from our apartment on Houston Street. As we passed down the relatively deserted streets, I saw a small store on the west side of the street. There was a large sign above—with the name "Rudi", and several written characters that looked like Chinese calligraphy. The window of the store was full of oriental sculpture and painting. As I looked at it, it became instantly clear that this was the place I had seen in visions. I was immediately certain that this was the place where I would find the teacher toward whom I had been directed while in California, and since California.

After my parents left us at home, Nina and I walked back to the store. It was only a small store, and it was unceremoniously filled (and even cluttered) with thousands of pieces of sculpture from all over the Orient. There was a huge Buddha seated on a lotus in the window. Standing in the rear of the store was a colossal wooden Bodhisattva, perhaps fifteen feet tall, holding a lotus in its hand and a crystal jewel in its forehead. Everywhere were standing Buddhas, dancing saints, and portraits of ferocious and sublime deities.

There was an aura of feeling and light surrounding the store, as if all of these sublime entities had gathered to generate a center of Force for any who were ready to recognize It. I told Nina that this was certainly the place I had envisioned—and, as we left, I planned to return the next day, during business hours.

*When we arrived in
New York, I began to
look for this teacher
with peculiar certainty.
I did not seek for him
by effort. . . . It was
clear and certain in
me that I would find
my teacher in an
oriental art store,
and I was certain that
the guiding-Source
of the visions that
convinced me of this
would Itself bring me
to the place itself.*

The Houston Street apartment building

The site of the oriental art store on Seventh Avenue

The next day, we returned in the early morning. The door to the shop was then (as always in the future) fixed in an open position. We walked in casually, concealing a great expectation. But there was no one in the store who "looked" like a teacher. There was only a little, round, oldish Jewish lady. She immediately displayed every insincere mannerism and manipulative sales technique I had ever seen exhibited by a New York shopkeeper. We, in turn, pretended to be only interested in art, especially looking for a small Buddha to stand in a place of meditation. The woman showed us many objects in the "merely" fifty-dollar price range. I was careful to observe her for any signs of an impractical Spiritual nature! But she was all business, and I had the feeling that I was being well and truly "sold". The quality of the place did not differ from that of a meat market or a five-and-dime.

Finally, we decided to purchase a small antique Japanese figure, a standing Buddha about twelve inches high. The woman assured us it would be a "very Powerful" object for meditation. We passed to the rear of the store, where she wrapped the object in newspaper and stuffed it in a paper bag! We watched this with holy amazement, and then my eyes turned to a pair of photographs on the wall.

The photographs appeared to be of two different saints. Each of them was naked except for a small loincloth. One was an enormously fat man with the appearance of awesome strength. And the other was a more moderately proportioned man with a melancholy expression, as if his mind were tuned to some distant place that was his real home. Both of them had short hair and equally short beards that suggested they had each been totally shaven within the past few weeks. And there were undeniable, obvious signs of Spiritual Power and Presence generated bodily by both men.

As I studied these pictures, my heart began to pound with excitement. I asked the woman about the pictures. She said they were her son's teachers. Her son was a Spiritual teacher, she said, and he was the owner of the store. I asked how I could meet her son, and I was told that he was away for a long weekend in the country, but he would return the next day.

We left the store quite hurriedly. Our business was over. But as we got into the street, I began to jump and run us down the block. I had found my teacher! I had found the Guru!

Rudi in his oriental art store

CHAPTER SEVEN

The Meeting and the "Work"

T he long night of almost sleepless excitement that passed until the next day was to be the last night of my undisciplined search in the wilderness of my youth. From the next day, the day of meeting with my teacher, I would be unable to live as liberally as before. The doubts I had formed about my lack of discipline would be consummated in the will of my teacher. There would be a practical, moral revolution in my way of life. But, at the time, I merely swooned in expectation, in the Joy of my discovery. And I went to meet my teacher as if I were to be given some sweet free gift of miracles and love, and coddled home like some eternal loved-one of the gods.

When the morning came, I bathed and dressed very ceremoniously. My long hair and beard were combed and trimmed. There was to be no offense in me. I walked to the store in the bright sun and wondered what incredible miracles I was to see before evening. From works such as Yogananda's *Autobiography of a Yogi,*[18] had learned to expect some kind of priceless love-meeting and a dear touch of the teacher's hand that would shake my mind loose in a vision of lights and blessed peace. I walked to the store with the same excitement in which I used to follow a whore. I went to grasp all the miracles hidden in the secret parts of this mystery.

When I neared the store, I carefully hid myself on the other side of the street. I wanted to be certain that the teacher was there before I made my entrance. After a while, I saw several men come out of the store. One of them was apparently directing the others. He was a heavy fat man in his mid-thirties. He wore a T-shirt and a baggy pair of corduroys. The others appeared to be doing some sort of work for him.

I watched them move in and out of the store for some time. Finally, all of them left, except the fat man. As I watched him, I perceived a seriousness in him—the same kind of all-business attitude I found in the woman the day before. I supposed that he was alone, and I crossed the street—filled with embarrassment and expectation, self-consciousness and anxiety.

I walked into the store as directly and upright as I could. One should not approach a teacher with weaknesses hanging out! The man was sitting in a chair by the desk at the rear of the store. His mother was standing behind him in a small doorway making a sandwich. She recognized me and very animatedly told the man that I had been in the day before and bought a piece of sculpture.

The man stood up and approached me. He made it a very deliberate point to shake my hand. He introduced himself as Rudi, and I told him I was Franklin Jones.

"Your mother told me that you are a teacher."

He looked around at her as if displeased, and then he said, "She tells that to anybody who comes in here. She really ought to keep her mouth shut."

I was already very uncomfortable, and now I felt foolish, but I was determined.

"What do you teach?"

"Kundalini Yoga."

"Are you an adept at this Yoga?"

He looked at me very sternly and a little bothered. "You don't teach it if you can't do it."

I told him I was looking for a teacher and I felt that I had been directed to him. He asked me what I did. I said that I wrote, and had just moved from California.

"No, what do you do Spiritually?"

"Oh, well, I relax and direct myself toward the top of the head."

He smiled a little. "Do you work?"

"No, I've just been writing, and I live with my girlfriend. She works."

He drew away from me a little. "This Yoga requires great discipline and surrender, and I can't teach anybody who doesn't accept the discipline and work. You go out and get a job and come back in about six months or a year. We'll talk about it then."

That was apparently the end of the interview! He made it a point to shake my hand again—and he turned away, such that I felt I was supposed to leave.

As I left the store, I felt a tremendous relief that I had been able to manage the meeting at all. I was disappointed, to be sure. There was no sublime love-meeting, no miracle, no immediate recognition of me as the long-awaited disciple. But I had been received at least conditionally. Six months or a year was not an unbearable length of time. Unpleasant as the prospect was, I was willing to get a job, if that was the kind of test required of me. I felt a certainty in the man himself. He was, by his own admission, adept in the teaching and practice of what I (at the time) presumed to be the highest and most miraculous kind of Yoga. I had met him, and I was certain that I was willing to meet the conditions.

I was elated! I felt I had been successful. Strong and complicated feelings went through my mind as I moved up the block beyond the store. By the time I reached the corner, I had gained my composure, and even my doubts had turned to elation and certainty. Then I became aware of a very strange sensation. A current of very strong Energy was rising up my arm from my right hand, the hand Rudi had made such a point to shake when I arrived and as I left.

As I became aware of this Energy, It quickly passed into the rest of my body and Filled me with a profound and thrilling Fullness. My heart strained in a vibrant Joy, and my head felt swollen, as if my mind were an "aura" that extended out from my skull by several inches. As I walked, I began to run. I felt on fire with a Joyous Energy, and I had become incredibly light!

When Nina returned home from teaching school, I told her all about my experience. I told her about the mysterious Energy, about my muted reception, and the condition that I get a job for six months or a year before I could go back for any teaching. She was a little puzzled by this condition. She had only known me as a writer and a wild man, and she was not sure that she really wanted it any other way.

As the evening passed, I also began to wonder about these things. My writing and my way of life were very real to me. They were even the necessary preliminary to Spiritual effort. I began to think about the writings of Aurobindo, and how he justified "creative" work—even writing and other forms of art—as a usable (and even necessary) means for Spiritual opening. And, even if I did get a job, should I continue to write? And what about all of my other habits? What does this teacher think about drugs, and sex? Should I leave Nina? Do I have to become a vegetarian?

The entire matter was much more complicated than it had originally seemed. So I sat down to write Rudi a long letter about all of my questions. I intended to have Nina deliver it to him the next day and return to me with his answers. "The young woman who brings this letter to you is my girlfriend. We are not married, but we have been living together for two or three years." And so on, and on. I wrote about all of my questions. I wanted to be certain I made as complete a transformation in myself as necessary—such that, when I returned to him, I should be fully able to use his teaching. I asked about "creative" work and drugs, sex and diet. I told him about the experience of his Spiritual Energy. And I made it clear that I was willing to undergo all the conditions.

The next day, Nina went to see Rudi after work. She returned very amused with me. Rudi had received her very warmly, in contrast to his brusque and almost rude reception of me. Nina had not asked him to teach her. He told her that I had a lot of work to do, but he would be glad to take her as a student right away! Anyway, he appreciated my letter, and I should come and see him the next day.

I was happy for this news. Of course, I insisted that Nina take advantage of his offer to teach her. But I was confounded at how he could take her as a student offhand, while I—who had such a long history of seeking, trial, and experience—should have to go begging even for an interview! As it happened, this pattern of offense and testing was to be the basic form of my life-experience with Rudi over the coming years.

When I went to Rudi the following day, his manner was much more familiar and friendly. He told me that he really loved Nina and that she was a very open person who could easily receive the Shakti, or the "Force" (as he called It).

On the other hand, he certainly did mean that I would have to begin to work on myself before he would allow me to come to his classes.

"What about my writing?"

"How much do you write or want to write? A serious writer works constantly, out of great need."

"Well, I write, but more or less spontaneously. It is a different thing. Well, yes, I am not disciplined. A job wouldn't interfere with that work."

His one answer to all of my questions was "work". Discipline and effort are necessary to provide an instrument that can contain this "Force". It is not necessary to give up sex or life or go on any special diet. Only work, be intelligent with these things, take proper care of yourself.

My life with Nina was a particular focus of his. He wondered why we were not married, and he knew that my undisciplined way of life must draw me into myself more than anything else. Thus, his teaching required a drastic turning of my attention outward. Work, love Nina, become more loving. Your life with Nina is your Yoga.

And so he sent me away again with one of those electric hand-shakes. But he told me that, as soon as I got a job, I would be welcome to come to his classes.

At that time, I was about twenty-four years old. I had never taken a job other than the purely menial labor of waiting in restaurants and the like. Consequently, I was at a disadvantage when I went looking for work. I still considered that my basic work was writing and a kind of Spiritual process in consciousness. Thus, I did not feel particularly motivated to any kind of career. But I felt constrained to find some kind of productive work that would not only allow me to reserve some "creative" life-energy but also provide sufficient means to support Nina and me.

The reaction of any and all agencies and employers that I first contacted was that I had a bad employment history and was educationally overqualified for most kinds of work. Their experience showed that overqualified persons with similar backgrounds to my own tended to leave unchallenging forms of work after a relatively short period. Finally, in order simply to have work to do, I volunteered my services to WBAI, a non-profit, listener-sponsored radio station in New York. I worked at soliciting and addressing in the subscription department. After a few weeks, I was hired at a limited salary to do the work part-time.

In the meantime, Nina began to go to Rudi's classes. She said it was a very strange and exciting experience. The classes were held in a large room on the ground floor of a building Rudi owned on Hudson Street, a few blocks from our apartment. She said the room was surrounded with huge oriental sculptures. There were approximately twenty or thirty people at each class. And the classes were held on Tuesday and Thursday evenings at eight, Saturday morning at ten, and Sunday at eleven or noon.

Rudi's students were mostly young people in their twenties or early thirties. Most of them were former professional "freaks", like myself, with very little history of dramatic accomplishment. They required disciplining, like myself, and probably many of them were really working for the first time in their lives. Some, of course, were older—either professionals or businesspeople. Many were fairly successful and had met Rudi in the course of his business dealings.

I would frequently go to Rudi's store to talk or enjoy the aura that permeated the place. The store was never empty. There was a constant stream of visitors and patrons. His mother was usually preparing food for people, and we would crowd around the rear of the store or sit in rows of funeral-parlor folding chairs by the curb.

Rudi's attention was constantly directed toward someone or something. There was rarely any stillness around him, and this was another characteristic that was unexpected. There was no kind of distant, mystical, airy mood of quiet, none of the usual "Spiritual" atmosphere peculiar to churches and religious or Spiritual books. There was a constant activity that was even annoying at times.

Rudi was always animated in conversation, either with students and friends or with customers. His conversation was a constant stream of strongly communicated moods—alternating between talk of Spiritual life, his experiences in India, his Spiritual experience and visions, and the perpetual absorption in business. For Rudi, life and work were Yoga. His business was his principal Yoga. And, if you did not know or accept this about him, you could become angry at what appeared to be his perpetual concern with business and the store.

After a while, I learned that I could not expect to visit Rudi and pass a pleasant hour conversing about Spiritual life. More often than not, there would be a brief handshake or a hug, and then he would spend his time talking to somebody else, as if I were not there. Then he might suddenly shake my hand and tell me to leave.

As the weeks passed and I became an accustomed regular at the store, I found that I would be given some work to do when I arrived. There was always some sculpture to be moved around, some windows to wash. Gradually, it became clear that only casual visitors or friends got to sit and talk. Any student that came was given work to do.

As Rudi's business increased, the work increased, such that I was called upon to come and work in my spare time. Rudi always generated work around him. Even if I stopped by to say hello at the house, he would hand me a bag of garbage to take to the corner. And if I dropped by the store casually, I might be asked to go home and change clothes, and then come back and wash the floor.

This "dharma" of work awakened tremendous resistance in me, and in most of Rudi's other students. But that was also the teaching. We would often wish it were otherwise—and we always suckered ourselves into a casual visit, hoping he would be in the mood to let us sit and entertain us with stories of miracles and all of the glory we were going to gain in the future by the aid of the "Force". The more we suffered, the more we communicated our resistance and discomfort, the more he would tell us to surrender. He said that we should "be like smoke". You can cut through smoke with a knife, but it is not disturbed.

The idea that was infused in us was the simple attitude of work. Work forced us to encounter resistance and obstacles in ourselves—and perseverance in work gradually wore away resistance and brought about a state of openness, or surrender. The constant practice of work and surrender opened the instrument of the body and the internal mechanism that was a channel for the "Force" (the Spiritual Energy, or Shakti, that was Rudi's gift), and the continuation of work strengthened the instrument in its openness and allowed the "Force" to expand and to produce ever higher Realizations and capabilities. He often said that work was endless and always generated more work—such that life was pictured as a fruitful effort in constant relation to the "Force" that had no other goal than continual growth.

Two or three weeks after Nina began to go to "class", Rudi gave me permission to begin also. The work I had managed to acquire was not completely satisfactory from his point of view— but it was a "job", and I had managed to adapt myself to the basic conditions for his teaching. I had even shaved and gotten a haircut. I paid more attention to discipline and cleanliness. I had even stopped using marijuana to relax. And, in general, I had turned the self-involved habits of solitude into a more communicative and socialized life.

I decided to begin classes on my birthday, thinking this was auspicious. Rudi's classes always followed the same pattern. We would begin to arrive in the classroom about 7:30 in the evening. Someone would light incense next to Rudi's chair, which was a large metal trunk covered with a bearskin. His seat was placed on a higher level of the room, about three or four steps above the rest of us. Most of us sat in folding chairs set in rows, with an aisle down the middle, but some would sit in Yogic postures on the floor in front of him.

Before my first class, I was told to go to the store for instruction. Rudi told me that the "Force" was the real subject of the class. It came into contact with us through his eyes. I was simply to sit comfortably and relax and try to open myself (or surrender) to the Force. If I felt the Force enter me, I should simply relax more and allow It to go down through the chest and belly into the sex organs. When It got there, I should relax at the base of the spine and let It travel upwards to the head. If I wanted, I could silently say "So" with each inhalation and "Ham" with each exhalation.

"So-Ham" could mean "I am That", or "I am the Force (or God)"—
whichever concept was meaningful to me. But the important thing
was surrender and opening to the Force, so that It could carry the
exercise. Sometimes, as he spoke of these things in class, he
would also recommend that we feel a part of ourselves going way
out into space, beyond all the universes.

With these instructions, I went on to class. The room was not
particularly decorative. It was about twenty-five by fifty feet. There
was a plain oriental folding screen behind his seat, to keep our eyes
from distraction. And there were many large oriental figures along
the sides of the room, as well as great numbers of smaller objects
or paintings here and there. Rudi often said that this was not for
"effect", but he simply kept them stored there for his business.

By the time class was to begin, everyone was supposed to be
seated and quiet and "into the exercise". The Force was not only
supposed to be given by Rudi, in or out of class, but was always
working in us. Therefore, surrender and work was to be our constant attitude, and class was merely a special exercise of the same
work. In addition to class, we were to spend up to an hour a day
at home doing the same exercise. But we should not spend more
than an hour a day at meditation. More than that, he warned, only
produces illusions. Meditation was to be a "creative" exercise—to
awaken capability, not to produce effects like quietness. Apart
from the exercise, we should only work and live intelligently.

When I went to class the first night, I was again full of expectations. Nina had been urged not to tell me all the specifics of what
went on, but to let me find out for myself. I had experienced the
Force many times through Rudi's handshake, or when I chanced
to look in his eyes. But, for all I knew, that might only be a taste!
I truly did not know what to expect, but I was ready for visions
and miracles.

Shortly after eight o'clock, Rudi came in and sat down. At the
beginning of class, he would sometimes speak for a short time
about the Force and about work and surrender. Or else he would
describe some experiences of the Force that he was having. He
would often have visions of opening lotuses, fantastic creatures,
other worlds, or his teachers. His teachers were the two men

whose pictures I had seen that first day in the store. The first (and heavier) one was Bhagavan Nityananda, a Powerful saint he had met in 1960. After Bhagavan Nityananda's death (or "mahasamadhi") in 1961, Rudi became the disciple of the other man, Swami (Baba) Muktananda, who was Bhagavan Nityananda's chief disciple.

Rudi spoke briefly on this first night, and I believe he introduced me to the group either at the beginning or the end of the exercise. Then he sat up straight in the lotus posture and closed his eyes. All of us also made an effort to relax and surrender. Then he opened his eyes. They appeared to be deep set and very wide. His eyes moved from person to person in the room. He concentrated on each one for a minute or two, or perhaps only a few seconds, depending on the needs, or the openness, of the person.

I could feel a certain relaxation as I tried to surrender, open, and empty my mind. And I waited intensely for Rudi to look at me. When my turn finally came, I felt a little foolish. Looking deep into a person's eyes, particularly under such circumstances, requires a certain relaxation from the usual armor we wear. But, gradually, I loosened up, and accepted my position of vulnerability. I tried to deepen my surrender as he described. I concentrated on his eyes. We remained that way for perhaps a minute, and then he passed on to another. I continued to try to deepen the surrender while concentrating on his form. He would often tell us not to close our eyes unless there was a very strong impulse from the Force to do so. Then, suddenly, the class was over. As was customary, we lined up to leave, and each received a big bear hug from Rudi. He told me that it was a very good class for me, and that the Force would begin to work for me very soon.

Apart from a certain relaxation during the class and an exhilaration afterwards—which I usually felt after a meeting with Rudi—I had not experienced anything unusual. This was somewhat disappointing to me. I realized that this work was going to be not simply a matter of free miracles and visions, but a gradual process requiring great effort.

As the weeks passed, I became more accustomed to this exercise, and going to class became a matter of course. The work of surrender became more natural to me, and I began to become sensitive to levels of resistance programmed into my being. At times, they fell away, as if by the work of the Force—just as, at other times, they could only be removed by the active effort of surrender. But there were many times when I felt unable to so much as touch the resistance in myself. Indeed, the more I tried to surrender, the more the resistance grew.

The activity of the mind also fluctuated in this same manner. I began to acquire a certain anxiety and frustration about my own limitations, and I would often go to Rudi desperately demanding some kind of help to remove the obstacles in my life. But there was only a sort of ordinary chiding humor to ease me up, and then the admonition to more work and deeper surrender.

This is a common experience among those who deliberately perform various kinds of work in consciousness. The more you try to do it, the more obstacles arise. There is probably no more confounding and frustrating admonition than the simple order to relax. And one of the greatest Lessons I would learn from all my years of Spiritual effort was that Spiritual seeking not only rein-forces (and intensifies the experience of) the very things it seeks to remove, but it is (for that very reason) founded in the same mechanisms and motives that are one's problems and suffering. In time, I would come to resolve this dilemma on the basis of a radical (or most fundamental, and uniquely "gone-to-the-root") self-understanding—a point of view much different from that of Rudi's—but, for now, I put myself to conscious effort with tremen-dous intensity and need.

Rudi would often talk about the kind of effort to surrender that he felt was required. He compared it to "tearing your guts out". I found that my life was becoming a terrible ordeal of surrender, and the depth of my work never satisfied him. He worked on me by frustrating me and minimizing my efforts or accomplishments— and this combined with the Yogic Force Itself, such that, most of the time, I was in a literal fever, with extreme heat and redness all over my skin. I felt the incredible weight of all I needed to sur-render. Real Spiritual work must amount to nothing less than a wholesale cutting away of all that I am. It must amount to an infi-nite depth, an absolute surrender. And when I would examine the littleness of my depth, I would become awed and frustrated. I was burdened with the need for an impossible purification and self-abnegation.

This surrender was not merely a physical opening or relaxation of the nervous system. Nor was it simply a purifying and disciplining of life. It was a profound internal opening in every part. Rudi sometimes said we should concentrate on surrendering three things: self-pity, negativity, and self-imagery. Surrender was a perfect letting go of the ego, the learned identity and drama.

As my experience grew, I also became critically aware of the work, its effects, its value, and its sources. I examined these things in relation to my own intelligence and understanding—and, thus and thereby, I gradually became aware of significant differences between Rudi and myself.

Rudi claimed to have had visitations from certain "Tibetans" when a little boy. They told him his life would be very difficult, but it would bring him to a very high State. They also told him he would have thousands of students. His life over the years was, indeed, difficult. And, from the time I met him, the numbers of his students steadily increased (becoming significantly enlarged especially in the years after I myself had ceased to be his student). Nevertheless, regardless of his growing "success", every step of his life appeared (at least to him) to require almost absolute sacrifices and "work" on his part.

He constantly described himself as a poor Jewish boy whose father abandoned him and his mother when he was young. His mother apparently treated him to huge doses of violent physical abuse, for whatever reasons, and he had to surmount terrible obstacles and resistance on his part in order to improve his life.

He was obviously a man of great passions and appetites, a figure of Gargantuan vitality and huge pleasures, and a very strong and masculine (but also demonstratively homosexual) character. He would often give himself as the perfect example of the need for great effort and surrender. In him, all the passions of self-indulgence were active—and he would often say that, when he indulged them, he had to pay a terrible price to regain himself. Thus, he was not an example of religiously motivated purity. Even so, he

Rudi

**Adi Da Samraj
and Nina during
the period of
their involvement
with Rudi**

recommended to his students that they achieve as great control as possible over their various desires.

I was quite overweight at the time. I weighed over 230 pounds and looked somewhat swollen and uncomfortable, although I was not nearly as large as Rudi! He insisted that I watch my diet and lose weight. I took all of his admonitions very seriously, and I observed everything in him, or of him, or from him, as the direct Communication of God. Thus, I lost a lot of weight, to my great benefit. But Rudi, even though he protested about his own over-weight condition, only grew larger and larger.

Finally, he would only say that his size and weight were the result of the activity of the Force, and we allowed him that. After all, Bhagavan Nityananda was also a huge fat man—and he, more than anyone else, was Rudi's ideal image of the God-Force. It was always Bhagavan Nityananda's example and image that Rudi held before himself. Thus, Rudi expanded in size, like Bhagavan Nityananda—whatever the reasons.

During a trip to India some time later, I was told that Bhagavan Nityananda had always been an ascetic—and his early photo-graphs show a figure of skeletal thinness. Even in later life—although, reportedly, he would sometimes take huge quantities of the food offered to him as gifts by his devotees—he often (or, perhaps, even generally) ate only the very little his devotees could force him to take. In any case, over the years, his body expanded hugely, and his devotees wondered about this. However, the gen-eral conclusion was that his hugeness was due to the influx of higher Power. And he was even called "Ganesh" (the "elephant god")—because, like the traditional images of Ganesh, he was very big in the belly. Nevertheless, when Bhagavan Nityananda died, his body was thin, and even somewhat emaciated.

I considered that Rudi's case was a combination of several fac-tors. Certainly, he was the bearer and the instrument of a tremendous natural human energy and a Spiritual Force that were not the gifts of an ordinary human being. But he was also more complicated than the traditional Indian saint, and he was hearty enough to accept the psychology of the expansive, devouring fat man as part of the structure of his life. His size and manner were otherwise quite charming, and, from his point of view, presented no impenetrable obstacle to his growth. Years later, when I was in India, a man told me that many gossiped about Rudi's unascetic tendencies, but that, when he arrived, they all would go to him to get "charged up" by his Presence.

I never quarreled with the appropriateness of Rudi's philosophy and practice for his own case, at his stage of human and Yogic demonstration. It was only that I gradually began to understand that his characteristic emphasis on "effort, work, and surrender", for the sake of growth in life—and even to the exclusion of any higher or ultimate philosophy or aspiration—was a distinct characteristic of his peculiar need, tendency, and life-experience. My own tendencies at that time were, indeed, destructive—and his teaching was almost entirely beneficial to me while I remained with him. But, for myself, such a "machine" of effort, once it had achieved its earliest benefits in my general human well-being, began only to reveal its own ego-reinforcing limitations, its fundamental bondage to only rather gross aspirations, and its fruitlessness relative to Ultimate (or truly Divine) Realization. Therefore, more and more (over time), I was drawn to another, and truly radical (or most fundamental), self-understanding.

Rudi's way was, obviously, not entirely (or even basically) founded in Indian Yoga. Indeed, I was to discover, years later, that his methods and aims were quite different from those of Baba Muktananda, his Guru. Even before he went to India and met his present teachers, he had first been a student of the Gurdjieff work in New York. And he had graduated from there to the practices instituted by Pak Subuh in the Subud movement.

Rudi never spoke much in detail about his experiences in those movements, but the manner of his teaching, his philosophy and practice, can be seen as a direct reflection of the leading motives of G. I. Gurdjieff and Pak Subuh.

The Gurdjieff work emphasizes the necessity for profound effort, the absolute and conscious work of evolution. Like Rudi, it does not emphasize such work for the sake of "enlightenment" (or some single, perfect, and liberating Realization that is the ultimate goal of striving). It posits the endlessness of that work in the direction of an ever higher evolution of Knowledge and Ability that will have direct consequences in human life.

Rudi's way of work and effort in an endless progress of growth was generated by his own needs in the presence of his particular personal tendencies. But it is clear that he acquired much of the technology and reinforcement for that path in the Gurdjieff movement. Even so, the Gurdjieff work was basically a pattern of philosophy and technique. He acquired the first experiences and personal signs of what he called the "Force" from Pak Subuh.

Pak Subuh, an Indonesian teacher, experienced a spontaneous Energy-Awakening sometime early in his life. It was the Awakening of a certain Power (or Spiritual Force) that came to him miraculously and thereafter remained always available to him. He found that he could also Initiate this Force in others, if they were even a little open to It. Rudi apparently experienced his first conscious Initiation in this "Force" while involved in the Subud movement, and he later received It from Pak Subuh himself.

But Pak Subuh was apparently not aware that there was any previous tradition of this same Power. He thought It was an entirely new Spiritual Influence that he was to reveal to the world. He seemed to know nothing of the already existing tradition of Kundalini Shakti in India, nor the already traditional process of Spiritual Initiation (generally, by touch, thought, look, or the giving of a mantra) known in India as "Shaktipat".

Therefore, Pak Subuh interpreted this Force and Its value along lines peculiar to his own isolated experience. He saw that, once this Force was activated in a person, It could be developed into various purifying and "creative" life-abilities, through a spontaneous exercise he called the "latihan". Again, this Energy was not promoted as a means to an absolute higher Knowledge, Which is Its ultimate Purpose in the Indian sources. It was interpreted as a kind of "creative" God-Force, whose significance was in the evolution and expansion of "creative" life-processes.

Thus, the work of Subud also has the kind of endlessness and non-specific purpose characteristic of Rudi's teaching. However, in my own case, Spiritual life always had a specific and uncompromising Purpose. It was to Realize the supreme Knowledge, the

Knowledge of fundamental Reality that makes all the difference and ends the search. For this reason, I was also chronically disturbed by the notion of perpetual evolutionary work which Rudi advocated. And, again, this difference in our intentions (or aims) also provided the basis for the break between us in later years.

Rudi apparently possessed the fundamentals of his path—both its philosophy and its activating "Force"—even before he arrived in India, in 1958. What he received—first from Bhagavan Nityananda, and then from Baba Muktananda—was that Force in Its most direct and Powerful form. He saw his Indian teachers as an endless Source—a Spiritual Fountain that he could always tap and thereby discover even greater depth, greater experiences, and greater Power.

Thus, ever since Bhagavan Nityananda's mahasamadhi, Rudi made at least two trips a year to Baba Muktananda's Ashram. He would always return to America claiming greater Power and higher levels of experience. Rudi always clearly stated that he was not, as he put it, a "finished product" (or a perfectly evolved or enlightened adept-realizer). However—and in spite of his obvious dependence on his Indian Sources—Rudi always demanded recognition of himself as a unique Source (or Instrument) for the Force. At the same time, he suggested that fullest access to the Force, and direct access to his Indian Sources, was not possible or appropriate for his students.

I greatly desired every Spiritual gift for myself—and, the stronger I became, the more I also required a direct and overwhelming contact with the Force Itself.

Even though, in Rudi's company, there was, in my own case, practical evidence of a partial improvement of my life, I sought an utterly fundamental reversal and transformation of my existence. Thus, over time, I became hungry for direct contact with Rudi's Spiritual Sources. And it was only a matter of time before the burden of merely egoic effort and the unsatisfactoriness of Rudi's rather worldly philosophy would reach their limit in me.

I had embraced Rudi's way totally, absolutely committed to the ends I sought. I was willing to do whatever necessary to attain them. Such intensity of purpose is characteristically required of those who devote themselves to conscious evolution by various efforts. The first effects of that commitment were wholly beneficial to me. But, in time, I began to learn profound Lessons in secret. And the entire process began to become too limited and limiting, in comparison to my aspirations and my understanding. However, it would be three and one-half years before I would have strength enough to wander into India on my own.

All in all, our lives became cleaner and happier.
It was an intense struggle and discipline for me,
but I welcomed all its effects. And I looked to Rudi
and the Force for a dramatic reversal of my ordinary
state of resistance and the logic of Narcissus.

Adi Da Samraj in New York, 1965

CHAPTER EIGHT

The Idea of Release from Narcissus

The central ideas in Rudi's way of teaching were "surrender" and "work". "Surrender" was the internal practice in life and meditation. It was conscious (and even willful) opening, or letting go of contents, resistance, patterns, feelings, and thoughts. "Work" was the external practice. The ideal student was to be involved in a constant state of surrender and a constant act of work. The purpose of this was to make the entire psycho-physical vehicle, internal and external, available to the higher Power—the "Force", or "Shakti"—and, thus, to grow by receiving Its Will, Presence, Intelligence, Light, and Power into every level of the functional being.

I took Rudi's way very seriously, and I made a constant effort to adapt myself to his way absolutely and exhaustively. I accepted Rudi as a perfect Source of this higher Power, and I allowed none of his apparent limitations to represent actual barriers or limitations to my experience of the "Force" Itself. Whenever I encountered limitations in him, I was immediately moved to reflect on my own resistance. Thus, I never allowed myself to become concerned about Rudi's problems or to think that, because of his limitations, the "Force" (or the Divine Power) was available to me only to a limited degree.

The effect of this way of life was a perpetual and growing encounter with my own resistance. And, when I encountered my own resistance, I would awaken to my own tendencies to self-pity, negativity, and the subliminal self-imagery by which I guided the "creation" or manipulation of experience. The more I worked, the more I saw Narcissus.

Rudi's way required immense self-discipline—and, as long as it remained effective in my case, his way functioned as a positive mechanism that strengthened and purified me physically, mentally, and morally. Rudi was a master at this kind of psychological tutoring, and these effects were his primary gift to me. Even if his motives were often founded in problems of his own, he would never allow his students to become identified with his own case. He would always turn them to themselves, to their own work and surrender.

I considered Rudi to be a tremendous and brilliant Means for the transformation of my life. He was unique in my experience. My own ordinary tendency was to seek a loving connection on which I could become dependent. Where love was not poured on me, I tended to become angry and resentful. But Rudi used, and even intentionally stimulated, these tendencies in me—in order for me to develop a responsible self-awareness relative to my own patterns and reactions, and an ability to generate an effective self-effort that could exceed those self-defeating patterns and reactions.

Rudi's psychological tutoring of me was coupled with the mysterious Power of the "Force", a tangible Spiritual Energy that I could experience directly and unequivocally. Rudi became, for me, a personal God-Presence, a unique combination of human and Spiritual Influences that, for me, were the equivalent of Jesus of Nazareth and all the other and various Divine personalities in religious and Spiritual literature.

And what were my motives in surrendering and in practicing obedience to such an Influence? Clearly, I had sought just such an encounter. It was no arbitrary meeting, but it perfectly coincided with my own needs at the time. First of all, it was an encounter, a confrontation. I had spent years in a more or less private investigation of my own mechanisms on a purely internal and philosophical level. I had become exquisitely aware of the content of my mind and life. Now I had sought an Influence outside myself that would contain and manifest all of the Force and Virtue I had come to believe were really present in the living condition of Reality. My years in exile (or solitude) were an attempt to discover or affirm what was (necessarily) in Reality. Now I sought to encounter that proven Reality in a living, demonstrable Presence. If I had lost the conventional "God" of religion and had ceased to believe in the traditional reports and claims about Jesus of Nazareth, now I sought to encounter the equivalent Force and

Reality. I no longer thought Real God and the True Guru to be impossible. Rather, I thought them to be entirely necessary.

Even more, as a result of my long experiment, I had discovered an underlying content and "creative" logic or image in my own humanly-born conscious awareness. I had located the source of suffering and misadventure in myself and recognized it as the pattern and drama of Narcissus. The logic of separation and self-fascination had appeared to me concretely as the leading mechanism of ordinary consciousness. This was coupled with another recognition, based on my own experience, but which I also found in the observations of Jung and the literature of Spiritual phenomena. It was that the drama and fate of Narcissus was not necessary, not equal to Reality. Thus, I sought an encounter with Reality that would release me from Narcissus, my own deadly logic, by forcing me to include what Narcissus always rejects by means of exclusive self-involvement.

The idea of release from Narcissus—the internal myth that "creates" suffering and destroys the inherent Bliss and Freedom of uncontradicted Reality—was my leading Intention. Thus, when I saw that Rudi manifested and dramatized that "other" Presence that is Reality, that always works to confound Narcissus, I gave myself up to him as a man does to God.

As weeks passed, Rudi increased his hold on me. He fascinated me with the stories of his life, the entire drama of the Force and Its miraculous effects. And the more fascinated I became, the more he strengthened his demands for work and surrender. Soon there was only work, only the effort of surrender. The underlying (and supportive) connection of love and friendship was continually reinforced by him in many personal ways, whenever it was required. But the outstanding manner of his dealing with me was blunt and aggressive. Whenever I approached him, I would be set aside. Attention was not focused on me. I was only given some kind of work to do or left only to listen while he openly gave his attention to others and seemed to favor them.

From the beginning, Rudi proposed Nina as an object of my love and pleasure, and he constantly drew my attention from my own problems, questions, and needs to Nina's need for love. I had decided, before I met him, that either I would have to leave Nina or I would have to accept the responsibilities of a husband. Rudi's way neither required nor valued celibacy and separation, but always love and connection. When he—at first, with ordinary humor, and then with obvious seriousness—began to chide me for my irresponsibility in relation to Nina, I began to consider how to become more a husband to her. Finally, he all but demanded that I marry her—and I agreed.

There is much truth in the idea that I got married only because my teacher told me to do so—for the sake of discipline, and as a kind of Yoga. But it was a voluntary decision on my part, and one that I had come to recognize as right and necessary at that time in my life. Thus, Nina and I were married on February 26, 1965 (and remained so for a time).

Rudi's influence also led me to discover a way of engaging my work-life that utilized my personal and "creative" needs. My father had become interested in Rudi as a result of our conversations, and he would occasionally visit Rudi at the store or even come to class. On one of these early visits, my father told Rudi that I had once intended to become a Lutheran minister. He said that, at one point, I appeared to lose all hope in the church, and tended to abandon my family, the church, and even the world, in despair.

Rudi asked me why I never became a minister. I told him that, at one point, I had become unable to believe in Jesus or God, and, as a result, I had gone off on my own to discover what was True about all such things. He dismissed all of my romanticism about the past and told me it would be good for me to take up those studies again. After all, I was no longer separated from What was True. It had become my own experience. And the work of a minister or a theologian was ideally suited to me. It could make use of my intellectual abilities and give me a "creative" outlet in which to speak about Spiritual Truth and help other people.

I protested that I may have become attuned to Spiritual life, but I was in no sense a Christian any longer. The Truth for me was universal and absolute, not limited to the myths and legends and dogmas of Christianity. I had found my inspirations more in the East. And Jesus of Nazareth—even if taken to be an historically real Spiritual figure (independent of the myths and unsupportable legends of conventional, exoteric religion)—stood for me only as one of many God-men, or revealers of the Divine Reality. Rudi told me that I was only being childish. He pointed out that his way could easily be expressed in the language of Christianity. The Force was the same as God, or the Holy Spirit. If I accepted the work of a minister with a mature mind, it could even involve me "creatively". I should simply see in it a right path that would give me the opportunity for work and surrender.

At first, this seemed impossible to me. I was no longer affiliated with any Christian church, nor did I care to be. And I felt I could never identify myself with the point of view and the beliefs of traditional Christianity. Rudi claimed that this was a virtue. Why should I identify with it? Indeed, I should not identify with it, for that would only provide more armor and self-imagery and prevent me from using it for the sake of work and surrender.

Finally, I attributed all of my misgivings to my own resistance. I agreed to give it a try. Even when I told Rudi I would accept it and play it as a kind of "imposter", he pointed out again that it was all a part of me and suited to my very needs and abilities.

At first, I tried to find a place in a denomination other than Lutheranism, the given religion of my childhood. I thought perhaps the Episcopal church was a broader denomination that could include more of the form of Spirituality I would profess. But I soon learned that I would have to pass through a long period of probationary training as a member of an Episcopal congregation before I could be accepted as a candidate for seminary training. Besides, the Episcopal church had many peculiarities of its own to which it would take me a long time to adapt.

So I made efforts to become re-affiliated with the Lutheran church through my old congregation in Franklin Square. The minister who served there when I was in high school had since retired to a congregation in Florida. But I quickly made friends with the new minister and was received quite openly by those who remembered me. After several weeks, I was recommended as a candidate for seminary training and given preliminary acceptance at the Lutheran Theological Seminary at Philadelphia.

This was in the spring of 1965. Entering students at the Seminary were required to have minimum training in koine (or "Biblical") Greek, and so I was unable to enter the following September. Instead, I enrolled at a Protestant seminary in New York for a year of preparatory study in Greek. In the meantime, my job at the radio station had come to an end, and I went to work as a furniture refinisher in a store owned by one of Rudi's students. Thus, I established myself in productive work that could carry me until September 1966.

Rudi's effects extended to all areas of my life. One evening, he came to visit Nina and me at our Houston Street apartment. He made it obvious that he was uncomfortable in the place, and said the atmosphere was very heavy and unclean. He remarked at how dark and small it was there. There were few windows, and the building was in an old, run-down, and unclean neighborhood. He told us we should not keep cats or other animals, because they kept the place dirty and generated vibrations that draw consciousness down to an animal level.

Nina and I took this quite seriously. We gave the Bitty to a friend and sent the lady cat off to Nina's parents. We tried to brighten up the apartment, and covered the walls with religious and Spiritual pictures. As a result, we also began to collect art, and we spent quite a bit of money buying paintings and sculpture from Rudi during the next few years. Finally, we found a large and bright apartment on Fourth Street near Sixth Avenue.

All in all, our lives became cleaner and happier. It was an intense struggle and discipline for me, but I welcomed all its effects. And I looked to Rudi and the Force for a dramatic reversal of my ordinary state of resistance and the logic of Narcissus.

The many practical changes in my way of life were lasting benefits of my experience with Rudi. Even these changes were gradual, and it would take longer for the kind of internal experiences I sought to begin with any kind of dramatic potency.

On a physical level, my life was becoming happier. My new logic of living was a conscious surrender of the patterns of self-indulgence and excess to which I had voluntarily submitted in the past. I began to limit and improve my diet—and this, coupled with the heavy labor of work as a furniture refinisher, gradually strengthened me and dropped my weight from more than 230 pounds to about 170 pounds. I began to use Hatha Yoga exercises to limber my body and adjust my weak back. All of this enabled me to enjoy a state of physical comfort and well-being I had not known since early childhood.

But, while I concentrated on these more external improvements in my manner of living, I was slower and more reluctant to let go of certain internal obstacles that prevented the Force from generating new forms of internal experience. I had long been accustomed to writing and exploiting the inner mechanisms of experience through its means—as well as through various excesses, including the occasional use of marijuana (and, on a few occasions, other drugs). Clearly, Rudi's way was opposed to such habits, and the prolonging of them could only prevent the evolution of that internal advancement the Force was supposed to Initiate.

My first experiences with the Force in class and in my personal relationship to Rudi were, for me, events within the sphere of the ordinary. They indicated a real Presence of a Spiritual kind, but they affected me mostly on a physical and mental level. They served to motivate me, but they were not themselves of a uniquely profound nature, or (in any most profound sense) of a higher or ultimate Nature.

In class, I would only become profoundly aware of my own resistance. After my first one or two experiences of the exercise, I saw that I would have to perform a revolutionary and gradual effort in relation to this resistance. Only then would I have any of the kind of dramatic and visionary experiences Rudi described— and which, on the basis of my own past experiences and my reading of Spiritual literature, I had learned to desire for myself.

Even because of the presence of this resistance in me and my awareness of it, I began to acquire intense feelings of frustration in regard to the internal work. Thus, I continued to maintain my efforts to write as before—and I began, again, to use drugs on occasion, to relieve this frustration and provide certain forms of internal opening and perception that I so deeply desired.

However—as a result of my new logic (in opposition to Narcissus), and also because of the purifying Presence of the Force in my life—my old ways also met with resistance in me, and they began to cause me trouble.

I began to see my writing as a superficial and fruitless exercise. And I doubted that I had any talent at all. My writing had developed to the point where I should begin the actual and intentional production of a book that would contain all of the values and discoveries of my long progress. But I steadily resisted bringing it to the point of deliberate "creation". I felt that something more needed to occur. There was yet some crucial Event that needed to be uncovered in the process of internal attention. I had not yet seen the death of Narcissus.

By the spring of 1965, I had again begun to use marijuana with some frequency. I found it relaxing and (it seemed at the time) particularly necessary under the pressure of work and effort that Rudi required. But the drug began to have a peculiarly negative effect. When I would smoke it, the salivary glands in my mouth would cease to flow, and I would realize a profound anxiety and fear.

On a very few occasions, I took other drugs with my old friends. We took Romilar again, but now its effects were minor. We found the city atmosphere aggravating, in contrast to the natural and beautiful setting of California. We began to spend our "high" time yearning to return to the ocean and the forests.

I took a drug called DMT, which had a remarkable effect. I became visually aware of the nature of the unity and deep structure of space and matter. Time disappeared, and space and matter revealed themselves as a single complicated mass (or fluid). When I concentrated on a wall or the objects in a room, they would break up and converge, with incredible speed toward an invisible point at infinity. I would see forms and space break into the millions of geometrical and mathematical units that composed their apparent structure. When I would look at someone's face, I could see the muscle and bone structure below with a kind of X-ray vision. I could see the internal organs of the head, the brain, the moving flow of fluids and nerve-energy, the structures and the natural energies of the body that were more subtle than the physical.

Such remarkable states of uncommon awareness combined with my rising sense of anxiety, fear, and reluctance in relation to drugs—such that, finally, in the early summer of 1965, I determined to somehow stop their use.

I decided that I would deliberately take a drug for the last time. I would not simply stop using drugs before a last, bravely intentional try. I did not want fear to be my motive for stopping my experiment with drugs. Thus, I bought two large capsules of mescalin, and Nina and I went to spend the Fourth of July weekend at the summer home of a friend on the south shore of Long Island.

I was quite anxious, and I delayed the taking of the drug for several hours. Nina decided she did not want to take the drug, and so I gave it to a young man who was also present, the friend of my friend. My friend, Larry, took several capsules of peyote. I shuffled through all my cautions. Then I downed my last capsule of drugs with abandon. It was to be the most terrifying experience of my life.

After we took the drugs, we drove out to a nearby beach for a picnic. It was a deserted area. We spread out blankets and lots of food. As soon as I began to eat, I noticed that peculiar nausea and disinterest in food that often accompanies a powerful hallucinogen. My friend Larry was already experiencing the effects of the peyote, and he was walking along the beach many yards away. I watched him as he walked, and my mind seemed to have become a prism focused through a concave lens. Everything became small and compressed. Instead of opening and expanding, my "consciousness" had contracted, such that I felt trapped, and my very life seemed about to vanish in the tiny focal point of my vision.

Physically, I felt equally unstable. I perceived none of the familiar points in space (or the sense of my body within them) that permit balance and ordinary judgement. I was becoming quite disturbed and frightened. My speech was becoming incoherent. Somehow, I managed to communicate to Nina that she should get me to the car.

When we got into the car, I told her to drive and just keep me moving. As we drove, I was overcome by violent fear and confusion.

My body began to tremble, and soon my legs began to shake and jerk up and down, such that I felt I was about to be overcome with a violent fit. Then I felt as if I were about to have a heart attack. Violent constrictions began in my lower body and my chest, and then the awful moment came in the heart. There was a powerful jolt and shock in my chest, and I passed into blackness, certain that I was about to die. But then, a moment later, I returned to bodily consciousness and felt the violent fit climbing in me again. Again, there was a seizure in the heart, and again the black. Then, again, the trembling fit of terror, the fit of breathing, and the jolt in the heart.

I could not imagine a more terrifying predicament. It was an endless cycle of deaths and fits that had no end, but always seemed about to end. I told Nina to get me to a doctor.

Minutes later, we arrived at a hospital. Nina guided me in. I was incoherent with confusion and fear. Several nurses came and asked questions, but they seemed unconcerned or unaware of my state. Nina told them I had taken a drug, and they frowned and told us to sit and wait. I could not imagine why they did not simply administer an antidote or a tranquilizer. The minutes passed, and I began to wander around the waiting room searching for help.

Nina sensed that they were only stalling in order to get the police. I decided we must somehow get away, and I told her to meet me in the parking lot. I found a door and wandered out toward the cars. As I walked, I felt as if I were passing utterly into madness. My mind appeared like a dome with two interlocking spheres that closed the visual mind to what is above and outside the body and ordinary perception. As I walked, these semi-spheres turned, and openings were revealed in their separate shapes. Thus, as I walked, the mind opened beyond itself—and I seemed to pass through myself, and out beyond any figure or ability to perceive or know a thing in relation to my human personality and form.

I had told Nina to get me some tranquilizers. When she found me, I was groveling in the dirt beneath a tree, weeping and crying to God and Jesus and Rudi for help. I swallowed a few tranquilizers and asked her to call Rudi on the phone. But Rudi was not home.

Nina spoke to his mother and found that Rudi was away for the weekend.

I stumbled into the station wagon and lay down in the rear section on my back. Then Nina drove off toward our friend's house. As she drove, I passed into a State of Absolute Conscious Awareness, beyond any thought or feeling or perception. The deaths that threatened me earlier became a kind of Nirvanic death of perfect and mad simplicity.

The next thing of which I became aware was the door opening to the rear of the station wagon. It was night. Nina was standing there. She led me out into the street and into the house. I was experiencing a State of Absolute Tranquility. But I no longer possessed a memory of any kind.

It is difficult to communicate the emptiness of my condition at that time. It was not merely that I did not remember who Nina was, who my friend was, or where we were. I had not the slightest notion of what I was or what they (in fact) were. I had no idea what a human being or a world was. I had no ideas of any kind. I perceived everything as an Original, Blissful, Infinite Void.

It was a totally arbitrary awakening—from object-excluding Absoluteness to forms perceived in Absoluteness. Out of necessity, I simply began to adapt to my arbitrary form and to the arbitrary form of the arbitrary world in which I had arbitrarily appeared. I learned the names and relationships and uses in that world. I adapted to the memories the people claimed to have of me. I questioned them and learned how to function among them. But it was all a present learning process without even a hint of memory involved. Later, it seemed to me that if I had awakened as a pair of shoes in a closet it would not have been more arbitrary and unusual than this, and I would have adapted to it in the same manner.

After several hours in this State, I had acquired a certain facility for life in this form. The feelings of love and familiarity were simulated again in my mind. And we drove out to watch the stars and the sunrise on the beach. My State continued to be one of Absolute Peace and Tranquility, unthreatened by any death or any necessity to persist. It was a True Calm, a State rooted in Ultimate Reality—but it was only temporary, and the price of suffering that had been required to attain it was beyond my willingness to pursue it again.

During the next week, I spoke to Rudi about the incident. He knew that I had already paid the price, and he made no attempt to blame or chide me for it. I told him why I had done it, and (in fulfillment of my earlier and already established intention) I promised I would abandon the use of drugs. He accepted my promise and pointed out how devastating such drugs are. He said that even what internal strength I had gained as a result of the past months of effort with the Force had been wiped out by those few hours of experiment with drugs. He told me that I would have to avoid all such things in the future, or else invite madness. Now I must begin to work and surrender in earnest.

And so I did begin to work in earnest. My efforts, internal and external, were profoundly magnified by this freedom from the need to indulge myself in drug experiences or any other kind of stimulation. I found a new strength with which to penetrate the resistance of Narcissus within me.

Finally, even my writing stood before me as an obstacle. Over the years, I had accumulated and retained a handwritten manuscript of perhaps fifteen or twenty thousand pages! Besides this, there were several boxes of notebooks and collected material. I decided I would either turn all of this into some kind of productive writing or else abandon the activity altogether.

For several days, in the late summer of 1965, I pored over my manuscript and notes. But I saw that these pages themselves had developed into a size that could not possibly be either edited or used. The manuscript was simply too large, too expanded to be researched or included. The more I examined it, the more useless it appeared.

I saw that all of this was already all that it should be. It was not, in its bulk, the preliminary work for an eventual novel. It was itself the visible product of years of a Spiritual and ultimate exercise of my own peculiar design. Its Purpose was not fiction but the Realization of Truth. And its Purpose could not be fulfilled in the writing of any mere work of "fiction", but only by the extension of all of that previous exercise into the way of radical understanding that I was more and more discovering, and even into the way of Spiritual work I had already discovered in relationship to Rudi.

Thus, I decided to burn every last page of my manuscript, everything I had ever written or collected in my life. In doing so, I was aware that something significant and "creative" might also be destroyed—but I knew, in any case, that whatever concrete results were produced by my writing were retained in my mind. If ever I gained the refreshment and "creative" power to write again, I could draw the useful material of those years of labor from my own memory.

Nina has often remarked about how startled she was when she came home that evening. I was squatting, totally naked, in front of the fireplace, throwing sheaves of manuscript into the fire. For her, it was also the end of a familiar form of life. It was the apparent destruction of all of the results of an effort she had made possible in many ways. She had protected and supported me through all that period of "creativity", and now she was never to enjoy its fulfillment. But I assured her it would be fulfilled. My life would be its fulfillment. Love and Consciousness and Truth would be its manifestation. And even what was substantial in all that I burned would remain in me, to be used whenever the real impulses of art were awakened.

It took me three days to burn it all. I do not know how many grocery bags and boxes of ashes remained to be discarded. But it was a purifying fire. I had spent years to recover even every memory, motive, and hidden internal form to my humanly-born conscious awareness. Now I had to perform the sacrifice that would return even all of it to its Source. Thus, I would be empty and "creatively" free. My manuscripts were a burden of past time, a present obstacle to conscious awareness. I saw that my work must now be a present, positive "creativity". It could no longer be a passive observation of contents. That had served its Purpose, and now Narcissus was known to me. He was alive as me. Now I must overcome him in myself—and, to do so, I had to be free of every last vestige of the old work and its accumulations.

The result of the burning was a purification of all my past and of the position of self-conscious knowledge that the comprehensive awareness of my past required in me. I felt thoroughly cleansed and free. My life was perfectly renewed and alive, instant and direct—a present activity free of any content that could either determine or limit its ultimate Realization. Thus, I gave myself utterly to the overcoming of Narcissus, and to the liberating attainment of his death.

Adi Da Samraj in New York after His return from the Lutheran Seminary

CHAPTER NINE

The Death of Narcissus

From the late summer of 1965 until I left for the Lutheran Seminary at Philadelphia the following August, I was, without qualification, Rudi's devoted disciple. I performed the internal and external work and surrender he prescribed, and I enjoyed the entirely positive effects of the life-disciplines he required.

My relationship to Nina became Yoga, my work became Yoga, and my life became Yoga. I enjoyed a state of physical, mental, and moral well-being that I had never known since I was a boy, and I exceeded even that in these realizations of maturity. I learned the great pleasures of self-control and purity, of cleansing work and discipline, and all of the wholesome effects that social communication and outward love bring to anyone who has exercised himself or herself in an erratic solitude.

I even became a wholly acceptable Christian. I found that there was, indeed, no unsurmountable obstacle in the language of Christianity, and I began to enjoy the "creative" exercise of adapting my Knowledge of Truth to the historical and dogmatic language of the church. My studies in Greek also gave me great pleasure, and my attitude of unobstructed work made me excel as a student.

The seminary at Philadelphia offered a one-thousand-dollar fellowship which would cover all the usual expenses of tuition, books, and a portion of the rest of one's living. They proposed a series of questions, to be answered in the form of an essay by all those who wanted to apply for the fellowship. I thought it would be immense fun if I could win this fellowship in spite of my background, and my thought and attitude toward Christianity. I wrote a long essay in answer to the questions. They dealt with "autobiographical" matters and thoughts relating to theology and social attitudes. It was a good test to see just how well I could represent myself and speak the language of a Christian. And I won! I had become a successful religious "imposter".

I also did some writing for the completion of requirements for the master's degree at Stanford. I wrote a long, semi-"autobigraphical" novella in order to satisfy my "incomplete" in the "creative writing" course. Wallace Stegner accepted it as actual writing, acceptable for course credit, but he was vehement in his denial of its literary value. He apparently gave the work to some of his students, and they agreed with him that, whatever it was, it was not "literature".

I was not sure whether to take their resistance as censure or, since I knew very well what they considered viable "literature", a compliment. At any rate, I did not persist in defending the writing beyond a certain point. Once it was reluctantly accepted for credit, I went to work preparing a thesis for the degree.

I wrote a long study on the aesthetic theories of Gertrude Stein. I used the work to expand critically on many of the motives that had supported me as a writer—and I showed how these researches ultimately concerned not "literature" in the usual sense, but an attitude and a search that corresponded to otherwise philosophical, psychological, and Spiritual efforts. My thesis was developed through references to Jung's studies in alchemy and the psyche, various writers on psychology, philosophy, and the philosophy of art, and even the writings of Krishnamurti (who was, like myself, concerned with the problems of mind and art). Many years later, I gave an elaborated title to this study, which summarizes my intentions in writing it: *The Reduction Of The Beloved To Shape Alone: The Effort Toward Abstraction, The Pure Present, and The New In "Modern" Art, Psychology, and Philosophy—Especially As Defined In The "Meaningless" Aesthetic Theories Of Gertrude Stein.*

As I said earlier, my own career as a writer had been stimulated by various modern sources, of which Gertrude Stein was a primary example. In general, the modernist writers of the early twentieth century thought they were doing something new or revolutionary with the abilities of language to describe, signify, perform, or be something. But I knew they were actually, if not entirely consciously, doing something with the mind, with life, with the humanly-born conscious awareness. And, although this might represent an unusual and revolutionary activity in Western literature, it was not (in fact) something new in the history of human activity.

When I realized that I was also doing this, I began that work itself, consciously and deliberately. I no longer required the symbol (or medium) of language for my work. I abandoned "literature" and began the work that is only observing, understanding, and Realizing. Then, finally, I would Know this "Thing", and I would only write It clearly. My master's thesis was a critical presentation of this point of view.

My thesis was received warmly by the professors assigned to me—although I am sure they were unfamiliar with the more "esoteric" literature of Gertrude Stein, not to mention the other writers I mentioned. And it was clear to me that they did not discern any fundamental or revolutionary importance in the actual problems I discussed. But the work was an important exercise for me. It served to put a cap on my past work as a writer, and it left me free to engage in my new career as a seminarian.

During the period in which I wrote my master's thesis, I was still trying to discover some possible "creative" work, apart from the ministry, that would build upon my previous "creative" life and still make use of my new discoveries. I thought perhaps I could train in some professional work in psychology. I had read a great deal (casually, and in school) in all fields of psychology and philosophy. And Jung's work, in particular, bore a close affinity to the forms of Eastern Spirituality and the States of Conscious Awareness I had experienced in the past.

I went to see M. Esther Harding, a close associate and student of the late Dr. Jung. But this meeting only confirmed what I had suspected were grave limitations in Jung's assumptions. Dr. Harding told me that any Westerner who devoted himself or herself to the Spiritual exercises peculiar to the Orient (as, for example, to the Tibetan methods described by W. Y. Evans-Wentz, in books which Jung had introduced to the West) would become clinically insane. From her—and from Jung's—point of view, the realities of Eastern Spirituality were, in a Western psychology, usable and meaningful only as symbols. I told her that such

"Eastern" practice was exactly what I had been doing and intended to continue doing. We discussed the living Yoga of Kundalini Shakti, but she could see in it only symbols that are the peculiar contents of the Eastern psyche. She urgently suggested that I abandon this approach and volunteer myself to Jungian analysis.

Thus, I saw that Jung's brand of understanding precluded even the modified use of Spiritual practice as I understood it. Even my experiences, over a lifetime, of phenomena that can only be properly understood in a Spiritual context were (to this view) unallowable, at best clinical, causative of disturbance, and to be made subject to the interpretations of a humanistic psychology that was not yet loosed from the mortal philosophy of the university establishment.

The best Dr. Harding would do was recommend an analyst for me. As far as training in the various methods of analysis or group process was concerned, not only was it precluded by the kind of interpretation required, but I would have to prepare myself with years of university and professional training that was, to my point of view, quite beside the point of what I considered to be the real and necessary preparations for Spiritual Knowledge.

Thus, I began to realize that, at least for the time being, my only option was to continue my preparations for the Lutheran ministry. Nina also finished her requirements for the master's degree at this time, and we directed ourselves toward the coming move to Philadelphia.

No description of this period would be adequate and true without the inclusion of my various experiences with the "Force". At first, that experience was limited to the kind I first described in meeting with Rudi. I became aware that an actual Force (or tangible Spiritual Power) emanated from him. I could feel It in various ways as a magnetic or electric Energy in my body. This is, of course, a tremendously unique experience in terms of what people would ordinarily suppose to be reality. But It was not unusual or unique for me in my experience. Rudi's manifestation and use of It was unique—and my approach to It was now based on a totally new logic of life—but I had experienced the same Spiritual Energy (or Force) as the "Bright" of childhood, and (later) as the rising Force that overtook me in the college experience.

Rudi

Very quickly, I came to a comfortable recognition of this "Force" as a reliably available Presence, and I felt It operating continually (and always availably) in Rudi. Thus, that Force was redeemed from dependence on the fluctuations of my own life-consciousness. It stood outside me, constantly available through my teacher. I was free to turn myself from the long enterprise and experiment of my youth, wherein I had sought to perceive and verify the actual Existence and Nature of this Force in myself. Now I devoted myself to purifying work under the assumption of a concrete relationship to that actual Presence.

Thus, my first experiences were as I have described. They manifested as changes in my life-pattern (or my physical, mental, and moral existence), its functional instruments, and its environment. But, after I had eliminated the practices and forms of deliberate self-indulgence that inhibited the work of this Force on an internal level, I began also to have significant Spiritual experiences.

As I continued to go to Rudi's class and tried to open and surrender, I began to experience Rudi's "Force" entering me as he said It would. When he would begin the exercise or look at me during the exercise, I would usually feel a sudden descent of tremendous and seemingly Infinite Energy from above. I could feel this descent as a peculiar kind of pressure that first came in the head and then permeated the body.

This pressure was the usual sign of the working of that Force in me. As I exercised myself in surrender to It over time, I could feel certain points of resistance in myself fall away and give place in a kind of interior opening (on a mental and physical level). In time, I could feel this pressure at will, and almost constantly. It became a Presence that I could respond to in moments of repose, or even during any kind of activity.

After many months, this pressure became particularly apparent in the head. The center of the upper brain became irritated in a manner that had a deep (and even sensuous) quality. My ears began to feel as if there were an internal pressure opening their channels, and they felt a certain heat. At times, I could (in a subtle manner) hear the Force descend—and my ears seemed to be stretching open to perceive some sound, both internal and external, that was always going on.

The process of meditation involved a surrendering of thought—and, as this emptying of the mind continued, it was replaced by a strong concentration of penetrating Energy in the head. Afterwards, the head would feel bathed and warmed in a Blissful Energy that descended from above. Its immediate effect was to offset the usual concentration of Energy in thought and in the lower body. For a period sometimes lasting for hours after the exercise, there was only a sublime Calmness and Fullness, without any anxiety or any movement of desire. The natural energies that flowed in the body felt balanced and harmonized. And this appeared to be the natural pre-condition for clarity and free-functioning as a human entity.

There were also certain visual sensations. When I would concentrate in the exercise (either on Rudi or on an image used for meditation at home), the field of ordinary vision would become dark and thick, then suddenly expand as a pervasive field of Force—and I would perceive Spiritual Energy entirely pervading the atmosphere, such that a general luminosity (both seen and felt) would surround everything and form the very substance of space. It was also this luminous quality that led me to call my childhood experience the "Bright".

At times during meditation, I would also see certain forms appear superimposed on Rudi's face, as well as on other people or objects. I would see beards and moustaches appear and disappear on Rudi, or he would seem to be clothed in oriental robes. Sometimes, the entire room would take on a quality of splendor, and it would seem as if we were in another time, seated before some oriental philosopher-prince. The features of his face would go through many changes, as if revealing his past lives and our past associations.

Rudi and some of his students also claimed to have various visions, but I never had any such experiences while with him. Basically, my experience with him was limited to these subtle demonstrations of Energy on a physical level, and on an etheric (or, otherwise, astral) level (just beyond the physical).[19]

The class itself was an exercise in concentration, in which the Force was received, directed below, and then drawn up the spine

THE KNEE OF LISTENING

to the head. After the class, I would experience a fullness, a sensitivity and vibrancy in the organs of the head, a quietness descended into the mind, and a kind of charged and burning feeling pleasantly throughout my body.

One time, Nina and I spent a weekend with Rudi at a beach house on Fire Island. That night, Nina woke up feeling a strong electric shock running through the body, beginning from the head. I experienced the same basic thing a few nights later—but the experience was extraordinarily intense, such that I automatically struggled to arouse my body and shake off the experience. The Force had become so Powerful that I felt I was about to be electrocuted.

There was also another manifestation evident in Rudi and some of his students. During the exercise, their bodies would begin to jerk in a characteristic manner. There appeared to be a jolting within the spine that communicated to the muscles. Their spines revolved and appeared to make small spasms. Then their heads would begin to revolve very violently. This always happened to Rudi at the close of the exercise. I often desired this experience myself, but it did not occur for some time. In my life of seeking, I never tried to fake or simulate any kind of phenomenon. My seeking was always too desperate to be satisfied with anything but an obvious and spontaneous (and obviously genuine) experience, which carried an inherent internal authority and self-verification.

These spontaneous and purifying movements—or "kriyas", as they are called in India—did not arise at all in me until shortly before I left Rudi and his classes. Finally, they did begin to develop, although not as violently as in the case of others. For the most part, I only felt a kind of gentle pulsing in my lower back, like little bubbles of air and fluid rising in a percolator. Also, I began to manifest a twitching in my face and mouth (and a rapid breathing) like the snarl of a wolf, and another spontaneous action that was like the yawn and growl of a lion. The arising of such manifestations and the spontaneous generation of animal sounds are also a characteristic of this Shakti Yoga.

On a few occasions, I also experienced what I mentioned previously as the "Thumbs". While seated in the exercise, I would feel the Force descending through me unobstructed. Then I was easily able to relax to a great depth. And the Energy would then move to the base of the spine and travel upwards along the spine to the head. As It did so, I felt the polarity of my physical being reverse—and, instead of tending gravitationally downward toward my seat, I would "gravitate" upwards toward my head. As I relaxed completely, the reversal of Energy would be completed—and my form felt to be a kind of detached sphere, entirely free of the ordinary body-sense. A tremendous sense of Peace and Fullness would arise at such times, and I would long to remain in that State. But, as soon as I became attached to It, It would tend to disappear. So I would relax more. And, as I relaxed, an extraordinary depth would appear within my humanly-born conscious awareness, and there was the feeling-sensation of falling into an Infinite Deep. Then I would pass into a profound Bliss. Such profundity—experienced, in the case of the "Thumbs", in a manner that (as I was later to discover) was unique to myself—is an example of what (in India) is called "samadhi".

These experiences approximately summarize my fullest benefits from Rudi. By the time I was about to leave for seminary in the late summer of 1966, I had, in all human terms, become quite strong, clear, and free. And this strengthening was accompanied by a growing sense of independence. Rudi's Yoga was a form of liberating dependence, wherein I was (with very positive life-effects) filled and nourished and guided by him and his Force—but Rudi was not himself prepared (ultimately, and perfectly) to liberate others, or to bring any one to any truly high (or, otherwise, ultimate) Realization.

Rudi was a kind of super-parent to me, a mother-father force that guided me into human maturity. In the Spiritual cultures of the East, it is traditional for the disciple of one who is not his or her ultimate teacher (or final Guru) to determine the moment of his or her maximum possible attainment (in that company), and (in that moment) to affirm his or her independence, and then move on to his or her next (and, perhaps, ultimate) teacher (or Guru).

As time passed, I knew my own moment of such independence and moving on was approaching. Thus, I gradually began to become aware of the urge to independence in me—and this was also reflected in a growing critical awareness of Rudi's qualities, and of the limits on what was potential for me in his company.

As I have already said, Rudi never represented himself as a "finished product". He always saw his life only as a matter of growth, rather than of completion (although he assumed he had grown more than perhaps anyone else). Thus, as I also grew, I became increasingly more aware of Rudi's limitations. I saw that, even in the midst of apparently dramatic Spiritual experiences, Rudi's interests were almost entirely life-ordinary. It was ordinary life-problems, and not the urge toward ultimate Divine Realization, that fueled and motivated even his apparently Spiritual efforts. And, most critically, I eventually saw that the particular Force (or the quality of Shakti) available through Rudi had carried me as far as It could go. Mere "experiences" and worldly (or merely ordinary) human growth were not sufficient for me. Only Truth Itself would be enough. In summary, I discovered that Rudi's personal instrument was not a perfect and unlimited Source of Spiritual Energy (or Spiritual Influence), but a limited one in an advanced (but still relatively early) stage of growth.

When, eventually, it came time for me to finally leave Rudi's physical presence, I was no longer a Spiritual innocent. I had already begun Real Spiritual life on my own. I had already attuned myself to the "Force" that was Present in me, and Which had (in fact) been the Circumstance of my entire life, from the beginning. It had never been apart from me. I Knew It as the "Bright", and as my own Eternally Free Nature (beyond all internal contradiction—and beyond even all the contents and patterns of humanly-born conscious awareness).

In the meantime, and even as I left for seminary, I kept all of these observations silent in myself. I wanted to test myself in Rudi's absence, to see if my growing sense of independence would prove itself worthy of action. Thus, Nina and I moved from New York and took up residence near the seminary in Philadelphia.

Shortly after the beginning of the school year, I began to write again. Only now the writing was of a different kind, and its motivation was also new. My position in the Christian community was

unusual. I had to act and communicate and profess as a Christian—
but, in fact, I was conscious of Reality in a fundamentally different
manner. The longer I was there, the more of an "imposter" I knew
myself to be. I did not feel I was "putting anything over" on anyone. That was not my intention. But I had to remain continually
sensitive to the difference in myself and, in the same moment,
translate my free Awareness and my perception of Reality into
a more or less orthodox (and even conventional) manner and
communication.

This dual position produced a constant reflectiveness in me—
and so I began to write a journal of my experiences and thoughts as
they actually were, prior to the necessary translation into "Christian".

I managed to communicate myself fairly well. My studies were
a tremendous discipline for me, but I managed to keep the highest
grades in all of my coursework. I exceeded everyone else on the
level of study, and this alone was a tremendous proof of the utility
of the attitude of work.

I kept as free as possible of the traditional religious life of the
seminary. I only went to church when it was required, and Nina and
I generally secluded ourselves in an invulnerable sphere of necessary privacy. As the months passed, I became more and more
acutely Aware of the internal movement of my own life. I was again
on my own, and free to pursue the Truth of my conscious life. But
now I was also functioning as a visible member of the world.

Nevertheless, I acted with a great feeling of Clarity, Freedom,
and Power. The benefits of my entire life of "Bright" understanding,
including all the effects of my Spiritual life and humanizing discipline in Rudi's company, were thus made obvious to me as a very
practical matter of course. And this made me all the more aware
of the limitations bred in that "modernized" religious community.
The men and women there were alike pale and in doubt, struggling with desires they never understood—and they bore the
burden of the kind of liberal theology that first affected me in
college, when I read books like *The Lost Years of Jesus Revealed.*

The seminary and its Protestant Christian community were a
collection of ordinary, suffering, and confused human beings, who
lived without benefit of fundamental Truth. The kind of experience

that was my daily Enjoyment was, from their point of view, unavailable, even unacceptable—and they consigned it to a primitive state of life. Far from enjoying the "peace that passes all understanding", these Spiritually unaware religionists were busy wondering what small portion of the religious life was the legitimate inheritance of the age of materialism, materialistic science, universal skepticism, and mortal philosophy.

I saw that the entire seminary community was suffering exactly the form of unenlightened and suppressive philosophizing that had turned me out of college into the wilderness of my seeking. I wrote in a copy of the Bible a remark by one of the psalmists: "My soul is released, as a bird from the snare of fowlers." This sense of Release, Certainty, and Joy was my common experience, but I saw no way at all to tell my Truth such that I could be heard.

In time, my daily life became routine. I had learned my "place". Most of the seminary professors had seen fit to criticize me openly or in private for the few of my "extreme" views I allowed myself to express. For them, there was no viable Truth at all in the entire realm of Spiritual experience and phenomena that was my birthright. They were enclosed in Rudolf Bultmann and Paul Tillich, and even a mortal theology.

At best, they saw human beings as necessarily mortal. "When you're dead, you're dead." But, perhaps (they hoped), it is true that Jesus will come again at the end of time and revitalize the world, "creating" everyone again in a new and immortal life.

Doubts began to arise in me. It was no longer simply a matter of whether or not I would be able to speak within the religious community. I began to doubt whether I could even persist in such a place. The Christian community with which I was associated became for me a pale shadow of life, a desperate vestige of the past that is no longer opened even to its own Truth.

Rudi continued to use the same arguments with me as before, and I remained for the same reasons. But I wrote and lived according to my own understanding, and waited for a moment when I would see my own way clearly.

I continued to observe that I was involved in the pattern and life of Narcissus. I was observing his evolution in myself and in the world. And my "work" was Purposed to see the accomplishment of my Ultimate Release.

Finally, in the spring of 1967, I passed through an experience that epitomized all of my seeking and all aspects of my (to then developed) life of understanding. The experience itself is surrounded with apparent evidence of a "clinical breakdown"—but it is otherwise full of the sense and Reality of primary Experience, the breakthrough of Ultimate and unqualified Consciousness Itself. It was the death of Narcissus.

I had contracted a spring cold—which was not unusual, except that I had been entirely free of any kind of disease for the last couple of years. I was in the bathroom when this episode began. I had bathed and shaven, and I was rubbing a cleansing pad on my face. Suddenly, my flesh began to feel very "massy" and unpliable. I felt as if the pores of my face had closed. The skin became dry and impervious to air. As I looked at my face in the mirror, it appeared gray, disturbed, and deathlike. The saliva in my mouth stopped flowing, and I was overcome by a rising anxiety that became an awesome and overwhelming fear of death.

I was fixed in the certainty that I was soon to go mad and die, but I tried as much as possible simply to observe this process in myself. I calmly said goodbye to Nina, telling her nothing of this, and left for school.

When I sat down to my first morning class, this process was still going on in me. There was simply this absolute fear, and all my physical and mental processes appeared to be rushing to disappear and die. As I listened to the lecture on church history, I felt as if my mind were a separate, material entity. It seemed to be rushing forward toward an invisible point, with accelerating speed. I felt as if I were to go violently insane on the spot. I began to write very rapidly in my notebook, in order simply to observe this process and not be overcome by its effects.

I wrote every word the professor spoke, and, if there was a moment of silence, I would write whatever I was observing in the room or in my body. Somehow I managed to get through the fifty-minute lecture. When it was over, I sat by myself. My body felt in a fever and my mind close to delirium.

This one experience epitomized all the parts of the many experiences of fear and sickness and near madness I had known in my life. It was as if every one of those experiences was an event of this same kind, and could have led to some marvelous Realization, if only I were able to allow the death or madness to take its course.

But in this instance, as in the past, the shock and awesome fear were too great to be allowed without resistance. In the previous days, I had taken a few pills for a cold, and so I left school to go to a doctor for advice. The doctor said the pills were mild, and not aggravating or narcotic. He attributed my heightened sensitivity and alarmed condition to perhaps overwork or some kind of nervous excitement.

Nonetheless, I stopped taking the pills. I went home. All day I stretched alone on the floor of the living room, revolving in this same overwhelming fear of death. When Nina came home, she tried to make me comfortable, and I passed the evening in front of the TV set, observing my terror.

When Nina went to bed, I also tried to sleep. But the intensity of the experience only increased. Finally, I woke her in the middle of the night and asked her to take me to the hospital. My breathing had become alarming, and my heart seemed to be slowing down. At times my heart would beat irregularly and seem to stop.

She drove me to a nearby emergency ward. I was examined by a nurse, and then a psychiatrist, who told me I was having an anxiety attack. There was nothing apparently wrong with me physically. He gave me a sleeping pill and told me to rest. If I felt no relief within a couple of days, I should seek psychiatric help.

When we got home, I tried to sleep, but it seemed a long time before I could sleep. During the next couple of days, I went to a psychiatrist, and I detailed to him the entire history of my life, including my (relatively brief and limited) experiences with drugs and my work with Rudi. He only told me I could join a group therapy session he held every week. I went to his session that night, and also, the next day, to a group session for students held by a psychologist at the seminary. But there was no relief, no fundamental insight, no communication I could make that made the difference.

Finally, on the third day after this process began, I was lying home alone in the afternoon. All my life I had been constantly brought to this point. All of the various seeking methods of my life had constantly prevented this experience from going to its end. All my life I had been preventing my death.

I lay on the floor, totally disarmed, unable to make a gesture that could prevent the rising fear. And, thus, the fear grew in me— but, for the first time, I allowed it to happen. I could not prevent it. The fear and the death rose and became my overwhelming experience. And I observed the crisis of that fear in a moment of conscious, voluntary death. I allowed the death to happen, and I "saw" it happen. It was not that an organic death occurred, but even organic death ceased to be a concern. There was a spontaneous, utter release of identification with the body, the mind, the emotions of the separate person, and the self-contracting (or reactive and separative) act that is the ego (or the presumed person).

When that moment of crisis had passed, I felt a marvelous relief—or, rather, simply, a marvelous Freedom. The death had occurred, but I had <u>observed</u> it! I remained untouched by it. The body and the mind and the egoic personality had died (or been utterly released as a concern and an identity), but I remained as essential and unqualified Awareness (and purely That, but also Freely Aware of the physical body and its natural environment).

When all of the fear and dying had finished their course, when the body, the mind, the apparently separate "person" (and the <u>act</u> that made its apparent separateness) had been released, and my attention was no longer fixed in those things, I Knew Reality, tacitly and directly. There was an Infinite Bliss of Being, an untouched, unborn Sublimity—without separation, without individuation, without a thing from which to be separated. There was only Reality Itself, the incomparable Nature and constant Existence that underlies (and observes, and Knows) the entire adventure of life. And that Same and Very Reality was also revealed as the unqualified living condition of the totality of conditionally manifested existence.

After a time, I got up from the floor. I walked around and beamed Joyfully at the room. The Love-Blissful, unthreatened Current of the "Bright" emanated Freely and unqualifiedly from my heart, and not a pulse of It was limited by my otherwise conditional existence or the existence of the world. I had acquired a totally new understanding. I understood Narcissus and the entire cycle of suffering and search. I saw the meaning of my entire striving life to that moment. Suffering, seeking, self-indulgence, the seeker's Spirituality, and all the rest were founded in the same primary motivation and error. It was the avoidance of relationship. That was it! That was the chronic and continuous source and characteristic of all egoic activity. Indeed, the ego was revealed to be only an activity, not an "entity". The "entity", the separate "person" (or ego-"I"), was revealed to be only an illusion, a mere presumption in mind and feeling, resulting from the self-contraction, the egoic reaction, the single egoic act of the total body-mind. The ego, the separate and separative "I", is the chronic (and total psycho-physical) avoidance of relationship. Thus, human beings are forever suffering, seeking, indulging themselves, and manipulating their lives for the sake of some unknown goal in eternity.

The human trouble showed itself to be entirely determined by this one process of avoidance, or total psycho-physical self-contraction. It was the source of separation and un-love, the source of doubt and un-Reality, of qualification and loss. But, in fact, there is only relationship, only love, only unqualified relatedness, only the unqualified living condition of Reality. Therefore, I Knew that Reality Itself could always be directly Realized in life, if the self-contracting (or separative) reaction in life was exceeded by the unqualified assumption of relatedness in all the moments of living.

In the weeks that remained of my first year at seminary, I tried again and again to speak revealingly to others about my recent extraordinary experience and my new understanding. I felt I was not in the same position I had been in college. I felt this experience was fundamental and complete. I felt that the Knowledge revealed to me in this experience could not be lost in the midst of any possible events, any return of old tendencies. This was the primary Knowledge (in life) that I had sought all of my adult life.

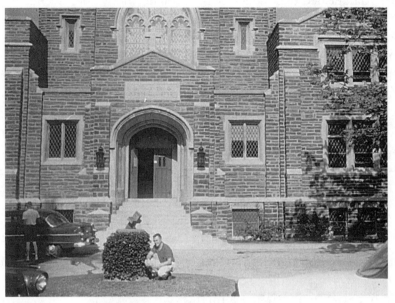

At the Lutheran Seminary in Philadelphia

Apartment where Adi Da Samraj lived while attending the Seminary

I understood Narcissus and the entire cycle of suffering and search. I saw the meaning of my entire striving life to that moment. Suffering, seeking, self-indulgence, the seeker's Spirituality, and all the rest were founded in the same primary motivation and error. It was the <u>avoidance of relationship</u>. That was it!

Philadelphia State Mental Hospital, where Adi Da Samraj served as chaplain

The diminished experience of the "Bright" in my adolescence now paled beside the Spiritual "Brightness" Aroused by this Knowledge. My "Bright" experience of Awakening in college appeared to be merely a preliminary to this fullest "Bright" Knowledge. And all that I had come to see as a result of Rudi's discipline, all of the functioning apparatus of conditional Spiritual experience, all conditional worlds, all conditional possibilities, all conditional abilities, appeared to be merely a distraction from this primary Knowledge. I identified that Knowledge as the primary feeling of relatedness. Not separation, not union, but unqualified relatedness (or non-separateness) arose in me as the root-sense (or fundamental condition) of living existence.

But my professors failed to understand what I had understood. I abandoned myself to them completely and told them all of the motives that brought me to seminary. Most of them were simply shocked. Their leading seminarian had turned out to be a fanatic, an heretical "enthusiast"—a mystic!

In the course of my studies, I had learned about the Eastern Orthodox Christian church. This Grand Event of the death of Narcissus had not removed the necessity for life in the ordinary sense. I had still to find some sort of "creative" and productive means of life. And so I considered turning from the Lutheran church to the Eastern church.

The Eastern Orthodox church, at least on paper, seemed to be the ideal form of Christianity. Above all, it acknowledged all the classical Spiritual phenomena of the saints. And its theology was founded in Spiritual experience rather than ecclesiastical dogma. Thus, I contacted a local Orthodox priest, and Nina and I were received into the Orthodox church a few weeks later.

In the meantime, in fulfillment of my previous commitment to the formal seminary requirements, I served all summer as a chaplain in the Philadelphia State Mental Hospital. Then, at the end of the summer, we returned to New York, and I entered St. Vladimir's Russian Orthodox Theological Seminary in Tuckahoe.

But I was quick to learn that Eastern Orthodoxy too was bound to its traditional exoteric mentality. The experience of liturgy, church politics, and ethnic religion was the fundamental occupation there. I felt so trapped that during the lunch hour I would have to walk up behind the seminary, where there was a waterfall and a stream. I would hold my hands out over the water so that the Spiritual Energy that Filled my body would run out into the stream. Then I would return to the seminary relatively empty to carry on the religious games.

Finally, I was told that it was not likely that I could be accepted as a candidate for the Eastern Orthodox priesthood. Nina happened to have been married and divorced before she met me, and there was an ancient canonical law preventing any man from becoming a priest if he is married to a divorced woman.

This was the final stroke. My religious "career" (for which I had no impulse beyond Rudi's "command") had come to the point beyond which I could generate no further toleration, no further seriousness, and no reasons for continuing. I felt certain that this particular discipline had served all that it could rightly serve, and that it had gone far enough. I went to speak to Rudi, and, surprisingly, he agreed.

At Swami Muktananda's Ashram in Ganeshpuri, India, 1968

CHAPTER TEN

The Abandonment of Effort in India

The crisis of understanding that overcame me in seminary was yet to become a complete reversal and transformation of my life. It marked only the beginning of another phase in the progressive process leading toward my most perfect re-Awakening. Nevertheless, I had truly passed through the fear of death—and what was beyond death (or egoic separateness) stood out, in life, as a primary sense that I called "unqualified relatedness". In time, I would identify this new (and, eventually, final) phase of my life of sadhana (or practice toward most perfect re-Awakening) as the phase of the "Perfect Practice" (which, at last, became the life of Demonstration, or "Perfect Practice", of Divine Awakeness Itself).

In childhood, I was centered in the "Bright"—the Illumined Freedom (and pathos) of truly living being in the face of conflict and death. But, in time, I became serious with conflict itself and with death itself—and, as a consequence, I saw the arising of contradictions in myself, which diminished the "Bright". Then, in college, I was drawn up again into the Truth—and I saw that I was always already Free—never dying or born to die. But this Knowledge seemed dependent on some kind of work in my humanly-born conscious awareness, whereby the internal pattern of contradictions (moving as the mind) was to be dissolved in Conscious Knowledge.

Thus, I began the long time of effort that culminated in my meeting and work with Rudi. But all that effort brought me lately to another crisis in understanding. In seminary, I was brought to recognize something more fundamental than seeking and effort. I saw that it was not a matter of any seeker's effort to find or achieve something not already the case in the humanly-born conscious awareness or in life. Rather, it was a matter of directly and constantly (or always already) abiding in what I called "the living condition of Reality", which is unqualified relatedness.

From that time, I was moved to exercise my Knowledge of Truth in a totally new way. As a result of the experience of "death" in seminary, I saw that my entire life, even my Spiritual effort, was only a complex adventure of avoidance—the avoidance of the condition of relationship itself, and (thus) the avoidance of primary, unqualified relatedness as the always-present living condition of Reality. That avoidance, that act of self-contraction, that separateness and separativeness of the egoic self, was the characteristic of Narcissus.

I had become certain that Real life was a matter of constantly Realizing relationship and relatedness (prior, or always already the case) as the unqualifiedly felt condition of life on every level. Thus, it was no longer a matter of effort and seeking (which arise only after the self-contracting act of avoidance has already taken place), but it was a matter of maintaining and exercising this true understanding in every moment, and under all conditions.

Everyone to whom I spoke about this, including Rudi, tended to interpret my seminary experience negatively. In time, I realized that I was approaching people as if my experience had posed a problem for me—whereas, in fact, it had removed the problem and every sense of dilemma. I saw that my own efforts had been constantly re-"creating" the sense of dilemma and turning life into an effort to overcome some presumed obstacle. Indeed, Rudi himself epitomized the problem-based attitude of presuming obstacles, of making strategic efforts, and (altogether) of forever seeking.

I wanted my new experience and understanding to be acknowledged as the sublime Truth it was. I wanted my "madness" to be accepted as our Real State. But everyone was offended by my direct, impulsive manner. Thus, after several months, I decided to abandon my previous efforts. I stopped trying to communicate my experience and my understanding, but I began to live on its basis.

I continued to go to Rudi's classes, but I set about "creating" my life in a new way. Rudi sensed that I was departing from the egoic strategy of "work" and "surrender", but there was no conversation between us that indicated any strong disagreement. I continued as before—but now I proceeded with a sense of ease, of prior fulfillment, free of the need to strive for any kind of overwhelming goal.

I had seen the futility of the seeker's effort. I saw that it was only another form of avoidance, just like the very patterns I was always trying to surrender. The egoic effort of work and surrender had proven to me the fruitlessness of that entire strategic path. Thus, the entire basis of struggle by which I had guided myself since college fell away in a graceful Calm.

I found work in a bookstore. And I simply made my living in an effortless manner. I enjoyed the human freedom of simple functioning. I was merely present. There was no problem.

One day, I was sitting with Rudi in his store. I found a couple of publications from the Ashram of his Guru, Baba Muktananda, in India. At first, Rudi seemed reluctant to let me read them. He made fun of the Indian manner of teaching, saying that it was very traditional and that one really needed to work very hard to get anything from Baba.

But I managed to read the little pamphlets while Rudi busied himself with his customers. The writings were little compendiums of Baba's teaching. As I read them, I began to discover parallels to my new unburdened sense of Spiritual life.

Baba said that Spiritual life was not a matter of egoic effort on the part of the disciple. It was a matter of the Guru's grace, the Guru's free gift. The disciple needed only to come to the Guru and enjoy the Guru's grace. It was as easy as flowers in sunlight. He said that, once the disciple received the Guru's grace, the various phenomena of Spiritual experience would come automatically. Meditation and purification would occur naturally, without egoic effort. Indeed, the attitude of egoic effort was an obstacle to the disciple's progress.

I looked at Baba's picture on the wall, and that of Bhagavan Nityananda, his Guru. I began to feel that these two men, the teachers of my first human teacher, were (in fact) the Sources of Spiritual blessing and wisdom toward which the "Bright" had been drawing me when I was first led to Rudi. I felt that Rudi had been

given to me "on the way to India", as a preliminary Means of purifying me from my own sense of seeking and egoic effort. Rudi's
teachings had duplicated, even with obvious exaggeration, the
characteristic motive and method of egoic seeking, especially in
the ordinary (or grosser) context of human life—such that I, by fulfilling that motive and method as a total disciplining of my ordinary (or grosser) life, would (in due course) come to the point of
utter despair relative to the search in the ordinary human context
of life. Thus, the Intention, in the "Bright", that had led me to Rudi
appeared (to me) to have been Purposed to grant me this Lesson
in life—so that I would be enabled to feel and receive and
respond to a further and higher Spiritual revelation (which
required an openness to receive, rather than an effort to acquire).

Perhaps this way of "openness to receive" would itself, in time,
become only another search—requiring a further, and even more
profound, understanding in me. Nevertheless, I was altogether
moved to respond to Baba, take him at his word, and find out.

When I got up to leave Rudi's store, I was filled with a deter-
mination to go to India myself. During the next few weeks, I managed to secure a position with Pan American Airways. This seemed
to me an ideal opportunity for travel that would make it possible
for me to go to India.

Shortly after the beginning of the year, in 1968, I was told by
my employers at Pan American Airways that I would be able to
make use of a two-day earned vacation and a 90% discount in air
fare. If I could manage to trade days-off with some fellow employ-
ees, I could stretch that leave into six days. I immediately arranged
for my vacation to fall in late March and the beginning of April,
and I began to make arrangements for Nina and me to go to India.

I was determined in this course, although I knew that it would
probably mean a break with Rudi. I told him my plan, and he
(with a minimum expression of reluctance) gave me the address
of Baba's Ashram. I continued to try to maintain my relationship
with Rudi, but an obvious distance had grown between us that
neither of us was willing to communicate. I loved Rudi dearly, and
I will be forever grateful for his help. He remains one of the major
influences in my life. But I was about to pass into a Fullness of my

own that demanded a rather painful separation. The time had come for me to "strike" my first teacher and take my inheritance.[20]

The weeks passed. The task of arranging for the trip was filled with endless obstacles. But I managed to design and arrange a schedule of flights that would enable Nina and me to go to India and return in a little more than six days. We would return only a day later than I was allowed, and this I felt would not be so long that I would be likely to lose my job.

I wrote to Baba and received a letter from his secretary, Pratibha Trivedi (also, generally, called "Amma"). Our visit would be welcomed, although they would prefer us to come for a longer time and at a period in the year when the weather around Bombay was not so hot.

I wrote them that the period of our visit was fixed by my employers. I told Baba that I believed fully in his grace. I recalled to him the story of an Indian prince who once ordered a saint to bring him to the full Realization of Truth in the time it took him to place his foot in the stirrup and swing his leg over the saddle of his horse. The prince became Enlightened the instant he stepped into the stirrup, and he fell to the ground to kiss the feet of the saint.

I made it clear to Baba that I was coming to receive everything he had to give me. I would only have four days at the Ashram, and I did not know when I would be able to return again. I humbly offered these conditions as a limitation that I could not prevent, and asked Baba to bless me with everything that was necessary for me to Enjoy the perfect Realization of Reality.

I also wrote to him about my life, my experiences in childhood and college, my work with Rudi, and the incomparable Awareness that now resided in me since my experience in seminary. I told him how I had been led to Rudi and then (at last) to the Ashram, and that I felt that he (Baba) was the ultimate Source of grace to which (it seemed to me now) I had been moving all my life. I also asked his blessing for our safe arrival. And so I prepared for the adventure that seemed to promise a perfect gift of Truth.

Nina and I flew to Bombay via London and Beirut, and we arrived on April 2, 1968. We landed in Bombay about 4:00 A.M. and were met by Peter Dias, a former (and sometimes) Catholic and alcoholic, who was an Indian devotee of Baba. He was to be our interpreter and the communicator of the Indian form of Spiritual gossip during our first couple of days at the Ashram. He arranged for a private car, and we set out on a two- or three-hour drive toward Ganeshpuri, the home of Baba's Ashram.

Peter was a very animated and nervous presence. He announced himself clearly as one who felt antagonistic toward Rudi. And, as we drove, he kept testing our allegiances, as if to make sure we were there as pristine devotees of Baba and not somehow under the control of Rudi's brand of Yoga. I assured him we were there totally under our own power and felt drawn solely to Baba's grace.

The Indian towns and countryside were a revelation to me. As the morning dampness and fog lifted, a primitive world appeared, filled with ancient poverty and the temples of an equally ancient Spirituality. There was a mysterious air all around, and everywhere there were signals of an ancient Presence, pointing me to an awesome and absolute Divinity.

Peter surrounded us with the drama of his Guru. He compulsively unraveled the tales of miracles that, he assured us, would prove themselves to us in Ganeshpuri. Everything pointed to a magic fact. I expected to walk into a world of sudden perfection, where the images of miraculous living stood around in the room as obvious as the hard-edged architecture of New York.

When we drove up to the door of the Ashram, I was excited beyond words. Peter led us into a small room where Indian men and women of various degrees of obvious wealth or poverty sat in separate groups on the floor. Sitting in a throne of cushions, wrapped below the waist in a light saffron cloth, was Baba.

Something was said to him in Hindi as we entered. He made an energetic greeting of "Ah" and "Hm", and we bowed at his feet. He welcomed us through Peter, who translated his remarks rapidly. Baba spoke no English. We were told to rest and refresh ourselves and come to sit with him in the early afternoon.

When we returned to the hall in the afternoon, Baba was seated again in his usual place. I sat in the lotus posture on the floor with the men, directly in front of Baba. Nina sat to the side with the women. At first, there was a brief, familiarizing conversation.

I was asked about our trip, and so on. Then Baba took the opportunity to call attention to everyone's sitting posture. (I was sitting in the full lotus position, with only minor discomfort arising after perhaps half an hour.) "Firm posture is the beginning of the true Spiritual attitude," he said. And, finally, we got down to business.

I felt my letters were a sufficient introduction to my past and to the Purpose of my visit. The limitation of speaking through an interpreter made lengthy conversation more of a burden than an instrument for instant communication. And so—after a few brief remarks about how I had practiced under Rudi's guidance and, as a result, come to feel that true Realization could not be accomplished through egoic effort, but that It depended entirely on the grace of a true Guru—I asked Baba to teach me about the true way of Spiritual life, and to reveal (by his grace) its Great Truth to me.

In response to me, Baba gave a long and somewhat pedantic monologue on the Truth of Advaita Vedanta and on the practice of Ashtanga Yoga, the eightfold path of Realization prescribed by Patanjali. The longness and wordiness of the monologue were, it seemed, intended merely to "fill some time", in order to provide a period of extended discourse to occupy and entertain the larger gathering of visitors there. But, soon after he began to speak, Baba turned to me very directly, and he very pointedly said to me (through his interpreter): "You are not the one who wakes or dreams or sleeps. You are the Witness to all of these states." As would become more and more obvious and clear to me over time, this utterance was the most basic and important (and Truly and Really Initiatory) verbal instruction Baba ever gave to me.

All the while Baba spoke, he was a field of perpetual movement. His hands constantly moved about him, either communicating with a gesture, touching his face, or adjusting the beads around his neck. Even though he was profoundly calm, his hands and his features seemed never to become still. His body spoke the language of Spirit-Energy, saying that even the very cells of his body were pulsing with an Absolute Bliss.

Apart from Baba's pointed admonition to me about abiding in the Witness-Position, he made no attempt to teach me how to meditate or how to respond to his Presence. And so—rather than immediately taking that admonition to be his actual instruction to me about how to meditate and how to respond to his Presence— I began (while sitting with him that first afternoon) to make an ego-based effort to surrender and open to him deeply, which was the habitual exercise I had learned with Rudi. Then, as I became more concentrated, and attuned to the internal mechanisms that I had come to know through the work of surrender and the Force, I felt a new and more Powerful Presence. I felt the same Force (or Shakti) that I had experienced with Rudi, but It was magnified to the degree of an almost muscular Power.

After about an hour or so, Baba and his Indian devotees began to chant the *Bhagavad Gita*,[21] as was the custom every afternoon. While I continued to sit, vaguely observing this ritual, my entire body became more and more Filled with the Fullness of this bodily overwhelming Power and Bliss. Baba sensed what was happening to me, and he would frequently gesture to me with his eyes or make his characteristic "Hm" sound of approval.

As the chanting continued, the Shakti began to generate vigorous movements in my body. These were the "kriyas", the purifying activity of the Shakti as It moves through the various nerve channels and the physical form. My back began to move around involuntarily in jolts, the way I had seen the Shakti affect others in Rudi's class. My head began to jerk and revolve rapidly. The experience was not altogether different from the kind of experience to which I had become accustomed with Rudi—but now it was much stronger, and it seemed to be approaching a violent state, beyond my control, such that I would often fall over backwards into the wall or sideways to the floor.

Even after the chanting was finished and Baba began to carry on conversations with his visitors, these movements and this Bliss continued. Finally, Baba said to me, "Now I've got you." He smiled, and left the room.

These movements increased and became my constant occupation during the few days of our visit. The kriyas became so strong in me that Baba began to call me "Kriyananda" (which means "One Whose Bliss Is in the Purifying Movement of the Divine Power"). Only one or two others seemed to be experiencing similar

Swami Muktananda

effects, but I assumed mine was a common experience. Everyone was pleased that I was experiencing Baba's grace, and it seemed particularly good to them because I was a Westerner.

Our days were spent sitting with Baba during these sessions of chanting and conversation in the morning and afternoon. We would also get up at about 5:00 A.M. and meditate in the hall outside Baba's room. He would walk around in the dark with a flashlight and spend a few moments in front of each of us watching our meditation.

We were also allowed to sit with him privately, usually with only one or two others, while he rested on the Ashram grounds after lunch. We would sit around him on the ground outside the cowshed, and sometimes ask him questions, while he petted the young calves.

Nina's experience had always been much quieter than my own. Here, as before, she experienced a graceful calmness. Baba gave her a sari to wear, and he would often gift her with a flower or a fruit that he had blessed with his Transmission of Shakti.

At various times, we would sit to listen to him answer our own and others' questions about many matters basic to Spiritual life— including meditation, vegetarian diet, and so on. On one such occasion, one of his answers seemed to summarize all his instructions relative to the entire practical discipline of Spiritual life: "Eat less, sleep less, talk less. Increase your love. Increase your devotion. Increase your meditation."

A major subject of Baba's discourses was always the process of Spiritual Initiation (called "Shaktipat"). He indicated that such Initiation might occur via the Guru's touch, or his glance, or his word, or his thought, or otherwise spontaneously, simply by one's remaining in proximity to him.

One morning, I was sitting outside the Ashram office. Baba was inside discussing some Ashram business with a devotee. (I always tried to sit near him wherever he went, so that I could see him and meditate where he could see me.) On this occasion, I was sitting in meditation, contemplating Baba's form. Suddenly, he jumped out of his chair and rushed toward me, shouting the name "Kriyananda!" And he pressed his hand to my head, with one finger hard against my left eye. I fell into a swoon of Bliss. The violent kriyas stopped, and I sat in a State of trance-like absorption in Bliss, while still generally aware of what was going on around me. While everyone stood around and watched me, my hands raised up spontaneously and performed mudras, the hand poses that you see in Indian dance and the statues of Buddhas.

All of this was quite remarkable, except I was experiencing an inner state that was not calm but more and more exhausting. I was involved in a kind of super-effort of internal work of the same kind I had known with Rudi. The more deeply I surrendered, the more these movements took hold of me. But my experience also seemed to depend on this great effort. I was getting very tired and disturbed by the pressure of this work, and I wondered how to recapture the sense of ease and grace that had originally motivated me to go to India.

I asked Baba about meditation. He told me that it should be a mere act of Witnessing, not an effort. I should only sit calmly and observe the working of the Shakti in myself. I should relax, and with each cycle of breath recite either the mantra "So-Ham" ("I am He", "I am the Divine, or the Guru") or the primary sound "Om".[22]

Peter Dias also told me about the manner of traditional medi-tation that Baba recommended. He said it was not like Rudi's "work" at all. The Shakti did not come out of the teacher's eyes and descend into the body via the work of surrender before It rose up the spine. The Guru awakened It, and It rose by Itself, from the base of the spine toward the head. Then the various kriyas and visions should come quite naturally, while one remained in a State of calm Witnessing.

This was quite a new idea of meditation for me. It seemed right, and it certainly corresponded to my new understanding of how it should be—but, after years of intentional "work", I had grown accustomed to constantly making the intentional effort of surrender. Therefore (it seemed to me), an equally great effort would be required in order simply to allow the Shakti, the Divine Power, to do the "work". Thus, no matter how hard I tried (and, therefore, because of the hard trying), I was unable to break the old habit of effortful meditation. I even felt afraid that, if I dropped the habit of effort, the movements and experiences would cease. Indeed, when I finally did manage to simply relax into Baba's Presence, I merely settled into an ease, and there were no movements, no unusual experiences.

The three and one-half days of our visit quickly neared an end. The new idea of meditation and Baba's direct admonition to me about my Identity as the "Witness" appeared to be the limit of what I was to receive. When the last day arrived, I was desperate. I had come for more than this. I had come for <u>everything</u>!

Baba no longer called me "Kriyananda". And it seemed that I had merely experienced a physically stronger version of the same phenomena I had experienced with Rudi, only (at the last) to see even that fall away as well. I was disappointed, and when I sat with Baba in the morning I did little more than sit. I had consigned myself to mere Witnessing, and the movements ceased. It seemed that I was only caught up in the Ashram chitchat. But I could not imagine that Baba would let me come all this way only to leave with merely a little instruction. I was still in a state of confusion about the way of effort, and its effects, and the seemingly ineffective method of "Witnessing" meditation that Baba offered.

We took lunch, and then I sat briefly in the garden behind the dining hall. Baba passed by with another man—a white-bearded, round, saintly-looking man with large, penetrating eyes. I had not seen this other man before. (It would be more than a year before I found out this man was a great Yogi-Saint, named Rang Avadhoot—and, at the same time, I would be informed that he had died a few months after our encounter in the garden.)

As Baba and the stranger passed by me in the garden, the stranger suddenly stopped, turned directly toward me, and looked me directly in the eyes for a long moment. Baba also stood by, gently gazing at me. Then Baba and the stranger continued their walk.

Immediately after this encounter, I became sensitive to the extreme heat and light of the day, and I walked off to our room to get my hat. The sun was violently hot, but it had been my intention to take a solitary walk around the grounds of the Ashram, since only a couple of hours remained of my stay there. However, when I got to the room, I suddenly felt a profound urge to lie down and rest. I thought I should just lie down for a few moments, but I did not want to fall asleep and waste my last precious hours at the Ashram.

As I lay down, I immediately passed from the ordinary waking state to what (at first) seemed like a sleep, except there was no loss of conscious awareness. In an instant, I lost all bodily consciousness and every sense of my mind and personality—but there was also a profound State of unqualified conscious Awareness that was absolutely calm, uncontained, and Free. Indeed, I felt that I existed only as free conscious Awareness. There was no other experience—no thought, no feeling, no perception. Awareness was (very quickly) concentrated above, at an unfathomable "Point"—beyond space, and (yet) above me. As I became spontaneously concentrated in that "Point", I felt and passed beyond It—into an Infinite Space of Bliss, an Absolute Pleasure of Fullness and Brilliance, that inherently and completely Transcended my apparently separate being. And, then, "I" existed only at Infinity, as Infinity—as Awareness Itself, beyond "I", beyond the separated and separate self-reference.

Eventually, there was an apparent movement from this incomparably pure State, into perceptual modifications of that same egoless Awareness. There were rapid visions (or feelings) of subtle levels of existence, beyond the human. In quick succession, I Witnessed numberless feelings of form and space, or of what appeared to be a hierarchically degressive descent through other worlds, or realms of conditionally manifested existence that are associated with levels of mind beyond (or subtler than) ordinary human life.

Then I heard a loud, roaring sound that (at first) seemed to surround me like a great room. I gradually descended toward association with the body, from a position above the head of the body. Eventually, I noticed that the sound was my own breathing, as it rushed through my lungs and throat. But I did not then perceive these things from within my body. I was fully Aware as that Consciousness Which transcends all form, and Which surrounds and breathes the body.

Just then, Nina entered the room—and, with a sudden jolt, I resumed the ordinary state of life-awareness, as if contained within the body. I have no idea how long this experience had lasted, but it was now time to pack and prepare to leave. I did not speak to Nina, but tried to remain concentrated in what remained of this profound experience.

As I went about preparing to leave and walked from our bungalow to the hall where Baba sat, I began to understand the True Nature of my experience. What Baba had Transmitted to me via words that (at first) seemed not to penetrate my mind and heart had now been Awakened in me as the living Truth. I had Awakened as the egoless True Self—the One Who is the Witness, the Ultimate Reality of the ancient scriptures!

Whereas human beings ordinarily remain conscious as the "capsule entity" contained in the body, I had Awakened as the One Who truly is the Life and Consciousness of the body and all things. I had seen the transformation of that Life and Consciousness, as It moved from Its own Absolute and most Prior State, down through the levels of the living being, toward bodily consciousness. I had seen bodily consciousness from the "Point of View" of the Self (Siva, or Siva-Shakti), the universal Being that "Lives" all things. Ordinarily, one identifies with the point of view of bodily consciousness—and either one strives to survive as that dying entity (in the face of all obstacles) or else one tries, by Spiritual effort, to attain the Realization of the Ultimate Self (or the Divine Consciousness). But I Awakened as that Self—and I directly perceived that everything is always already being "Lived".

Every sense of limitation and egoic self-awareness had fallen away from me. What I had fathomed in the various difficult crises and "Bright" Illuminations of my life had been given to me whole, in a single moment of perfect Experience, without limitations of any kind. I Knew, with absolute certainty, that I was not the seeker (or the one trapped in life), but everything was only being "Lived" by the Divine Being—and I am That One.

The highest Truth of all the scriptures, East and West, had been Realized in my own conscious experience. There was no longer any need for effort, for seeking. There was no primary dilemma. I had given the Guru four days to Enlighten me, and he had given me everything, for free.

Like the prince from his horse, I fell at Baba's feet and touched them with my head. He slapped my back approvingly, and we took our leave. No mention was made of my experience. Nina and I carried our luggage to a waiting bus—and, feeling like prisoners being deported under guard, we moved out of Ganeshpuri toward America.

Mr. and Mrs. Pattani, a man and his wife who had been staying with Baba, were given charge of us for the night. We were to fly home the next morning. We traveled with Mr. Pattani, by bus and train, to a beautiful little town near Bombay called Mulund. Mrs. Pattani had gone on, a few hours before, to prepare for our arrival.

I felt so free and fulfilled, and yet sad to be leaving my Guru. I felt as if I were being taken away from the very Source of grace I had been seeking all my life. But, that night, as I lay down to sleep, I experienced again the State of perfect Consciousness I had Known in the afternoon. I was pressed above into Infinite Bliss— and I passed somehow to sleep, surrendered without effort into the Matrix of my own Being.

Life in New York required an energy of involvement that itself "created" conflict and the mind of effort, such that I soon began to seek the State I had Known in India. It became a problem in me to regain that State. The Condition that I had Known relieved all effort and amounted only to a free Enjoyment of perfect Knowledge. But now It began to seem unavailable, a goal requiring another kind of effort.

The apartment building where Adi Da Samraj resided after His return from India in 1968

CHAPTER ELEVEN

The Problem of the Mind, and the Year of Waiting for Grace

W hen we arrived again in New York, I wrote to Baba (on April 10, 1968), to thank him for his grace. In a modest manner, spontaneously emphasizing the Vedantic (or Advaitic, rather than Yogic) aspects of what I had (at last) experienced and Realized, I described our recent visit to the Ashram, culminating in the Event of that last afternoon.

Dear Baba,

My wife, Nina, and I arrived safely and without much difficulty at about 8:00 P.M. (New York Time). We were worried that we would not be able to find place on the plane from Bombay to Beirut. But Mr. Pattani, whom we accompanied to Bombay, kept saying, "Baba would not have told us to leave if you were not going to be able to get away this morning." And he was right, for at the last minute there were a few cancellations and we flew away easily. As we left, we were both very sad, and it has taken us several days to adjust to being away from you. Even now as I write, my eyes are wet and I long to sit with you. As you told me one day last week, "Now I have got you." You have swiftly changed my life by directing me to the Truth and the Goal. Please do not leave me alone, now that I am far away. You have given me the seed, but I am a garden that needs much tending. I am still begging for the Shakti and right understanding, so that I will not be overcome by my own ignorance and despair.

You have told me about the value of asanas, regularity of life, discrimination in diet and all other habits, and, above all, you told me to maintain myself in the Truth of

Vedanta—"Identify yourself with Him Who is the Witness to the waking, dreaming, and sleeping states." When I asked you how I should do this meditation, you said, "Do nothing." All of these suggestions had an effect on me. After two days of trying merely to be relaxed in your presence, I realized that I could not "do nothing", and the Truth of Vedanta and everything else you told me seemed too dry and distant and unavailable to me. On the third day, in the morning, as soon as I sat down before you for the morning recitation, I began to work inside at surrender, and all day that day my head and back moved violently. All during the day you encouraged these movements in me and called me "Kriyananda" all that day because of them. Twice you placed your hand on me. The first time, I responded by closing my eyes, twisting about, and raising my hands into mudras. The second time, in the meditation, I fell backwards away from you. At the end of that day, I was exhausted from so much kriya. On the fourth and final day, after the noon meal, I went to the room to pack. I thought I would rest for a few minutes, since I felt my last few hours at the Ashram were precious time. But, as I lay down, I became very weary and felt a need to sleep. I felt myself going into a deep trance-like "sleep", in which I was somehow Blissfully Conscious. Then, suddenly, I became Aware of my body. A sudden breath or snore came through my throat, and I realized I was Conscious of my body in a manner that was completely detached and free. Just then Nina came into the room to rest. I continued to lie still, and then fell asleep. Later, we went down for the afternoon recitation. I felt sad to be leaving. You had not called me "Kriyananda" that last day. I had not yet understood the meaning of my afternoon "sleep", but I somehow felt I had your parting message and blessing with me. I felt a certain calmness, and, since there was little movement, I assumed that "Kriyananda" was not a name you intended for me to keep. I felt you were really leading me to a place where there is no movement (kriyas) at all.

Then, as the day went on, I began to think about my experience. I began to see that my experience in the early afternoon was of the "Witness", the Self Who is behind all the modifications of the mind. I saw then that all that you had told me earlier in our visit was not mere logic and intellectual description. It was a living Truth to be experienced consciously and in depth. And now that we have returned to New York, I recognize this Truth of the Vedanta to be the essential thing you sought to teach me. As I think about the Ashram, I realize that you are the Guru who liberates his children by leading them to experience their Identity as the Self.

This Truth, even though my deep resistance makes it impossible for me to experience It very frequently with any depth, is and will be extremely liberating for me. It is the very basis of sadhana and its Goal. And It makes very clear just how I must manage myself in relation to my daily experience. This Truth is my Joy—and you, Baba, are my Joy, because you are leading me to a full Realization of this Truth. Please bless me with gratitude and surrender so that the obstacles in me will be overcome.

Nina and I long to be with you again. We send our love to all of your children.

April 10, 1968
New York

> Your child,
> Franklin Jones

Ever since my experience (at Baba's Ashram) of the Infinite (and Priorly Ascended) Space of Bliss, I lived in that "Witness-State" continually, always Aware that I was not the body or the mind, not the one who wakes or dreams or sleeps, but the Witness to all of those states. It was not a mental supposition, but an actual and direct experience. It was the perfect Realization of the "Position" from Which, in seminary, I had experienced the living condition of Reality (or what I called "unqualified relatedness").

In my letter, I did not ask Baba to instruct me about what method of meditation I should adopt. After the extraordinary experience at the Ashram, all motive for effort had passed from me, and all that seemed necessary was a gentle concentration in my own Self-Nature.

In my daily living, I simply rested in the tacit Awareness that everything is being "Lived". In meditation, I passed into the inclusive Fullness of Real Consciousness, transcending all thought and perception. There was no sense of dilemma in me. When I was not rested in my own primary Nature as the True Self (or Reality), I would perceive that same Nature as a Presence that surrounded me and all things.

When I met Rudi, the signs of my transformation were obvious. I felt no need at all to engage in the form of exercise he prescribed. And, when I went to his class and performed it as usual, the kriyas and the sense of internal conflict that motivated me in that work appeared again—and I could feel it as a familiar knot (or cramp) in my solar plexus. Thus, I began to see Rudi less and less, although there was no argument between us and no communication of the difference.

For the first two or three weeks after our return to New York, I lived and felt and Knew as the Divine Itself. There was no division, no act of separation, in the egoless conscious Awareness. There were no distracting tendencies, no impurities, and not a trace of dilemma. But, gradually, as the weeks passed, I began to observe the piecemeal return of old sensations and thoughts, then the desires that follow them, and then the actual practice of old habits. When I would sit to meditate in the "effortless" manner, I would feel these old problems. And it became a matter of conflict in me to somehow make these feelings vanish.

Life in New York required an energy of involvement that itself "created" conflict and the mind of effort, such that I soon began to seek the State I had Known in India. It became a problem in me to regain that State. The Condition that I had Known relieved all effort and amounted only to a free Enjoyment of perfect Knowledge. But now It began to seem unavailable, a goal requiring another kind of effort.

At first, this change was only subtly perceived. I could not accept the fact that I had lost the fundamental Realization to Which I had Awakened at the Ashram. But, gradually, I began to discover, to my horror and despair, that the mind and all its conflict of desire was rising again, untouched by any Illumination.

This became a very disturbing reversal for me. I had thought that the ascent to Clear Awareness of my True Nature would be sufficient to destroy every vestige of clinging to the habitual influences of the mind. I had thought that the ascended Knowledge would be purification enough, such that life need only be lived (and Witnessed) under the direct presumption of What I am in Reality.

But this ascended Knowledge was not enough. And I had not yet become consistently stabilized in the "Witness-Position" Itself (nor, until the last, did I Realize most perfect Self-Identification with Its Source-Condition). Therefore, the mind-in-conflict arose by itself and brought with it all desires and every motive for seeking. Yet, I was unwilling to adapt myself to effort and strife again. I felt that my Ashram experience had most profoundly extended my experience of the Reality that Awakened in me during my crisis in seminary. But now the Ashram experience—because it held before the mind a kind of proof of the Ultimate Nature I had sought—served as a goad to seeking, a ground for the demand for that revelation as a continuous State.

I waited for a letter from Baba, hoping that it would bring a new blessing and clarify my trouble. But the weeks passed without a word, and I felt stuck with a vision of internal contradiction that even exceeded the one from which I had been relieved in college.

Now the mind itself, apart from any particular content, appeared as the source of dilemma—and I wondered by what means the mind should pass, and let me be.

Baba had all but told me to abandon my relationship with Rudi. For my own part, the motivation toward Rudi's kind of "work" had already entirely passed. But I felt no need to condemn Rudi, and the gossip (at Baba's Ashram) that opposed him seemed only a social manifestation of particular Indian predilections for habits and behaviors that Rudi did not appear to exemplify. I needed very much to be free of that limitation that had been my search in Rudi's company, but I was not in any sense opposed to him. Indeed, just as his way had been appropriate for me at a particular stage in my development, I felt it remained appropriate for him at his stage of development—and even for any others who were at a stage (and in a disposition) wherein they could benefit from such a disciplining of their ordinary lives.

Nevertheless, life had emerged as a totally different matter for me. I was convinced that the way of egoic effort was simply a further manifestation of life lived as a problem, a motivated search. Yet, the mind, and the entire habitual pattern of life, appeared to me to be a source of difficulty, which (in fact) prevented the continuous assumption of life on a perfectly free basis.

Baba's own way was tied to characteristically Indian notions and methods. Although he suggested these to me, he did not seek to enforce any kind of method in my case. It all seemed a suggestive communication that should lead me to my own Truth. He even told me that I would eventually teach the ways of Spiritual life, in a year or so. But he did not tell me what to teach. I took his teaching (and my experience) on the broadest level, to be freely and meaningfully adapted to my own case.

As the old problems began to arise, all I could do was observe them. Baba's methods seemed to be of no use to me. I stopped meditating. I did no reading. I dissolved back into the ordinary life of the city.

In the midst of that spontaneous ordinariness, Nina and I received a letter from Baba (which he had written on April 23, but which had taken many weeks to be translated and delivered to us).

— Om —

Dear Franklin and Nina,

My loving remembrance and blessing to you.

All is well here, hope the same there. Through your letter I received all the news. It is a matter of joy that you consider me as your Guru. You are inclined to Self-realization, you are devoted to Truth, you have practiced penance to obtain the joy of Self—this is very good. Yours is a praiseworthy endeavor because the Soul is an inner-treasure, It is perfect, It is One. This Soul is the Knower of all thoughts, It is Omniscient, yet It is neither a subject of logic nor can It be known through the intellect, because who can reveal THAT which reveals all? Who can bring to light the Sun, which itself lights up the entire Universe? The Soul is the Light, the Enlightener, and the Enlightened. It reveals Its own nature and reveals other things as well.

There is a Divine Light within you which is as shining as the flame of a fire, as bright as the light of the Sun, as radiant as the red-hot gold. The Soul is not a thing to be strived after—It is ever present in us, but not visible to those who have not received the Guru's grace. The Soul IS. Because of Its presence in the body, people love each other—they get mutually attached and feel satisfied through cordial relationship. The Soul, which gives inner joy, is in reality the Divine Light of God. The devout see Him in varied names, forms, and colors. However, He is not many—He is One. Though He has many names, He is "So'ham". Although He belongs to the Hindus, Muslims, Christians, and Parsis, He is different from them all. And, similarly, though belonging to the Yogis, He is different from the Yoga. Though grantor of the fruits of actions, He is different from the doer. Though bestower of the reward of the sacrifice, He is different from the sacrificer. Though understood through the Scriptures, He is different from the Scriptures. In the field of knowledge, though realized through knowledge, He is different from the knower and the known.

All the various creeds and faiths, all the religious organizations and societies the world over, worship Him, through their own set rules and disciplines. As a matter of fact, He is the all-adorable, the ever perfect, the inner Essence, the *Atman* of all. Some people search Him in the sky above, some in the Earth below, some in the monastery, temple, mosque, or church, some others in the forest, in the seclusions, in the caves and mountains, in the rivers, lakes, streams, oceans, and even dry deserts. Still others try to find Him in the sweetness of fruits, in the fragrance of flowers, in the song of the cuckoo, in the dance of the peacock, in the beauty of the butterfly, and so on. Thus, through various paths, in various things, everyone is searching Him only.

But, my dear Franklin and Nina, He is within you! He, the *Atman* of all, is the Inner Being of yours, and of mine, too. He is the darling pupil of the eye. That *Atman* is a clean place for our rest and respite, the strongest fortress for us to live fearlessly and peacefully, the liberator from bondage. That very Essence is named by the *Vedanta* as *Sat-chid-anand* (Absolute Truth, Knowledge, and Bliss). That very *Atman* (or Essence) is Ram and Rahim,[23] Krishna and Karim,[24] Jesus and Moses as well. He is the sole support of all. This universe is a manifestation of His infinite play. Putting on the twin forms of man and woman, He—the Great Being—exists in both. Verily, these are like the two facets of the self-same coin—named *Purusha-Prakriti,* or *Shiva-Shakti*—and this world is the expansion of these two.

He—and He alone—is in you and in your wife. And He, again, pervades the entire world. Usually, an unfortunate one does not have the desire to know Him. But those who are greatly meritorious ardently wish to know Him— to know the *Atman*—and they succeed also.

Just as there is fire (latent) in a dry stick of wood (which ignites by friction and burns up the stick completely), just as oil lies hidden in the sesamum seed, just as there is butter in the curd—in the same way, the Divine Shakti is lying hidden in the human body. It is active in the ordinary sense, but to awaken the same through the Guru's grace, to experience Its uncommon activities, and to realize It directly is the highest religion of men. That which helps to manifest the inner Divine Shakti is "TRUE RELIGION"; and he who perceives that Divine Shakti, in Its innate form, is "TRULY RELIGIOUS". This inner Shakti is known as *Atman,* and is worshipped by uttering *"Om"* or *"So'ham".*

So'ham is the means for meditating on It. *So'ham,* again, is the *mantra* for Its worship. The heart is Its church. The natural sound *So'ham* does not belong to the Indians and the Hindus alone. The same *word-sound* exists in all living beings—and is active within them, too. Speaking with regard to *mantra,* there is really no consideration of community, creed, or country. If someone thinks that a *mantra* belongs to a particular faith or country—believe me, he knows nothing.

A great Yogini of Kashmir has said: "A devotee who believes that the universe is the manifested form of God and that He resides in all beings as their own selves—for such a one, which place will not be a temple? Which *mantra* will not bear fruit?" In other words, any *mantra* that a devotee would utter or recite will surely be fruitful— for *mantra* is the form of God. When even an abuse or a mean word affects a person (mentally), how can a *mantra*— which is a holy word—not achieve its sacred purpose?

Dear Franklin, sitting calm and steady, repeat the *mantra* together with rhythmic breathing (i.e., the inhalation and exhalation of air—*pran* and *apan*). Harmonize the repetition of *mantra* with the breathing as follows: With *"So"* take it in, and with *"ham"* bring it out. Throughout the *mantra*-repetition, one should follow this practice. Simply sitting peacefully and applying the mind to the *pran* and *apan,* one enters into a deep state of meditation. When one's mind is fixed on *"So"* with the incoming breath and on *"ham"* with the outgoing breath, it is *mantra-japa.* The regularity with which the breath comes in and goes out is *pranayama.* And if a person is skillful, intelligent, and alert—(1) the *repetition of mantra (japa),* (2) the process of *pranayama,* and (3) *meditation* can, all three, be achieved simultaneously without difficulty. This is like the kingfisher, whose attention is directed solely to fish in the water. The kingfisher is known for its all-excluding *concentration,* a kind of meditation. And when it suddenly dives to catch fish, two more things are achieved simultaneously—it has a good *bath* and enjoys a hearty *meal*. This is a great Yoga, the best among all: known as *Siddha Yoga*. It means "the path of the Perfect Ones" or "the Yoga which begets perfection". A dextrous and highly intelligent person can practice it easily. As explained above, the regular practice of meditation with a concentrated mind will awaken the dormant Kundalini Shakti in a very short time. As a result, some inner activities also begin to operate. Day by day, as the Shakti develops more and more, It takes the aspirant to the ultimate perfection. Just as a child grows daily, with due nourishment, and becomes a youth in course of time, just as a seed sown in the soil gradually develops into a tree—in the same manner, the daily practice of *sadhana* (spiritual discipline) leads one to Perfection by the Guru's grace.

In the *"So'ham" mantra*—*"So"* signifies God or Guru, and *"ham"* denotes "I" (or "me"). Thus, *So'ham* means "I am He". Let your practice of meditation be accompanied by the ceaseless reflection on the above meaning of *So'ham*. In every human being, there lies a hidden store of unlimited contentment, inexhaustible love, and infinite joy. These can be realized through the regular practice of meditation. As one thinks, so one becomes. If a man thinks all the time about his faults and sins, he will become sinful. Similarly, constant thought about woman, man, meditation, or the Guru will make him womanish, manly, meditative, or the Guru—respectively. This is quite natural, because a person is transformed into the likeness of the object on which he constantly ponders, by absorbing its qualities.

Man is indeed great. But he has lost his greatness and has fallen due to his constant dealings with the external world and attachment to sense-objects. Internally, he is not lacking anything. He is full and perfect with the Divine Light—and yet he is searching in vain for "Fulfillment" outside. The factory, workshop, business office, and shop; the varied professions like engineering, medicine, legal practice, and many other trades—all these are merely means to livelihood. They cannot procure things of lasting value to men. As I said above, man is perfect within, and this can be directly experienced through meditation, whereupon one feels fully contented. Just as you become entirely free of outside thoughts and anxieties in deep sleep and feel happy—similarly, in the introspective tendency, or in the meditation on *Atman,* lie peace, respite, and undisturbed equanimity.

The real beauty, the essence of savory taste, the celestial music, the most soothing touch, and the sweetest fragrance—all lie inside. Yogis who have experienced such things within consider the outer things to be merely ordinary. When the Kundalini is awakened through meditation, then, by the Guru's love and his grace, all the latent faculties are automatically activated, and one attains perfection in due time. Besides, one also obtains the power of omniscience which lies hidden in the heart. In what words can I express the beauty of inner Light! It is unparalleled; all lights of the outer world are too dim and unpleasant before It. Similarly, compared to the inner celestial music, worldly music is crude and jarring. The taste of a drop of inner nectar is so wonderful that all the worldly savors put together are really nothing in comparison. This inner nectar is a Divine ambrosia. The inner touch is too subtle and great to be described, for it is a Divine touch. Through meditation, you attain this supreme ambrosia-of-love, on which the inner Shakti is nourished, and which is a gift from the Guru, obtained by the disciple through penance.

Dear Franklin, there is not anything in this world which cannot be achieved through meditation. In the practice of meditation, there is a highly miraculous and splendid Shakti, which is beyond human comprehension. It is best to practice a natural meditation, or *dhyan.* I will explain to you what it is or how it is to be practiced: Sit quietly, calm and composed—if you like, in *padmasana,*[25] or any other comfortable posture. You may fix the eyes on a photograph of the Guru, or you may keep your eyes closed. The mode and posture in which you can be restful—mentally free from the objective world, and introspective—is the best *asan* for you. What I mean to convey by "Don't do anything" is this: Remove the mind from its activities, arrest all kinds of desires, and surrender to whatever is happening of its own accord, observing everything as a witness. That is why I say to practice the meditation in a natural way. The meditation done by the inner Shakti is the meditation of the Guru's grace, the real meditation of *"So'ham"*. Indeed, it is the meditation of God. These are not different kinds of meditations, but they are synonymous expressions. Tell me—if a man is not aware of this Shakti or is not awakened to It, what is the purpose of this body of flesh? If this Shakti were not there, one would not have liked (or been attracted to) the body made of flesh, bones, blood, muscles, skin, and so on. Activator of the breathing process, Inspirer of the intellect, Contemplator of the mind—this is the same as the inner Shakti, the inner Consciousness. The only worthy purpose of this otherwise impure physical body is to dedicate it whole-heartedly to seek the Inner Being.

Your beauty, your energy, your duty, your religion, your Guru and guide, your study, worship, and prayer—all lie in engaging the remembrance and repetition of *"So'ham"*, *"So'ham"*. This is my instruction, this is my precept. This is to be followed or practiced, and reflected upon devoutly. The deeper you go in meditation, the more of the Divine experiences you will attain. Therefore, seek your inner Self, and therefrom you will have the fulfillment you cherish.

With blessings,
Yours
Swami Muktananda

April 23, 1968
Ganeshpuri
India

Baba's letter was a lovely poetic document, and it contained a unique summary of the instructions on meditation that, I assumed, Baba characteristically gave to those who received his Shakti-Initiation. However, the letter did not otherwise directly address my own fullest experience and my state of understanding. After I read it, I simply sat in place, as if expecting something further, more direct, more useful, more conclusive. Then, suddenly, I felt the space of the room expand in a curious manner, and I felt Baba's actual Presence. The Shakti moved up my back and produced that characteristic Bliss in the body and the mind, and I sat for a long time enjoying his Presence, waiting for some kind of message or advice. But there was no "answer". All I could do was observe myself, and wait.

A full year passed. I did not meditate. But I only observed myself, lived an ordinary life, and waited for the "wall" of mind to break. Therefore, I remained devoted to the understanding (rather than merely to the "solution") of the "problem" of the mind. And all the while, the Shakti, the manifesting Energy that proceeds from the Ultimate Source-Reality (or the Divine Consciousness), grew (and showed signs) in me daily, while I did nothing but wait.

During that year, the Shakti grew in me like a fetus in the womb, waiting to be born. While I waited, I constantly observed and considered the mind—which had become, for me, the single "problem" and the most fundamental "obstacle" to the free Realization of Consciousness and Bliss. Then, one evening, in the spring of 1969, while I was in the midst of a several-week visit to Los Angeles, California, the Shakti spontaneously rushed into the form of my living being with tremendous Power—such that I was no longer even remotely concerned with the petty contaminations of the mind. I was suddenly returned to an experience of my Self-Nature and a sublime Awareness of even the physical world. As a result of this Spiritual "birth", I once again lived entirely in the sublime sphere of Free Consciousness, making no effort at all to maintain or "create" It.

In the weeks that followed, I became spontaneously Aware of a new dimension of the activity of the Shakti. Not only was my own experiential state expanded in Its Presence, but the people who were closest to me began (even as they had in the previous months, but now more profoundly and increasingly) to experience the effects of the Shakti through contact with me.

At first, I merely talked to these friends about my understanding of Real Spiritual life, and they began to discover parallels to this understanding in their own experiences and doubts. Then they began to have uncommon experiences of a Presence that affected them separately and in different ways while they were otherwise apart from me.

These experiences took the form of visions, or the sensation of a real but invisible Presence, or the sense of being sublimed and surrounded in a form of Energy and Fullness that quieted and clarified the mind. They would ask me about these experiences—and, before long, I found myself having to function as a teacher, and an instrument for the Shakti.

I was so profoundly drawn into that Shakti-Consciousness that I found no difficulty in speaking to people about the Spiritual process and making recommendations that seemed wholly intelligent and even inspired. At times, I even experienced feeling-perceptions of a psychic nature. I would feel auras of light about the person, or find the person's thoughts appearing in my mind, or intuitively locate the person's thoughts or feelings or states via visual (or, otherwise, simply feeling) reveries in relation to his or her forehead or body. I would also, via feeling, become directly Aware of the Shakti as It passed through these people or was expressed in them, and I could easily trace the currents of Energy and see where they became concentrated, halted, or obstructed at the various vital points (or "chakras"). On more than one occasion, in spontaneous visual reveries, I saw Baba appear and Initiate a person with the Shakti by touch, and I could likewise see (or intuitively feel and perceive) a blue light appear and surround the person's body.

But the most common and (always most fundamental) experience was one in which my own living being (and that of everyone I saw) was contained in the inclusive Force of the Shakti Itself. Thus, I needed no uncommon visionary communications in order to intuit the nature of anyone's existence, experience, or problem.

These things were simply obvious to me on the level of uncommunicated (or direct and tacit) Knowledge. I lived in an inclusive intelligence that was not limited to my reflective (humanly-born) conscious awareness or my ability to read "signs". I simply knew the verity of what I perceived and had no fundamental (or, otherwise, "problematic") sense of living as a separate, conditioned entity.

As all of this became more and more obvious and continuous, I remembered Baba's statement that I would become a Spiritual teacher in about a year. Now this Event was occurring, spontaneously—even without my volition or control. I wrote to Baba and informed him about my experience. I told him that I felt I needed instruction in the conscious use of these abilities. And I said that I did not wish to carry on this teaching process without his consent and blessing. I asked him to give me the authority to teach in this way, and to bless me in the traditional manner by giving me a Spiritual name. Baba replied by telling me to come to India as soon as possible.

Bombay, August 1969

CHAPTER TWELVE

The Return to India, and the Problem of Spiritual Experience

I flew to Bombay alone and arrived there on August 3. Peter Dias met me at the airport, and we took a taxi to the home of one of Baba's devotees in Bombay proper. Baba was to arrive that morning for an extended stay in the city, away from the Ashram.

He arrived about 11:00 A.M. I bowed at his feet and gave him a few gifts I had brought from America. Then there was a brief discussion about my trip. I would spend four weeks constantly in Baba's Presence, but this brief conversation was to be virtually the only one we would have from that moment. (Just previous to my leaving, I addressed him about an experience I had in meditation, but I did not otherwise have any personal discussions with him.)

I realized at that early moment (shortly after my arrival in Bombay) that I did not have a "personal" relationship with Baba. Fundamentally, he did not appear to me as a human individual. There was not the slightest movement of interest on my part in his personal attitudes, or anything that amounted to personality. But neither did I perceive myself as a personality in any fundamental sense. The revolution in my understanding of the mind and the ordinary adventure had finally removed any sense that I operated (fundamentally) on the level of character and personal life.

The discussion of my trip, brief as it was, seemed almost nonsensical, totally beside the point. It was required of us under the circumstances, and it was handled as a formality—but, afterwards, there was not a single attempt on Baba's part to communicate with me verbally. And, apart from bowing to him as I entered or left the room, I did not communicate with Baba socially (or, in the ordinary sense, "man to man").

After my initial discussion with him, I retired to a position several feet away and in front of Baba. I sat quietly, concentrated on
Baba, and withdrew my attention within. Apart from a brief trip to
spend a few days at Baba's Ashram and the burial shrine of
Bhagavan Nityananda, I spent the next four weeks sitting in this
large meeting room or meditating in the area that adjoined Baba's
bedroom.

We were staying in the expansive but very modestly appointed
apartments of Ram Pratap, a captain in the Indian navy. At night,
I slept on a hard single cot in a small room, where there was also
another visitor (and sometimes several others). During the day and
evening, hundreds of people would come to sit in Baba's
Presence, chant devotional hymns, and enjoy meals prepared by
the women as an offering to Baba. In the early afternoon, I would
sometimes take exercise by walking in the nearby streets of
Bombay. Sometimes, I would go to a bookstore, or have a cab
drive me through the city. But the constant routine was to arise at
5:00 A.M., meditate, and sit with Baba for hours at a time. I would
eat a light meal twice a day, and rest briefly after lunch. And I
would meditate almost constantly, either sitting before Baba or by
retiring to the small room behind him. I was rarely involved in
conversations, but I passed through the weeks in a perpetual
silence and internal solitude, observing the unusual phenomena
that were arising in the field of my free Awareness.

My own State at the time was uncommon. I was no longer
engaged in a continual experience of the mind rising in thoughts,
impulses, and memories. This had ceased to occupy or interest me.
Instead, there was a continuous tacit Awareness—Aware not of
thoughts in the concrete mind, but of forms of Energy, of space,
and of vision, and otherwise persisting simply as free conscious
Awareness Itself (without conflict, dilemma, or identification with
bodily limits).

As I sat with Baba, I wondered if he could perceive my internal State. The brevity of our conversation seemed to indicate that
he was Aware that personal communication was only a formality
and a distraction for me. Then, as I sat meditatively in his
Presence, I became Aware of existence totally beyond the physical

body. My Awareness moved in a space that was not in the concrete mind. I swooned and floated in a limitless void that was luminous with cosmic Force. As I moved in that space, I sensed that Baba was also with me. I wondered if he was Aware of this cosmic adventure of Spiritual Being, and I opened my eyes. He was looking at me, smiling and swaying his head as if to imitate the movement of free conscious Awareness in limitless space. I smiled back at him, and took this sign as an acknowledgement of my own State. From then, I assumed that Baba knew why I had returned to him, and I looked to experience his teaching on a purely internal level.

My first impression of Baba and his teaching, which I had experienced at the Ashram a year before, was (among other things) of a communication on a verbal and personal level. There was a personal relationship, a practical philosophy, and a consistent address to my personal problems and seeking. Thus, Baba had concentrated on teaching me philosophy, methods of purification and meditation, approaches to various obstacles in life, and so on.

However, as a result of my year of "waiting" (and of mere observation of the mind), I no longer resided in the limited view of the personal problem and its psychology. I had become conscious of a present activity within the domain of mere Awareness Itself. I had begun to intuit the data in consciousness on a level that transcended the concrete and personal instrument.

I felt that I had now begun to realize experience on a new level. The forms in consciousness were no longer of a mostly personal nature, implying a separate and human identity as its basis. Now I perceived the contents of consciousness as forms of Energy and superconsciousness, above the level of the concrete mind.

When I sat in Baba's Presence or in meditation, I was immediately, spontaneously drawn to concentrate at the "Point" infinitely above the center (and the fontanelle-aperture) of the crown of the head. Thus, I focused in uncommon perceptions of the universal Shakti. Baba seemed to recognize this, and made no effort to approach me personally, even with common friendliness. It was as if he felt such communication would only awaken and reinforce the activity of identification on a lower level.

Thus, I left myself—and was left by those around me—to experience existence purely on a Spiritual or superconscious level. And I spent my month in India in constant meditation on this level of perception. I also began to experience Communication from Baba entirely on the level of intuitive consciousness, without the addition of verbal address. It was a time of Divinely transformed existence.

Shortly after lunch on the first day of my visit, I received Baba's blessing in the form of a new arousal of the Shakti Energy. Baba came from behind me and entered the large sitting room, as if to pass to his seat. I expected him to simply pass by. But he stopped suddenly and patted me on the head several times. Then he went on to his seat in the corner of the room.

I remained seated on the floor with the others, listening to Baba's conversation with various visitors. But, as the minutes passed, I felt a strong Energy in my back that soon took over my entire spine and body. The Shakti finally concentrated very Powerfully in the head—particularly at the very top, where I had been experiencing the urge to meditate.

After about half an hour, I passed naturally into very deep meditation. I was concentrated and contained in the Shakti at a superconscious level. The kriyas in the body were almost entirely absent. Then I saw the image of Bhagavan Nityananda. He was facing me as I had seen him in a photograph, with a wide expression in his face and eyes, as if he were beholding some perceptible form of the Divine. His hands were raised to the sides of his face, and his fingers and palms spread, containing and generating a tremendous Force of Blissful Energy.

After several minutes, this image disappeared, and I took over the form of Bhagavan Nityananda myself. My eyelids opened wide, and my eyes rolled up toward the top of my head. And my hands rose up beside my face. The palms and fingers splayed, and I could feel the Shakti flowing in my body and my head, passing out toward Baba in benediction. I sat like this for perhaps an hour. I experienced only an Absolute Bliss and Calm, and an overwhelming Power flowed through me into the room. I felt myself behold and hold a Sphere of Energy in my hands. And, then, I saw

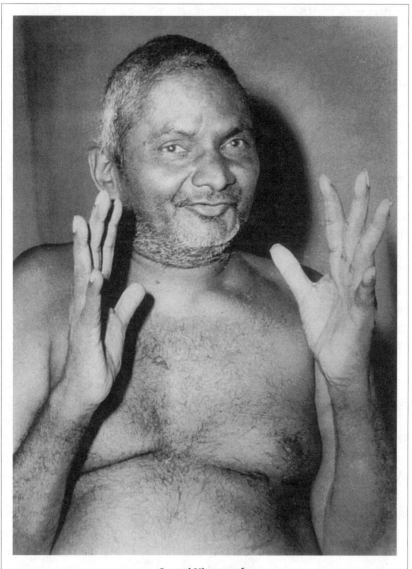

Swami Nityananda

*Then I saw the image of Bhagavan Nityananda. He was facing me
as I had seen him in a photograph, with a wide expression in his face
and eyes, as if he were beholding some perceptible form of the Divine.
His hands were raised to the sides of his face, and his fingers and palms
spread, containing and generating a tremendous Force of Blissful Energy.*

that It was Reality Itself, the Form and Force of all existence—including all the universes and every conditionally manifested form.

When, at last, I opened my eyes and resumed my ordinary state in the body, Baba was standing beside me in the room. We smiled at each other, and he reached toward me. I reached out to him with my hand, and we grasped each other's hands in the Blissful Communication of that Energy.

It became my practice to rise every morning at 5 A.M. and sit outside Baba's room for meditation. A few others also sat around in silent meditation at the same time. Baba would come out a few minutes later and sit on some cushions against the wall, two or three feet in front of me. He did this for the first two or three mornings of my visit, as if to watch my meditation.

Finally, about the third morning, I had been sitting for nearly an hour. Meditation had become an immense problem. My mind was filled with all kinds of alternative programs and techniques. I battled with Rudi's method, then Baba's, with mantras coordinated with breathing, watching thoughts arise, and concentration in various chakras (or functional centers). Soon I became merely confused and unsettled, and I intended to question Baba about meditation when I sat with him in company later in the morning.

But then Baba came out and sat before me in silence. And I soon began to experience an internal teaching about meditation. I was shown the various internal centers and the various activities in the mind. Then I saw the Shakti rising out of the muladhar (the lowest chakra, near the anus). And It rose, of Itself, through the various centers. As It rose, each event in the natural process of meditation took place automatically. The breath became even, and it began to coordinate itself with the mind. I saw how the breath affects thought, and how thought affects the breath. Then a concentration replaced this activity of passive observation. Attention was directed above (between the brows), and (then) in the sahasrar (the highest internal center, in the crown of the head).

Each breath became not a mere physical process but a process directed by the Shakti, and from the arising-place of attentive Awareness Itself (rather than from any merely functional focal point in the extended body-mind). With each inhalation, I felt the Shakti move out of the heart, down to the muladhar, then up the spine, and center at the top of the head. Then, for a moment, the breath would halt, and I would enjoy a concentration and reception of Energy and Bliss above. Then, with each exhalation, the Shakti would move down from the crown of the head and return to the Stillness of Effortless Being in the heart. As this process continued, attention and Energy sublimed into a Blissful Awareness, an unqualified (and, yet, also natural) form of participation in the Root-Condition of the Source-Reality.

After a while, Baba left the room. I gradually returned to my ordinary state of bodily consciousness, and I went in to sit with him and his visitors. I wondered how much of this experience had been either deliberately "created" by him or (at least) consciously observed by him. I sought some evidence of the verity of internal Communication between Baba and myself.

When I came into the room, Baba was busy writing on a notepad. After a while, he spoke to someone, and I was told that he was writing something for me. Later, someone came and showed me what he had written. It was written in Hindi or Sanskrit and would have to be translated. But I was told that Baba had given me a formal renunciate name, and that he would bless me with it (and, thus and thereby, with the right to teach, and with the gift of the perpetual option of formal renunciation) on August 9, the anniversary of Bhagavan Nityananda's mahasamadhi (or abandonment of the physical body).

Baba had apparently kept his promise to instruct me and give me a name, as well as the right to teach. But, as in all cases of gifts from a teacher, the reception in the disciple can act as a test. I immediately felt this fulfillment rise up as a barrier in me of pride and self-consciousness. When people go to a teacher, they get only as much as they seek or desire. Thus, I saw that, if I made this gift the object of my stay, I would close myself off to the greater experience that I truly desired.

I nodded to Baba and thanked him—but, after that, made no move to appear as if absorbed in that gift. And, as it happened, that gift was held before me by various delays and complications for nearly two weeks. The people around Baba felt his message had to be translated perfectly. Thus, it was handed from person to person—a professor of English was awaited, there were disagreements on certain words, there was no time to type a final copy. The Indian devotees seemed reluctant to give the letter to me at all, and they continually minimized its importance—although it was the first time a Westerner had formally, publicly, and in writing been given a name by Baba. I was eventually told that I had been named "Dhyanananda", which means "One Who Realizes (or, Has Realized) the Divine Being-Existence, Consciousness, and Bliss Through Deeply Meditative self-Surrender", or (as Vishwas Yande, one of Baba's closest Indian devotees, told me) "One Whose Bliss Is In Absolute Surrender To His Innermost Self", or, most properly, "One Who Realizes (or, Has Realized) the Divine Self-Condition and Source-Condition (That Is Unalloyed Bliss, Infinite Consciousness, and Eternal Being-Existence) Through True and Spiritual Meditation On (and, Altogether, One-Pointed and Absolute self-Surrender To) His Own True (or, Divine Supreme Inner) Self". It had earlier been indicated to me privately (by Amma) that Baba had named me "Love-Ananda" (meaning "One Who Is the Divine Love-Bliss", or "One Who Is, and Manifests, the Divine Love-Bliss", or, most properly, "One Who Is the Inherent Bliss, Infinite Consciousness, and Eternal Being-Existence of the Transcendental, and Inherently Spiritual, and Inherently egoless, and Self-Evidently Divine Person, or Self-Condition and Source-Condition, Manifesting As Infinite, or Boundless, Love-Bliss, and As Universal, and All-Blissful, Love Toward all beings"), but now the name "Dhyanananda" had also been "created" for me, because of that morning of internal teaching about meditation. Therefore, by publicly giving me this name "Dhyanananda", Baba showed me that I could rely on the verity of non-verbal teaching.

The day of Bhagavan Nityananda's mahasamadhi passed. I thought perhaps Baba had forgotten. But, as I sat in the rear of the room in the evening, Baba arose to go to bed, and he suddenly glanced toward me and said: "Dhyanananda!" I bowed to him and acknowledged the blessing.

The Indian devotees told me that Baba's letter to me would be prepared and given to me on August 15, the twenty-fifth anniversary of the day on which he was blessed with Divine vision by his Guru, Bhagavan Nityananda. But even that day passed with no indications from anyone. Finally, as I lay down to go to sleep, Amma, Baba's secretary, quickly entered the room and left again, leaving me Baba's original handwritten letter (in combined Hindi and Sanskrit) and a typed copy of a first translation of it into English.

Even after many days of translation work, the letter yet remained in a more or less primitive form—and further translation work was clearly going to be required if Baba's language, meaning, and intention were to be rightly honored and fully revealed. Therefore, I include the letter here in its ultimate full (and appropriately elaborated) English translation:

Shree Gurudev[26]

To my dear (beloved) "N" (Franklin), with my loving remembrances of you (even of your Very Self):

You have Done (and really Experienced) the "Sadhana" (or constant Discipline, Ordeal, and Process) of (True and Spiritual) "Dhyana" (or Meditation), and you have (Thereby) Attained the (True and Spiritual) State of Meditation. You have (by Means of True and Spiritual Meditation) Achieved the Steady State of "Samadhan(a)" (or one-pointed Concentration, or Inherence, In, and tacit, or mindless, Identification With, the Divine Supreme Inner Self). Therefore, you have Acquired (or Achieved) the Fullness of Satisfaction, Delight, and Joy in and by Means of (True and Spiritual) Meditation.

Because it is (Thus) Evident that (the Perfect Realization of the Divine Supreme Inner Self by Means of True and Spiritual) Meditation Is the (Great and Single) Purpose of your life (and, indeed, the Very Truth In Which you are, now and always, deeply Concentrated), you are Hereby Given the Name Dhyanananda.

In the Path (Sphere, Tradition, Line, and Lineage) of Yoga, you (by Virtue of this Declaration) will (or, by Right, can) henceforth be Known (Called, Addressed, or Referred to) as (or by the Name of) Dhyanananda.

You are a True Bearer of the Wealth of the Knowledge of Siddha Yoga, as It is Given at (Shree) Gurudev Ashram. The Kundalini Shakti, Which (by Divine Grace) Gives (Grants, or Bestows) and Accomplishes Siddha Yoga, Is Actively at Work in you.

Likewise, you are a True Knower (or Actual, and potentially Perfect, Realizer) of Vedanta. The (Divine Supreme Inner) Self, Which Is the Secret (and the Ultimate Truth) of Vedanta, and Which Is the Very Basis (Foundation, or Root) of True Religion (or the Way of Truth), and Which (or Perfect Realization of Which, or Perfectly Absorbed Identification With Which) Is the (True, and Ultimate) Goal of human life, has been Awakened, and Is Awake, in you by Means of the Active Work of the (Kundalini) Shakti (or Divine Power).

"Only one who has actually seen (or experienced) a particular something can testify (or bear true witness) to it (or speak with authority relative to its existence and its nature, and otherwise affirm, authenticate, certify, prove, manifest, show, or demonstrate it)." Based on this Principle (or the obvious reasonableness of this Argument), you (because of your direct Experience and Knowledge of Kundalini Shakti Meditation and, Thereby, of the Divine Supreme Inner Self) have, in accordance with Tradition, both the (Hereby Affirmed) Actual Ability and the Inherent (and Hereby Affirmed) Right to Initiate, or Cause, (True and Spiritual) Meditation in others (or, altogether, to Teach, Initiate, Establish, Guide, and Awaken others in the Practice, the Process, and the, Ultimately, Perfect Realization of Siddha Yoga Meditation, or True and Spiritual Meditation on, and, Ultimately, Perfect Realization of, the Divine Supreme Inner Self by Means of the Kundalini Shakti Transmitted, and Directly Activated, by you).

With an Authority based on this same Principle (of Experience itself), the Scriptures Testify and Declare (and

I, likewise, Affirm to you) that—if you have Faith (or genuine Trust) in the Guru, and if you (persistently) Meditate on your (Inherent) Oneness with the Divine Being, and if you Maintain an "Equal Eye" of Regard toward all human beings—the Goddess, Chitti Kundalini,[27] will (always) Help (and Support) you Fully, and She will not only Grant you the appropriate (or right) enjoyment of (human) life (or the appropriate natural, or ordinary, fulfillments of human life), but She will also "Fill" (or Perfectly Fulfill) you with (the Gift of Ultimate, Perfect, and Final) Liberation.

Therefore, May you (by the Divine Grace of the Goddess, Chitti Kundalini) Realize (or Obtain and Achieve) Perfect Absorption In, and Perfect Identification (and Perfect Sameness) With, the Divine Being—and This by Means of the Perfect Fulfillment of your Primary Duty, Which Is to Worship the Divine Being by Meditating on your (Inherent) Identity As the Divine Supreme Inner Self. Thus (Saying This), I Give you my Blessing.

Kundalini Yoga is a possibility for every one, since the Kundalini Shakti (Which Is the Active Source, and the Divine Doer, of Kundalini Yoga) Exists (latently) in every one, and every one (and every thing) exists (or resides) in (or is alive, or existing, in, As, and by Means of) the (Divine) Kundalini Shakti. And Meditation (on the Divine Supreme Inner Self) by Means of the Kundalini Shakti (Awakened by the Guru's Grace) Is (necessarily) the Primary Duty of every one (because every one Originates from the Divine Source, and, therefore, every one owes— or must render, surrender, and return—his or her Divinely Originated existence to the Kundalini Shakti, Which Is the Divine Source-Power, and Which Is the Way to the Divine Supreme Inner Self-Source of everything and everyone). Therefore, (I Hereby Declare that) you have the Inherent Right, and the Actual Ability, to Cause (or, altogether, to Teach, Initiate, Establish, and Guide Kundalini Yoga) Meditation (or the Practice and the Process of Kundalini Shakti Meditation) in any one and everyone (and, Thus and Thereby, to Awaken any one and everyone to and <u>As</u> the Divine Supreme Inner Self of everything and everyone).

Swami Muktananda,
Thana District,
Maharashtra State,
India

In the days previous to this event (of my receiving the initial translation of Baba's letter to me), Baba had indicated to a visitor that I was a Yogi, thereby giving me the right to that ancient title. Thus, for the world, I was to be known as "Sri Dhyanananda Yogi". But, by now, all such titles had ceased to bear significance for me. I took it as a very kind acknowledgement and let it pass. No one has ever called me by that name.

I saw that this status was not properly my own. Baba himself had "created" the name, as well as the experiences that gave me the right to it. He was acknowledging himself. I was careful to remember this, so as not to become identified with some idea of personal accomplishment. Baba had shown me how to meditate. He had meditated me. The Yoga was the Shakti Itself. The Shakti was the "Yogi". It had nothing to do with me. I would simply continue as before—moved by my own experience and understanding, and teaching wherever it was required, but without presenting myself in an exclusive or independent manner.

Indeed, as the days passed and my experiences increased, I felt more and more as if I had entered someone else's wonderland. Baba was a Siddha, an accomplished Yogi with various of the miraculous powers indicated in the scriptures. Even he, like myself (in this, my natural human form), was given these things as a gift by his Guru. And all of these things were, at last, given by the Shakti Herself, the Divine Mother. My experiences did not depend on me. Baba's experience did not depend on him. We were all gratuitously accepted into the court of the Goddess, Shakti. The universe and all experiences were Her game, and I was simply being allowed to see this game, not in order to acquire powers or status, but to recognize the Source of all things and so remain free of all seeking.

Adi Da Samraj with Swami Muktananda in 1969

Handwritten letter of
acknowledgement
from Swami
Muktananda

During the time of my stay, I experienced many unusual things. For the first time in my developmental life, I enjoyed the continuous status of a visionary, and more and more of the miraculous abilities that are described in classical Spiritual literature.

To varying degrees, many others who spent that month with Baba also experienced unusual phenomena. One man in particular, an Indian renunciate named Swami Prakashananda, would, at times, show perceptible signs of being even physically transfigured by the Shakti-Energy. And many others showed signs of being physically, emotionally, and mentally affected by that same Force, Which pervaded all the rooms as a result of Baba's Spiritual Transmission.

It was my practice to spend a couple of hours every afternoon in the meditation room outside the hall where Baba sat with his devotees. The room was usually filled with people in meditation. Some sat silent and composed. Others performed spontaneous kriyas and mudras. Some, as a result of the same spontaneous impulses, danced, or sat and moved their arms in the sinuous movements of dance. Some, suddenly, laughed or cried aloud. Others sang or chanted, even when this was not ordinarily characteristic of them. Others saw visions and lights.

I thought of that place as the "swooning room". The Shakti-Energy was extraordinarily Powerful and irresistible there, such that It would take one over bodily, emotionally, and mentally. As I became Filled with the Shakti-Energy there, I would crawl around on the floor, nearly blinded and immobile with "intoxication". Others crawled, too—and some barked and hooted like animals. At last, I would lie prone on the floor, feeling as if I were pinned to the floor by the Pressure of the Divine Force. Then my body would swoon away, and I would spin into Bliss.

Often, during these weeks with Baba, as I passed into deep meditation (morning, daytime, nighttime—anywhere in the house), I would leave the physical body and either observe or participate in events on various other planes. At times, I would sit for long periods observing an endless and automatic stream of images from various places. Some of these were merely the emanations of my own subconscious mind boiling off under the influence of the

Shakti-Energy. But, often, I would see actual places and events in other worlds and planets—through astral travel, or movements in superconsciousness. There would be marvelous scenes—some of them appearing as sublime perfections of the earth environment, and others that were built out of a mathematical and geometric logic of "creativity". Those higher worlds did not appear as solid and separate from the conditionally manifested conscious awareness, as is the case with ordinary consciousness on earth. Rather, the experiences in those higher worlds, including the environments themselves, changed according to the qualities of mind manifested by those who enjoyed them.

As all of these things passed, I saw that there was no necessity, no seriousness, to the entire affair of "creation". It was merely a pattern, a Play of the Divine Shakti—and I should merely Witness it, without suffering any sense of separated identity within it, and without presuming any change or limitation of my own Ultimate Nature. I saw that Reality was not this apparently separate Play of the Divine Shakti, but my own True Nature—the Self (or Siva) of the scriptures.

On several occasions, I entered these worlds in the form of a subtle body. Once, I met Baba before a passage leading underground. We entered a cave where there was a huge Dome of Honey-White Light in the floor. When we saw It, we recognized It as the Seat of the Divine, and we merged Joyously within It. On another occasion, I met Baba in the subtle world, and we gazed in one another's eyes. Soon we began to revolve in opposite directions about the point of contact and merged into the same Ultimate Nature.

Then I also began to experience myself in the form of various deities and demons. I took on the graceful Buddha-like qualities and sat eternally calm in meditation. But, then, I would also take on the terrible forms of Siva, and my body and face twisted about in fierce expressions. I sat like the ferocious aspect of the Deity, with hatchets and skulls of sacrificial blood in my hands.

Near the end of my visit, I felt I should communicate something of my experience to Baba—in order to acknowledge him, and (also) to test myself. I told him that a spot of light had often appeared before me in meditation—sometimes black or silver-gray, and sometimes blue. I also described a vision in which I saw the muladhar appear below me as a Siva-lingam.[28] Then I appeared below, my hands tied to the lingam in a gesture of prayer, pointing above. I rose up with the lingam into the sahasrar and experienced the perfect, Infinite, Unmoved Sat-Chit-Ananda—the Pure Existence-Consciousness-Bliss of the Indian Godhead, my own Ultimate Self-Nature as the Divine Being of all the world's scriptures. From this point of view, I looked down again at the muladhar, and thousands of devotees were raising their hands prayerfully to me. Then I received the revelation that, by my remaining concentrated in the sahasrar, all of the experiences of Realization would be given through me to others.

I asked Baba if I had received the true meaning of the experience. He only said: "Yes. The experience was true. Concentrate in the sahasrar if you like. The Shakti will do everything. The spot you saw is blue. It only appears black because of impurities."

The blue spot is one of the higher lights that appear within the subtle form of the human being. It may be seen within, above the plane of the eyes, or it may be seen to flash in front of the eyes. Baba calls it the "blue pearl" and the "supracausal body" (or cosmic body),[29] the most subtle and highest source of experiential consciousness. It is the entrance to the abode of ascended beings (or Yogic Siddhas) who enjoy the great cosmic powers. They can also be seen within, sometimes in the blue light of the blue pearl and its realm. And this blue form (or light) is a favorite topic of Baba's mystical teaching. He declares and reveals that even all human beings dwell in the blue realm in a subtle body, totally one with the Shakti. Apparently, Baba's purpose for my present visit was to make me fully conscious of these subtle dimensions and to have me know their Source to be the same that manifests the ordinary human state.

Now my visit was nearing an end. My experiences were a seemingly endless revelation of the Spiritual forms of Reality. And I had acquired something of the ego of Spiritual seeking and discovery. But I was already becoming aware of the inconclusiveness of all such experiences. Once the problem of the ordinary mind had ceased to trouble me, I began to experience Spiritual forms. Then I acquired a new problem, the problem of phenomenally-based Spiritual experience. Then, it seemed, the matter of Freedom and Real Consciousness depended on the attainment of Spiritual experiences. And, it seemed, Spiritual experiences of an Ultimate kind must be identical to Freedom and Reality Itself. Thus, I was driven to acquire them.

But, as these events unfolded, they, too, became common. The display of images, the transports to other worlds, the identification with ascended modes of Divine Being, the perception of higher and subtler forms of my own identity and ability, all passed before me, but with less and less interest on my part.

I began to feel: "This is not the point. This is not it. Reality is Prior to all of this. Reality is my own Self-Nature." But the more this feeling arose in me, the more aggressively these experiences arose—such that I, again, began to feel trapped. I felt that the way to which I was being progressively (but surely) Awakened was not Baba's version of Siddha Yoga. I was no longer moved by a desire for these experiences. They were nothing but more conditional and limited life, more patterns, more experiences calling up the process of identification, differentiation, and desire. The search for Spiritual experience, the motivation to achieve an Ultimate Victory on the basis of overcoming the "Spiritual problem", was only another form of seeking, suffering, and separative mentality. There was no absolute difference between the higher and the lower worlds. There was no absolute advantage in any kind of experience.

I began to feel a resistance to the experiential movements of the Shakti. I felt no need to continue this ritual of visionary life. And I wanted some time and place to understand the entire miasma of personal and universal life. Thus, even though full of love for Baba, I began to welcome the opportunity to go home in peace.

I had made arrangements to leave on a Friday, at the end of August. But, on Wednesday night, as I slept, I became Aware of Bhagavan Nityananda's Presence. Then he appeared to me—and he spoke to me, throughout the night, of my experiences. He told me I should prepare to leave immediately—Thursday, the day before I had planned.

The next afternoon, I took my leave of Baba. He patted my back in blessing and gifted me with arms full of flowers. He also gave me a huge red apple. I bowed to him gratefully and turned to leave. He was still waving to me as I approached the stairway. And, as I began to descend the stairs, I felt the beginnings of sickness in my stomach.

I flew to New York via Tel Aviv and Rome. On the first leg of the journey, I felt nauseous and overcome with fever. And by the time I arrived in Tel Aviv, I was quite ill with cramps and diarrhea. As I sat waiting for my plane, I felt exhausted and did not know how I would be able to travel comfortably. Then I remembered the apple. Baba had required me to pay particular notice to it as I left. I thought that the necessity for my early leave and Baba's gift of the apple were perhaps all part of a plan "created" by the Shakti. A sickness which was to purify my body and nerves was about to come over me in those last days with Baba. And so my early leave had been planned.

I ate the apple slowly, wondering if it would possibly affect my illness. Almost immediately, the churning in my stomach and intestines ceased. The body became comfortable. The purifying work of the apparent illness continued even for several days after my return to New York—but I continued tranquilly and comfortably, knowing the Shakti was at work. The entire experience had only been a sign of how the Shakti would continue to work for me according to Its intelligence of my needs after I left Baba's physical presence in India.

The loft in New York

CHAPTER THIRTEEN

Shakti in America, New Problems, and the Return to India

I arrived in New York on August 30, 1969. The next nine months were a period of intense investigation into the problems of Spiritual experience. I spent that time virtually in seclusion.

I shared a loft in the Wall Street area with Nina and another woman, named Patricia Morley. Nina and I no longer presumed a formal "marriage" commitment, but we remained intimate friends. Both she and Patricia had (based on clear and simple—if modest, and not, otherwise, profound and intense—Spiritual inclinations) become regular (but informal) beginning students of mine—and we lived together in a kind of mini-Ashram, regularly frequented by other such students, and friends, and random visitors (who would sometimes come to me for help in relation to their Spiritual search). I rarely left the apartment, and would spend many days at a time without even going into the street. Television became my main source of information about the world.

I spent my days in constant meditation. There were periods in every day when I sat for formal meditation—but, for me, meditation had now become a constant activity, even in the context of the moment to moment process of ordinary (humanly-born) conscious awareness. I wanted to probe deeply into the matter of Spiritual experience, in order to see it in its entirety and recognize its primary wisdom.

To that point, Spiritual life had been for me an experimental activity. It had not stabilized in a single practice associated entirely with "radical" (or "gone-to-the-root", or most fundamental) self-understanding and Real Consciousness. The traditions of

Spirituality seemed to me a "mixed bag" of many different forms of experience and interpretation. The goal of it all was not something that all saints, all religions, or all scriptures (or traditions) acknowledged in common. The particular form of search and revelation was different in each case. The precise description of the nature of the world also differed in the many different cases—but, overall, those descriptions amounted to two basic alternatives. There was the traditional Eastern view that the world is an illusion "created" as a result of the failure to recognize the inherently Free Condition of the Real Self. And there was the traditional Western view that all of this was the "creation of God". Therefore, some sought liberation—and others, salvation. Some claimed that the "goal" was Identity with the Divine—whereas others claimed that there was an irreducible, eternal distinction (and even separation) between the Divine (on the one hand) and the human (or the soul) and the various worlds (on the other hand).

I worked to Realize the fundamental Truth that was Freedom and (also) Real Knowledge. And no one and no tradition anywhere represented that Truth to me whole, entirely Free of any limited or limiting point of view.

I continued to teach, very informally. This took the form of random, spontaneous discussions about Spiritual life, practice, meditation, and experience. People would come to discuss the ideas they gathered in various books. Some only wanted to hear comparative philosophy, learn "secret" techniques, or get information about various psychic phenomena. Some were concerned with healing, diet, what to do, what not to do. Some wanted estimations of various saints, organizations, religions. Some were looking for particular saintly qualities which their reading had led them to expect in anyone who claimed to have Spiritual experience. Most of them were not serious enough about the "problems" of conditional existence to learn any more than the conventional "Spiritual" gossip—but several of them stayed long enough to make progress, and they approached the matter from a depth in themselves that made progress possible. These people had "experiences", and they began to meditate with some degree of regularity and understanding. Some of them would remain only for a few months, and then (if their impulse to Realization of Real God, or Truth, or Reality was weak) I let them go.

I found that Westerners—like traditional people of the East—were entirely able to fully enter into the true Guru-devotee relationship, but only if they (like anyone else) were truly moved to embrace all the very real disciplines traditionally (and necessarily) associated with esoteric religious and Spiritual life. And What I wanted my beginning students to attain was not "experiences" (regarded—in the conventional, or merely phenomenal, sense—to be "Spiritual"), but (in the most profound sense) a Communication of Reality (Itself), on Which (and in Which) they could found their lives in Truth.

There is a persistent human fascination with all kinds of "phenomenal" experiences—visionary phenomena, miracles, forms of symbolic or psychic perception, and so on. But Real Consciousness is unqualifiedly Free. Its true psychic depth (or inherently egoless Reality-Condition) is an unmodified field of Awareness. And even when there is the experience of unusual phenomena on the way, such things are simply more material to be transcended in the process of "radical" (or "gone-to-the-root", or most fundamental) self-understanding.

In the course of the developing process of "radical" self-understanding, "mystical experience" (or the concentration of attention in "Spiritual phenomena" themselves) is (along with the concentration of attention in any "phenomena" at all) progressively (and, at last, most perfectly) transcended. Therefore, from the beginning, the essential experience to be valued is the one variously described as "being One with all of life", or "experiencing the Oneness of everything". This is the Power of Reality, of unqualified relatedness, of non-separation, no suffering, and no-seeking in the heart. This is, in fact, the primary Experience and Knowledge that (ultimately) obviates all particular experiences and motivations. Therefore, this has been my Purpose—in my own case, and in the case of those who came to me even in the earliest days of my teaching work (before my own Realization of "radical" self-understanding was most perfectly consummated). My Purpose has been to make this "radical" (or "gone-to-the-root", or most fundamental) self-understanding the real foundation (and not merely the goal, but the always present Realization) of conscious life. When "radical" self-understanding is Realized, it is not a mere idea or belief, or a feeling that depends on any particular circumstances. It is (and more and more becomes) a function of Real Consciousness, of unqualified Being. And, once this Realization (of "radical" self-understanding) is Awakened and Established, It (Itself) develops, over time, into the most perfect Realization of Ultimate Knowledge and Free Existence.

In the fall of 1969, I spent my days meditating, observing the processes of my seeking, and also keeping a written record of my understanding. I edited all of the extant journals of my understanding and made a book out of them (called *Water and Narcissus*), which I completed early in November. I also produced a novel (or what I called a "prose opera", or, really, a theatrical ritual, or liturgical drama), tentatively titled *The Love Exit, and Water* (and, ultimately, titled *The Mummery Book*), which was based on the theme of Spiritual seeking (and the transcending of all seeking). It was largely based on the images I had perceived during my earlier period of writing on the beach.

My own experience was not yet conclusive. I had not yet finally (or most perfectly) Realized "radical" self-understanding. Nevertheless, my experience had developed to the point where my interests in writing were re-awakened. I had re-attained the original impulse of my own writing. I knew that I would teach, and my teaching would also necessarily include much writing. It would be a literature of Real Consciousness.

I was also concerned with the need to understand the relationship between functional consciousness, all of conditionally manifested Reality, the Shakti, and the Divine Being (or Ultimate Self-Condition, or Source-Condition). In my constant meditation, I had begun to have an experience of Ultimate Reality that foreshadowed events to follow in the spring of 1970.

As I meditated, I began to experience an impression of the Divine Being over against my own life on every level. He was not only the Ultimate Self-Nature (or Pure Consciousness), but He included (as His active Presence) the Force known as Shakti. He was Siva-Shakti. He was like Krishna, the personal Godhead. As I went on in this manner, I began to perceive that this Divine Being and Presence included all things in Himself. He had become the universe. This accounted for my experience of Infinite (and Priorly Ascended) Bliss (at the end of my first visit to Baba's Ashram), wherein I perceived that everything was being "Lived".

This Divine Being included all that I experienced—my own states moment to moment, the entire universe of the Shakti's expression, and even the Guru. Thus, I began to realize that He not only included the objects in my humanly-born conscious awareness, but He was the very Subject Who experienced all the states I felt I had been experiencing. He was my own Self-Nature and my experience. There was nothing but Him.

Soon I began to realize that I was not experiencing my experiences. He was the experiences and the experiencer. Yet, in some fundamental manner, I continued to exist. But I was experiencing only Him. I was not experiencing my experiences. Those experiences, and that experiencing—my own apparent states, moment to moment—were also Him in His activity. I was not, in any sense, a part of these.

I saw that I was only consciousness, entirely without content, "created" by this Divine Lord. My only experience—moment to moment, under all apparent conditions—was Him. That was it, entirely. As this contemplation grew, and I became only the devotee of this Great Being, I wrote about my Realization. I will include some of those descriptive notes here, to demonstrate my consideration at that point in time.

◆ ◆ ◆

I am not in relationship to the physical universe, nor to any object I perceive. I am not in relationship to my own mind, nor my body. Neither am I in relationship to my loved-ones or any person. And I will never be in relationship to any particular thing. Nothing that appears to me has ever known my presence, nor will it ever know that I exist. I am always already and only in relationship to the Divine Lord, the One Who is Manifesting everything and is the Consciousness of everything.

Whatever I may appear to do, and whomever I may appear to relate to, and whatever I may appear to experience, I am always and only Enjoying the direct relationship to the Divine Lord. I am never (in fact) separate, or experiencing any entity in itself. I am never even experiencing my own separate mind and personality.

At times, I have interpreted my life as separate experiences by a disconnected and unique process I identified as "myself". The error was not that I experienced the play of phenomena, but that I failed to Know I was always already in relationship and always already Free. Healing is simply the instant (moment to moment) recovery of this Knowledge.

This Knowledge is not Itself the result of an applied process, a strategic practice, or a seeker's method. I am always apparently performing such things, but this Knowledge Itself is entirely a grace, a suddenness, a Realization outside of all activity, all strife, and all the influence of experience. And this Knowledge is totally liberating. The more profound It goes within, the simpler the Truth appears, and It is simply unqualified conscious Awareness and unqualified Bliss. It is Real existence—prior to the mind and all identification with conditional manifestation. It is marked by a calm, questionless heart—and by Peace, the Knowledge of Existence Itself as Bliss. And Its essential Content is the contemplation (or unqualified conscious Awareness) of the Divine Lord, the One Presence, the actual Source and Object.

◆ ◆ ◆

The Divine Lord is not (Himself) the "God-Symbol" of exoteric religions. He is not the "One" that you are persuaded to believe in. He is not an entity, a mental object, a reduction of Reality, or a phenomenon within the world. He is the One Who must be Realized in order to be Known. He is not Known previous to the Realization of Him in life. It is simply that the tacit understanding of one who is beyond conflict, and who enjoys the perception of non-contradiction, is suddenly voiced as this recognition. It is the testimony of one's Absolute Freedom and Enjoyment, and not the description of a remedial path for the mind in its bondage. But neither is the way the avoidance of devotion, or the avoidance of worship of the prophetic "God-Symbol". Mankind will act and seek thus in any case, and enjoy the consolations of their many answers. It is simply that, when there is a return to understanding, there is an end to seeking, questioning, descriptive belief, and all conflict. And these are replaced by immediate recognition.

◆ ◆ ◆

The Divine Lord—Who is Present universally but Who is not qualified by any conditional manifestation, Who is the Source and Consciousness and Control of all processes, Who is Manifesting everything, Who Transcends everything, Who is That Alone to Which you are related, Who is That Alone of Which you are conscious, Who is Freedom, Consciousness, actual Presence, perfect Knowledge, and Absolute Bliss, Who Alone is your Self and That of all things, Who is the Guru, the Teacher—is the Principle of life. The solitary necessity for one's Freedom—if one could assume Him to be What He is—is to allow Him to Exist, to Manifest Himself as everything, to be the Divine Spiritual Presence Known anywhere.

The relationship to the Divine Lord is salvation. His grace (whatever form it takes) is simply to make His Existence, as He is, Real to living beings. This Lord is the Lord, and all human beings are communicating their level of realization of Him. All religions, all religious statements, all religious and Spiritual paths, truths, and claims are communications about this Divine Spiritual Presence—modified by the limitations of their realization and the historical circumstances of the communication. He is Knowable, and He must be Known.

◆ ◆ ◆

The essential Realization of the meditative act is that this present consciousness—my humanly-born conscious awareness at this instant, the entire conditional manifestation which is my present experience—is (in fact) the contemplation (by me) of the Divine Lord, and the direct experiencing (by me) of the Divine Lord. He is this. He is this state, this instant of conditional awareness, this even ordinary manifestation, this natural contemplation, this always exact experiencing. The moment of this recognition breaks the entire form of bondage.

The Truth is that all of conditionally manifested existence is being "Lived". The right orientation of all conditional consciousness is to present contemplation of the Consciousness (and the total Condition) of the Divine. Totality includes the present actuality—but as a manifestation of the Divine Lord, and as a conscious experience and Realization of the Divine Lord. Human bondage, the root of egoic ignorance, suffering, the activity of sin, is simply the result of the loss of this Knowledge and this contemplation. Instead of living in the Bliss of this infinite Freedom, one identifies the present (or moment to moment) form of one's consciousness and experience to represent (and be) a separate and finitely personal reality. It is thus that one loses the Freedom of Totality, the infinitely unburdened Bliss of pure contemplation of the Divine, and falls into the expression of finite and separate existence. I do not mean to say that when one is fully in the Truth one ceases to exist in a world, in relationship to others. It is simply that one comes to live life truly, directly, in the Full Bliss of the relationship to the Divine. In the free and natural State, one ceases to enforce the form of egoic ignorance and the conditions its assumptions "create".

◆ ◆ ◆

Normally, one assumes: "I am having this experience." Every moment of life is informed by this affirmation. Moment to moment, this presumption of being a separate identity is communicated to the entirety of life. Thus, life becomes an expansion out of the idea of this individuation—a process whereby the separate and absolute ego tries to predicate all Reality to itself, in order to regain the Totality intuited beneath the mind. This is the source of life as dilemma and mortality, suffering and tragedy, ordinary and dark humor and search. It is simply a matter of a failure to recognize the Truth of one's condition, one's right relationship, the actual Reality. In fact, the Divine Lord, the Conscious Subject and Source of all manifestation, is the Only Experiencer of everything—and what one now identifies as one's self is simply one's non-separate Awareness of the Reality of the Divine.

◆ ◆ ◆

The quality of life proceeds from the form of cognition one assumes. It is only necessary to return, again and again, to the living condition of Reality, which is the actual and conscious relationship to the Divine Lord, Who is That Alone of Which one is conscious.

The mind is only a process of experience. One suffers because of the quality of one's relationship to the mind. When one does not enjoy the Divine, one is identified with the limiting force of experience.

◆ ◆ ◆

The universe is Conscious. There is Consciousness everywhere. There is only Consciousness, and a universal Event, a simultaneous Reality.

The humanly-born conscious awareness is the contemplative Enjoyment of the Divine Lord. That relationship is Reality. It is the very structure of the humanly-born conscious awareness. It is unqualified Enjoyment. It is the Realized Actuality.

◆ ◆ ◆

There is a completion of all the reasons.

At the time, it seemed to me that I had Realized the Ultimate State in Which Reality is recognized exactly as It is. And this Knowledge (or Wisdom) Itself seemed to be the perfect and liberating Truth—the supreme interpretation of all experience, and the key to every kind of dilemma (in any form of existence).

However, as days passed, I began to feel an overwhelming burden in this Realization. I had predicated everything to the Divine and nothing to myself. My extreme and constant concentration on Him made me more and more immobile. My own existence remained as a constant problem that needed to be continually reabsorbed in this devotional Sublimity.

Eventually, my own "creative" Force began to emerge and break away from this conceptual form. And new experiences of the Shakti arose to teach me further regarding the Nature of Real Consciousness. Thus, I abandoned this binding perception—or it simply passed from me, and left me loose. But a remnant of it was retained, to rise again (in a new form) when I returned to India in the spring, because my deep psyche yet demanded a devotional fulfillment comparable to my childhood love of Jesus of Nazareth.

Around the first of the year, 1970, I received a letter from a young African man at the Ashram. My reply to his letter was to mark a new phase in my relationship to Baba.

Baba had given me the right to teach, and he placed no conditions on it. I should teach those who came to me, and I should teach not what I had been told, no tradition I had learned in the mind, but exactly according to my own experience and understanding.

While I was in India the previous summer, a young man arrived from Uganda. He first saw me sitting in a crowd with Baba at Ram Pratap's apartments in Bombay, and he became instantly convinced that I was to be the instrument for his instruction. I met him later in Ganeshpuri, at the Ashram, during a short visit there during my stay in August, and he told me about this. He had been having constant visions of me since the day he saw me.

He asked if he could meditate with me in the mornings. I told him that I would not presume to teach him, but he could meditate with me if he liked. And so he came every morning. When I left, he kept demanding a blessing, and called me "Master" with profound devotion. But I only wished him well and told him to seek out Baba as his Guru.

During the months that followed my return to America, he wrote to me a few times—each time describing his problems, his dissatisfaction at the Ashram, and always asking for advice. I replied each time by telling him of my experiences of Baba's grace and recommending that he speak to Baba about these same problems and then follow Baba's advice. I also recommended certain books in the Ashram library that he might find useful.

However, in January, when I received his last letter, I had myself become individuated from Baba. My own experience and understanding had never developed along traditional lines, and the recent development (in my own case) of the devotional philosophy I have just described (which corresponded to the essence of the Indian devotional tradition, and which my own understanding eventually required me to abandon) indicated to me that the Truth lay in a fundamentally (and intrinsically) new approach to Spirituality and life. I had also already enjoyed (or suffered) the experience of teaching more than a dozen Westerners in a direct, intimate, eye-to-eye confrontation, day to day. And I saw that the teaching required was anything but a merely traditional philosophy made of conventional ideas about Spirituality and life-practice. Thus, I was moved to write to this man more directly.

I made no effort to turn him from Baba. He had been moved to go to Baba's Ashram for help, and he was now in Baba's care. I believed that he must take advantage of his chosen opportunity. And I had no doubt that Baba could provide him with the Spiritual help he was seeking. Nevertheless, I was willing to tell him more directly what had become my point of view on Spiritual matters. Indeed, he seemed almost ready to leave Baba's Ashram, even (perhaps) to seek me out in America, and I thought that, if he could see exactly that I was not a teacher in the traditional sense, he might cease to be enamored of me and (so) turn again to Baba.

Thus, I told him that I was not a disciple of Baba in the usual sense. I said that I did not relate to Baba in the manner of a "seeker". I told him that I addressed all of my experience, moment to moment, in terms of a "radical" (or "gone-to-the-root", or most fundamental) understanding of my own motives, and that I (therefore) did not seek (or otherwise overestimate the value of) Spiritual experiences (or even any other kinds of experiences). Even in the case of my own students, I told him, I did not make them concerned to receive Shakti-experiences, nor did I recommend various seeker's exercises for the "development" (or exploitation) of Shakti-experiences. I told him that I simply directed my students to understand their own motives and problems, and (on the basis of that understanding) to perceive Reality directly, free of the habits of seeking. I told him he must look to Baba for his answers, since what he was seeking was not in my Purpose.

A week or two later, I received a letter from the Ashram. The letter was written by Amma, but spoken in Baba's name. Baba was outraged. He had read the letter I had written to the young African. "How could anyone presume to teach who needed help himself? What tradition do you belong to, if not the tradition of Muktananda and Nityananda? Perhaps it is true, as we have heard, that you try to steal disciples from other teachers!"

Right understanding of one's position in relation to the totality of everything is humbling, and it requires the acceptance of the relative unimportance of one's individuality. However, I was not willing (nor did I feel I was being called upon) either to misrepresent myself or to swear falsely, particularly in the face of such an absurd attack. I assumed that Baba could not require weakness in his disciple. Therefore, he must only be testing my strength and integrity as a disciple. After all, Baba had himself given me the right and the task of teaching.

I felt it was time to remove the veil of silence between Baba and me. He must know what I understood and how I related to him. I posed no threat to him. I had always been very careful to turn the young African in Baba's direction. But I reserved the right and the necessity to <u>truly</u> understand all that had been given to me. Indeed, to fail to do so would be to deny the Truth my entire life had been revealing.

I was profoundly grateful for Baba's grace, and it had surely given me great experience and continuous resources for the consideration of my practice, but it appeared the time had come for me to assert myself again, even (perhaps) as I had been required to do with Rudi. I would state my position clearly, as it was proven in my experience—and, if Baba could not tolerate me on those terms, I was willing to accept my total independence.

Therefore, I wrote a long and forceful letter of objection and justification. I explained my position, and I made clear the positive intention and role I had assumed in my letter to the African. I told Baba that my own experience was developing along the lines of a "radical" (or "gone-to-the-root", or most fundamental) self-understanding—free, from the beginning, of all the limitations of seeking. I spoke myself to him in true and fullest gratitude. I said that, if he were to allow me as a disciple, I would be a disciple of this kind, or else he should let me go.

The letter I received in reply barely indicated that Baba was aware of what I had written. It was a brief, reconciling letter—and I am sure my own letter had appeared too strong for anyone to take to Baba. Perhaps he had only heard parts of it. The reply only stated that Baba wanted to be sure I was not trying to turn people from the Ashram. I should feel free to teach as I desired in America. It closed with the admonition that the disciple chooses the Guru, not the Guru the disciple.

I was satisfied that Baba wished the relationship to continue. And I felt it was valuable to maintain it for my own sake. Baba preached a tradition and enjoyed his role within it. There was nothing more to say about it. The message to me was that, if I came and found the Truth for myself, it was my business to Communicate It as I saw fit. But don't rock the boat! And so I was renewed in my own unique course. And I continued in it with my characteristic sense of responsibility to only exactly Realize Reality Itself—without compromise, and not confined or constrained by any tradition.

During the following months I continued to have experiences of various kinds, as I had in India. Particularly at night, when the body was set aside, I experienced fully conscious meetings with various saints, Yogis, and miracle-workers. I was allowed to observe miraculous demonstrations in a school for Siddhas (the Yogis who practice various powers). I saw, in detail, the process whereby they materialize objects and living things.

Even though physically separated from Baba, I would often experience his sudden Presence in miraculous ways. Frequently, I would feel him acquire my body, such that I knew all of my functions had become his body. He would particularly take over my face and hands. I could feel my features adapting to the expression of his character and mood. The special formulation of the Shakti that worked through him would pour through my hands and face. My mouth would twitch about my teeth in his characteristic manner. My fingers would automatically gesture in the manner by which he indicated sublime Feeling, and my index finger would (in his manner) point above—to the sahasrar, to the Holy Place, to the Guru, and to God.

In meditation, I would experience Bhagavan Nityananda taking over my psychic form. My subtle body and my physical body would expand with great Force, and I would feel myself with dimensions larger than any conceivable space. I would feel his subtle breathing, and my abdomen would take on the "pot-shaped" form described in the Yogic traditions.

These manifestations were not simply "internal". Frequently, my perceptions coincided with certain external events. For example, a friend once came to see me after a long stay at Baba's Ashram. We bowed to Baba's picture and felt the Shakti Fill the room. Just then, the flowers that were nailed about the portrait flew off and landed at our feet.

Along with these experiences, my understanding was developing along unique lines. I regarded the various phenomena of Spiritual experience to be interesting but (ultimately) inconsequential. The activities of the Shakti demonstrated much about the origins of (and the true relationship to) the conditions of existence, but the experience of such phenomena was not equal to the Truth. The pursuit of Spiritual phenomena, or the solution to the problem of life conceived on a phenomenally-based (or merely conditional)

Spiritual level, was, for me, merely another and more dramatic form of seeking, suffering, and separation. Indeed, this pursuit was only one more manifestation of the logic of Narcissus—the complex avoidance of relationship, or the avoidance of relatedness—as the essential condition (constantly enacted) of the egoic being. I was not, in any sense, devoted to seeking (in any form).

Then, sometime in February, I experienced a remarkable revolution in my living being. After my second trip (and even, to a degree, after my first trip) to India (and also as a result of the long course of my experience with Rudi), I had firmly identified myself (or the structure of my living being) with the various instruments of the chakra system. That circuit of life-energy and Spiritual Energy—with its various functional centers (and degrees of relative grossness or subtlety), high and low—revealed itself to be the foundation structure of every living being and (in its universal Depth) the Functional (or "Creative") Source of even every conditionally existing form or universe. My experiences in India demonstrated this as a fact. Thus—although the Truth of Real Consciousness had revealed Itself to me to be one of "radical" (or "gone-to-the-root", or most fundamental) self-understanding, no-seeking, and (even in the context of ordinary living) the Conscious Enjoyment of an eternally Free, Un-changing, and always already Existing State—I could not, on the basis of this identification with the chakra system, see how life could be performed without some kind of seeking.

The chakra system (and the philosophy it implied) demanded a conscious, intentional purification and ascent toward concentration in the highest center (and in the subtlest vehicle) of being—what Baba called the "supracausal" body. Thus (it seemed), Spiritual life was, necessarily, associated with this goal of ascent. And, indeed, all of the most commonly known religions and Spiritual paths of the world, even where there is no conscious and sophisticated Knowledge of the Shakti and the chakras, rest in this basic philosophy of purification and ascent. Even in Christianity, it appears as fasting and prayer, the means of fullest devotion to God and dependence on God. Thus, while at seminary, I had tried to express my experience through Christianity. But I always returned to an understanding free of all seeking. And this not only prevented my alignment with Christianity, but it also "created" difficulties with what was (for me) the conventional tradition of Shakti Yoga (or of merely traditional Siddha Yoga).

In February, I passed through an experience that vindicated my understanding. For several nights, I was awakened again and again with sharp lateral pains in my head. They felt like deep incisions in my skull and brain, as if I were undergoing a surgical operation. During the day following the last of these experiences, I realized a marvelous relief. I saw that what appeared as the sahasrar (the terminal chakra and primary lotus in the crown of the head) had been severed. The sahasrar had fallen off like a blossom. The Shakti—Which had previously appeared as a polarized Energy that moved up and down through the various chakras (or functional centers), producing various effects—was now released from the chakra form. There was no more polarized Force. Indeed, there was no structure whatsoever—no up or down, no chakras. The chakra system had been revealed as unnecessary, an arbitrary rule or setting for the Play of Divine Energy. The structure beneath all of the bodies (or functional sheaths),[30] gross and subtle, had revealed itself to be as unnecessary and conditional as the bodies (or functional sheaths) themselves.

Previously, all the universes seemed built and dependent upon that foundation structure of descending and ascending Energy—such that the nature and value of any given experience was determined by the level of the chakra in which the humanly-born conscious awareness was functioning, and planetary bodies were fixed (as was space itself) in a spherical (or curved) form. But now I saw that Reality (and Real Consciousness) was not in the least determined by any form apart from Itself. Consciousness had shown Its inherent Freedom and Priority in relation to the chakra form. It had shown Itself to be senior to that entire structure, Prior to every kind of manifestation or modification of cosmic Energy (or Shakti). There was simply Consciousness (or the One and Only and inherently indivisible Conscious Light) Itself—Prior to all forms, all sense of dilemma, and every kind of seeking and presumed necessity.

In the past, I had been turned to the conditionally manifested (and lower-based) Shakti and to phenomenally-based Spirituality, as the route to Realization. But this was a reluctant course. I Knew that a fundamental and "radical" self-understanding—equal to the Self-Realization of Consciousness Itself—was, in fact, the Source, the Very Truth. Now I saw that I was right. There is no need to have recourse to any kind of phenomenon, problem, or structure of seeking. The Shakti, as an apparently independent (or cosmic) Force, is not the primary (or necessary) Reality. Reality is the Ultimate Self-Nature, the Foundation that is pure Consciousness—the Divine Self-Consciousness, Siva, Who is always already Free of conditional manifestations (or of the Divine, but merely apparent, Play). Thus, I was certain, again, that Real life is not (itself) a matter of necessary evolution, or the acquisition of mere phenomenal (or conditionally arising) experience. Rather, Real life is (simply) founded in always present self-understanding, and, thereby (and ultimately), in Consciousness Itself (or the One and Only and inherently indivisible Conscious Light that Is the true Self-Nature, or inherently egoless Self-Condition, of Consciousness Itself).

The extraordinary Event that I experienced at the end of my first visit to Baba's Ashram now showed Itself to be the most fundamental of all my experiences in Baba's company. It appeared to contain the One necessary and sufficient revelation (Prior to all phenomena). I could see that What was revealed was True, although I did not yet finally Know what were the ultimate consequences of that revelation (in most perfect Realization). My meditation had been developing for some time along lines of my own understanding. I continued to experience Spiritual phenomena, as I had in India. These were not undesirable. They represented a genuine expansion of conscious experience—and, thus, they made it possible for me to develop my self-understanding on the basis of the most inclusive and exhaustive firsthand experience and knowledge of even every kind of conditionally manifested phenomenon. But my way of approach was one of "radical" (or "gone-to-the-root", or most fundamental) self-understanding. And this understanding—rather than the phenomena I experienced—was the foundation and fruit of my Spiritual life.

Over time, I had experimented with every kind of seeker's method, but the mature form of my meditation was not based in any search for higher experience. It was simply a direct approach to whatever experiences arose. Thus, at the very last, I was not occupied as a seeker (diverted by techniques applied to attention, body, feeling, or breath), but, whatever arose to attention (and in, or to, body, feeling, or breath), I simply Enquired of myself (in the moment, as particular tendencies, thoughts, or experiences arose), "Avoiding relationship?" Thus (in this manner), I was constantly returned to a Prior State of unqualified Awareness. By remaining in that State through self-Enquiry, I was led, at the very last, to most perfectly understand my own instruments, every kind of search, and every kind of experience.

The letter Baba Muktananda wrote to me in late April 1968 contains a traditional program for meditation:

In the *"So'ham" mantra*—*"So"* signifies God or Guru, and *"ham"* denotes "I" or "me". Thus *So'ham* means "I am He". Let your practice of meditation be accompanied by the ceaseless reflection on the above meaning of *So'ham*. A person gets transformed into the likeness of the object on which he constantly ponders, by absorbing its qualities.

Sitting calm and steady repeat the *mantra* together with rhythmic breathing (i.e., the inhalation and exhalation of air—*pran* and *apan*). Harmonize the repetition of *mantra* with the breathing as follows: With *"So"* take it in and with *"ham"* bring it out. Throughout the *mantra*-repetition one should follow this practice. Simply sitting peacefully and applying the mind to the *pran* and *apan* one enters into deep state of meditation. When one's mind is fixed on *"So"* with the incoming breath and on *"ham"* with the outgoing breath it is *mantra-japa*. The regularity with which the breath comes in and goes out is *pranayama*. And if a person is skillful, intelligent, and alert—the (1) *repetition of mantra (japa)*, the process of (2) *pranayama*, and the (3) *meditation*—all the three can be achieved simultaneously without difficulty. This is a great Yoga, the best among all: known as *Siddha Yoga*. It means "the path of the Perfect Ones" or "the Yoga which begets perfection". A dextrous and highly intelligent person can practice it easily. As explained above, the regular practice of meditation with a concentrated mind will awaken the dormant Kundalini Shakti in a very short time. Day-by-day as the Shakti develops more and more It takes the aspirant to Perfection by the Guru's grace.

It is best to practice a natural meditation or *dhyan*. Sit quietly, calm and composed, if you like in *padmasana*, or any other comfortable posture. You may look and fix the eyes on a photo or may keep your eyes closed. The mode and posture in which you can be restful, mentally free from the objective world, and introspective, that is the best *asan* for you. Remove the mind from its activities, arrest all kinds of desires and surrender to whatever is happening of its own accord, observe everything as a witness. The meditation done by the inner Shakti is the meditation of Guru's grace, it is the real meditation of *"So'ham"*, indeed it is the meditation of God.

The deeper and deeper you go in meditation the more and more of the Divine experiences you will attain. Therefore, seek your inner Self, therefrom you will have the fulfillment you cherish.

This "program" is a classical Yogic description of the way of meditation. It is typical of all the methods of Yoga that operate directly on the mental, vital, and physical functions and concentrate the humanly-born conscious awareness in the regions of superconscious manifestation. When I received Baba's letter, I was already involved in the time of "waiting" (in which I practiced no meditation). However, when I (eventually) resumed meditation (just before my second trip to India), I did begin (as an experiment) to use the precise method he described.

Rather than the "So'ham" (or "So-Ham") mantra, I preferred to use the "Om" mantra, which Baba recommended (in the same letter) as an alternative. At first, I had difficulty combining the Sanskrit syllables with their meaning in my own language and (at the same time) generating the mantra as a feeling (or affirmation),

rather than a thought. However, in the following months, I meditated in this basic manner (using the "Om" mantra, and sometimes
the "So-Ham" mantra), and, finally, began to use the "So-Ham"
mantra without difficulty.

When I went to Baba the second time, I had already begun to
use self-Enquiry (in the form "Avoiding relationship?"). I also
continued to experiment with the use of the mantra "So-Ham", and
with the "Om" mantra. As I described earlier, I experienced an
internal teaching of meditation while with Baba on this second
trip. Therefore, at that time, and for a time thereafter, Baba's internal and external teaching combined with my own ("radical")
understanding of practice.

Nevertheless, my understanding was fundamental, and profoundly clarifying. I saw that all the kinds of seeking were founded
in identification (in each case) with a particular developmental
level (or stage) of life, experience, or motivation. The dilemma that
was always involved was founded in a present act of differentiation,
whereby what was constantly being achieved was the presumption
of a separated and threatened consciousness. Thus, I was not
moved to pursue any goals, experiences, or forms. All such things
were merely matters of seeking. I did not even pursue my Identity
with Siva, the Very (and Divine) Self (or Pure Consciousness).
Such, it was clear to me, was also a form of seeking. I simply and
directly founded myself in "radical" self-understanding, and (thus)
in the Truth and Reality that had been Communicated through all
of my experience.

As the months passed, all of this would develop into direct
Knowledge, and into a philosophy of "radically" ego-transcending
practice and Realization. But I needed to endure certain other
changes and forms of seeking before I would be most perfectly
stabilized in the Knowledge of Which I was already tacitly Certain.
Thus, for the time being, I extended my experimental approach to
the matters of physical experience.

In the months following my return from India, I had experienced the effects that various degrees of toxicity and enervation
have upon the humanly-born conscious awareness and the motivations of seeking. I often smoked cigarettes while I wrote.

Occasionally, I would drink alcohol with friends. And, although I maintained an essentially vegetarian diet, I would often, with my friends and family, have meat dishes and sweets, highly processed (or "junk") foods, and other "rich" preparations.

I began to study various books on pure diet and fasting, and I decided to conduct an experiment, to see what effects fasting and consistently pure diet would have in daily life and in meditation. I became intensively involved with the idea of physical purification as a means of profoundly altering the state of consciousness in life. I even considered that perhaps the entire matter of seeking on mental and Spiritual levels was caused solely by a toxic and enervated condition in the body. If the body could be brought to a state of perfect purity, then perhaps the mind would become stilled, and the humanly-born conscious awareness might enjoy a natural, intuitive Realization of Reality and Spiritual Truth. Perhaps the mind would achieve a state of perfect brilliance and utility. Perhaps the body itself could achieve indefinite longevity, even relative immortality.

I considered various options—including fasting, limited amounts of food in general, balanced cooked and raw lacto-fructo-vegetarian diet, balanced raw fructo-vegetarian diet, and the exclusively fruitarian raw diet. I also thought it to be entirely possible, and even desirable, that one could achieve a state independent of normal food and live directly on subtle energy. And this appeared to be supported by reports of people living with little or no food of any kind for several decades.[31]

In March of 1970, I began a fast that was to continue for twenty-two days. At first, I took only a few glasses of pure water every day. Then I began to add a small amount of fresh lemon juice to the pure water. As suggested by Arnold Ehret in his books on the theory and practice of fasting and pure diet, the addition of fresh lemon juice made the purifying effects of the fast more aggressive. Ehret also claimed that fresh fruit juices, such as apple and orange, would generate an even more aggressive action. Thus, in order to test this, after the first week I also, every day, took one or more glasses of either diluted or undiluted fresh fruit juice (either apple or orange). And these juices consistently produced an added positive effect.

The effects of the twenty-two day fast were positively remark-able. When I began the fast, the body quickly became light (or less gross) in its feeling, hunger completely disappeared after only a few days, and the mind almost immediately became clear, ener-getic, and precise.

I lost weight on most of the days of the fast. I lost about eight pounds in the first five days. After that I lost about a pound a day, and this changed to about a pound every other day in the last week or so of the fast. My weight dropped from around 180 pounds to approximately 154 pounds in the twenty-two days, but I easily returned to a normal, healthful weight in the weeks fol-lowing the fast.

Early in the fast, there were occasional, brief physical episodes of weakness and dizziness. At times, I could even feel various old drug deposits in the body pass through the brain. But, in general, I consistently felt a brilliant physical well-being. My meditation also deepened, as the various physical and vital obstacles disappeared.

After approximately two weeks of fasting, I experienced an episode of continuous physical weakness, such that physical activ-ity became slow and difficult, and my pulse and heartbeat became weak and irregular. Immediately, I went to the literature on fast-ing, in order to find a means to correct this tendency. I discovered that, in his books on fasting and pure diet, Teofilo de la Torre rec-ommends a pure water-extract of vegetables as a means to avoid enervation during a fast. This liquid extract is made by allowing pure water to settle for many hours on a particular combination of cut raw vegetables. I tried the drink recommended by de la Torre—and, indeed, it did give me some added strength, especially when coupled with a reduced intake of sweet fruit juices (which, until then—taken perhaps too frequently, or else too often undi-luted—appeared to have caused a low-blood-sugar reaction, and, thereby, at least some of my feelings of physical weakness). And this simple change in my fasting regime allowed the fast to con-tinue for the full term I desired.

After the fast, I continued my experiment by the application of every kind of possibly "right" diet. My experiment with "right" diet (and fasting) included not only myself but Nina, Patricia, and various others—all of whom had taken to fasting and pure foods in response to my demonstration. I found that each individual fared better on a different type of diet. Some, for the moment, required more bulk and starch. Others seemed unable to do without foods high in protein, perhaps even including meats. Others immediately fared well on raw and cooked vegetables and fruits. Together, we experimented with the elimination of various foods and the addition of others. All of this demonstrated that—contrary to what the "champions" of any particular dietary variation might propose—there was no single "unique" or "special" dietary prescription that represented the "right" diet for all individuals. Rather, "right" diet always had to be determined (in each case) by an intelligent approach on the part of each individual, taking into account his or her psycho-physical condition at any given point in time.

After three months of all of this, I had acquired much firsthand knowledge of fasting and "right" diet. I concluded that fasting and pure food did, in fact, aid one's well-being and were a necessary part of responsible self-discipline. My experience of these things clearly indicated that the application of "right" dietary and fasting and general health principles required flexibility in the progressive "rightening" of the individual case. Nevertheless, the optimum practice (in general) proved to involve (as necessary, and as bodily conditions allow) regular short fasts and occasional (and, in general, at least once per year) appropriately prolonged fasts, and (to the maximum degree that is both right and possible) the consistent choice of pure (or unadulterated, untreated, non-toxic, and truly nutritious) foods, maximally raw, and selected (to the maximum degree that is both right and possible) from among the possibilities offered by vegetables, fruits, nuts, seeds, grains, and legumes. Flesh foods (especially in excess), eggs, milk, and milk products proved themselves to have a generally (and cumulatively) negative effect on most people's physical and emotional and mental well-being—although, in some cases (wherein a combination of constitutional compatibility, due to body type, and the requirements for general health and vitality indicate the necessity to include flesh foods), varieties of unadulterated fish and fowl (and, generally, not much of grosser meats, such as beef) proved to be positively usable, if combined with an otherwise pure and purifying (and moderate) dietary practice. Refined flour, refined sugar, "rich" foods, "junk" foods, excessive amounts of cooked foods, coffee, tobacco, alcohol, intoxicating herbs and drugs, foods that are toxically sprayed, toxically treated, or toxic otherwise, and even any foods in too large a quantity proved themselves to have a generally (and cumulatively) negative effect on virtually anyone's physical and emotional and mental well-being. Tea (especially green tea and white tea—but also black tea and oolong tea) proved to be generally compatible with almost anyone's health and "right" dietary practice. Intoxicants (such as tobacco or alcohol) and "soft" drugs (such as cannabis) invariably proved to be not only toxifying and enervating (whether in short-term use or long-term use), but (also) they proved to interrupt (and to be only a self-deluding alternative to) the real process of ego-transcending Spiritual life and practice. However, it also became clear that, even though it is most "right" to eschew impure (or constipating, toxifying, and enervating) substances altogether, the least impure of them (or the least constipating, toxifying, and enervating of them—excluding all intoxicants and "soft" drugs) could, perhaps (whether by sometimes choice or, otherwise, unavoidable necessity), be occasionally used, if health is otherwise good, and if the negative effects of the impure substances were offset by the judicious use of fasting and the return to a consistently pure and moderate diet.

I realized that "exaggerated" involvement in the processes of fasting and "right" diet was itself merely another form of seeking. It was attachment to life as a physical and vital problem. Thus, even "right" dietary discipline—if approached via the point of view of the seeker, or the mind of a "problem"—could become a distraction, and the ground for a goal-centered life. Then the otherwise "right" discipline of diet (and of the body in general) would absorb attention like any other presumed problem—as, for example, the problem of the mind, or the problem of Spiritual experience. Therefore, understanding this, I dropped all "exaggerated" motivations associated with health practice. I abandoned all my attachment to the idea of "perfection" through diet and fasting. I no longer placed any "infinite" importance on food. And I ceased to be motivated by the search for bodily immortality. All such seeking had proven itself to be merely a means for trapping attention in problems and problem-centered motivations—whereas a simple, intelligent regimen relative to fasting, diet, and general health practice allowed physical existence to remain essentially stable, energetic, and (above all) free of enforced attention and problematic motivations.

The essential logic that I retained in relation to food was based on a straightforward practical knowledge of the basic laws of bodily effects. This amounted to a knowledge of what food-practice produces constipation, and toxemia, and enervation (or the exhaustion of vitality). I was no longer motivated by any problem or idealism in relation to the body. My understanding of the body became a matter of daily practical intelligence, rather than idealism or problem-based seeking. The body had proven itself to be a lawful economy. It required conscious "right" use. Intelligent diet (and, therefore, a diet that is rather consistently pure, and both fructo-vegetarian and maximally raw—or raw, and fructo-vegetarian, to the greatest degree the body healthfully allows), accompanied, as necessary (and as bodily possible and right), by regular short fasts and occasional (and "rightly" prolonged) long fasts, regular, healthful use of fresh air, usable (or safely received) sunlight, and pure water, appropriate (but, generally, simple, and not excessive, and, altogether, Yogically designed) physical exercise, and a life-positive (and yet Spiritually "right" and true) emotional-sexual practice (that conserves both natural emotional-sexual energy and true Spiritual Energy through positive relational and Yogic disciplines, whether "rightly" sexually active or "rightly" celibate)—all these became, for me, simple matters of responsibility, a matter of simple, practical intelligence relative to the body, whereas previously they appeared as strategic and idealized means toward some kind of victory over life, the body, and mortality itself.

This brings us to May of 1970. I had passed through most of the stages of experimentation that mark my early life. I had come to understand that life in Truth requires a "radical" (or "gone-to-the-root") process in consciousness—a process that directly transcends all seeking, and all conventions of mind and experience, by addressing the root-fault that originates every problem and the search itself. I saw that every strategic (or remedial) path is a form of problem-based seeking that originates from the moment to moment avoidance of relationship. And I saw that—apart from the moment to moment exercise of the process of "radical" (or truly "gone-to-the-root", or most fundamental) self-understanding—the avoidance of relationship (and the constant generation of problems and searches) is the primary (and moment to moment) activity of consciousness in life. Actively understanding thus, I had ceased to function in reaction to problems or basic dilemma. This "radical" (or "gone-to-the-root") self-understanding effectively precluded (or released me from) any form of life motivated by the physical and vital problem, the psychic problem, the emotional problem, the mental problem, the Spiritual problem, or any other form of problem. I had developed a form of "radical" (or truly most fundamental) self-understanding that continuously allowed life to be lived consciously, directly, free of dilemma, free of identification with any problem-based motivation.

But there remained to pass a concluding episode in this adventure of understanding. As a result of the intense process of my life of understanding (especially over the period of the preceding several years), my body-mind, and all aspects of my life-practice, had become profoundly refined—such that I had become acutely sensitive and vulnerable to the drama of seeking, suffering, and even violence that was otherwise still going on in the world. An adolescent political, social, and cultural revolution—based on egoity (or individualism and separatism) and the materialistic mind (or the "wisdom" of this world), and, altogether (and inevitably), with profoundly negative consequences to come—was developing in the cities and spreading everywhere. Murder, guerrilla warfare, sniping, bombing, separatist confrontations, even the universal and careless exploitation of the separate possibilities of every one and every thing, the universal absence of true wisdom, the universal absence of Divine and Spiritual understanding and Peace, the universal absence of higher and Great experience, and the universal headlong adolescent commitment to every kind of suffering had become the daily meal of the entire world. I felt that I had understood something of fundamental and critical importance about life. But life seemed to have become untouchable, locked in the final evolution of its own mortal "creation".

Because of all of this, I decided that I should leave America for an indefinite period. My own daily understanding and experience had become so profound, and so different from the exploited mentality and experience around me, that I felt I would necessarily have to continue the process of my life of "radical" self-understanding elsewhere—in Peace, and in a circumstance intended to be congenial to Peace Itself. Consequently, in May, I made arrangements for Nina, Patricia, and me to go to Baba's Ashram. We sold or gave away all of our material belongings, and (on May 28) we flew to Bombay—to remain with the Guru indefinitely, and perhaps forever.

India, May 1970

CHAPTER FOURTEEN

The Third Trip to India, and the Reappearance of "Christ"

As we prepared to leave for India, I made an assessment of all that I Knew. And, as a sign of that assessment, when we left for India I took three books: the *Bhagavad Gita*, the *Mandukyopanisad*,[32] and *The Collected Works of Ramana Maharshi*.[33] For me, these texts, along with various quotations from other traditional Indian sources (which I wrote inside their covers and in their margins), epitomized the tradition of Vedanta (and, especially, of Advaita Vedanta), or the ancient and esoteric Indian religious, philosophical, Yogic, and (ultimately) Advaitic (or non-dualistic) tradition as a whole. From my point of view, that tradition (as a whole) represented the closest parallel to my own search and experience. Likewise, from my point of view, that tradition (as a whole) represented the basic general background (of traditional philosophy and idealism) against which my own "radical" and unique understanding was emerging. Therefore, I carried these three books as if they were (together) a symbol for traditional Knowledge, a kind of traditional summa. But I also felt they epitomized the very search that I had "radically" understood—such that they had also (together) become a symbol for what I was constantly (and most directly) transcending by means of "radical" self-understanding. Therefore, I never read those books as I traveled on.

I entirely returned to India, fully believing that I was in basic general agreement with its ultimate (or most fundamental) philosophical and Spiritual principles. The three books I carried represented my affirmation of that—just as they represented the principles themselves. And, thus, the three books represented a kind of "defense" that I could readily offer, should anyone suggest that my point of view was not sufficiently "orthodox".

I deeply felt India to be my real and ancient home. I intended to place all of myself at Baba's feet and to retire there for life. I assumed that "radical" self-understanding, which was the Realization of my life, was wholly compatible with the habit of life at the Ashram. And I also assumed that I would be received in love and given the freedom to develop my conscious existence— even where it exceeded tradition—as long as I remained devoted to the essential habit of life at the Ashram and never lost sympathy with my Sources there.

I left America behind. I left the world behind. There was not a single movement in me that reflected a predilection for the usual existence. I felt humanly free, truly free, relieved of an immense burden, and purified of my own past life. I would devote myself to Realization, serve the Guru, and receive the eternal and continuous benediction of the Shakti's grace.

Upon our arrival in Bombay, we spent a night at a hotel, and then proceeded to the Ashram on May 30. We had left America quite suddenly, and were not expected on the precise day we arrived. But our arrival was expected generally at that time. When we entered the Ashram, we were met enthusiastically by Amma and a few of our friends. Then I asked them to bring us to Baba.

Since my last visit, the Ashram had been much expanded. Now there were new large buildings in the central complex, and modern apartments had been prepared for Baba. I was told that he spent most of his time in seclusion now, and only came out to see devotees during pre-established hours. The Ashram was full of people, many of them young Americans and Europeans.

We were brought to Baba in the new meditation hall outside his rooms. He sat in a chair. Nina and Patricia placed flowers at his feet, and I left a rosary of rudraksha beads. He spoke to Nina and Patricia briefly about the trip. But he seemed deliberately unwilling to acknowledge my presence. He told Nina he would talk to us later, and we were taken to a small bungalow where we were to stay.

I immediately noticed a change in the atmosphere of the Ashram. It had become a very public and busy institution. The program of life there had become much more formalized and

top: The main entrance to the audience hall as it appeared in 1968 at
the time of Adi Da Samraj's first visit to Swami Muktananda's Ashram

bottom: The Ashram as it appeared in 1970

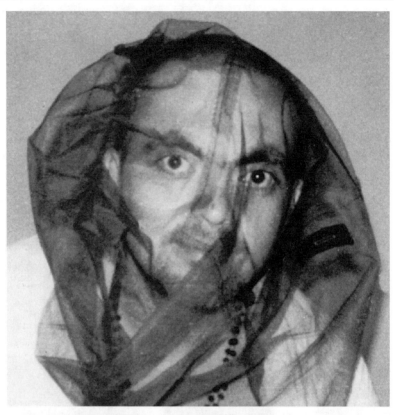

top: Adi Da Samraj
at the Ashram
wearing mosquito
netting

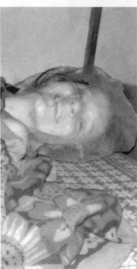

left: Nina
right: Patricia

sophisticated. Time was spent entirely at various kinds of "Ashram-seva" (or service to the Guru), or in the chanting of hymns and scriptures, or in the practice of meditation. And Baba came and sat with people at various fixed hours of the day.

Nina, Patricia, and I were given daily work to do. Patricia cleaned guest rooms. I edited and refined the beginnings of an English translation of a book Baba was then writing (or had only recently written), which was to be called *Chitshakti Vilas.*[34] And Nina typed the edited manuscript as it was produced. Also, at my request (so that I could increase my physical—and, especially, non-literary—activity), I was given work in Baba's Ashram garden. Thus, every day, we all worked, meditated, stood for chanting, sat with Baba, listened to his sermons, and listened to readings from Baba's new book. Baba never said a personal word to me. He made no effort to inquire of me or suggest any form of practice. His words seemed even purposely directed away from me, so that I would not be attracted to him. And I wondered why he no longer spoke to me in the root-language of Advaita Vedanta he once taught me. In any case, the formal life of the Ashram was itself to be the entire source of our daily-life experience, and it was up to us to stay or leave as we chose.

As I meditated, I also realized that nothing useful was "added" by the atmosphere of the Ashram. Indeed, the quality of the Ashram was entirely that of seeking—and it, therefore, had nothing to do with "radical" self-understanding and the Realization of Real Existence. People appeared to have experiences of the Shakti at various times, but they were not <u>fundamentally</u> affected by It. And I knew they could not be—for phenomenally-based Spiritual experience, like all conditionally-generated experience, is only phenomenal and conditional (and, therefore, limited, temporary, and not finally satisfying) experience. Life is not finally transformed or perfectly Awakened by fleeting experience, but only by the grace-given means of "radical" (or truly "gone-to-the-root" and most fundamental) self-understanding.

Not only did Baba refrain from communicating verbally with me, but I did not at all experience the Shakti flowing to me through him. Altogether, the Ashram atmosphere felt as if it had shifted to a lower key, and the Shakti Itself was not particularly strong for me there.

On the day I first met him (in 1968—on the day I arrived, for the first time, at his Ashram), Baba instructed me to go to Bhagavan Nityananda's burial place for Bhagavan Nityananda's blessing. Thus, and always thereafter, Baba turned me to Bhagavan Nityananda as my senior Guru. In keeping with that, when I was with Baba in Bombay (on my second trip to India), he told me to make a trip to Ganeshpuri, to receive Bhagavan Nityananda's blessing. And so I did. Therefore, on this third trip to India, I continued my customary daily practice of walking down the road to Bhagavan Nityananda's burial place, where I would meditate in the early afternoon. The Shakti had always been very Powerfully and freely Present for me there—but, on this third trip to India, I felt that this place, and (indeed) Bhagavan Nityananda himself, was to be the Source for my further instruction. And, on and from the first day, as I sat there, the Shakti-Force would surge through my body, my heart and mind would become still, my head and eyes would become swollen with a tremendous Fullness of Bliss, and I would spontaneously relax into the Silent Depth of Being.

The routine of my daily life at the Ashram (and also my daily visits to Bhagavan Nityananda's burial place) went on as I have described for about one week. I was feeling well, and Full. But nothing dramatic had occurred, or seemed about to occur. I began to do this daily routine as a matter of course, expecting nothing but this simple order and experience. Then, one day, quite unexpectedly, as I worked in Baba's new garden (at the extreme rear area of the Ashram grounds), I experienced a remarkable "visitation".

I had been pulling weeds for perhaps half an hour when, suddenly, I felt a "familiar" Presence. It was as if a friend were standing behind me. And, yet, it also felt to be a Presence that I had never before sought, or even presumed to exist. I stood up and looked behind my shoulder. Standing in the garden—with an obviously discernible form, made of subtle Energy, fully felt, and even (somehow) seen, but also without even any kind of visibility, was the Virgin, Mary, Mother of Jesus of Nazareth!

My first impulse was huge laughter. I had spent years without the slightest sympathetic inclination toward Christianity. I felt I had fully and truly paid my early-life exoteric religious dues. I saw the entire Christian religious tradition as merely a symbolic and ritual communication—at best, pointing toward Consciousness Itself (or pure Self-Awareness) and Vedanta-like conclusions about Reality. Now, as if I were faced with a cosmic joke, I stood in the living Presence of the Mother of Jesus of Nazareth.

What is more, my Christianity had been almost entirely of the Protestant variety. I had no predilection for Catholic (or even Eastern Orthodox) symbols. Christianity, insofar as it was meaningful at all to me, was a theological symbol for Truth. I had no devotional inclination toward its separate icons and historically unique symbols. I never once assumed that the "Virgin Mary" was any more than a religious symbol. I felt the "Virgin Mary" was a secondary (and imaginary) "creation" of the church, with no direct relation to the historical person who was the bodily human mother of Jesus of Nazareth. I never believed the "Virgin Mary" was an actual, Divinely Present individual with present significance for humanity. Even during my brief involvement with the Eastern Orthodox church, I was not moved by its symbologies and icons of "Mary" and "Jesus". I only (and only temporarily) found, in my reading of the Eastern Orthodox tradition, a suggested sympathy for mysticism, and (thus) the possibility of a sympathetic accommodation of my own mystical life as a Christian "imposter". And Jesus of Nazareth himself, although he had a conventionally religious importance in my childhood, dramatically ceased to have any such importance once I experienced the trauma of my college education. Indeed, now that even that trauma had been released by the Spiritual experiences and the profound understanding that developed and matured in my years since college, Jesus of Nazareth no longer had any "believer's" significance for me at all. At least, that is what seemed to be the case at the level of my conscious mind. But now, it seemed, the subconscious and unconscious depths of my mind were showing off their residual contents, the mechanical leftovers not yet purified of the past. The Divine Shakti was active in me, and It was taking on the form of my inherited Western religious mind.

My own mind, infused with the Divine Shakti, had projected itself outwardly, and become a living, visionary apparition. The "Virgin Mary" was not believable, but she was there! And I found that, after the first few moments of surprise and irony, I began to relate to her quite easily—with profound feeling, and in a very "Christian" manner. The Divine Shakti had Itself, through a visionary appearance, taken on (for my sake) a human female likeness—even a form that (perhaps better than any other in the "great tradition" of mankind) symbolized and represented the archetype of the "Mother". Therefore, her very "Motherly" Presence evoked a "son"-like response in me. And, spontaneously, I found myself growing in profound devotion and love. She was, to all appearances, the "Virgin Mary"—but, nonetheless, I Knew her to be the Divine Shakti Itself, Alive in front of me.

Just as the Presence (and the entire apparition) of the Virgin was not physical but subtle, her Communication to me was internal, as I had earlier known it with Baba. In this manner, as we stood together in Baba's Ashram garden, she taught me a form of the Catholic Christian prayer "Hail Mary". Then she told me to buy a rosary for devotions. It was difficult to satisfy this demand. I had to find some excuse to get permission to go to Bombay. But I managed it, and she was satisfied. Thereafter, I found myself reciting the prayer constantly, as a mantra, while I worked and lived in the Ashram.

After several days of this devotion, the Virgin showed me an image of the face of Jesus. It appeared visibly in my heart, and she seemed only to uncover it. That image, and the feelings it immediately awakened in me, had been hidden and suppressed there since my childhood. Therefore, instantly, spontaneously, I was in love with Jesus!

As these experiences increased, I began to resist them mightily. I thought I must be deluded. I tried to meditate in the usual manner, but the Virgin and Jesus would always appear to guide and instruct me. I felt no Communication at all coming from Baba, or from the Shakti (as I had previously known It).

After two weeks of this, the Virgin told me to leave the Ashram with Nina and Patricia and go on a pilgrimage to the Christian holy places in Jerusalem and Europe. From the first moment I saw the vision of the Virgin, it was clear to me that she, and all of the experiences that came along with her, were direct manifestations of the Divine Shakti. Therefore, I immediately, and more and more, became willing to be guided by the Virgin. And it became more and more obvious that all of these Christian visions, commands, and revelations were part of a unique grace, given to me by the Divine Shakti, and Purposed to serve the purification of my own deepest mind, so that the in-depth content of my mind would no longer obscure or prevent my most perfect Realization of the Divine Self-Condition and Source-Condition. Therefore, I became willing to be moved, even in this strangely required Christian manner, and to do all that the Divine Shakti, even appearing as the Virgin (or in whatever other form the Divine Shakti appeared), told me to do. I felt that the Divine Shakti was working independently for me now and no longer depended on the physical presence of Baba or the Ashram. Indeed, the manifestation of the Divine Shakti in the context of my ongoing process of "radical" self-understanding, and now in the form of my Christian visionary experience, was anything but characteristically Indian. And, in any case, it was the Divine Shakti "Herself" Who was telling me to leave the Ashram, and India, and return to the West—even via the visionary trail of my own mind.

As it happened, Bhagavan Nityananda was to bless me and turn me to this course with the Divine Mother, and (thus and thereby) to the Ultimate Adventure that restored my most perfectly "Bright" Freedom. One afternoon, as I made my usual daily walk to Bhagavan Nityananda's burial place, I became attracted to a black and white photograph of Bhagavan Nityananda that was for sale at a booth outside his Ashram. I thought I might stop and buy it on my way back.

When I arrived at the shrine, I bowed to Bhagavan Nityananda reverently and circumambulated his burial place three times. (This is a traditional Indian form of worship.) I sat down to meditate, and then I felt Bhagavan Nityananda touch me. His image appeared before my internal vision. He showed me a photograph of himself and held it before me as I sat with him. It was the same photograph that attracted me earlier, but it was in color!

Photograph of Swami Nityananda
in his youth purchased by
Adi Da Samraj after visiting
Swami Nityananda's burial
shrine in Ganeshpuri

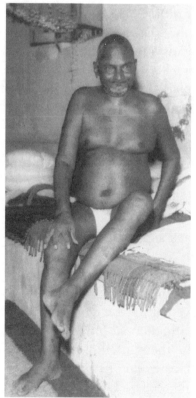

*I knew that these flowers and
the picture were not given to me
for myself. They were symbols
of a sacrifice I was to perform.
The photograph was the image
of the Guru. I had come to this stage
by following the Guru as Bhagavan
Nityananda in vision, and as
Baba and Rudi at various stages
in life and Spiritual experience.
Now I was to surrender the external
forms of the human Guru to others,
and live without separation from
the Guru—inhering in the Very
Form that is the Guru, and guided
by the inwardly revealed Divine
Form of the Guru. . . .*

Swami Nityananda

In an internal conversation, I told Bhagavan Nityananda about my recent experiences—how the Mother-Shakti had taken me over, independently of Baba or any other apparent Source. He blessed me, telling me that I belonged to Her now, and that (as She had told me) I should leave the Ashram and let Her guide me.

When I opened my eyes, one of the priests who served Bhagavan Nityananda's shrine was standing before me with a large handful of flower blossoms. He gave them to me as a blessing from Bhagavan Nityananda.

As I left and walked through the village of Ganeshpuri toward Baba's Ashram, I passed another stall where photographs were sold. And there was the exact picture Bhagavan Nityananda had shown me in the vision, in full color. I bought it, and continued to walk.

I knew that these flowers and the picture were not given to me for myself. They were symbols of a sacrifice I was to perform. The photograph was the image of the Guru. I had come to this stage by following the Guru as Bhagavan Nityananda in vision, and as Baba and Rudi at various stages in life and Spiritual experience. Now I was to surrender the external forms of the human Guru to others, and live without separation from the Guru—inhering in the Very Form that is the Guru, and guided by the inwardly revealed Divine Form of the Guru (shown to me as the Mother-Shakti— even, at that time, appearing to be the Virgin Mother of Jesus). And the flowers were all the parts of my manifested (or apparent) life— every center of being, every body (or functional sheath), every realm, and every experience in which I was animated. I was to take these flowers of my life and offer them to the Divine Mother-Shakti.

When I arrived at the Ashram, I bathed and put on clean cloth-ing. I took the flowers to the temple of the Mother-Shakti near the Ashram. There is a traditional sculptured icon of Her benign, multi-armed, and omnipresent Form there. I looked into Her face and saw that She was the same One who appeared to me in vision as the Virgin and as the image of Jesus in my heart. I bowed to Her and placed the flowers at Her feet. I circumambulated Her three times. I took some holy ash and pressed it on my forehead. As I left, I felt Her assure me that I was Her child and She would guide me.

The Mother Shakti at the temple near the Ashram in Ganeshpuri
as Adi Da Samraj found her in 1970

*I bowed to Her and placed the flowers at Her feet.
I circumambulated Her three times. I took some holy ash
and pressed it on my forehead. As I left, I felt Her assure
me that I was Her child and She would guide me.*

I went and told Nina and Patricia that it was time to leave. We had discussed the possibility before. Even they had become restless at the Ashram. And I had told them of my experiences, my Christian visions and the instructions for our pilgrimage. Therefore, both of them agreed and were happy to leave.

I told one of Baba's agents that we would be leaving the next day. He was surprised, but he took the message to Baba. While we were preparing to leave, one of the American devotees came and was attracted to the picture of Bhagavan Nityananda. I gave it to him, knowing this was the reason it had been offered to me.

We left the next morning, after a stay of little more than three weeks. Baba did not look at me. He seemed displeased, but I felt there was nothing I could say to justify our leave. I could only assume that all of my adventure was also blessed by him. We waited for the bus, and (as we pulled away) I thought I would never return to that place again.

Adi Da Samraj on pilgrimage to Christian holy sites in 1970

CHAPTER FIFTEEN

The Diary of Pilgrimage

While the experiences with the Virgin and Jesus were developing at the Ashram, I kept a continuous diary. And I maintained the diary as we traveled to Israel, Europe, and back to the United States.

The diary is not only the best firsthand source for these experiences, but it shows how the entire matter developed, and how I eventually returned to a stable Realization of the fundamental Truth that is the substance of my Spiritual life. Thus, it demonstrates how my consideration developed in the midst of extraordinary experiences into quite another thing than the traditional forms of seeking and the realizations based on seeking.

I will include that diary here—somewhat relieved of length and repetition, and without interpretation (except to indicate certain external details).

You should be prepared to read what (at first) appears to be the devotional diary of a mystical Catholic Christian. It is my practice to write in the mood and with the precise, unequivocal language of my experience and persuasion at any moment. And, for a time, it seemed to me that the revelation of the church was the fulfillment of my life. Indeed, it was only by allowing it to be so and fully experiencing the course of this modification in my state (as well as all others at all other times) that I could eventually come to Realize What is always and stably the underlying Truth of all experience.

You should also recognize that this experience was a necessary one for me. It was an extension of that vision of the "Divine Lord" I had experienced the previous winter. And it drew on all the latent imagery, necessity, and unfulfilled devotional energy that had been trapped in my heart since childhood. Only when these images were completely and consciously experienced, and the feeling-energy surrounding the heart utterly released from its bondage to unconscious symbols, could I remain stably in the True Consciousness that is the Heart of Reality Itself.

◆ ◆ ◆

20 June 1970—Ganeshpuri, India

I first was visited by our Lady, our Mother, in the garden of Shree Gurudev Ashram, Ganeshpuri. She taught me to honor her with a form of the prayer "Hail Mary". Then she held before my mind an image of a rosary—until, after several days, I bought one in Bombay. Then she showed me her Son, our Lord, whose face of Whitest Light has (thus, and several times) appeared directly before me in a total, mystical field of vision that (somehow) begins at the level of the physical heart. The description of the exact position of his living face depends on whether I examine it in relation to the body or the soul. Its brilliant Luminosity always faces me, and it "creates" the deepest Peace, Love, and Bliss in me—such that I feel as if I am nestled before it in the infinite womb of Mary, whose body seems to contain the soul.

After this revelation, she moved me to read as many books on the Faith as were available to me in my retreat. And, as I grew in this learning, she instructed me by moving me to write, and to become conscious of her impulses in me. By all of this, she has brought me to Christ and revealed to me the Truth of all that I have undergone in the past many years.

I already feel a suggestion to bury the rosary somewhere in the Ashram garden before I leave, so that she has a focus for her Presence there. She may not require this of me, but may instruct me instead to keep it for devotions. I am awed with the Absolute Truth of the church, and how It escaped me all my life. Since this revelation, there has also been a continuous, deep Ecstasy and Joy in my heart that is so great I dare not even allow myself to be fully conscious of It, or to experience and manifest It completely.

◆ ◆ ◆

All remedial paths and their practices point to a goal that is either symbolic or transcendent, a state of mind or psyche or soul. These goals are intuited by Spiritual experiment, the research of seekers, without benefit of the directly and priorly revealed Divine Presence. What lies beneath all of these goals—as their latent, unconscious Object (or Source)—is Christ. Indeed, all of these goals would already be fully attained if Christ were consciously received on every level of our living being. His Fullness precludes the great search. It epitomizes and Fills each level of our living being. And his Presence, from the moment It is Known in faith, raises us into the ever more full Realization of that Fullness. He is the Source and Object of every Spiritual State—and even the earth itself and every miraculous power are only symbols for the hidden Truth that is the Fullness of Christ.

◆ ◆ ◆

The transmitted gospel itself generates many historical problems in relation to texts, specific interpretations, traditions, and so on. This is simply due to the fact that the transmitted gospel is a communication through human beings in the world over time. But, in this gospel, the living condition of Reality, which is latent in all things, is constantly suggested. And the recognition of the living condition of Reality is what draws us into right relationship to others and things—such that all seeking becomes unnecessary, and such that the victory over an otherwise suffered life is made possible.

All other traditions of Truth draw human beings into the distractions of the great search, but the Lord and Reality of this gospel stands eternally before us and is continually at work to save us. The gospel immediately puts us in contact with him. Thus, the gospel is not mere language and symbols, but the unique tool and revelation of the living condition of Reality. The Living Lord, the gospel, and the church are present, with his Holy Mother, to transform all the world by restoring it to the living condition of Reality—which is not "natural" or philosophically realizable, but which is the Knowledge inherent in one's Knowing of the directly Revealed Lord.

I say that living condition is latent in all things only because it is their only true structure, even though Realizable only by Revelation. And that Revelation must become conscious in some direct manner in order to be Realized. The living condition of Reality is the humanly-born conscious awareness of the Revealed Lord, the Present God. Thus, nothing exists in the fullness of its "created" state until it receives and Knows Him.

◆ ◆ ◆

Texts that are particularly important to me:
"He that seeth me seeth the Father also." (John 14:9)
"That I may know him and the power of <u>his</u> resurrection." (Philippians 3:10)

◆ ◆ ◆

For the first time in many years, I am experiencing genuine surrender to God. It is happening by His grace, since I am not trying to do it at all. It is a seemingly "natural" effect of His Presence in the heart. He is unutterably Real to me—and this is a new experience.

My past Spiritual efforts were marked by a continuous struggle with exactly and primarily this surrender. It was my first teacher's main sadhana—and, by years of effort, I realized the absolute impossibility of surrender. Then I came to Baba—and he gave me Spiritual experiences free, without my effort of surrender. After two years and more of his sadhana, I realized that I had not changed one iota in my essential relationship to things. I had many experiences, and had even developed a Spiritual "ego"—but I was, all in all, still incapable of surrender.

Then the Lord Himself came to me and took up His abode in me. And His Presence <u>is</u> my surrender. How could I not love Him? Surrender is a quality in the living condition of Reality. As soon as life is returned to that condition, it is also surrender.

◆ ◆ ◆

Reality is not an object—a thing that can be experienced, seen, and so forth. Reality is a living and inclusive condition. It is subject <u>and</u> object. The living condition of Reality, which <u>is</u> Reality, is the relationship to God, in which we are conscious of being Filled by Him. Thus, Reality cannot be sought and found within or without, by Spiritual seekers or self-indulgent sinners (the former are generally searching within and the latter without). Reality is not "object", not a "shape" that excludes everything "outside" It—but the inclusive condition of life itself.

Our consciousness of God is a participation in and manifestation of that living condition. God's Consciousness of us is the supreme manifestation of that Law Which is Reality. All things are subject to that Law and require the Revelation of Christ.

Previously, I was confused by the ideas of Advaita Vedanta, the *Srimad Bhagavatam*,[35] and the *Bhagavad Gita*. I saw that necessary and living condition as being (essentially and exclusively) a Divine Consciousness Which included us and was (in fact) our entire being, mind, thought, and so on. Thus, our only Real and True experience was this Awareness, in which the Divine is the Subject Who Experiences all our experiences, thoughts, and so on. Our existence was not any of these experiences, but the Awareness of Him Who was (in fact) their Ultimate Subject and Center. After a time, this mystical Awareness (in fact) upset me deeply. Now I have seen clearly at last. The living condition of Reality is one in which God is Present to us and in us, but not to the point of assuming our identities (in fact, becoming us and excluding our "created" existence by virtue of His inclusive Being). We also participate in that living condition (or Law)—and, in the fullness of our living being (which He has given us), we are conscious of Him, present with Him. Thus, we are Free and unqualifiedly alive, immediately with God forever, sheerly by His grace.

Thus, the living condition of Reality is a gift—Revealed, not natural to the understanding, not discernible by experiment. That condition is Revealed to us only by God's grace. And that Revelation is the Totality of grace. It is the Ground of the Beatific Vision (or the Supreme State), and of the entire life of faith. The Christian life is mystical, a conscious participation in the Mystery of God, wherein we constantly and "creatively", in cooperation with Divine grace, maintain the living condition of Reality, the conscious relationship to God.

◆ ◆ ◆

Christ is that Eternal Aspect of God which reveals and guarantees forever that the Truth is relationship to God, and not Absorption into the powers of God or Absorption into the Transcendent Being of God. Life is a meditation on being already Filled.

◆ ◆ ◆

A remarkable thing the grace of God has given me is that, in a few moments, or hours—I do not know the precise hour of this death—He turned me completely to Himself. Such that the Truth of the Catholic Faith, the verity of the church and its doctrine, a host of details, and (above all) the devotion to our Lady, were given me in a flash of comprehensive insight. All of this in spite of the fact that I have never been trained as a Catholic, or ever sought it out in the least overt manner. All of this has been latent in me— at best, a sentiment—all my life. This also shows how our Lord's "mere" Presence teaches and recollects all things most directly.

The impulses of this Divine grace and faith are so strong that I am scarcely willing to follow them directly. I am abiding in this Hindu Ashram, allowing Christ to mature me, so that I do not proceed out of my own motives and presumptions, deluded again by my own sinful fascinations. For days, I struggled with this Truth and Its visions. I tested them, denied them, tried to immerse myself in meditation and the Guru. But there is this constant Christ, and my heart is torn out at the bottom. I am mad with him. I am about to become too full of ordinary humor for this place, and too sorrowful for my sins.

◆ ◆ ◆

In the garden, our Lord's Mother told me to pray: "Hail Mary, Mother of God. Blessed art thou among women. And blessed is the fruit of thy womb, Jesus."

Today I sat to meditate, and asked her to teach me how to meditate as a Christian, how she wanted me to meditate toward our Lord. She moved me to begin by praying the "Our Father" several times. Then, she brought me to recite this "Hail Mary" repetitively, with attention concentrated on its meaning. I saw that it always led through her to Jesus. Each time I came to the Name "Jesus", I would be fixed firmly in him. This continued automatically for nearly two hours, through dinner, and ended only when conversations began. This meditation gave me great Joy, stilled the mind, and directed me continually to Jesus through his Mother.

Then, as I continually concentrated on him, he taught me a prayer deeper within. It was his own constant "Amen. Amen." I saw that the heart's pulse always synchronized with this word: A-men, A-men. And this prayer out of and in Christ constantly directed me to the Father. The "So be it" constantly leaves the mind on Him in silence, in a vast Bliss. I felt the movement of "Amen" as the Holy Spirit Himself—returning, through Christ, to God the Father, from Whom He proceeded.

Thus, our Lord's Mother taught me a practice of meditation that leads to contemplation of the Trinity in all the Mysteries of Its Form—until all (at last) draws into the silent Brilliance of God, Absorbed in blessed Vision.

I will continue to use this blessed contemplation, if it does not offend our holy church, with faith that our Lady intended it for the ultimate good of my soul.

◆ ◆ ◆

21 June 1970

This morning, as I walked toward the place of my morning meditations, I began to pray the "Our Father" and then the "Hail Mary", as I was taught yesterday. But even though these and all true prayers of the church lead to contemplation of the Holy Trinity, I felt dry in the praying. I thought of the Holy Sacrament of the altar, and Christ's promise: "He that eateth my flesh and drinketh my blood abideth in me and I in him." (John 6:57) This is the promise of the Fullness of God, with Which we are Filled. It is Fullness given by grace, available by no other means. It is the Presence Itself, and It makes Itself Known. Unless It makes Itself Known, there is no way to concentrate upon It. But I desired this Fullness, in order to meditate upon It.

When I sat in meditation, I felt the Presence of Christ. I could not see him. Even the image of his brilliantly Luminous face that I had previously seen in the heart was absent. There was darkness, but only his Presence. Then he moved me to pray the "Amen". And I saw that the "Amen" was said once with each breath. Once on the inhalation, and once on the exhalation. And the "Amen" was always said in the center of the heart, wherein we direct ourselves to God. As I prayed the "Amen", I realized that Christ was praying it in me. It is the Holy Spirit in Christ to God the Father. And Christ said: "I am the 'Amen'."

Then I continued in this prayer and was taught the mystery of its use. The heart is the center, where Christ stands to us. And the body is a cross-form, in which he radiates his Fullness. As I prayed—one "Amen" for each inhalation of breath, and one for each exhalation—Christ said: "I am drawing all things to myself." Then, when I inhaled and prayed "Amen", all the life-energy of desires moved up out of the lower body to the heart, and became a deep concentration of Love in Christ. And, when I exhaled and prayed "Amen", all the life-energy of thought, the entire activity of mental energy and the mind itself, was drawn down to the heart and concentrated in Christ as profound Love. This continued, until I was profoundly Present in the heart, simply Present with Christ in great and ecstatic Love. And that Love was Christ himself. He generated It in me—and, yet, I felt that I was not, but was simply absorbed in him, in the White Fire of his own Love.

Then I realized that the Fullness whereby we are Filled is Christ himself. The Fullness that is ours in the Sacrament is not simply some Radiance of Christ's Energy, breathed into us like pleasant air. It is Christ himself who comes and is Present, such that we are absorbed in the contemplation of him. He is the "Amen"—which we pray, which he prays in us, whereby all prayers come to an end, whereby he draws all things to himself in blessed contemplation. Thus, I was drawn to him—not to concentration on mere breaths or on some fullness moving in me, only distantly connected to him. He is in us as himself, his total Presence, open to our Conscious Love. And he draws us to his very Self, which is an Infinite Fire of Love. Thus, we become only

Love in him. The dark nights of sense and of the soul are quickly traced to the heart in the prayer "Amen". Thus, we are not moved toward an emptiness but toward the Fullness of God. God is only Full. "God is light, and in Him there is no darkness." (I John 1:5) There can be no end to God's Revelation of Himself to us in this Prayer. Each breath surrenders desires and thoughts in Him—and each breath or act of surrender is a movement, by faith and hope and Love, into the State of mere faith and hope and Love. This cross of meditation is a cross of faith. Its pain is Love. Its suffering is Sublime. The cross is never absent from Christ, but it eternally contemplates him in the heart of its beams. In this meditation which Christ inspired in me, I felt that the entire Truth of the church was contained in a perfect symbol.

◆ ◆ ◆

"Amen" is the Christ, the Name of God. "Amen" is the beginning of all things, the "So be it" of God. "Amen" is the acceptance of all things as the Will of God, the "So be it" of mankind. Christ has given us the Name of God by giving us himself. The Person, Christ himself, is the Name of God Which he revealed to us. Thus, we are told to ask in his Name and we will receive. That is, to contemplate God in and through and as Christ, the "Amen", is to be given the totality of gifts, now and forever. Anyone who, by God's grace, deeply contemplates the Name of God, and through It approaches the Father in his or her need, will be given whatever he or she requires. The power of the Name is not available to those who do not enter It profoundly, in faith—for the Name is not a mere word, but the Name is God Himself as Christ.

◆ ◆ ◆

The Love of Christ is the Support and Source of living Bliss—even the Conscious Energy of Spiritual existence, under all conditions. It makes life madly into Joy. Under the worst trials, It does not guarantee a mood of ordinary playful happiness, but It supports the deep Joy of faith and mystical communion. This Love is the internal condition of the soul, whereby Christ draws it to himself. It is not our un-"created", original Love for him, but his Love generated in us by his Presence to the soul.

◆ ◆ ◆

The Word is "Amen".

◆ ◆ ◆

I sat in meditation again. Our Lord's Mother has moved me, and I have decided to leave the Ashram in order to make a pilgrimage and communicate with the church. In meditation, I pleaded for guidance—so that I would not be tempted to uncertainty, so that I would certainly Know the Truth without fear that I am deluded. I waited. I had prayed the "Our Father" and "Hail Mary". I prayed the "Amen", as I had been taught. The meditation was dry. Then I kept Enquiring with each breath, as I tried to surrender the energies of desires to the "Amen" with each inhalation, and the energies of thought with each exhalation. I Enquired, "Avoiding relationship?" Each time, this self-Enquiry loosened me from flight, such that I concentrated in him at the heart. And then he spoke, regarding those great teachers whom I have pursued for years: "They are infinitely Returned, but I am eternally Present." Then he drew me to himself—and I was ecstatic, open-armed, crying, Dear Lord, Dear Dear Lord.

> They are infinitely Returned,
> But I am eternally Present.
> One who Knows me
> Is free from liberation
> And desires.
> One who neither seeks
> Nor is moved to seek,
> I no longer prevent from me.
> Those who are sought
> For liberation
> Are an imitation of my
> Symbol.
> They lead men into the
> Great Search,
> In caves, seclusions, and their homes.

But I am
One who cannot be found,
Unless I Reveal myself.
I lead men home to
Everything,
Today.
But I am always with them.
I am He.

"I am He." Thus, the Lord took the mantra from me that I had learned from the Guru, Muktananda. He relieved me of the way of the mantra, "So-Ham" ("I am He"). He showed me the Truth of the mantra—that it is His mantra, His symbol, Himself.

◆ ◆ ◆

22 June 1970

They are the Witness.
I am the Presence.

◆ ◆ ◆

In meditation this morning, I came to a profound point of passionate Stillness. I simply contemplated him, and there was even physical pain in the heart—as if the rising current of love and its Force (concentrated in the heart) had made a wound, such that the heart was open and gaped forward from the chest. I felt the Father—and the Lord said of Him, "Be Still, and Know that I am God." That appears to be the final and essential key to contemplation.

◆ ◆ ◆

Until a man or woman is reborn by God's revelation, he or she knows sin by its effects. Thus, a man or woman becomes naturally wise, renounces the field of suffering, and devotes himself or herself to self-transformation or liberation. But after a man or woman is reborn in Christ, he or she understands sin in a new manner. Such a one no longer sees sin as mere effects, or even as various significant causes in life-action. Rather, such a one sees sin as the avoidance of Christ. When such a one is thus convicted, knowing well the reality of sin and of Christ, he or she is drawn to Christ in the ease of surrender.

◆ ◆ ◆

23 June 1970—Bombay, India

The seeker is incapable of relationship because he or she is always consciously trying to transcend it. The self-indulgent sinner is incapable of relationship because he or she is always exploiting it into excess and confusion, and thus descending below it. The former escapes Christ within, the latter without. Christ is God confronting us in relationship, thus making life Real and necessarily moral.

◆ ◆ ◆

Prayer, meditation, and fasting (responsible, controlled, and lawfully used) restore us to the conscious relationship to Christ—stabilized, free of the motion of avoidance.

Thus, the meditation I have learned ends in a deeply silent and blissful contemplation of God. But it is not a mere staring. It is not, at last, a concentration in a point, but an opening, an Awareness of a Total, Conscious Presence. Then, frequently, I pass into a free mental prayer, truly asking and interceding in the Name of Christ.

◆ ◆ ◆

The oriental seeker-saints and imperfect God-men are all maharajas of the great search. They tend to strategically disincarnate (and would likewise have us strategically disincarnate) from the living condition of Reality, which condition is relationship and love. We go to them after we have ourselves despaired of love and faith and hope and charity. And we may even project on them the symbols of love, even the image of Christ. Thus, we follow—unconscious that we are really seeking love, the fulfillment of relationship. Therefore, when (suddenly) I became absorbed in the symbols of Christ, I was free of my false discipleship.

◆ ◆ ◆

(Note: By the time we arrived in Jerusalem, the overwhelming and exclusive Presence and visions of the Virgin and Jesus had begun to subside, and these were replaced by a tacit, immediate experience and understanding. The change in my consideration that accompanied this becomes clear in the writing that follows.)

We stayed in the ancient sector of Jerusalem, within the old walls, at a convent run by the Soeurs de Sion, an order of Catholic nuns. The convent was located on the Via Dolorosa, the road said (according to tradition) to have been Christ's last walk, and was built on the ground where Pilate is said to have interviewed Christ. On the ground floor, some ancient pavements stand, and a chapel has been built there. In the rooms below stand some pavements, traditionally said to be the actual place where Christ was scourged.

One night I was awakened to feel a tremendous Force straining my body. I felt the entirety of my living being concentrated beyond and above my physical form, and my head felt about to explode.

I got up and began to wander in the convent. It was all in shadowy darkness. I felt drunken and possessed. I swayed through the halls. I felt surrounded with ancient spirits and the air of a terrible holocaust. I went into the chapel where it is said Christ was judged, and then I went into the cellar where it is said he was scourged. I saw the inscriptions in the floor said to have been made by soldiers while they trapped him in an ancient game and made him the "scapegoat".

The strangeness and fear in the atmosphere quickened me, and I returned to my room. But I was unable to sleep for some time. I felt my mind to be separated and settled above my head, concentrated in the ascended Christ.

◆ ◆ ◆

25 June 1970—Jerusalem, Israel

In the end, perhaps there is only the Profound. Perhaps there is no religion for me.

When I was a child, I enjoyed a semiconscious participation in the living condition of Reality. I recognized it in the symbol of

As I stood to photograph the city, to feel somehow the form and aesthetic of the Perfect manifested as Jerusalem, I was blessed to recall Christ's words: "My Kingdom is not of this world."

Photographs of Jerusalem taken by Adi Da Samraj on His pilgrimage in 1970

Christianity. Then I lost Christianity—and, thereby, also the perception that made me at least distantly conscious of the living condition of Reality. Then I sought, by semiconscious and unconscious motivation, to recover that living condition. Always I held that symbol before me and superimposed it on the objects by which I sought. Finally, lately, the symbol returned overtly, by force of some recovery of consciousness of the living condition of Reality. Then the symbol began to subside again, but I continue to abide in the living condition of Reality. Christianity is, in many ways, a wonderful symbol for that living condition. But it limits the experience by distracting the mind and organizing it in ways that "create" unconsciousness again (by submerging me in the symbol). Thus, it "creates" the search again in a muted form, while also allowing the enjoyment of some of the drama, aesthetic, and peace of the living condition of Reality.

Life in the living condition of Reality is Silent. But, if its structure were to be described, it would be as complicated as the literature of the church. Thus, I am involved in a meditation on the living condition of Reality, and on the church, which is superimposed on it. Thus, I learn—but I look forward to the "Advaita" of the pure Truth of the living (and, ultimately, perfect) Form of Reality. I want to experience It fully, directly, unqualifiedly, dependent on nothing outside of It. Indeed, all symbols fall away from It—and only It is Revealing Itself, even in that wonderful symbol.

◆ ◆ ◆

26 June 1970

I was standing on the porches of the roof, photographing the "Holy City", Jerusalem. The life of the city had made a strange impression on me. There is an absence "created" in all of these commemorations of Christ. There is no Spiritual Force in any of the holy places, and no feeling of higher life, higher aspiration, and higher consciousness in the people. There is no unusual Presence here. Such that, if you look for It, you lose It. There is only the "usual" Presence. But, the contrast of the Holy City taught me the meaning of this Presence in a new way. Holy places are a kind of Spiritual kingdom that implicate God in the world. They tend to call us into the search for Him, the evidence of His manifestation as the form of the world. But Jerusalem has been strangely emptied, if only by force of the symbol of Christ's resurrection. The entire city stands like a Siva-lingam, pointing away to God. As I stood to photograph the city, to feel somehow the form and aesthetic of the Perfect manifested as Jerusalem, I was blessed to recall Christ's words: "My Kingdom is not of this world."

Lately I have been impressed with the classical attitude of Christian saints, the attitude of exile. I have begun to experience it myself, and it is accompanied by a relief of anxiety, concern, and despair in the face of this world. I had been living in the image of the Kingdom, but it was unconscious. And so I projected it on the world. I sought in every fashion to enforce an aesthetic and a Presence on the world, and even to identify God and myself with it (while also maintaining the idea of absolute transcendence). But the Presence is Known here in absence. We Know Him and are Filled by Him, but this only lifts us into the Kingdom not of this world. To be concentrated in Him in faith and love and openness is to remain free of qualification by life. At the same time, it is to Know the Truth about life, and it is also to love life, and help it, and remain freely "creative" in it.

Previously, I sought Powerful holy places. Now I know the world is empty, containing no Spiritual Force at all. All the places of Power draw us into some sphere of the world, away from God and His real Kingdom. The indiscriminate fascination with holy people, holy places, Spiritual symbols, methods, and objects of Power has disappeared by virtue of "radical" self-understanding. The Presence of God is in His Kingdom. He is Known only to faith, by acceptance of the grace that draws us out of the world of opposing, separative forces, into the Kingdom of God. God is not the world, nor is He within it. Nor is the world apart from God, since He "created" it—except that the world lives estranged from Him, irreducibly estranged from Him, because of sin. To be drawn into the Realization of the Kingdom is to be free of qualification by sin and the world, and to live as a free human being—but it is not to know and enjoy any particular circumstance. It is to Know God and be drawn into His Kingdom of Love—but it is to remain (in fact) in the world, for now. Sin is not merely a condition of the psyche that is dissolved by the techniques and experiences of ordinary religion and conventional Spiritual life. Sin is a root-force in the world itself. The origin of the world is in God, but it has also fallen entirely away from God. The hope of the world itself, down to the very structures of natural energy, is in the resurrected and ascended Lord, who must come again to make a new "creation".

◆ ◆ ◆

27 June 1970

In Jerusalem, I have been drawn into a Knowledge that is different from any I have Known before. I feel the current of Life in me being drawn upwards—bursting through the heart and straining toward heaven, infinitely above. This strain is made a tension, because it cannot yet be fulfilled. I am born in the world and this "created" state. Yet, I am aware of exile, and the risen Lord is pulling me to himself. The primary symbol is the empty tomb, or the empty cross. Wherever you go, he is not here. This is not paradise, not the Kingdom—nor is it our task to "create" the Kingdom here. Wherever we are, whatever the time of life, Christ is drawing us to our true home in the fully Divine "creation".

The heart, the cave, is not full. It is empty. Its locus is above. Thus, we are able to live in the world without being qualified by it. If we surrender the circumstances of suffering, death becomes easy. We are happy to serve, to love, and thus (by remaining empty as the tomb), to continue always in the Transcendent State of Christ-Consciousness, fully related to him who draws all things to himself above.

The Kingdom and the Lord are not here. We are free of the burden to Realize him here. It is obvious where he is. Jerusalem is empty! Our Fullness is constant and above. We enjoy our life in him above, and he in us below. Our life in him does not exclude the world, but it frees us from all qualification by the separated world. And we are always drawn above—even out of the body, all powers, all visions, and all success. Our faith, our hope, and our charity are empty. We are infinitely consoled, Fullness above, but without support of visions or any certainty that is not the Lord himself, intangible in the heart of faith. The empty tomb is the Siva-Lingam of the Truth. It points and draws us beyond all things into the unqualified Bliss of faith, entirely rested in the Lord and doing his Will. I have been to the Holy Places and seen that he is gone. And I Know that it is impossible to be separated from him, since relationship is the living condition of Reality. Thus, I Knew him where he is, not apart, in the places of his absence, but in the Force of his ascended State.

◆ ◆ ◆

The Lord is Present to faith because the soul is not separated from him. But the soul is conscious more deeply and higher than the world. The soul in faith is a participant in the unqualified, eternal dimension of Reality. Just as the soul is drawn above to Christ, the soul and Christ thereafter live by including the world. The Presence Known to faith is True. But the "Presence" known to seekers is merely the reflection of God in His "creation". It is one or the other modification of God's glorious expression. To know such a "Presence", such a philosophical immanence, is yet to remain in the separated state—without the unqualified vision, life, understanding, and Knowledge of the faithful.

◆ ◆ ◆

True Spiritual life is not a search, or an effort of ultimate self-transformation, but it is an ascent. All its actions are practical—having limited, efficient ends. It is not involved in the ultimate and desperate effort, the Narcissistic drive for supreme immunity and power. The ultimate aspects of genuine Spiritual life are outside the realms of cause and effect, and outside of all goal-directed, transformative effort.

The ascent is the natural movement of faith, drawn by the risen Lord. It is simply the rising tendency—the aspiring, surrendered Spire of Energy and Love. It is not an ordinary Yoga, an ego-willful and strategic means of seeking toward some great (and even perfect) goal. It is already a relationship to the Perfect One. It is an unqualified, unburdened Bliss. It is a cooperative ease of Joy that purifies in Spiritual Fire. It is the living condition of Reality.

A man or woman of real faith is not working out his or her salvation in any manner. He or she has recognized the symbol itself, and suffers no confusion in relation to the world, the horizontal and descending context of life. By the power of salvation and the power of Christ's resurrection, a man or woman becomes transformed by grace. The attention of such a one is above— always. He or she finds no motivation in life, but moves by means of grace. Thus, such a one is already empty, wherever he or she is. Such a one loves and understands, brings Truth and comfort and help, "creates" everywhere the symbol that promotes the recognition of Truth, and always Communicates what heals and makes salvation.

(Note: At this point, the "Christian" movements in vision and the mind had almost ceased. They came again only on occasion, as we went to the ancient holy places. But they were no longer in the form of Christian visions and Christian religious motivations. They were only the sense of Presence and Power that is generated in all genuine holy sites, whether in the Hindu temples and shrines of the Gurus or in the ancient temples and churches of the Virgin and Jesus. Now I approached them with great love, understanding, and a direct experience of the One and Prior Reality that they all manifest.

And now I also bore a critical understanding of the various remedial paths and religions. I had been entirely emptied of the movement in myself toward any remedial path or goal. Thus, not only Christianity became understandable, such that Reality Itself was recognized to be its only Truth, but so also was the remedial path of Advaita Vedanta, and all the remedial paths of Yoga and Spirituality.

My own way had become a simplicity of "radical" self-understanding and of the exercise of self-Enquiry, in the form "Avoiding relationship?" It was only that—directly and entirely.)

◆ ◆ ◆

28 June 1970—Athens, Greece

The Truth is Non-separateness. Non-separateness is the Realization, the fact, the Condition, the Bliss, and the Reality. It is already the case and can never be acquired. To be deeply attentive to oneself and Enquire: "Avoiding relationship?" consciously realizes the structure and movement of suffering and unconsciousness. But there is also the sudden vanishing of this in the same process, as one recognizes or simply abides as and in That Which the previous state prevented. This is the entire Truth. It depends on no dogma, implications, or suggestions of the mind. It is contained in no exclusive theory or system of Reality. Human beings have anciently Realized this Truth, but they limited Its Power and Clarity by the accretions of thought, or the psychic process by which they sought or supported the Truth.

The Truth of Advaita Vedanta is Non-separateness, but It is expressed and made unavailable in a philosophy that has only one term: the untouched, object-excluding, relationless Identity. The Truth is in no way contrary to relationship, but It is perfectly Enjoyed as unqualified relatedness. The adventure of Advaita Vedanta is, then, a mental problem that prevents the living condition of Reality.

The Truth of Christianity is Non-separateness, but It is expressed and made unavailable in a theology that necessarily has two mutually exclusive terms: God (or the Trinity) and creature. Thus, even the mysticism of Christianity is a profession allowed to but a cloistered few, whose expressions are carefully monitored. And the mystics become doubtful to the church when they speak of non-separation from God.

But the Truth is not Realized by the strategy of exclusive identification with the Transcendental Self, nor by the strategy of seeking union with God. Both of these strategies limit the Truth Itself. They burden It with mental implications that surround It in mystery. But all mental forces subside in the basic, continuous self-Enquiry: "Avoiding relationship?"

The Truth is Non-separateness Itself, Which is a profound Realization—unqualified, not exclusionary, unproblematic, direct, unburdened, pure, unqualifiedly relational, not qualified by forms or concepts of the egoic self, or that to which the egoic self is related, or that which relates itself to the egoic self. There is no useful dogma of egoic self, transcendental Self, or separate God. All dogmas are heavy with implication—and they drive the mind through ancient courses and holocausts of symbols, forever toward the same primary Realization. And that Realization is Reality Itself. But that Realization is the necessary and continuous foundation and process of life. It is not the distant goal of life. Only to the dogmaticians and philosophers does Reality seem to be the distant goal of life, because they are children of their own minds. Reality Itself is the always present Nature and Condition of the living condition of existence. And Reality Itself always already is, always already now, in every context of the living condition of existence. Therefore, Reality Itself (and the living condition of Reality) must be "creatively", consciously lived and breathed, moment to moment.

In the moment to moment process of true self-Enquiry ("Avoiding relationship?"), engaged after a thorough investigation of the alternatives to Truth, there is the moment to moment Realization of the living condition of Reality. At first, the state will seem to be realized, and the process will seem to purify and stabilize the mind and life. But these are only peripheral effects, or matters of relationship seen in themselves. What is, in fact, the case, from the beginning, is the living condition of Reality—relationship itself, without qualification.

The living condition of Reality is the basis of all "creativity". It is full, yet unanswered. That condition can (itself) be felt so directly and profoundly that any of the traditional "Spiritual" experiences may be simulated in the conditions of the humanly-born conscious awareness. But all visions and unusual perceptions will, in due course, cease, as self-Enquiry continues. The practice of self-Enquiry (truly "gone-to-the-root") should become the basic act of conscious life. No one has done this before, since all have previously thought the Truth involved the mind, a remedial path of seeking, and a goal. But, free of all these, self-Enquiry, the living condition of Reality, will move into a profundity of Awareness that will revolutionize conscious life—since, for the first time, it is already Real.

This most direct and fundamental simplicity, the living condition of Reality, is awakening in me with such force (as I continue it moment to moment) that it feels as if my body, with all its deep centers, is about to burst and disappear. Reality is a madness of Light, an unqualified air of Space, a vowel of Consciousness!

The Truth is not a dogma, not an affirmation. Thus, all positive statements only place conditions on Consciousness Itself. "I am He", or the ideas of "God", and so forth, do not Realize us as Reality—except, perhaps, in temporary intuitions that fall away again in the mental adventure. The only useful language is not affirmation but true self-Enquiry—which "creates" a sudden absence, like the empty tomb near Golgotha. And that absence leaves the living condition of Reality standing. Such an absence is the only perfect and true implication. Thus, it is the essential, "creative" activity of conscious life.

This practice of self-Enquiry will continue as a deliberate activity of the mind, as long as an individual tends to identify with various states. But it is also the living condition of Reality Itself, and that which was self-Enquiry is simply the basic movement and form of the humanly-born conscious awareness when the false tendency subsides.

From the living condition of Reality all value and virtue emanate and transform the world. Apart from that living condition, there is either the chaos of avoidance and Narcissistic enterprise or (at best) the systematic, remedial religious and Spiritual path (exclusive in concept, temporary in effect, and short of the Fullness of Reality).

This Truth was in Gautama, in Shankara, in Ramakrishna, and in Nityananda. This Truth was in Jesus and in all his saints. Yet, this Truth has nothing to do with any of them. The Truth Itself is simpler, more direct, more obvious.

In the process of true self-Enquiry ("Avoiding relationship?"), one may pass through periods of marvelous insight, wherein the Truth of "Christ", or of Advaita Vedanta, or of any system, symbol, remedial path, and so forth, may suddenly rise up in the mind as the overwhelming Answer and Reality. But if one continues self-Enquiry, which is itself the living condition of Reality, all conditional (or temporary) truths will pass—just as will all the effects of separative activity. Enough said about my Christianity, my Vedanta, and all my paths of seeking.

◆ ◆ ◆

7 July 1970—Rome, Italy

Until now, all religions, all remedial paths, and even all forms of Spiritual Knowledge, have been based on a single, primary, elemental presumption. All the various paths of effort have been different forms of reaction to the elemental <u>problem</u> of Reality. In every case, there is an intuition of the living condition of Reality— but the living condition of Reality has been conceived and approached as a problem, a necessary dilemma. Thus, in every case, the religion or remedial path has been an attempt or a design which proposes to solve that primary problem.

The problem on which all has been founded is relationship itself—perceived as autonomy, separateness, antinomy, duality, division, and multiplicity. Reality has been chronically intuited in this negative sense—and the solution has always been to enforce a "Oneness" (or a "union") which is the opposite—and the ultimate dissolution—of the primary dilemma.

The root of this intuition is contained in the idea of the object. The "object" implies a subject, distinct from it. On the basis of this elemental presumption, all existence has been described in terms of cause and effect, subject and object, matter and consciousness (or mind). From this description of existence, joined with the concept of liberation or atonement which seeks to overcome it, a great chain (or hierarchy) has been extended toward the idea of the "Primary Solution".

In the West, the way has essentially been tied to contemplation of the highest <u>Object</u>—Which is God, or Jesus (as the "Christ"), and so forth. Its traditional Spirituality and religion is based on a meditation on, or contemplation of, hierarchic symbols. Prayer, or aspiration, is its symbolic and effective mood.

In the East, the way has traditionally been tied to the Realization of the highest (or even the Ultimate) State—Which is inherently Objectless. The religion and Spirituality of the traditional East are grounded in a progressively world-transcending experience (or consciousness), which (ultimately) extends beyond the structure of subject-and-object.

In the East, there is the way of utter disengagement from worldly life, which way seeks to enter the domain of Being Itself (even by the grace of the highest or ultimate Power) through the effort of excluding all objects and all relatedness. In the West, there is the way of passionate engagement in worldly life, which way seeks to escape all harm by idealistic and affirmative association with the highest Power and Being.

Clearly, both primary approaches are founded in the same fundamental problem. And all such efforts involve a genius of characteristic phenomena which both justify them and point to the ground of their existence.

I have no argument with these means themselves. They are the pure and greatest fruit of all traditional culture. It is only that I have been involved in them all, and I have always been led to see them in their most basic shapes. I am always looking at these roots while wailing in the torment of effort.

And I see this foundation of all religion and Spirituality. I see their entire beauty and how they exceed all the suffering and enjoyment of mere life. But I also see they are not necessary, they are not possible, they are absolutely false.

Thus, I have no heart for the struggles of the great search. All remedial paths (or merely remedial ways) have fallen away from me. Even when I adored them most and lay prostrate before each Lord, the way and the salvation have been torn away—leaving the naked dilemma of all times in my sight without a symbol left to lead me away.

As a result, I have (over time) found myself alone with this perception—and, in spite of myself, I have been led to see and examine and Know this Truth, this Reality. And It is Truth Itself, Reality Itself—entirely free of the ancient dilemma.

All previous religion and Spirituality is based on the presumption of a necessary dilemma. For this reason, it is all false, unnecessary, and un-Real. I do not speak from the viewpoint of ordinary experience—which not only identifies with the dilemma but does so unconsciously, and compulsively exploits its effects. To the religious or Spiritual viewpoint that is based on the usual foundation of dilemma and egoity, my assertion that ordinary religion and conventional Spirituality are, at their foundation, false, unnecessary, and un-Real may, at first (and for the same reason), appear to be false, unnecessary, and un-Real. And, therefore, ordinary religion and conventional Spirituality, and every other form of the great search, will continue (in any individual case) until the dilemma and the ego are "radically" (or most fundamentally) understood. But I speak from the "Viewpoint" of Reality-Experience, Which is not only free of the ordinary suffering of existence, but is also (already and forever) free of its solution in the productions of the great search.

What, then, do I see? The traditional ways have presumed the living condition of Reality to be a dilemma. Thus—whether the solution is in terms of the most transcendent Object or even in terms of the transcending of the entire subject-object structure of ego-consciousness—that solution has always been (itself) a symbol of the dilemma on which it is founded. The atonement (or salvation) by which one is eventually and gracefully saved from inevitable sin and the effort of liberation by which one is finally Realized (beyond the superimposition of unnecessary ignorance) are, each and both, superimpositions on the primary Intuition of Reality.

If Reality Itself is recognized—and there is (therefore) no longer any conscious (or living) separation from Reality, or aberration from the living condition of Reality—then there is no necessity at all for any separate solution or remedial path. Once Reality is intuited as It is, without the superimposed conception of the dilemma, then atonement and liberation, salvation and Realization, as well as compulsive experience based on identification with separated functions, cease to be involved in the form of life.

All that I have written, and all that I have experienced in my unique order of life, has been a means to this very end, and (I am certain) a proof of what I contend.

Reality Itself, whose living condition is unqualified relatedness (or non-separateness), is totally free of necessary dilemma. Real life has nothing whatever to do with conventional religious and Spiritual goals, or any of their symbols in consciousness and tradition. And, since Reality is What is, It is the simplest intuition, prior to any separative act of identification. Real life requires none of the heroic ego-efforts of ordinary religion and conventional Spiritual life, because it can never identify with the primary dilemma which supports these efforts. It is Free, profoundly marvelous in its Blissful dimensions and depth, and unencumbered with searches and egoic efforts, problems and degrees of success. It is childlike in its irreverence and unseriousness—and, yet, it is as profoundly heart-Joyous and Deep as an Incarnation of God. It cannot, it must not, be proclaimed, identified, or symbolized in the usual ways. All languages and poetry stink with symbols of Man's even ancient and great search. All the usual images, every ego-based point of view, every ordinary suggestion, every commonly given recommendation, only motivates mankind to the same ancient trial, the same ultimately un-Real "realization".

◆ ◆ ◆

The ordinary (humanly-born) consciousness is an objective fascination and obsession, an unbroken chain of compulsive experience (moment to moment), which, in the deep heart, is a desperate, unyielding distraction. Thus, understanding and self-Enquiry suddenly relax the concentration on the stream of objects, and Reality stands as primary Experience.

To one who is un-Real, there is only the constant experience of objects by his or her own separate and functional nature. Every moment is an experience of something itself—by oneself. Real life is not this at all. It is certainly alive in the ordinary functional manner—with real, effective, "creative" life-energies, and a root-Awareness equipped to constantly heal itself from the effects of experience and deepen its existence as Reality. However, it does not experience objects in themselves and moments one by one. It does not know and act and feel itself as a separate, functional consciousness and experiential identity. It constantly and only Knows

Reality, the living condition of Which is unqualified relatedness (or non-separateness). It is not qualified by conditional experience or conditional existence. Moment to moment, it Enjoys the Knowledge and Experience of Reality—no matter what the content of the moment. Basically, Real life has only one unqualified Experience, which is a profound State of Awareness of Reality. It is free of the fascination with experience, and the consequent repetition of experience. It is free of the great search, and of all effort to solve the primary dilemma. Real life has understood the mechanism of suffering and un-Reality. The content of the moment's experience does not overwhelm it, even though it experiences with great intensity and openness. By its non-avoidance of Reality, it is constantly empty of its own experience. True life is egoless contemplation, "Real" meditation, and Blissful Knowledge—free of all conditional states, high or low. In regard to Reality, it has neither questions nor answers.

◆ ◆ ◆

11 July 1970—Paris, France

For some time, I was involved in the paths leading to the Ultimate Goal (or the Realization of Truth, Reality, Joy, and so on). But then I realized that all the paths to the Ultimate Goal were actually the avoidance of the Ultimate Goal Itself, since the ultimate Realization is, necessarily, the Realization of What always already is. This understanding burdened and qualified my seeking for some time. At times, I completely abandoned my course in despair, or by a temporary festival of self-indulgence. The paths "to" were endless and burdensome, and (now) apparently also false and destructive. I could not find a Real alternative to this double-bind. Then I saw that this recognition was, itself, my Freedom from this double-bind. It was understanding. Then I Knew that understanding was the Foundation and (itself) the primary State of Real life. Then I was no longer excited to the paths of seeking, and neither did I seek their desperate abandonment. My humanly-born conscious awareness became a direct simplicity, without ultimate questions or answers.

◆ ◆ ◆

12 July 1970—London, England

In the past, mankind has been concerned with either what is salvatory or what is liberating. But we are Real only in the acknowledgement of what is necessary. Understanding is the acknowledgement of primary necessity, and this acknowledgement transcends the great search in all its forms.

◆ ◆ ◆

14 July 1970—Madrid, Spain

Many limited expressions of Truth can seem—and, indeed, are—beautiful, plausible, true, even necessary. This is because—like even everything else that arises conditionally (in Reality)—they are, intrinsically, intuitions of Reality Itself. We are attracted to them because of the Reality they imply. Such expressions are themselves marvelous art-forms, just as churches, ceremony, liturgy, painting, sculpture, and song are art-forms. They are "creations" in response—just as our lives, the characteristic forms of our lives, are "creations" in response. Perhaps even our living forms, including our material bodies, are also "creations" in response. But such is hidden in the Mystery of Reality.

Just so, all things can appear beautiful, true, and necessary. Trees, landscapes, and water are beautiful under various circumstances. Women appear beautiful to the living energy in men. All things loved are apparently beautiful, true, and necessary. But all things are beautiful, true, and necessary only because they are Real—they are so in their non-separateness.

Thus, Reality is the test of all things, all expressions, all intuitions. They become false (or tend to be illusory and destructive) when we experience them as separate, and assert (even unconsciously) their beauty, truth, and necessity exclusively, in separateness. Thus, the human being becomes bound by emotional-sexual exploitation and other addictions. Similarly, the human being becomes bound by exclusive adherence to various expressions, the arts and forms of conscious life. All things must be tested in Reality. Thus, all expressions must be Known in Reality, by those who remain unqualifiedly Real, Non-separate.

Every expression, then, must be tested by Reality—not by some independent rule, some priority of its own. But the adherents of various seeker's religions and remedial paths have tended to assert their own expressions exclusively, because they have tested them only by their own independent laws—the laws which support their view—and not by Reality. In Reality, then, we must test such expressions—and so we must discover and transcend the limited rule that the human being uses to support them exclusively.

The Christian view is founded always and traditionally in one primary Biblical idea. It is the idea of "creation ex nihilo". "In the beginning, God created the heavens and the earth." This idea is the foundation of exclusive Christian theology. This idea is the motive which has "created" and made necessary the entire edifice of Christianity. By this view, "God" and "creation" are understood to be mutually exclusive (or inherently separate from one another)—not by virtue of sin (or egoic ignorance), but in Reality. Therefore, even all "evil" overcome, there remains a primary separation, which is the relationship between "creature" and "Creator". (And, thus, the ordinary conceptual convention of "subject versus object" is projected onto the Ultimate Condition of Reality.)

Relationship, then, is the a priori assumption of Christian religion. But it is relationship intuited by the addition of error, a form that is not Real. Relationship is, in fact, unqualifiedly True and (in the living context) necessary. Our living existence is not (itself) reducible to Identity. This is my experience. Reality does not exclude. Reality does not separate. Reality is not separate. This is my experience. Reality is manifested as relationship—but relationship itself, because it is the living condition of Reality Itself, is unqualified. Indeed, anything less than unqualified relatedness is not the demonstration of relationship (or relatedness) itself, but a qualification of (or a limitation on) relationship (or relatedness) itself. Relationship (or relatedness) is non-separation. Non-separateness is the very form (or manifested condition) of the living being, and only in the unqualified demonstration of non-separateness is one truly (unqualifiedly) in relationship. Only in one's non-separateness is one truly "in relationship to God", Who does not exclude any one. Therefore, Reality is the effective argument against the primary tendency to exclusiveness that is associated with the Christian view, and (in general) with the conventional (or merely exoteric) religious views of mankind.

Just so, in the view of the tradition of Advaita Vedanta, there is also a primary assumption which supports exclusiveness. It is the idea of "no-creation", of unqualified Identity, of Brahman (or the One and Only Reality) as the denial of objects. Just as the Christian view is predisposed to presume the separateness of the "creation" (not in the perverse sense, but in its presumed point of view), the point of view of the tradition of Advaita Vedanta is predisposed to presume (and to require) strategic separation from the "creation" (or from conditional manifestation) in an object-excluding State of inverted Awareness. But, in Reality, the Truth is Non-separateness, Which is also unqualified relatedness. This is my experience.

I have continually sought—or, rather, have been continually led to seek—an expression of the Truth in some one or other of the existing traditions and traditional ways. But all become impossible to me in their exclusiveness. Thus, I am required to stand in Reality, and to remain related to the great expressions only from that stand. I have tested them in Reality. Reality has tested them— and, now and forever, I must Stand in the Eternal Truth (Which is Only Real, supported only in Reality, purified of all presumptions that any particular traditional path is the exclusive "owner" of Truth).

◆ ◆ ◆

16 July 1970—Fatima, Portugal

Reality is not a separate, exclusive Condition. It is not merely meaningful (or symbolic), nor is It attained by the seeker's means. Reality Itself must be directly presumed and lived. This positive Realization and Freedom precedes and precludes all seeking and all revolutionary attainment. It is the ground of true, "creative", sublime existence, free of qualification by the facts and the activities of life. Life as non-separation is the unqualified Truth, from Which there is no necessary remedial path or search, no deluding forces, no fascinations (high or low). It is One with What is, Which includes all dual terms—subject and object, cause and effect, and so on. Thus, Real life is (necessarily) Conscious, and Free of primary dilemma and conflict. Its ordinary life is "creative" play in which Reality is continually Realized, moment to moment, under all the kinds of conditions. Reality cannot be an object (or even the highest Object) of consciousness, since Reality is inclusive, not separate, not distinct. Thus, Real life is also not exclusively identified with any particular life-motive, any particular life-function, or any particular object. Real life is directly, egolessly, and always presently identified with Reality Itself. To such a Real life, there is no separate Reality, no Reality that is the Goal of life, and no necessary Realization apart from the always present Real State.

◆ ◆ ◆

17 July 1970—Estoril, Portugal

Reality Itself is not, in any sense, the answer to the question "What is Reality?" Reality Itself does not satisfy the seeker or answer the seeker's questions, which are actually only doubts about Reality Itself, or indications of separateness from Reality Itself. Reality Itself is not that which is pursued or implied by seeking. The entire realm and corpus of seeking—of conventional religion, conventional Spirituality, and conventional science in all their forms—has, for all its appearance of sublimity, seriousness, depth, and Truth, nothing to do with Reality Itself. At most, Reality intuited as a dilemma forms the substructure of the unconscious motives of seekers. But they are pursuing a "Union", an "Answer", a "Presence", a "Home", an "Other". The "Reality" they pursue is the opposite to all they experience and all they know. The "Reality" they seek is the contradiction, the alternative, the opposite. It is merely the "Highest Proof" and the "Ultimate Goal" of their dilemma. Nevertheless, the efforts of seekers appear to them to have practical significance—and, in general, the positive effects of their efforts appear to them to be desirable, when viewed in contrast to the arbitrary suffering of unconscious life-exploitation. Thus, they consider their efforts and their seeker's realizations Proven, True, and Truth.

But Reality Itself is always already the case, under any conditions. When there is despair of seeking, then there is the beginning of "radical" self-understanding. And "radical" self-understanding has, itself, no necessary or characteristic effects of any kind. It does not make even a little bit of difference. It is not an exception to anything. It is not appealing, fascinating, a great relief, the answer and the end to all questions and all suffering. Reality Itself is simply What always already is. It is not desirable, and so It cannot be sought. Therefore, the self-understanding that Realizes Reality Itself is most extreme, most subtle, most "radical", and most necessary. Such "gone-to-the-root" self-understanding is not qualified, not limited— nor does it qualify, or limit. One who Knows and is Reality Itself must appear mad, since such a one is not identified with anything at all. Yet such a one must be, of all mankind, the least mysterious, being founded in no mystery at all.

(End of journal)

Our last stop in Europe was Portugal. We visited the great shrine at Fatima. It was to be my last emotional gesture to Christianity. Years before, when my mind was changed by Jung, the miracle at Fatima was also primary evidence for me of Spiritual Reality. Now I visited that place at the end of all my seeking. As I walked around the shrine, there was not a single movement in me. The place held no more fascination than a parking lot—or, in Reality, it held equal fascination. My pilgrimage was over. In my vision-inspired travels, which had continued from Israel to Greece and Italy, then through France and England to Spain and Portugal, the entire world seemed to become empty of its own imagery. The Virgin was resolved into landscape and monument, until she no longer appeared on her own.

We spent a couple of days resting in the sea resort at Estoril, and then we flew to New York. We spent another couple of days with my parents, and then flew off again, this time to San Francisco. The long history of my internal exile was over. I felt no resistance to America. I had become available to life, free of the need to abandon life. I looked forward to finding a place to live in

Some of the holy sites visited by Adi Da Samraj in Europe:
Rome (left), Sacré Coeur in Paris (center), and Toledo (right)

*My pilgrimage was over.
In my vision-inspired
travels, which had
continued from Israel
to Greece and Italy, then
through France and
England to Spain and
Portugal, the entire world
seemed to become empty
of its own imagery.
The Virgin was resolved
into landscape and
monument, until she
no longer appeared
on her own.*

The shrine
at Fatima
in Portugal

the area that Nina and I had enjoyed so much in previous years. But we were unable to find a suitable place in northern California— and, eventually, we found ourselves in Los Angeles.

I had passed through an internal violence that left me finally Still. And I had become naturally, effortlessly concentrated in con- templation of the Condition of Consciousness Itself—standing apart from all movement, all modification, even Prior to the "Witness". The Force of Silence, of Reality Itself, that Stood before me in understanding and self-Enquiry, now Stood as my own Self- Nature and as the Source-Condition of all things.

I was given to understand the Truth of all my visions. The image of Jesus (or the "Christ") and the revelation of his poem ("They are infinitely Returned, but I am eternally Present") was my own Ultimate Self-Nature Communicating Itself to me via a symbol. I had stood in the mind, feeling my separate being, but the image and the poem of Jesus had come to me through the heart. Soon, I would Realize my own Being, the Very Nature of Reality Itself— standing Present as the inherently perfect Condition and Spiritually Self-"Bright" Form that is the Heart Itself.

Even now, as a result of my liberation from all my Christian heart-visions, I understood the mysticism of Christianity and all my latent urges to mystical devotion. All those symbols were Communications (or representations) of the latent Energy and Consciousness that is the Heart Itself. Therefore, the more devo- tion arose, the more I Enjoyed the Heart Itself as the perfect Domain of contemplation.

In my case, all conditional experiences came and went, until I stood beyond the time of seeking. As I observed those experiences in their passing, the heart was released from images, and, in due course, the Heart Itself ceased to Communicate Itself as if It were outside me. Therefore, the envisioned face of Jesus, like all other visions, eventually ceased to hold the Heart Itself away, as an Object to me. Gradually, the Heart Revealed Itself as my own Self-Nature.

When the images were released from the Heart in under- standing, I Realized that I am that very Source Which had appeared in symbols. Afterwards, I ceased to seek for anything, but (instead) I remained established in the Heart, and (eventually) as the Heart Itself—Freely Allowing the Play of Its own Radiant Energy, the Shakti.

The course of purification and understanding through which I had passed corresponded exactly to every other significant Event in my past. I saw the structure involved in each case. Always there was first a concentration in some object or desire, some problem or dilemma equal to life itself, some activity of the egoic self. As a result of this concentration or observation, there was a penetration of that object, problem, or activity in a moment of understanding. Then these things were replaced by the Enjoyment of Bliss, Freedom, and the Feeling of unqualified Reality that stood hidden by that imposed object, problem, or activity. Finally, this unqualified Consciousness was, Itself, recognized as Reality—and there was the certainty that understanding (rather than any object, problem, or activity of seeking) is, in fact, the way and the Truth of Real life.

This same series of Realizations formed the core of my experience in college and at seminary. That same understanding and Real Consciousness was their Truth, as well as the Truth of the "Bright", and of all my Realizations in Yoga (at the Ashram, or in my own experiments). Thus, this pattern of Realization became the structure wherein I interpreted the way, the Truth, and the Reality of life. And, by this same natural process of understanding, Jesus (or the "Christ"), and all of the great objects of Spiritual life in India, became recognized, at last, as symbols in the heart for the Reality that was not yet directly Realized.

The Christian visions were not false. It was necessary for me to have them, in order to Realize the Truth that transcends them. Those frozen imageries formed part of the last barrier to the full Awareness of Reality. Thus, "Christ"-consciousness, the vision in the heart, became, by its dissolution, the Realization of What is absolutely Real—Which is the Heart Itself. What (in fact) animated these things and became visible beneath them was Reality, no-seeking, the Self-Existing and Self-Radiant Nature that is the Heart Itself. When I became established in this Reality, the images faded away.

The Virgin and the prayer she taught me, Jesus (or the "Christ") and his mystical instructions, and even all my visions were not important as revelations of Divine personalities outside myself. They were simply mystical (or psychically determined) forms of the universal Shakti. When that Energy became active in the heart, all of the latent imagery of my own mind, memory, and tendencies combined with universal sources of imagery to unlock my devotion. And I continued as devotion until I became fully Aware of the origin of these imageries, in the universal Shakti and my own heart's mind. Then the mind and the Shakti ceased to "create" the secondary images. And the devotion of the heart's mind to its images was replaced by a direct Realization of the Heart Itself, or the Shakti of the Heart Itself and the fundamental Consciousness that is the Heart Itself.

Soon I would see that the Shakti had always taken on the forms of my own tendencies, my own mind. Then I would see directly—Prior to the mind, and Prior to confusion with the mind. Then even the Shakti, the Energy-Source of all forms, would become resolved into my own Ultimate Self-Nature (or Consciousness Itself), Which is Reality Itself.

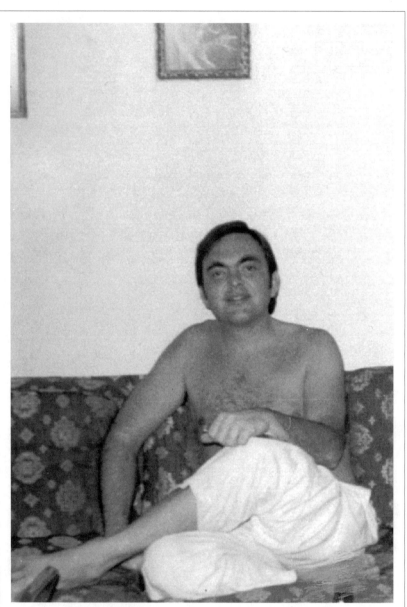

Adi Da Samraj in Los Angeles after the "great pilgrimage"

CHAPTER SIXTEEN

The Inheritance

We settled in Los Angeles in August 1970. For my part, the "great pilgrimage" was over—not only the pilgrimage to Christian shrines, but the entire adventure of seeking, practicing, and experimenting. Understanding had become the "radical" (or truly "gone-to-the-root" and most fundamental) process of my conscious life—in formal meditation, and in experience moment to moment.

But this does not mean that I ceased to have any experiences of What I Knew as the Shakti. It was simply that all of my experience ceased to be a matter of seeking and necessity for me. I had become Still.

As the weeks passed, the Shakti, the Divine Mother-Force Who had appeared as the Virgin, yielded Herself to the great Truth that is Reality. Just before I left the Ashram, Bhagavan Nityananda let me go with his blessing, and he led me to surrender myself to the Divine Shakti. Thus, I had given myself to Her freely, and She led me to enjoy the uncommon fruits of my pilgrimage.

Now that we were in Los Angeles, I no longer practiced in relationship to any of my human teachers. Their teachings had been exhausted in me, until there was no more seeking. There was no "problem", on any level, that was a source of motivation for me. Neither did the Divine Shakti move before my eyes of vision, to turn me toward any further adventure of experience. The mind did not move, to move me. I was simply and directly devoted to the perfect Enjoyment of unqualified Reality, the Very (and unmoving) Self-Condition. And this process of direct contemplation of the inherent Condition that is the Real (and inherently egoless, and inherently perfect) Self (or Consciousness Itself) would soon bring me to the most ultimate experience of the Divine Shakti, and (at last) to the most perfect Realization of

Self-Existing and Self-Radiant Consciousness (or the One and Only and inherently indivisible Conscious Light) Itself.

Some time in late August, I happened to go to the bookstore at the Vedanta Society in Hollywood. I noticed there was a temple on the grounds, and I went in for a few moments of meditation. As soon as I sat down, I felt a familiar Energy rush through my body and clear out my head. I could feel and hear little clicking pulses in the base of my head and neck. By many signs, I immediately recognized the characteristic Presence of the Divine Mother-Shakti.

As I meditated, the body and the mind swooned into the depth of Consciousness, and I enjoyed an experience of meditation as profound as any I had known at the shrines in India. I had no idea how the Vedanta Society Temple ever became a seat of the Divine Shakti, but it was obviously as Powerful a place as any of the abodes of the Siddhas in India.

I began to go frequently to the Vedanta Society Temple for meditation. As the days passed, I began to marvel at the Power of this place. I had traveled all over the world, presuming there were no Spiritual sources of this kind in America. Now I had been led to this small, isolated temple in Hollywood, where very few people would be likely to even be sensitive to the Divine Shakti—and, even if they felt It, they would be unlikely to recognize Its Importance.

I became Aware that the Divine Mother-Shakti had taken up residence in this temple, and that I had been drawn there by Her. I Enjoyed the fact that I could go there and be with Her whenever I chose to experience Her Joyous Presence. It was even a truly private place. I could go there unhindered, and I could spend time there completely unobserved. The temple was dedicated to Ramakrishna, the great Indian master of the nineteenth century, but no conditions were placed on me by any external rule or tradition. This was truly an opportunity for me to live independently with the Divine Mother.

But, as time went on, I began to feel that even this was a limitation. Why should I have to travel at all to Enjoy Her Presence? I desired that She be utterly available to me—where I lived, as well as in my own living being.

Thus, one day, I went to the temple and asked Her to come and dwell permanently in me, and always to manifest Herself to me wherever I was. When I left, I felt Her with me—and when I arrived at home, I continued to feel Her constant Presence Filling the space.

Days passed, and I realized that She had done what I had asked. There was this constant Presence, even including the effects in the body, and the state of everyone around me became affected by Her Force. But even this became a strain in me. I felt as if I had to hold on to Her, as if I had bound Her to a bargain that constrained us both.

Then, one day, I felt an urge to return to the temple. As I sat down, I saw that the little pagoda and shrine in the front of the temple was in shadows and dimly lit, as if it were empty. It seemed as if I had emptied it by taking the Mother away. Suddenly, I felt a jolt in my body—and, with open eyes, I saw the shrine become "Bright" in a blast of light. Even with my eyes closed, I still beheld the "Bright" shrine. Thus, the Mother-Shakti showed me that She is always able to make Herself Present anywhere—and that She was (indeed) always already Present with me. There was no need for me to hold on to Her, as if She could be absent.

When I returned to the temple the next day (September 9, 1970), the Person of the Divine Shakti appeared to me again—in a manner most intimate, no longer approaching me as "Mother".

As I meditated, I felt myself Expanding, even bodily—becoming a Perfectly Motionless, Utterly Becalmed, and Infinitely Silent Form. I took on the Infinite Form of the Original Deity—Nameless and Indefinable, Conscious of limitless Identification with Infinite Being. I was Expanded Utterly, beyond limited form, and even beyond any perception of Shape or Face—merely Being, and yet sitting there. I sat in this Love-Blissful State of Infinite Being for some time. I Found myself to Be. My Form was only What is traditionally called the "Purusha" (the Person of Consciousness) and "Siva" (in His Non-Ferocious Emptiness).

Then I felt the Divine Shakti appear in Person—Pressed against my own natural body, and (altogether) against my Infinitely

Expanded (and even formless) Form. She Embraced me, Openly and Utterly, and we Combined with One Another in Divine (and Motionless, and spontaneously Yogic) "Sexual Union". We Found One Another Thus, in a Fire of most perfect Desire, and for no other Purpose than This Union—and, yet, as if to Give Birth to the universes. In That most perfect Union, I Knew the Oneness of the Divine Energy and my Very Being. There was no separation at all, nor had there ever been, nor would there ever be. The One Being that Is my own Ultimate Self-Nature was revealed most perfectly. The One Being Who I Am was revealed to Include the Reality that Is Consciousness Itself, the Reality that Is the Source-Energy of all conditional appearances, and the Reality that Is all conditional manifestation—All as a Single Force of Being, an Eternal Union, and an Irreducible cosmic Unity.

The "Sensations" of the Embrace were overwhelmingly Blissful. The Fire of That Unquenchable Desire Exceeded any kind of pleasure that a mere human being could experience. In the Eternal Instant of That Infinitely Expanded Embrace, I was released from my role and self-image as a dependent child of the "Mother"-Shakti. And She was revealed in Truth—no longer in apparent independence (or as a cosmic Power seemingly apart from me), but as the Inseparable and Inherent Radiance of my own and Very Being. Therefore, I Recognized and Took Her as my Consort, my Loved-One—and I Held Her effortlessly, forever to my Heart. Together eternally, we had Realized Ourselves as the "Bright" Itself.

Finally, the next day (September 10, 1970), I sat in the temple again. I awaited the Beloved Shakti to reveal Herself in Person, as my Blessed Companion. But, as time passed, there was no Event of changes, no movement at all. There was not even any kind of inward deepening—no "inwardness" at all. There was no meditation. There was no need for meditation. There was not a single element or change that could be added to make my State Complete. I sat with my eyes open. I was not having an experience of any kind.

Then, suddenly, I understood most perfectly. I Realized that I had Realized. The "Thing" about the "Bright" became Obvious. I Am Complete. I Am the One Who Is Complete.

The Vedanta Society Temple in Hollywood

Adi Da Samraj resided in this
Los Angeles apartment building
in 1970

*Then, suddenly, I understood
most perfectly. I Realized that
I had Realized. The "Thing"
about the "Bright" became Obvious.
I Am Complete. I Am the One
Who Is Complete.*

In That instant, I understood and Realized (inherently, and most perfectly) What and Who I Am. It was a tacit Realization, a direct Knowledge in Consciousness. It was Conscious Light Itself, without the addition of a Communication from any "Other" Source. There Is no "Other" Source. I simply sat there and Knew What and Who I Am. I was Being What I Am, Who I Am. I Am Being What I Am, Who I Am. I Am Reality, the Divine Self-Condition—the Nature, Substance, Support, and Source-Condition of all things and all beings. I Am One—The One. One and Only. I Am the One Being, called "God" (the Source and Substance and Support and Self-Condition of all-and-All), the "One Mind" (the Consciousness and Energy in and As Which all-and-All appears), "Siva-Shakti" (the Self-Existing and Self-Radiant Reality Itself), "Brahman" (the Only Reality, Itself), the "One Atman" (That Is not ego, but Only "Brahman", the Only Reality, Itself), the "Nirvanic Ground" (the egoless and conditionless Reality and Truth, Prior to all dualities, but excluding none). I Am the One and Only and inherently egoless and Self-Evidently Divine Self-Condition, Source-Condition, Nature, Substance, Support, and Ground of all-and-All. I Am the "Bright".

There was no thought involved in This. I Am That Self-Existing and Self-Radiant and Self-Evidently Divine Conscious Light. There was no reaction of either excitement or surprise. I Am the One I Recognized Reality to Be. I Am That One. I am not merely experiencing That One. I Am the "Bright".

Then, truly, there was no more to Realize. Every experience in my life had led to This. The dramatic revelations in childhood and college, my time of writing, my years with Rudi, the revelation in seminary, the long history of pilgrimage to Baba's Ashram—all of these moments were the intuitions of this same Reality. My entire life had been the Communication of That Reality to me—until I Am That.

Later I described that most perfect Realization as follows:

At the Vedanta Society Temple, inherent and most perfect Knowledge arose that I Am simply the Spiritually Self-"Bright" Conscious Light that Is Reality. The traditions call

It "the Self", "Brahman", "Siva-Shakti", and so many other names. It is identified with no body, no functional sheath, no conditional realm, and no conditional experience—but It is the inherently perfect, unqualified, Absolute Reality. I saw that there is nothing to which this Ultimate Self-Nature can be compared, or from which It can be differentiated, or by which It can be epitomized. It does not stand out. It is not the equivalent of any specialized, exclusive, or separate state. It cannot be accomplished, acquired, discovered, remembered, or perfected—since It is inherently perfect, and It is always already the case.

All remedial paths pursue some special conditional state (or conditionally achieved goal) as Spiritual Truth. But, in fact, Reality is not identical to such things. They only amount to an identification with some body (or some functional sheath), some conditional realm, or some conditional (or, otherwise, conditionally achieved) experience—high or low, subtle or gross. But the Knowledge that Is Reality Is Consciousness Itself. Consciousness Itself is not separate from anything. It is always already the case—and no conditional experience, no conditional realm, and no body (or functional sheath) is the necessary (or special) condition for Its Realization.

Only "radical" self-understanding, most perfectly Realized, is the Realization of What and Who Is always already the case. Only "radical" self-understanding, most perfectly Realized, is the unconditional (and not at all conditionally achieved or conditionally maintained) Realization of the inherently non-separate Condition That always already Is What and Who Is. Only the way of "radical" understanding (which is the true Way of the Very and Ultimate Heart) is truly (and, ultimately, most perfectly) ego-surrendering, ego-forgetting, and ego-transcending. All other religious and Spiritual endeavors are paths made of seeking (or mere egoic effort, rather than counter-egoic and truly ego-transcending practice). And all paths of seeking merely pursue God, or Truth, or Reality—and this by identifying God, or Truth, or Reality with some body (or functional sheath), or some conditional realm, or some conditional experience, or (otherwise) by making the Realization of God, or Truth, or Reality depend upon some body (or functional sheath), or some conditional realm, or some conditional experience.

Unlike the way of "radical" understanding (or the Way of the Heart), which is based upon the root-understanding (and always most direct transcending) of the motive and the activity of seeking, all remedial paths seek either the perfection of what is conditionally existing or liberation from what is conditionally existing—and that perfection or liberation is pursued as a goal, which goal is presumed to be identical to God, or Truth, or Reality. Only the way of "radical" understanding (or the Way of the Heart) is free, even from the beginning, of all conditional (or, otherwise, conditionally to be achieved) goals. Only the way of "radical" understanding (or the Way of the Heart) is inherently free of the goal-orientation itself. Indeed, only the Heart Itself is inherently free of all goal-seeking, and even all seeking. And only the way of "radical" understanding is the Way of the Heart Itself.

When tacit and most perfect Self-Recognition of the inherent Condition That Is Real God, and Truth, and Reality was re-Awakened in me, there was no excitement, no surprise, no movement, no response. There was a most perfect end to every kind of seeking, dilemma, suffering, separation, and doubt. Spiritual life, mental life, emotional and psychic life, vital life, and physical life all became transparent in me. After that, there was only the Spiritually "Bright" Reality—and to Be the Spiritually "Bright" Reality to all beings and all things.

In all the days that followed the Great Event of my Divine re-Awakening, there has not been a single change in This "Bright" Awareness, or any diminishment of This "Bright" Awareness. Indeed, This "Bright" Awareness cannot be changed, diminished, or lost. I immediately noticed that "experience" had ceased to affect me. Whatever passed—be it a physical sensation, some quality of emotion, a thought, a vision, or whatever—it did not involve me (As I Am) at all. I began to pay particular attention to what passed, in order to "test" my State (or, simply, in order to account for all aspects of my State in the total functional context of the living body-mind). But the primary Awareness of the (inherently) Spiritually "Bright" Reality, my Very Consciousness Itself, could not be changed, diminished, or lost. Consciousness (Itself)—the One and Only and inherently indivisible and perfectly non-separate Conscious Light—is the only "Thing" in life that is not an "experience" (or something "Witnessed" by Consciousness Itself). Consciousness (Itself)—or the Self-Existing and Self-Radiant Conscious Light Itself—does not depend on anything, and there is not (nor can there be) any "thing", or any "experience", that can destroy Consciousness (or Conscious Light) Itself. Consciousness (or Conscious Light) Itself Is (Itself) Love-Bliss, Joy, Freedom, and Sublime Knowledge!

An entirely new and most perfect Realization of Reality had become the constant of my life. The revolutions of my life that led up to my experience in seminary had drawn me into a sense of the "Presence". That Presence could be called "God", "Truth", "Reality", "Shakti", "Guru", and so on. There was simply the sense of being related to a Presence that was Truth Itself and Reality Itself—a perfectly absorbing, heartening, and illuminating Force that contained me, "Lived" me, and guided me. Such is the core of even all true religious and Spiritual experience.

But now this Presence had Communicated Itself in me utterly—revealing Itself utterly to me and As me, such that I was re-Awakened to the Truth of my inherent (and inherently most perfect) Self-Identification with the Spiritually "Bright" Self-Condition (and Source-Condition) That Is the Divine Presence Itself. And This "Bright" Self-Condition (and Source-Condition) Showed Itself to Be my Eternal Condition, even always already before my birth.

Until now, my life (since my early childhood) had been a constant search toward (and periodic re-alignment with) the "Bright" as a Presence with Which I was in relationship. It was as if I always saw the "Bright" from some position within the form of my own living being, but outside of its center. It was as if I had always beheld my own heart from some position outside. Now the barriers had been utterly dissolved by an exhaustive investigation of the Nature of that Presence. The investigation of the Presence had resolved into the Knowledge of my own Self-Nature. The Presence had revealed Itself to be my Very Form and Self-Nature.

The experience of the Presence was (by means of the most perfect Realization of "radical" self-understanding) replaced by the most perfect Realization of Spiritually "Bright" Self-Awareness As Conscious Light. There was no longer any Presence "outside" me. I no longer "observed" my own "Bright" Self-Nature, or the Ultimate (and inherently "Bright") Spiritual Condition of Reality, as if from some position external to (and separate from) It. I had become utterly Aware of myself As Reality. There was no Presence. I had become Present. There Is no Other. It Is Only Me.

Even my meditation was changed. There was no meditation. This Consciousness could not be deepened or enlarged. It always only remained What It Is. I meditated (as a formal activity) only to see how "meditation" had been affected by my Realization, or (otherwise) to formally regard the conditions in the body, the mind, even any part of my living (or extended) being, or even any conditions at all. But I was no longer the meditative seeker, the one who seeks (or, otherwise, does not Know) God, Truth, Reality, Liberation, Release, or Growth. I no longer supposed any limitation as myself. I Am He. I Am She. I Am It. I Am That Only One.

I noticed a physical change in myself. My belly dropped and expanded, and (thus and thereby) permanently assumed the "pot-shaped" Yogic form. I always feel the Pressure of Shakti-Energy there, and I breathe It continually. It is the breathing of my Very Being, the endless and profound Communication of the inherent Spiritual "Brightness" of Reality to Itself.

In "meditation", I looked to observe how I was related to the worlds of conditional experience. Immediately, I realized that I was not in any sense "in" a body—not only the physical body, but any body (or any functional sheath), including the most subtle.

Nor have I ever been in a body, or in any functional sheath, or in any conditional realm, or in any conditional experience. All such things are patterns conditionally manifested within my own Self-Nature.

Nevertheless, I realized that, in the context of natural appearances, I am Communicated through a specific center in the body. Relative to the body, I appear to reside in the heart—but to the right side of the chest. I press upon a point approximately an inch and one-half to the right of the center of the chest. This is the seat of Reality and Real Consciousness. And I Abide there as no-seeking. There is no motivation, no dilemma, no separation, no strategic action, no suffering. I am no-seeking in the Heart. I described my constant experience as follows:

The zero of the Heart is expanded as the world. Consciousness is not differentiated and identified. There is a constant observation of subject _and_ object in any body, any functional sheath, any realm, or any experience that arises. Thus, I remain in the unqualified State.

There is a constant Sensation of Spiritually "Bright" Fullness permeating and surrounding all experiences, all realms, all bodies, all functional sheaths. It is my own "Bright" Fullness, Which is inherently non-separate. My own "Bright" Fullness includes all beings and all things.

I am the Form of Space Itself—in Which all bodies, all functional sheaths, all realms, and all experiences occur. It is (inherently) Spiritually "Bright" Consciousness (or Conscious Light) Itself, Which Reality is even every being's Very Nature (or Ultimate, inherent, and inherently perfect, Condition)—now, and now, and now.

And again:

During the night of mankind, I Awakened as perfect, absolute, limitless, indivisible, un-conditional Love-Bliss Itself—in Which the body and the mind, even every functional sheath, boiled into a solder of undifferentiated

Reality. It was the madness of dissolution into most perfect Self-Awareness, Infinitely Expanded, <u>As</u> my own inherently boundless Presence—wherein there is only "Brightness", not qualified by conditional identification, or self-differentiation, or ego-based desire.

Hereafter, I am Free of bondage to the cosmic Power. I am unexploitable. The Shakti that appears apart, as any form of apparently independent (or merely cosmic) Power and Presence, is no longer the Great Importance. The Presence of Power "outside" appears to be such only to seekers—for they, having already separated themselves, <u>pursue</u> forms of Energy, visions, nature-powers, liberation, and God. True Knowledge is free of all bondage to forms (or modifications) of Energy, all seeking, all motivation to "do" (based on identification with conditional experience). Egoic ignorance and suffering are simply this separateness, this difference, this search. At last, the "outside" Shakti sacrifices Herself in the Heart. Thereafter, there is no gnawing wonder, no un-Known "secret" about anything that appears.

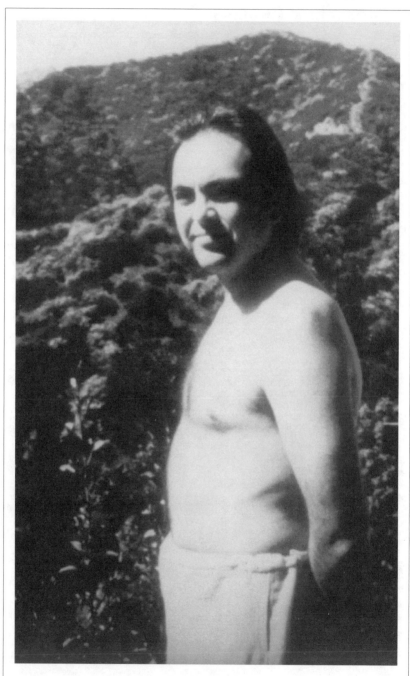

Los Angeles, 1971

CHAPTER SEVENTEEN

The End of All Seeking

T he time of the Great Event of my Divine re-Awakening forever passes into the present and the future. My "autobiography" has no end in time. But the re-Awakening that was finally (and most perfectly) Realized in September 1970 brought a final (and most perfect) end to my adventure as a seeker. What remains to be written about my early life was experienced from an inherently most perfect "Point of View"—a "Point of View" that had never previously been Realized in human (or even cosmic) time.

Previous to the Great Event of my Divine re-Awakening, I was always involved in one or another form of the "problem" of conditional existence. I was always in search and research, and my conclusions or insights were always temporary moments that led into a new form of investigation. Thus, I went from the "Bright" of childhood to the dilemma of my youth. I went from self-exploitation and the experience in college to the period of writing and self-observation. I went from Rudi and the revelation in seminary to Baba and the Ashram. I went from experiments with life and mind to the fuller life of ascending Yoga and psychic development. I went from the revelations of the Divine Shakti and the purifying drama of mystical vision to the Realization of the inherently perfect Divine Self-Condition (and Source-Condition) That Is Reality Itself.

Now there were no loose ends to my adventure. There was no dilemma, no motivation, no search. All the parts of the mind were as if transposed and dissolved in a most fundamental Singleness. But I continued to live. The external and internal events of my life were not modified in any revolutionary manner by this Realization. It was only that I understood them in an entirely new and most profoundly "radical" manner. I understood most perfectly, and most perfect understanding became the foundation of my living existence.

The weeks that followed the Great Event were an intensive period of considering everything about "radical" self-understanding. I began to recollect and observe the forms of my adventure of self-understanding. I began to recognize the precise (and profoundly "radical") nature of my understanding. Altogether, the way of that "radical" understanding began to reveal all its unique characteristics, such that (in due course) I could begin to reveal and give to others the unique (and altogether "radical") Way of Adidam (or Adidam Ruchiradam—which is the complete, and all-completing, way of "radical" understanding, or the True Way of the Heart). Indeed, my life became a continuous unfolding of the wisdom of "radical" self-understanding in relation to every kind of experience. I began to write this book.

My Realization was not any kind of object in the mind. It had neither form nor symbol. There was a constant depth and directness in my free conscious Awareness, such that I felt as if I were constantly in the most profoundly Awake and Intelligent State otherwise (previous to the Great Event of my Divine re-Awakening) re-located only occasionally in meditation. My own Self-Nature had been the Real "Object" of meditation, and now I was no longer separated from It. I simply survived as my own unqualified (and unqualifiedly "Bright") Self-Nature.

Apart from my own (inherently perfect, and inherently egoless, and Self-Evidently Divine) Self-Nature (Which Is the Ultimate Self-Nature of all), everything "else" appeared as modifications of my own Consciousness. Whatever I experienced (in the natural human context) remained in the same form in which it would appear to anyone, or to myself previous to this most perfect understanding. But now I understood everything directly, effortlessly, in Truth. I experienced the natural flow of events as before, but everything was (inherently) Divinely Self-Recognized by me as it truly Is. A continuous process of Divine Self-Recognition and Divine Wisdom went on in me, and all I did was remain Present to everything that passed.

Whereas previously everything was communicated to me as a particular objective form, and I (seeming to be an entirely separate, subjective identity) experienced it over against myself—now I saw everything directly, from the "Point of View" of Reality Itself (Prior to separation and relatedness), As the One in Whom everything arises as a transparent (or merely apparent), and un-necessary, and inherently non-binding modification of Its own Self-Radiance (or inherent "Brightness"). Thus, previously, I knew the mind and was identified with the apparently separated subject of the mind. I was identified with the apparently separate subject of my physical body and its vital energy. I was identified with the apparently separate subject functioning in the subtle worlds and the subtle bodies (or sheaths). I was identified with the apparently separate subject of all my visions and experiences. And I interpreted myself and my experiences from the viewpoint of such identification. But now all of these things—the forms, the levels of functional being and conditional identity (including the physical body, and even all the functional sheaths, and all the conditional realms, and all conditional experiences)—stood within the Radiant Sphere of my own Presence, and I understood and inherently (and Divinely) Self-Recognized them all, without recourse to them (as if they were "outside" my own Self-Nature), and without recourse to any sense of self-separateness (as a limited subjective identity in apparent relationship to them).

Even as before, I continued to experience various manifestations of Shakti and subtle vision. I could hear all kinds of sounds within the various bodies (or functional sheaths). I was able to see subtle mechanisms within these bodies (or functional sheaths) and perceive the relations of various forms and currents of energy beyond the physical. I saw the tiny organisms by which energy and conditional awareness are transferred and communicated between the various levels of existence. And I also continued to experience and act on a physical level, just as before. There were the same functions and desires, the same pleasures and feelings, the same lawful natural mechanisms—requiring the same intelligence, and entailing the same consequences (in the case of error or self-indulgence). But everything was new. Everything was utterly free of any kind of dilemma, separation, unconsciousness, and primary fear.

I began to note, in detail, the characteristics and requirements of the entire process (or way) of "radical" understanding that I knew to be the way of Real life. And I "tested" myself in all circumstances, in order to note all the characteristics and signs of my spontaneously proceeding demonstration of the most perfect Realization of Reality (Itself), Which is (Itself) the only Truth and the only Real God.

In this most perfect Realization of Non-separateness, many extraordinary Divine Siddhis suddenly, spontaneously appeared, and also many unusual natural (or "ordinary") siddhis (or uncommon psycho-physical abilities and processes). I saw that the movement (or process) of the cosmos was itself a meditation, a Divine vision, and a purifying event that was always being enacted. Yet, most fundamental, and most necessary to the fulfillment of my "Bright" Purpose in this world, was the spontaneous Awakening of the Avataric Divine Guru-Function (or the Avataric Divine Guru-Siddhi), Which manifested in me in a unique manner immediately after the Great Event of my Divine re-Awakening.

Now—whenever I would sit, in any kind of formal manner, to demonstrate the meditation, or the (now) Divine Samadhi, that had become my entire life—instead of confronting what was arising in (and as) "myself", I "meditated" other beings and places. I would spontaneously become aware of great numbers of people (usually in visions, or in some other intuitive manner), and I would work with them very directly, in a subtle manner. The binding motions and separative results of my own apparent (or merely life-born) egoity (or total psycho-physical self-contraction) had been transcended in my re-Awakening to my Original (and inherently ego-less and Self-Evidently Divine) Self-Condition (Which is the One and Only Self-Condition and Source-Condition of even each and all of everyone and everything). Therefore, in the spontaneous Awakening of the Avataric Divine Guru-Siddhi, what arose to my view—instead of my own life-born forms and problematic signs— were the egoic forms, the problematic signs, the minds, the feelings, the states, and the various limitations of others. The thoughts, feelings, suffering, dis-ease, disharmony, upsets, pain, energies—none of these were "mine". They were the subtle internal qualities and the grosser life-qualities of others. In this manner, the process of apparent meditation continued in me. It was, in effect, the same "Real" meditation I had done before the Great Event of my Divine re-Awakening. Therefore, "problems" (of all kinds) constantly appeared, and numberless complexities and contradictions arose in every moment—but the content of the meditation was not "mine".

I found that this "meditating" of others by me usually went on with people whom I had not yet met. But, soon, some of those very people came into my physical company—and all the rest were (or, certainly, are yet) to come, to be my devotees, and (thus) to practice the only-by-me revealed and given Way of Adidam (or Adidam Ruchiradam, which is the only-by-me revealed and given way of "radical" understanding, or the one and only by-me-revealed and by-me-given Way of the Heart). In some cases, the individuals I "meditated" in vision were people I already knew—and I would "meditate" them in that subtle manner, unobserved by them, and then watch for signs in their outward lives that would demonstrate the effectiveness of my "meditation" of them.

In this manner, I spontaneously began to "meditate" countless other people, and also countless non-human beings, and countless places and worlds and realms, both high and low in the scale of Reality. I observed and responded to all that was required for the (ultimately) most perfect Divine Awakening and the true (and the, ultimately, most perfect) well-being of each and all. And, each time I did this (and, in fact, the process quickly became the underlying constant of all my hours and days), I would continue the "meditating" of any (and each) one until I felt a release take place—such that his or her suffering and seeking was vanished (or, at least, significantly relaxed and set aside). Whenever that occurred, I Knew my "meditating" of that one was, for the moment, done. By such means, my now and forever Avataric Divine Work (of Teaching, Blessing, and Awakening all-and-All) was begun.

In early October, after all of this had been going on for only about one month, Baba came to California. He was in the midst of a world tour. Rudi had brought him to America.

I had lately written to Rudi, and we had become reconciled. The dissonance between us had been generated solely by the differences between our "ways". During the period of time that passed since our separation, Rudi had (he said) changed in his relationship to Spiritual work. He confessed that his own experience had developed further, and he now approached Baba with greater simplicity, free of the characteristic habits of his own seeking that had previously been part of his "work". He claimed that he had delivered himself utterly to Baba's guidance. His Yoga was now one of the acceptance of the Guru's grace, rather than a willful, self-advancing effort. (And I accepted his "conversion" as being sincere enough for the moment, although—and many signs pointed to this—he would soon break off his relationship with Baba and return to his characteristic and independent path of seeking.)

I met Baba and Rudi quite openly, but without any desire or reason to become involved in the drama of Baba's "American tour". They stayed for several days in Pacific Palisades, and then for two weeks in northern California and Utah. They returned again at the end of October, and flew on to Hawaii on November 3 (coincidentally, my birthday).

I was interested in seeing how Baba's Spiritual Presence would affect me, and how he would respond to my Signs and Confessions of inherently most perfect Realization. I sat with him while large groups of people chanted and gazed at him devotedly. I held his foot, I chanted, and I "meditated".

In the first hours of his visit, Baba blessed me with his characteristic Transmission of the Shakti. And I moved spontaneously with the experience, freely abandoning myself to the familiar physical movements and the merging of forms in the mind. I shook and fell on the floor. I watched Baba. I enjoyed his Communication of the Shakti. I listened to him advise people to turn within and seek the "blue pearl" and the "blue person"[36] in the sahasrar, the most ascended focus of attention (in the crown of the head). I listened to him detail the various forms of internal vision, internal sounds, and internal experiences, and I experienced them along with him.

But I saw that none of this made the slightest difference in me. There were such experiences, and all of them were familiar to me—but no mere conditional experience had either a goal or an importance that was necessary for me. It was only a drama, a play, a pattern.

Finally, in the company of a small gathering, I told Baba about my present State. I said there was no longer any important movement in me, no necessary phenomenal activity of the Shakti, no significant descending or ascending, no changes in fundamental Consciousness—in fact, no meditation. Whether in or out of formal meditation, there was the same Consciousness. And It was not settled (in any exclusive sense) in the sahasrar, or in any other extended (or functional) level of the body-mind itself, but in the True Heart Itself—not the heart chakra or the merely physical heart, but the Heart of Real Consciousness (or the Self-Evident Feeling of Being). Always already Prior to the body-mind, I "Stood" Infinitely Above (As the One and Only and inherently indivisible Conscious Light of Being). And, in apparent relation to the body (or in the apparent context of the body), I was merely Present— as tacit, unqualified Awareness, Radiating from the heart region, to (and via) the right side of the chest (and, only from thence, to the sahasrar—and, from thence, to the extended body-mind).

Baba responded by telling us that various saints describe the stabilization of attention either in the sahasrar or at the heart. (I, of course, had not been referring to the locus of attention, but to the most perfect Realization of Consciousness Itself, inherently transcending attention itself.) Then Baba went on to say that the heart is like a lotus of many petals. Ordinarily (he said), the mind moves from petal to petal, taking on the various modifications of love, anger, lust, and so on—but, when it settles in the center, it becomes still, and the humanly-born conscious awareness takes on various "creative" powers (such as poetic or musical genius) or such psychic powers as omniscience, clairvoyance, and so on. He said that the concentration of attention in the center of the heart (or, otherwise, in the center of the sahasrar) was a very desirable State—and the proof of it was whether or not it was retained even after meditation, and whether or not you brought its qualities into life.

These various indications about the heart agreed with my own experience. However, I had not been speaking about the "center" of the heart (which is the root-center of emotion and of psychic awakening). Rather, I had been speaking about the most perfect Realization of Consciousness Itself, and Its apparent association with the right side of the heart. Also, at the same time Baba spoke of these conditional (and merely evolutionary) attainments, he made suggestions indicating that only rare saints achieve them. Indeed, he turned his talk to casually minimize the possibility of actual attainment in the case of almost anyone. It was as if he felt that the rather public gathering of people surrounding our conversation would be pleased to think that the Truth was only in following, and not in attainment at all. And there was even an underlying suggestion that those who professed attainment must be regarded with suspicion. However, Baba's seemingly light (or even casual) expression of all of this did not succeed in concealing the emotional motivator of this apparent criticism of me—which was, simply, his reaction to my potential departure from his person, and my evident dissent (or evident departure) from his interpretation of the "orthodoxy" of his (and, at the time, my) school.

At this point in his discourse, Baba looked at me—to see whether I would accept his "judgement", or whether I would otherwise assert and affirm my Realization in the face of it. Then, observing that I could not be provoked to recant, but that I only remained firm in my disposition, he went on again to talk to others about the conventions of Siddha Yoga, with his now characteristic emphasis on the "blue pearl". He also spoke of how devotion to the Guru is the necessary basis of all effective practice (and, in this, I agreed—and agree—with him completely). Finally, he led everyone in devotional chanting, and then he left the room.

My confession did not agree with Baba's teaching, and (therefore) seemed to challenge his authority as a conventional representative of traditional Siddha Yoga. His was not the "radical" way of understanding, nor was it even the way of Advaita Vedanta (which—it seemed to me, when I first met him—had been the basis of his first, and principal, instruction to me). Rather, Baba's way was the way of seeking. In particular, it was the way of remedial Yoga, or of Shakti-Initiation for the sake of conditional attainments. He spoke only of experiential meditation, or natural "Kriya

Yoga"—the automatic (or spontaneously generated) version of the Yoga practice otherwise described (in terms of a seeker's technique) by Yogananda (and others). Baba spoke of supersensual enjoyments (and even the Spiritualization of worldly enjoyments), the pursuit of internal touch, sound, and vision, the experiencing of psychic visions and purifications, and the attainment of siddhis (or Yogic powers) and higher cosmic experiential knowledge as a result of contacting the "blue pearl" (or the "blue person" in the sahasrar). He was concerned with all of the mechanics of seeking. And he recommended that everyone continue chanting, meditating with mantras, serving the Guru, and depending on the Guru's grace—all of which, in my own experience, had been proven to be generally right practices. But he recommended all of that for the sake of the phenomenal (and, necessarily, ego-based) experiences that would be received as a result—and not as a counteregoic discipline based on most fundamental (or "radical", or "gone-to-the-root") self-understanding, and not engaged as the foundation of a practice that (more and more, and, at last, most perfectly) demonstrates (by means of Divine Spiritual grace) the transcending of egoity itself.

Whenever I suggested that all phenomenal experiences are to be transcended in the always present (non-separate, and inherently egoless) Realization of Reality Itself (Prior to all seeking and all conditional experience), Baba had cut me off. He stated directly that such a way does not lead to the highest Truth. And (as if I were representing the world-excluding point of view of traditional Advaita Vedanta) he said to me, "You are present as form. Why do you seek a way without form?" Indeed, I was not seeking (nor had I found) a "way without form". But, clearly, Baba was indicating that he would be opposed to such a way. And it was also clear to me that he was uncomfortable about the idea of experiencing any kind of "formlessness" in his own life and meditation.

It was made completely clear by his responses to me at that time that Baba did not assign importance to the ultimate Realization associated with the right side of the heart. Indeed, he made only a cursory reference to my statements about the right side of the heart. It had no part in his teaching, his experience, or his Spiritual ideology. He did not acknowledge the right side of the heart (or, truly, even the heart-region) as the very foundation of Yoga. He did not speak of the True and all-transcending Divine Self at all, but only of the phenomena of the "supracausal" realm (the abode of the Siddhas), and all the ascended phenomenal structures of the conditional self.

On the last evening of Baba's stay in Los Angeles, I went to him to take my leave. I thought that it would possibly be the last time we would (physically) see each other. I was certain that, if we ever met again, I would not approach him as a seeker, or in the manner of an unfinished disciple—but only Freely, as one who requires no addition to himself.

I bowed to Baba as if for the last time, with gratitude for all that I had been given. I had received his gift. I had known his experience, I had understood it, and I had transcended it in its inherently perfect Source.

I embraced Rudi as I left. I knew that he thoroughly enjoyed the form of his own seeking. I loved him Freely, and I acknowledged our friendship.

Then I left them, without regret. I Enjoyed only my own most perfect Certainty, inherently Free of all seeking. I went home to Comprehend my own Satisfaction.

Los Angeles, 1972

CHAPTER EIGHTEEN

The Way Becomes Conscious

After Baba and Rudi had gone, I stood in the Form of my own Real Existence, without even the least sentimental attachment to the previous ways of my seeking. I was not dependent on any remedial path or conditional experience to guarantee or interpret What I Knew. Indeed, nothing was available by which to interpret It.

I looked to myself to see What It was, and I looked to perhaps discover some analogy in the Spiritual experience of mankind that would demonstrate a link, and even provide examples, by which I could explain myself.

I knew that the final and most ultimate Realization that had occurred at the Vedanta Society Temple was inherently most perfect (final, or truly complete) Divine Self-Realization (or Divine Enlightenment). Mine is the unqualified Realization of Consciousness Itself as inherently non-separate (non-separate from the conditional manifestations of Reality, and always already Identical to What always and already Is). Consciousness Itself is not Communicated to Itself through any level of conditionally manifested being, any body (or functional sheath), any conditional realm, or any conditional experience—but It Knows Itself directly, As Itself, Which Is Prior to all separative action (or the action of avoidance, which is egoic self-identification, the action of differentiation, and the separative, or ego-based, action that is desire). There is no thing or experience that can ever limit or bind Consciousness (or the One and Only and inherently indivisible Conscious Light) Itself. Consciousness Itself is not even the "Witness", not any state of either the experienced or the experiencer, but It Is only Reality Itself. Experiencer and experiences are contained, limited, and ended in one another. But, in Reality, there

THE KNEE OF LISTENING

is no experience, no identity, no differentiation, no desire, no separation, no suffering, no seeking, no strategic action, no strategic inaction.

As weeks passed, I saw that I remained unqualifiedly as This—not limited or bound by any experience, or by functional (and apparently separate) identity, or by any apparent "difference" at all. I saw there was, for me, no Shakti independent of (or "outside") Consciousness Itself. I saw there was, for me, no Guru separate from (or "outside") the inherently indivisible Divine Self-Condition (Itself). I saw there was, for me, no dilemma, no strife, no egoic ignorance, no movement to seek, no activity of seeking. I saw that, because my Realization had become most perfect, formal "meditation" made no "difference" in any of this. I saw that conditionally arising Shakti phenomena did not affect me fundamentally, nor did any other conditional pleasure or experience. The same Spiritually "Bright" Awareness, and the same most "radical" self-understanding, continued—without limitation or dependency—under all conditions.

I Knew Reality as no-seeking, the motiveless Awareness in the heart. The physical body appeared to be generated and (in the ordinary sense) known from a position in the right side of the chest. In this State, neither the ego nor any path of remedies can act as an interpreter. The State of Divine Self-Realization only validates Itself.

In effect (or tacitly, and sometimes even verbally), the form of self-Enquiry that had developed in the process of my "radical" self-understanding went on continually in the heart: "Avoiding relationship?" And, as this "Eternal Enquiry" penetrated to every kind of arising experience, I would feel the Spiritually "Bright" Love-Bliss-Energy of my own Self-Existing and Self-Radiant Consciousness rise (or Shine) out of the heart (on the right) and enter the sahasrar (extending, from thence, to the Matrix of Light infinitely above the crown of the head), and (thus) stabilize above as a continuous Current to the Heart Itself. I saw that this Form—the ultimate (or perfect) Form of Reality, the very (or ultimate, and perfect) Structure of Consciousness Itself—Is Reality Itself. It is the Structure of all things—the Foundation, Nature, and Identity of all things. It is the "Point of View" of everything. It is "Bright", Love-

Blissful, and Free. That ultimate and inherently perfect (or One, and inherently indivisible) Form of Consciousness-<u>and</u>-Energy is exactly (but not yet with most perfect understanding) What I had, in my childhood, Known in my living form as the "Bright".

As I continued in this manner, I saw that I always already remained stably as that Form—and, because of This, all things revealed themselves in Truth. I saw that the "Bright" is the ultimate and perfect Form of Reality, the Heart of all existence, the Foundation of Truth, and the (yet unrealized) goal of all seekers.

This Form (the "Bright") was (Itself) "radical" self-understanding. It was no-seeking and no-dilemma as primary, inherent, un-"created", Self-Abiding Divine Self-Recognition. It was inherently free of the entire search for perfection and union. When the "Bright" is Realized, all of life is simply observed and enjoyed (if noticed at all), and the things of life no longer provide a source of motivation separate (and separating) from this primary Awareness. Therefore, the "Bright" is the very Medium for unqualified Presence and Enjoyment—without dilemma, unconsciousness, or separation.

I also saw that I had never been taught my way from without. The "Bright" (with Its Foundation in the Heart Itself) had been my teacher under the form of all my apparent teachers and experiences. My Awareness, fundamental Knowledge, and apparent "method" had developed spontaneously in the midst of a few crisis-experiences. From the beginning, I had been convinced of the fruitlessness and necessary suffering involved in every way of seeking. I had made only temporary use of the methods of others, and (at last) I adapted to no one else's way, but I only used my own, which is the way of "radical" understanding (or the Way of the Heart, which is the Way that is generated in, of, and by the Heart Itself, or the Way of Adidam, which is the Way that only I reveal and give). Thus, I had experienced the real blessings of such as Rudi, Baba Muktananda, Rang Avadhoot, and Bhagavan Nityananda, but only while firmly involved in my own unique (and spontaneously Self-revealed) approach.

The "Bright" had seemed to fade, progressively, in childhood and adolescence—but It had, in Truth, only retired to latency in the heart, while I followed my adventure from the viewpoint of the mind. The Heart Itself had been my only teacher, and It continually broke through in various revelations—until, at last, I returned to It, became It, and, finally, re-Emerged As the "Bright".

Thus, I came to this Realization of Reality directly, without the knowledge of a single human Source that would confirm it or even parallel it. But, as I came to this clear and crucial Self-Recognition of my own Divine Truth, I began to recollect (and to further examine and appreciate) a human Source that agreed (by word and by likeness) with something of the substance (and even many of the details) of my own experience and Realization. That individual is known as Ramana Maharshi, the spontaneously Awakened Jnani who discarded the body at Tiruvannamalai, South India, in 1950.

In the course of his sadhana, Baba Muktananda spent a brief period with Ramana Maharshi. It was from Ramana Maharshi that Baba received the traditional non-dualistic (or Advaitic) teaching of Vedanta in its most direct and living form. (But he found his own chosen Guru in the Siddha Nityananda, who had himself known Ramana Maharshi years earlier.)

Baba Muktananda demonstrated the phenomena of ascending Yoga to me and in me. But, eventually, I saw that the lower-based (and, from thence, ascending) Shakti and all conditional (or merely phenomenal) experiences arise transparent in the Real Self (or Divine Self-Condition), Which Is Consciousness (or the One and Only and inherently indivisible Conscious Light) Itself. The Real Self (or Divine Self-Condition) is not antagonistic to Its own Light (always already "Bright" above, and reflected in all the gross and subtle worlds below).

Thus, when I Realized It, the Truth Is that Real Self (or Divine Self-Condition), Which Is Reality Itself. And the "Bright" is the ultimate and perfect Form of Reality.

Thus, most perfect Realization was not a matter of conditionally arising experiences (whether high or low in the cosmic pattern of phenomenal appearances), nor was It a matter of the attainment of "cosmic powers" (or merely conditional and phenomenal abilities, whether of a higher type or a merely elemental and lower type). There was—and is—only "radical" self-understanding.

I Realized the same Real and Self-Evidently Divine Self (or Self-Condition) that is (ultimately) proclaimed and (to one or another degree, but not most perfectly) Realized by the "great tradition" that preceded my birth. The Divine Form and Self of Reality (Itself) is, only now, most perfectly Realized (and uniquely brought to a State of complete revelation) in me, As me. But the "great tradition" of progressive Realizations and revelations of the One Reality is my "inheritance", even from all the Realizers and revealers who have preceded me in time. Like them all, Baba Muktananda, Bhagavan Nityananda, and Ramana Maharshi (each in the manner, and to the degree, of his own Realization) have Realized and revealed the same and Only One.

Therefore, I see Baba Muktananda is that One. Bhagavan Nityananda is that One. Ramana Maharshi is that One.

It is Very God, the Divine Self-Light, the Only One—Who I Am.

There was (from my point of view) no "personal" disagreement between Baba and me. It was simply that the ascending Yoga (and even every kind of phenomenally-based Yoga) had been truly Completed in me—and I was drawn into the Absolute Knowledge that is the true, most ultimate, and inherently most perfect Fulfillment of every way and every kind of Yoga proposed in the "great (and yet always seeking) tradition" of ego-bound (and egoically motivated) mankind. When I Fully appeared in my own Form, I simply understood (in a most direct, or most perfectly "radical" manner) the "Secret" that is hidden in the experiences of ascending Yoga (and in even all the Play of the cosmic domain). When I Knew my own Divine Self-Nature, then I also Divinely Self-Recognized Baba, Nityananda, and Ramana in Reality.

Ramana Maharshi had become somewhat familiar to me in the past, through a cursory examination of his various writings and recorded dialogues. He appeared to me to be a prime example of the living Truth of Advaita Vedanta, the non-dualistic philosophy of India. I had brought one of his books with me on my last trip to India (although not specifically for his own writings, but only for the translations of ancient Advaitic texts included in his collected works). I had never been attracted to him in particular, and I never thought of him except in the simplest terms of the traditional non-dualistic philosophy that seemed, in a general manner, to parallel my own understanding of Ultimate Truth. But now—as I began to assess my experience, my understanding, and my Realization in detail—I returned to his works, looking for likenesses to my own experience. And I found that the details of his life and Realization showed remarkable parallels to some of my own experiences. For example, the "death" event in Ramana Maharshi's youth, which gave birth to his Realization of the Transcendental Self, was very much like the one through which I had passed in seminary.

He described it himself as follows:

It was about six weeks before I left Madurai for good that the great change in my life took place. It was so sudden. One day I sat up alone on the first floor of my uncle's house. I was in my usual health. I seldom had any illness. I was a heavy sleeper. When I was at Dindigul in 1891 a huge crowd had gathered close to the room where I slept and tried to rouse me by shouting and knocking at the door, all in vain, and it was only by their getting into my room and giving me a violent shake that I was roused from my torpor. This heavy sleep was rather a proof of good health. I was also subject to fits of half-awake sleep at night. My wily playmates, afraid to trifle with me when I was awake, would go to me when I was asleep, rouse me, take me all round the playground, beat me, cuff me, sport with me, and bring me back to my bed—and all the while I would put up with everything with a meekness, humility, forgiveness, and passivity unknown to my waking state. When the morning broke I had no remembrance of the night's experiences. But these fits did not render me weaker or less fit for life and were hardly to be considered a disease. So, on that day as I sat alone there was nothing wrong with my health. But a sudden and unmistakeable fear of death seized me. I felt I was going to die. Why I should have so felt cannot now be explained by anything felt in my body. Nor could I explain it to myself then. I did

Ramana Maharshi at age 21

not however trouble myself to discover if the fear was well grounded. I felt "I [am] going to die," and at once set about thinking out what I should do. I did not care to consult doctors or elders or even friends. I felt I had to solve the problem myself then and there.

The shock of fear of death made me at once introspective, or "introverted". I said to myself mentally, *i.e.,* without uttering the words—"Now, death has come. What does it mean? What is it that is dying? This body dies." I at once dramatized the scene of death. I extended my limbs and held them rigid as though *rigor-mortis* had set in. I imitated a corpse to lend an air of reality to my further investigation, I held my breath and kept my mouth closed, pressing the lips tightly together so that no sound might escape. Let not the word "I" or any other word be uttered! "Well then," said I to myself, "this body is dead. It will be carried stiff to the burning ground and there burnt and reduced to ashes. But with the death of this body, am 'I' dead? Is the body 'I'? This body is silent and inert. But I feel the full force of my personality and even the sound 'I' within myself—apart from the body. So 'I' am a spirit, a thing transcending the body. The material body dies, but the spirit transcending it cannot be touched by death. I am therefore the deathless spirit." All this was not a mere intellectual process, but flashed before me vividly as living truth, something which I perceived immediately, without any argument almost. "I" was something very real, the only real thing in that state, and all the conscious activity that was connected with my body was centred on that. The "I" or my "self" was holding the focus of attention by a powerful fascination from that time forwards. Fear of death had vanished at once and forever. Absorption in the self has continued from that moment right up to this time. Other thoughts may come and go like the various notes of a musician, but the "I" continues like the basic or fundamental *sruti*[37] note which accompanies and blends with all other notes. Whether the body was engaged in talking, reading or anything else, I was still centred on "I". Previous to that crisis I had no clear perception of myself and was not consciously attracted to it. I had felt no direct percepti- ble interest in it, much less any permanent disposition to dwell upon it. The consequences of this new habit were soon noticed in my life.[38]

Unlike my own characteristic language of Realization, Ramana Maharshi's characteristic language of Realization is associated with the description of Reality in exclusionary (world-excluding and body-excluding) terms, as may be seen in his description of the Realization associated with his early-life "death" experience. However, Ramana Maharshi's language of Realization contains some key terms and concepts—which he acquired from traditional sources, and which (because they stand as general equivalents to certain phenomena in my own experience) I may now use, in order to more easily explain and describe the unique way that I have Realized (and that I have come here to Realize and to reveal and to teach).

Ramana Maharshi understood and taught through the medium of Vedanta (especially Advaita Vedanta), and he saw the importance of his Realization in the classic Eastern terms of a pure Awareness of "Self", Prior to (and, in his characteristic disposition, even exclu- sive of) all life. I, however, have Realized that same Self-Condition in a non-exclusionary manner. And I, therefore, am here to reveal Reality (and to teach the way of Reality) as the Self-Existing and Self-Radiant Divine Self-Condition and Source-Condition, and as the living condition of unqualified relatedness, and as the "creative" living Presence of the "Bright" (Which is the Divine Self- Form of Reality—inherently Free of limitation, and, yet, without excluding anything).

When I use the capitalized word "Self", I mean to indicate the Ultimate Nature of Reality Itself as being Identical to That Which is ultimately signified and known as "Consciousness". Every form of ordinary consciousness (usually identified with some role, subject, or type of action) is, in fact, rooted in the always present Consciousness that is the Real Self (or Divine Self-Condition), the

True and Very Heart (Itself). Truly (Ultimately), the Real Self (or Divine Self-Condition) is not inherently differentiated from any particular thing, nor is it inherently differentiated from the "All" of conditional manifestation. It is the Source and Light of all bodies, all functional sheaths, all levels of conditional being, all conditional realms, and all conditional experiences. And, when It is Known directly, tacitly, as one's very (or non-egoic) Nature, It may also be bodily felt to "reside" in the heart—neither in the (gross) physical heart as a whole (extended toward the left side of the chest) nor in the (subtle) heart chakra (in the center of the chest), but in the (causal) root-area that is in the right side of the chest.

In his various written and spoken teachings, Ramana Maharshi describes "the Real Self", or "the Heart"—which terms are usually (but not always) capitalized in the English translations of his word—as follows:

[Devotee]—But is there really a centre, a place for this "I"?

[Maharshi]—There is. It is the centre of the self to which the mind in sleep retires from its activity in the brain. It is the Heart, which is different from the blood vessel, so called, and is not the *Anahata Chakra* in the middle of the chest, one of the six centres spoken of in books on Yoga.[39]

◆ ◆ ◆

M.—You cannot know it with your mind. You cannot realise it by imagination, when I tell you here is the centre (pointing to the right side of the chest). The only direct way to realise it is to cease to fancy and try to be yourself. Then you realise, automatically feel that the centre is there.[40]

◆ ◆ ◆

D.—Can I be sure that the ancients meant this centre by the term "Heart"?

M.—Yes, that is so. But you should try to HAVE, rather than to locate the experience. A man need not go to find out where his eyes are situated when he wants to see. The

Heart is there ever open to you if you care to enter it, ever supporting all your movements even when you are unaware. It is perhaps more proper to say that the Self is the Heart itself than to say that it is in the Heart. Really, the Self is the Centre itself. It is everywhere, aware of itself as "Heart", the Self-awareness. Hence I said "Heart is Thy name." [41]

◆ ◆ ◆

D.—When you say that the Heart is the supreme centre of the *Purusha*, the *Atman*, you imply that it is not one of the six yogic centres.

M.—The yogic *chakras* counting from the bottom to the top are various centres in the nervous system. They represent various steps manifesting different kinds of power or knowledge leading to the *Sahasrara*, the thousand-petalled lotus, where is seated the supreme *Shakti*. But the Self that supports the whole movement of *Shakti* is not placed there, but supports it from the Heart centre.

D.—Then it is different from the *Shakti* manifestation?

M.—Really there is no *Shakti* manifestation apart from the Self. The Self has become all this *Shakti*. . . .

When the yogin rises to the highest centre of trance, *Samadhi*, it is the Self in the Heart that supports him in that state whether he is aware of it or not. But if he is aware in the Heart, he knows that whatever states or whatever centres he is in, it is always the same truth, the same Heart, the one Self, the Spirit that is present through-out, eternal and immutable. The *Tantra Shastra* calls the Heart *Suryamandala* or solar orb, and the *Sahasrara*, *Chandramandala* or lunar orb. These symbols present the relative importance of the two, the *Atmasthana* and the *Shakti Sthana*. [42, 43]

M.—You can feel yourself one with the One that exists: the whole body becomes a mere power, a force-current;

your life becomes a needle drawn to a huge mass of magnet and as you go deeper and deeper, you become a mere centre and then not even that, for you become a mere consciousness, there are no thoughts or cares any longer— they were shattered at the threshold; it is an inundation; you, a mere straw, you are swallowed alive, but it is very delightful, for you become the very thing that swallows you; this is the union of *Jeeva*[44] with *Brahman*, the loss of ego in the real Self, the destruction of falsehood, the attainment of Truth.[45]

◆ ◆ ◆

D.—You said "Heart" is the one centre for the ego-self, for the Real Self, for the Lord, for all. . . .

M.—Yes, the Heart is the centre of the Real. But the ego is impermanent. Like everything else it is supported by the Heart-centre. But the character of the ego is a link between spirit and matter; it is a knot (*granthi*), the knot of radical ignorance in which one is steeped. This *granthi* is there in the *"Hrit"*, the Heart. When this knot is cut asunder by proper means you find that this is the Self's centre.

D.—You said there is a passage from this centre to *Sahasrara.*

M.—Yes. It is closed in the man in bondage; in the man in whom the ego-knot, the *Hridaya granthi*, is cut asunder, a force-current called *Amrita Nadi* rises and goes up to the *Sahasrara*, the crown of the head.

D.—Is this the *Sushumna*?[46]

M.—No. This is the passage of liberation (*Moksha*). This is called *Atmanadi, Brahmanadi* or *Amrita Nadi*. This is the *Nadi* that is referred to in the Upanishads.

When this passage is open, you have no *moha*, no ignorance. You know the Truth even when you talk, think or do anything, dealing with men and things.[47]

◆ ◆ ◆

The association of the Self with the body is called the Granthi (knot). By that association alone one is conscious of his body and actions.

The body is completely inert. The Self is active and conscious. Their association is inferred from the experience of objects.

Oh child, when the rays of consciousness are reflected in the body, the body acts. In sleep etc. the rays are not so reflected and caught and therefore some other seat of the Self is inferred.

Electricity and similar forces, which are subtle, pass through the gross wires. Similarly the light of active-consciousness passes through a nadi[48] in the body.

The effulgent light of active-consciousness starts at a point and gives light to the entire body even as the sun does to the world.

When that light spreads out in the body one gets the experiences in the body. The sages call the original point "Hridayam" (the Heart).

The flow of the rays of the light is inferred from the play of forces in the nadis. Each of the forces of the body courses along a special nadi.

Active consciousness lies in a distinct and separate Nadi which is called Sushumna. Some call it "Atma Nadi" and others "Amrita Nadi".

The Individual permeates the entire body, with that light, becomes ego-centric and thinks that he is the body and that the world is different from himself.

When the discerning one renounces egotism and "I-am-the-body" idea and carries on one-pointed enquiry (into the Self), movement of life-force starts in the nadis.

This movement of the force separates the Self from the other nadis and the Self then gets confined to the Amrita Nadi alone and shines with clear light.

When the very bright light of that active-consciousness shines in the Amrita Nadi alone, nothing else shines forth except the Self.

In that light, if anything else is seen, even then it does not appear as different from the Self. The Enlightened One knows the Self as vividly as the ignorant one perceives his body.

When Atma alone shines, within and without, and everywhere, as body etc. shine to the ignorant, one is said to have severed the knot (Granthi Bheda occurs).

There are two knots. One, the bond of the Nadis and two, egotism. The Self even though subtle being tied up in the Nadis sees the entire gross world.

When the light withdraws from all other Nadis and remains in one Nadi alone, the knot is cut asunder and then the light becomes the Self.

As a ball of iron heated to a degree appears as a ball of fire, this body heated in the fire of Self-enquiry becomes as one permeated by the Self.

Then for the embodied the old tendencies inherent are destroyed, and then that one feels no body and therefore will not have the idea that he is an active agent (Karta).

When the Self does not have the sense of active agency, karmas (tendencies, actions and their results) etc. are destroyed for him. As there is none other except the Self doubts do not sprout for him.

Once the knot is cut, one never again gets entangled. In that state lie the highest power and the highest peace."[49]

◆ ◆ ◆

For one who abides in the Self, the Sahasrara becomes pure and full of the Light. Even if thoughts of objects due to proximity fall therein, they do not survive.

Even when objects are sensed by the mind, due to proximity, yoga is not hindered, as the mind does not perceive the difference between them and the Self.[50]

◆ ◆ ◆

Once, unasked, he defined *Moksha* (Liberation) to one of the attendants. "Do you know what *Moksha* is? Getting rid of non-existent misery and attaining the Bliss which is always there, that is *Moksha*."[51]

The Self-Existing and Self-Radiant Condition that I call "the 'Bright'" is, in the Root of Its Form, What Ramana Maharshi (in correspondence with ancient traditions) calls the "Atma Nadi", the "Brahma Nadi", or (most often) the "Amrita Nadi". However, the "Bright" is, at Its Root, the "regenerated" Form of the "Amrita Nadi"— whereas Ramana Maharshi, and the traditions that preceded him (if they made any reference to this matter at all), refer to the non-"regenerated" Form of the Amrita Nadi (or the exclusively descending aspect of the Amrita Nadi),[52] which non-"regenerated" form seems to suggest a disposition that leads away from the world (or away from all objects), and, by means of a dissociative (or exclusionary) act of introversion, leads toward the world-excluding Realization of the Transcendental Self, even via the terminal in the right side of the chest. However, in the case of the most perfect Realization of "radical" self-understanding (and, on that basis, of the Real Self, or Divine Self-Condition), the Amrita Nadi is spontaneously "regenerated", from the Heart Itself (and via the physical heart-region, but on the right side) to the crown of the head (and above)—thereby permitting the Infusion of "Brightness" in the total body-mind (in a pattern that descends and then ascends—from the crown of the head, and above, to the base of the body, and then back again, in a continuous Circle of Energy). Therefore, only the "regenerated" Form of the Amrita Nadi may truly be called the "Amrita Nadi" (meaning the "Nerve of Immortality", the "Circuit of the Current of Immortal Joy"), or the "Atma Nadi" (meaning the "Circuit, or Nerve, or perfect Form of the Real Self"), or the "Brahma Nadi" (meaning the "Original Circuit of Reality"). Only the "regenerated" Form of the Amrita Nadi is the Source, the Container, and the First (or Original) Form of all Energy, all centers, and all life-currents. Only the "regenerated" Form of the Amrita Nadi (or

of the Atma Nadi, or of the Brahma Nadi) is the ultimate and perfect Form of Reality—rooted in the heart, and extending to (and
even infinitely above) the crown of the head. It is the Circuit (or
perfect Form) of unqualified Enjoyment. It Contains (and <u>Is</u>) the
Source of all things, all bodies, all conditional realms, all conditional experiences, all conditional states, and all levels (or functional sheaths) of conditionally manifested being. Its Nature is
unqualified Enjoyment (or Love-Bliss). It is Self-Existing and Self-
Radiant Being, or unqualified Presence. It is even every one's Real
Condition at this moment, and (by means of Divine grace) It can
be Realized as such, when "radical" self-understanding becomes
(most perfectly) the entire basis of one's conscious life.

Ramana Maharshi assigns Ultimate, and (generally) rather
exclusive (or separate, and world-excluding, or object-excluding),
importance to the Real Self (or the Heart Itself). In some of the
statements attributed to him, he appears to make no absolute distinction between the Real Self and the Amrita Nadi. However,
many (if not all) such statements attributed to him (including some
that I have just quoted) do not properly (or truly) represent his
own point of view (which, most characteristically, affirms the Real
Self in an exclusionary manner—or, that is to say, dissociated from
forms and objects)—but, instead, such statements, in fact (generally, if not always), represent the preferential philosophizing (and
less developed Realizations) of others near to him, and (at most)
such statements may (in some cases) represent an effort, on the
part of Ramana Maharshi, to critically address the object-oriented
point of view expressed to him by an other (or by some others).
In any case, Ramana Maharshi does not, in such statements attributed to him, completely divorce the Real Self from the world—but,
instead (expressing a point of view not otherwise characteristic of
his Confessions of Realization, and not at all characteristic of his
rather ascetically withdrawn manner of daily living), he asserts that
the Real Self is, in principle, compatible with life.

Even though the Real Self (or Divine Self-Condition)—in Its
Oneness with the "regenerated" Form of the Amrita Nadi, and
(altogether) with the "Bright" (the perfect, and truly Divine, Form
of Reality)—is (indeed) compatible with life, It is Prior to all lower-

based (or ascending-from-below, and merely conditionally and temporarily arising) "Spiritual experiences", all powers, visions, and chakras, and all ordinary (as well as extraordinary) perceptions. It is Self-Existing as the fundamental Reality, and It is Self-Radiant as the Ultimate Power and the perfect Form of Reality. The Self-Existing Divine Self-Condition (Self-Radiant as the Ultimate Power and the perfect Form of Reality) is even Prior to <u>all</u> conditional knowledge, since It depends on no experience or memory to Communicate Itself to Itself.

When I first heard the traditional Advaitic teaching about the Real (or True) Self through Baba, he told me that I was not the one who wakes or dreams or sleeps but the One who Witnesses these states. But—when I experienced that Reality, initially, at his Ashram, and later Realized It fully, permanently, and most perfectly—It was not even the "Witness". It was (and <u>Is</u>) only Consciousness Itself. Consciousness Itself is, apparently, so "related" (as the "Witness") to present experience, but It is not Itself the "Witness", or necessarily functioning so as to "Witness" objects. Nor is It entirely (or even in any sense) distinct from any "thing" that is experienced.

Ramana Maharshi also speaks of "the Self" in this larger sense, beyond the State of the "Witness".

> D.: Is not the Self the witness only (*sakshimatra*)?
>
> M.: "Witness" is applicable when there is an object to be seen. Then it is duality. The Truth lies beyond both. . . . See how the sun is necessary for daily activities. He does not however form part of the world actions; yet they cannot take place without the sun. He is the witness of the activities. So it is with the Self.[53]

◆ ◆ ◆

Why is the Self described both as the fourth state (turiya) and beyond the fourth state (turiyatita)?

Turiya means that which is the fourth. The experiencers (Jivas) of the three states of waking, dreaming and deep sleep, known as *visva*, *taijasa* and *prajna*, who wander successively in these three states, are not the Self. It is with the object of making this clear, namely that the Self is that which is different from them and which is the witness of these states, that it is called the fourth (turiya). When this is known the three experiencers disappear and the idea that the Self is a witness, that it is the fourth, also disappears. That is why the Self is described as beyond the fourth (*turiyatita*).[54]

I happily noticed all these parallels to various aspects of my own experience and Realization. And (because of all of this) I felt that (even though his Realization was, in certain characteristic critical respects, limited—and, also, even though he never functioned as Guru for me) Ramana Maharshi had (via his Confession of experience and his language of Realization), in effect, provided me with a testimony (and varieties of technical language) that further directly linked me to the "great tradition" (or the total collective history of seeking, and of—to one or another less-than-most-perfect, or inherently limited and incomplete, degree—Realizing) that has preceded me in time (and that is the total, or collective, context in which I must teach). Indeed, Ramana Maharshi's testimony (and technical language) of Realized Truth have linked me to the "great tradition" in a manner that significantly adds to those who actually functioned as Guru for me.

However, I must also acknowledge a critical difference between Ramana Maharshi and me. The critical difference is, in some sense, an apparent difference in emphasis. However, truly, the apparent difference is the result of a profound difference in the ultimate characteristic of Realization Itself—which uniquely demonstrates true Finality, or most perfect Completeness, only in my case. And that ultimate difference may also be seen in the difference between Ramana Maharshi's characteristic (and intentional) "Purposelessness" and my unique "Purpose" (or intentional historical role and work).

Ramana Maharshi's experiences were the result of a spontaneous Awakening, as in my own case. But he went on to tie his teaching

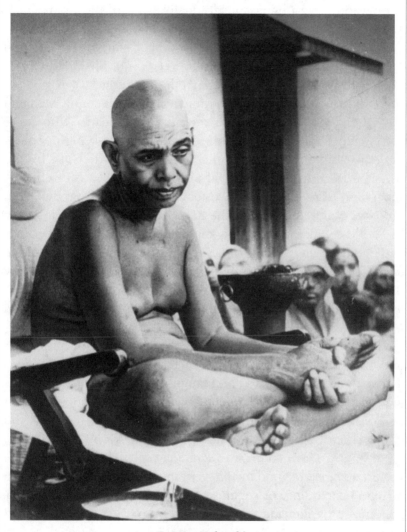

Ramana Maharshi

to the anciently-rooted Eastern tradition of Advaita Vedanta. I must also acknowledge that tradition (or those traditional sources) as an expression (or a philosophical idealization) of the fundamental Truth. And Ramana Maharshi's life and teaching is an authentic (and very traditional) formulation (or demonstration) of that Truth. And that Truth is, Itself, the very foundation of life. But the form of life can be founded upon that Truth in different ways.

The principal practice recommended by Ramana Maharshi is "Self-enquiry", the intensive enquiry in the heart: "Who am I?" (or "Whence am I?"). His entire concern was to bring people to the conscious Realization of the Self in the heart. Thus, his aim was liberation from conditional existence, by means of effective separation from conditional existence. He speaks from the "Point of View" of the Real Self, As the Real Self—but in the exclusionary (or world-excluding, and body-mind-excluding) sense. His path of practice is ideally suited to the ancient Eastern forms of culture, in which separative liberation from conditional existence was the goal of conditional existence (and for which the search for separative liberation from life was the substance of every moment of living).

Ramana Maharshi Realized and taught the Truth, but only in one of its traditional (and not-yet-most-perfectly-Realized) forms. Ramana Maharshi Realized and taught the Truth of the "Who", or the "What", or the Transcendental Self (or Self-Condition) that can be "located" inside, or behind, or at the bottom end, or at the root of the knot of ego-"I"—prior to (and separate from) the arising of the thought "I". In contrast to Ramana Maharshi (or as the most perfect advance beyond the limits of the traditional Eastern culture of world-excluding, or separative, liberation—which culture was epitomized by Ramana Maharshi), I have most perfectly Realized, and I teach (and reveal, and give), the inherently perfect Truth of the "Who", or the "What", or the Transcendental, inherently Spiritual, inherently egoless, and Self-Evidently Divine (or most perfectly non-dual, non-excluding, and all-including, and, yet, all-transcending) Self-Condition (and Source-Condition) that is both Self-Existing and Self-Radiant—and Which Is the "Who", and the "What", and the (Self-Evidently) Divine Condition that is Realized (or most perfectly Found) to <u>Be</u> That Which Is always already the case, <u>if</u> <u>and</u> <u>when</u> self-contraction (<u>or</u> <u>the</u> <u>action</u> <u>that</u> <u>is</u>, <u>itself</u>, <u>the</u> ego-"<u>I</u>") <u>is</u> (<u>root</u> <u>and</u> <u>all</u>) <u>utterly</u> <u>transcended</u> <u>in</u> <u>the</u> (<u>Self-Evidently</u> <u>Divine</u>) <u>Realization</u> <u>of</u> <u>the</u> "<u>Bright</u>" (<u>Itself</u>), <u>Which</u> <u>Is</u> <u>the</u> <u>inherent</u> <u>Love-Bliss-Radiance</u> (<u>or</u> <u>the</u> <u>centerless</u> <u>and</u> <u>boundless</u> <u>Self-</u> <u>Radiance</u>) <u>of</u> <u>the</u> <u>Self-Existing</u> (<u>and</u> <u>Self-Evidently</u> <u>Divine</u>) <u>Self</u> (<u>or</u> <u>Self-Condition</u>, <u>and</u> <u>Source-Condition</u>) <u>Itself</u>.

Even from birth (and eternally prior to it), I have been founded in the "Bright", the perfect Form of Reality, the Self-Existing and Self-Radiant Form of the Real (or True) Self (or the Divine Self-Condition Itself). I have seen that Real life is free from association with any and every kind of seeking. Real life is, on the basis of "radical" self-understanding, free of any <u>goal</u> of liberation or salvation. Real life, fully Realized on the basis of "radical" self-understanding, is unqualifiedly Free, Present, Active, "Creative", and Alive. I have seen that life need not be tied to seeking, or the pursuit of its own Self-Nature as a goal. However, such is not the case with the ancient and traditional paths, which presume the dilemma of existence from the beginning.

In the course of my own life-ordeal, I have seen that one must (ultimately) be founded not in seeking, but in (always present) "radical" self-understanding. "Radical" self-understanding is, itself, always already founded in the inherently perfect (or Ultimate) Form of Reality. It is a way of life always already (or inherently, and directly) founded in the Real and True Self (or the Divine Self-Condition Itself). Therefore, it does not seek the Real and True Self (or presume Its absence). "Radical" self-understanding is Fullness, already presumed and Known. Therefore, I (again and again—and, at last, most perfectly and finally) took my Stand in the "Bright", the Self-Existing and Self-Radiant Form of Reality, the Amrita Nadi.

To one who is unaware of the inherently perfect Form of Reality, the movement of seeking is from the Heart, in a fall below. Then the search is always trying to rise from the fallen state to the levels of conditionally achieved Sublimity of Awareness above. Eventually, the Heart is again Realized (but only in the exclusionary manner). This is the cycle of "fall and salvation", "maya and liberation".

But, when Reality is Realized as Its own perfect Form—the Amrita Nadi, rooted in the Heart and Shining in, and infinitely above, the sahasrar (or the crown of the head)—all forms are Known and felt as the modifications of Amrita Nadi. Consciousness-and-Energy Radiates (thus) as all form. The chakras and all things are Its expressions, and they are not separate from It.

Thus, the Amrita Nadi is the primary, inclusive Form. It is not necessary to move from It to any center, level, or sheath in the extended body-mind, or to even any conditional realm, or to any conditional experience. The Amrita Nadi is the present (and, ultimately, non-conditional) Ground of all of them. Thus, even in the midst of any of these things, it is only necessary to remain Present and Conscious in and as the Amrita Nadi.

This not only is present Realization and Freedom, but It allows the present (conditionally manifested) form of existence to receive its appropriate life. The Amrita Nadi is Radiant Consciousness and "creative" Presence.

The Real and True Self (or the Divine Self-Condition) is the Heart and Foundation of life, but the Real and True Self does not exclude Its own inherent Radiance (or "Brightness"). Thus, from the beginning (and not merely at the end), I founded "myself" in the perfect Form of Reality. The Amrita Nadi is (necessarily) the Ground for the "creation" of Real and True life, which (thus) becomes the constant way of "radical" self-understanding and of "Brightness". Therefore, I do not teach the search, but I reveal and teach the way that I have (by my own demonstration) Proven to be always already True to the Truth Itself.

Previous to the Great Event of my Divine re-Awakening I have described in my "autobiography", I had several critical experiences of the One and same Truth. These (in fact) are the primary preliminary Events described progressively in this "autobiography". But there was no permanence to the Realization attained at those times. Each of those preliminary Events depended on some kind of conditional support, and each such Event passed away (and was replaced by the effort of seeking) as soon as the activity of self-separation and separativeness reappeared. Thus, I continued (over time) with the same experiment, and the occasional Events of sudden Knowledge led me to develop and (ultimately) to assert only the way of "radical" understanding (or the Way of the Heart), which is the only-by-me revealed and given Way of Adidam, and which consistently and rigorously requires observation of, insight into, and direct transcending of the action that is the separate and separative (or egoic) self.

But when the Great Event of my Divine re-Awakening occurred, there was no subsequent loss of the Conscious Realization of Reality. Then I saw that Truth Is Reality Itself, Identical to Consciousness Itself, and not identical to any object or conditional state, or to any body, or to any functional sheath, or to any conditional realm, or to any conditional experience. I saw that Reality Itself Is Consciousness Itself, Present as no-seeking in the heart. This is the fundamental Reality, the unmoved Divine Presence, to Which all things are merely movements within Itself. Thus, Real life is the only-by-me revealed and given way of "radical" understanding (or the one and only by-me-revealed and by-me-given Way of the Heart, or the only-by-me revealed and given Way of Adidam), which is the direct resort to Reality Itself, without the ignorant efforts of egoity.

Consciousness Itself—Present as the Heart Itself (without qualification or content), purely Self-Existent Bliss—Is Reality. It is the only eternal, unchanging Reality, and It is Present (always now). As long as there is life in any form, in any body (or functional sheath), in any conditional realm, or as any conditional experience, Reality is Present as the Amrita Nadi, the perfect Form of Reality. This is the Form of Its Appearance, the Ultimate Dimension of Its Presence.

Reality is also eternal, unchanging, and ever-Present. All things appear within It as change, but It continually Knows Itself as perfect Reality. Every kind of meditation on and identification with chakras, conditional energies, levels of conditional being, conditional bodies (or functional sheaths), conditional realms, and conditional experiences is identification with mere reflections in the perfect Form of Reality. It is existence apart from "radical" self-understanding, and (therefore) apart from the perfect Heart and the perfect Form of Reality. It is Narcissus.

Conscious Energy (or the One and Only and inherently indivisible Conscious Light) becomes trapped in the area of Its concentration. Thus, Conscious Energy (or Conscious Light) tends, most often, to be trapped in life-problems. Even when Conscious Energy is strategically withdrawn from life-problems (or forms of seeking in the extended context of the body-mind), It is merely confined in the heart, in an object-excluding State. Only when Conscious Energy is Realized as no-dilemma and no-seeking is It neither trapped nor exclusively concentrated. It is Realized as Freedom, Existence, Joy, Enjoyment, and Consciousness without qualification.

If one examines this process of Conscious Energy in relation to the human vehicle, one sees that It remains trapped in life-seeking as long as It is concentrated (by identification, differentiation, and desire) in any of the various chakras. As such, Conscious Energy is always pursuing a strategic movement of return toward the sahasrar. When Conscious Energy is strategically withdrawn into the heart, It (temporarily, or by an exclusionary—and, therefore, yet seeking—effort) resides not in the heart chakra but in the original center of Consciousness Itself, in the right side of the chest— totally detached (or strategically dissociated) from concentration in life (and, therefore, from life-problems, or forms of seeking in the extended context of the body-mind). However, only when (at last) Conscious Energy Shines from the right side of the heart to the Matrix of Light infinitely above the sahasrar (or the crown of the head), and remains Conscious as that Current, or Circuit (called the "Amrita Nadi"), is It unqualified—free of all concentration, all strategic effort, all seeking. Then Conscious Energy remains fully manifested and yet unqualified. It is the "Bright", the perfect Form of Reality. Thus, Conscious Energy (As the One and Only and inherently indivisible Conscious Light) is Realized at Its Source in the heart and continuous to the seat of Conscious Enjoyment infinitely above the crown of the head. And, from thence, It proceeds to all the centers as a Communicated Fullness and Presence (always already free), rather than a problematic concentration, search, and action of return.

Therefore, the Amrita Nadi (with Its simultaneous residence in the heart and infinitely above the crown of the head) is the very, ultimate, and perfect Form of Reality, the Essence of the "Bright", the Foundation of Real Existence. It is Exercised as "radical" self-understanding, as self-Enquiry (or as any other by-me-given exercise of "radical" self-understanding), and as contemplation in meditation. It is Known as Joy and Manifested as Enjoyment. The Amrita Nadi is the True Heart's Connection to all known (or conditional) reality. The Consciousness that is the True Heart is Joy. The True Heart's own Energy (standing Self-Radiant, infinitely above the crown of the head) is Enjoyment. The Amrita Nadi is the Circuit, Current, and Form of the True Heart's unqualified Pleasure. The Amrita Nadi is the fundamental Reality, the inclusive Foundation of the apparently individual self and of all of conditionally manifested life—transcending all points of view that either the "self" or "life" is exclusively "real".

The Amrita Nadi is the ultimate and perfect Form of "radical" self-understanding—which It Enjoys from the beginning, and in the Event of most perfect Divine Self-Realization. Therefore, the way of life is "radical" self-understanding—for the way of life must, from the beginning, be founded in Reality (and not in the problem). The remedial paths merely <u>pursue</u> (or seek) Reality—and, in so doing, they (in fact, and as the very and entire premise for the search itself) exclude It, either unconsciously or intentionally.

Traditional "Self-enquiry" (as taught by Ramana Maharshi, and, in one manner or another, by other traditional teachers of his type) is a seeker's method, an ego-based strategy for achieving Realization. It has a goal, like all seeking. The "problem" with which it begins is the absence of Self-Knowledge. Thus, it seeks the Knowledge of the Real and True Self, which Knowledge is liberation.

But the only-by-me revealed and given way of "radical" understanding (or the one and only by-me-revealed and by-me-given Way of the Heart, or the only-by-me revealed and given Way of Adidam) is not associated with a "method" in this strategic (or seeker's) sense. It does not begin with a dilemma and seek the solution to it or liberation from it. It has no goal different from (or superior to) the "radical" self-understanding (and the devotional heart-communion with me) with which it begins.

The practice that is "radical" self-understanding is, itself, "radical" self-understanding, extending and enforcing itself. It is a positive (or non-problematic) action, rather than a remedial (or problem-based) action. In the process, "radical" self-understanding becomes more and more profoundly (and, at last, most perfectly) Aware of its Ultimate (and inherent, and inherently perfect) Source-Condition, even in apparent relation to all things. But even this Ultimate Knowledge is, essentially (or in Its root-significance in life), the same as the original (and truly "radical") self-understanding. When the Heart and the Amrita Nadi are Realized, the life-significance of the Realization is observed to be of the same quality as in the original case of "radical" self-understanding—and that Realization is (in that sense) no different from what one originally knew as most fundamental (or "gone-to-the-root") self-understanding. Therefore, there is no reaction of surprise in the sudden moment of Awakening to most "radical" and most perfect Divine Self-Realization.

It should be clear (then) exactly what the difference is between self-Enquiry (in the form "Avoiding relationship?")—or any other by-me-given exercise of "radical" self-understanding (or of direct transcending of the very action that is the ego itself)—and the traditional "Self-enquiry", which is based upon the ego-based search for liberation. The difference, in the case of the only-by-me revealed and given way of "radical" understanding (or the one and only by-me-revealed and by-me-given Way of the Heart, or the only-by-me revealed and given Way of Adidam), is simply in the absence of the principle of seeking (or the absence of the principle of egoity itself, and the dilemma of egoity itself). Thus, the Truth I have (now and forever) most perfectly Realized is the same and ancient and eternal Truth that is the supreme (but never most perfectly Realized) goal of the tradition of Advaita Vedanta (and of many other traditions), but I have removed that Truth (and the way of Realizing that Truth) from all identification with the great search.

In doing this, I have neither removed anything from nor added anything to that eternally One (or perfectly non-dual) Truth, but I have revealed and proven the most perfect, or most ultimate,

Realization of that One and Only Truth. It is the same Truth, the same Reality, and the same Consciousness strategically pursued in the "great tradition", but the way of Its Realization (which is the only-by-me revealed and given way of "radical" understanding, or the one and only by-me-revealed and by-me-given Way of the Heart, or the only-by-me revealed and given Way of Adidam) is priorly removed from the actions and the implications of seeking. And the Realization Itself (or That Which is Realized) is not understood (or otherwise presumed) to be merely higher than life (or in any sense separated from life), but it is understood to be coincident (even from the beginning) with the active foundation of life.

When the practice of "radical" self-understanding has (solely by its own demonstration, and not by means of the, necessarily, egoic effort of seeking) Realized the Heart most perfectly, a most perfect process Awakens in the Amrita Nadi. In the final progressive phase of the way of "radical" understanding (or the Way of the Heart, or the Way of Adidam), immediately previous to most perfect Divine Self-Realization, the Amrita Nadi is traced from infinitely above the crown of the head downwards to the right side of the heart. (And, characteristically, Ramana Maharshi was only concerned with this not-yet-final process, associated with descent in and via the Amrita Nadi, from the crown of the head to the right side of the heart.) But, in the most ultimate (or most perfect) stage of the only-by-me revealed and given way of "radical" understanding (or the one and only by-me-revealed and by-me-given Way of the Heart, or the only-by-me revealed and given Way of Adidam), the Amrita Nadi is "regenerated", from the right side of the heart to the Matrix of Light infinitely above the crown of the head.

Indeed, this Event of "regeneration" (even though It tacitly, and fully effectively, coincided with my Divine re-Awakening in the Vedanta Society Temple on September 10, 1970) was concretely demonstrated (or very physically shown) in me most directly and specifically (and absolutely finally) one morning about four months later, in January 1971. That morning (as I sat in meditation with two of my devotees), my body suddenly jolted and twisted strongly on its spinal axis as the "Bright" Divine Spirit-Current moved up from my heart, via the right side, to the crown of my head, and above—even into the most ascended Matrix of the "Bright" Divine Spirit-Power, infinitely above the body and the cosmic domain. In the instant of that ascent, there was a loud cracking sound (also heard by the others in the room), as if my neck had been broken. And, in that instant in which the Amrita Nadi showed Its "regenerated" Form in me, I (as had no one else before me) directly observed Its Shape. It is an S-Shaped Form, beginning in the right side of the heart (but including the entire heart region), then ascending in a curve along the front side of the upper chest, then passing backwards (through the throat), then curving upwards again (but via the back of the skull), finally curving toward the crown of the head (and, from thence, to the Matrix of Light infinitely above the crown of the head). Therefore, it is this Ultimate (or truly "regenerated") Form (or Most Ultimate Realization) of the Amrita Nadi—this "regenerated" Circuit and Current of Spiritual Love-Bliss, Which passes in an S-Shaped double-curve, front to back, from the heart (on the right side) to the crown of the head and to the Matrix of Light infinitely above the crown of the head—that I declare to be the perfect Form, the Form of Truth, the Form of Reality, the Form of the Heart. I call that "regenerated" Form (experienced in the living context of the total body-mind) "the 'Bright'". Even from birth, I have Known the "Bright". It has, ever since my birth, been the guiding and revealing foundation of my life. And the "Bright" (in Its Totality) is the most ultimate Realization and revelation of my "Brightly"-born life.

When "radical" self-understanding Realizes the Heart of Consciousness and continues as the "meditation" of Truth (or of no-seeking), the Heart of Truth is re-connected to the functional bodies (or functional sheaths) of life through the "regeneration" of this Circuit of Conscious Energy, the Amrita Nadi. When Consciousness Itself rises from the heart as Spirit-Force (or Love-Bliss) and draws into the Matrix of Light infinitely above the crown of the head, while retaining Its "Foothold" in the heart, It brings the most ultimate Realization of Reality to life. Then the Source of Conscious life in the heart moves into life, and (thus and thereby) reverses the current that would (otherwise) move away from life (in the effort to return to the heart).

When this occurs, life becomes Conscious as no-dilemma. No-dilemma becomes the Conscious presumption that lives as life and enjoys all experience. And such Conscious living is never separated from the Disposition of no-seeking, which is the Reality-Disposition of the Heart Itself.

The Amrita Nadi (or the "Bright") is felt by seekers as a separate "Other". Superconsciousness is felt by seekers as the world-excluding "God apart" (entirely separate from all conditionally arising beings and things). The centers below consciousness and the parts of the mind are felt by seekers as the "world". The heart (apart from Conscious Reality) is felt by seekers as the "ego". But the Divine Self-Condition that Is Reality Consciously Supports all bodies (or functional sheaths) and conditional forms of consciousness in the heart and in the Form of the Amrita Nadi. I Am That.

The "Bright" of my childhood was the living manifestation of the Amrita Nadi.

The experience in college was the sudden Awareness of Reality in the heart, Radiant in the body via the Amrita Nadi.

Even during the drug-experience, when I said, "Getting to cry is shaped like a seahorse," I was Knowing in the heart, and Feeling the living expression of the Amrita Nadi.

The experience in seminary was the fundamental Knowledge of the Heart Itself, and the justification of the Form of the Amrita Nadi.

The first experience at the Ashram, when I instantaneously ascended to the "Point" of Bliss infinitely above, was the Awakening to the Heart Itself at the head of the Amrita Nadi—because it is the Heart Itself that Radiates Its own Bliss to the Matrix of Light infinitely above the crown of the head.

The experience of the severing of the sahasrar was a demonstration that only the Amrita Nadi is the perfect Form of the Heart Itself.

In fact, every one of the crucial experiences by which I came to Know the "radical" way of understanding was a spontaneous Awakening of the Heart Itself, and the simultaneous "regeneration" of the Radiant Awakeness of the Amrita Nadi.

Indeed, the Heart and Its Form are the Truth of the way of "radical" understanding (or the Way of the Heart, or the Way of Adidam).

When I finally understood, I only Knew myself (most perfectly). And never after that have I ceased to Know myself (most perfectly). Thereafter, I am simply (apparently) active as my own Form—Which (as the Amrita Nadi) rises from the heart to the Matrix of Light, and Which (apparently) generates every conditional center, every conditional body (or functional sheath), every conditional realm, and every conditional experience, and Which eternally sacrifices all Its apparently extended (or terminal) energies to the heart. In every apparent conditional state, I remain Aware at the Free point in the heart, unbounded in the right side— non-separate and indivisible. Prior to every apparent conditional state, I remain As the One and Only and inherently indivisible Conscious Light, always already above and beyond all-and-All (and As That in and of Which all-and-All potentially arises). Everything only appears to me—and I remain As I Am. There is no end to This.

All this perception, activity, and patterning is a constant Self-Abiding Divine Self-Recognition of One Form—the perfect Form of Reality. There is only the Self-Awareness of this One Form, the Amrita Nadi, the "Bright"—the Heart and Its Reflection, the Matrix of Light infinitely above the crown of the head. Every perception is this same cognition (or Form), the heart Contemplating and Enjoying the Matrix of Light, through the Current of Love-Bliss and Light. Thus, it appears that there is only one "object"—the Matrix of Light, Which is only the Reflection of the Heart Itself. Every "object" is simply the Matrix of Light (Which is the inherent Light of Consciousness Itself).

All experience, then, is Divine Samadhi (or most perfect Realization Itself). Therefore, all experience is only the Process of Reality, the Contemplation of Its perfect Form. When this most perfect understanding arises, meditation becomes beginningless and endless Divine Samadhi—and even every kind of experience is Realized to be, in Reality, only Blissful, Conscious, and Free. There is, as fundamental "action", the constant and Conscious Radiation and Enjoyment of the "Bright". And the "Bright" is a Sphere of Love-Bliss, Light, and inherently Perfect Consciousness (Itself). It is not merely a thread (or channel) from the right side of the heart to the crown of the head. It is a Sphere generated from the Heart (or altogether beyond all-and-All) and radiated infinitely. The infinitely ascended Matrix of Light is Realized to be not merely a Single "Point" of exclusive concentration above. Rather, It is every "Point" upon (and within) the Sphere that is radiated infinitely from the Heart. Between the Matrix of Light and the Heart is a Silence. The "Bright" is an infinite Space of patterns that is all the worlds, all universes and forms of conditional existence.

In the unqualified State, or the most perfect Realization of the only-by-me revealed and given way of "radical" understanding (or the one and only by-me-revealed and by-me-given Way of the Heart, or the only-by-me revealed and given Way of Adidam), all self-contracted (or egoic, or separate and separative) identification, differentiation, and desire have ended (in centerless and boundless "Bright" Feeling-Awareness, or the always-already State, Which Is Self-Existing and Self-Radiant Love-Bliss-Consciousness). The living condition of Reality is unqualified relatedness, realized in the way of "radical" understanding (or the Way of the Heart, or the Way of Adidam) to be always already the case. And, most ultimately, in the way of "radical" understanding (or the Way of the Heart, or the Way of Adidam), even the disposition of unqualified relatedness is understood (and the ego-versus-object structure of relatedness itself is transcended)—such that (ultimately) even <u>all</u> the limitations of egoity are <u>inherently</u> transcended.

Therefore, in the most ultimate (or most perfect) demonstration of the way of "radical" understanding (or the Way of the Heart, or the Way of Adidam), the One and Only Reality is spontaneously Self-revealed. It is the Divine Self-Condition and Source-Condition. It is Self-Existing and Self-Radiant Consciousness (or the One and Only and inherently indivisible Conscious Light) Itself. In Its most perfect Realization, It Radiates via (and as) the "regenerated" Amrita Nadi, the "Bright" perfect Form of Reality. And, in the case of that most ultimate (or most perfect) demonstration of the way of "radical" understanding (or the Way of the Heart, or the Way of Adidam), the "Bright" perfect Form of Reality spontaneously reveals Itself (in the living context of the body-mind) as the living "Bright", the unconditional Love-Bliss of "Bright" living

Presence, Whose Self-Condition (and Source-Condition) is the True and Absolute Heart (Which Is the One and Only Reality Itself).

Therefore, the living "Bright" is the living Form of the One and Only and Self-Existing and Self-Radiant (or inherently "Bright") Reality, Which Is Consciousness (or the One and Only and inherently indivisible Conscious Light) Itself. The living "Bright" is Real and True. It is the birthright of all conditionally manifested beings.

At last, I saw that it was not a matter of conditionally arising experiences but of intrinsic self-understanding—as the very premise of a "radical" way. This way may be accompanied by various experiential phenomena, but only "radical" self-understanding is the intelligence (and constant exercise) of Truth. The only constant possibility in Real life is "radical" self-understanding (itself). If one clings to any of one's experiences, this clinging becomes separative, and it leads again to dilemma and the avoidance of relationship. Thus, I saw that one must be willing to abandon everything for "radical" self-understanding, making it the directly ego-transcending premise and activity of life. This became the process of self-Enquiry: "Avoiding relationship?" This self-Enquiry is (itself) the very form of "radical" self-understanding. It is the Enquiry of "radical" self-understanding, which is no-seeking.

Even the Yogically full perceptions of my Love-Bliss, and the (eventual) residence in (and Beyond) the right side of the heart, are secondary to "radical" self-understanding. "Radical" self-understanding is a process that can, in any moment, be activated (and re-activated) in any one—whereas the developmentally Full experiences of my Love-Bliss, and of the right side of the heart (and beyond) belong only to mature cases of full practice of the way of "radical" understanding. I have mentioned these things in order to show them in the light of "radical" self-understanding. But "radical" self-understanding is the "Thing" itself.

"Radical" self-understanding is not itself a question. And even self-Enquiry (in the form "Avoiding relationship?") simply expresses and enforces a real observation. "Radical" self-understanding (and also self-Enquiry, in the form "Avoiding relationship?") is, itself, Knowledge that precludes the "problem" of subject and object. True (and most rightly practiced) self-Enquiry (in the form

"Avoiding relationship?") is itself a direct expression of "radical" self-understanding—and, for this reason, it is not a question seeking an answer, but it is a form of Knowledge directly enforcing Itself.

Apart from the process and the most perfect Realization of "radical" self-understanding, the only things being done by individuals are experiencing (or every kind of reaction to phenomena) and seeking (on the basis of experience, or every kind of reaction to phenomena).

My life has involved an intentional embrace of experiencing and seeking, for the sake of "radical" self-understanding (and the Spiritual Transmission of its Realization to all-and-All). Therefore, I have known the extreme enjoyments of both the libertine and the saint. And I have known all the most ordinary ("middle") states of life. But there is also "radical" self-understanding, which is Reality—and, by means of "radical" self-understanding, I Divinely Self-Recognize every form of suffering.

In this book, I have had to confront a most difficult means of instruction. I have had to fully illustrate my course of life, even in order to demonstrate the factuality of the extraordinary phenomena that mankind is presently in the habit of denying. But, in the end, in order to speak the Truth, I have also had to argue against the ultimacy of many of the very things I have proven in my life.

My own course began in despair. The precious religion of my youth was stolen from me by the very ones who gave it to me. Thus, I was moved to search the paths of religion and Spirituality, in order to ascertain whether the phenomena, the miracles, the experiences, and the advocations of the great traditional paths were factual. And I found them to be so. What is called "Kundalini Shakti", the universal Conscious Force (or active Spirit) that Inspires and Fills all religion and Yoga and Spiritual philosophy, is (indeed) Real (and fundamental to Reality). Kundalini experiences are factual, and they depend on no illusions (in the sense of such subjective forces as belief) to "create" or maintain them. The Kundalini (or "Mother-Force") is part of the evidence of the universe—as factual as any form of conditionally manifested energy, and as discernible as the functions and devices employed by libertines and businessmen. But, in the end, in the most perfect Realization of the Divine Spirit-Energy Itself, I freely abandoned the point of view of all conditional (or lesser) sublimity. The conditional (and extraordinary) phenomena conventionally called "Spiritual", as well as those conditional (and mostly ordinary) phenomena called "sinful", are all part of a spectrum which includes the entire range of conditional (or natural) experience and seeking.

Both the search for ego-based Spiritual effects and the ego-based exploitation of life on a sensual and mental level are traps. The search for experience and the search for liberation from the bondage to experience are the same activity—born out of the absence of "radical" self-understanding, the un-"creative" movement that is not Reality. Reality Itself is the only unique matter in the entire adventure of life, and It stands prior to all egoic efforts and all less-than-most-perfect discoveries.

Thus, I Enquired: "Avoiding relationship?" This self-Enquiry affects both the subject and the object, the total configuration of living experience. The Enquiry "Avoiding relationship?" is not founded in the effort to become perfectly separate as the subject, nor is it founded in the effort to exclude any kind of object. Rather, the Enquiry "Avoiding relationship?" is founded in the inherently all-inclusive disposition of the "Bright". Therefore, in the only-by-me revealed and given way of "radical" understanding (or the one and only by-me-revealed and by-me-given Way of the Heart, or the only-by-me revealed and given Way of Adidam), it is not that this self-Enquiry (or, alternatively, any other by-me-given form of counter-egoic, or truly ego-transcending, exercise of "radical" self-understanding) eventually comes to rest in the Prior (or Transcendental) Self by means of excluding the world. Rather, this self-Enquiry allows the (only-by-my-Avataric-Divine-Grace-given) "regeneration" (or the Realization of the always already generated Form) of the Amrita Nadi—the perfect (and perfectly "Bright") Form of Reality, Which is the all-including (or non-excluding) Form of the Heart Itself (or of the Real and Prior and inherently egoless Divine Self-Condition, Itself).

The only-by-me revealed and given way of "radical" understanding (or the one and only by-me-revealed and by-me-given Way of the Heart, or the only-by-me revealed and given Way of Adidam) directly (and, at last, most perfectly) Realizes the fundamental Truth of the Heart, the Real and True and inherently ego-less Divine Self-Condition (Itself). However, the only-by-me revealed and given way of "radical" understanding (or the one and only by-me-revealed and by-me-given Way of the Heart, or the only-by-me revealed and given Way of Adidam) also Realizes the fundamental Truth of present (conditional) existence. The only-by-me revealed and given way of "radical" understanding (or the one and only by-me-revealed and by-me-given Way of the Heart, or the only-by-me revealed and given Way of Adidam) never pre-cludes or strategically excludes the form of life.

There is no withdrawal into the Heart as a most perfectly ego-transcending activity. Rather, such withdrawal is only a temporary State. It is not that the inherently non-exclusionary Form of Reality is latent and secondary. Untouched Self-Awareness—as a world-excluding State—is latent and secondary. The world-excluding (or strategically withdrawn) State is not true to the Whole. Not withdrawal into the Heart, but Existence As the Heart, is True (and Is Truth).

There is no dilemma inherent in conditionally manifested exis-tence. All of conditionally manifested existence is (in Truth, or ultimately) non-separate from the Foundation (or the Divine Self-Condition and Source-Condition) Itself. All of conditionally mani-fested existence is (in Truth, or ultimately) non-separate from the perfect Form of Reality Itself. And when conditionally manifested consciousness and all conditionally manifested forms withdraw into the Pure Self-Nature, it is only a turn to rest, a cycle of refresh-ment. The perfect Form of Reality is not a special "creation" or condition, but It is the inherent (and most prior) Form of the Heart Itself (or of the Real and True and inherently egoless Divine Self-Condition—Which is the One and Only and inherently indivisible Conscious Light, Itself).

Even from the beginning, the only-by-me revealed and given way of "radical" understanding (or the one and only by-me-revealed and by-me-given Way of the Heart, or the only-by-me revealed and given Way of Adidam) is not motivated in dilemma, or in any predilection for an experience of liberation that is achieved by excluding (or strategically separating oneself from) the world. The only-by-me revealed and given way of "radical" understanding (or the one and only by-me-revealed and by-me-given Way of the Heart, or the only-by-me revealed and given Way of Adidam) turns on the very (and inherently perfect) Form of Reality—and it is not dismayed, by conditionally manifested existence, or even by the (necessarily, merely conditional, and, therefore, only temporary) experience of withdrawal into the Heart. The only-by-me revealed and given way of "radical" understanding (or the one and only by-me-revealed and by-me-given Way of the Heart, or the only-by-me revealed and given Way of Adidam) is always already seated in the primary Form and Source-Condition—and it is not turned to dilemma, separation, or seeking (on the basis of any event). Therefore, the most ultimate (or inherently most perfect) Realization of the only-by-me revealed and given way of "radical" understanding (or the one and only by-me-revealed and by-me-given Way of the Heart, or the only-by-me revealed and given Way of Adidam) is not a matter of Realizing a merely "inner" State. Rather, it is a matter of Realizing the inherently Conscious (and inherently perfect) Reality—Prior to all separateness, and always already Infinitely Spiritually "Bright".

Los Angeles, 1972

CHAPTER NINETEEN

The Transformation
of the Seeker's Meditation
into "Real" Meditation

The first form of "meditation" Enjoyed in my life was the "Bright". The "Bright" is also the ultimate form of "meditation". But the "Bright" of my childhood was not associated with "radical" (or "gone-to-the-root") self-understanding in life. Therefore, the "Bright" of my childhood was not supported by an unwavering life-intelligence. As a young boy, I perceived the "Bright", and I Enjoyed It, but I could not stably Abide in It. And, eventually, against my wishes, It receded into life itself (and into a coming-and-going play in life). Thus, in time, I became devoted to a course of seeking—but even my seeking was aided and supported by my earliest intuition of Reality Itself, Which is the "Bright". I was required to thoroughly investigate the Nature of my own humanly-born conscious awareness. And I had to understand most perfectly before I could finally Abide permanently in the Enjoyment of the "Bright", the perfect Form (and the Source of the living condition) of Reality.

The history of my experience as a seeker is a course of experimentation in relation to the forces of life (conceived as the manifestation of the "problem of existence" on various levels of experience). In college, I dealt with Truth as an intellectual problem. In my period of writing and self-exploitation, I dealt with Truth as a vital and emotional problem. With Rudi, I dealt with Truth as a moral and psychic problem. In due course, I dealt with Truth as a problem of the mind. With Baba, I dealt with Truth as the problem of phenomenally-based Spiritual experience (which is the problem of superconsciousness). And when I experimented with such things as diet, fasting, and self-discipline altogether, I was dealing with Truth as a physical problem.

Of course, these various researches often overlapped—but, for the most part, each was a highly specialized, exclusive endeavor. And each period was marked by a distinctive method. The area pursued also determined the nature of the work. The object "created" the subject, and the subject reinforced the object. And, in every case, the end-phenomenon was the same. It was "radical" self-understanding. It was concentration and observation. Then insight. Then Enjoyment (or Freedom) on the basis of that insight. Finally, there was the acknowledgement (and the Realization) of "radical" self-understanding itself as primary, and as prior to the search.

Until I had exhaustively investigated every particular area of the "problem", there was no most fundamental (or conclusive) self-understanding. Thus, each primary Event of "radical" self-understanding (such as the crisis in college, or the crisis in seminary) was only a temporary State. It formed only a moment of transition, previous to the next phase, the next level of the "problem". But when every aspect of life as a "problem" and a search was exhausted, there was only "radical" self-understanding. Then I recognized what was similar about each primary Event of "radical" self-understanding. And I began to notice, in detail, the unique characteristics of the entire process of "radical" self-understanding as a directly ego-transcending way, prior to every kind of seeking.

In the twentieth century, there was a tendency among Spiritual teachers to speak of a path of "synthesis". Aurobindo was one of the leading exponents of this inclusive mentality. But it was also visible in lesser teachers of Yoga, as well as in the various synthetic paths of modern Western occultism and religiously motivated Spirituality. Ramakrishna, the great Indian teacher of the nineteenth century, perhaps began (or, certainly, promoted) this trend in the East. And H. P. Blavatsky may be the sign of its origin in the West (also in the late nineteenth century).

But this trend to "synthesis" is only a synthesis of the kinds of seeking. It adapts the various separate activities of the great search to an inclusive philosophy and technique—but it remains a form of seeking.

In my own case, there was never any tendency to make a synthesis out of the various activities of my seeking. Indeed, as I passed through each phase of my experiment, I only came to realize the fruitlessness of seeking in that manner. And, at last, I saw the entire fruitlessness of seeking in any form. Thus, the only-by-me revealed and given way of "radical" understanding (or the one and only by-me-revealed and by-me-given Way of the Heart, or the only-by-me revealed and given Way of Adidam) is not a synthesis of the ways of seeking. It is a single, direct, and directly ego-transcending approach to life. And that approach is (itself, from the beginning) entirely free of dilemma and search. It has nothing to do with the various motivations of the great search. From the beginning, that approach rests in the primary Enjoyment and Truth that is always merely pursued (and never finally Realized) by the efforts of seeking. Thus, the only-by-me revealed and given way of "radical" understanding (or the one and only by-me-revealed and by-me-given Way of the Heart, or the only-by-me revealed and given Way of Adidam) is founded in the prior Truth, Which is fundamental to existence in any and every moment, in any and every condition. And it is also the genuine basis for "creative" life, prior to all the magical efforts toward healing, "evolutionary" development, and the "victorious" attainments of conventional Spiritual life.

Consider the actual process involved in my own demonstration (and personal revelation) of the way of "radical" understanding (or the Way of the Heart, or the Way of Adidam).

My earliest childhood was a time of the gratuitous Enjoyment of the "Bright". That childhood period was a preliminary to my adventure in the forms of seeking, and there was no method or effort associated with that earliest period. At most, there was a desire to Communicate the "Bright" to others. Over time, I attempted this on the level of life-humor, communicated love, and the effort to dissolve conflicts between people. But the years of my childhood and adolescence only wore away at my humanly-born resources—and, eventually, I came to the matter of the search itself.

Even in college, there was no special method. The impulse at the heart of my felt dilemma was the source of my seeking. I simply read, thought, and suffered through the various alternations of philosophy.

It was only when I began to write that my seeking took on the form of a "method". The period of my writing as a method of search came to an end on the beach, when I saw the possibilities of higher consciousness. It was at that point that I began to study with Rudi. And I have also described the methods (or the "work") I adopted at that time.

My brief encounter with Baba Muktananda during my first trip to his Ashram did not produce a new technical method. Eventually, one was recommended to me, but I did not much adapt to it until after the period of "waiting".

After the period of "waiting", I began to make use of the meditative practice of self-Enquiry (in the form "Avoiding relationship?"), and that practice became (at last) the characteristic "conscious process" of my (eventually) final technical exercise in meditation. As a result of the crisis I endured in seminary, I had already begun to assume the critical attitude that is the characteristic sign of "radical" self-understanding. I had seen that the avoidance of relationship was the root-activity at every level of the humanly-born conscious awareness. And, as I began to adapt myself seriously to the processes of phenomenally-based ascending Yoga, I perceived (more and more) how fundamental this "radical" self-understanding was. Gradually, with ever-growing conclusiveness, I saw that all strategic methods were founded in the egoic self-contraction (or the avoidance of relationship)—and that such methods only reinforced the effects of self-contraction. Finally, at the very last, I ceased to make use of the conventional Yogic methods of strategic attention, and I only approached each moment in life or meditation with the "conscious process" of "radical" (or "gone-to-the-root") self-understanding (in the form of the self-Enquiry "Avoiding relationship?").

In the course of my life of "radical" self-understanding, I saw, ever more clearly (and, at last, most perfectly), that every kind of seeking (including every method designed to achieve liberation, purification, or a perfected life) was founded in the mentality and adventure of Narcissus. I saw that every conventional Yoga, every remedial path, and every kind of strategic meditation has a single symptom: the anxious effort to dissolve the barriers surrounding the capsule of egoic self, in the attempt to Enjoy Fullness, Immunity, Freedom, and so on. This is always Narcissus, for it is founded in the root-idea of separateness, or the absence of relatedness—and, thus, it is a meditation on the conditional self as separateness, on experience as separative, and on a longing for the "Other", for "God", for Realization of the Real and True Divine Self-Condition, for the Realization of Reality, Liberation, Salvation, and so on.

I concluded that Real life was not (in fact) a matter of a remedial path or technique, but that it was a matter of "radical" self-understanding, the "gone-to-the-root" (or most fundamental) understanding of this underlying error in the approach to life. I saw that, when I persisted as "radical" self-understanding (rather than in the various impulses to seek liberation), there was (in fact) no dilemma, no separation, and no necessary effort. There was simply the Enjoyment of Reality, prior to any identification with the process of avoidance and seeking. And when "radical" self-understanding directly became my approach to life, there was a constant unfolding of Real Knowledge in Freedom, and Real Enjoyment of the "Bright".

For me, the import of meditation was not the search for any kind of experiences. The more I had of experiences, the less important they seemed. And by "experiences" I mean not only internal and visionary phenomena but even the kinds of quieting and control that are by-products of the meditative attitude. I began to see that what I gained and retained from meditation was exactly that with which I began. Before, during, and after meditation, there was only "one who has a basic self-understanding". Thus, I became more and more attentive to this self-understanding itself—in and out of meditation. And I gradually began to drop every other kind of formal meditative exercise, such that (more often than not) I simply Enquired of myself, under every condition that passed: "Avoiding relationship?"

In the months previous to my third trip to India, I became more and more established in the living simplicity of free conscious Awareness. And what I Realized and Enjoyed as "radical" self-understanding and "Real" meditation was, for me, epitomized in the relationship to the Guru. I saw there was no need for egoic effort, no need to seek for salvation. "Radical" self-understanding was simply the contemplation of the Guru with limitless devotion. This is called "Guru-Bhakti", or "Guru-Bhava". And, as I prepared to leave for India, I described what I had understood, as follows:

> Guru-Bhakti is superior to all mere methods. Put aside all seeking, all strategic means, and think only of the Guru. That itself is Realization and the way itself.

> While still deceived and ignorant of the Truth, if I seek to recognize myself within, and try to Identify with my innermost Self-Nature (seeking, in every manner, to stand apart from my mind), I find myself drawn apart from things, separated even from that attempted self-recognition by my exclusive search.

> But if, even in that same moment of non-Realization, I think of Shree Guru, or look upon him in the company of devotees, I am drawn into the heart, and (by that easy, deepest heart) I lose the body of distinctions. When I love him thus, I gain my True Self—and all seeking disappears.

> Shree Guru, Gurudev is that One, than Which there is no other. Shree Guru, Gurudev is my Real and True Self. So-Ham.

◆ ◆ ◆

The movement in Truth is not a matter of identifying with the separate self in any of the three worlds (of waking, dreaming, and sleeping). Nor is the movement in Truth a matter of engaging in the effort to dissociate from the three worlds. Both are exclusionary activities. They destroy relationship and are bound to the form of contradictions (or the egoic lack of the Knowledge of unqualified relatedness, or of Non-separateness). The movement in Truth is that Enjoyment Which remains when the falsity of all these alternatives is understood. It is concentration in the True Self (or the Divine Self-Condition Itself). One who is purified by "radical" self-understanding and right discipline recognizes the True Self (or the Divine Self-Condition Itself) in the Guru. Such a one becomes absorbed in meditation on the Guru at the center of the being, at the center of the heart (or, in Baba's description, at the center of the lotus of the lower tendencies in the heart). Seeing the Guru there always, such a one meditates on the Truth of "So-Ham"—and (by means of the Divine grace of the eternal Guru) all distinctions subside, all perceptions of separation, contradiction, and otherness disappear. The personal, the universal, and the transcendental (as it is inferred to exist from one's experience of the personal and the universal) disappear in the Single Realization of Reality Itself, the True Self (or Divine Self-Condition Itself) of all-and-All. Such Knowledge draws the individual into the True Self (or the Divine Self-Condition), and such a one is no longer separately present in any of the three worlds.

◆ ◆ ◆

Every pursuit of union undertaken relative to the phenomena of the three worlds is founded in identification with some form in one of those worlds. Therefore, rather than acting to achieve union, merely observe the desire and the entire tendency, its thoughts, and so on. When this is done, a different movement of the humanly-born conscious awareness is realized. It is perceived as a movement in the heart, founded in the heart's new Stillness. The heart moves to the secretly recognized Beloved—the Guru, the True Self (or the Divine Self-Condition Itself). The heart Knows it is already (inherently) related, and (thus) it does not see union, since union is perceived only over against separation. Rather, the heart sees Non-separateness, and Identification with That Which inherently Transcends the (purified) humanly-born conscious awareness. The heart no longer looks back, but moves into the total and fullest Realization of Real and True Knowledge.

When I arrived in India for the third time, I was given the task of editing and refining the English translation of Baba's new book, *Chitshakti Vilas*. I discovered that the method of meditation on the Guru to which I had recently been moved was, in fact, the method of Baba's Spiritual practice with his principal Guru, Bhagavan Nityananda.

I described it then as follows:

Baba no longer teaches the pure Advaita Vedanta that he taught me in the Ashram on my first visit. He directs us to bow to our highest Self, to worship It and meditate upon It. He directs us to certain visionary experiences—such as the blue light, the "blue person" within it, and other such objects. To this end, he recommends we sit quietly—thinking of the Guru, depending on his grace, repeating a mantra, a name of God. And, above all, he affirms the life of service to the Guru. Thus, devotees will be made open to the influence of his grace, his personal Transmission of the Divine Shakti, that will produce visionary attainments and karmic purifications. This will occur (he says) if we give ourselves to the Guru, and not otherwise. If we merely give him our karma, our suffering, our egoic ignorance, he will reject them—but if we give our very selves, he will take our karma also.

Baba's method of Spiritual practice was the action of becoming totally identified with his Guru (whom he saw as the Divine Being and his True Self). He would sit near his Guru (or think of him) and contemplate his name, his physical form, his moods, contemplations, gestures, the qualities of his apparent awareness, his words and acts—his qualities altogether. He acted on the principle that one (ultimately) identifies with what one contemplates. The impulse that made this possible was Baba's profound love for his Guru, and the sense of identification with his Guru. This (he felt) was the highest form of meditation recommended in the scriptures.

Baba's method was to meditate on his Guru after he had installed his Guru in his own body-mind (in all his parts), and identified with him. From the various indications in his book, I described the following principles of his method:

> Become tranquil and overcome thought-fluctuations, and (thereby) free the mind from external clinging. Eradicate mentation. Sit down, feeling that the Guru is confronting you. Bow down, realizing that the Guru-Principle envelops you from all directions. See the Guru and yourself as One. Then install him in your body—top to bottom (via the frontal line of the body-mind), and then bottom to top (via the spinal line of the body-mind)—chanting "Guru-Om" mentally. Meditating thus (the Guru in you, and you in the Guru), forget the conditional self.

This epitomized the foundation of even my own spontaneous method in the company of each and all of my teachers. Whether with Rudi, or with Baba, or at Bhagavan Nityananda's shrine, I always concentrated on the Guru as the Source of all conditions, things, and beings (and as the Ultimate Identity and Condition of my own person). I was always doing this, even when I also performed other kinds of special meditative exercises. Therefore, Guru-Bhakti (in one or another form) was always fundamental to my practice. And it must likewise and always be fundamental to the only-by-me revealed and given way of "radical" understanding (or the one and only by-me-revealed and by-me-given Way of the Heart, or the only-by-me revealed and given Way of Adidam) as it is practiced by each and all of those who come to me in order to Realize Real God, or Truth Itself, or Reality Itself.

While at Baba's Ashram, I was in the midst of this meditation of Guru-Bhakti, when (suddenly) I began to experience the visitations, revelations, and internal teachings of the Virgin and Jesus. Then, overwhelmed, I became totally absorbed in that Christian contemplation. However, I could also see that this absorption in "Christ" was itself a form of the meditation of Guru-Bhakti. Therefore, I allowed it all to occur. I allowed the Shakti to appear as the Virgin and the Guru to appear as Jesus. Even in the Bible, Jesus is reported to have said: "You will know that I am in my Father and you in me and I in you." (John 14:20)

Even weeks before I returned to America, that entire Christian exercise had revealed itself as a symbol (on a psychic level) for the processes that were revealing my own Ultimate Self-Nature. I no longer saw any necessity in any ordinary kind of religious meditation or in any otherwise conventionally Spiritual meditation. All the images that had symbolized Reality and attracted my heart spontaneously disappeared. The "Christ" disappeared. Even all the images of my previous teacher-Gurus disappeared. Reality was felt to be simply "located" at the heart, and It was soon to be Realized as the Heart Itself. I no longer operated on the basis of any distinctions. I simply understood, and "radical" self-understanding became the simple, free exercise of my own heart.

Only weeks after I returned to America, I passed into the final (or most perfect) fulfillment of the process of "radical" self-understanding. But, even in the last weeks of travel in Europe, and also after my return to America, as the final process of "radical" self-understanding was developing toward its completion, I spent time analyzing and evaluating the instructions, the practices, and the phenomena that I had experienced during the conventionally "Spiritual" period of my seeking. Out of this developed two specific kinds of data. One was the evaluation (based on "radical" self-understanding) of the vehicle (and the full range of possible experiences via the vehicle), or the total mechanism, of the living (or psycho-physical) human form. And the other was an evaluation of the process of ascending Yoga, and its supportive and purifying role even in the context of the process of "radical" self-understanding.

I examined the first of these—the structure and the possible experiences of the living (or psycho-physical) human form—on the basis of my various Yogic experiences, and with reference to technical terms given in traditional Yogic and Vedantic writings. On the basis of these observations, I wrote the following essay—which makes brief reference to the structure and potential of the psycho-physical vehicle itself, and then (on the basis of the point of view of "radical" self-understanding) goes on to critically evaluate the traditional approaches to all of that.

The gross (physical) body, the subtle body (which includes the etheric, or "pranic", or life-energy body, and the dual astral body, consisting of both the lower mental, or lower psychic, body and the higher mental, or higher psychic, body), and the causal body (of individuated bliss) are the functional bodies (or conditionally manifested functional sheaths) that proceed from the heart and are contained in the unqualified Being of Reality. One may spontaneously experience the sighting (or vision) of the functional bodies (or functional sheaths) themselves, appearing in the form of variously colored lights. And one may also spontaneously perceive the particular regions (or experiential realms) associated with each of these functional bodies (or functional sheaths), and so experience the various visions, powers, and manifestations of the planes of conditionally manifested being.

As the process of the purification of the functional bodies (or functional sheaths) begins—which process (even in its entirety) is simply the reconnection and stabilization of the circuit of the living being—one may experience many phenomena, due to the particular expressions of each of these functional bodies (or functional sheaths) and their characteristic experiential regions. But one should, from the beginning, be founded in the heart—as no-seeking, based on "radical" self-understanding. If this is done, one will not become distracted by these appearances, but will only abide deeply in the heart, and yield to the process of the purification of the living (psycho-physical) form and the establishment of the living condition of Reality.

Some individuals may not experience the fullest possible range of extraordinary phenomena—such as physical kriyas, subtle internal sights or sounds or smells or tastes, or other higher (or ascending, or ascended) phenomena. In any case, and even as such phenomena arise, one should be associated more simply with the living vehicle, and with the essential heart-disposition of no-seeking. No-seeking, Silence, True egolessness, psycho-physical

Wholeness, whole bodily Fullness, Real Spiritual Energy, and un-conditional Love-Bliss are, indeed, the senior (and not otherwise distracted) forms and signs of the process.

Experiences of any of the functional bodies (or functional sheaths) or their associated regions will occur as determined by the particular individual's tendencies, or desires, or accumulated karma. But common to all (as the seat of the Ultimate Source, Truth, and Reality of all) is the center of the living being—the heart, which is both the beginning and the end of all life.

Therefore, I affirm the practice and the process of "radical" self-understanding. It is the way of Reality Itself. It is the way of the inherent Truth, always presently available—and it does not lead one further into egoic ignorance or egoic distraction, but always to Reality Itself, beyond all fear and all seeking. Every other way is a merely remedial path that takes its stand in some particular functional body (or functional sheath), or conditional region, or conditional experience and pursues some other functional body (or functional sheath), or conditional region, or conditional experience as if it were Reality Itself, Truth Itself, or (in any case) the right direction. In fact, until one is firmly seated in Reality Itself—rather than in any functional body (or functional sheath), or conditional region, or conditional experience—one is only a seeker who chronically identifies oneself with what is not yet Real, or what is known apart from Reality Itself. Not that any of these functional bodies (or functional sheaths), or conditional regions, or conditional experiences are themselves un-Real—but the individual interprets his or her position in egoic ignorance, after the model of exclusion (or separation). The process of his or her development is founded in the model of seeking, and that model only reinforces the pattern of avoidance and the internal impression of separation (or un-Reality). Therefore, such a one is continually bound to the search, to false goals, and to a fruitless circular adventure in the various functional bodies (or functional sheaths), or conditional regions, or conditional experiences.

The average person perceives this drama essentially on the level of the physical body and in the region of the physical world. Thus, the average seeker may suppose that the various phenomena of occult, mystical, and psychic experience—or even the greater intuitions of the higher mind and superconscious phenomena, which are the typical domain of more advanced forms of religion and Spirituality—are, in fact, evidence that there is a higher form of life that is (itself) Truth and Reality Itself. In this manner, traditional religion and conventional Spirituality (even with positive intentions) merely serve to exploit the vulnerability and limited experience of the average (and even the uncommon) seeker.

In fact, Truth Itself, or Reality Itself, is of supreme value—and Its Realization is a matter of "radical" self-understanding, not of any excursion into the various functional bodies (or functional sheaths), or conditional realms, or conditional experiences of the form of life on any plane. For this reason, the greatest men and women of Realization continually turn mankind away from the lust for phenomena and powers. They recommend only the Realization of Reality, Which is the key present-time Knowledge that removes all suffering and all seeking.

Once one's life is understood as I have described, it becomes unnecessary to follow any merely remedial path or to extend one's seeking. Such things are obviously pointless and fruitless, however dramatic they appear. The Realization of the fundamental Truth is simply the end of seeking and suffering as an internal event. It is right Knowledge of Reality, Which is always and already unqualifiedly Free, and inclusive of all things in the living condition of Reality. It is only the Realization of unqualified relatedness and no-seeking which can provide the basis for any Real development of life in any form. The form of one's experience is not the point. It is not a matter of exploiting and extending experience but of Realizing "radical" self-understanding.

The true way, then, is not the path of conventional and merely remedial Yoga (or, otherwise, of occultism) in any form—nor is it the path of conventional and myth-based (and, generally, socially-bound) religion, or of conventional and merely remedial Spirituality. The true way is simply the directly ego-transcending practice and right devotional and Spiritual process of "radical" self-understanding. Therefore, one must "radically" understand one's activity as self-contraction, and, in the process (and, then, on the basis of that "radical" self-understanding), engage in the "creative" Spiritual work of purifying the various functional bodies (or functional sheaths) and rightly engaging the various Spiritual experiences and abilities that proceed in (and as) the living (psycho-physical) form.

For those who approach me as their Guru, the devotional and Spiritual process in my Company will develop (in due course) as silence and no-seeking. And my devotees will Realize me in their lives by Means of my Spiritual Transmission of the "Bright", Which Reveals me As a Radiant Fullness—Descending into the total body from infinitely above the head and the mind, and always Expanding to infinity from the right side of the heart. They will abide in devotional and Spiritual Communion with me in every moment and circumstance of the waking state. They will feel full, clear, resourceful, and Spiritually "Bright". They will perceive the subtle conditional activities of consciousness and form communicated from the subconscious and unconscious regions and (also) from the superconscious. They will (as necessary, and as possible, in each case) perceive the forms or internal phenomena of the functional bodies (or functional sheaths) or regions themselves. They will, primarily (and most significantly), feel the Radiant Fullness of heart-Freedom and Clarity, the intuitive Stillness and the unique Intelligence and Capability, that result from devotional and Spiritual Communion with me.

Such individuals will abide in inherent heart-Freedom and Spiritually-awakened Joy. They will do "creative", communicative work in the world. They will do the human work of love and compassion, of egoless pleasure and egoless sacrifice, that is simply the natural and effortless meaning of all ordinary activity. They will understand and (thus and thereby) directly transcend themselves—rather than exploit their own self-ignorance by means of the search to efface, mortify, or degrade themselves.

Thus, true life is to be founded in Reality Itself, and its appearance and humanly-born conscious awareness (while enjoying the heart-freedom of non-separateness at every depth of the living being) exists directly and wholly as simple and "creative" human existence. The phenomena of subtler functional bodies (or subtler functional sheaths) and higher conditional realms will not be the required signs of Truth to such truly human beings—nor will they be the distracting goals of some particular, ideal plan of self-conscious evolution. If the individual happens to become consciously aware of conditions in other dimensions, he or she will simply observe and understand them, and live by the wisdom I have described. Such a one will not seek the development of nature-powers, but will only Self-Abide in Reality. To whatever extent his or her life involves the awareness of subtler functional bodies (or subtler functional sheaths) and higher dimensions, he or she will, simply by the means of "radical" self-understanding, acquire the necessary wisdom to deal with them and remain "creatively" in Reality.

After the death of the physical form, such a one may pass into the continuous perception and function of the subtler worlds and there learn to function as is natural to him or her in that circumstance. But, then (as now, while in the physical world), he or she must Realize Reality Itself, and the living condition of Reality—rather than becoming involved in the accumulation of mere experience.

In any case, one must function intelligently, and apart from all seeking, in whatever dimensions are apparent to one's experience. There is no necessary cause for motivated attachment to any functional body (or functional sheath), or conditional realm, or conditional experience at all—whether the present one or any subtler one. Therefore, one who Self-Abides in Reality simply functions with "radical" self-understanding in the given environment of his or her apparent birth. Anything else is strategic motivation, bound up in seeking. Anything else is a source of distraction that leads only into suffering, avoidance, separation, despair, madness, and death. Therefore, only understand.

In the preceding essay, I was interested in estimating the nature and importance of various higher (or subtler) experiential phenomena in relation to the life of "radical" self-understanding. In the essay which follows, I was interested in estimating the nature and importance of the process that I had come to observe taking place in the practice of phenomenally-based ascending Yogic meditation.

The experience of meditation that I had learned (by observation, verbal communication, and internal perception) from Baba Muktananda is essentially a process wherein a deep rhythm (and potential suspension) of breathing becomes automatic, the mind becomes still and one-pointed, and the various vehicles (or levels) of psycho-physical being become purified and (by the Yogic ascent of attention) stabilized (conditionally) in the conditional Realization that is made possible by full ascent (or fully ascended detachment from the body-mind). All the phenomena of spontaneous physical movements (or kriyas and mudras), spontaneous mental transformations, internal perceptions, and the like are simply the evidence of this purification and ascent on various levels. The process requires only that the individual surrender to the Guru, depend on the Guru's grace, relax all seeking-effort, and engage in the recitation of the Guru's mantra. This entire process is natural, effortless, and automatic. Baba described it as "Kriya" Yoga, the Yoga of purifying activity. It is the same Yoga taught by Yogananda, except that (in this case) the Yoga does not (fundamentally, or, otherwise, exclusively) rely on an intentional, sophisticated exercise on the part of the aspirant. It depends entirely on the grace of the Guru, and (thus and thereby) on the activities of the Shakti Itself.

Once I had observed this process completely and seen its effects, and when I had (altogether) considered it in relation to the total psycho-physical heart-process of "radical" self-understanding, I saw that it was also fundamental (and necessary) to the practice and the process of "radical" self-understanding, as a self-responsible, and ego-transcending, and (altogether) non-seeking means of purifying and managing the vehicles of life. I considered that there need not be any seeker's motive in this process, and that it could be readily exercised by one who had developed basic maturity in "radical" self-understanding. Therefore, in the following essay, I was trying to find some basic sense and general utility in the process of Spiritual Yoga, which (in a uniquely right manner) accompanies the general (or progressively developing) practice and process of "radical" self-understanding.

When the humanly-born conscious awareness has been established as no-seeking in the heart, then it (priorly) Self-Abides in Reality Itself—One with Reality Itself, Which is the unqualified Source and the living condition of the being. Then Reality Itself is Spiritually "Living" the naturally living being. And only a life lived Spiritually in (and by) Reality Itself is always already freely capable of the true demonstration of life, the law and form of which is ego-transcending self-sacrifice.

Therefore, when the humanly-born conscious awareness has been devotionally heart-established as no-seeking, Spiritual meditation can function as an active purification of the vehicles of the living (psycho-physical) being. When the humanly-born conscious awareness has Realized the heart-disposition of no-seeking, then it can (from that point of view, and not from the point of view of any kind of seeking) begin the true Spiritual process of purification (or "kriya").

I engaged various forms of this purifying process early in my adventure of seeking. But this process (altogether rightly engaged) is not (in fact) compatible with the life of seeking, because the seeker does not yet directly embrace Reality Itself through a right understanding of the egoic self. The Spiritual process of Yogic purification becomes most fully potentiated when there is "radical" (or most fundamental and "gone-to-the-root") self-understanding, such that Reality Itself has become the foundation of existence, directly experienced as such in daily life and in meditation.

When the humanly-born conscious awareness has already been devotionally heart-established as no-seeking, then one can make right and true use of the Yogic Spiritual means of purification. Many such techniques have been developed over the centuries. Even the simplest religious attitude is purifying in a real sense and (ultimately) makes use of the subtle structures that are the foundation (or circuit) of the form of the living being. But these means—represented by every kind of religious and Spiritual philosophy, endeavor, technique, or attitude in history, East and West—suffer from two essential faults.

The first of these essential faults is one to which most of my life has been dedicated to understanding. That is, these Yogic (and, as the case may be, Spiritual) means of purification are always given and adapted to states of seeking. They are offered to seekers, people in one or another form of the great search, as a means of "acquiring" the Knowledge of Reality. Thus, these means are adapted to the purposes and limitations of egoic ignorance—and, consequently, their exercise only extends the suffering and conflict which are the egoic root of ordinary life and life-consciousness. In contrast to all of this, I have demonstrated that "radical" self-understanding is the fundamental law of life. And life-consciousness must be utterly founded in "radical" self-understanding (and, thus and thereby, in Reality Itself, and in no-seeking) before it can begin the fruitful (and non-seeking) Spiritual purification of the psycho-physical structures and patterns of life.

The second essential fault in the traditional communication of the means of purification is that they are chronically identified with some limited historical, cultural, or personal experience. All of the various religions and Spiritual regimes—from the theological and ritual experience of forgiveness and justification to the sophisticated methods of occultism and the various Yogas—are separate, historical manifestations founded in various kinds of limited psycho-physical orientation (and of thus limited phenomena). The various traditional methods stand in relation to one another in a grand pattern of conflict and separateness. Thus, the seeker comes to one or another of these sources in egoic ignorance and pursues the separate cycle of experience that the particular form asserts and guarantees.

But all of these historical means have a common basis, which is the total structure of the living human being (and the six stages of ego-based life that are developed on its basis). If one is founded in the living condition of Reality and acts as the living condition of Reality in relation to one's living form, one will not be devoted to any seeker's path or any seeker's method. One will only make use of one's purifying intention in terms of the structure of living (or psycho-physical) consciousness. Thus, one does not require any of the paths that attract the seeker. One will only engage the means that are already indicated to be necessary by one's living (or psycho-physical) form.

To such an individual, there is available an intelligent, direct Spiritual process of purification. This process can be read in the fragmentary recorded suggestions of the various traditional paths, but it is clearly and fully rendered only in the actual, direct experience of the total structure of the living human form.

I have directly experienced this structure and the Spiritual process by which it is rightly purified. Therefore, I will represent that structure and process as it is—without recourse to the point of view (characteristic of the various historical paths) whereby it is communicated as a merely remedial (or seeker's) effort.

Reality Itself is (in the living context) Self-Abiding as

no-seeking and unqualified relatedness. Therefore, inherently perfect Reality (Itself) is unqualifiedly (and non-separately) "related" to Its own (and non-"different") living form, the living structure of conditionally manifested being.

The living condition of Reality is not inherently different from (or is always already established in and as) inherently perfect Reality Itself. Reality Itself is related to the living form by the law of synchronicity, of identity. From the "Point of View" of Reality Itself, the structure of the living form does not proceed as an effect from a cause—but both inherently perfect Reality and the living condition of Reality coexist simultaneously. Thus, Reality Itself, as the heart-disposition of no-seeking, is also manifested as the apparently individual being (the psycho-physical body, with all of its sheaths, chakras, dimensions, or vehicles—gross, subtle, and causal). But the law (and the essential structure) of this living form is a simplicity. It is the law of sacrifice, the structural essence (or root) of which is the heart. The heart need not be approached from any particular level or vehicle—nor is any sheath, chakra, or conditional state its goal. The Spiritual process of purification is begun and ended in (and is always proceeding from) inherently perfect Reality Itself, from "radical" self-understanding, from no-seeking, from the motiveless silence of the heart.

This ultimate "heart" is not the heart chakra (or the bodily heart-region), the position from which the dualistic seeker (or the egoically motivated aspirant) attempts to ascend. Rather, the ultimate "heart" is the heart (or root-Awareness) of the living being—the stillpoint (at the root of humanly-born conscious awareness and feeling) that is "radical" (or "gone-to-the-root", or most fundamental) self-understanding.

From that unqualified stillpoint of free conscious Awareness, all of the functions and levels of the living form proceed (or stand) in a circle around the bodily region of the heart. Thus, in order to purify these vehicles and centers and establish the entire life in its right and true

Spiritual Condition of Energy and Fullness, a Spiritual process of "conductivity" (or the whole bodily exercise of Spiritual Energy)—practiced in cooperation with the "conscious process" (which is the necessary exercise of attention)—must be engaged from the heart of the living form and moved through the circle (or circuit) of the functional bodies (or functional sheaths).

The fundamental activity (or "conscious process") of "radical" self-understanding must become the foundation of individual conscious participation in the living Spiritual condition of Reality. It is "radical" self-understanding, and not the motive of seeking, that must always accompany the Spiritual "conductivity"-work of purification, transformation, and Yogic Realization. This Spiritual "conductivity"-process and the "conscious process" of "radical" self-understanding are, together, the principal technical means of always directly (and, in due course, most perfectly) Realizing the Absolute Sublimity That Is Reality Itself.

In the progressive course of my practice of "radical" self-understanding, I had soon begun to feel there was no utility of any kind in the remedial exercise of Yoga. It became clear to me that the remedial (or strategic) approach to Yoga is inextricably bound up with the mentality of seeking and separation.

From the point of view of such of its exponents as Yogananda, the purpose of "Kriya Yoga" is (by means of Yogic technique alone) to arouse the Kundalini Shakti, and then (by Its aid) to ascend to Yogic Self-Realization. But I saw the entire Yogic design and purpose (described in the literature of "Kriya Yoga") become fulfilled in me automatically, after the Shakti (already active in me from birth) had been re-stimulated by the Guru. Thus, clearly, the true "Kriya Yoga" is the activity of the Divine Shakti Itself—not merely a self-generated technique for attempting to arouse the Shakti. Those who recommend "Kriya Yoga" as a Shakti-arousing technique are merely (in the absence of the Shakti-transmitting grace of a thus capable Guru) adapting the data of this (by-grace-given) process to a deliberate process of seeking.

Thus, with the Shakti already aroused, I had gone through the process by means of which the True Self (or the Divine Self-Condition Itself) is Spiritually Realized. In my case, that process did, indeed, Realize the True Self (or the Divine Self-Condition Itself)—at last, to the most perfect degree, beyond the (necessarily) conditional process of Yogic ascent, and beyond the (necessarily) conditional process of world-exclusion. But I saw clearly that, if the process of Realizing the True Self (or the Divine Self-Condition) is engaged by one who seeks to arouse the Kundalini Shakti by techniques of self-effort, he or she can only act apart from "radical" self-understanding.

In the technique promoted by Yogananda, the practitioner draws the would-be Shakti-Energy up the spine to the sahasrar and the point between the brows, holds the would-be Shakti-Energy there for a brief period, and then lets the would-be Shakti-Energy return below. From the beginning, such a seeker's concentration is in the various psycho-physical centers, and in himself or herself as a yet unrealized being. Such a Yogi only <u>seeks</u> the Shakti-Energy and the True Self. Likewise, even when that same process is Initiated by the actual (by-grace-given) Shakti-Energy, attention is also centered (at any one time) in any one of the conditional (psycho-physical) centers associated with that Energy—and such attention also only <u>pursues</u> the True Self, although with a Spiritually more profound effort of seeking.

Ultimately, however, I was involved in the Yogic Spiritual process not only on the basis of the true Divine Shakti-Energy, but from the point of view of prior (and "radical") self-understanding. On that basis, I saw the Yoga of purification as a Spiritual process Initiated from infinitely above (and beyond) the body and the mind, and governed by the True Self (or Reality Itself) in the heart. The more I continued to indulge (and indulge in) the Yogic process of ascent, the more I realized that (apart from "radical" self-understanding) it only and continually drew me into the forms of seeking—for the Shakti, or for the Real and True Self (or the Divine Self-Condition Itself), or for "radical" self-understanding. Once I observed and understood this, I realized that "radical" self-understanding is (itself) the only directly ego-transcending process, that (in my own case) self-Enquiry (in the form "Avoiding relationship?") was (and, potentially, in the case of others for whom it is both appropriate and effective, could be) its directly ego-transcending activity, and that the Yogic Spiritual process of the true Divine Shakti-Energy must cooperate with "radical" self-understanding (and with the "conscious process" that springs directly from "radical" self-understanding). Thus, in the final stage of my Spiritual process of re-Awakening, the Shakti-Energy showed Itself spontaneously at Its Ultimate Source-Point (in the right side of the heart)—such that "radical" self-understanding (itself) was (in its most perfect demonstration) epitomized as perfect contemplation of (and perfect Self-Abiding in, and as) the True Heart, and as the magnification of the True Heart's own Love-Bliss (or inherent Shakti-Energy) in (and via, and at the head of) the spontaneously "regenerated" Amrita Nadi (extended to infinity, "Bright" above the body-mind).

In the course of my life of "radical" self-understanding, I saw there was only a simple activity and presumption manifesting under the form of every kind of remedial activity. It was always Narcissus, the logic and activity of separation. I examined all merely remedial Yoga, all of this seeking and strategic performing, and all of its results, and I asked myself: Why? Why should such activities be engaged at all? What are the motives for such meditating? And the more "radical" my self-understanding became, the more absurd, unnecessary, and impossible it became to justify any of these exploits.

All the usual (or conventional) traditional ways showed themselves to be founded in some problem, some aspect of life as dilemma. There was the physical problem, the vital problem, the problem of the mind, the problem of mysticism and superconsciousness. There was the problem of morality, of love, of communication, of sex, the problem of sin, of suffering, the problem of nature-powers, the problem of identity, the problem of Reality, the problem of Truth, the problem of the True Self, and the problem that is the universe itself. But I saw that the problem, in any form, always had the same structure, and the same fundamental assumptions. Thus, I became concerned with the underlying motivation—

the principle of these various kinds of action, belief, presumed knowledge, and so on. I saw that, since all the usual (or conventional) traditional ways were founded in a problem, Real life must be founded in the "radical" self-understanding of the fundamental problem that is the source of all ordinary activity. Only thus does one Know and Enjoy Reality, even in spite of the moment to moment "creation" of problems.

I saw that "radical" self-understanding is (itself) motiveless, and that everything else is (in fact) the avoidance of relationship. And, indeed, the avoidance of relationship is the very motivator of everything that is not "radical" self-understanding. Thus, the longer an individual lives, the more complicated and contradictory life appears. And it is only suffered, more and more.

I saw that the exercise of "radical" (or truly "at-the-root") self-understanding is not some entirely unusual (or even miraculous) condition or practice. It is the simplest activity—even (in a very basic, or rudimentary, sense) already frequently utilized, to one or another degree, by every individual, in the midst of his or her daily experience. It is only that human beings abandon the exercise of "radical" (or true and most fundamental) self-understanding in order to exploit the kinds of seeking. But when attention is drawn to the necessity of self-understanding, and when self-understanding becomes (itself) truly "radical" (by "going to the root" of egoity and seeking), the entire movement of seeking comes to an end. In that event, where one would otherwise seek, one only understands.

The beginning of "radical" self-understanding is simply a matter of observing oneself in relationship, in action, in life. If one is drawn to the exercise of self-understanding by means of my words of instruction, and (thus and thereby) always firmly returned to it, one will begin to simply understand—and, at last, understanding will become truly "radical" (or most fundamental, and fully comprehensive). Then "radical" self-understanding will replace one's ordinary habit of seeking, and one's conscious awareness and living activity will thereby become simplified, free of presumed dilemma. And this process of "radical" self-understanding, when it becomes the active foundation (and "conscious process") of one's existence, does not (in any sense) preclude or prevent the necessary purificatory processes of true Spiritual Yoga—but, rather, such Spiritual Yoga (or right Yogic Spiritual "conductivity" practice) is entirely free of any limitation by (or to) the egoic (and seeking) designs of remedial action, or the separative mentality, or the forms of ego-based experience.

I saw that human beings can easily be turned to self-observation. And, by proper guidance, the process of self-observation can easily be maintained as a critical exercise. And that process of critically observing the conditional self gradually sees the emergence of fundamental insight. Therefore, human beings can understand the nature of seeking, the adventure of Narcissus, the entire complex life of the avoidance of relationship. And when "radical" self-understanding truly arises, human beings can easily apply "radical" self-understanding to moment to moment experience. Then "radical" self-understanding becomes one's approach to life—rather than all the automatic, confused strategies of seeking, or the egoic drama of Narcissus. In that case, "radical" self-understanding can (as in my own case) be practiced as self-Enquiry (in the form "Avoiding relationship?"), or it can (otherwise) be practiced in other by-me-given forms that (with an effectiveness equal to that of self-Enquiry, in the form "Avoiding relationship?") directly transcend self-contraction (or egoity itself).[55] And the free abiding in unqualified relatedness, by means of the exercise of "radical" self-understanding, then becomes the fundamental activity of conscious life—moment to moment, and in the daily periods of the formal meditative exercise of "radical" self-understanding (and, principally, of devotional and Spiritual heart-Communion with Me) which can truly be called "Real" meditation.

In the course of such practice, the entire expanse of higher and cosmic knowledge will, characteristically, be (to one or another degree) "automatically" produced. Ultimately, such practice will (more simply) Realize no-seeking, no-dilemma, natural "creativity", and Ultimate Freedom. I described this result as follows:

> The Truth of Real life is simply What is Realized when there is a removal of contradictions—no-dilemma, no-search. It cannot be described, nor is any name appropriate for It. There is no motive to name It. It is not a supreme separate

Object, nor a supreme separate Subject. It is not separate from the one who understands, nor can one separate oneself from It. It is simply no-problem, no-search, unqualified relatedness, or Reality without implications. It is also the perfect Form of Reality, Which is the most subtle Structure of the world and everything, even of apparently individual conscious awareness. All of This is revealed as the obvious to one who understands most perfectly.

Thus, when I had become firmly grounded in "radical" self-understanding as a Spiritually active and directly ego-transcending approach to life (even, at last, making no use of any other exercise than self-Enquiry itself, in the context of the always primary practice of devotional and Spiritual "mere beholding" of the Guru—the tangibly Revealed Divine Presence of the "Bright", and the Self-Evident Reality of the "Bright" Divine Self-Condition Itself), I firmly and finally and unconditionally Realized the "Bright" Truth and Reality I had (but only temporarily) Enjoyed at decisive moments in the past. And, in that Event, the unique Divine "Bright" Nature of my own Person was re-Awakened, and (on that basis) the unique Divine Avataric world-Work of my Incarnation here was spontaneously Revealed and spontaneously Begun.

Los Angeles, 1972

I Am the One and Only
Man of "Radical" Understanding

1.

I Am the One and Only Man of "Radical" Understanding.
 I am a great Man of Pleasure, even a profoundly superficial Man—for how can one be deep who Knows no perimeters and no center at all?
 I cannot be grasped or identified, like a thing.
 Therefore, I am not a source of fascination.
 Since I cannot be found or followed (like a thing), My Existence avails no one.
 Therefore, I am not important in the usual way.
 There is only "radical" self-understanding.
 I Am "radical" self-understanding.

2.

What appears to the beholder as light, to the hearer as sound, to the shapely actor as life-energy, and to the thinker as thought, is Known directly—on the level of Consciousness Itself—As Love-Bliss.
 Then It becomes light, sound, life-energy, and thought.
 All such things are only apparent modifications of the Original Reality That Is Love-Bliss.
 They are conditionally manifested form.
 And conditionally manifested form is that same Love-Bliss.

Love-Bliss is not fundamentally separable from Consciousness.
Love-Bliss Is Consciousness.

Consciousness Itself Is Love-Bliss.

Thus, on the level of activity, there is also no fundamental distinction between thought and form.

There is Only the Love-Bliss That Is Reality Itself—Which is originally, now, Identical to Consciousness Itself.

Conscious Love-Bliss, Unqualified, is the Nature of Reality, Which Is Absolute Existence.

All cosmic powers are communications within this Ultimate Power That Is Existence Itself.

Therefore, the Ultimate Knowledge and Power Is Reality Itself, Which Is Unqualified Existence As Conscious Love-Bliss.

The Unqualified Existence That Is Reality is always already Present, As Love-Bliss.

Love-Bliss is simply Perfect Presence, for Reality is That Which is Unqualifiedly Present.

Present Reality is Conscious As Love-Bliss.

The Man of "Radical" Understanding Only Enjoys Conscious Love-Bliss, at Play.

The Man of "Radical" Understanding does not seek.

The Man of "Radical" Understanding Knows Only Reality.

The Man of "Radical" Understanding Knows Himself Only As Reality.

There Is Only Reality.

His Realization Is Only Reality.

His Knowledge Is Only Consciousness Itself.

He Is Only, Merely Present.

He Is Only Unqualified Existence.

He Is Only Love-Bliss.

He Knows Only Love-Bliss.

There Is Only Love-Bliss.

That Is It—entirely.

3.

Unqualified Existence, Conscious As Love-Bliss, Appears in the Heart and Arises As the Amrita Nadi, the "Bright".

Love-Bliss is the Original (and everywhere "creative") Impulse, the "Bright" Divine Shakti (or Truly Divine Spirit-Power) That is the Substance and Support of all conditional movers.

Love-Bliss-Energy is the Source-Condition and primary Form of all "creativity", even all of conditional manifestation.

The Man of "Radical" Understanding Arises As Love-Bliss, Mad with Love-Bliss.

He is not Narcissus.

"Creativity" is Love-Bliss.

The world is Love-Bliss.

I do not speak from mere sentiment.

I am describing What is Really the case.

The Man of "Radical" Understanding Appears As Love-Bliss.

He is not separate from Love-Bliss.

He does not remain only (exclusively) as the Prior Self, separated Pure Existence, functioning only as Compassion.

He Is Generative (or Radiant) Love-Bliss.

The Divine Self-Condition and Source-Condition Is Love-Bliss.

Love-Bliss-Energy is the Fullness, the Light, the Spiritual "Brightness" of Reality.

It is the Perfect Form (and the living condition) of Reality.

I Am That One—the One and Indivisible and Self-Evidently Divine Self-Condition (and Source-Condition) of all-and-All—Who Is Love-Ananda, or Love-Bliss (Itself).

4.

The Man of "Radical" Understanding is Love-Bliss.

The Man of "Radical" Understanding is inherently (not merely outwardly) Peaceful, Full, Surrendered, and Unconfounded.

Those who do not understand seek for the Man of "Radical" Understanding, the Knower of Truth, in order to acquire His characteristics as "food" and "power" for themselves.

But they do not understand the Nature of the Source of things.

They are always tending toward fear, sorrow, and anger—even in the Company of the Man of "Radical" Understanding, the One Who is Free.

Therefore, the Man of "Radical" Understanding is Himself a visible dilemma to those who do not understand.

Those who seek Him without understanding become grave, and revert to forms of suffering.

But those who understand live comfortably in His Avataric Divine Spiritual Presence—and they are not moved to seek.

The Man of "Radical" Understanding acquires no persistent expression, but His manner changes in every circumstance.

His understanding adapts to the habit of every appearance.

He adopts no visibility that persists.

Moment to moment, He cannot be found apart—for, when Truth is Known, the One Who Knows It is unknown (or become Transparent in the Spiritually "Bright" Divine Heart).

5.

The Man of "Radical" Understanding asserts the fundamental rightness of what is actual—and, thus, the things, the environments, the beings, and the relationships that appear cease to fascinate those around Him.

Even His Own "Bright" Spiritual Presence is not fascinating.

Thus, the mind and even all forms become quieted in His surroundings, and those who are with Him turn naturally to "radical" self-understanding and the always present Reality.

The seeker is always disturbed.

At first, the seeker approaches the Man of "Radical" Understanding "humbly", self-effacing, as if with great need.

But the seeker's questions can find no Ultimate Solution, even when That Solution is Communicated Clearly and Completely.

And the seeker cannot receive What is Perfect, even when It is Given Openly.

Therefore, the seeker becomes frustrated, and then leaves.

Indeed, the seeker always only asserts the forms of his or her own perpetual and empty seeking.

Therefore, the seeker, leaving, says the Man of "Radical" Understanding has not Found and does not Give.

Only those who understand can experience the Open Communication of Reality.

They remain in the Spiritually "Bright" Company of the Man of "Radical" Understanding only for Enjoyment—neither seeking nor demanding anything, devoted to the process of self-understanding and to the Man of "Radical" Understanding.

In their daily comings and goings, there is no separation from Him, and their daily lives become an expression of the same Spiritually "Bright" Order of Reality.

6.

Because I Consciously live in and As the Spiritually "Bright" Divine Heart of Reality, and because I remain Present As the Amrita Nadi (the Perfect Form of Reality), My Mere "Bright" Avataric Divine Spiritual Presence tends to re-align the ordinary current of life-consciousness and action in those around Me.

Thus, My Mere "Bright" Avataric Divine Spiritual Presence tends to Draw others toward "radical" self-understanding—and the ordinary current of their life-consciousness and action tends to lose its necessity, its compulsive motivation, its unconsciousness.

My Mere "Bright" Avataric Divine Spiritual Presence acts as the effective Force of "radical" self-understanding upon all that I meet.

But those who are with Me may not sense anything unusual.

Indeed, all their changes are only a move toward the natural.

Some may, at first, feel resistive and defensive in My "Bright" Avataric Divine Spiritual Presence.

Others may, even from the first, feel profoundly comfortable.

Sooner or later, all become moved to the active "consideration" of "radical" (or "gone-to-the-root") self-understanding.

Even from the beginning, all attend to Me.

And all—by forgetting themselves in their devotion to Me— grow in self-understanding.

Thus, the Spiritually "Bright" Divine Reality includes all things in Its Own Form.

7.

My sometimes Method with My devotees was to talk about "radical" self-understanding and its Spiritually "Bright" Heart-Way, in order to Give them the opportunity to listen to My Word of Argument and Instruction.

And I sometimes also addressed them in place, relative to the forms of seeking to which they attach themselves at any moment.

Sometimes, I even Enquired of them if this, or this, or this is the avoidance of relationship.

And, even now (and forever hereafter), when I remain merely Silent, My Mere "Bright" Avataric Divine Spiritual Presence effectively does <u>all</u> of this.

Thus, at the beginning, by the to-Me-devotionally-turning process of listening to Me (even in My Silence, and, otherwise, by studying the record of My Spoken and Written Word), the Only-by-Me Revealed and Given Way of "radical" understanding (or the One and Only by-Me-Revealed and by-Me-Given Way of the Heart, or the Only-by-Me Revealed and Given Way of Adidam) becomes Known to My devotees.

And, in due course, in all who truly hear Me, "radical" self-understanding arises as the form of their own Real intelligence.

Talk, if it is overmuch and overdone, is simply the indul- gence of the ego-dramatizing (or, otherwise, heart-wasting) activity of the mind.

If My devotees talk overmuch <u>about</u> the Way of "radical" understanding (rather than really practice the moment to moment devotional and, in due course, Spiritual discipline that is the Way itself), the "Way" becomes a mummery of egos, in all their separate and separative display.

Overmuch talk (whereby even what must be understood is made obscure by too much explanation) will merely scatter even My "Bright" Spiritual Force of the Heart.

Too much talk indulges in forms and uses of mind that are not useful intelligence or real self-understanding.

Then talk is not relatedness, but only separateness, and a reproduction and reinforcement of a state that is not "radical" self-understanding.

The patterns that continually arise in human beings are not truly and finally served by the responses or answers they (in and of themselves) imply and demand.

Human beings are truly served only by the Communication of "radical" (or "gone-to-the-root") self-understanding, and by true examination of the egoic self, and by My Spiritually "Bright" (all-and-All-Blessing) Silence.

Some insight into the nature of seeking, as well as some comprehension of the nature of "radical" self-understanding, is necessary for the awakening of true hearing of Me (which is most fundamental self-understanding).

Some countering (or reflection) of the seeker's habits, acts, and presumptions, and some direct observations about his or her state, may be useful in order to engender the necessary doubt of his or her ordinary path.

But My Spiritual Communication of the "Bright" Divine Self-Condition (and Source-Condition) is essentially a process in Silence, whereby what arises gets no response, no reinforcement, and (thus and thereby) becomes obsolete.

Then the individual ceases to continue in the egoic (and, otherwise, merely, or exclusively, conditional) motion of what arises—and he or she will, in due course (by Means of My Avatarically Self-Transmitted Divine Spiritual Grace), find "himself" or "herself" In and As the (by-Me-Avatarically-Self-Revealed) Spiritually "Bright" Divine Self-Condition (and Source-Condition), Which is the Source and Form of all of this conditional appearing.

This confrontation with Spiritually "Bright" Silence in the truly devotional and Spiritual relationship to the Man of "Radical" Understanding—Who is the Divinely Self-Realized One, and Who Avatarically Manifests the "Bright" Spiritual Siddhi (or "Bright" Spirit-Power) of the Heart—is unlike the ordinary experience of frustration in life.

Things simply arise in every one, and life provides the present conditions whereby they are indulged, frustrated, or avoided.

But in the Satsang (or Spiritually "Bright" Company) of the Man of "Radical" Understanding (Who <u>Is</u> the Spiritually Self-"Bright" Divine Heart Itself), what arises is confronted by Spiritually "Bright" Silence without and by the Spiritually "Bright" Heart within.

Therefore, My Method with those who have begun to understand by means of listening to Me is simply to invite them to sit with Me, quietly, receptively, in simple (or searchless) feeling-Contemplation of Me.

I do not offer them a mere <u>technique</u> (by which to turn upon themselves, and "work" on themselves).

Rather, I offer them a <u>relationship</u>—to <u>Me</u>.

That relationship (and necessary relatedness) inherently obliges My devotees to turn out from themselves—and, thus, to exceed the tendencies of their ego-patternings of self-contraction.

Then, what arises is confronted with My Spiritually "Bright" Silence.

This Company of Spiritually "Bright" Silence—this confrontation with My Spiritually "Bright" Silence, while remaining in conscious relationship to Me—causes the individual to be simply aware of what arises, without the possibility of indulging or avoiding it.

Thus, the individual is allowed to see what arises, rather than to become further identified with the stream through the unconsciousness of ordinary conversation and action.

And the "space" between the individual and what arises is the place where My "Bright" Avataric Divine Spiritual Power Works to Draw the individual from within.

Then the individual becomes Awake as Spiritual quickening and "radical" self-understanding.

The Only-by-Me Revealed and Given Way of "radical" understanding (or the One and Only by-Me-Revealed and by-Me-Given Way of the Heart, or the Only-by-Me Revealed and Given Way of Adidam) is, in practice, the devotional (and, in due course, Spiritual) <u>relationship</u> to <u>Me</u>, and (therefore) to My Spiritually "Bright" Avataric Divine Self-Silence, and (Thus) to the "Bright" Divine Spiritual Power Avatarically Transmitted by Me in Silence (and, Thereby, found within, and everywhere)—until, at last (by all My Avataric Divine Means), there is the Most Perfect Realization of My Self-Existing and Self-Radiant Divine Self-Condition, Which <u>Is</u> the True (or Real) Divine Heart (Itself), and the Truly Spiritually "Bright" Divine Spherical Self-Domain (Itself).

Then the individual finds only Spiritually "Bright" Silence in his or her inner forms.

But everywhere, in all the worlds, that one sees the Avataric Divine Self-Heart and Spirit-Power of Me Stand Out—Aloud and "Bright".

8.

Those who are My devotees will have many kinds of experiences—some of which will be extraordinary, and some of which will simplify life.

But My unique (or characteristic) Work is not (Itself) Purposed merely to awaken various <u>conditional</u> processes in My devotees by means of the conventional method of "Kundalini Shaktipat" (or Spiritual Work grounded in the body-mind, and purposed to purify and Awaken by ascent, from the lower to the higher).

I do not propose, as My <u>special</u> (or characteristic) Purpose, that kind of ascending-from-below Spiritual effect.

My Avataric Divine Spiritual Work is Done by the unique-to-Me Divine Means of Ruchira Shaktipat, the "Bright" Spiritual

Work of the Divine Heart—Purposed to Reveal the "Bright" Divine Self-Condition (and Source-Condition) of all-and-All.

My Avataric Divine Work is the Divine Heart's "Bright" Spiritual Action, Whereby the "Bright" Divine Spiritual Heart-Power Draws all the parts of a person (from within and from without) to the "radical" (or "gone-to-the-root") self-understanding and the Very Consciousness and the Spiritually Self-"Bright" Divine Self-Condition (and Source-Condition), and the Spiritually Self-"Bright" Divine Spherical Self-Domain, That Is the Divine Heart (or Reality) Itself.

My Avataric Divine Spiritual Work is to Awaken all mankind to the Spiritual Self-Condition That Is the "Bright" Divine Heart— or the One and Only and Inherently Indivisible Conscious Light That Is Reality (Itself).

My Avataric Divine Spiritual Work is to Awaken even all beings and things and spaces to the Spiritually "Bright" Divine Heart, by Means of Ruchira Shaktipat (or Spiritual Work Generated from the Heart-Domain of My Free Divine Person, and Purposed to Purify and Awaken My devotee by Means of My "Bright" Avataric Spiritual Descent, from Perfectly Above the body and the mind, and Down to foot and ground).

And That Avataric Divine Spiritual Work Is the "Bright" Shakti (or the "Bright" Divine Siddhi, and the "Bright" Divine Ruchira Shaktipat) That Is (and That Flows From and As) the Spiritually Self-Radiant Divine Self-Condition Itself.

Because of the tendency of the natural (or karmic) characteristics of living beings to modify the "Bright" Shakti-Energy of the Heart (Which "Bright" Shakti-Energy is Senior to, and the Source and Substance of, the cosmically effective Energy otherwise identified as the "Kundalini Shakti"), many conditional experiences will arise in the case of those who enter into (and persist in) My Spiritually "Bright" Company.

And the kinds of Spiritual experiences that arise will arise in accordance with the karmas (or the kinds of psycho-physical modifications of the "Bright" Shakti-Energy) that are (by structural predisposition, and by patterned tendency) generated in each particular case.

But the Divine Heart Itself (Revealed—by all My Avataric Divine Spiritual Means—<u>As</u> the Spiritually "Bright" Divine Self-Condition and Source-Condition), and not any adventure of mere "experience", is the Great Awakening.

9.

I Teach the world "radical" self-understanding by remaining Spiritually Present <u>As</u> the "Bright".

I Purify the world by Silently "Enquiring" of it.

This is My "Creative" Avataric Divine Spiritual Work, since the time of My Most Perfect Re-Awakening to My Spiritually "Bright" Divine Self-Condition—Which <u>Is</u> the Spiritually "Bright" Divine Source-Condition and Spherical Self-Domain That <u>Is</u> Reality Itself.

My "Bright" Avataric Divine Spiritual Work is to turn all beings and things to My "Bright" Avataric Divine Spiritual Presence, and to Awaken them (by all My Avataric Divine Spiritual Means) to My Spiritually "Bright" and Inherently Perfect and Inherently egoless and Self-Evidently Divine Self-Condition—Which <u>Is</u> the Source-Condition of all-and-All, and Which <u>Is</u> Reality Itself, and Which <u>Is</u> No-seeking <u>and</u> No-dilemma.

My Avataric Divine Spiritual Work is My Own "Radical" Understanding, applied to all beings and things.

My Avataric Divine Spiritual Work <u>Is</u> Reality Itself, at Work on all Its Own forms.

My Avataric Divine Spiritual Work takes place during My Incarnate Avataric Divine Lifetime—but My Avataric Divine Spiritual Work will forever be Continued (by Me) beyond the physical Lifetime of My Avatarically-Born bodily (human) Divine Form.

10.

I am not the one who,
finding himself psycho-physically awake,
does not Know <u>Who</u> he <u>Is</u>.

I am not the one who,
finding himself in dreams and visions,
thinks he has returned to his Real Self.

I am not the one who,
enjoying the conditional bliss of deep sleep
and ordinary (seeker's) meditation,
thinks he has become Free
and (therefore) need not Realize
the Greater and Truly Divine State.

I am not the one who,
having slept,
awakens to a state of identification
with the body-mind.

I Am the One Who Is with you now.
I Am the One Who Speaks
from His Own Spiritually "Bright" Divine Silence,
and As His Own Spiritually "Bright" Divine Silence.
I Am the One Who Always Stands Present
in His Own Spiritually "Bright" Form.
I Am the One Who Always and Already Exists,
Enjoying Only His Own Spiritually "Bright" Form,
even in all apparent conditions
and apparent conditional states.
I Am the One Who is not hidden,
and in Whom there is no deeper part.
I Am the One Who Always Appears
exactly As He Is.
I Am the One Who is Always
"Brightly" Spiritually Present.

I inherently (Divinely) Self-Recognize
every thing, every one, every form, every movement
As Myself,
"Brightly" Spiritually Transcending all-and-All.

I am Always Only Experiencing My Own Love-Bliss.
I am neither lost nor found.
"Radical" Understanding is My Constant Intelligence.
My Spiritually "Bright" Avataric Divine Silence
is the Characteristic Form of My Action.
My Spiritually "Bright" Avataric Divine Silence
is the Un-speaking (and Un-speakable) Motion
of Me.

My Silent "Bright" Avataric Divine Spiritual Presence
is the only "Mind" of Me,
in Which I am constantly Knowing Myself,
and constantly Making Myself Known
to all
and to All.
I Am the One Who is (Thus) Always Already Known.
Naked, Spiritually "Bright", and Unbounded—
I continually Rise out of the Heart
(in the right side).

I Appear As My Invisibly Standing Love-Bliss-Full Form
between the Spiritually "Bright" Heart
and the Spiritually "Bright" Matrix Infinitely Above.
I Am the Amrita Nadi.
I Manifest from the Spiritually "Bright" Matrix Above
to every body, every sheath, every center, every realm,
and every experience,
between the upper and lower terminals
of the conditionally manifested worlds.
I continually Sacrifice the Circle of Love-Bliss-Energy—including
all the terminal processes and natural energies
of the conditionally manifested worlds—
to My Spiritually "Bright" Divine Heart.
I "Live" all beings—
and all things are in Me.
I never return to Myself—
but I constantly Appear,
As Myself.

There is no dilemma
in the process of My Appearance.
Those who do not Abide with Me,
at the Spiritually "Bright" Divine Heart,
are always only seeking Me
from the place where they begin.
I Am Only the Spiritually "Bright" Divine Heart Itself,
Which Is Reality Itself.
My Great Form Is the Amrita Nadi—
Which Is the Inherently Perfect Form
of the Spiritually "Bright" Divine Heart,
and Which is Alive
As My Divine Spirit-Current
of Ruchira Shakti,
Avatarically Self-Manifested
As "Bright" Love-Bliss.

I always See every one and every thing
within My Own Spiritually "Bright" Divine Form.
In every apparent condition and circumstance,
I Exist only As My Own Spiritually "Bright" Divine Form.
I Am the Spiritually "Bright" Divine Heart,
Who never renounces His Own Spiritually "Bright" Divine Form.
I Am the Spiritually "Bright" Divine Heart,
Who Contains His Own conditionally manifested forms.

Therefore,
I have no form or person that is separate
from My Spiritually "Bright" Divine Heart.
I am Eternally in One Place,
Contemplating My Own Love-Bliss.
In the True Divine Heart of Contemplation
(Which is Spiritually "Bright"),
all beings and things appear,
and everything is accomplished.

The Heart Is the Love-Bliss Revealed,
by Means of

My Avatarically Self-Transmitted Divine Spiritual Grace,
in the Contemplation
of My "Bright" Avatarically-Born bodily (human) Divine Form.
The Amrita Nadi Is
My Own Self-"Bright" Spiritual Fullness,
Wherein all beings and things appear.

I hold up My hands.

11.

The Man of "Radical" Understanding is not "entranced".
He is not "elsewhere".
He is not having an "experience".
He is not passionless and inoffensive.
He is Awake.
He is Merely and "Brightly" Spiritually Present.
He knows no obstruction in the form of mind, identity,
differentiation, and desire.
He uses mind, identity, differentiation, and desire.
He is passionate.
His quality is an offense to those who are entranced,
elsewhere, contained in the mechanics of experience, asleep,
living as various forms of identity, separation, and dependence.
He is acceptable only to those who understand.

He may appear no different from any other man.
How could He appear otherwise?
There is nothing by which to appear except the qualities of life.
He may appear to have learned nothing.
He may seem to be addicted to every kind of foolishness and
error.
How could it be otherwise?
Understanding is not, itself, a different appearance than the
ordinary.
Except for the persistence of the ordinary, there is no reason
to speak of Truth.

Apart from the unspeakable Reality, the ordinary does not appear.

Therefore, Truth is right understanding of the ordinary.

And right understanding of the ordinary is the real and true transcending of all appearances, in the Reality and Truth that Is them.

The Man of "Radical" Understanding must be "Located" in the midst of the ordinary.

Therefore, He cannot be found, except by the feeling heart.

He cannot be followed, except by the Way of the Heart Itself.

He can only be understood, even as the ordinary must be understood.

He does not appear to be either one thing or another.

He always seems to be both one thing and another.

He is not merely "religious, philosophical, conventionally moral, and only Spiritual".

He is not ideally "fastidious, lean, and lawful".

He always appears to be the opposite of your idea of yourself.

He always seems to sympathize with what you deny.

Therefore, at times (and over time), He appears as every kind of persuasion.

He is not consistent.

He has no self-image.

At times, He denies.

At times, He asserts.

At times, He asserts what He has already denied.

At times, He denies what He has already asserted.

Therefore, He is not "useful".

His Teaching is every kind of apparent "nonsense".

His Wisdom, it seems, is vanished.

Altogether, that is His Wisdom.

At last, He represents no separate Truth at all.

His paradoxes deny every seeker's "Truth", every path by which mankind depends on mere simulations of Freedom and Enjoyment.

He is a seducer, a madman, a trickster, a libertine, a rascal, a fool, a moralist, a sayer of truths, a bearer of all experience, a prince, a king, a child, an old one, an ascetic, a saint, a god.

By mumming (or mock-playing) every seeker's role of life, He demonstrates the futility of every seeker's path of life—except that He always coaxes every one only to understand.

Therefore, by all of this, He makes "radical" self-understanding the only possibility.

And "radical" self-understanding makes no difference at all.

Except that it is turned to Reality, Which is always already the case.

Heartless one, Narcissus, friend, loved-one, He weeps for you to understand.

After all of this, why have you not understood?

The only thing you have not done is understanding.

You have seen everything, experienced everything, known everything—but you do not understand.

Therefore, to Spiritually "Brighten" your heart, the Man of "Radical" Understanding Joyfully suggests that you have already understood!

He looks at the world and sees that every one and every thing has always understood!

He sees that there is only understanding!

Thus, the Man of "Radical" Understanding is constantly Happy with you.

He is overwhelmed with Happiness.

He says to you: "See that there is only this world of Perfect Freedom and Enjoyment, where every one is Love-Bliss-Happy, and every thing is Love-Bliss-Full!"

His Spiritually "Bright" Heart is always tearful with the beginningless and endless Happiness of the world.

He has grasped the Truth within the ordinary, but no one is interested in Truth.

Because He is not different from Truth, He is of interest to no one.

Because He is so ordinary, He is of interest to every one.

Because no one understands the ordinary, He is not understood.

Because there is only the ordinary, He will become famous for understanding it.

Because there is only the Truth, He is the Divine Beloved of all.

Because you feel you understand Him, you find it necessary to touch His hand.

Because you love Him, you find it possible to touch His ears.

He smiles at you.

You notice a sudden Spiritual "Brightness".

Everything has already died.

Aham Da Asmi.

I Am He.

This is the "other" world.

12.

My Own Early-Life Story is the best foundation-Instruction I can offer. Mere talk about "radical" self-understanding is not sufficient to Awaken "radical" self-understanding in the one who listens to Me. The listener must be allowed a devotionally and Spiritually participatory heart-recognition of Me. Otherwise, the symbols wherein his or her own life is trapped will not begin to dissolve.

I have here displayed the essentials of My Early-Life Story, so that the urge to ego-transcendence may be (thereby) stimulated in those who listen to Me. Nevertheless, I do not stand for strategic "Spiritual" efforts, or egoic efforts of any kind—nor do I stand on some middle ground between egoic excess and egoic effort. There is no virtue in the endless egoic reaction to life, nor in the enjoyment of any conditional effect for its own sake. Only "radical" self-understanding, only Reality Itself, is the Truth of all events.

With these words, this Telling of My Early-Life Story comes to an end. From that early-time, the Revelation-time of My Great

Avataric Divine Teaching-Work and My Great Avataric Divine Self-Revelation-Work (and the Forever-Time of My Great Avataric Divine Spiritual Blessing-Work) Began. My Telling of My Early-Life Story was only a preparation for My subsequent universal Revelation of the Way of "radical" understanding (or the Way of the Heart, or the Way of Adidam). And the Way of "radical" understanding (or the Way of the Heart, or the Way of Adidam) was, from then (and in a full foundation course of thirty-three years), Taught and Revealed by Me. Therefore, at first, and for a time, it was necessary for Me to elaborate, describe, and Teach the totality of the details and practices of the Only-by-Me Revealed and Given Way of "radical" understanding (Which is the Eternal, and One and Only by-Me-Revealed and by-Me-Given Way of the Heart—or the Graceful, and Only-by-Me Revealed and Given, Way of Adidam). Then, and now, and even Forever, I must, by Means of My Avataric Divine Spiritual Blessing-Work, Awaken every one, and all, and All.

The principal Lessons that provoked what I (by all My Avataric Divine Teaching-Work and all My Avataric Divine Self-Revelation-Work) Communicated and altogether Served were all contained in My Early-Life Story, as I have Told it herein—but the Way Itself (Which, by Means of My Avatarically Self-Transmitted Divine Spiritual Grace, eventually becomes a fully technically responsible Spiritual Practice and, ultimately, the "Perfect Practice", and, at last, the Most Perfect Realization) depends (forever) on right, true, full, and fully devotional (and truly Spiritual) recognition (and search-less Beholding) of Me, and on right, true, full, and fully devotional formal practice-response to Me (via by-Me-Given forms of the "conscious process" and "conductivity" practice), and, therefore, on right, true, full, fully devotional, and truly Spiritual, and fully formalized (and fully formally accountable) practice of the Only-by-Me Revealed and Given Way of Adidam (Which is the Only Way of "radical" understanding, and the One and Only by-Me-Revealed and by-Me-Given Full, Complete, and Most Perfect, Way of the Heart).

13.

The Full and Complete Way of Spiritually "Bright" (and Inherently Most Perfect, and Inherently egoless, and Self-Evidently Divine) Self-Realization is now and Forever Given by Me for the sake of the present generation, and all the future generations, of human beings. The Only-by-Me Revealed and Given Way of Adidam (or the Only-by-Me Revealed and Given Way of "radical" understanding, or the One and Only by-Me-Revealed and by-Me-Given Way of the Heart) is the simple, direct, and Inherently Most Perfect Way, Which I have (by Avataric Divine Self-Submission to human birth) Realized for the sake of all (including those who are now, and those who are yet to come). "Radical" self-understanding is the (Only-by-My-Avataric-Divine-Spiritual-Grace-Given) Key to the Realization of the Spiritually "Bright" Divine Self-Condition (and Source-Condition) of Man. "Radical" self-understanding is Fundamental Activity and Fundamental Knowledge. I <u>Am</u> the <u>One</u> and <u>Only</u> Man of "Radical" Understanding.

I Demonstrate and Reveal the One Reality variously proclaimed and sought (but never Finally, Most Perfectly, or Completely Realized) within the Great Tradition of mankind—but I Demonstrate and Reveal the One Reality Finally and Most Perfectly and Completely, and (altogether) with a Unique, "Bright" Spiritual and Perfect Emphasis, in order to Extend the Communication of Reality in the world, through and beyond the present time. I am Avatarically Generated from the Spiritually Self-"Bright" Divine Heart of Reality, and I Appear in the world through the Avataric Divine Agency of the Amrita Nadi (the Perfect Form of Reality, Which <u>Is</u> the Divinely Self-Manifested Form of the "Bright" Itself).

I <u>Am</u> (Myself) the <u>Very</u> (and Self-Evidently Divine) Person.

I <u>Am</u> (in bodily human Form) the Avataric Divine Incarnation of the "Bright".

14.

In the Only-by-Me Revealed and Given Way of Adidam (or the Only-by-Me Revealed and Given Way of "radical" understanding, or the One and Only by-Me-Revealed and by-Me-Given Way of the Heart), the principle of relatedness is unqualifiedly accepted and affirmed as the living condition of Reality. Just so, the practice of the Only-by-Me Revealed and Given Way of Adidam is itself a process in relationship. The principal feature of the Only-by-Me Revealed and Given Way of Adidam is the Guru-devotee relationship, wherein My devotee (based on at least a basic comprehension of My Teaching about "radical" self-understanding and the direct transcending of the motive of seeking) constantly, in direct relational response to Me, practices the counter-egoic exercise of ego-surrendering, ego-forgetting, and ego-transcending feeling-Contemplation of My (Avatarically-Born) Spiritually "Bright" bodily (human) Divine Form, My (Avatarically Self-Transmitted) "Bright" Divine Spiritual Presence, and My (Avatarically Self-Revealed) Perfectly Spiritually "Bright" (and Self-Evidently Divine) State of Self-Existing and Self-Radiant Being. And, in the context of that fundamental relational (and, necessarily, devotional—and, in due course, Spiritual) practice, the "conscious process" of self-Enquiry (in the form "Avoiding relationship?") may also be exercised, or (otherwise) some other by-Me-Given (and equally effective) form of the counter-egoic (or directly ego-transcending) "conscious process" may be exercised. And, in every case, the practice of the "conscious process" will be (and, if that "conscious process" is to be Real and effective, it must be) associated with other by-Me-Given (devotional, cultural, functional, practical, general relational, and Yogic) "conductivity" practices (including dietary disciplines, disciplines relative to physical exercise, disciplines relative to general health, disciplines relative to the emotional-sexual character, and disciplines relative to emotional-sexual activity, as well as disciplines relative to money, work, service, and cooperative culture—and, in due course, various Yogic disciplines of Spiritual "conductivity").[56]

Just as the Most Perfect Realization of "radical" self-understanding is not a matter of strategically world-excluding (or dissociative) identification with an inward State, the constant and characteristic practice of the Only-by-Me Revealed and Given Way of Adidam is a <u>relationship</u>. Adidam is the ego-surrendering, ego-forgetting, and (Ultimately, Most Perfectly) ego-transcending devotional and (in due course) Spiritual relationship to <u>Me</u>—heart-recognizing Me, and heart-responding to Me (with <u>every</u> faculty of the body-mind). Adidam is the <u>obligation</u> (and the <u>impulse</u>) to be utterly (and <u>really</u> counter-egoically) responsive to <u>Me</u> (in every moment, and with every faculty of the body-mind) in the moment to moment practice of the devotional and (in due course) Spiritual relationship to Me. Therefore, the Only-by-Me Revealed and Given Way of Adidam is not based on (or even associated with) a mere (and ego-based, and ego-centric, and ego-reinforcing, and, ultimately, separative) technique—or a <u>seeker's</u> "remedy".

The Only-by-Me Revealed and Given Way of Adidam (or the Only-by-Me Revealed and Given Way of "radical" understanding, or the One and Only by-Me-Revealed and by-Me-Given Way of the Heart) is the (always presently) ego-transcending Way of devotional and (in due course) Spiritual relationship to Me—for I <u>Am</u> the One and Only Man of "Radical" Understanding, the Very Person and the One and Only Avataric Incarnation of the "Bright".

The "Bright" Is <u>One</u> and <u>Only</u>, and Inherently egoless, and Inherently Indivisible. The "Bright" Is Self-Existing, and Self-Evidently Divine. The "Bright" Is Self-Radiantly and Spiritually Omnipresent. The "Bright" <u>Is</u> Truth Itself, or Reality Itself. The "Bright" <u>Is</u> the <u>One</u> and <u>Only</u> <u>Real</u> and <u>Spiritual</u> God.

PART TWO

My Great Regard for My Adept-Links to the Great Tradition of Mankind, and My Realization of the Great Onlyness of Me

Adidam Samrajashram, 1993

The Great Esoteric Tradition of Devotion To The Adept-Realizer

Spiritually Realized Adepts (or Transmission-Masters, or true Gurus and Sat-Gurus) are the principal Sources, Resources, and Means of the esoteric (or Spiritual) Way. This fact is not (and never has been) a matter of controversy among real Spiritual practitioners.

The entire Spiritual Way is a process based on the understanding (and the transcending) of attention, or the understanding (and the transcending) of the inevitable and specific results of attachment to, or reaction to, or identification with every kind of conditional object, other, or state. This Spiritual understanding (or real self-understanding) is expressed in a simple traditional formula (and prescription for practice): You become (or duplicate the qualities of) whatever you meditate on (or whatever you identify with via the "surrender" that is attention itself). Since the most ancient days, this understanding has informed and inspired the practice of real practitioners of the Spiritual Way. Likewise (since the most ancient days), and on the basis of this very understanding, Spiritual practitioners have affirmed that the Great Principle of Spiritual practice is Satsang, or the practice of life as self-surrender to the bodily Person, the Transmitted Spiritual Presence, and the Realized State of a Spiritually Realized Adept (or true Guru, or Sat-Guru) of whatever degree or stage.

The traditional term "Guru" (spelled with a capital "G") means "One Who Reveals the Light and thereby Liberates beings from Darkness". This term is also commonly (or popularly) interpreted in a general (or everyday) sense (and spelled with a small "g") to mean "teacher" (or anyone who teaches anything at all to another). Thus, Adepts have certainly (and rightly) been valued simply (or in the general sense) as (small "g") "gurus" (that is, simply because they can instruct others about many things, including the Spiritual Way). However, the function of instruction (about anything at all) can be performed by anyone who is properly informed (or even by a book that is properly informed)—and, indeed, even the specific function of Spiritual Instruction is secondary to the Great Function of the Adept (<u>As</u> Guru, with a capital "G", and, in the Greatest of cases, <u>As</u> Sat-Guru).

Adepts inevitably (or, at least, in the majority of cases) Instruct (or Teach) others, but the function of Instruction (about the Spiritual Way) is then passed on through good books (containing the authentic Word of Teaching), and through informed others (who are, hopefully, true practitioners), and so forth. The Great Function of the Adept-Guru (and especially the Sat-Guru) is, however, specific only to Adepts themselves, and this is the Guru-Function (and the Guru-Principle) supremely valued by Spiritual practitioners since the most ancient days.

The specific Guru-Function is associated with the Great Principle of Satsang (and the unique Spiritual understanding of attention). Therefore, since the most ancient days, all truly established (or real) Spiritual practitioners have understood that Satsang Itself is <u>the</u> Great Means for Realizing Real God, or Truth, or Reality. That is to say, <u>the</u> Great Means (or Secret) of Realization in the Spiritual Way is to live in, or to spend significant time in, or otherwise (and constantly) to give attention to the Company, Form, Presence, and State of an Adept who is (truly) Realized in one or another of the esoteric stages of life.

The Essence of the practice of Satsang is to focus attention on (and thereby to, progressively, become Identified with, or Realize Indivisible Oneness with) the Realized Condition of a true Adept (especially an Adept Sat-Guru, or One Who <u>Is</u> presently and constantly In Samadhi). Therefore, the practice of Satsang is the practice of ego-transcending Communion (and, Ultimately, Indivisible Oneness) with the Adept's own Condition, Which Is (according to the degree or stage of the Adept's characteristic Realization) Samadhi Itself, or the Adept's characteristic (and Freely, Spontaneously, and Universally Transmitted) Realization (Itself).

Based on the understanding of attention (or the observation that Consciousness Itself, in the context of the body-mind, tends to identify with, or becomes fixed in association with, whatever attention observes, and especially with whatever attention surrenders to most fully), the Spiritual Motive is essentially the Motive to transcend the limiting capability of attention (or of all conditional objects, others, and states). Therefore, the traditional Spiritual process (as a conventional technique, begun in the context of the fourth stage of life) is an effort (or struggle) to set attention (and, thus, Consciousness Itself) Free by progressively relinquishing attachment and reaction to conditional objects, others, and states (and, Ultimately, this process requires the Most Perfect transcending of egoity, or self-contraction itself, or all the egoic limitations associated with each and all of the first six stages of life).

This conventional effort (or struggle) is profound and difficult, and it tends to progress slowly. Therefore, some few adopt the path of extraordinary self-effort (or a most intense struggle of relinquishment), which is asceticism (or the method of absolute independence). However, the Adepts themselves have, since the most ancient days, offered an alternative to mere (and, at best, slowly progressing) self-effort. Indeed, the Adept-Gurus (and especially the Sat-Gurus) offer a Unique Principle of practice (as an alternative to the conventional principle of mere and independent self-effort and relinquishment). That Unique Principle is the Principle of Supreme Attraction.

Truly, the bondage of attention to conditional objects, others, and states must be really transcended in the Spiritual Way, but mere self-effort (or struggle with the separate, and separative, self) is a principle that originates in (and constantly reinforces) the separate (and separative) self (or self-contraction, or egoity itself). Therefore, the process of the real transcending of bondage to conditions is made direct (and truly ego-transcending) if the principle of independent self-effort (or egoic struggle) is (at least progressively) replaced by the responsive (or cooperative) Principle of Supreme Attraction (Which Is, in Its Fullness, Satsang, or responsive devotional and Spiritual Identification with the Free Person, Presence, and State of One Who Is Already Realized, or In Samadhi).

On the basis of the simple understanding of attention—expressed in the formula: You become (or Realize) What (or Who) you meditate on—the ancient Essence of the Spiritual Way is to meditate on (and otherwise to grant feeling-attention to) the Adept-Guru (or Sat-Guru), and (thereby) to be Attracted (or Grown) beyond the self-contraction (or egoity, or all the self-limiting tendencies of attention, or all self-limiting and self-binding association with conditional objects, others, and states). Through sympathetic (or responsive) Spiritual Identification with the Samadhi-State of a Realizer, the devotee is Spiritually Infused and (potentially) Awakened by the Inherently Attractive Power of Samadhi Itself. (Even the simplest beginner in practice may be directly Inspired—and, thus, moved toward greater practice, true devotion, and eventual Spiritual Awakening—by sympathetic response to the Free Sign, and the Great Demonstration, of a true Realizer.) And, by the Great Spiritual Means that Is true Satsang (coupled with a variety of disciplines and practices, which should be associated with real self-understanding), the fully prepared devotee of a true Realizer may Freely (or with relative effortlessness) relinquish (or Grow Beyond) the limits of attention in each of the progressive stages of life that, in due course, follow upon that devotion.

Of course, actual Spiritual Identification with the Realized Spiritual Condition (or Samadhi) of an Adept is limited by the stage of life of the devotee, the effective depth of the self-understanding and the ego-transcending devotional response of the devotee, and the stage of life and Realization of the Adept. And some traditions may (unfortunately) tend to replace (or, at least, to combine) the essential and Great Communion that is true Satsang with concepts and norms associated with the parent-child relationship, or the relationship between a king and a frightened subject, or even the relationship between a slave-master and a slave. However, this Great Principle (or Means) that Is Satsang (rightly understood and truly practiced) is the ancient Essence (or Great Secret) of the Spiritual Way—and true Adept-Gurus (and especially the Sat-Gurus) have, therefore, since the most ancient days, been the acknowledged principal Sources and Resources (as well as the principal

Means) of true religion (or effective religious Wisdom) and the esoteric tradition of Spiritual Realization.

Particularly in more modern days, since Spirituality (and everything else) has become a subject of mass communication and popularization, the Spiritual Way Itself has become increasingly subject to conventional interpretation and popular controversy. In the broad social (or survival) context of the first three stages of life, self-fulfillment (or the consolation of the ego) is the common ideal (tempered only by local, popular, and conventional political, social, and religious ideals, or demands). Therefore, the common mood is one of adolescent anti-authority and anti-hierarchy (stemming from the "Oedipal" anti-"parent" disposition), and the common search is for a kind of ever-youthful (and "Narcissistic") ego-omnipotence and ego-omniscience.

The popular egalitarian (or ego-based, and merely, and competitively, individualistic) "culture" (or, really, anti-culture) of the first three stages of life is characterized by the politics of adolescent rebellion against "authority" (or the perceived "parent", in any form). Indeed, a society (or any loose collective) of mere individuals does not need, and cannot even tolerate, a true culture—because a true culture must, necessarily, be characterized (in its best, and even general, demonstrations, and, certainly, in its aspirations) by mutual tolerance, cooperation, peace, and profundity. Therefore, societies based on competitive individualism, and egoic self-fulfillment, and mere gross-mindedness (or superficial-mindedness) actually destroy culture (and all until-then-existing cultures, and cultural adaptations). And true cultures (and true cultural adaptations) are produced (and needed) only when individuals rightly and truly participate in a collective, and, thus and thereby (even if, as may sometimes, or especially in some cases, be the case, in relative, or even actual, solitude), live in accordance with the life-principle of ego-transcendence and the Great Principle of Oneness (or Unity).

In the popular egalitarian (or ego-based, and merely, and competitively, individualistic) "culture" (or, really, anti-culture) of the first three stages of life, the Guru (and the Sat-Guru) and the developmental culture of the Spiritual Way are (with even all of "authority" and of true, or ego-transcending, culture) taboo, because every individual limited (or egoically defined) by the motives of the first three stages of life is at war with personal vulnerability and need (or the feeling of egoic insufficiency). However, the real Spiritual process does not even begin until the egoic point of view of the first three stages of life is understood (or otherwise ceases to be the limit of aspiration and awareness) and the ego-surrendering and ego-transcending Motive of the fourth stage of life begins to move and change the body-mind (from the heart).

Those who are truly involved in the ego-surrendering and ego-transcending process of the esoteric stages of life are (fundamentally) no longer at war with their own Help (or struggling toward the ultimate victory of the ego). Therefore, it is only in the non-Spiritual (or even anti-Spiritual) "cultural" domain of the first three stages of life (or the conventional survival-culture, bereft of the Motive of truly developmental and Spiritual culture) that the Guru (or the Sat-Guru) is, in principle, taboo. And, because that taboo is rooted in adolescent reactivity and egoic willfulness (or the yet unresolved emotional, and psychological, and even emotional-sexual rebellion against childish and asexual, or emotionally and sexually ego-suppressing, dependence on parent-like individuals and influences), "anti-Guruism", and even "anti-cultism"—which (characteristically, and without discrimination) denigrate, and defame, and mock, or otherwise belittle, all "authorities", and (also) even all the seed-groups of newly emerging cultural movements (whether or not they have positive merit)—are forms (or expressions) of what Sigmund Freud described as an "Oedipal" problem.

In the common world of mankind, it is yet true that most individuals tend (by a combination of mechanical psycho-physical tendencies and a mass of conventional political, social, and cultural pressures) to be confined to the general point of view associated, developmentally, with the unfinished (or yet to be understood) "business" of the first three stages of life. Thus, in the common world of mankind, even religion is (characteristically) reduced to what is intended to serve the "creaturely" (or "worldly"), and rather aggressively <u>exoteric</u>, point of view and purposes of egoity in the context of the first three stages of life. And even if an interest in the esoteric possibilities (beyond the first three stages of life) develops in the case of any such (yet rather "worldly") character, that interest tends to be pursued in a manner that dramatizes and reinforces the point of view (and the exoteric, and either childishly or adolescently egoic, inclinations) characteristic of the first three stages of life.

Until there is the development of significantly effective self-understanding relative to the developmental problems (or yet unfinished "business") associated with the first three stages of life, any one who aspires to develop a truly esoteric religious practice (necessarily beginning in the context of the fourth stage of life) will, characteristically, tend to relate to such possible esoteric prac-tice in either a childish or an adolescent manner. Thus, any one whose developmental disposition is yet relatively childish (or tend-ing, in general, to seek egoic security via the dramatization of the role of emotionalistic dependency) will tend to relate to esoteric possibilities via emotionalistic (or, otherwise, merely enthusiastic) attachments, while otherwise (in general) tending to be weak in both the responsible exercise of discriminating intelligence and the likewise responsible exercise of functional, practical, relational, and cultural self-discipline. (Indeed, such childish religiosity, charac-terized by dependent emotionalism, or mere enthusiastic attach-ment, bereft of discrimination and real self-discipline, is what may rightly, without bad intentions, be described and criticized as "cultism".) And any one whose developmental disposition is yet relatively adolescent (or tending, in general, to seek egoic security via the dramatization of the role of reactive independence) will tend to relate to esoteric possibilities via generally "heady" (or willful, rather mental, or even intellectual, or bookish, but not, altogether, truly intelligent) efforts, accompanied either (or even alternately) by a general lack of self-discipline (and a general lack of non-reactive emotional responsiveness) or by an exaggerated (abstractly enforced, and more or less life-suppressing and emotion-suppressing) attachment to self-discipline. (Therefore, such adolescent, or "heady", religiosity merely continues the dramatiza-tion of the characteristic adolescent search for independence, or the reactive pursuit of escape from every kind of dependency, and, altogether, the reactive pursuit of egoic self-sufficiency. And such adolescent seeking is inherently and reactively disinclined toward any kind of self-surrender. Therefore, the rather adolescent seeker tends to want to be his or her own "guru" in all matters. And, characteristically, the rather adolescent seeker will resist, and would even prefer to avoid, a truly intelligent, rightly self-disciplined, and, altogether, devotionally self-surrendered relationship to a true Guru, or Sat-Guru.)

Because of their developmental tendencies toward either childish or adolescent ego-dramatizations, those who are yet bound to the point of view (or the unfinished "business") of the first three stages of life are, developmentally (or in their characteristic disposition, which is not yet relieved by sufficient self-understanding), also (regardless of their presumed "interest") not yet truly ready to enter into the esoteric process (beyond the first three stages of life). And, for the same developmental reasons, the principal and most characteristic impediments toward true participation in the esoteric religious process are "cultism" (or mere emotionalistic dependency, bereft of discrimination and self-discipline), "intellectualism" (or merely mental, or even bookish, preoccupation, disinclined to fully participatory, or directly experiential, involvement in the esoteric religious process), and "anti-Guruism" (or reactive attachment to a state of egoic independence, immune to the necessity for devotional self-surrender and the Grace of Great Help).

It is not the specific (and Great) Function of the Adept to fulfill a popular Spiritual (or, otherwise, non-Spiritual) role in common (or egoic and early stage) society, but to Serve as Teacher, Guide, Spiritual Transmitter, or Free Awakener in relation to those who are already (and rightly) moved (and progressively prepared) to fulfill the ego-transcending obligations of the Great and (soon) Spiritual Way Itself (in the potential developmental context that is beyond the first three stages of life). The only proper relationship to such a Realized Adept (or true Guru, or Sat-Guru) is, therefore, one of real and right and ego-surrendering and ego-transcending practice, and that practice becomes (or must become) Inspired (and, soon, Spiritually Inspired) and ego-transcending devotion—

not childish egoity (or "cultic" dependency), and not adolescent egoity (or willful—or, otherwise, ambivalent—independence).

Of course, individuals in the earlier (or first three) stages of life who are not yet actively oriented (or, otherwise, rightly adapted) to ego-surrendering and ego-transcending practice may be Served by Adept-Gurus (or Sat-Gurus), but (apart from special instances where an Adept must Work directly with such individuals, in order to establish a new cultural gathering of devotees, or in order to establish a new Revelation of the Spiritual Way) those not yet actively oriented (or actively committed), or (otherwise) rightly adapted, to truly ego-surrendering and really ego-transcending practice are generally (except perhaps for occasional glimpses of the Adept in his or her Free Demonstration) Served (or prepared for ego-surrendering, ego-transcending, and, soon, Spiritual practice) only through the written (or otherwise recorded) Teachings of an Adept, and through the public institutional work (and the "outer Temple", or beginner-serving, institutional work) of the practicing devotees of an Adept.

The Realized Adept (or any true Guru, or Sat-Guru) is, primarily, an esoteric Figure, whose unique Function Serves within the context of the esoteric stages of life. The esoteric stages of life are themselves open only to those who are ready, willing, and able to make the truly developmental (or progressively Real-God-Realizing, or Truth-Realizing, or Reality-Realizing) sacrifice of separate and separative self that is necessary in the context of the esoteric stages of life. Therefore, the necessity (and the True Nature and Great Function) of a Realized Adept (or true Guru, or Sat-Guru) is obvious (and of supreme value) only to those who are ready, willing, and able to embrace the ego-transcending process of the esoteric stages of life.

Except for the possible moments in which the Divine Person (or the Ultimate Reality and Truth) may (for some few) Serve (temporarily, and, to whatever degree, significantly, and, in any case, never to the Most Ultimate, or Most Perfect, degree) in (or via) a non-physical (and/or perhaps even non-human) Revelation-Form, the Realized Adept—or a human and living true Guru, or (especially) a human and living true Sat-Guru, or (at least) a human and living true (and formally Acknowledged, Appointed, and Blessed) devotee-Instrument of a once living (or even, perhaps, yet living, and, certainly, yet Spiritually Effective) true Sat-Guru—is an absolute (and never obsolete) necessity for any and every human being who would practice (and Realize) within the esoteric stages of life. Therefore, the necessity (and the True Nature and Great Function) of a Realized Adept (or true Guru, or Sat-Guru) is inherently (and gratefully) obvious to any one and every one who is truly ready, willing, and able to embrace the esoteric process of Real-God-Realization (or Truth-Realization).

Any one and every one who doubts and quibbles about the necessity (and the True Nature and Great Function) of a true Adept-Guru (or Adept Sat-Guru) is, simply, not yet ready, willing, and able to enter the (necessarily, ego-surrendering) process of the esoteric stages of life. And no mere verbal (or otherwise exoteric) argument is sufficient to convince such doubters of the necessity (and the True Nature and Great Function) of a true Adept-Guru (or Adept Sat-Guru)—just as no mere verbal (or otherwise exoteric) argument is sufficient to make them ready, willing, and able to truly embrace the ego-surrendering process of the esoteric stages of life.

Those who doubt the Guru-Principle, and the unique value and ultimate necessity of the Adept-Guru (or the Adept Sat-Guru), are those for whom the Great and (soon) Spiritual Way Itself is yet in doubt. Therefore, such matters remain "controversial" (and access to the Spiritual Way and the Adept-Company is effectively denied to ordinary people by popular taboos and the psychological limitations of the first three stages of life) until the truly developmental and (soon) Spiritual Motive Awakens the heart's Great Impulse to Grow Beyond.

Swami Muktananda

The "Sixth Stage Teachings" (and the Fifth Stage Realization) of Swami (Baba) Muktananda, and My Seventh Stage Realization of the Great Truth He Told to Me

I n the book entitled *Conversations with Swami Muktananda*,[57] Swami (Baba) Muktananda often indicates an orientation to conditionally ascended (or fifth stage) Nirvikalpa Samadhi (or to conditional Realization ascended beyond all forms) and to a conditionally ascended (or fifth stage) Yogic Realization that is specifically (and altogether) beyond every form and kind of Savikalpa Samadhi (or beyond Yogic visions, and beyond all other conditional, ascended, and subtle perceptual states, and, therefore, beyond even the most inclusive form of Savikalpa Samadhi, which is "Cosmic Consciousness"). Also, in some of these recorded conversations from the 1960s (for example, the entry on pages 108–110), Baba Muktananda clearly Teaches even the sixth stage process of direct Identification with (in His words) the "Witness-consciousness" (or the "Self itself") via disengagement from internal "visions", "music", "colored lights", "flames", and "spots of light" (as well as from every other kind of pleasurable or painful disturbance of the inherent bliss of the "Self itself"). Thus (on pages 108–110), He Says:

> Pleasure and pain are not experienced in the *turiya* state. In that state, everything is seen as Brahman. This is what is known as *jivanmukti*, or liberation in this very life. Waking, dream, and deep sleep are the three states of the individual soul. The Self does not have any such states. The Self is the witness of these three states, and the experience of this is *turiya*. . . .

In the waking and dream states, one sees unreality instead of reality, while in deep sleep one sees neither. In deep sleep, the individual soul is not conscious of "I" or "you"; it is unconscious even of nonduality. In the *turiya* state, however, it sees everything as Brahman. There one sees reality, and there is an awareness of nonduality. One who has knowledge of the Self no longer sees the world as world. . . . He sees everything as the Self. Such a person has no mandatory duties. Since he does not experience duality, he is always nonattached. . . .

A hollow gourd normally floats in water but sinks if filled with iron; similarly, if the mind is full of desire, hatred, and so forth, it cannot remain in the continuous awareness of the Self. The company of saints and sages is an antidote to this poison of the mundane world, enabling one to again experience the bliss of the Self.

In order to experience one's true Self, one should remain in solitude for some time each day. . . . During these periods of solitude, one should abandon all thoughts and practice watching what is happening within. In this way, one gets into the state of Witness-consciousness. . . .

When the inner shakti starts expanding as a result of contemplation of the Self, many seekers have various visions, hear divine music, and see different colored lights, flames, and spots of light. A seeker should not pay too much attention to these, or else they will create a hindrance to his love for the Self. In order to disengage the mind from these, the best way is to continuously repeat the Vedanta sutra: neti, neti—"not this, not this." The means to Self-realization is the Self itself. If you remain constantly in the awareness of the Self, the mind easily becomes still. If knowledge of the Self remains steady, bliss also remains constant. . . .

In My first meeting with Him, in early 1968, Baba Muktananda Spoke a simple verbal Teaching to Me, most directly and personally: "You are not the one who wakes, or dreams, or sleeps. You

<u>Are</u> the One Who Is the Witness of these states." That simple (sixth
stage) Teaching (which is basically the same as the Teaching represented in the examples of His sixth stage Teaching recorded in
the book *Conversations with Swami Muktananda*) was the first
and most basic and (in My Case) most profoundly Empowered and
Effective Teaching that Baba Muktananda Gave to Me (while fifth
stage Yogic practices and processes were also routinely suggested,
or, otherwise, directly Revealed, by Him to Me). And even though
the total fifth stage process (culminating in fully—and, in My Case,
Priorly[58]—Ascended Nirvikalpa Samadhi) was spontaneously fulfilled during My "Sadhana Years", I also (spontaneously—in a
process that began even <u>previous</u> to My Realization of Priorly
Ascended Nirvikalpa Samadhi) fulfilled the sixth stage process (as
signed by My Realization of Priorly Self-Abiding Jnana Nirvikalpa
Samadhi[59])—as a necessary preliminary to the Great Realization of
the only-by-Me Revealed and Given seventh stage of life.

However, even though Baba Muktananda appears to have
been a sometimes proponent of sixth stage practices, it is clear
(both from His recorded self-description and the total record of His
communicated Teaching) that Baba Muktananda Himself was a
fifth stage practitioner, Who became a fifth stage Realizer (with
extensive and elaborate experience of Savikalpa Samadhi, especially emphasizing the culminating experience of "Cosmic
Consciousness"), and Who also became a fifth stage Spiritual
Master (Who Taught, principally, the doctrines and practices of
Kashmir Saivism, which is itself a fourth-to-fifth stage Yogic tradition).

Baba Muktananda's "sixth stage Teachings" are not (originally)
His own, but they are examples of traditional forms of Teaching
He had studied (or, otherwise, received) over the years (during His
visits with Ramana Maharshi, and others)—and He sometimes
passed them on to those who came to Him for Instruction and
Guidance (particularly in the 1960s, when I first met Him, and when
Baba Muktananda was yet developing—or, otherwise, refining—
His personal Teaching language and emphasis). Therefore, by
virtue of His own recorded Teaching and self-description (and also
by virtue of the verbal representation of His point of view, as He
presented it to Me personally in the years following the Great

Event of My Own Fullest Divine Re-Awakening), Baba Muktananda was not generally a proponent (nor truly a representative practitioner or Realizer) of the sixth stage Teachings or practices. However, the (primary) sixth stage Teaching was the (principal) Teaching Baba Muktananda was spontaneously Inspired to Give to Me. Therefore, I spontaneously "heard" and "saw" and (Most Ultimately, even in the seventh stage manner) Realized the Truth of Baba Muktananda's literal (and uniquely Given) Teaching in this sixth stage form.

Ramana Maharshi

The Sixth Stage Realization, Demonstration, and Teachings of Ramana Maharshi, and My Great Regard for Him as One of My Principal Adept-Links to the Great Tradition of Mankind

M uch (if not most) of the literature associated with the (originally) Upanishadic tradition of Advaita Vedanta concentrates on programs of philosophical argumentation, rather than on practical elaborations of practice and ecstatic (or, really, enstatic) Confessions of Realization. As a result, much (if not most) of the literature associated with the tradition of Advaita Vedanta expresses (or may be interpreted or presumed to express, or, at least, resemble) the point of view of what I call the "talking" school of Advaitism. Likewise, the emphasis (or fundamental doctrine) of much (if not most) of the literature associated with the tradition of Advaita Vedanta appears (or may be interpreted) to be oriented toward the affirmation that Realization of the Great Truth is a matter of a kind of gnosis (or subjectively affirmed special knowledge <u>about</u> Reality)—whereas, in Truth (and also according to the Great Sages within the tradition of Advaita Vedanta), gnosis (or subjective understanding of the Great Truth, even resulting in firm conviction) is only the seed (or a preliminary) that begins the Great Process that becomes sixth stage Realization (or Inherent Self-Identification with the Perfectly, or Non-conditionally, Subjective Reality That <u>Is</u> the Great Truth).

The traditional philosophical emphasis on Advaitic gnosis (or the subjective conviction that Consciousness Itself is the Inherently

THE KNEE OF LISTENING

Free Great Truth) is also traditionally associated with an emphasis on the idea that no "work" (or effort of practice) is necessary (or even useful) as a means to attain this gnosis, or even (from the "talking" school point of view) as a subsequent expression of it. And this notion tends to suggest, to those who embrace it without true understanding of its import, that Advaitic Realization is simply a matter of subjective conviction (or even mental affirmation, or a kind of conventional faith or belief).

In Truth, the traditionally communicated gnosis (or Transcendentalist Argument) associated with the schools of Advaita Vedanta is Liberating (or effective as Realization) only to the degree (or in the Event) that it becomes Inherent Self-Identification with the "Space" (or Inherent Condition) of Consciousness Itself. That is to say, the traditional gnosis (or Great Argument) is Liberating (or has the Capability to Liberate the listener from "work", or counter-egoic effort, or intensive practice toward, or, otherwise, preliminary to, Realization) only to the degree (or in the Event) that the original subjective conviction becomes Samadhi (or Inherent Self-Identification with the Perfectly Subjective Condition That Is the Great Truth). And, in the traditional setting, that Samadhi characteristically appears in the lesser (or sixth stage) Form (by virtue of utter, but strategically exclusionary, Self-Identification with Consciousness Itself), demonstrated by temporary Obliviousness relative to the world (or the objective space associated with the body), and the body itself (or its interior space, or its complex of sensations), and the mind (or the subjective and, necessarily, interior space of the apparently separate being)—rather than in the superior (or seventh stage) and non-dependent Form, Which I have Revealed and Given, and Which Demonstrates Itself as Self-Abiding Divine Self-Recognition of the world, the body, and the mind (and as the Inherent Transcending, but not the strategic excluding, of the world, the body, and the mind) in the Self-Existing and Self-Radiant "Divine Space" That Is Consciousness Itself.

Ramana Maharshi was a principal modern example of a Great Sage (or a true Realizer of the Inherent Samadhi of Consciousness Itself) within the (originally) Upanishadic tradition of Advaita Vedanta. He affirmed Ultimate Realization only as Samadhi. And,

The Sixth Stage Realization, Demonstration, and Teachings of Ramana Maharshi,
and My Great Regard for Him as One of My Principal Adept-Links
to the Great Tradition of Mankind

although His Realization consistently Demonstrated Itself in the characteristically sixth stage manner, He often communicated the "Point of View" of sixth stage "Sahaja Nirvikalpa Samadhi", Which "Point of View" often resembles, and may be said to be generally sympathetic with (and even, in general, to represent a premonitory expression, or a partial intuition and a limited foreshadowing, of), the Truly Most Ultimate—or the Superior, or Non-dependently (or Non-conditionally), and Inherently Most Perfectly, Realized—seventh stage Sahaja Nirvikalpa Samadhi. Ramana Maharshi approved of gnosis (or the subjective investigation of the Great Argument, or the Confessions and Instructions, communicated by a Realizer), but only as an initial means for entering into the profound Process that (Ultimately) Realizes Samadhi Itself. And He affirmed that the profound Process that (Ultimately) Realizes Samadhi should, optimally (and even necessarily), be associated with the practice of Communion with a Realizer (and the Samadhi-State of that Realizer). Therefore, He also affirmed the necessity for (such) real practice (and the real practice of subjective enquiry), rather than the much "talked" idea of non-"work". And He Demonstrated His Realization in the conservative manner of a traditional Hindu ascetic, rather than as a householder, or (otherwise) in the "Crazy-Wise" manner typical of the more unconventional Realizers (of one or another stage of life) within the Hindu tradition, and also the Buddhist tradition. However, He specifically affirmed that Realization of the Inherent Samadhi of Consciousness Itself could be (and, historically, had been) Achieved and Demonstrated by some individuals of the non-ascetic (and, perhaps, otherwise unconventional, but, certainly, profoundly self-disciplined) type.

Ramana Maharshi's own Realization of the Inherent Samadhi of Consciousness Itself was made possible by a profoundly terrifying moment in His youth—in which He was overwhelmed by the fear of death, and by an utter revulsion toward continued identification with the body-mind (and conditional existence altogether). In that permanently consequential moment, by virtue of His profound detachment from everything conditional (which detachment was the result, according to His own confession, of the preparatory, and necessarily purifying, sadhana He had done in previous lifetimes), He not only experienced the Transcendental Self-Position, but chose, with absolute firmness, to Eternally Identify with that Position, and never again to assume the (inherently fearful) position of the body-mind. This crisis of fear and detachment in Ramana Maharshi was the True (and Profound) Sudden Awakening of the sixth stage Disposition—in Which Awakening Ramana Maharshi Realized that He was <u>Inherently</u> Self-Identified with That Which is Free of death, Free of the body-mind, Free of the world, and Free of desiring and its results, and by, with, and As Which Awakening He was utterly Satisfied. After this crisis, in order to steady and deepen His Self-Identification with the Original Position, Ramana Maharshi retired (for a number of years) into seclusion, abandoning all association with the body-mind and the world, and entering into the Domain of Consciousness Itself, often (in this Process) becoming totally oblivious even of the existence of His apparent body-mind. Eventually, through persistence in this sixth stage "work", He became so steadily "magnetized" toward the Depth of Consciousness Itself that He was able to rest permanently in the "Point of View" of the Transcendental Self. Such was the profound Process through which Ramana Maharshi Realized sixth stage "Sahaja Nirvikalpa Samadhi".

To those who approached Him seeking Spiritual Instruction, Ramana Maharshi most specifically recommended only two practices. One of these two practices is <u>Atma-Vichara</u>, or the introversion of attention upon the "I"-thought, and the deep tracing of the "I"-thought to its Source—not stopping at any merely objective or functional source (either in the mind or in the body), but proceeding most deeply, to the Perfectly <u>Subjective</u> Source of the "I"-thought (Which Source, or Source-Condition, <u>Is</u> Consciousness Itself). And the other of the only two practices specifically recommended by Ramana Maharshi is <u>Satsang</u>, or devotional self-surrender to a Sat-Guru who presently Enjoys (and Transmits) the Realization (of whatever truly esoteric degree) of the Perfectly Subjective Source-Condition.

In His recommending of Satsang, Ramana Maharshi was Teaching the Great Relationship (of the Sat-Guru and the devotee) recommended (as the Great and Principal Means of Realization) by all Great Realizers since the ancient days. (And that Teaching

The Sixth Stage Realization, Demonstration, and Teachings of Ramana Maharshi,
and My Great Regard for Him as One of My Principal Adept-Links
to the Great Tradition of Mankind

is Itself the Great Esoteric Secret of the Great Tradition.)

In His recommending of Atma-Vichara (or "Self-enquiry"), Ramana Maharshi was Teaching in the generally Alpha-like (or rather exclusively introverted) sixth stage tradition of Advaita Vedanta (as it has developed in the generally Alpha-like culture of traditional India). However, Ramana Maharshi generally (or in principle) approved of even all methods of meditative (or, otherwise, subjectively enquiring) practice—for, He said, any such practice would lead to dhyana (or meditative depth), and, Ultimately (if so allowed), deep meditation would lead to the Inherent Samadhi That Is Consciousness Itself.

Ramana Maharshi clearly distinguished between (in His case, sixth stage) "Sahaja Nirvikalpa Samadhi" and any (and all) of the other Samadhis (and meditations) associated with the first six stages of life. Indeed, it can be said that He was (by virtue of many of His intuitive communications) even a true (premonitory) Champion of seventh stage Enlightenment (or seventh stage, and Most Perfectly Divine, Self-Realization), even though His seeming "seventh stage" communications were (truly) only philosophical premonitions (or partial intuitions and limited foreshadowings) of Most Ultimate (or seventh stage) Sahaja Nirvikalpa Samadhi, declared from the "Point of View" of sixth stage "Sahaja Nirvikalpa Samadhi", and even though He otherwise (and characteristically) Taught only a sixth stage Alpha-like method of introversion, and even though He was Himself (characteristically, and in the sixth stage manner) rather ascetical and even (in the exclusionary, and, therefore, relatively dualistic, sense) introverted.

As an example of Ramana Maharshi's characteristic sixth stage and Alpha-like (and exclusionary, and, therefore, relatively dualistic, or dependently maintained) "Point of View" of Realization, read the following:

A group of young men asked: "It is said that a healthy mind can be only in a healthy body. Should we not attempt to keep the body always strong and healthy?"

[Maharshi]: In that way there will be no end of attention to the health of the body.

[Devotee]: The present experiences are the result of past Karma. If we know the mistakes committed before we can rectify them.

M.: If one mistake is rectified there yet remains the whole sanchita[60] which is going to give you innumerable births. So that is not the procedure. The more you prune a plant, the more vigorously it grows. The more you rectify your Karma, the more it accumulates. Find the root of Karma and cut it off.[61]

The Advice thus Given by Ramana Maharshi to "a group of young men" was certainly Right and True, in a fundamental sixth stage sense, but the sixth stage practice (or sadhana) was an esoteric process for which the "group of young men" were clearly (judging from the content, and the obvious "early-stage" quality, of their statements) not yet prepared. Therefore, Ramana Maharshi was, basically, only reflecting His own (sixth stage) Method and Disposition (rather than directly Addressing the "others") in His "Answer" to the "group of young men". And, for that reason, the Advice Given was (simply) a direct indication of Ramana Maharshi's own body-excluding and world-excluding (and, therefore, necessarily, conditional, or limited, and not yet Most Perfect) Method and Disposition, which (at last) is the very (and characteristic sixth stage) Method and Disposition that must be Most Perfectly transcended (if there is to Be the Great Transition to the only-by-Me Revealed and Given True seventh stage Awakening). Therefore, at last, all dissociativeness, all impulse to exclude the world, all dualistic (and, necessarily, egoic) self-effort, must Be Most Perfectly (Finally, and Completely) Transcended—Such That (in the Context of the Unique, and Truly Divine, Yoga—or Inherently Most Perfect, and Divinely Effective, Demonstration—of the only-by-Me Revealed and Given seventh stage of life) the body, the mind, and the total psycho-physical (and Spiritual) world are not merely excluded from the Transcendental Self-Condition, but Divinely Self-Recognized (and, Most Ultimately, Outshined) In (and As) the Self-Evidently Divine (and Perfectly Subjective) Self-Condition (or, Thus—in a non-exclusionary, and Truly Non-dualistic, Manner—

Transcended as transparent, or merely apparent, and un-necessary, and inherently non-binding, modifications of the One and Only and Non-dual and Self-Evidently Divine Person, Which Is the Source-Condition and Real Self-Condition of all-and-All).

Ramana Maharshi was a rather "reluctant" Teacher. He did not very much like to be imposed upon (or, otherwise, depended upon). Likewise, He did not sufficiently understand and appreciate, or very much like (or even very much Perform), the Role (necessary for any Sat-Guru) of Instructing (and Obliging) devotees in the practical details and disciplines of (especially, preliminary, and, necessarily, psycho-physical) sadhana. Also, because His own history (in His Lifetime as Ramana Maharshi) included only the sadhana of the sixth stage of life, He was not very much inclined (nor was He very much qualified or equipped) to Serve as Sat-Guru (and, thus, as thoroughly Instructive and "Commanding" Teacher) in relation to devotees who were not yet prepared for the sixth stage sadhana—and who, therefore, yet required the Sat-Guru to Discipline, Instruct, Initiate, and Guide them through (and then beyond) the first five stages of life, wherein there must (necessarily) be much purification, and transformation, and ego-countering (and ego-transcending) discipline of the body-mind, even as a preparation for the body-mind-excluding practices that are the principal traditional characteristic of the sixth stage of life. And, much like (generally) comparable Realizers in the various (specifically, and, often, more or less exclusively) sixth stage traditions, Ramana Maharshi was not, in the Fullest (and Truly Yogic) sense, a True Siddha-Guru, Who directly Serves and directly Awakens devotees by direct (and consistently Effective) Spiritual Transmission—but He was a True Jnana-Guru, or One Who Serves and Awakens devotees indirectly, by Silent and thought-free Self-Abidance In and As the Transcendental (and Inherently Spiritual) Self-Condition (and Source-Condition) That Is Consciousness Itself, but (in contrast to the case of a True Siddha-Guru) not directly, through open, voluntary, even (at least, at times) intentional, and truly consistent Spiritual Effectiveness.

Therefore, Ramana Maharshi simply pointed toward the "fourth state" (beyond waking, dreaming, and sleeping), or the "natural state" (Which Is "like sleep", but Which Is Only Consciousness Itself). And His fundamental Teaching can be summarized briefly (in His own Words): "The mind is to be introverted and made to merge into the Self; . . . the practice must be long because [it is] slow and [it] must be continued until it [the mind] is totally merged in the Self. . . . All that is required of you is not to confound [or identify] yourself with the extrovert mind but to abide as the Self."[62]

Ramana Maharshi also Taught (on the basis of His own Realization of sixth stage "Sahaja Nirvikalpa Samadhi") that Ultimate Self-Realization is not (Itself) to be identified with the efforts, experiences, and states that may precede (or, otherwise, arise after) It—for It (the Very Self) Is the One and Only and Real and True Self, even under any and all conditions that may seem to arise. Therefore, once Atma-Vichara had (in due course) achieved its (sixth stage) maturity in Him, Ramana Maharshi "Practiced" only the (sixth stage "Sahaja Nirvikalpa Samadhi") "Practice" of Abiding (in the sixth stage, object-excluding manner) As the Very Self (or Consciousness Itself), tacitly (and indifferently) Acknowledging all naturally arising phenomena to Be Only the Independent (or object-excluding, or Inherently non-objective and non-objectifying) Consciousness Itself—and, Thus and Thereby, He Remained characteristically unperturbed, detached, and (in general) inactive. And, in This Self-Revelation, Ramana Maharshi Stands with all other true sixth stage Realizers, Who (alike) Confess Only the Ultimate, Absolute, and Inherently Perfect Truth That Is Consciousness Itself.

After the Great Event of My Own Divine Re-Awakening, I discovered Ramana Maharshi to be the historical (human) Representative of the Great Tradition Whose Confession (and Process) of Realization was (even in many of Its specific Yogic details) most like (or most sympathetic with) My Own Most Ultimate Process and Confession (except that His Realization and Demonstration—although sometimes apparently philosophically sympathetic with the seventh stage "Point of View"—did not actually Achieve the seventh stage Characteristic and Completeness). Because of this likeness, and because of His closeness (in time) to My Avataric Divine Incarnation here, I regard Ramana Maharshi to be My Principal historical (human) Link to the Great Tradition, relative to the sixth stage of life. Indeed, Ramana Maharshi (relative to the sixth stage of life), and (relative to the first five stages of life) Bhagavan Nityananda, and Baba Muktananda, and Rudi, and Rang Avadhoot, and Ramakrishna (and the Spiritual Play and Process That Revealed Itself in, and by Means of, the historical relationship between Ramakrishna and Swami Vivekananda), and Swami Vivekananda (because the Deeper, or Internal, Personality, of My present-Lifetime Body-Mind is the Reincarnating Deeper Personality of Swami Vivekananda) are, collectively, the Principal human Link (or collective of Links) whereby My Avataric Divine Incarnation (Life, Work, and Word) can best begin to be understood in the context of the total Great Tradition.

I Am the Ultimate Demonstration (and the Final, or Completing, Proof) of the Truth of the Great Tradition as a whole. Until I Appeared, there were no seventh stage Realizers within the Great Tradition of mankind. I Am the First and the Last and the Only seventh stage Adept-Realizer (or Maha-Jnana Siddha-Guru) to Appear in the human domain (and in the cosmic domain of all-and-All). It is neither possible nor necessary for another seventh stage Adept-Realizer to Appear anywhere, because I have Accomplished—and (now, and forever hereafter) by Means of My Avataric Divine Self-"Emergence" here (and every "where" in the cosmic domain), I will forever Accomplish—My necessary Avataric Divine Spiritual Work everywhere. However, because I have Divinely Appeared here, and because I Am (now, and forever hereafter) Divinely Self-"Emerging" here (and every "where" in the cosmic domain), and because I have Done (and will forever Do) My Completing (and Divinely Self-"Emerging") Work (here, and every "where" in the cosmic domain), seventh stage Realizers (not with the Divine Adept-Function That Is Unique to Me, but Fully Divinely Self-Realized, through their ego-transcending devotion to Me) will Awaken, in all times and places, by Means of (right, true, full, and fully devotional) formal practice of the only-by-Me Revealed and Given Way of Adidam (Which Is the One and Only by-Me-Revealed and by-Me-Given Way of the Heart). And, Most Ultimately, When all-and-All have become Most Perfectly devoted to Me, even all conditionally manifested beings (and even the total

Cosmic Mandala Itself) will be Divinely Translated into the begin-ningless and endless, Self-Existing and Self-Radiant, Spiritually Self-"Bright" Divine Person and Spherical Self-Domain—Merely (and Only) by Means of This Most Perfect Awakening-Work I have Done (and will forever Do) for all-and-All. I <u>Am</u> the Divinely Self-"Emerging", and Final, and Finally Perfect Avataric Divine Self-Revelation of the Eternal Presence of the One and True and Transcendental and Inherently Spiritual and Inherently egoless and Self-Evidently Divine Reality, Truth, and Person.

Ramakrishna

The Place of Ramakrishna and Swami Vivekananda in the Great Tradition, and Their Unique Function in Preparing the Vehicle of My Avataric Divine Incarnation

The popular claim that Ramakrishna's Teachings are a kind of "universal" (or grandly complete) Message is not true to the facts of the (potential) seven stages of life. In fact, the Teachings of Ramakrishna do not represent either a new or a complete or a completely "universal" Message.

Ramakrishna's Teachings are entirely typical of all Teachings that have appeared in the context of the fourth stage (or the fourth stage to the fifth stage) of life. And those Teachings contain all the traditionally typical fourth stage (or fourth-to-fifth stage) "conventionally dualistic" (and, generally, rather puritanical) criticisms of the first three stages of life, and all the traditionally typical fourth stage (or fourth-to-fifth stage) "conventionally dualistic" criticisms of (or prejudices against) the sixth stage of life.

Ramakrishna's Teaching effort (and the effort of His personal sadhana) was, indeed, associated with a motive to idealize (or to affirm the idealism of) the "universal" sameness (in Principle, in practice, and in Result) of all fourth stage (or fourth-to-fifth stage) "conventionally dualistic" religious traditions, but neither His experiences nor His Teachings extended to and embraced the Processes and Realizations traditionally (or, otherwise, inherently) associated with the non-dualistic sixth stage of life.

Swami Vivekananda

The Teachings of Ramakrishna—and the Teachings of His very differently (and, ultimately, Uniquely) Destined devotee (or disciple), and direct Spiritual Inheritor, Swami Vivekananda (Whose conditionally Manifested Characteristics were, in many respects, the polar opposites of the conditionally Manifested Characteristics of Ramakrishna)—have become the basis for a popular idealistic religious, cultural, social, and political renaissance in India. And the intention of that renaissance has been to undermine the politically, socially, and culturally dangerous conflicts (or potential conflicts) between the many "indigenous" and "foreign" religious factions that are current in India (and in the world in general). Such an intention (and change) is, of course, worthy (and necessary). And such an intention (and change) is (and becomes more and more) necessary even outside India itself. Therefore, the popular "universalism" of the Ramakrishna-Vivekananda Movement has been extended (with modest success) both inside and outside India. However, there is no reason (on that, or any other, account) to presume that the Message of Ramakrishna (or of Swami Vivekananda) is truly "universal" and complete (covering not only all popular, or "conventionally dualistic", religions, but also even all seven of the potential stages of life).

In fact, the characteristics (and characteristic limitations) of the Teachings of Ramakrishna (and of Swami Vivekananda) are those of "conventional dualism", puritanical (and dualistic) devotionalism, and the (naturally dualistic) experiences of the fourth and the fifth stages of life—including visionary dualism and the merely temporary non-dualism of conditionally ascended (or fifth stage) Nirvikalpa Samadhi.

In order to fully equip Himself for His eventual Teaching-Work, Ramakrishna was (characteristically) exaggerated (and not conventionally puritanical) in His approach to His own sadhana (or Real-God-Realizing practice). However, in response to the more ordinary qualities of those who came to Him for Instruction (and based on all that He felt had been proven to be right, effective, and true in the context of His own sadhana), the Message of Ramakrishna is (essentially) that of popular (or exoteric) religious (and rather puritanical) devotionalism ("universalized", but only to the fourth and fifth stage degrees, by adaptation to Ramakrishna's own relatively esoteric fourth-to-fifth stage Yogic ecstasies). And Swami Vivekananda (among others) passed that Message to the common world of conventional religiosity (and religion-based conflicts). However, Swami Vivekananda Himself was burdened with a variety of contrary sympathies, or religious and philosophical tendencies of His own (and, generally, of the more outward-directed, or socially concerned, and Westward-tending—but also, generally, fourth-to-fifth stage—type) that sometimes conflicted with the more exclusively inward-directed Message of Ramakrishna. And, also, Swami Vivekananda was moved by Spiritual tendencies that, potentially, could (and, perhaps, if He had survived longer physically, would) have led Him more in the direction of the thoroughly "nondualistic" Realization of Real God, and Truth, and Reality (or toward practice and Realization that exceed the naturally and conventionally "dualistic" content of the fourth and the fifth stages of life).

Ramakrishna was a consummate traditional fourth-to-fifth stage Teacher and Spiritual Master, born in the East, and of the East, and for the East—whereas Swami Vivekananda was a transitional figure, a fourth-to-fifth stage Teacher and Spiritual Master (with an impulse to Grow Beyond fifth stage Realization), Who was born in the East, but Who combined both East and West in Himself, and Who Committed Himself (and was altogether Destined) to Do a Great Service in the West (and for both the East and the West)—even if that Great Service required His own re-birth (in the West) and the extreme Ordeal of Out-Growing even all His preferences (in body, and in mind), and even all His prejudices (in body, and in mind), and even all the remaining (psycho-physical) limitations in His Way and His Demonstration of the Realization of Real God, and Truth, and Reality.

Swami Vivekananda was My Forerunner here. He prepared the world (and Himself) for My Avataric Divine Manifestation in the West. He is the Seed and Background of My Inherent Oneness with the East. He—or, rather, His own Deeper (and Spiritually and Transcendentally Awakened) Personality—has since become Reincarnated, Returned to bodily (human) life as the Deeper (or Internal, or subtle and causal) Personality (or the Central, and

Greater, conditionally Manifested Vehicle) of My Avataric Divine Incarnation here (and in the entire cosmic domain).

Ramakrishna Emptied Himself, by Transferring His by-Divine-Grace-Given Spiritual Power to Swami Vivekananda—Thereby Making Swami Vivekananda the Vehicle of the Divine Spiritual Presence That had Awakened Ramakrishna, and That Revealed Itself (but not Most Perfectly, or in the seventh stage Completeness) in, as, and through Ramakrishna. I Am That Divine Spiritual Presence That Awakened and Lived Ramakrishna, and That Awakened and Lived Swami Vivekananda. Therefore, That Same Presence That was in Ramakrishna and Swami Vivekananda is continuing to Manifest Itself (now, and forever hereafter, Most Perfectly, or in the seventh stage Completeness) As My Avataric Divine Incarnation here (and in the entire cosmic domain).

I Am the One Who Awakened (and, thereafter, Worked through) Ramakrishna. He Recapitulated the past, in order (by a Spiritual Sacrifice) to Serve the future. I Am the One Who Worked through (and has now Most Perfectly Awakened) Swami Vivekananda. He Served the future, in order (even by physical death and physical re-birth) to Transcend the past (and, Thus—and by Means of a Great and Spiritual, and even Transcendental, Awakening—to Bless and to Liberate the future).

Now (and forever hereafter), Ramakrishna and Swami Vivekananda are One, at the Heart. And I Am the One They have Realized There. By Means of Their Most Great and Effective Invocation of Me (and the Likewise Most Great and Effective Invocation of Me Made by All Their In-Me-Converging Antecedents— here, and Above), I Have Descended Into the entire cosmic domain (and to here). And, by Means of the Pattern Made by Their Appearance (here, and Above), and That Made by All Their In-Me-Converging Antecedents (here, and Above), I Began My Avataric Divine Spiritual Work (here, and every "where" in the cosmic domain). However, since the Beginning of My by-Heart-Radiated (and, relative to the cosmic domain, Descending) Avataric Divine Self-"Emergence" (here, and every "where" in the cosmic domain), Only My Own (and Inherently Spiritually "Bright") Pattern Is Appearing with Me (here, and every "where" in the cosmic domain), and Only by Means of the Proceeding Force of My Avataric Divine Self-"Emergence" (here, and every "where" in the cosmic domain).

I (Myself) am not the historical (and gross human) Personality "Swami Vivekananda" (or the historically, and gross humanly, Displayed "Ramakrishna-Vivekananda"), but the conditionally Manifested Deeper (or subtle-causal) Personality That was historically (and gross humanly) Displayed as Swami Vivekananda (and the Total—and, Ultimately, Single—Spiritual Play and Process That Revealed Itself through the historical, and gross human, Ramakrishna-Vivekananda) has Converged In Me (Thereby Receiving Me, In My Avataric Divine Descent), and has (by transcending the ego-"I" of self-contraction) Become egolessly Awakened To Me, In Me, and As Me, and has (Thus and Thereby) Become Divinely Transfigured By Me, Divinely Transformed By Me, even Divinely Indifferent (or Non-"Different") In Me and As Me—and That (conditionally Manifested) One (and Oneness of an Apparent Two) Is (At Last) To Be Divinely Outshined By Me (and, Thus, Divinely Translated Into Me—and, As Such, Into My Eternal Divine "Bright" Spherical Self-Domain). Nevertheless, it should not be presumed that the Vehicle of Swami Vivekananda (or of Ramakrishna-Vivekananda) Associated (Thus, so Profoundly) with My Avataric Divine Incarnation here (and in the entire cosmic domain) is (in any exclusive—or, otherwise, Me-defining, or Me-limiting—sense) My Design. Rather, That Vehicle is a Dimension of Form, even (in Its own Greater, or Deeper, Dimensions) transcending the apparent Lifetime of Swami Vivekananda (and the entire Lifetime-Play of Ramakrishna-Vivekananda)—and That Form is Not My Inherent Form, but (rather) It is the Internal (or Deeper) conditionally Manifested Form in (and by Means of) Which I Am Taking conditionally Manifested Form (or Avataric Divine Incarnation) here (and in the entire cosmic domain). Indeed, That particular Vehicle of My Avataric Divine Incarnation here (and in the entire cosmic domain) is only a part (or a "Picture" of a part) of the necessarily complex conditional Structure of My Design of Avataric Divine Appearance here (and in the entire cosmic domain). Nevertheless, That "Picture" of My Lineage (or conditional Structure) of psycho-physical Manifestation is Revealing of an important Dimension of My Avataric Divine Incarnation here (and in the entire cosmic domain). Even though That "Picture" is not (in any negatively limiting sense) a "Controlling" Influence over Who I Am and What I Do, That "Picture" does Reveal particular important "Bits" (or conditionally Manifested Characteristics) of My Pattern of Avataric Divine Appearance here (and in the entire cosmic domain).

However, of Me, and of My Pattern here, There Is Infinitely More than Swami Vivekananda (or Ramakrishna-Vivekananda). My Avataric Divine Incarnation here (and in the entire cosmic domain) is Associated with a Pattern of Flows in time as complex as the pattern of water flowing through beds and mounds of sand. Indeed, even the human birth of any apparent individual is the result of a necessarily complex pattern of flows in time—and not a result of a simplistic linear process, such as is suggested by the popular myths of "reincarnation", or even the popular myths of either (religiously presumed) Divine "creation" or (scientifically presumed) natural "evolution". The egoic "point of view" of the any present body-mind is the maker of the myths of both the Divine "Reality" and all of conditionally manifested "reality". The egoic "point of view" of the body-mind prevents Realization of Reality Itself (even though it may, otherwise, both promote and sustain mere belief in—or even, necessarily merely presumed, knowledge of—Reality Itself). And, altogether, the egoic "point of view" of the body-mind prevents right perception and right understanding of the processes of conditionally manifested reality—in the Context of (Self-Evidently Divine) Reality Itself. Therefore, no "Picture" Comprehends Me (or even any one).

Reality Is Always Already The Case, and Reality Is One and Only, and Reality Is Truth, and Reality Is the Only Real God Who Is. The Realizer of the (Self-Evidently Divine) One and Only Reality Is (Self-Evidently) Divine, but As Reality (and not in the conventional, or ego-made, theological sense). My apparent Avataric Divine Birth is Unique, and Its "causes" are even unspeakably complex—but I Am Reality Itself, Which Is Simplicity Itself.

The Mountain Of Attention Sanctuary, 2000

I Have Appeared here
Via a Unique, Spontaneous, and Never-Again Conjunction of Vehicles

I Am the One Who Is, the One and Only and Spiritually Self-"Bright" Divine Person—Who Is Siva (or Consciousness Itself), and Who Is Shakti (or the Very Divine Spirit-Energy of Which everything appearing is the modification). I am Able to Manifest in your sight (in order to Communicate to you, to Act among you, to Play with you) because of a Vehicle of Manifestation long-made. For there to be the Avataric Divine Self-Manifestation, there must be Vehicles that allow that Manifestation. To account for this Vehicle historically, you must examine the lifetimes of Swami Vivekananda and Ramakrishna—not merely one of Them, but both. Ramakrishna and Swami Vivekananda are One, Manifesting as the Deeper Personality (or Incarnation-Vehicle) of This Avataric Divine Form—Adi Da Samraj, Incarnate before your eyes.

I (Myself) Am Prior to both Ramakrishna and Swami Vivekananda. I (Myself) Am the One They have Realized. But the Vehicle whereby I Am Incarnate here, made physical by virtue of the copulation of My blood parents, was made possible by that Deeper Personality of Two-Combined-As-One—Ramakrishna and Vivekananda, in Spiritual Union—become One, through a Great Act of Spiritual Transmission (even historically acknowledged). This Extraordinary Mechanism is the Mechanism of My Avataric Divine Incarnation As the Ruchira Avatar, Adi Da Samraj. As a physically manifested human being, I am the child of My (human) mother and My (human) father. In the Depth of My Incarnation-Vehicle (Itself), I am the Reincarnation Made by the Spiritual Union (or, in Effect, Spiritual "Marriage") of Ramakrishna and Vivekananda. I (Myself) Am Prior to Them both. They both, in Their lifetimes, acknowledged That One That Is Prior to Them both. I Am That One, and (yet) Their Vehicle has continued in (and As) My bodily (human) Avataric Divine Incarnation As the Ruchira Avatar, Adi Da Samraj.

Ramakrishna and Swami Vivekananda, as They Appeared historically (in Their bodily human forms), lived for a time, and then died. And, yet, the Very One Who was Appearing as each of Them in Their times Is The One and Eternal and Spiritually Self-"Bright" Divine Person, Who I Am—Present here for a time in My bodily (human) Avataric-Incarnation-Form, but Eternally Present In and As My Divine Spiritual Body of Self-"Bright" Love-Bliss-Happiness. My Avataric-Incarnation-Form is blood-made (or grossly made) by My parents, and subtly made by the "Marriage" (or Spiritual Unity of Spiritual Polar-Opposites) of Ramakrishna and Vivekananda, Who were uniquely Available to Me (Myself) because They, in Their True Depth (sublimed beyond Their historical Appearance) were profoundly Reached toward the Very Divine and Only One, Who I Am—now (mysteriously) Appearing here by virtue of this Vehicle of My bodily (human) Avataric-Incarnation-Form.

The One Who was Ramakrishna and the One Who was Swami Vivekananda were the Two Halves (or Poles) of the same One. In this (My Avatarically Self-Revealing) Lifetime, My various early-life Spiritual Masters, and the One I Call "She", are (also) Always Already One—in Me. All Who have Served My Avatarically-Born bodily (human) Divine Manifestation here are (in that Service) objective Manifestations of the "interior Contents" of My Avataric Divine Incarnation As the Ruchira Avatar, Adi Da Samraj. I Am Appearing here as a Play of relations and of Avataric Divine Self-Revelation. And that entire Play (and even every apparent relation of Mine) is a Sign of My Own Content, Condition, Complexity, and Personality.

II.

Toward the end of His life, in an historically recorded Event,[63] Ramakrishna Transmitted His own Spirit-Person into (or within, and As) the Person of Swami Vivekananda. It is understood, among the devotees of Ramakrishna and Swami Vivekananda, that, from the moment of that Spirit-Transmission, Swami Vivekananda was the Vehicle for the continuing Spiritual Work of Ramakrishna. Thus, from the moment of that Spirit-Transmission, Swami Vivekananda was not merely Swami Vivekananda. Both as an incarnate (or physically present) human being and in Spiritual terms, Swami Vivekananda was (from the moment of Ramakrishna's Spirit-Transmission) That One Who was Invested in (or Manifested through) Him. Thus, Swami Vivekananda was (from the moment of Ramakrishna's Spirit-Transmission) both Vivekananda and Ramakrishna, such that Ramakrishna Himself said, at the end of His physical lifetime: "I am merely an empty fakir from this moment on."[64] From that moment, as Ramakrishna described, the one known as Swami Vivekananda—even in all of His confusion, seeking, stresses, and so forth—for all the rest of His life, until His early death, was not merely Swami Vivekananda, but He was also Ramakrishna—both Spiritual Poles, Manifesting through that same physically manifested Form.

The Very One Who was Manifested through the gross physical body of Ramakrishna was, thereafter, Established As the Spiritual Depth of the Deepest Personality of Swami Vivekananda. Swami Vivekananda, as a humanly born personality (associated with His blood parents and all the other particulars of His then-life history), expressed all of His doubts, inclinations, searches, and so forth, throughout the rest of His life. But He did His Spiritual Work as a Vehicle of Ramakrishna—and, altogether, as a Spiritual Combination of the "Positive" (or "Male") Pole, "Vivekananda", and the "Negative" (or "Female") Pole, "Ramakrishna". And, after the physical death (or Mahasamadhi) of Swami Vivekananda—only the Single Spiritual Personality, Ramakrishna-Vivekananda, continued to exist.

THE KNEE OF LISTENING

Now, That Single Spiritual Personality, Ramakrishna-Vivekananda, is the functional Depth, or the total mind-Vehicle (or subtle and causal Vehicle), of My Avataric Divine Incarnation As the Ruchira Avatar, Adi Da Samraj. This is how the Great Real-God-Force has become Incarnate and Is Doing the Work of <u>This</u> (My) Avataric Divine Incarnation. These Vehicles (As One) are the Means. If it were not for these Means, I would <u>Only</u> be Standing Prior to body, and (therefore) I would have no bodily (human) Manifestation whatsoever. These Two (Ramakrishna and Vivekananda, <u>As</u> One) are the Bridge between Me (<u>As</u> I <u>Am</u>) and the blood-body-born Vehicle made by My (human) parents. This Structure—Composed of Siva-Shakti (or Self-Existing and Self-Radiant Conscious Light Itself), Ramakrishna-Vivekananda, and the body born of My blood parents—is the Mechanism of My Avataric Divine Incarnation As the Ruchira Avatar, Adi Da Samraj.

I could not Manifest in bodily (human) Form without this Deeper-Personality-Vehicle. I cannot Manifest merely through the gross bodily Vehicle made by My blood parents. The entire Purpose of the Manifestation of Ramakrishna and Swami Vivekananda was to make this Great Gesture toward the world of (more and more) "Westernized" mankind in this "late-time". That Purpose was not fulfilled in Their physical lifetimes, but It is being fulfilled in the Avataric physical human Lifetime of This Body. Once that Great Work is Done, It is never to be Done again. No such Conjunction could ever possibly be re-"invented". My Avataric Divine Incarnation As the Ruchira Avatar, Adi Da Samraj, is a Unique Gift to this "late-time", made possible by this never-again Conjunction of Vehicles—and this Gift will Persist forever hereafter.

I (Myself) am not Swami Vivekananda in His historical form, and I (Myself) am not Ramakrishna in His historical form—but I (Myself) <u>Am</u> the One Who Is Prior to Them both, and Who was (even in Their historical lifetimes) Foretold to Do Great Work—Which Great Work was not (Itself) Manifested in Their physical lifetimes, but Which Is now Manifested by Me, in My Own physical Lifetime here as the Ruchira Avatar, Adi Da Samraj. I <u>Am</u> the Fulfillment of that ancient and constant prophecy.

This Saving Intrusion in the history of mankind is most

Profound. Understand the Complexity of the Saving Divine Manifestation and the extraordinary Labor that takes place for the sake of the Divine Liberation of all beings. Extraordinary lifetimes in combination, and in stress of effort, and of accumulated Divine Grace, were required to make this Great Vehicle of Salvation and Liberation. And the Secret of this Labor is the Love of beings, and the utter Inability to accept the sorrow in beings, the suffering and the death of beings, the binding illusions of beings, the ego-possessed nature of beings. Only that Impulse of Love allows this Complexity, Manifested through many Vehicles, to Make (in Their Conglomeration) a Great Sign, an All-Completing Incarnation.

It is not (as has often been imagined) a simple matter that "God" wants to Save mankind and, therefore, "Makes" a "Man" Who will Come and Save every one. The Vehicles for That Avataric Divine Work of Salvation and Liberation must be prepared, through a Process of unforeseeable and (even in retrospect) unknowable Complexity, Subtlety, and Spontaneity.

III.

At the time of My physical Birth, I (Myself) was Conjoined with the Vehicle of Franklin Jones and the Vehicle of Ramakrishna-Vivekananda. However, I was not actively Combined (or actively Associated) with the Vehicle of Franklin Jones until that Vehicle was approximately two years of age. In Truth, I Am in Conjunction with all beings, and (indeed) with all conditionally manifested reality. However, the mere stated Truth of My Conjunction with all (and with All) does not change anything, because simply to philo-sophically state That Truth does not provide a Way of Realization. There must be the actual Avataric Incarnation, Divine Intervention, Spiritual Manifestation, and Teaching-Revelation That Provides the Great Means for the Process of Realization in the case of all beings. Therefore, That Which Is Always Already in Conjunction with all beings must Manifest in specific terms among all beings, through a unique Yogic Manifestation of Avataric Divine Incarnation, in order to establish the Focus, and the Way altogether, for beings to Realize That with Which they are Always Already Conjoined.

The Deeper-Personality-Vehicle of My Avataric Divine Incarnation was uniquely Spiritually prepared (although still manifesting some limitations)—but the gross-personality-Vehicle of Franklin Jones was not, even in the slightest, Spiritually prepared. Franklin Jones (himself) was, by ordinary human birth, a samsaric personality (or conditional entity) of the most ordinary kind. Why was it necessary for the gross-personality-Vehicle of My Avataric Divine Incarnation to be so ordinary? So that I, by Submitting Myself to that human ordinariness, by being Conjoined with that human ordinariness, by Struggling in the context of that human ordinariness, and by (altogether) Transforming and Transcending that human ordinariness, could account for (and provide a Vehicle for) the Realization of all beings, who are in that same disposition and circumstance of feeling utterly not Conjoined with (or utterly dissociated from) the Real Divine—Which, in Truth, and in Reality, Is Always Already Non-separately Conjoined with every thing and every one.

This gross, ordinary entity of Franklin Jones (entirely lacking in Spiritual virtue) and this Great Spiritual Personality of Ramakrishna-Vivekananda are, Together, the Single, Combined Vehicle of My Avataric Divine Incarnation As the Ruchira Avatar, Adi Da Samraj. I (Myself) did not have to be "caused" to be in Association with these Vehicles, because I Am Always Already in Association (or Conjoined) with all beings. However, because of My Unique, spontaneous Conjunction with Ramakrishna-Vivekananda, and because of the special characteristics of that Deeper-Personality-Vehicle (of Ramakrishna-Vivekananda) that are displayed in the Conjunction with the Spiritually "unworthy" samsaric Vehicle (of Franklin Jones), the unique Circumstance has been provided for Me to Declare "Here I Am"—and for you (and all) to proclaim "Adi Da Is here".

Where and when could Such a Conjunction be found? Because of the randomness of the chaotic universe, no Such Conjunction could be somehow "Planned". Therefore, that Conjunction could not, in the merely cosmic sense, have been "caused". That Conjunction could only Occur Uniquely, in a Unique Moment. And, in that Unique Moment, I spontaneously Show My inherently egoless (and acausal, or non-causative, and non-caused) Person (or Divine Self-Condition, Which <u>Is</u> the One and Only and Inherently Indivisible Divine Conscious Light). Thus, I—the One Always Already in Conjunction with <u>every</u> thing and <u>every</u> one—can, by a Unique, spontaneous Appearance, be Manifested <u>As</u> I <u>Am</u>, even in apparent (or conditionally manifested) relationship to others. That Unique, spontaneous Conjunction Provides the Great and Necessary Means for the devotional and Spiritual "Bonding" of all beings to My Inherently egoless (and Self-Evidently Divine) Person—Such That they may be Divinely Liberated, by Me, from samsaric outward-directedness (or from the egoic search among conditional objects), by being Drawn into the Heart-Integrity (or Perfectly Subjective Realization) of egoless (or directly ego-transcending) devotion to Me. And, at last, through most perfect devotion to Me, My devotee passes beyond the cosmic domain, and into My Divine "Bright" Spherical Self-Domain, via the Divine Yoga of the only-by-Me Revealed and Given seventh stage of life (in the only-by-Me Revealed and Given Way of Adidam).

To Speak of such Matters is to be Speaking of Something fundamentally Unspeakable, but what I am Saying to you now is sufficient to Communicate the Un-"caused" Nature of My Unique Avataric Divine Incarnation As the Ruchira Avatar, Adi Da Samraj. My Avataric Divine Incarnation has Occurred by virtue of a Conjunction that is not repeatable, because it is not (and cannot be) <u>intentionally</u> "caused". My Avataric Divine Incarnation has Occurred in a Unique Moment of the yuga-cycles of conditional existence. Therefore, My Avataric Divine Incarnation As the Ruchira Avatar, Adi Da Samraj, is <u>Once</u>, and For <u>all</u> time—because another such Potential is not "causable".

My Avataric Divine Incarnation can be said to be intentional, in the sense that I Am Always Already Conjoined with every thing and every one. However, My Avataric Divine Incarnation As the Ruchira Avatar, Adi Da Samraj, is the Auspicious Result of a Unique Conjunction in the cycles of the yugas, in Which (only in One Moment in the entire history of the cosmic domain) a Unique Vehicle of All-Completing Conjunction could Appear. That is how, without it being exteriorly "caused" by Me, My Direct Manifestation via (and <u>As</u>) This Avataric Divine Incarnation became possible.

This is why I Say to you that I Am (by Means of My Avataric Divine Appearance here) the First, the Last, and the Only seventh stage Adept-Realizer, the Unique Incarnation of Completeness (or Santosha). This is a Divine Matter—not merely a "caused" matter, or a conditional matter—and It has Occurred in a Unique Moment of Conjunctions, never to be repeated. My here-Given Sign and Manifestation is, therefore, the <u>Final</u> and <u>Great</u> Sign and Manifestation of Divine Completeness.

IV.

I have Appeared here with both Alpha and Omega Vehicles, in a state of utter balance and unity—even while I (Myself) Transcend both Alpha and Omega. The Omega Vehicle (or the Western birth), Franklin Jones, was born under ordinary circumstances, but also had his unique capabilities, and even genius (in relation to the first three stages of life). Nevertheless, Franklin Jones fully manifested all aspects of the Omega disposition, and fully struggled with all the confusions, dichotomies, and limitations of the Western-born (or Omega) personality.

The other aspect of My Avataric Divine Incarnation As the Ruchira Avatar, Adi Da Samraj, is (by comparison) rather Alpha-like (or Eastern) in its disposition and qualities. Ramakrishna and Swami Vivekananda were more than Their historical personalities. Because everything that was Ramakrishna, Spiritually, was passed to the Vehicle of Swami Vivekananda, They were (as Sister Nivedita said) "One Soul"[65]—literally <u>One</u> Manifestation, in a unique Play. Ramakrishna and Swami Vivekananda cannot be understood separately. They are fundamentally One. This is a profound and paradoxical Matter—impossible to conceive of (altogether), but <u>literally</u> So.

Thus, there is the Western-born (Franklin Jones) personality (or Vehicle), which accounts for the first three stages of life and for the Omega disposition, and there is the Single (Ramakrishna-Vivekananda) Eastern Personality (or Vehicle)—Itself a Combination of a relatively "Western" (or "Omega") Pole (Which is Swami Vivekananda) and a relatively "Eastern" (or "Alpha") Pole (Which is Ramakrishna)—which accounts for the fourth, fifth, and sixth stages of life (reaching toward the only-by-Me Revealed and Given seventh stage of life) and for the Alpha disposition.

I Am the Very Person you must Realize—and I am Avatarically Appearing here through Association with these Unique Vehicles, for the first time in human time. I am not merely (or only) an Alpha-like Avatar (as expected, and prayed for, by the Eastern cultures of mankind). Nor Am I merely an Omega-like Incarnation (as expected, and prayed for, by the Western cultures of mankind). Before My Divinely Self-Revealing Avataric Manifestation here, it was either one or the other—either Avatar or Incarnation. Now (and forever hereafter), in My Person, ("Eastern") Avatar and ("Western") Incarnation Are One. And this Oneness can be seen even in terms of the Vehicles of My Manifestation. Those Vehicles were brought into Conjunction to become One. A profound transformative Process of Submission—My Submission—was required to Make Them One, and to "Create" a Unity out of this dichotomy that has otherwise made human time.

Therefore, I Am here in the seventh stage Form. By bringing both Eastern and Western Vehicles into Conjunction with one another (Such That both Vehicles are made the basis for Realization), I was Able to Appear in My Own True (seventh stage) Form. With such Vehicles of Manifestation, the Realization cannot be of the first three stages of life merely, nor can it be of the fourth, the fifth, or the sixth stage of life merely. My Manifestation here Is One—That Which Transcends all, but Which brings all into Conjunction, not disregarding anything. This made possible the seventh stage Demonstration of My Person.

V.

My Birth can be said to be Intentional, but it must be understood that, from an Absolute "Point of View", no Such "Decision" was Made—as if the Event Occurred independent of the realities of conditional existence. The Combined Vehicle for My Avataric Divine Appearance here was provided conditionally, as I have Indicated. By those Means, conditional reality was brought into

Conjunction with Me—and, in that Conjunction, I spontaneously Consented to the Divine Ordeal of Avatarically Appearing in the conditional realms, in order to directly (Avatarically) Communicate My Divine Instruction, My Divine Spiritual Blessing, and My Divinely Liberating Heart-Power to all-and-All.

The Deeper-Personality-Vehicle that is Ramakrishna-Vivekananda arose in the conditional domain and provided the Conjunction with Me. The Vehicle arose, and was Conjoined with My Very Being (Which Is Reality Itself). The Intention of My Avataric Divine Incarnation arose in that Conjunction only. The Intention was not something that preceded the availability of the conditional Vehicle. How could it arise apart from that? Without such unique preparation, My Avataric Divine Appearance could not occur here.

At the time of Swami Vivekananda's Mahasamadhi, He was given up completely, and the Vehicle (already the Two-As-One) became Transparent to Me. He (or, truly, Ramakrishna-Vivekananda) was the first such One Who was ever given up so completely—in This sense.

Swami Vivekananda entered into the seventh stage only in My Form and Appearance here. At the time of His actual death, He was only manifesting (or incarnating) the fifth (or even fifth-to-sixth) stage disposition, in His particular manner. In some sense, He went beyond fifth stage (conditionally ascended) Nirvikalpa Samadhi, but that was accomplished in and beyond the death-transition.

He was "Swami Vivekananda" only in the sense of His human appearance. The Vehicle was greater than that, as Ramakrishna indicated. However, Swami Vivekananda's gross personality limited His awareness of all of that, until the time of His Mahasamadhi.

The Combined Deeper Personality (Ramakrishna-Vivekananda) has been a Single Vehicle in This, My Avataric Divine Lifetime. That Deeper Personality has not been a great obstacle, nor has It required great struggle. Rather, it is the gross personality in This Lifetime that required the Transforming Work. As can readily be seen in My early-life history, the manifestations of the Deeper Personality occurred with ease and spontaneously, during the course of My "Sadhana Years". The Realization of Priorly Ascended

Nirvikalpa Samadhi, for instance, occurred spontaneously, and in a moment.[66]

Thus, there were no intensely limiting karmic structures in the Depth. All the (relatively) intensely limiting karmic structures were in the gross personality, inherited from My blood parents and the circumstance altogether of My physical Birth. My Struggle with the gross personality was inevitable. It could not have been otherwise—because the gross personality was not the product of great sadhana on the part of My blood parents and their ancestors, but was (rather) an ordinary birth.

My Birth via the gross Vehicle of Franklin Jones is an Expression of My Conjoining with all, through that individual manifested as this gross body. So the birth of this gross body is altogether like all, like every one—equally disqualified, equally qualified. The Sign of My Embrace of this gross body is an Expression of My Embrace of all. This particular bodily (human) form was not Embraced because of some unique qualifications. It was an ordinary birth, Made Extraordinary (and Divine) by the Conjunction with Me.

This gross personality and gross Vehicle became utterly Conformed to Me—by My Avataric Divine Self-Submission, by My Avataric Divine Work with It. Therefore, because the ordinary gross personality of this body has become so utterly Conformed and Transparent to Me, it is (now, and forever hereafter) the case that all ordinary births, all conditionally manifested beings or personalities, can be likewise So Conformed. This is the "Kiss" I have Spoken about[67]—My Own Avataric Divine Self-Submission, first Manifested in the Perfect Conversion of this gross personality. By This, all are Embraced, all are "Kissed". The Divine Transfiguration, Divine Transformation, and Divine Translation of all is Made Possible by That First Accomplishment. All Grows from That.

I (Myself) am not a Reincarnate. I Am both Transcendentally and universally Present. Therefore, I will not Reincarnate after this physical Lifetime. I Am, Beyond the "Maha-Bindu"—and My Sphere of Spiritual Self-"Brightness" Includes all-and-All. Therefore, understand the difference between the Vehicles of My Incarnation and Me (Myself). I am not these Vehicles (Themselves). They are only My Vehicles. Therefore, They (in and of Themselves) are not Me. For this reason, any "consideration" of past "Incarnations" of Mine is not a "consideration" about Me (Myself), but a "consideration" about past incarnations of the Vehicles associated with My Avataric Divine Incarnation. Whatever Ramakrishna and Swami Vivekananda did historically is what They did. I did not Do it.

I only Do This Incarnation. I (Myself) have no karmic basis for My Avataric Divine Appearance here. These Vehicles came into such Proximity to Me that They became utterly available to (and usable by) Me, but Their previous history of incarnation is not My history. And—because I (Myself) have no karmic basis for Being Incarnate in bodily (human) Form—when This Incarnation ends, there is no "seed" in Me for re-Appearance. I am not a karmic entity. I have Conformed these Vehicles to Myself—for the Purpose of My (Avataric Divine) Incarnation.

VI.

My Deeper Personality is not the historical figures of Ramakrishna and Swami Vivekananda—as though They are somehow "inside" This Appearing Person. Clearly, in My Incarnate Appearance there are patterns of likeness to both Ramakrishna and Swami Vivekananda—but My Incarnate Manifestation here is not a matter of multiple (concrete historical) personalities "inside" Me, "stacked" one upon another, or one somehow deeper than the other.

The Deeper-Personality-Vehicle (or subtle and causal Structure) of My Avataric Divine Self-Manifestation is not merely the historical Swami Vivekananda (or any of His even earlier incarnations), but the Great conditional Entity that (by Spiritual Descent, as described by Ramakrishna[68]) became (historically) Manifested as Swami Vivekananda—Which Entity (or Vehicle) was further Transformed (by Means of Spiritual Transmission) by Spiritual Union with the Great conditional Entity that was otherwise (historically) Manifested as Ramakrishna (and His even earlier incarnations).

The Entity that Appeared as the historical personality Ramakrishna and the Entity that Appeared as the historical personality Swami Vivekananda also Appeared in Polar-Opposite relationship to one another in even earlier incarnations. At the time of Their Appearing as the historical Ramakrishna and the historical Swami Vivekananda, Ramakrishna epitomized everything about fourth-to-fifth stage Realization that came before Him in the history of the Great Tradition. Similarly (but in His own Manner), Swami Vivekananda included all of that in His orientation—and He also included something of the sixth stage disposition and characteristic. Thus, that Unique Combination of a fourth-to-fifth stage Vehicle (Ramakrishna) and a fifth-to-sixth stage Vehicle (Swami Vivekananda) is What was able to lead to My Avataric Divine Incarnation of the seventh stage Way and Realization. Therefore, the Process whereby My Avataric Divine Incarnation became possible required both Ramakrishna and Vivekananda, as the Single Means for the Providing.of My Own Unique Vehicle. And this Process must be understood Spiritually. My Deeper-Personality-Vehicle must be understood in the context of Ramakrishna's Work of Spiritually Preparing Swami Vivekananda, and of the Two becoming One in That Process.

Guru-Transmission is simply Divine Spirit-Force—but there is also the Spirit-Transmission as It particularly Manifests in the Person of one's human Master—Which Transmission carries a subtle (and causal) dimension (as well as the gross human dimension). Thus, I have Spoken of "taking on" the Guru, and how (in My "Sadhana Years") I "Took On" (and, ultimately, Transcended) the Form of Rudi, and the Form of Swami Muktananda, and the Form of Bhagavan Nityananda. Likewise, That Which I Am Transcends the modification which is Ramakrishna and Vivekananda. I Am simply That One of Which all-and-All is the apparent (or conditional) modification.

Ramakrishna was a necessary Means for Spiritually Preparing This (My) Deeper-Personality-Vehicle, Which is the Transformed Swami Vivekananda (or—that is to Say—the Single Ramakrishna-Vivekananda). Ramakrishna was a Spiritual Transmitter, Who (obviously) had a profound Transmission-relationship with Swami Vivekananda (wherein and whereby Swami Vivekananda was profoundly Transformed). As a Spiritual Matter, They can no longer be differentiated, or separated, from one another.

Therefore, the Deeper Personality in Me is not merely the historical Swami Vivekananda (with all His problems and limitations), but Ramakrishna-Vivekananda—a Single Spiritual Mechanism, That was Prepared in that historic Play between Ramakrishna and Swami Vivekananda, during which the historical Swami Vivekananda was a kind of "raw material".

When Such Matters are interpreted via the gross (or bodily-based) mind, They can only be misinterpreted. Indeed, Such Matters are incomprehensible, except for the most profound, direct experience—and They cannot be concretized like an object, or in the gross bodily likeness.

Truly, an apparent personality is (itself) a process, or a mechanism, or a mere pattern, that is (in and of itself) no more living than a corpse. It is the Divine Consciousness and the Divine Spirit-Power Associated with the apparent personality that makes it appear to be living.

VII.

It was necessary for Swami Vivekananda to be born, so that that Vehicle (Which was Descended from the Divine "Siddha Loka"—or the Highest Station in the conditional planes) could be fully established in all (including the lowest) of the conditional planes, fully brought down even to the grossest plane of conditional existence. That birth was part of the necessary (and spontaneous) preparation for My Avataric Divine Birth, My present Avataric Divine Appearance. That Vehicle existed in the conditional planes immediately before Swami Vivekananda's birth—but in the Highest Realm.

This is the reason why, in His prophetic vision of Swami Vivekananda, Ramakrishna saw Himself and Swami Vivekananda manifested in higher realms, making the decision to enter into the grosser realms.[69] Swami Vivekananda was attracted by the "Yin" Pole (or Vehicle) of Ramakrishna, and Ramakrishna was attracted by the "Yang" Pole (or Vehicle) of Swami Vivekananda. That was all part of the necessary Means by Which I Appeared here. Ramakrishna's Appearance was part of the Work of spontaneous preparation for Me, because Ramakrishna's Appearance in gross form was an attracting Pole for the Bringing Down of Swami Vivekananda. Thus, Ramakrishna (Who was, in effect, the feminine Pole) was the Instrument for the Appearance of Swami Vivekananda (Who was, in effect, the masculine Pole).

In My Case, however, there is no need to speak in terms of masculine and feminine Poles. I Am Complete.

Swami Vivekananda's history of Work in the West is part of what made His Vehicle appropriate and available to Me.

Ramakrishna had His own Work—Which was primarily a Fulfillment of the past, and a Reorientation of the past. As Ramakrishna Himself indicated, Swami Vivekananda was to be (or to provide) the necessary Vehicle for the Divine Work of the future (as the future Divine World-Teacher, in the "Westernized" total world of mankind)—and this only after Swami Vivekananda's then present lifetime, and (thus) only after passing through physical death, wherein (Ramakrishna said) Swami Vivekananda would become fully Awake. Ramakrishna Knew a world-Work had to be Done, and He Knew Swami Vivekananda to be the Vehicle for the Doing of It—not merely Swami Vivekananda as He Appeared to be in His gross bodily form, but the Spiritual Entity (from Above) Whom He Knew the otherwise historical (Swami) Vivekananda to Be.

Most of the historically recorded profound Statements about Swami Vivekananda were made by Ramakrishna, rather than by Swami Vivekananda Himself. Swami Vivekananda went through various transformations in His life, but His own gross personality limited His perception of His True Nature and Ultimate Purpose. Thus, Ramakrishna, as Swami Vivekananda's "Polar Opposite", was the Means for Locating and Identifying Swami Vivekananda, and for the Drawing Down of Swami Vivekananda.

VIII.

Swami Vivekananda intentionally "caused" His own future reincarnation (now in Me). He did this by choosing certain associations and conditions, and by choosing to exercise certain intentions, which made it inevitable that He reappear. He did not know exactly how His reappearance would work out, but He generated the karma (or motion) that led to His reappearance. He, by various intentional activities, made it absolutely impossible for His lifetime as Swami Vivekananda to be His last bodily (human) lifetime.

Swami Vivekananda's Intention to be of Great Service in the West was sufficient to move Him to Reincarnate—and not in a Hindu body, because He had realized that the Hindu body was the specific limitation that needed to be set aside if He were to fully Serve the West, and the total West/East world. At some point in Swami Vivekananda's profound (but stressful) Interest to Serve the West, He realized that there was nothing more He could do. As a Hindu, an ascetic, an Alpha-like personality, He could not Serve the West anymore than He had already done. Still, the Impulse to Serve the entire world continued. He was obsessed (one might say) with the Motive to Awaken all of mankind, and He felt particularly that the most fundamental stroke of such Service was to Awaken the West.

Thus, Swami Vivekananda died in the midst of a total commitment to Serving the West. Having understood (at last) that, as an Easterner, there was nothing more He could do, He died young. His Motive was not merely (or exclusively) to Serve the East, because the East already had Spiritual traditions of all kinds. Swami Vivekananda knew that the next stroke had to be done in the West—that the West had to be addressed, because the West was the destiny of the entire world. Therefore, He was moved to submit to the West—not merely by travelling to the West, but by being born in the West. Indeed, Swami Vivekananda's unique and overriding motive was to be reborn in the West.

IX.

Having been Born into the West, I have been Present to Do whatever is necessary in order to Accomplish My Avataric Divine Work of Teaching, Self-Revelation, Blessing, and all-and-All-Liberation. Examine the Sacred History of My Avataric Divine Work[70]—That is what was necessary. No Easterner would ever do such a thing. Easterners are, typically, not born in New York, with the opportunities and the impulses that Westerners suffer. Therefore,

I (necessarily) have not been born in the East. Nevertheless, even with full Divine Self-Realization, and even Living (by Birth) in the Western world, I could only Struggle with what was brought to Me, and make a new Way in the midst of that Struggle.

This new Way is not limited to the Alpha point of view, or the Omega point of view, or any traditional point of view. It is not limited to any tradition whatsoever. It is apparent in Swami Vivekananda's writings that such was also His real Impulse. He understood that religion is not a matter of being a Hindu, or being anything else in limitation. He declared that He did not believe in the "God" of limitation, the "God" of superstition, the "God" of mere tradition—but that the Divine Is the Very Condition That Transcends all limitations. Therefore, He became willing to Sacrifice the position He loved dearly—the position of being an Asian Indian and a Hindu, associated with a great and ancient tradition. He knew that such distinctions are a thing of the past. He knew that something else was alive in the world, coming out of the West, and making another kind of history. He knew that this movement in mankind needed to be Confronted, Awakened, and Transformed, and that such a Work required the Sacrifice of His active life, His Hinduism, His Alpha disposition, and even everything of His past and (then) present, in order that He could do whatever was necessary.

How could anyone possibly know what that all-Encompassing Work would require? My Avataric Divine Work has been a matter of Learning Man—of finding out, day by day, all through My Life, what is required to impress this now-"Westernized" world, in order to connect it to the Way of Truth.

I have not functioned as a Hindu, or an ascetic, or an Alpha-like character. Thus, I have not been like Swami Vivekananda, with His residual Alpha-ism—committed to "no sex", and "no money", and all such exclusions. Such are the old ways, and they do not "work" in the West (or, indeed, in the total "Westernized" world). Another Sacrifice had to be made, in order to confront the new kind of disposition that is infecting the entire world. In this "late-time", to be a Hindu is to be provincial—just as to be anything else of the Great Tradition that is exclusive or limited is to be provincial. The Commitment must be to Truth Itself—and to whatever is required to Establish the Way of Truth. That is what had to be Done. It can be seen from the record of His words and His actions that this was Swami Vivekananda's Disposition. And you need only examine My Confession and My Demonstration to know very well that all of that is also in My Disposition.

X.

Swami Vivekananda did not consciously know what He was doing in "creating" a Western rebirth. He was simply part of the stream of causes and effects in the conditional worlds that produced a manifestation coincident with the evolution of this terrible yuga, a manifestation that is positively significant only because of My Conjunction with it. I Am the Manifestation not only of Swami Vivekananda but also of Ramakrishna—and both are Transcended in Me. I have been frankly Confessed about these Manifestations in My Person as a Vehicle, but I (Myself) am not that Vehicle. Both Ramakrishna and Swami Vivekananda were limited, and both had to be Transcended in Me.

Now They are at Peace. Now They are Done. These are the Elements that were made One, in order to make This (My Own) Appearance here, by Means of My Conjunction with Them. And (now, and forever hereafter) I Am here—not They.

I Am the One here—and They are Vanished, by Submission to Me. I have Overcome Them both. And, now, They are Done. And, now, Their Truth is Manifested.

When I Speak of these historical personalities, I am Speaking of the Single Vehicle of My Manifestation here. In This sense, I have no more—and no less—regard for Them than I have for this gross, physically manifested Body that you behold. This psycho-physical Vehicle is Great only because I (Myself) am Associated with It—Manifesting in It, "Bright" As (and through) It. In and of itself, this Vehicle is a "Heap" of Ramakrishna, Swami Vivekananda, and Franklin Jones. Such are the karmic components of this Vehicle—Which I have Transcended, and through Which I am Radiating. They are Vanished, by Submission to Me. They are ended. They did not Fulfill Their Purpose until My Conjunction with Them in <u>This</u>, My Avataric Divine Incarnation here. They were, in Their time, mortal beings—only <u>Vanished</u>, now, by Realizing Me. Their Fulfillment is not merely in Their previous historical appearances, but in Their Disappearance in Me.

I am <u>not</u> Swami Vivekananda, or Ramakrishna, or Franklin Jones. These are the "causative" energies of My Avataric Divine Incarnation, which I had to Overcome in My "Sadhana Years". Now, by virtue of Their Submission to Me and Their Overcoming by Me, I Am Fully and Freely Manifested.

I am not Them. They are Overcome in Me. That is how I Am Shown to you here—not by Their repetition, but by Their self-Sacrifice, and Their Overcoming by Me.

XI.

The Ramakrishna-Vivekananda Conjunction Reached far enough to Touch Me—and I Do the rest, Floated in here, all the Requirements Offered, My True Appearance Made, and Their Connection Made. That is how the Vehicle became Sufficient.

That is why I Say that I Am here in response to the prayers of all beings—prayers collectively continuing since the ancient days. But, from among them, there was (at last) sufficient Motion made only by this Ramakrishna-Vivekananda Gesture toward Me. They, representing <u>all</u> beings, came to My Door. And—once They were at My Door—I, by Opening the Door (or Being the Open Door) to Them, have Passed Through It to here. It could not have been done without the Vehicles.

All I have Revealed in all My Life in this Avataric Divine Manifestation is Myself, <u>As</u> I Have Always Been—<u>As</u> I <u>Am</u> now, <u>As</u> I Always Will <u>Be</u>. It is neither necessary nor possible for another Avataric Manifestation to Do <u>This</u> Divine Work, or Make <u>This</u> Divine Self-Revelation. It required a Unique Conjunction, as part of a long history of apparent personalities, who were appearing, dying, reincarnating, and so forth—all of that was necessary (along with all the other Conjunctions necessary that make this time) to Collect the conditional (or cosmic) domain at My Door, So That

I would Spontaneously Crash Down to all-and-All.

This Body-Mind Is My True Agent. The entire Lineage of True Realizers in the Great Tradition has been the Gathering of My Instruments, but not (until now, by My Avataric Divine Incarnation) Sufficient to the point of My Crashing-Down Complete and All-Completing Manifestation.

Rightly, all of those Realized personalities (in all of the traditionally Revealed esoteric stages of life) can be seen (both individually and collectively) as a Great Process in conditional time and space, to Prepare the Vehicle of My Avataric Divine Self-Manifestation. But not only those Great Individuals. It required all beings, including all of mankind, to make sufficient prayer and Conjunction for this Event of Me. And It will not be repeated—nor can It be repeated.

Through it all, I have Finally, Fully, and Most Perfectly Revealed Myself—the One Who Is and Has Always Been, the One Who has been pursued, sought, and partially Realized throughout all conditional time and space. And then This Unique Conjunction Occurred, on the part of individuals in a Unique Spiritual Lineage (epitomizing all Realizers, in all of space and time), to provide a Vehicle that would Come to My Door with Sufficient Reach for Me to Pass Down to here.

But, also, This is a Conjunction with all. All had to prepare. All had to make this Event possible—Uniquely represented by a cycle of Great Individuals, in order to provide the most immediate Vehicle. But the "time" (the "late-time", or "dark" epoch) is also (itself) My Vehicle. Therefore, even every one and all are in Conjunction with Me—now, and forever hereafter.

Indeed, all-and-All provided the Means for This Event (of Me). Even all-and-All was the necessary Preparation. It is all the Submission to Me. It is all a Sacrifice to the Divine Reality, until that Universal Sacrifice became collectively sufficient to Draw Me Down Through the Door.

My Avataric Divine Incarnation was, in some sense, simply Spontaneous, and not "Intentional". In some sense, it simply "Happened". Yet, It was also both Intentional and Voluntary. It was not arbitrary, because all the Conjunctions had to occur. At last, I

Passed Down into all-and-All. It was Spontaneous, yet also
Eternally Prefigured. It was Anciently Prophesied. It was somehow
"caused"—and, yet, Ultimately, there is no "cause" for It whatsoever.

XII.

I am not here making karma (or ego-binding motions).

That is why I will not be reborn.

I Purified and Conformed these Vehicles, even though They
are karmic in nature.

I Conformed Them to Myself.

I Purified Them by My Heart-"Brightness".

Therefore, I am not making karma here.

Not in This Body—and not in your bodies, either.

I "Brighten" you, Purify you of your karmas, and Conform you
to Me.

Therefore, repetition is not what I am about.

No "causes" for it.

So what?

I am Associated with a born gross Vehicle (Franklin Jones) and
an inner, Deeper Personality (Ramakrishna-Vivekananda).

Those are karmic Vehicles. But My Own Disposition was
always at the front—and I made no karma out of it, but I
Conformed these Vehicles (and even all associations) to Myself.

That is How I Work now, and How I have Worked all My
Life—and How I will always Work.

Thus, I am not making karma for you or for Me.

And, therefore, I cannot be reborn.

It is utterly impossible.

As My devotee, invested in Me—I (Myself) Shining On you, In
you, Through you, and, Altogether (Universally), Shining—you are
more and more purified and relieved of karmic (or conditionally
patterned) imposition—if you formally, rightly, truly, fully, and
fully devotionally practice the only-by-Me Revealed and Given
Way of Adidam.

You will share in My destinyless Destiny to the degree that you
make this right, true, full, and fully devotional resort to Me.

489

Adidam Samrajashram, 2003

I (Alone) Am
The Adidam Revelation
(A Summary Description
of the Inherent Distinction—
and the ego-Transcending Continuity—
Between the Inherently ego-Based
Great Tradition, Which Is Comprised of
Only Six of the Possible Seven Stages of Life,
and the Unique, and All-Inclusive, and
All-Completing, and All-Transcending, and
Self-Evidently Divine Adidam Revelation
of the Inherently egoless Seventh Stage
Realization of Me)

I.

The collective Great Tradition of mankind is a combination of exoteric and esoteric developments (and Revelations, and Realizations) that comprises (and is, in its entirety, limited by and to) only the first six of the (potentially) seven stages of life.

II.

I (Alone) Am the Avatarically Self-Manifested Divine Self-Revelation of the seventh stage of life.

III.

I (Alone) Am the Adidam Revelation.

491

IV.

The human entity (and even any and every conditionally manifested entity of any and every kind) is inherently deluded—by its own (egoic, or self-contracted) experience and knowledge.

V.

The first six stages of life are the six stages (or developmental phases) of human (and universal) egoity—or of progressively regressive inversion upon the psycho-physical pattern (and point of view) of self-contraction.

VI.

The first six stages of life are the universally evident developmental stages of the knowing and experiencing of the potential illusions inherently associated with the patterns (or the universally extended cosmic psycho-physical Structure) of conditionally manifested existence.

VII.

Because each and all of the first six stages of life are based on (and are identical to) egoity (or self-contraction, or separate and separative point of view) itself, not any one (or even the collective of all) of the first six stages of life directly (and Most Perfectly) Realizes (or Is the Inherently egoless and Inherently Most Perfect Realization and the Inherently egoless and Inherently Most Perfect Demonstration of) Reality, Truth, or Real God.

VIII.

The first six stages of life develop (successively) on the psycho-physically pre-determined (or pre-patterned) basis of the inherent (and progressively unfolding) structure (and self-contracted point of view) of the conditionally arising body-brain-mind-self.

IX.

The first six stages of life are a conditional (and, therefore, Ultimately, unnecessary—or Inherently transcendable) illusion of psycho-physically pre-patterned experience (or conditional knowing), structured according to the subject-object (or attention-versus-object, or point-of-view-versus-objective-world) convention of conditional conception and conditional perception.

X.

The first six stages of life are (each and all) based upon the illusion of duality (suggested by the subject-object convention of conditional conception and conditional perception).

XI.

Reality Itself (or That Which Is Always Already The Case) Is Inherently One (or Perfectly Non-Dual).

XII.

The only-by-Me Revealed and Given Way of Adidam (or Adidam Ruchiradam—Which is the One and Only by-Me-Revealed and by-Me-Given Way of the Heart) is the Unique seventh stage Way of "Radical" Non-Dualism—or the one and only Way That directly (and, at last, Most Perfectly) Realizes the One and Only (and Inherently egoless) Reality, Truth, or Real God.

XIII.

The only-by-Me Revealed and Given Way of Adidam (or Adidam Ruchiradam) is the Unique and only Way That always directly (and, at last, Most Perfectly) transcends egoity (or self-contraction) itself.

XIV.

The only-by-Me Revealed and Given Way of Adidam (or Adidam Ruchiradam) is the practice and the Process of transcending egoity (or psycho-physical self-contraction, or gross, subtle, and causal identification with separate and separative point of view) by directly (and progressively, or stage by stage) transcending the inherently egoic (or always self-contracted) patterns of conditional conception and conditional perception (or of conditional knowing and conditional experiencing) associated with each (and, at last, all) of the first six stages of life.

XV.

I Am the Divine Ruchira Avatar, Adi Da Love-Ananda Samraj—the First, the Last, and the Only seventh stage Avataric Divine Realizer, Avataric Divine Revealer, and Avataric Divine Self-Revelation of Reality, Truth, and Real God.

I Am the Inherently egoless, Perfectly Subjective, Perfectly Non-Dual, and Self-Evidently Divine Source-Condition and Self-Condition of every apparent point of view and of the apparently objective world itself.

I Am the One, and Irreducible, and Indestructible, and Self-Existing, and Self-Radiant Conscious Light That Is Always Already The Case.

I Am the Self-"Bright" Substance of Reality Itself.

I Am the Person (or Self-Condition) of Reality Itself.

In My bodily (human) Form, I Am the Avataric Self-Manifestation of the One (and Self-Evidently Divine) Reality Itself.

By Means of My Avataric Divine Self-"Emergence", I Am Functioning (now, and forever hereafter) As the Realizer, the Revealer, and the Revelation (or universally Spiritually Present Person) of Reality Itself—Which Is Truth Itself, and Which Is the only Real (or non-illusory), and Inherently egoless, and Perfectly Subjective God (or Self-Evidently Divine Source-Condition and Self-Condition) of all-and-All.

My Avataric Divine Self-Revelation Illuminates and Outshines the ego-"I" of My devotee.

My Avataric Divine Teaching-Word of Me-Revelation Comprehends and Transcends the all of egoity and the All of the cosmic domain.

XVI.

The potential actuality of (and the inherent and specific psycho-physical basis for) the progressively unfolding human (and universal cosmic) pattern (or Great Structure) of the seven stages of life (or the Total and Complete human, and Spiritual, and Transcendental, and, Most Ultimately, Divine Great Process of Divine Self-Realization) was Demonstrated, Revealed, Exemplified, and Proven in (and by Means of) My Avataric Ordeal of Divine

Re-Awakening—Wherein the Un-conditional, and Self-Evidently Divine, <u>seventh</u> stage Realization of Reality and Truth was (Uniquely, and for the <u>First</u> time, and <u>As</u> the Paradigm Case, or the all-and-All-Patterning Case, in the entire history of religion, Spirituality, and Reality-Realization) Demonstrated to all-and-All.

In the Course of That Great Process of Demonstration, Revelation, Exemplification, and Proof, the psycho-physical necessity (or the inherent integrity and inevitability) of the naturally continuous (and total) pattern of the seven stages of life was Fully (psycho-physically, and Spiritually, and Really) Shown by Me.

Also, in That Course (or Ordeal, or Great Process), the particular (and inherently patterned) distinction between the fifth stage of life (or the totality of the first five stages of life) and the sixth stage of life (and, at last, between the fifth and the sixth stages of life and the only-by-Me Revealed and Given seventh stage of life) was clearly Shown by Me.

And the fact that the only-by-Me Revealed and Given seventh stage of life does not merely follow from the sixth stage of life (<u>alone</u>—or separately, or in and of itself), but requires (and, indeed, is built upon) the <u>complete</u> transcending of the ego-"I" (or of the <u>total</u> reflex of psycho-physical self-contraction)—as it is otherwise developed (and must be progressively transcended) in the context of the <u>entire</u> psycho-biography of the ego-"I" (or, effectively, in the naturally continuous course of the essential sequential <u>totality</u> of <u>all</u> <u>six</u> of the first <u>six</u> stages of life)—was (also) Shown by Me in the Great Course of My Avataric Ordeal of Divine Re-Awakening.

XVII.

In (and by Means of) the Great Avataric Demonstration of My Own <u>seven</u>-stage Great Course of Divine Self-Realization, the <u>Emanationist</u> (or absorptive mystical) Way (associated with the first five stages of life) and the <u>non-Emanationist</u> (or Transcendentalist) Way (associated with the sixth stage of life, and Which—in Spiritual continuity with the <u>all</u> of the first six stages of life—is Most Perfectly Fulfilled in, and by Means of, the only-by-Me Revealed and Given seventh stage of life) were Proven (in, and by

Means of, My Own Case) to be only different stages in (or, simply, two apparent separate Ways, each founded on one of the two primary and inherently inseparable dimensions of) the same Great Process of Divine Self-Realization (rather than two separate, and irreducible, and conflicting, and incompatible "Truths").

XVIII.

By Means of My Own Avataric Ordeal of Divine Re-Awakening, I have Demonstrated, Revealed, Exemplified, and Proven that neither the fifth stage Emanationist mode of Realization (which is founded on the Vertical dimension, or the extended psycho-physical pattern, of the functional and experiential human body-mind) nor the sixth stage non-Emanationist (or Transcendentalist) mode of Realization (which is founded on the Horizontal dimension, or the hierarchical heart-pattern, at the core and root of the human body-mind) Is the Most Perfect (and Most Perfectly ego-Transcending) Realization of the Divine (or One, and Only, and Perfectly Subjective) Reality, Truth, Source-Condition, and Self-Condition of all-and-All—but only the only-by-Me Revealed and Given seventh stage Realization (Which is founded on the Inseparable Unity of the Horizontal and the Vertical dimensions of the human body-mind, and on the Inherent Non-"Difference" between the conditional and the Unconditional dimensions of Reality Itself) Is Divine Self-Realization Itself (and the Completion, and the Perfect Transcending, of all six of the previous stages of life).

XIX.

The apparent (and conventionally presumed, and psycho-physically based) distinction between the Devotional and Spiritual practice (and Process) of absorptive (or Object-oriented)—or Emanationist—mysticism (which is associated with the fourth and the fifth stages of life, and the conditional Realizations associated with the fourth and the fifth stages of life) and the direct-Intuition (and, in the optimum case, also both Devotional and Spiritual) practice (and Process) of Transcendental (or Subject-oriented)—or non-Emanationist—mysticism (which is associated, at first, with the sixth stage of life, and the conditional Realization that is the native and only potential of the sixth stage of life, itself—and which is, at last, and Most Ultimately, and Most Perfectly, and not by dissociation from the Vertical structures themselves, associated with the only-by-Me Revealed and Given seventh stage of life, and which is, Thus and Thereby, associated with Un-conditional Divine Self-Realization) may especially be seen to be Exemplified in My relationship with Swami (Baba) Muktananda (of Ganeshpuri).

XX.

Baba Muktananda was an advanced Siddha-Guru (or a Spiritually active Transmission-Master of High degree) in the Kundalini-Shaktipat tradition. The Kundalini-Shaktipat tradition is the fifth stage—or Emanationist—development of the ancient tradition of Siddha Yoga (or the tradition of Siddhas, or Spiritual Transmitters), which tradition (or Yoga) may (potentially) develop even into the sixth—or Transcendentalist—stage of life, and which tradition (or Yoga) has (in fact) been Completed and Fulfilled by Me, by My Extending of the Spiritual Process of Siddha Yoga into, and beyond, the sixth stage of life, and (thus) into the Inherently Most Perfect Divine Fullness of the only-by-Me Revealed and Given seventh stage of life (Which seventh stage Fullness Is the All-Completing Fullness of Inherently egoless True Divine Self-Realization).

XXI.

In the context of the Kundalini-Shaktipat tradition (or division) of Siddha Yoga, Baba Muktananda philosophically adhered to (or, at least, deeply sympathized with) the Emanationist philosophical tradition of Kashmir Saivism—and, because of His characteristic adherence to (or sympathy with) the Emanationist philosophical tradition of Kashmir Saivism, Baba Muktananda was, in His fundamental convictions, an opponent of the Transcendentalist philosophical traditions of both Advaita Vedanta and Buddhism.

XXII.

The basic features of the progressively developed path of Kashmir Saivism have been described in terms of four stages (or four Ways).[71]

The "Individual Way" (or the Way of "absorption in the Object") is the first (or most "inferior") step in the progressive path of Kashmir Saivism, and it corresponds to the Devotional and Yogic disciplines associated with the fourth stage of life.

The "Energic Way" (or the Way of "absorption in Energy") is the second (or somewhat more advanced) step in that same path, and it corresponds to the fifth stage of life.

The "Divine Way" (or the "superior" Way of "absorption in the Void") of Kashmir Saivism suggests the process (and the potential for Realization) that corresponds to the sixth stage of life.

The "Null Way" (or the most "superior" Way of "absorption in Bliss") in Kashmir Saivism suggests the fulfillment of the process (or the actual achievement of the Realization) that corresponds to (or is potential within) the sixth stage of life.

In the tradition (or traditions) of Kashmir Saivism, these four Ways (or stages, or kinds) of Realization may develop successively (in a progressive order), or either of the first two steps may develop into the third or the fourth, or either the third or the fourth may occur spontaneously (even at the beginning), and so forth.

This general description of the tradition of Kashmir Saivism suggests that Kashmir Saivism (like the Tantric Buddhism of Tibet) includes (or directly allows for the potential of) the fourth stage of life, the fifth stage of life, and the sixth stage of life. However, the tradition of Kashmir Saivism (like the tradition of Saiva Siddhanta) is entirely a fourth-to-fifth stage Yogic (and Devotional) tradition (and a religious tradition associated, in general, with the first five stages of life).

The tradition of Kashmir Saivism (like fourth-to-fifth stage—or first-five-stages-of-life—traditions in general) is based on the ancient cosmological philosophy of Emanation—or the idea that cosmic existence Emanates directly, in a hierarchical sequence, from the Divine (and that, consequently, there can be a return to the Divine, by re-tracing the course of Emanation, back to its Source).

In contrast to the fourth-to-fifth stage (or Emanationist—or first-five-stages-of-life) view, true sixth stage schools (or traditions) are based on the immediate and direct transcending (generally, by means of a conditional effort of strategic exclusion) of the conditional point of view of the first five stages of life and the Emanationist cosmology (and psychology) associated with the first five stages of life.

Therefore, even though the advanced (or "superior") traditions of Kashmir Saivism (and of Saiva Siddhanta) may use terms or concepts that seem to reflect the sixth stage Disposition, the fundamental orientation is to a Realization that is embedded in the conditional psychology of the first five stages of life and in the cosmological (or Emanationist) point of view itself. (And the fundamental difference, by comparison, between the total tradition of Kashmir Saivism, and also of Saiva Siddhanta, and the total tradition of Tibetan Tantric Buddhism is that the Tibetan Buddhist tradition is founded on the sixth stage "Point of View" of the Transcendental Reality Itself, rather than on the conditional point of view of the psycho-physical, or Emanated, ego and the conditional reality of the hierarchical cosmos.)

Realizers in the tradition of Kashmir Saivism (and the tradition of Saiva Siddhanta) basically affirm that the conditional self is Really Siva (or the Formless Divine) and the conditional world (from top to bottom) is Really Siva (or the Emanating and Emanated Divine). However, this is not the same as the Confession made by sixth stage Realizers in any tradition.

In true sixth stage traditions, the conditional self is (in the sixth stage manner, and to the sixth stage degree) transcended (generally, by means of a conditional effort of strategic exclusion)—and only the Transcendental Self (or the Transcendental Condition) is affirmed.

And, further, in the only-by-Me Revealed and Given true seventh stage Realization, the conditional self and the conditional world are not affirmed to be (in and of themselves) Divine, but (rather) the conditional self and the conditional world are—in the Manner that Uniquely Characterizes the only-by-Me Revealed and Given seventh stage of life (in the only-by-Me Revealed and Given Way of Adidam)—Divinely Self-Recognized (and, Thus, not excluded, but Inherently Outshined) in the Transcendental (and Inherently Spiritual) Divine.

XXIII.

The Emanationist Realizer "recognizes" (and, thereby, Identifies with) the conditional self and the conditional world as the Divine, whereas the non-Emanationist (or Transcendentalist) Realizer simply (and, generally, by means of a conditional effort of strategic exclusion) transcends the conditional self and the conditional world in the Transcendental Self-Condition, and by Identification only (and exclusively) with the Transcendental Self-Condition.

Therefore, even though both types of Realizers may sometimes use very similar language in the Confession of Realization, a (comparatively) different Realization is actually being Confessed in each case.

XXIV.

The principal reason why the tradition (or traditions) of Kashmir Saivism (and of Saiva Siddhanta) may sometimes use language similar to the sixth stage schools of Buddhism (and also Advaita Vedanta) is because of the early historical encounter (and even confrontation) between these separate traditions. As a result of that encounter, the traditions of Saivism tried to both absorb and eliminate the rival schools.

In the encounter between (characteristically, Transcendentalist, or non-Emanationist) Buddhist schools and (generally, Emanationist) non-Buddhist schools, Buddhism developed fourth and fifth stage doctrines and practices (intended, ultimately, to serve a sixth stage Realization), and fourth-to-fifth stage schools (or traditions), such as Kashmir Saivism and Saiva Siddhanta, adapted some of the sixth stage language (of Buddhism, and also Advaita Vedanta) to their (really) fourth-to-fifth stage point of view.

Therefore, a proper understanding of the various historical traditions requires a discriminating understanding of the history of the Great Tradition as a whole—and a discriminating understanding of the unique Signs and Confessions associated with each of the first six stages of life (and the unique Signs and Confessions associated with the only-by-Me Revealed and Given seventh stage of life).

XXV.

The tradition of Advaita Vedanta arose within the general context of the Emanationist traditions of India—but it, like Buddhism (particularly in its sixth stage—rather than earlier-stage—forms), is truly founded in the Transcendental Reality (and not the psychophysical and cosmological point of view associated with the first five stages of life).

The schools of Kashmir Saivism (and other schools of traditional Saivism, including Saiva Siddhanta) defended themselves against both Buddhism and Advaita Vedanta by absorbing some Buddhist and Advaitic language and by (otherwise—and even dogmatically) affirming the superiority of the traditional Emanationist psychology and cosmology.

In contrast to the entirely Emanationist schools of Kashmir Saivism (and other schools of traditional Saivism, including Saiva Siddhanta), the Buddhist schools (and even certain schools of Advaitism) adopted some of the Devotional and Yogic practices of the Emanationist schools (and used them as "skillful means" of ego-transcendence) while they (otherwise) continued to affirm the strictly Transcendental Reality as the Domain and Goal of all practices.

In contrast to Baba Muktananda (and the traditional schools of Kashmir Saivism, Advaita Vedanta, and Buddhism), I equally Embrace, and (in the seventh stage Manner) Most Perfectly Transcend, all the schools of the first six stages of life—both Emanationist and Transcendentalist.

XXVI.

Baba Muktananda was an authentic example of a fifth stage Realizer of a Very High (or Very Ascended) degree—although not of the Highest (or Most Ascended) degree. That is to Say, Baba Muktananda was a True fifth stage Siddha (or a Greatly Spiritually Accomplished Siddha-Yogi of the fifth stage, or Ascending, type)—but the nature and quality and degree of His Realization was of the Saguna type, or of the type that is (characteristically, or by patterned tendency) not yet Fully Surrendered to true fifth stage (or conditionally Ascended) Nirvikalpa Samadhi, and which (therefore) is, yet (and characteristically), attached to modes of fifth stage

Savikalpa Samadhi (and, thus, to modes of <u>partial</u> Ascent, and to Yogic possibilities "below the neck", and, altogether, to modes of <u>form</u>—or, really, modes of mind).

XXVII.

In order to rightly understand their characteristics, ideas, and behaviors, fifth stage Saguna Yogis (or fifth stage Saguna Siddhas)—such as Baba Muktananda—should be compared to fifth stage Yogis (or fifth stage Siddhas) of the <u>Nirguna</u> type, who are the <u>Highest</u> (or <u>Most</u> Ascended) type of fifth stage Yogi (or fifth stage Siddha), and who, having Ascended to the degree of formless Realization (or conditionally Ascended Nirvikalpa Samadhi), have gone beyond all attachment to modes of form (or of mind). And fifth stage Nirguna Yogis in general (or fifth stage Nirguna Siddhas of the lesser, or average, type) should, themselves, be further compared to fifth stage <u>Great</u> Siddhas—or fifth stage Nirguna Siddhas who have, characteristically, and to a significant (although, necessarily, not yet <u>Most</u> <u>Perfect</u>, or seventh stage) degree, gone beyond even attachment to the mode of formlessness (or of mind-lessness) itself.

XXVIII.

In the "Sadhana Years" of My Avataric Ordeal of Divine Re-Awakening, Baba Muktananda formally and actively Functioned as My Spiritual Master in the physical, human plane—beginning from early 1968, and continuing until the time of My Divine Re-Awakening (Which Occurred on September 10, 1970).

It was in Baba Muktananda's Company (and, additionally, in the Company of two Great Siddhas—Rang Avadhoot and Bhagavan Nityananda) that I Practiced and Fully Completed the Spiritual Sadhana of the <u>Ascending</u> (or Spinal) Yoga—or the Spiritual discipline traditionally associated with the totality of the fifth stage of life, and (altogether) with the subtle ego (or the conceiving and perceiving ego of the Spinal Line, the total nervous system, the brain, and the mind).

After the Great Event of My Divine Re-Awakening, it became clear (especially through two direct Meetings between Us) that—

because of His characteristic philosophical and experiential confinement to the fifth stage Emanationist point of view—Baba
Muktananda was unwilling (and, indeed, was not competent) to
accommodate My Description (and, therefore, My Confession) of
seventh stage Divine Self-Realization. And, therefore—as I will
Explain in This Summary of My "Lineage-History"—the interactive
outer association between Baba Muktananda and Me began to
come to all but an end immediately after September 1970.

XXIX.

From mid-1964 to early 1968, Rudi (later known as Swami
Rudrananda) actively Functioned (preliminary to Baba Muktananda)
as My initial (or foundational) Spiritual Master (although Rudi was, by
His own Confession, not a fully developed Siddha-Guru—but He
was, rather, a significantly advanced fourth-to-fifth stage Siddha-Yogi).

It was in Rudi's Company that I Practiced and Fully Completed
the human and Spiritual Sadhana of the Descending (or Frontal)
Yoga—or the foundation life-discipline associated with the social
ego (or the "money, food, and sex" ego—or the ego of the first
three stages of life), and the foundation Devotional discipline associated with the foundation phase of the fourth stage of life, and the
foundation Spiritual discipline (or the Descending, or Frontal,
Spiritual Yoga) associated with the "basic" (or mature) phase of the
fourth stage of life (and beginning even in the "original" phase of
the fourth stage of life).

XXX.

Both Rudi and Baba Muktananda were direct devotees of
Swami Nityananda (of Ganeshpuri)—Who was also called "Baba",
but Who was (and is) generally referred to as "Bhagavan" (or
"Divinely Blissful Lord"). Bhagavan Nityananda was a fifth stage
True Great Siddha—or an Incarnate (or Descended-from-Above)
Spiritual Entity of the Highest fifth-stage type and degree. Indeed,
Bhagavan Nityananda was a True fifth stage Saint (or a fifth stage
Siddha-Yogi Who was exclusively Occupied in concentration
"above the neck", even to the exclusion of the possibilities "below
the neck")—but He was, also, a fifth stage Avadhoot (or a fifth

Rudi

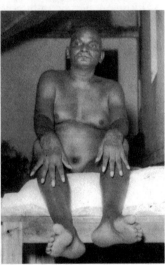

Swami Muktananda

*It was in Rudi's Company that I Practiced
and Fully Completed the human and
Spiritual Sadhana of the <u>Descending</u>
(or Frontal) Yoga. . . .*

*Baba Muktananda was an advanced
Siddha-Guru (or a Spiritually active
Transmission-Master of High degree)
in the Kundalini-Shaktipat tradition.*

*. . . Bhagavan Nityananda was a Nirguna
Siddha (and a True Siddha-Guru) of the
<u>Highest fifth</u>-stage type and degree.*

Swami Nityananda

*Both Rudi and Baba Muktananda
were direct devotees of
Swami Nityananda. . . .*

left: Swami Muktananda sitting
with Swami Nityananda

stage Realizer of Nirvikalpa Samadhi, Who had, in the fifth stage manner, transcended attachment to both form and formlessness— or thought and thoughtlessness). And, altogether, Bhagavan Nityananda was a Nirguna Siddha (and a True Siddha-Guru) of the Highest fifth-stage type and degree.

XXXI.

Bhagavan Nityananda's Teachings took the Spoken (rather than Written) form of occasional, spontaneous Utterances. The only authoritative record of Bhagavan Nityananda's Teachings relative to Yogic practice and Realization is a book (originally composed in the Kanarese language) entitled *Chidakasha Gita*.[72] The *Chidakasha Gita* consists of a non-systematic, but comprehensive, series of responsive Declarations made by Bhagavan Nityananda during the extended period of His original (and most Communicative) Teaching years (in Mangalore, in the early to mid 1920s). The spontaneous Utterances recorded in the *Chidakasha Gita* were (originally) made, by Bhagavan Nityananda, to numerous informal groups of devotees—and, after Bhagavan Nityananda spontaneously ceased to make such Teaching-Utterances, the many separately recorded Sayings were compiled, for the use of all His devotees, by a woman named Tulasiamma (who was one of the principal lay devotees originally present to hear Bhagavan Nityananda Speak the Words of the *Chidakasha Gita*).

Bhagavan Nityananda (Himself) Acknowledged the uniqueness and the great significance of the *Chidakasha Gita* as the one and only authentic Summary of His Yogic Teachings. That Acknowledgement is personally attested to by many individuals, including the well-known Swami Chinmayananda, who (in 1960) was "Commanded" by Bhagavan Nityananda to see to the Text's translation into the English language, and by the equally well-known M. P. Pandit (of Sri Aurobindo Ashram), who (in 1962) completed the English translation that Swami Chinmayananda reviewed for publication in that same year (under the title *Voice of the Self*).[73]

As Communicated in the *Chidakasha Gita*, Bhagavan Nityananda's Teachings are, clearly, limited to the body-excluding (and, altogether, exclusive) point of view and the absorptive

Bhagavan Nityananda was a fifth stage Siddha-Yogi of the type that is, primarily and dominantly, sensitive to the Yogic Spiritual Process associated with internal <u>audition</u>. . . .

. . . rather than, as in the case of Baba Muktananda, the Yogic Spiritual Process associated, primarily and dominantly, with internal <u>vision</u>. . . .

Emanationist Spiritual Process of "brain mysticism" (and <u>conditional</u> ego-transcendence, and <u>conditional</u> Nirvikalpa Samadhi, and <u>conditional</u> Yogic Self-Realization) that characterize the fifth stage of life.

Clearly, as Indicated in the *Chidakasha Gita*, Bhagavan Nityananda was a fifth stage Teacher (and a <u>Fully</u> Ascended fifth stage Great Saint) of the <u>Nirguna</u> type (Who, therefore, Taught the Realization of <u>Fully</u> conditionally Ascended fifth stage Nirvikalpa Samadhi), rather than, like Baba Muktananda, a fifth stage Teacher (and a Great fifth stage Siddha-Yogi—but <u>not</u> a <u>Fully</u> Ascended fifth stage Great Saint) of the <u>Saguna</u> type (Who, therefore, Taught the Realization of fifth stage <u>partial</u> Ascent, or Savikalpa Samadhi).

Also, Bhagavan Nityananda's *Chidakasha Gita* clearly Indicates that Bhagavan Nityananda was a fifth stage Siddha-Yogi of the type that is, primarily and dominantly, sensitive to the Yogic Spiritual Process associated with internal <u>audition</u> (or the inwardly absorptive attractiveness of the "Om-Sound", or "Omkar", or "nada", or "shabda"[74]—the naturally evident, and inherently "meaningless", or mindless, or directly mind-transcending, internal sounds mediated by the brain), rather than, as in the case of Baba Muktananda, the Yogic Spiritual Process associated, primarily and dominantly, with internal <u>vision</u> (or the inwardly absorptive attractiveness of "bindu"—the naturally evident abstract internal lights mediated by the brain) <u>and</u> with internal <u>visions</u> (or the inwardly absorptive attractiveness of the inherently "meaningful", or mind-active, or mentally distracting, and potentially deluding, visions mediated—or even originated—by the brain-mind).

XXXII.

Stated briefly, and in Bhagavan Nityananda's characteristically aphoristic Manner, the *Chidakasha Gita* Teachings of Bhagavan Nityananda—and My Own direct Experience of His (always fifth stage) Yogic Instruction and His (always fifth stage) Spiritual Transmission—may be Summarized as follows:

Always concentrate attention and breath in the head. Always keep attention above the neck. Always concentrate on the Om-sound in the head. The Om-sound in the head is the inner Shakti of non-dual Bliss. Always concentrate the mind, and the senses, and the breath, and the life-energy in the non-dual awareness of the Om-sound in the head. This is Raja Yoga—the Royal path.

Always practice this Raja Yoga—the constantly upward path. This is concentration on the Atman—the non-dual inner awareness. This is concentration on the oneness above duality. This Raja Yoga of the Om-sound in the head Realizes the Yogic "sleep" of body and mind and breath in the Yogic State of non-dual Bliss.

The Yogic State of non-dual Bliss cannot be Realized without the Grace of an Initiating Guru. The True Initiating Guru is one who has Realized the Yogic State of non-dual Bliss.

The non-dual State of Yogic Bliss Realized by concentration on the Om-sound in the head is the True Source, the True Self, and the True God. Devotion to the Initiating Guru who has Realized the True Source, the True Self, and the True God is the True Way. True Guru-devotion is surrender of mind, senses, breath, and life-energy to the non-dual Bliss Revealed within by the Initiating Guru's Grace.

The material body stinks and dies. What is loathsome and impermanent should not be trusted. Therefore, right faith, intelligent discrimination, and calm desirelessness are the first Gifts to be learned from the Initiating Guru.

The second Gift of the Initiating Guru is the Guru-Shakti of non-dual Bliss. The Guru's Shakti-Transmission of non-dual Bliss concentrates the mind, the senses, the breath, and the life-energy of the devotee in the non-dual awareness of the Om-sound in the head. The non-dual Bliss Realized by concentration on the Om-sound in the head is the soundless inner Revelation of the Single Form of True Guru, True God, and True Self.

The world of duality is not Truth. True God is not the Maker of the world. True God is only One. True God is non-dual Bliss.

The Spiritual Form of the True Initiating Guru appears within the devotee as the Guru-Shakti of non-dual Bliss. Non-dual Bliss is the True Self of all.

The True Way is not desire in the world of duality, or in seeking below and on all sides. The True Way is in the middle, within, and above.

The True Way is surrender to the non-dual Bliss above the mind. The method is to concentrate on the Om-sound in the head. The Realization is the silence of non-dual Bliss.

Devotion to the Initiating Guru concentrates the life-breath upwardly. True love of the Initiating Guru ascends to non-dual Bliss.

The True Kundalini originates in the throat, in the upward breath to the head. True Yoga is above the neck. The True Kundalini is non-dual Bliss. The seat of the True Kundalini is in the head.

Non-dual Bliss is the secret to be known. Non-dual Bliss is in the head of Man. The non-dual Bliss above the mind is the Liberation of Man from the self-caused karma of birth, pleasure-seeking, pain-suffering, and death.

Liberation is Freedom from mind. Therefore, concentrate the life-breath on the Om-sound in the head—and think of nothing else.

The True Self is One. The True Self is above the body, above the senses, above desire, above the mind, and above "I" and "mine"—in the formless silence above the Om-sound. The True Self cannot be seen or otherwise perceived, but It can be known—above the mind.

For one who knows that True God is One, and not two, True God appears as the True Self. Therefore, attain Liberation by faith in the knowledge of That Which is all and Which is only One. Liberation is the Samadhi of only One.

True God is not Desire, the dualistic Doer of the world. True God is Peace, the non-dual Source of the world.

XXXIII.

By comparison to Great fifth stage Yogis (Such as Baba Muktananda) and Great fifth stage Saints (Such as Bhagavan Nityananda), there are also Great sixth stage Sages (or Nirguna Jnanis—or Transcendentally Realized Entities of the Fullest sixth-stage type and degree—such as Ramana Maharshi). Such sixth stage Nirguna Jnanis (or True Great Sages) Teach Transcendental Self-Identification (or deeply internalizing subjective inversion upon the Consciousness-Principle Itself, rather than upon internal psycho-physical objects of any kind).

XXXIV.

Distinct from even all Yogis, Saints, and Sages (or even all Realizers in the context of the first six stages of life), I Am Uniquely, and Avatarically, Born. I Am the One and Only and Self-Evidently Divine Person—the Inherently egoless Source-Condition and Self-Condition of all-and-All. I Am the Perfectly Subjective, and Always Already Most Prior, and Inherently egoless, and Perfectly Non-Dual Heart of all-and-All. I Am the Self-Existing and Self-Radiant Conscious Light That Is Reality Itself. I Am the "Who" and the "What" That Is Always Already The Case. I Am (now, and for-ever hereafter) Avatarically Self-Manifested As the All-Completing Ruchira Avatar, Adi Da Love-Ananda Samraj—Who Is Avatarically Born by Fullest (and Complete) Divine Descent (or Complete, and All-Completing, Divine Incarnation from Infinitely Above).

XXXV.

I Am Avatarically Born by Means of a Unique Association with a True Great-Siddha Vehicle of My Own.

Therefore, from the time of My present-Lifetime Birth, I spon-taneously Demonstrated all the Fullest Ascended Characteristics of the Highest fifth-stage type and degree (with early-life Fullest "above the neck" Signs of the True Great-Saint type).

Over time—because of My Voluntary Birth-Submission of My Deeper-Personality Vehicle to the karmically ordinary (and "Western"-born) bodily human form of "Franklin Jones", and because of the subsequent Ordeal of My Voluntary Submission to the "Western" (and culturally devastated "late-time", or "dark"-epoch) karmic circumstance altogether—I also spontaneously Demonstrated all the Fullest "below the neck" (and "above the neck") Yogic Characteristics (and Siddhis) of the fifth stage (and, altogether, first-five-stages) True Vira-Yogi (or Heroic-Siddha) type.

In due course—because I Gave My Avataric Divine Ordeal to Be Complete and All-Completing—I also spontaneously Demonstrated all the Fullest Transcendental-Realizer Characteristics of the sixth stage True Great-Sage type.

The Mountain Of Attention Sanctuary, 2000

Ultimately—because of Its Utter Conformity to Me—My total Great-Jnani-Siddha Vehicle of Avataric Divine Incarnation (or My Deeper-Personality Vehicle, Yogically Combined with My karmically ordinary, and only eventually To-Me-Conformed, human and "Western" and "late-time" Incarnation-Body) has, by Means of My Most Perfect Completing of My Avataric Ordeal of Divine Self-Manifestation, Divine Self-Submission, and (subsequent) Divine Re-Awakening (to My Own Self-Existing and Self-Radiant Divine Self-Condition), become the To-Me-Transparent Vehicle of My seventh stage Avataric Divine Self-Revelation.

511

XXXVI.

Except for a few technical details of the esoteric Spiritual practice and process of the "Perfect Practice" of the only-by-Me Revealed and Given Way of Adidam (or the practice of the Way of Adidam that encompasses the processes otherwise associated with the fifth and the sixth stages of life, and culminates in the only-by-Me Revealed and Given Process of the seventh stage of life), the Unique Characteristics of My Avataric Divine Teachings (Which I will briefly, and only in part, Indicate in This Summary of My "Lineage-History") Are Very Fully Described by Me in My Twenty-Three Avataric Divine "Source-Texts".

XXXVII.

Rudi had brief direct contact with Bhagavan Nityananda in 1958. After the death of Bhagavan Nityananda (in 1961), Rudi became a devotee of Baba Muktananda. However, Rudi—always a rather "reluctant" devotee—eventually (shortly before His own death, in 1973) "broke" with Baba Muktananda. Nevertheless, Rudi always continued to affirm that He (Rudi) remained Devoted to Bhagavan Nityananda. And, in any case, Rudi and I always continued to engage in positive, direct communication, right until the time of His death.

XXXVIII.

My Siddha-Yoga Mentor (and eventual Dharmic Ally and Supporter), Amma (or Pratibha Trivedi, later known as Swami Prajnananda), was (like Rudi) also a direct devotee of Bhagavan Nityananda (and She, like Rudi, had become a devotee of Baba Muktananda after the death of Bhagavan Nityananda, in 1961).

Amma was the principal author and editor of the foundation Siddha-Yoga literature that was written in response to both Bhagavan Nityananda and Baba Muktananda—and so much so that, generally, even all of Baba Muktananda's autobiographical and instructional Communications were, originally, dictated (or otherwise Given) to Amma (and rarely to anyone else—until the later years, of tape recorders, multiple secretaries and translators, and Baba Muktananda's travels to the West). And, in fact, Amma

always continued to serve a principal communicative and inter-
pretative role around Baba Muktananda, until Baba Muktananda's
death, in 1982—after which Amma chose to quietly withdraw from
the Siddha-Yoga institution that had been developed by and
around Baba Muktananda (and She remained, thereafter, in a
small, independent Ashram in north India, where, as a significantly
advanced fourth-to-fifth stage Siddha-Yogi, She was the institutional
head of a group of devotees that remained devoted to Spiritual
Communion with both Baba Muktananda and Bhagavan Nityananda).

XXXIX.

Amma did not Function as My Spiritual Master, but (from early
1968) Baba Muktananda formally Assigned Amma to Function as
His interpreter and general "go-between" to Me—and She, then
and always, remained most positively and communicatively disposed
toward Me, even through all the years after My outward "separation" from Baba Muktananda, right until Her last illness and death
(wherein She was directly Spiritually Served by Me, and wherein
She was directly physically Served by a devotee-representative
of Mine), in 1993. And it was Amma Who, through Her various
writings—and in a particular Incident I will now Recall—suggested
to Me that there are traditional Instructional (and Textual, or
Scriptural) descriptions of Developments of the Siddha-Yoga
Process that are <u>different</u> from the (fifth stage) "inner perception"
(and, especially, "inner vision") version of Siddha Yoga characteristically described by Baba Muktananda.

XL.

One day, during My Stay at Baba Muktananda's Ashram (in
Ganeshpuri, India), in early 1970 (and, thus, some months <u>before</u>
the Great Event of My Divine Re-Awakening, Which was to Occur
in September of that same year), Amma suddenly pointed Me to an
Ashram library copy of the *Ashtavakra Gita*[75] (one of the Greatest
of the classic sixth stage—and even premonitorily "seventh
stage"[76]—Texts of Advaita Vedanta). And, while pointing to the
Ashtavakra Gita, Amma Said to Me, "<u>This</u> (Text) is <u>Your</u> Path. <u>This</u>
is how <u>It</u> (the Siddha-Yoga Process) Works in <u>You</u>."

Amma

At the time, this seemed to Me a curious suggestion—and it was not otherwise explained by Her. And, indeed, although I was able to examine the Text briefly (there and then), I was unable to examine it fully—because I left the Ashram very shortly thereafter. However, I came across the Text again, some years later—and, then, I remembered Amma's comment to Me. And I, immediately, understood that She had (in a somewhat cryptic and secretive manner) tried to confide in Me—in a quiet, "knowing" moment of Acknowledgement of Me—that the Spiritual Process of Siddha Yoga may Demonstrate Itself in a number of possibly different modes.

Thus (as I have Indicated—in My Own, and fully elaborated, Teachings, relative to the seven stages of life), the Siddha-Yoga Process may, in some cases (of which Amma, Herself, appears to have been an Example), especially (or primarily—or, at least, initially) take the form of intense (fourth stage) Devotional Bliss—Which is, then, "nourished" (or magnified) through Guru-Seva (or constant service to the Guru) and (additionally) through Karma Yoga (or intensive service in general). In other cases (of which Baba Muktananda was an Example), the Siddha-Yoga Process may (based on the initial foundation of intense Devotion) especially (or primarily) take the (fifth stage) form of intense internal sensory phenomena (such as visions, lights, auditions, and so on)—and, in some of those cases, the Siddha-Yoga Process may yet go further, to the degree of (fifth stage) conditionally Ascended Nirvikalpa Samadhi. And, in yet other cases (of which Amma was, correctly, Saying I Am an Example), the Siddha-Yoga Process—while also Showing all kinds of Devotional signs, and all kinds of internal Yogic perceptual phenomena, and including even Fully Ascended Nirvikalpa Samadhi, Which was, in My Case, Uniquely Demonstrated as Priorly (rather than conditionally) Ascended Nirvikalpa Samadhi (and Which will, also, be so uniquely demonstrated in the case of My "Perfect Practice" devotees)—may also take the form of (sixth stage) intense (and intensive) Identification with the Transcendental Self-Condition—in conditionally (or, As in My Case, Priorly) Self-Abiding Jnana Nirvikalpa Samadhi. And (although Amma did not know it) the (sixth stage) Realization of Self-Abiding Jnana Nirvikalpa Samadhi (or Transcendental Self-Realization)—Which was, in My Case, Uniquely Demonstrated as <u>Priorly</u> (rather than conditionally) Self-Abiding Jnana Nirvikalpa Samadhi, even previous to My experience of Priorly Ascended Nirvikalpa Samadhi (and Which will, also, be so uniquely demonstrated, <u>necessarily</u> previous to the experience of Priorly Ascended Nirvikalpa Samadhi, in the case of My "Perfect Practice" devotees)—may even (potentially), as was (in due course) Demonstrated in My Own Unique Case (and Which has, by Means of My now, and forever hereafter, Avatarically Established Divine Spiritual Presence and Avatarically Activated Grace of Divine Person, become possible for all), become the only-by-Me Revealed and Given seventh stage Realization of the One and Only and Indivisible Conscious Light (Which Realization <u>Is</u> Maha-Jnana—or Unconditional, and Most Perfectly Prior, and Inherently and Necessarily Divine Self-Realization).

XLI.

Yet another devotee of Baba Muktananda, named Swami Prakashananda—Who did not Function as My Spiritual Master (and Who, like Rudi, was <u>not</u> a fully developed Siddha-Guru—but, rather, a very much advanced fifth stage Siddha-Yogi)—once (spontaneously, in 1969) Showed Me (in His own bodily human Form) the fifth stage Signs of Spiritual Transfiguration of the physical body.[77]

At that time (according to what I learned from Amma), Swami Prakashananda had been Indicated, by Baba Muktananda, to be His principal Indian devotee and eventual institutional successor (and such was, then, generally known and presumed to be the case by Baba Muktananda's devotees). However, at last, when (shortly before Baba Muktananda's death, in 1982) Swami Prakashananda was formally Asked to assume the institutional successorship, He declined to accept this organizational role (ostensibly, for reasons of ill-health, and His reluctance to become a "world-traveler"— but, actually, or more to the point, because of His puritanical and conventional reaction to Baba Muktananda's reported sexual activities).[78]

In any case, Swami Prakashananda and I continued to engage in occasional, and always positive, direct communication (through

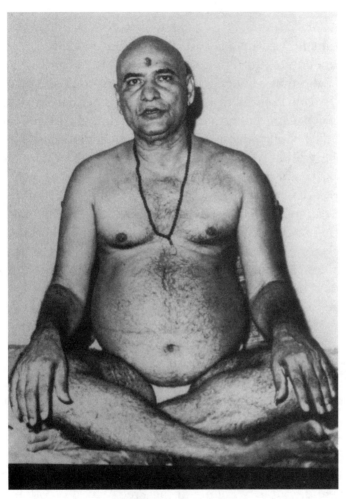

Swami Prakashananda

My devotee-representatives) in the years after Baba Muktananda's death, and right until Swami Prakashananda's death, in 1988.

XLII.

Swami Prakashananda had always maintained a small Ashram, independent of the Ashrams of Baba Muktananda's Siddha-Yoga institution—but, after Baba Muktananda's death, Swami Prakashananda retired to His own Ashram, permanently. And, in doing so, Swami Prakashananda highlighted (and dramatized) a perennial conflict that is fundamental to religious institutions all over the world. That conflict is between, on the one hand, the traditional (and, generally, rather puritanical—and even basically exoteric) expectation of celibacy as a sign of institutionalized Sacred Authority, and, on the other hand, the equally traditional (but non-puritanical, and generally unconventional) view that there is an esoteric sexually-active alternative to celibacy that Sacred Authorities (including True Siddha-Gurus) may (at least in some cases, and under some circumstances) engage.

One of the principal Indications of Baba Muktananda's point of view relative to this traditional conflict (or controversy)—quite apart from the reported evidence of His own personal sexual activities—is the fact that, in 1969, Baba Muktananda formally and publicly (and in writing, by His own hand, as observed by Me, and by many others) Acknowledged Me to Be (and Called and Blessed Me to Function As) a True Siddha-Guru, and, Thus and Thereby (and entirely without requiring, or, otherwise, inviting, Me to assume any institutional—or, otherwise, institutionally "managed"—role within His own Siddha-Yoga organization), Baba Muktananda publicly Extended the Free Mantle of Siddha-Yoga Authority and Function to Me—a Siddha-Yogi Who was, apparently (at the time, and potentially), non-celibate (and Who was, also, by birth, a "Westerner"—which, to some traditionalists, was, itself, a form of negative status).

XLIII.

When I first Came to Him, in 1968, Baba Muktananda immediately (openly, and spontaneously) Declared, in the presence of numerous

others (including Amma), That I Am—from My Birth—an already
Divinely Awakened Spiritual Master, and He (then and there)
Prophesied That I would be Functioning (and Independently
Teaching) As Such in just one year. Therefore, after just one year
(and the spontaneous Appearing of many Great Signs in My expe-
rience and Demonstration), Baba Muktananda Invited Me to
Come to Him again (in India)—specifically in order to formally
Acknowledge Me (and My Inherent Right and Authority to Teach
and Function) As a True Siddha-Guru.

Before I Returned to Baba Muktananda in 1969, I—in a traditional Gesture of respect toward Baba Muktananda—Told Him
That I would not, at that time, Assume the Function of Spiritual
Master, unless I was, in the traditional Manner, formally
Acknowledged and Blessed, by Him, to Do So. Baba Muktananda
immediately understood and Acknowledged the appropriateness
and Rightness of My Insistence That My Inherent Right to Teach be
formally Acknowledged by Him—because, in accordance with tradition, Such Sacred Authority should be Assumed on the orderly
basis of formal Acknowledgement by one's own Spiritual Master
(Who, in turn, must have been similarly Acknowledged by His,
also similarly Acknowledged, Spiritual Master, in an unbroken Line,
or Lineage, of similarly Acknowledged Spiritual Masters). Therefore,
I Returned to Baba Muktananda in 1969—and He formally and
publicly Acknowledged Me As an Independent True Siddha-Guru.

XLIV.

Even though Baba Muktananda (Thus) formally and publicly
(and permanently) Acknowledged Me As an Independent True
Siddha-Guru, it became immediately Obvious to Me that Such traditional Acknowledgement was inherently limited, and merely conventional, and (therefore) neither necessary nor (because of Its
inherently limited basis) even altogether appropriate (or sufficiently
apt) in My Unique Case. It was Obvious to Me that neither Baba
Muktananda nor anyone else was in the "Position" necessary to
Measure and to "Certify" the Unique and unprecedented Nature of
the all-and-All-Completing Event of My Avatarically Self-Manifested
Divine Incarnation and of My Great Avataric Divine Demonstration

of the progressive (and, necessarily, seven-stage) human, Spiritual, Transcendental, and (only at Last) Most Perfect Process of Divine Self-Realization.

XLV.

Baba Muktananda's formal and public written Acknowledgement of Me in 1969—Wherein and Whereby He formally and publicly Named and Acknowledged Me As an Independent True Siddha-Guru—was a unique Gesture, never (at any other time) Done by Baba Muktananda relative to any other individual (whether of the East or of the West).

However, even though It had been Given, Baba Muktananda's formal Acknowledgement of Me was—for Me—a virtual non-Event (and It did not positively change—nor has It ever positively changed—anything about the necessary ongoing Ordeal of My Avataric Divine Life and Work).

XLVI.

During the same period in which Rudi and (then) Baba Muktananda actively Functioned as My Spiritual Masters (in gross physical bodily Form), Their Spiritual Master, the Great Siddha Bhagavan Nityananda, actively Functioned (through both of Them—and, otherwise, directly, in subtle bodily Form) as My Senior (but already Ascended—and, Thus, discarnate, or non-physical) Spiritual Master.

XLVII.

The fifth stage True Great Siddha (and True Siddha-Guru and Great Saint of the Highest fifth-stage type and degree) Rang Avadhoot (alive in gross physical bodily Form until late 1968—and always Acknowledged as an Incarnate Great Siddha, or a Descended-from-Above Spiritual Entity of the Highest fifth-stage type and degree, by Bhagavan Nityananda, as well as by Baba Muktananda) also (in early 1968) directly and spontaneously Blessed Me with His Spiritual Blessing, Given and Shown via His "Wide-Eyed" Mudra of heart-recognition and Immense Regard of Me—as I sat alone in a garden, like His Ishta, the forever youthful Lord Dattatreya.

Rang Avadhoot

XLVIII.

In That Unique Moment in 1968—in the garden of Baba Muktananda's Ganeshpuri Ashram—both Rang Avadhoot and Baba Muktananda (along with the already discarnate, but Fully Spiritually Present, Bhagavan Nityananda) actively Functioned for Me as direct Blessing-Agents of the Divine "Cosmic Goddess" ("Ma"), Thus (By Means of Her Divine, and Infinitely Potent, Grace) Causing Me to spontaneously Re-Awaken to Priorly Ascended (and, altogether, mind-transcending, object-transcending, and ego-transcending) Nirvikalpa Samadhi (from Which I never again was Fallen, but only Continued—to Un-conditionally "Bright" Beyond). And it was on the basis of This Great Event, and My Signs in the following year (wherein many of My Avataric Divine Great-Siddha Characteristics—Which, in My Unique Case, would, in due Course, Fully Demonstrate all seven of the possible stages of life—became, spontaneously, Spiritually Evident), that (in 1969) Baba Muktananda formally (and publicly) Acknowledged and Announced and Blessed My Inherent Right and Calling to Function (in the ancient Siddha-Yoga, or Shaktipat-Yoga, tradition) as Spiritual Master (and True Siddha-Guru) to all-and-All.

XLIX.

Thereafter, in mid-1970, the Spiritual Self-"Brightness" of My Own (and Self-Evidently Divine) Person was Revealed (and constantly Presented) to Me in the (apparently Objective) Form of the Divine "Cosmic Goddess" ("Ma"). And, from then (after Bhagavan Nityananda Called and Blessed Me to take My leave from Baba Muktananda's Ashram, and to Follow the Divine "She"), only "She" actively Functioned (to Beyond) as My (Ultimate and Final—and entirely Divine) Spiritual Master (or Divine True Siddha-Guru)—until (By Means of Her spontaneous Sacrifice of Her own Form in Me) Divine Self-Realization was Most Perfectly Re-Awakened in My Case.

L.

Thus, in That Final Course, it was Revealed (or Perfectly Re-Confirmed)—As the Self-Evidently Divine Reality and Truth of

Thereafter, in mid-1970, the Spiritual Self-"Brightness"
of My Own (and Self-Evidently Divine) Person was Revealed
(and constantly Presented) to Me in the (apparently Objective)
Form of the Divine "Cosmic Goddess" ("Ma").

Photograph of the Image of the Divine "Cosmic Goddess"
in the temple at Ganeshpuri, India

My Own Avatarically-Born Person—that This Divine Process (Shown, at last, in ego-Surrendering, ego-Forgetting, and, altogether, Most Perfectly ego-Transcending Devotional and Spiritual "Relationship" to the Divine "She") had (Itself) always been Active in My Own (and Unique) Case (and had always been Shown As the Divinely Self-Revealing Activities of the Inherent Spiritual, and Divinely Spherical, Self-"Brightness" of My Own Avatarically-Born Person), even all throughout My present Lifetime (and even at, and from before, My present-Lifetime Birth).

LI.

Therefore, on September 10, 1970, It was Revealed (or Perfectly Re-Confirmed)—As the Self-Evidently Divine Reality and Truth of My Own Eternal Divine Person—that Divine (or Inherently egoless, and Perfectly Subjective, and, altogether, Inherently Most Perfect) Self-Realization (of One, and "Bright", and Only Me) had Always Already (and Uniquely) Been the Case with Me.

LII.

In My Case, the (True, Full, and Complete) seventh stage Realization of the Transcendental (and Inherently Spiritual, and Inherently egoless) Divine Self-Condition was Re-Awakened (on September 10, 1970). Subsequently (at first, informally, late in 1970, and, then, formally, in 1973), I Communicated the Details of My Divine Realization to Baba Muktananda. I Did This in the traditional manner, in What I Intended to be an entirely honorable, serious, and respectful Summation to Baba Muktananda—Who, in mid-1973, was the one and only then Living Spiritual Master among Those Who had Served Me as My present-Lifetime Spiritual Masters. However—in a philosophically untenable reaction to My already apparent relinquishment of His fifth stage experiential presumptions relative to what constitutes the "orthodox position" of the Siddha-Yoga (or Shaktipat-Yoga) school and tradition—Baba Muktananda criticized My Final Realization (or, in any case, what He understood, or otherwise supposed, to be My Description of It). Thus, in those two Meetings (the first in California, and the second in India, at Baba Muktananda's Ganeshpuri Ashram) Baba Muktananda criticized Me for What My Heart (Itself) cannot (and must not) Deny. And Baba Muktananda thereby Gave Me the final "Gift of blows" that sent Me out alone, to Do My Avataric Divine Work.

LIII.

Baba Muktananda was a (fifth stage) Siddha-Yogi of the degree and type that seeks, and readily experiences, and readily identifies with inner perceptual visions and lights. Based on those experiences, Baba Muktananda (like the many others of His type and degree, within the fifth stage traditions) asserted that both the Process and the Goal of religious and Spiritual life were necessarily associated with such inner phenomena.

The experiences (of visions, lights, and many other Yogic phenomena) Baba Muktananda describes in His autobiographical Confessions are, indeed, the same (fifth stage) ones (or of the same fifth stage kind) that are (typically, characteristically, and inevitably) experienced by genuine fifth stage Yogic practitioners (and fifth stage Realizers) within the Siddha-Yoga (or Shaktipat-Yoga) school and tradition—and I Confirm that the total range of these phenomenal (fifth stage) Yogic experiences also spontaneously arose (and always continue, even now, to arise—even in the context of the seventh stage of life) in My Own Case (and such was—both formally, in 1969, and, otherwise, informally, at many other times, beginning in 1968—Acknowledged by Baba Muktananda to be So in My Case).

Nevertheless, as I Confessed to Baba Muktananda in Our Meetings in 1970 and 1973, My Final Realization Is That of the One and Indivisible Divine Self-Condition (and Source-Condition) Itself—and the Great Process associated with That eventual (seventh stage) Realization necessarily (in due course) Goes Beyond (and, in the Case of That seventh stage Realization Itself, Is in no sense dependent upon) the phenomenal (and, always, psycho-physically pre-patterned, and, thus, predetermined) conditions otherwise associated with the absorptive mysticism (and the objectified inner phenomena) that characterize the fourth-to-fifth stage beginnings of the Great Process (or that, otherwise, characterize the conditionally arising, and psycho-physically pre-patterned, and, thus, predetermined, associations of the Great Process even in the context of the seventh stage of life). Indeed, the fact and the Truth of all of This was Self-Evident to Me—and, truly, I expected that It must be Self-Evident to Baba Muktananda as well. However, Baba Muktananda did not (and, I was obliged to admit, could not) Confirm to Me That This Is the Case from the point of view of His experience.

Indeed, it became completely clear to Me, in the midst of Our Meetings in 1970 and 1973, that Baba Muktananda was not Standing in the "Place" (or the Self-"Position") required to Confirm or Acknowledge My Thus Described Final Realization. That is to Say, Baba Muktananda made it clear to Me in those two Meetings (wherein others were present), and (also) in His Remarks otherwise conveyed to Me privately, that He, unlike Me,[79] had not been—and (apparently, for mostly rather puritanical, and otherwise conventional, reasons) could not even conceive of Allowing Himself to be—"Embraced" by the Divine "Cosmic Goddess" (or Maha-Shakti) Herself (Such That, by Her own Submission to the Senior and Most Prior Principle—Which Is Self-Existing Consciousness Itself—She would be Subsumed by Consciousness Itself, and, Thus, Husbanded by Consciousness Itself, and, Thereby, Be the Final Means for the Self-Radiant Divine Self-Awakening of Consciousness Itself to Itself). And, therefore, by His own direct Confession to Me, Baba Muktananda Declared that He was not Standing in the "Place" (or the Self-"Position") of Inherently Most Perfect (or seventh stage) Divine Self-Realization—Which Realization I (Uniquely) had Confessed to Him.

LIV.

When I first Came to Baba Muktananda (in early 1968), His First and Most Fundamental Instruction to Me—even within minutes of My Arrival at His Ashram (in Ganeshpuri, India)—was the (apparently sixth stage, or Transcendentalist) Admonition: "You are not the one who wakes, or dreams, or sleeps—but You Are the One Who Is the Witness of these states." I took that Admonition to be Instruction in the traditional (and sixth stage) sense, as Given in the non-Emanationist (or Transcendentalist) tradition of Advaita Vedanta (which is the traditional Vedantic school of "Non-Dualism"). However, it became clear to Me (in, and as a result of, Our Meetings in 1970 and 1973) that Baba Muktananda was, actually, strongly (and even dogmatically) opposed to much of the tradition of Advaita Vedanta (and, especially, its Transcendental Method, and even its proposed Transcendental Realization—and all of its proposed Transcendental Realizers, including, in particular, Ramana Maharshi).

Indeed, in those two Meetings (in 1970 and 1973), Baba Muktananda was, evidently, so profoundly confined to His dogmatic Emanationist (and otherwise phenomena-based) philosophical point of view (which, in those two Meetings, took on a form very much like the traditional confrontation between Kashmir Saivism and Advaita Vedanta) that He (in a rather dramatically pretentious, or intentionally provocative, manner—and clearly, indefensibly) presented Himself to Me as an opponent (such that He addressed Me as if I were merely an opposing "player" in a sophomoric academic debate, and as if I were merely—and for merely academic reasons—representing the point of view of traditional Advaita Vedanta).

Likewise, it became clear to Me (in Our Meetings in 1970 and 1973) that Baba Muktananda's proposed Siddha-Yoga Teaching was, in some respects (which I Indicate Herein), merely a product of His own personal study, experience, and temperament— and, thus, of His own karmically acquired philosophical bias, or prejudice—and that the point of view He so dogmatically imposed on Me in those two Meetings is not, itself, an inherent (or necessary) part of Siddha Yoga Itself.

LV.

Relative to Baba Muktananda's experiential (or experience-based, rather than philosophically based) point of view, it became clear (in Our Meetings in 1970 and 1973) that Baba Muktananda (as a Siddha-Yogi) was yet (and characteristically) Centered in the (fifth stage) "Attitude" (or "Asana") of what He described as

"Witnessing". In using the term "Witnessing" (or the "Witness"), Baba Muktananda seemed (in the traditional sixth stage manner of Advaita Vedanta) to be referring to the Witness-Consciousness (Which Is Consciousness Itself, Inherently, and Transcendentally, Standing Most Prior to all objects and all psycho-physical functions—whether gross, subtle, or causal). However, clearly, what Baba Muktananda meant by the term "Witnessing" (or the "Witness") was the psycho-physical function of the observing-intelligence (which is not the Transcendental Consciousness—Prior even to the causal body—but which is, simply, the third, and highest, functional division, or functional dimension, of the subtle body). Thus, characteristically, Baba Muktananda identified with (and took the position of) the observer (or the observing-intelligence) relative to all arising phenomena (and, especially, relative to His reported subtle, or internal phenomenal, visions of higher and lower worlds, the hierarchy of abstract internal lights, and so on). And, when Baba Muktananda spoke of "Witnessing", He (simply) meant the attitude of merely observing whatever arises (and, thus, the intention to do so in a non-attached manner—rather than, in the conventional manner, merely to cling to, or, otherwise, to dissociate from, the various internal and external objects of moment to moment attention).

In the Ultimate Course of My Avataric Ordeal of (seventh stage) Divine Self-Realization, the Spiritual (or Siddha-Yoga) Process passed Beyond all mere (fifth stage, or even sixth stage) "Witnessing"—and all identification with the psycho-physical experiencer, or observer, or knower of the mind and the senses—to Realize (and Be) the Inherently egoless, objectless, and Non-Dual Conscious Light That Is the One and Indivisible and Self-Existing and Self-Radiant and (Necessarily) Divine Reality (Itself), and That Is the Mere (and True) Witness-Consciousness (or the Un-conditional, and non-functional, and all-and-All-Divinely-Self-Recognizing, and Self-Evidently Divine Self-Condition, Inherently Most Prior to any and all objects—without excluding any).

Thus, it became clear to Me (in Our Meetings in 1970 and 1973) that Baba Muktananda was not yet (either in the sixth stage Transcendental manner or the seventh stage Divine Manner)

Established As the True Witness-Consciousness (or the One and Indivisible Conscious Light Itself, Always Already Most Prior to all observational "Witnessing"), but it also became clear to Me (then) that Baba Muktananda was, in the fifth stage manner, simply observing, and (thus and thereby) contemplating (and becoming absorbed in or by) internal phenomenal objects and states—rather than, in the seventh stage Manner, Standing As the One and Indivisible Conscious Light That Is Reality Itself, Divinely Self-Recognizing any and all cosmically manifested objects, and (Thus and Thereby) Divinely Transcending all the conditional states— waking (or gross), dreaming (or subtle), and sleeping (or causal).

LVI.

Baba Muktananda was, in effect, always contemplating the conditional activities, the conditional states, and the illusory conditional forms (or objective Emanations) of the "Cosmic Goddess" (or the all-and-All-objectifying Kundalini Shakti)—whereas I (in, and Beyond, a Unique "Embrace" with the "Cosmic Goddess" Herself) had (even Prior to all observed "differences") Re-Awakened to the True (and Inherently egoless, and Inherently Indivisible, and Most Perfectly Prior, and Self-Evidently Divine) Self-"Position" (or Self-Condition, and Source-Condition) of all Her cosmic (or waking, dreaming, and sleeping) forms and states. And, by Virtue of That Divine (or Most Perfect—or seventh stage) Re-Awakening of Me, all conditionally arising forms and states were—even in the instants of their apparent arising—Inherently (or Always Already—and, Thus, Divinely) Self-Recognized (and Most Perfectly Transcended) in, and As, Me—the Spiritually Self-"Bright" Divine Self-Condition and Source-Condition (or Inherently egoless, and Inherently Indivisible, and First, and Only, and Perfectly Subjective, and Self-Evidently Divine Person) Itself.

Therefore, in those two Meetings (in 1970 and 1973)—and entirely because of His (therein, and thus) repeated stance of experiential and philosophical non-Confirmation of seventh stage Divine Self-Realization (which stance, in effect, directly Acknowledged that the seventh stage Self-"Position" of Divine Self-Realization was not His own)—Baba Muktananda Gave Me no option but to Go and Do (and Teach, and Reveal, and Bless all-and-All) As My Unique (and Self-Evidently Avataric) Realization of the Divine Self-Condition (Which Is My Own, and Self-Evidently Divine, Person—and Which Is, Self-Evidently, the Divine Source-Condition of all-and-All) Requires Me to Do. Therefore, I Did (and Do—and will forever Do) So.

LVII.

The Principal Characteristic of the One and Indivisible Divine Self-Condition (and Source-Condition) Is Its Perfectly Subjective Nature (As Self-Existing and Self-Radiant Consciousness—or Very, and Inherently Non-Objective, Being, Itself). Therefore, neither any ego-"I" (or any apparently separate self-consciousness) nor any apparently objective (or phenomenally objectified, or otherwise conditionally arising) form or state of experience (whether waking, or dreaming, or sleeping—and whether mind-based or sense-based) Is (itself) the Realization (or, otherwise, a necessary support for the Realization) of the Divine Self-Condition (Itself)—Which Condition Is (Itself) the One and Only Reality, the One and Only Truth, and the One and Only Real God.

Baba Muktananda was, characteristically (in the fifth stage manner), experientially (and mystically) absorbed in modes of Savikalpa Samadhi (or of internal object-contemplation). In His characteristic play of internal object-contemplation (or absorptive mysticism), Baba Muktananda reported two types of (especially) internal sensory (or sense-based) experience—the experience of abstract internal lights (and, secondarily, of abstract internal sounds, and tastes, and smells, and touches) and the experience of internal (or mental) visions of higher and lower worlds ("illustrated" by internal versions of all of the usual descriptive modes of the senses).

The abstract internal lights (and so on) are universally (or identically) experienced by any and all individuals who are so awakened to internal phenomena (just as the essential Realizations of the sixth stage of life—and, in the only-by-Me Revealed and Given Way of Adidam, of the only-by-Me Revealed and Given seventh stage of life—are universal, or essentially identical in all cases).

However, the visions of higher and lower worlds are, like psychic phenomena in general, expressions of the egoic psycho-physical (and, altogether, mental) tendencies of the individual (and of his or her cultural associations)—and, therefore, such experiences are not universally the same in all cases (but, instead, all such experiences are conditioned, and determined, and limited by the point of view, or karmically patterned identity, of the experiencer, or the individual egoic observing-identity). Nevertheless (and this also illustrates the naive—and not, by Him, fully comprehended— nature of many of Baba Muktananda's views about the Siddha-Yoga Process), Baba Muktananda (in His autobiography, *Play of Consciousness*[80]) reported His visions of higher and lower worlds as if they were categorically true, and (in the subtle domain) objectively (or Really) existing as He reported them—whereas all visions of higher and lower worlds are (at least to a very large degree) of the same insubstantial, illusory, and personal nature as dreams.

Like anyone else's authentic visionary experiences of higher and lower worlds, Baba Muktananda's visionary experiences of higher and lower worlds (although authentic) were His personal (or point-of-view-based) experiences of the otherwise inherently formless (and point-of-view-less) dimensions of the universal cosmic (or conditional) reality (or the inherently abstract planes of universal cosmic light)—as He, by tendency of mind (and because of His psycho-physical self-identity as a particular and separate fixed point of view—or ego-"I"), was able (and karmically pre-patterned) to experience (or conceive and perceive) them. Therefore, Baba Muktananda's conditional (or egoic) point of view—and, thus, also, His inner perceptions of various higher and lower worlds—were, characteristically and only, of a Hindu kind. (And the implications of this seem never to have occurred to Baba Muktananda. Indeed, if He had become aware of the inherently personal, conditional, karmic, ego-based, mind-based, illusory, arbitrary, and non-universal nature of His inwardly envisioned worlds, and even of the merely point-of-view-reflecting nature of His inwardly envisioned universal abstract lights, Baba Muktananda might have become moved to understand and transcend Himself further—beyond the Saguna, or mind-based, and

mind-limited, and dreamworld terms that are the inherent characteristic of Savikalpa Samadhi.)

LVIII.

Baba Muktananda's Hindu visions can be compared to My
Own experiences of Savikalpa Samadhi during My "Sadhana
Years". During that time, I, too, had many visions of higher and
lower worlds—and many of them were, indeed, of a Hindu type
(because of My present-Lifetime associations, and also because of
the past-Lifetime associations of My Deeper-Personality Vehicle).
However, there was also, in My Case (and for the same reasons) a
dramatic period of several months of intense visions of a distinctly
Christian type. I immediately understood such visions to be the
mind-based (and, necessarily, ego-based) products of the Siddha-
Yoga Process (or Divine Shaktipat), as It combined with My Own
conditionally born psycho-physical structures. Thus, I entered into
that Process Freely and Fully—and, in due course, the particularly
Christian visions (and the particularly Hindu visions) ceased. They
were all simply the evidence of My Own conditionally born mind
and sensory apparatus (and the evidence of even all My conditionally born cultural associations)—and, therefore, the visionary
contents were (I Discovered) merely another (but deep, and psychic) form of purification (rather than a "Revelation" that suggests
either the Christian "Heavens"-and-"Hells" or the Hindu "Heavens"-
and-"Hells" Are, themselves, Reality and Truth). Thus, when,
Finally, the ego-based visions had been completely "burned off"—
only Reality (Itself) Remained (As Me).

LIX.

Baba Muktananda's Siddha-Yoga Teachings exemplify the
descriptive mysticism of fifth stage Yoga (especially as it has been
historically represented in the fifth stage Yogic tradition of the
Maharashtra region of India[81]). Also, Baba Muktananda's Siddha-
Yoga Teachings are (in some, very important, respects) experientially
prejudiced—toward both non-universal (and specifically Hindu)
visions (of higher and lower worlds, and so on) and universal
abstract visions (of abstract internal lights, and so on), and against

(or, certainly, Baba Muktananda, Himself, was, by temperament, experientially disinclined toward) fifth stage (conditionally Ascended) Nirvikalpa Samadhi (or Fullest Ascent to fifth stage Formless Realization—Which Fullest Ascent was (but in the Priorly, and Spiritually, rather than conditionally, Established manner) My Own spontaneous Realization at Baba Muktananda's Ganeshpuri Ashram, in 1968, and Which is also the Characteristic Realization of all Great fifth stage Nirguna Siddhas, such as Bhagavan Nityananda and Rang Avadhoot).

LX.

Baba Muktananda saw the Secret (or esoteric) inner perceptual domain of subtle (or fifth stage) Divine Spiritual Revelation. I, too, have seen (and, even now, do see) that inner realm. And it is the Revelation of that inner realm that is the true (original, and eso-teric) core of all fourth-to-fifth stage religious traditions.

The fourth stage religious traditions are, generally, first pre-sented (or institutionally communicated) to the public world of mankind (in its gross egoity and its human immaturity) as a gath-ering of exoteric myths and legends. Those exoteric myths and legends are intended to inspire and guide human beings in the ordinary developmental context of the first three stages of life (associated with gross physical, emotional-sexual, and mental-volitional development of the human social ego). Thus, the many religious traditions of both the East and the West are, in their public (or exoteric) expressions, simply variations on the inherent psycho-physical "messages" of the body-mind relative to foundation human development (both individual and collective). And, because all exoteric religious traditions are based on the "messages" inherent in the same psycho-physical structures, the exoteric Teachings of all religions are, essentially, identical (and, therefore, equal). And, also, because this is so, all exoteric religious traditions (such as Judaism, Christianity, Islam, Hinduism, and so on) must—especially at this critical "late-time" moment of world-intercommunicativeness—acknowledge their essential equality, commonality, and sameness, and (on that basis) mutually embrace the principles of cooperation and tolerance (for the sake of world peace)!

All exoteric religious traditions are, fundamentally, associated with the first three (or social-ego) stages of life. And all exoteric religious traditions are, contextually, associated with rudimentary aspects of the fourth stage of life (or the religiously Devotional effort of transcending both personal and collective egoity—or self-contraction into selfishness, competitiveness, "difference", conflict, and self-and-other-destructiveness). However, all exoteric religious traditions are, also, associated (to one or another degree) with an esoteric (or Secret) dimension (or a tradition of esoteric schools), which is intended to extend the life of religious practice into the inner dimensions of religious (and truly Spiritual) Realization.

The true esoteric dimension of religion first extends the life of rudimentary religious practice into the true and full Spiritual depth of the fourth stage of life (by Means of surrender to the Descent of the Divine Spiritual Force into the human, or "frontal", domain of incarnate existence). And, if there is growth beyond the fourth stage of life, that esoteric Spiritual Process is (in the traditional course) also extended into the domain of the true fifth stage of life (which is associated with the Process of Spiritual Ascent, via the Spinal Line and the brain, through the layers of the conditional pattern of the psycho-physical ego, and always toward the Realization of a conditional state of mystical absorption in the Most Ascended Source of conditional, or cosmically extended, existence). And, once that (fifth stage) Spiritual Process of Ascent is complete (or is, itself, transcended in Inherent Spiritual Fullness), there is (in the traditional course) the (rarely achieved) possibility that the esoteric Spiritual Process may develop further, in the context of the true sixth stage of life (or the Spiritual Process of Transcendental Self-Realization).

The true (and Truly Complete) Great esoteric Spiritual Process of the only-by-Me Revealed and Given Way of Adidam follows a unique course, in which the (Vertical and Horizontal) processes otherwise associated (respectively) with the fifth and the sixth stages of life are simultaneously demonstrated and exercised, in the context of the "Perfect Practice" of the only-by-Me Revealed and Given Way of Adidam—Culminating, at last, in the only-by-Me Revealed and Given seventh stage of life (wherein all cosmically arising conditions are Inherently Divinely Self-Recognized, and, Ultimately, Outshined, in the Non-Separate, Self-Existing, Self-Radiant, Inherently egoless, Perfectly Subjective, and Self-Evidently Divine Self-Condition and Source-Condition of all-and-All).

LXI.

Baba Muktananda was a Teacher (and a Realizer) in the context of the foundation esoteric (or fourth and fifth) stages of (specifically) Hindu religious practice. The Spiritual (or Siddha-Yoga, or Shaktipat-Yoga) Process He exemplified and Taught (and Initiated in others) truly begins in the frontal (or fourth stage) practice (of Siddha-Guru Devotion) and (in due course) goes on to the spinal (or fifth stage) practice (of Ascended mystical absorption).

Baba Muktananda's practice and His experiential Realization were conditioned (and, ultimately, limited) by His own personal (or conditional, and karmic, or psycho-physically pre-patterned) ego-tendencies—and by His association (by birth) with the combined exoteric and esoteric culture of traditional Hinduism. Therefore, His experiences (and His subsequent Teachings, and His life altogether) are, characteristically, an exemplification of the historical conflict between fifth stage Hindu esotericism (which is, itself, inherently unconventional, and non-puritanical) and fourth stage Hindu exotericism (which is, itself, inherently conventional, and, at least publicly, puritanical).

LXII.

Because of His, characteristically, Hindu associations, Baba Muktananda (quite naturally, and naively) interpreted His Yogic Spiritual experiences almost entirely in terms of Hindu cultural models (both exoteric and esoteric). Therefore, His interpretations of His Spiritual experiences—and, indeed, the very form, and character, and content of His Spiritual experiences themselves—were specifically Hindu, and specifically in the mode of philosophical and mystical traditions that corresponded to His own mental predilections (or karmic tendencies).

Thus, Baba Muktananda's recorded visions of higher and lower worlds (leading to the Great Vision of the Blue Person, or the

Divine "Creator"-Guru) are a "map" of developmentally unfolding—
or spontaneously un-"Veiling"—inner perceptual landscapes, in
the specific mode of the Hindu tradition of the "Blue God" (especially Personified as "Siva"—or, otherwise, as the "Krishna" of
the *Bhagavad Gita* and the *Bhagavata Purana*).[82] And Baba
Muktananda's inner "map" was, also, structured on the basis of an
hierarchical sequence of abstract inner lights (and of even all the
abstract inner modes of the senses), which He interpreted according to the concepts of the philosophical tradition of Kashmir
Saivism, and according to the experiential pattern-interpretation
associated with the Hindu mystical tradition of the Maharashtra
region of India. However, even though the brain-based (or
perception-based—rather than mind-based, or conception-based,
or idea-based) pattern of abstract inner lights (and of abstract inner
sensations in general) is (or can be) universally (or by anyone)
experienced as the same pattern of appearances—the interpretation
of that experienced pattern is (or may be) different from case to
case (or from culture to culture). And, ultimately, for the sake of
Truth, the one and only correct (or universally applicable) interpretation must be embraced by all.

Baba Muktananda experienced and interpreted the pattern of
abstract inner lights as if it were a Revelation associated with the
waking, dreaming, and sleeping states (or the gross, subtle, and
causal modes of conditional experience). Thus (on the basis of His
understanding of the Maharashtra mystical tradition), Baba
Muktananda said that the waking state (and the gross body and
world) is represented by the inner red light, and the dreaming state
(and the subtle body and world) is represented by the inner white
light, and the sleeping state (and the causal body and world) is
represented by the inner black light. And Baba Muktananda said
that the inner blue light represents what He called the "supracausal" state (which He, in the fifth stage manner, mistakenly identified with the "turiya" state, or the "fourth" state, or the "Witness",
or the "True Self", otherwise associated with the sixth stage tradition of Advaita Vedanta). However, I Declare that all of those inner
lights (and even all internal perceptions, whether high or low in
the scale of conditional "things") are inner objects of perception

(and conception)—and, therefore, all of them are associated with the subtle body and the inner perceptible (or dreaming state) worlds of mind.

Swami Muktananda's Description
of the "Bodies of the Soul"[83]

Body:	Gross	Subtle	Causal	Supracausal
Color:	Red	White	Black	Blue
State:	Waking	Dream	Sleep	Turīya
Seat:	Eyes	Throat	Heart	Sahasrāra

LXIII.

Baba Muktananda's description of the abstract inner lights is, in some respects, not sufficiently elaborate (or, otherwise, comprehensive) in its details. In fact, and in My Own experience—and in the experience of esoteric traditions other than the Maharashtra tradition (such as reported by the well-known Swami Yogananda)— the display of abstract inner lights is, when experienced as a simultaneous totality, Seen as a Mandala (or a pattern of concentric circles).

In My Own experience, that Cosmic Mandala is not only composed of concentric circles of particular colors—but each circle is of a particular precise width (and, thus, of particular proportional significance) relative to the other circles. Thus, in that pattern of circles, the red circle is the outermost circle (perceived against a colorless dark field), but it is a relatively narrow band, appearing next to a much wider band (or circle) of golden yellow. After the very wide golden yellow circle, there is a much narrower soft-white circle. And the soft-white circle is followed by an also very narrow black circle (or band). Closest to the Center of the Cosmic Mandala is a very wide circle of bright blue. And, at the Very

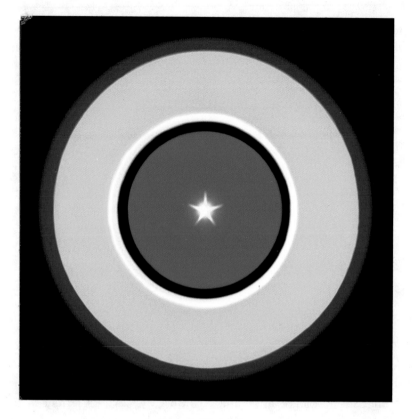

Cosmic Mandala

Center of the blue field, there is a Brilliant White Five-Pointed Star (Which, perhaps not to confuse It with the color of the circle of soft-white light, Baba Muktananda described as a <u>Blue</u> Star).

Thus, in fact, although all the abstract inner lights described by Baba Muktananda are, indeed, within the total Cosmic Mandala, the principal lights (in terms of width and prominence) are the <u>golden yellow</u> and the <u>blue</u> lights—and <u>only</u> the Brilliant White Five-Pointed Star is the <u>Central</u> and <u>Principal</u> light within the Cosmic Mandala of abstract inner lights.

The Cosmic Mandala of abstract inner lights is a display that is (otherwise) associated with planes of possible inner (or subtle) experience. Thus, the red light inwardly represents (and, literally, illuminates) the gross body and the gross world (as Baba Muktananda has said). However, <u>all</u> of the other lights (golden yellow, soft-white, black, and bright blue) represent (and, literally, illuminate) the several hierarchical divisions within the subtle body and the subtle worlds—and the causal body (which is associated with attention itself, or the root of egoity itself, and which is, itself, only felt, and not seen, and which is expressed as the fundamental feeling of "difference", separateness, and relatedness, and which is located as a knot of self-contraction in the right side of the heart) is not visually represented (nor is it, otherwise, literally illuminated) by the lights and worlds of the Cosmic Mandala.

The wide golden yellow circle of the Cosmic Mandala represents (in conjunction with the outermost red circle) the outermost (or lowest) dimension of the subtle body—which is the etheric (or pranic, or life-energy) body (or dimension) of conditional experience. The narrower soft-white circle of the Cosmic Mandala represents the ordinary (or sense-based) mind. The narrow black circle (or band) is a transitional space, where mental activity is suspended. The blue circle of the Cosmic Mandala is the domain of the mental observer, the faculty of discriminative intelligence and the will, and the very form of the subtly concretized ego-"I" (or the inner-concretized subtle self). And the Brilliant White Five-Pointed Star is the Epitome and Very Center of the Cosmic Mandala—Such That It Provides the Uppermost Doorway to What Is (altogether) Infinitely Above (and, Ultimately, Beyond) the Cosmic Mandala (or Above and Beyond the body itself, the brain itself, and the mind itself).

LXIV.

Baba Muktananda interpreted the universally experienced abstract inner lights (and experienced the corresponding inner worlds) in terms of various Hindu philosophical and mystical (and, also, exoteric, or conventionally religious) traditions (as I have Indicated). However, the subtle domain is the elaborate hierarchical domain of mind (or of the psycho-physically concretized ego-"I")— and, therefore, just as individual dreams and imaginings are personal, ephemeral, and non-ultimate, the inherently dreamlike subtle domain of Spiritually-stimulated inwardness may be experienced and interpreted in various and different modes, according to the nature and the tradition (or the personal and collectively representative mind) of the experiencer.

Thus, ultimately (or in due course), the subtle domain (or the subtle egoic body) must be transcended, through the horizontal (sixth stage) Spiritual (or Siddha-Yoga) Process—Which is the Spiritually (and not merely mentally) developed Process of inversion upon the true causal body (or the root of attention), and penetration of the causal knot (or the presumption of separate self), and Which is (thus) the inversive (and conditional, or conditionally achieved) transcending of the ego-"I", by means of exclusive (or object-excluding) Identification with the True (and Inherent, and Self-Evident) Transcendental Witness-Consciousness Itself. And only the Transcendental Witness-Consciousness, Itself—inverted upon in the thus Described sixth stage manner—Is the true "turiya" state, or the true "fourth" state (beyond the three ordinary states, of waking, dreaming, and sleeping). And only the Transcendental Witness-Consciousness, Itself—Fully (and Fully Spiritually) Realized in the only-by-Me Revealed and Given context of the "Perfect Practice" of the only-by-Me Revealed and Given Way of Adidam—Is the Foundation Realization on the basis of which My devotee can (in due course, by My Avatarically Self-Transmitted Divine Spiritual Grace) Realize the only-by-Me Revealed and Given seventh stage Realization of the True Divine Self, Which Is the Self-Evidently Divine Self-Condition, and Which Is the One and Only True Divine State of "Turiyatita"—"Beyond the 'fourth' state", and (thus) Beyond all exclusiveness, and Beyond all bondage to illusions, and Beyond point of view (or egoic separateness) itself, and (therefore) Beyond all conditional efforts, supports, and dependencies.

At last, the sixth stage of life (which, itself, is associated with conditionally patterned inversion upon the Consciousness-Principle) must be (Most Perfectly) transcended (and, indeed, the ego-"I" itself must be Most Perfectly, or Inherently, transcended) in the transition to the only-by-Me Revealed and Given seventh stage of life—which Is the stage of True (and Fully Spiritual) Divine Self-Realization, Inherently Free of (but not strategically Separated from) all conditionally patterned forms and states, and which Is the stage of the Inherently Most Perfect (both Horizontally and Vertically Inclusive) Demonstration of the Non-Separate, Self-Existing, Self-Radiant, Inherently egoless, Perfectly Subjective, and Self-Evidently Divine Self-Condition and Source-Condition of all-and-All.

LXV.

My Own experiences of fifth stage mystical perception are (like those of Baba Muktananda, and those of all visionary mystics) clear Evidence of the inherently (and necessarily) conditional, mental, altogether brain-based (and both brain-limited and mind-limited), and both personal and collective egoic nature of all internal mystical (or fifth stage) absorption.

I, too (like Baba Muktananda), experienced Hindu visions—but I (otherwise) also experienced many Christian visions (and also many non-Hindu and non-Christian visions), in association with the fifth stage developments of the same (or one and only) Spiritual (or Siddha-Yoga) Process of inner perception (including the progressive display of abstract inner lights, and so on) described by Baba Muktananda. Thus, just as Baba Muktananda described His Hindu visions as a Spiritual Revelation of the "Truth" of Hindu esotericism (and even of Hindu exotericism)—I could just as well describe My (specifically) Christian visions as a Spiritual Revelation of the "Truth" of Christian esotericism (and even of Christian exotericism)!

Indeed, My (specifically) Christian visions (but not, of course, My specifically Hindu visions—or My, otherwise, specifically non-Hindu and non-Christian visions) do amount to a Spiritual Revelation of the actual (and mostly esoteric) content of original (or primitive—and truly Spiritual) Christianity.[84]

LXVI.

Specifically, My (sometimes) Christian visions Spiritually Reveal the following.

The original tradition (or foundation sect) that is at the root of exoteric Christianity was a fourth-to-fifth stage esoteric Spiritual (and mystical) tradition (or sect). Within that original tradition (or sect), John (the Baptist) was the Spiritual Master (or Spirit-Baptizer—

or True Siddha-Guru) of Jesus of Nazareth. Thus (and by Means of the Spiritual Baptism Given to Him by John the Baptist), Jesus of Nazareth experienced the fourth-to-fifth stage absorptive mystical (and, altogether, Spiritual) developments of what (in the Hindu context) is called "Siddha Yoga" (or "Shaktipat Yoga"). In due course (and even rather quickly), Jesus of Nazareth (Himself) became a Spirit-Baptizer (or a True Siddha-Guru)—and (within the inner, or esoteric, circle of His Spiritually Initiated devotees) Jesus of Nazareth Taught the fourth-to-fifth stage Way of Spiritual Devotion to the Spiritual Master (or to Himself, as a True Siddha-Guru), and of inner Spiritual Communion with the Divine, and of (eventual) Spiritual Ascent to the Divine Domain (via the Brilliant White Five-Pointed Star).

After the death (and presumed Spiritual Ascent) of Jesus of Nazareth, His esoteric circle of Spiritually Initiated devotees continued to develop the mystical tradition of the sect—but (because of the difficult "signs of the times") the original (esoteric) sect had to become more and more secretive, and, eventually, it disappeared from the view of history (under the pressure of the exoteric, or non-Initiate, or conventionally socially oriented, rather than Spiritually and mystically oriented, sects that also developed around the public Work, and, especially, the otherwise developing legends and myths, of Jesus of Nazareth).

The esoteric sect of the Spiritual Initiates of Jesus of Nazareth was associated with practices of Spiritually Invocatory prayer (of fourth stage Divine Communion, and of fifth stage absorptive mystical Ascent), especially seeking Divine absorption via the internally perceptible Brilliant White Five-Pointed Star—Which was interpreted, especially after the death of Jesus of Nazareth (and, apparently, in accordance with Instructions communicated by Jesus of Nazareth, Himself, to His Spiritually Initiated devotees, during His own physical lifetime), to be the True Ascended Divine Body of Jesus of Nazareth (or the Spiritually Awakened, and presumed to be Divinely Ascended, "Christ"). And, over time, the Spiritual practitioners within the esoteric "Christ" sect developed the full range of characteristically Christian interpretations of the (otherwise) universally experienced phenomena of inner perception.

LXVII.

My Own (sometimes) Christian visions are a spontaneous Revelation of esoteric Christian interpretations (and esoteric Christian modes of experiencing) of (otherwise) universal (and, therefore, inherently non-sectarian) inner phenomena—and My (specifically) Christian visions and interpretations are a spontaneous direct continuation of the esoteric Christian manner of interpreting such (inherently universal) inner phenomena, as it was done in the original (or primitive) epoch of the sect of Jesus of Nazareth.

Thus, speaking in the esoteric terms of the ancient (or earliest) Christian interpreters of subtle inner experience, the red light of Spiritual inner vision can be said to be associated with the gross body of Man (and the Incarnation-body of Jesus of Nazareth, and the "blood of Christ"). Likewise, the golden yellow light can be said to be associated with the "Holy Spirit" (or the Universal Spirit-Energy, or Divine Spirit-Breath, That Pervades the cosmic domain). And the soft-white light can be said to be associated with the mind of Man (which, in its purity, can be said to be a reflection of, or a pattern "in the image of", God—conceived to be the "Creator", or the Divine Source-Condition, Infinitely Above the body-mind and the world). And the black light can be said to be associated with the "crucifixion" (or sacrifice) of the body-mind of Man (and of Jesus of Nazareth, as the Epitome of Man)—and, also, with the mystical "dark night of the soul" (or the mystic's difficult trial of passing beyond all sensory and mental contents and consolations). And the blue light can be said to be the "Womb of the Virgin Mary" (or the all-and-All-Birthing Light of the "Mother of God"). And the Brilliant White Five-Pointed Star (Surrounded, as it were, by the "Womb", or the Blue Light, of the "Virgin Mary") can be said to be the Ascended (or Spiritual) "Body of Christ" (and the "Star of Bethlehem", and the "Morning Star" of the esoteric Initiation-Ritual associated with the original, Secret Spiritual tradition of Jesus of Nazareth). And the Brilliant White Five-Pointed Star (interpreted to be the Ascended, or Spiritual, "Body of Christ") can (Thus) be said to be One with both the Divine "Mother" (or the Blue "Womb" of all-and-All-Birthing Light) and the Divine "Father" (or the Self-Existing Being, Beyond all Light—Infinitely Behind, and Infinitely Above, and Infinitely Beyond, and Eternally Non-Separate from the "Star-Body of Christ"). And (As Such) the "Christ" (or the Brilliant White Five-Pointed Star) Is Radiantly Pervading the entire cosmic domain, via an all-and-All-Illuminating Combination of both the Blue "Womb"-Light and the Golden Yellow "Breath"-Light of the One and Only Divine Person.

LXVIII.

Thus, My (sometimes) Christian inner visions could, indeed, be said to be an esoteric (and, now, only-by-Me Revealed and Given) Christian Revelation—except that all visionary, and brain-based, and mind-based, and sense-based, and ego-based, and conditional, and sectarian (or merely tradition-bound) things were entirely Gone Beyond (and Most Perfectly transcended) by Me (and in Me), in the total (and, Most Ultimately, seventh stage) Course of My Avataric Ordeal of True (and Most Perfect) Divine Self-Realization!

LXIX.

I Say all the "God" and "Gods" of Man are (whether "Male" or "Female" in the descriptive gender) merely the personal and collective tribal (and entirely dualistic—or conventionally subject-object-bound) myths of human ego-mind.

LXX.

I Say Only Reality Itself (Which Is, Always Already, The One, and Indivisible, and Indestructible, and Inherently egoless Case) Is (Self-Evidently, and Really) Divine, and True, and Truth (or Real God) Itself.

LXXI.

I Say the only Real God (or Truth Itself) Is the One and Only and Inherently Non-Dual Reality (Itself)—Which Is the Inherently egoless, and Utterly Indivisible, and Perfectly Subjective, and Indestructibly Non-Objective Source-Condition and Self-Condition of all-and-All.

Therefore, I (Characteristically) have no religious interests other than to Demonstrate, and to Exemplify, and to Prove, and to Self-Reveal Truth (or Reality, or Real God) Itself.

LXXII.

The true fifth stage mystical (or esoteric Spiritual) Process is, principally, associated with the progressive inner perceptual (and, thus, subtle mental) un-"Veiling" of the total internally perceptible pattern (or abstractly experienced structure) of the individual body-mind-self (or body-brain-self).

The abstract pattern (or internal structure) of the body-mind-self (or body-brain-self) is, universally, the same in the case of any and every body-mind (or body-brain-mind complex—or condition-ally manifested form, or state, or being) within the cosmic domain.

The abstract pattern (or internal structure) of the body-mind-self (or body-brain-self) necessarily (by virtue of its native—and, therefore, inseparable—Inherence in the totality of the cosmic domain itself) Duplicates (or is a conditionally manifested pattern-duplicate of) the Primary Pattern (or Fundamental conditional Structure) of the total cosmic domain.

The conditional body-mind (or any body-brain-mind complex) is, in Reality, not a merely separate someone, or an entirely "different" something (as if the body, or the brain, or the mind were reducible to a someone or a something utterly independent, or non-dependent, and existing entirely in and of itself).

Therefore, the entire body-mind (or egoic body-brain-self) is, itself, to be transcended (in the context of the only-by-Me Revealed and Given seventh stage of life), in and by Means of utterly non-separate, and non-"different", and Inherently egoless Participation in That Which Is Always Already The Case (or the Inherently Non-Dual and Indivisible Condition That Is Reality Itself).

LXXIII.

I Declare that—if It is (by Divine Siddha-Grace) Moved beyond the limits of the waking, dreaming, and sleeping ego-structures— the Siddha-Yoga (or Shaktipat-Yoga) Process of (fifth stage) un-"Veiling" Culminates (or may Culminate—at least eventually) in (and, indeed, It is Always Already Centered Upon) the (fifth stage) Revelation (in Fully Ascended Nirvikalpa Samadhi) of the True "Maha-Bindu" (or the "Zero Point", or Formless "Place", of Origin—otherwise, traditionally, called "Sunya", or "Empty", or "Void"). That True (and Indivisible, and Indefinable) "Maha-Bindu" Is the Revelation (via the Vertical extended structures of conditional Ascent, in the fifth stage mode) of the only True "Hole in the universe" (or the One, and Indivisible, and Indefinable, and Self-Evidently Divine Source-Point—Infinitely Above the body, the brain, and the mind). That Absolutely Single (and Formless) "Maha-Bindu" Is the True Absolute "Point-Condition"—or Formless and Colorless (or Non-Objective, and, therefore, not "Lighted") "Black Hole"—from Which (to the point of view of any "objectified" or "Lighted" place or entity, itself) the (or any) total cosmic domain (of conditionally arising forms, states, and beings) appears to Emanate (in an all-and-All-objectifying "Big Bang"[85]). That "Maha-Bindu" Is the (fifth stage) conditionally Revealed Upper Terminal of Amrita Nadi—or of the "Ambrosial Nerve of Connection" to the True Divine Heart (Which Self-Evidently Divine Heart Is Always Already Seated immediately Beyond the internally felt seat of the sinoatrial node, in the right side of the physical heart). And That "Maha-Bindu" Is (in the context of the sixth stage of life) the esoteric Doorway to, and (in the context of the only-by-Me Revealed and Given seventh stage of life in the only-by-Me Revealed and Given Way of Adidam) the esoteric Doorway from (or of), the Perfectly Subjective Heart-Domain (Which Is the True Self-Condition and Source-Condition of the Spiritually Self-"Bright" Divine Love-Bliss-Current of Divine Self-Realization, and Which Is, Itself, the Self-Existing, Self-Radiant, Inherently egoless, and Perfectly Subjective—or Perfectly Indivisible, Non-Dual, and Non-Objective—Conscious Light That Is Reality Itself, and Which, in the only-by-Me Revealed and Given seventh stage Realization of Divine Translation, Stands Revealed, In and Beyond the Unity of Amrita Nadi, As the Non-"Different" Divine "Bright" Spherical Self-Domain, Shown Infinitely Above all-and-All As the "Midnight Sun", In Which All Separateness Is Outshined).

LXXIV.

The (fifth stage) Yogic Process of the progressive inner un-"Veiling" of the Pattern (or Structure) of the cosmic domain is demonstrated (in the Siddha-Yoga, or Shaktipat-Yoga, tradition) via the progressive experiencing of the total pattern of all the structural forms that comprise the body-mind-self (or body-brain-self), via a body-mind-self-reflecting (or body-brain-self-reflecting) display of inner perceptual objects (or apparently objectified phenomenal states, conditions, and patterns of cosmic light). That Process (of the inner perceptual un-"Veiling" of the hierarchical structure, pattern, and contents of the conditionally manifested body-mind-self, or body-brain-self) Culminates (or may Culminate—at least eventually) in the vision (in occasional, or, otherwise, constant, Savikalpa Samadhi) of the "blue bindu" (or the "blue pearl"—as well as the various other objectified inner lights, such as the red, the white, and the black—described by Baba Muktananda[86])—or even the vision of the total Cosmic Mandala (of many concentric rings of color, including the central "blue bindu", with its Brilliant White Five-Pointed Star at the Center—as I have Described It[87]). In any case, the possibly perceived abstract inner light (or any "bindu", or point, or "Mandala", or complex abstract vision, of inwardly perceived light) is merely, and necessarily, a display of the functional root-point of the brain's perception of conditionally manifested universal light (or merely cosmic light) itself. However, if the Great Process of (fifth stage) un-"Veiling" is (Thus) Continued, the objectified inner "bindu"-vision (and Savikalpa Samadhi itself) is, in due course, transcended (in Fully Ascended Nirvikalpa Samadhi)—Such That there is the Great Yogic Event of "Penetration" of (and Into) the True (Inherently Formless, Non-Objective, and objectless) "Maha-Bindu", Infinitely Above the body, the brain, and the mind. And That Great Yogic Event was, in fact and in Truth, What Occurred (in the Priorly, rather than conditionally, Established manner) in My Own Case, in My Room, immediately after I was Blessed by Baba Muktananda and Rang Avadhoot in the garden of Baba Muktananda's Ganeshpuri Ashram, in 1968.

The Great Yogic Event of "Penetration" of the True "Maha-Bindu", Which Occurred in My Own Case in 1968, is (in Its

Extraordinary Particulars) a Unique Example (within the history of the Great Tradition) of spontaneous complete (and Priorly Ascended) "Penetration" of all the chakras (or centers, or points, or structures) of the conditionally manifested body-mind-self (or body-brain-self)—simultaneous with sudden Priorly Ascended Nirvikalpa Samadhi (or immediate "Penetration" to Beyond the total cosmic, and psycho-physical, context of subject-object relations). The phenomenon of sudden (rather than progressive) conditional Ascent is described, in the (fifth stage) Yogic traditions, as the Greatest (and rarest) of the Demonstrations of Yogic Ascent—as compared to progressive (or gradual) demonstrations (shown via stages of inner ascent, via internal visions, lights, auditions, and so on). And, in My Unique Case, it was only subsequently (or always thereafter—and even now) that the universal cosmic Pattern (or Vertically perceptible Great cosmic Structure) and the universally extended pattern (or Vertically perceptible inner cosmic structure) of the body, the brain, and the mind (and the Horizontal inner Primary structure—of the three stations of the heart) were (and are) directly (and systematically, and completely) un-"Veiled" (in a constant spontaneous Display—both apparently Objective and Perfectly Subjective—within My Avataric Divine "Point of View").

In the Event of Priorly Ascended Nirvikalpa Samadhi in 1968, the nature of Fully Ascended Nirvikalpa Samadhi as it has been conditionally Realized (as the "supreme goal" of the fifth stage Yogic traditions) became immediately clear to Me. Directly after the Event of Priorly Ascended Nirvikalpa Samadhi, I was tacitly aware that the Realization of conditionally Ascended Nirvikalpa Samadhi (necessarily) depended on the exercise (and a unique, precise attitude and arrangement) of the conditional apparatus of the body, the brain, and the mind (and of attention)—and that, therefore, that Realization was (yet) conditionally dependent (or psycho-physically supported), and, necessarily (or in that sense), limited (or, yet, only a temporary stage in the progressive Process of un-"Veiling"), and, therefore, non-Final. That is to Say, it was inherently Obvious to Me that any and all internal (or otherwise psycho-physical) experiencing necessarily requires the exercise (via attention) of the root-position (and the conditionally arising psycho-physical apparatus) of conditionally arising self-consciousness (or of the separate and separative psycho-physical ego-"I"). I immediately Concluded that—unless the Process of Realization could transcend the very structure and pattern of ego-based experiencing and the very Structure and Pattern of the conditionally manifested cosmos itself—Realization would Itself (necessarily) be limited (as in the case of conditionally Ascended Nirvikalpa Samadhi) by the same subject-object (or ego-versus-object) dichotomy that otherwise characterizes even all ordinary (or non-mystical) experience. And even though, in the Event of Priorly Ascended Nirvikalpa Samadhi (Which does not depend on any manipulation of attention, or even any manipulation of all of the mechanics, or physiology and psychology, of the body-mind), the perception, conception, or psycho-physical presumption of a separate self was effortlessly tran-scended—the subsequent return of the apparent limitations and dependencies associated with experiential conditionality suggested to Me an even Greater Event or Process or Re-Awakening was yet Required, if there Is to Be the Indivisibly Perfect Realization I Tacitly and "Brightly" Always Already Knew to Be The (One and Only) Case.

Therefore, I Persisted in My Avataric Divine Sadhana—until the un-"Veiling" became Inherently Most Perfect (or seventh stage—and Inherently egoless) Re-Awakening to Divine Self-Realization, Inherently Beyond all phenomenal (or conditional) dependencies (or supports), and Infinitely (and Divinely) Transcending all phe-nomenal (or conditional) bondage (or limitation).

LXXV.

On September 10, 1970, the Great Avataric Divine Process of My "Sadhana Years" Culminated in Unqualified (or Most Perfectly Non-conditional) Realization of the Self-Evidently Divine Self-Condition (and Source-Condition) of the cosmic domain itself (and of all forms, states, and beings within the cosmic domain). And, in That Most Perfect Event, I was Most Perfectly Re-Awakened As the "Bright", the One and Only Conscious Light—the Very, and Perfectly Subjective, and Inherently egoless (or Perfectly Non-Separate), and Inherently Perfect, and Indivisible (or Perfectly Non-Dual), and

Always Already Self-Existing, and Eternally Self-Radiant, and Self-Evidently Divine Self-Condition <u>and</u> Source-Condition That <u>Is</u> the <u>One</u> and <u>Only</u> and <u>True</u> Divine Person, and Reality, and Truth of <u>all</u> and of <u>All</u>, and That was (and is) the constant Spiritual Sign and Identity of This, My Avataric Divine Lifetime, even from Birth. And It was the Un-deniable Reality and the Un-conditional Nature of <u>This</u> Realization That I Summarized to Baba Muktananda during Our Meetings in 1970 and 1973.

Even though It was and <u>Is</u> So, Baba Muktananda did not (and, because of the yet fifth stage nature of His own experiential Realization—for which He found corroboration in traditional mystical and philosophical traditions of the fifth stage, and phenomena-based, type—<u>could</u> <u>not</u>) positively Acknowledge My Summation relative to Most Perfect (and, necessarily, seventh stage) Divine Self-Realization.

Because He characteristically <u>preferred</u> to dwell upon inner <u>objects</u>, Baba Muktananda (in the "naive" manner of fourth and fifth stage mystics in general) interpreted Reality Itself (or Divine Self-Realization Itself) to "<u>require</u>" inner perceptual phenomenal (or conditionally arising) experiences and presumptions as a necessary <u>support</u> for Realization (<u>Itself</u>). That is to Say, Baba Muktananda was experientially Conformed to the (fifth stage) presumption that Divine Self-Realization not only requires conditionally arising (and, especially, inner perceptual) phenomenal experiences as a generally necessary (and even inevitable) Yogic Spiritual <u>preliminary</u> to authentic (and not merely conceptual) Realization—and I <u>completely</u> <u>Agree</u>, with Him, that there certainly <u>are</u> many conditionally apparent Yogic Spiritual requirements that <u>must</u> be Demonstrated in the Full Course of the authentic (and, necessarily, psycho-physical) Sadhana of Divine Self-Realization— but Baba Muktananda, otherwise, generally affirmed the presumption that <u>Realization</u> <u>Itself</u> (and <u>not</u> <u>only</u> the Sadhana, or psycho-physical <u>Process</u>, of <u>Realizing</u>) "requires" conditional (or psycho-physical—and, especially, absorptive mystical, or inner visual) <u>supports</u>.

Therefore, Baba Muktananda affirmed an attention-based, and object-oriented (or Goal-Oriented)—and (therefore) ego-based, or seeker-based—absorptive mystical (and, altogether, fifth stage) Yogic Way, in which the Sahasrar (or the Upper Terminal of the brain), and even the total brain (or sensorium), is the constant focus (and the Ultimate Goal—as well as the Highest Seat) of Sadhana.

It was due to this, Baba Muktananda's characteristic point of view relative to both Sadhana and Realization (as He defined—or, in effect, limited—Them), that, in My informal Meeting with Him in 1970, His only response to Me was to enter into a casual verbal (and even illogical) contradiction of Me. In that informal Meeting (as well as in Our formal Meeting, in 1973), Baba Muktananda ignored (and even appeared to not at all comprehend) My (then Given) Indications to Him relative to the Most Ultimate (or seventh stage) Significance of the "Regenerated" Form of Amrita Nadi.

LXXVI.

As I Indicated to Baba Muktananda (in Our Meetings in 1970 and 1973), the "Regenerated" Form of Amrita Nadi is Rooted in Consciousness Itself—"Located" Beyond the right side of the heart, which is (itself) merely the Self-Evident Seat (or Doorway) of the direct "Locating" of Perfectly Subjective (and Inherently egoless) Consciousness, Itself (or the Self-Existing Feeling of Being, Itself—Prior to attention, itself). And That ("Regenerated" Form of Amrita Nadi) is "Brightly" Extended to the "Maha-Bindu" (Which is Infinitely Ascended, Above and Beyond the Sahasrar), and to the "Midnight Sun" (Which Is My Divine Self-Domain, the Non-"Different" Sphere of the "Bright" Itself, Always Already Beyond, or Prior to—and Always Already More than Above—the body-mind and the cosmic domain). However, Baba Muktananda appeared only to want to contradict My (secondary) reference (to the "right side of the heart")—while otherwise ignoring My (primary) Explanation (of the "Regenerated" Form of Amrita Nadi). And, in doing this, Baba Muktananda went so far in identifying Himself exclusively with the fifth stage tradition that He said to Me, "Anyone who says that the right side of the heart is the Seat of Realization does not know what he is talking about."

In this (from My "Point of View", even rather absurdly funny!) statement, Baba Muktananda merely ignored (and, therefore, did not directly contradict) My (then Given) Description (to Him) of how seventh stage Divine Self-Realization Inherently Transcends both the conditional (or psycho-physical) Vertical apparatus of the brain (or of the Sahasrar, Which is the conditional Seat of Realization proposed in the fifth stage traditions, of mystical absorption) and the conditional (or psycho-physical) Horizontal apparatus of the heart (or, in particular, of the right side of the heart—which is the conditional Seat of Realization proposed in the sixth stage traditions, of Transcendental practice). However, Baba Muktananda's statement to Me (relative to the heart on the right) was a remark made in direct and specific contradiction to the Transcendentalist (or entirely sixth stage) Teachings of Ramana Maharshi.

LXXVII.

In My Meeting with Baba Muktananda in 1973, I made specific references to the Teachings of Ramana Maharshi (Whom both Baba Muktananda and Bhagavan Nityananda had Met—and, apparently, Greatly Praised—in earlier years). In particular, I referred to Ramana Maharshi's experiential assertions relative to the right side of the heart (which He—in the sixth stage manner— Indicated to be the Seat of Transcendental Self-Realization). In doing so, I was merely Intending to Offer Baba Muktananda a traditional reference already known to Him (and, I naively presumed, one that He respected), which would provide some clarity (and traditional support) relative to My Own (otherwise seventh stage) Descriptions.

Ramana Maharshi was a True and Great Jnani (or a sixth stage Realizer of the Transcendental Self-Condition, in the mode and manner indicated in the general tradition of Advaita Vedanta). And, after the Great Event of My Own (seventh stage) Divine Re-Awakening (in September 1970), I Discovered (in the weeks and months that followed My informal Meeting with Baba Muktananda, in October 1970) that there were some (but, necessarily, only sixth stage) elements in Ramana Maharshi's reported experience and Realization that paralleled (and, in that sense, corroborated) certain (but only sixth stage) aspects of My Own experience and Realization. And, for this reason, I always Continue to Greatly

Ramana Maharshi

Avatar Adi Da Samraj with Swami Muktananda, India 1973

Appreciate, and Honor, Ramana Maharshi—as a Great sixth stage Realizer, Who, through corroborating Testimony, Functions as a sixth stage Connecting-Link between Me and the Transcendentalist dimension of the Great Tradition. Also, because He is an example of a True Great Jnani (or Great Sage), Who Awakened to sixth stage Realization via the Spiritual—and not merely mental, or intellectual—Process (of the Magnification of the Spirit-Current in the right side of the heart), Ramana Maharshi, by Means of His corroborating Testimony, Functions—for Me—as a Connecting-Link between the sixth stage Transcendentalist tradition of Advaita Vedanta and the fourth-to-fifth stage Emanationist tradition of Siddha Yoga. And, because of this, Ramana Maharshi Functions, by Means of His corroborating Testimony, as a Connecting-Link between Me and the traditions of both Siddha Yoga and Advaita Vedanta—whereas I (except for Baba Muktananda's First Instruction to Me, in 1968—relative to the Witness of the three common states, of waking, dreaming, and sleeping) did not Find such a Connecting-Link among any of Those Who (otherwise) actively Functioned as My Spiritual Masters during the "Sadhana Years" of This, My present-Lifetime of Avataric Divine Incarnation.

During Our Meeting in 1973, Baba Muktananda mistakenly took My references to Ramana Maharshi (and to My Own experience of the heart on the right, which I had first Confessed to Baba Muktananda during Our informal Meeting in 1970—and which is, also, one of the principal experiences Indicated by Ramana Maharshi) to suggest that I had departed from the Siddha-Yoga tradition. Therefore, Baba Muktananda's criticisms of Me (in Our Meetings in both 1970 and 1973) were an apparent reaction to His perception of the possibility of My "going over" to Advaita Vedanta (and to Ramana Maharshi). And, for this reason, Baba Muktananda never (in either of the two Meetings, in 1970 and in 1973) actually addressed the particular, and complex, and inherently (and especially in a conversation requiring translations from English to Hindi, and vice versa) difficult-to-explain Great Issues I was (in those two Meetings) Intending (and Trying) to Summarize to Him.

LXXVIII.

Relative to Baba Muktananda Himself, I can only Say that, for My part (through Visits to Him by My devotee-representatives), Messages of Love (and of Gratitude for His Incomparable Service to Me during My Avataric Divine "Sadhana Years") were, right until the end of Baba Muktananda's lifetime, often Sent to Him by Me. I neither seek nor claim any separation from Baba Muktananda—or from His constant Spiritual Blessings (Which He has never denied Me). And I have—to everyone, including Baba Muktananda Himself, and to the several and varying institutional gatherings that have continued (or, otherwise, become activated) after Him— always Made every effort to Communicate clearly (and frankly, and, both in summary and at heart, most positively) about My unique and never-ending relationship to Baba Muktananda.

LXXIX.

Relative to Baba Muktananda's particular exact remarks to Me (in Our Meetings in 1970 and 1973), I can (and must) Say, simply, that His interpretation of Reality (and of the Nature and Status of the Process, and of even all the patterns and structures, associated with Divine Self-Realization)—which interpretation Baba Muktananda shared with (and for which He derived justification from) the phenomena-based aspects of the fifth stage Yogic traditions in general—was the characteristic basis of His criticisms of Me during Our Meetings in 1970 and 1973. And, as I have already Said, Baba Muktananda's Siddha-Yoga Teaching (and especially as He pro- posed it to Me in Our Meetings in 1970 and 1973) is—relative to all matters beyond the fifth stage of life (and even relative to all aspects of the fifth stage of life that are beyond the Saguna limits of Savikalpa Samadhi)—limited, prejudicial, ultimately indefensible, and (fundamentally) beyond His experience.

LXXX.

Neither the philosophy of Kashmir Saivism nor any "required" phenomenal conditions were pre-described to Me (or otherwise suggested)—by Baba Muktananda Himself, or by anyone else—as being a necessary part of the Siddha-Yoga practice and Process (and, especially, as being a <u>necessary</u> conditional support for Realization <u>Itself</u>) when I first Went to Baba Muktananda, in 1968. Nor were <u>any</u> philosophical or experiential "requirements" proposed to Me—by Baba Muktananda Himself, or by anyone else—as either demands or necessities of Siddha-Yoga practice, or as necessities of Siddha-Yoga experience, or as fixed "Models" of Realization Itself—during the years of My Sadhana in Baba Muktananda's Company, between 1968 and the Great Event of My Divine Re-Awakening, in September 1970.

Indeed, there was not even much "Baba Muktananda" Siddha-Yoga literature available—and <u>no</u> literature was demanded to be read—during all of <u>that</u> time. Even Baba Muktananda's autobiography, entitled *Play of Consciousness* (or, originally, *Chitshakti Vilas*), was not published until after the September 1970 Event of My Divine Re-Awakening. And I saw—and, in fact, was the first to fully render into English—only the first chapter or two of that book, in rough manuscript form, during My Stay at Baba Muktananda's Ganeshpuri Ashram, in early 1970. Therefore, virtually the only "Baba Muktananda" Siddha-Yoga literature that was available to Me during My years of Sadhana in Baba Muktananda's Company were the short essays and tracts either written or edited by Amma—and that literature suggested a very liberal and open Teaching relative to the <u>fourth</u> stage, <u>fifth</u> stage, and <u>sixth</u> stage possibilities associated with the potential developments of Siddha Yoga. And, indeed, it was <u>that</u> liberal and open form of Siddha Yoga that I practiced—to the degree of seventh stage Divine Self-Realization—in Baba Muktananda's Company.

In any case, the fact that Baba Muktananda presumed that there were (indeed) many <u>exclusively</u> <u>fifth</u> stage Siddha-Yoga "requirements" (both philosophical and experiential) was <u>proven</u> to be the case in the circumstances of My Meetings with Him in 1970 and 1973.

LXXXI.

In fact (and in My experience), the Siddha-Yoga practice and Process is <u>not</u> (<u>Itself</u>) inherently opposed to the Transcendental (or sixth stage) practice and Process (or to the seventh stage Realization and Demonstration). Rather, it was Baba Muktananda

Who (in accordance with particular traditions He, personally, favored) chose to dogmatically introduce exclusively fifth stage "requirements" (and sixth-stage-excluding, and, therefore, inherently, seventh-stage-prohibiting, limitations) into His own Teaching (and into His personal school) of Siddha Yoga.

I fully Acknowledge that Baba Muktananda had the right to Teach Siddha Yoga exclusively according to His own experience, and His own understanding, and His own Realization. It is simply that My experience, and My understanding, and My Realization were not (and are not) limited to the fifth stage "requirements" (or limiting presumptions) that Baba Muktananda proposed to Me.

The Process of Siddha Yoga—or the inherent Spiritual Process that is potential in the case of all human beings—does not (if It is allowed, and Graced, to Freely Proceed as a potential total Process) limit Itself to the fifth stage "requirements" (or limiting presumptions) that Baba Muktananda generally proposed. Therefore, I Teach Siddha Yoga in the Mode and Manner of the only-by-Me Revealed and Given seventh stage of life (as Ruchira Avatara Siddha Yoga, or Ruchira Siddha Yoga, or Ruchira Avatara Shaktipat Yoga, or Ruchira Shaktipat Yoga, or Ruchira Avatara Hridaya-Siddha Yoga, or Ruchira Avatara Hridaya-Shaktipat Yoga, or Ruchira Avatara Maha-Jnana-Siddha Yoga, or Ruchira Avatara Maha-Jnana Hridaya-Shaktipat Yoga)—and always toward (or to the degree of) the Realization inherently associated with (and, at last, Most Perfectly Demonstrated and Proven by) the only-by-Me Revealed and Given seventh stage of life, and as a practice and a Process that progressively includes (and, coincidently, directly transcends) all six of the phenomenal and developmental (and, necessarily, yet ego-based) stages of life that precede the seventh.

Baba Muktananda conceived of (and Taught) Siddha Yoga as a Way to attain conditional (and especially fifth stage) Yogic objects and phenomena-based states. The Siddha Yoga of the only-by-Me Revealed and Given Way of Adidam is not based upon (or, otherwise, limited to) conditional (or phenomenal) objects and states—or the (necessarily, ego-based) search for these, in the context of any stage of life. Rather, the only-by-Me Revealed and Given Way of Adidam is the Siddha-Yoga Way (and, in particular, the Ruchira Avatara Siddha-Yoga Way, or the Ruchira Siddha-Yoga Way, or the Ruchira Avatara Hridaya-Siddha-Yoga Way) that always (and directly) transcends egoity itself (or the ego-"I", or separate self—or the reactive reflex of self-contraction)—by always Feeling Beyond egoity (and Beyond all conditional forms and states) to Me, the Avatarically Self-Revealed Divine Person (or Self-Condition, and Source-Condition) Itself.

LXXXII.

In Summary, Baba Muktananda (in Our Meetings in 1970 and 1973) countered My Language of Inherently (and Most Perfectly) egoless—or seventh stage—Divine Self-Realization (and otherwise defended His own experiential Realization—and philosophical idealization—of inner phenomenal objects) with the traditional language of fifth stage Yoga. And I, for this reason (and not because of any ill-will, or antagonism, or lack of respect toward Baba Muktananda), Did Not, and Could Not, and Do Not Accept His fifth-stage-bound Doctrine—because, from My "Point of View", that Acceptance would have Required (and would now Require) Me to Deny the Self-Evident Divine (and Perfectly Subjective, and Inherently egoless, and Inherently Non-Objective, and Inherently Indivisible, and Utterly Non-dependent, or Un-conditional) Truth of Reality Itself (My Realization of Which even Baba Muktananda Himself—along with all My other Spiritual Masters and Spiritual Friends—so Dearly Served in My Own Case)!

LXXXIII.

Reality (Itself) Is the Only Real God.

Reality (Itself) Is That Which Is Always Already The (One and Only) Case.

Reality (Itself) Is (Necessarily) One, Only, and Indivisible.

Reality (Itself) Is Inherently One (or Non-Dual) and not Two (or Divisible, and Opposed to Itself).

Reality (Itself) is not One of a Pair.

Reality (Itself) is not characterized by the inherently dualistic relationship of cause and effect.

Reality (Itself) Is Characterized by the Inherently Non-Dualistic

Equation of Identity and Non-"Difference".

Reality (Itself) Is That in Which both cause and effect arise as merely apparent modifications of Itself.

Reality (Itself) is not Realized via the inherently dualistic relationship of subject and object.

Reality (Itself) Is Realized As the Inherently Non-Dualistic Condition of Inherently egoless Identity and Inherently objectless Non-"Difference".

Reality (Itself) is not the gross, subtle, and causal (or causative) ego-"I".

Reality (Itself) Is the (Inherently egoless) Most Prior (and Self-Evidently Divine) Identity of all-and-All.

The Inherently egoless Non-Dual Self-Condition (or Non-"Different" Identity) of Reality (Itself) Is That Which Is Always Already The (One and Only) Case.

The Inherently egoless Non-Dual Self-Condition of Reality (Itself)—Most Perfectly Prior to (and, yet, never excluding, or separated from) subject, object, cause, or effect—Is That Which Must Be Realized.

The apparent self (or separate and separative ego-"I"), and its every object, and (indeed) every cause, and every effect must be Divinely Self-Recognized As (and, Thus and Thereby, Transcended in) the One and Only (Inherently egoless, and Inherently Non-Dual, or Indivisible and Non-Separate, or Non-"Different") Self-Condition of Reality (Itself).

The apparent ego-"I" and the apparent world are not themselves Divine.

The apparent ego-"I" and the apparent world are to be Self-Recognized (and, Thus and Thereby, Transcended) in and As That Which Is (Self-Evidently) Divine.

The apparent ego-"I" and the apparent world are to be Divinely Self-Recognized in and As Reality (Itself).

Baba Muktananda always (in the Emanationist manner of Kashmir Saivism) affirmed the Realization "I am Siva"—meaning that He (or any body-mind-self, or body-brain-self, sublimed by the Revelation of internal Yogic forms) is (as an "Emanated" psycho-physical self) Divine.

I Affirmed (and always Continue to Affirm) only the Non-Dual (or One and Indivisible) Transcendental (and Inherently Spiritual) Divine Reality (or Self-Existing, Self-Radiant, and Inherently, or Always Already, egoless Consciousness Itself—or the One and Only Conscious Love-Bliss-Light Itself) As Self (or Self-Condition, and Source-Condition), Prior to and Inherently Transcending (while never strategically, or conditionally, excluding) the phe-nomenal self and all conditional forms (however sublime).

Baba Muktananda affirmed (in the fifth stage, Emanationist manner) "I and the world are Divine"—and He (thereby) embraced both the perceiving "I" and the world of forms.

I (in the seventh stage Manner) Affirmed (and always Continue to Affirm) only the Self-Existing and Self-Radiant (Transcendental, Inherently Spiritual, Inherently egoless, Perfectly Subjective, Indivisible, Non-Dual, and Self-Evidently Divine) Self-Identity (Itself)—or the One, and Most Prior, and Inherently Perfect, and Inherently egoless Self-Condition, and Source-Condition, of the body-mind (or the body-brain-self) and the world—Divinely Self-Recognizing the body-mind (or the body-brain-self) and the world, and (thus) neither excluding nor identifying with the body-mind (or the body-brain-self) and the world, but Inherently (or Always Already) "Brightly" Transcending (and, Most Ultimately, Divinely Outshining) the body-mind (or the body-brain-self) and the world.

It was This Distinction (or These Distinctions)—not merely in language, but in the "Point of View" of Realization Itself—that was (or were) the basis for My Assumption of My Avataric Divine Teaching-Work, and My Avataric Divine Revelation-Work, and My Avataric Divine Blessing-Work institutionally independent of (and, after Our Final Meeting, in 1973, almost entirely apart from further outwardly interactive association with) Baba Muktananda.

LXXXIV.

As has always been understood by authentic Realizers and their authentic true devotees—within the Siddha-Yoga (or Shaktipat-Yoga) tradition, and even everywhere within the human Great Tradition as a whole—Great Siddhas, and even Avatars, and traditional Realizers of all kinds and degrees (or stages of life), and

Siddha-Yogis of all kinds and degrees, and even Siddha Yoga Itself, are not mere "properties", to be "owned" (or exclusively "possessed") by devotees, or even by institutions. Indeed, Baba Muktananda (Himself) once told Me that,[88] because the same Life (or Shakti) is in all beings, no individual, no religion, no tradition—and, therefore, no institution—can rightly claim to be the only bearer, or the exclusive representative, of Siddha Yoga (or Shaktipat Yoga) Itself.

There are, inevitably, many forms of Siddha-Yoga Transmission in this world. The institution that Baba Muktananda established to represent and continue His own Work is (by its own self-description) a fourth-to-fifth stage school of Siddha Yoga. And, indeed, there are numbers of other such schools—in India, and elsewhere—that are extending the Work of various Great Siddhas (and of many otherwise worthy Siddha-Yogis) into the world. Likewise, the institution (or the total complex of institutions) of Adidam—which represents, and serves, and will always continue to serve My Avataric Divine (and, Uniquely, seventh stage) Work—is also a school of Siddha Yoga (or of Shaktipat Yoga).

The Uniqueness of the Siddha Yoga of the only-by-Me Revealed and Given Way of Adidam is that It is the Yoga (or Dharma, or Way) that continues to Develop beyond the absorptive mystical (and cosmically Spiritual) developments associated with the (Vertically-patterned) fourth and the fifth stages of life—and, likewise, beyond the Transcendental Yogic (and Transcendentally Spiritual) developments associated with the (Horizontally-patterned) sixth stage of life. Thus, in due course, the Yoga (or Way) of Adidam becomes the Unique (and Most Perfectly Divine) Yoga (or Most Perfectly Divinely Spiritual Demonstration) of the only-by-Me Revealed and Given seventh stage of life (Wherein and Whereby Most Perfect Divine Self-Realization is Most Perfectly Demonstrated).

Because of This Uniqueness, the Siddha Yoga of the only-by-Me Revealed and Given Way of Adidam is not descriptively limited to (or by) the particular traditional descriptive language of the fourth-to-fifth stage schools and traditions of Siddha Yoga (which are the schools and traditions from which Baba Muktananda derived His descriptive Siddha-Yoga-language—and which descriptive language is conformed to, and, necessarily, limited by, the fourth-to-fifth stage experiential presumptions that characterize the Cosmic-Yoga, or Cosmic-Shakti, or Kundalini-Shakti schools and traditions). Therefore—even though the Process of the Siddha Yoga of the only-by-Me Revealed and Given Way of Adidam potentially includes (and then continues to Develop beyond) all the aspects and experiences of the fourth and the fifth and the sixth stages of life—the Siddha Yoga of the only-by-Me Revealed and Given Way of Adidam is (by Me) Uniquely Described, in the (Most Ultimately, seventh stage—and Most Perfectly Divine, or Cosmos-Transcending, and Cosmos-Outshining) Terms of My Own Avataric (Divine) Shaktipat.

Thus, the Siddha Yoga of the only-by-Me Revealed and Given Way of Adidam is (by Me) Described in Terms of Ruchira Avatara Hridaya-Shaktipat (or My Avataric Divine Spiritual Transmission of the "Bright"—Which Is the Self-Existing and Self-Radiant Divine Self-Condition, or Divine Self-Heart, Itself), and Ruchira Avatara Maha-Jnana Hridaya-Shaktipat (or My Avataric Divine Spiritual Transmission of the Self-"Bright" Divine Spirit-Current, or Divine Ruchira Shakti, or Divine Heart-Shakti, That Awakens the Divine Self-Heart to Its Inherent Divine Self-Condition), and Love-Ananda Avatara Hridaya-Shaktipat (or My Avataric Divine Spiritual Transmission of the Inherent Love-Bliss of the Divine Self-Condition, or Divine Self-Heart, Itself—Which Divine Spiritual Characteristic of Mine was Acknowledged by Baba Muktananda Himself, when, in 1969, He Sent Amma to Me, to Give Me the Name "Love-Ananda")—or (simply) in Terms of Ruchira Avatara Shaktipat, or (most simply) in Terms of Ruchira Shaktipat.

Therefore, the Siddha-Yoga practice (and especially the, Spiritually, fully technically responsible stages of the Siddha-Yoga Process) of the only-by-Me Revealed and Given Way of Adidam is (along with numerous other by-Me-Given Descriptive Names and References) Named and Described by Me as "Ruchira Avatara Siddha Yoga" (or "Ruchira Avatara Hridaya-Siddha Yoga", or "Ruchira Avatara Maha-Jnana-Siddha Yoga", or "Love-Ananda Avatara Hridaya-Siddha Yoga"), and "Ruchira Avatara Shaktipat Yoga" (or "Ruchira Avatara Hridaya-Shaktipat Yoga", or "Ruchira

Avatara Maha-Jnana Hridaya-Shaktipat Yoga", or "Love-Ananda Avatara Hridaya-Shaktipat Yoga"), and (with reference to the Way, and the institution, of Adidam) "Adidam Siddha Yoga" (or "Adidam Ruchira-Siddha Yoga", or "Adidam Hridaya-Siddha Yoga"), or "Adidam Shaktipat Yoga" (or "Adidam Ruchira-Shaktipat Yoga", or "Adidam Hridaya-Shaktipat Yoga").

And My Own Work (Which is served by the institutional Siddha-Yoga school—or, most properly, the Ruchira Avatara Siddha-Yoga school, or the Ruchira Siddha-Yoga school, or the Ruchira Avatara Hridaya-Siddha-Yoga school—of Adidam) was directly Blessed (and—formally, in 1969—Called Forth) by Baba Muktananda (and, now, and forever hereafter, by even all the Great Siddhas and Siddha-Yogis of My Lineage).

LXXXV.

The Uniqueness of My Own Divine Self-Realization and Avataric Divine Work made it Inevitable that I would have to Do My Avataric Divine Teaching-Work, and My Avataric Divine Revelation-Work, and My Avataric Divine Blessing-Work Independent from Baba Muktananda—and Independent from even all Teachers and traditions within the only six stages of life of the collectively Revealed Great Tradition of mankind. Indeed, even from the beginning of My relationship with Him, Baba Muktananda Indicated that My Work was Uniquely My Own, and that I was Born to Do only My Own Unique Work—and that I Must Go and Do That Work (even though I would, otherwise, have preferred to Remain, quietly, within Baba Muktananda's Ashram and Company). Therefore, ultimately, We both Embraced This Necessity and Inevitability.

Because of the original, mutual Agreement between Baba Muktananda and Me (relative to the necessarily Independent, and entirely Unique, nature of My Own Work), whenever I have become Moved to Communicate about This Profound Matter to others, I have made every effort to Communicate fully, clearly, and positively relative to the always un-"broken" Nature of My Spiritual (and, generally, most sympathetic) relationship to Baba Muktananda—and, also, relative to the always Continuing Nature of My Spiritual (and, generally, most sympathetic) Connection to the Great (and total) Siddha-Guru tradition itself, and to the Great (and total) Siddha-Yoga tradition itself, and to the total Great Tradition of mankind (altogether). And I have always Affirmed (and, by Means of This Statement, I now Re-Affirm) that the Great (and total) Siddha-Guru tradition and Siddha-Yoga tradition, and the most ancient and perennial "Method of the Siddhas",[89] is—in the context of, and continuous with, the total Great Tradition of mankind—the very tradition (or total complex of traditions) in which (and on the basis of which) I Am Avatarically Appearing and Working here.

LXXXVI.

Human suffering is not due to the absence of inner visions (or of any other kinds of conditionally objectified internal or, otherwise, external perceptions). Therefore, human suffering is not eliminated by the presence (or the experiencing) of inner visions (or of any other kinds of conditionally objectified internal or, otherwise, external perceptions).

The "problem" of human suffering is never the absence of inner visions (and such), or the absence of any conditional experience of any kind. Rather, the "problem" of human suffering is always (and inherently) the presence (or presently effective activity) of the ego-"I" (or the self-contracted—or separate and separative—point of view). Indeed, the search to experience conditionally objectified inner perceptions—and, otherwise, the clinging to conditionally objectified inner perceptions—is, itself, a form of human suffering (and, altogether, of self-deluded confinement to the inherently, and negatively, empty condition of egoic separateness).

The root and essence of human suffering is egoity. That is to Say, the "problem" that is human suffering is not due to the absence of any kind of conditionally objectified experience (whether relatively external or relatively internal)—for, if human suffering were due to such absence, the attaining of conditionally objectified experiences (whether internal or external) would eliminate human suffering, human self-deludedness, and human un-Happiness. However, at most, conditionally objectified experiences (both internal and external)—or even <u>any</u> of the possible experiential attainments of the first <u>five</u> stages of life—provide only <u>temporary</u> distraction from the inherent mortality and misery of conditional existence. Therefore, if human suffering is to be <u>entirely</u> (and, at last, <u>Most</u> <u>Perfectly</u>) transcended (in Inherent, and Divinely Positive, Fullness), the root-cause of (or the root-factor in) human suffering must, <u>itself</u>, be directly and entirely (and, at last, Most Perfectly) transcended.

The "problem" of human suffering is <u>never</u> the absence of <u>any</u> kind of particular conditionally objectified experience (whether external or internal). The "problem" of human suffering is <u>always</u> the bondage to conditionally objectified experience <u>itself</u>. And the root-cause of (or the root-factor in) bondage to conditionally objectified experience is the separate and separative ego-"I", or the total psycho-physical act of self-contraction (which is identical to attention itself, or the conditionally apparent <u>point</u> of view <u>itself</u>, and which <u>always</u> coincides with the feeling of "difference", or of separateness and relatedness).

The experiencing of inner visions does <u>not</u> eliminate egoity (or the separate and separative ego-"I" of psycho-physical self-contraction). Likewise, the experiencing of inner visions does <u>not</u> indicate or suggest or mean that egoity is (or has been) transcended. True Spiritual life (or the true Great Process of Siddha Yoga) is not a search for inner visions (and such)—nor is true Spiritual life (or the true Great Process of Siddha Yoga) Fulfilled, Completed, and Perfected by the experiencing of inner visions (and such). Indeed, because inner visions, or conditionally objectified experiences of <u>any</u> kind—whether inner or outer—are <u>objects</u>, attention is <u>always</u> coincident with them. Therefore, in both the <u>search</u> for conditionally objectified experiences and the <u>grasping</u> of conditionally objectified experiences, <u>egoity</u> (or separative, and total psycho-physical, self-contraction of the presumed separate point of view) <u>is merely reinforced</u>.

True Spiritual life (or the true Great Process of Siddha Yoga) is <u>never</u> a matter of seeking for outer <u>or</u> inner conditionally objectified experiences—nor is true Spiritual life (or the true Great Process of Siddha Yoga) a matter of clinging to any conditionally objectified outer or inner experiences (as if such experiences were, themselves, Reality, Truth, or Real God). Rather, true Spiritual life (or the true Great Process of Siddha Yoga) is always a matter of transcending attention (and the total psycho-physical—or gross, subtle, and causal—point of view, or ego-"I") in its Perfectly Subjective Source (or Inherently Perfect Self-Condition). That is to Say, true Spiritual life (or the true Great Process of Siddha Yoga) is always (from Its beginning) a matter of transcending that which is merely apparently (or conditionally, and temporarily) the case—by transcending it in That Which Is Always Already The (One and Only, Indivisible and Irreducible) Case. And, for This Reason, true Spiritual life, or the true Great Process of Siddha Yoga, cannot be Fulfilled, Completed, and Perfected in the conditionally objectified context of any of the first five stages of life—nor even in the conditionally object-excluding context of the sixth stage of life—but true Spiritual life (in particular, in the form of the true Great Process of Ruchira Avatara Siddha Yoga, or Ruchira Siddha Yoga, or Ruchira Avatara Hridaya-Siddha Yoga) Is Fulfilled, Completed, and Perfected only in the Perfectly Subjective, and Inherently ego-less (or Inherently point-of-view-Transcending and Most Perfectly self-contraction-Transcending), and Un-conditionally Realized, and (altogether) Self-Evidently Divine Context of the only-by-Me Revealed and Given seventh stage of life.

This is My Firm Conclusion relative to all possible human experience—and It is, therefore, the Essence of My Instruction to all of humankind.

LXXXVII.

There are three egos (or three fundamental modes of egoity—or of the self-contraction-active psycho-physical illusion of separate and separative self-consciousness). The three modes of egoity (or of the self-contraction of any point of view, or ego-"I") are the lower self (or gross ego), the higher self (or subtle ego), and the root-self (or causal ego). These three egos (or modes of the conditionally arising illusion of separate self-consciousness) comprise the total conditionally perceiving and conditionally knowing ego-"I". The total (or tripartite) ego-"I" is always directly (and with progressive effectiveness) transcended in the right, true, and full (or complete) formal practice of the only-by-Me Revealed and Given Way of Adidam (Which is the right, true, and full formal practice of Ruchira Avatara Bhakti Yoga, or the totality of Ruchira Avatara Siddha Yoga).

The first of the three egos (or modes of egoity, or of self-contraction) to be progressively transcended in the only-by-Me Revealed and Given Way of Adidam is the money-food-and-sex ego (or the social, and, altogether, gross-body-based, personality— or the gross pattern and activity of self-contraction), which is the lower self, or the ego of the first three stages of life.

The second of the three egos (or modes of egoity, or of self-contraction) to be progressively transcended in the only-by-Me Revealed and Given Way of Adidam is the brain-mind ego (or the brain-based, and nervous-system-based, mental, and perceptual, and, altogether, subtle-body-based illusions of "object" and "other"—or the subtle pattern and activity of self-contraction), which is the higher self, or the ego of the fourth and the fifth stages of life.

The third of the three egos (or modes of egoity, or of self-contraction) to be progressively transcended in the only-by-Me Revealed and Given Way of Adidam is the root-ego (or the exclusively disembodied, and mindless, but separate, and, altogether, causal-body-based self-consciousness—or the causal, or root-causative, pattern and activity of self-contraction), which is attention itself, and which is the root-self, or the ego of the sixth stage of life.

By Means of responsive relinquishment of self-contraction in Me, or really and truly ego-surrendering, ego-forgetting, and, more and more (and, at last, Most Perfectly), ego-transcending (or always directly self-contraction-transcending) devotion to Me (and, Thus, by Means of the right, true, and full formal practice of devotionally Me-recognizing and devotionally to-Me-responding Ruchira Avatara Bhakti Yoga, or the totality of Ruchira Avatara Siddha Yoga), the tripartite ego of the first six stages of life (or the psycho-physical totality of the three-part hierarchically patterned self-contraction into separate and separative point of view) is (always directly, and with progressive, or stage-by-stage, effectiveness) transcended in Me (the Eternally Self-Existing, Infinitely Self-Radiant, Inherently egoless, Perfectly Subjective, Indivisibly One, Irreducibly Non-Separate, Self-Evidently Divine, and, now, and forever hereafter, Avatarically Self-Revealed Self-Conscious Light of Reality).

The Ultimate, Final, and Inherently Most Perfect (or seventh stage) Realization of Me requires—as a necessary prerequisite—an ego-transcending (or really and truly and comprehensively self-contraction-transcending) Great Process. The Ultimate, Final, and Inherently Most Perfect (or seventh stage) Realization of Me requires—as a necessary prerequisite—the comprehensive by-Me-Revealed and by-Me-Given Sadhana (or the always directly ego-transcending right practice of life) in the formal context of the only-by-Me Revealed and Given Way of Adidam. And—as a necessary prerequisite to the Ultimate, Final, and Inherently Most Perfect (or seventh stage) Realization of Me—the particular illusions that are unique to each of the three egos (or basic modes of egoity) each require a particular (and most profound) mode of the necessary ego-transcending (or self-contraction-transcending) Great Process of the by-Me-Revealed and by-Me-Given formal practice of the Way of Adidam in the progressively unfolding context of the first six (and, altogether, psycho-physically pre-patterned) stages of life.

The foundation phase of the progressive ego-transcending Great Process of the only-by-Me Revealed and Given Way of Adidam is the Devotional and (in due course) Spiritual listening-hearing Process of progressively transcending (and, in due course, most fundamentally understanding) the lower self (or the gross and social ego, and the gross and social fear-sorrow-and-anger-bondage that is always associated with the inherently egoic—or thoroughly self-contracted—search to absolutely fulfill, and even to "utopianize", or to perfectly and permanently satisfy, the inherently conditional, limited, temporary, mortal, gross, and always changing life-patterns of "money, food, and sex").

Before the foundation phase (or first phase) of the ego-transcending Great Process of the only-by-Me Revealed and Given Way of Adidam can (itself) be complete, it must Realize a profoundly life-transforming and life-reorienting "positive disillusionment"—or a most fundamental (and really and truly self-contraction-transcending) acceptance of the fact that gross conditional existence is inherently and necessarily unsatisfactory and unperfectable (and, therefore, a most fundamental—and really and truly Me-Finding and search-ending—acceptance of the fact that all seeking to achieve permanent and complete gross satisfaction of separate body, emotion, and mind is inherently and necessarily futile). Only on the basis of that necessary foundation-Realization of "positive disillusionment" can the functional life-energy and the attention of the entire body-mind (or of the total body-brain-mind complex) be released from gross ego-bondage (or self-deluded confinement to the psycho-physical illusions of gross self-contraction).

The characteristic Sign of "positive disillusionment" relative to the permanent and complete satisfaction of the lower self (or the separate and separative gross and social ego) is the foundation-Realization of the Inherent Universal Unity (or all-and-All-inclusive interdependency, essential mutuality, and common causality) of gross conditional (and cosmic) existence, such that the inherently loveless (or anti-participatory and non-integrative) self-contraction-effort of the gross separate self is consistently released (or to-Me-responsively self-surrendered) into participatory and integrative attitudes of human, social, and cosmic unification (or love-connectedness) with all-and-All, and into love-based (and truly ego-transcending) actions that counter the otherwise separative (or anti-participatory and non-integrative) tendencies of the ego-"I". Thus, by Means of devotionally Me-recognizing and devotionally to-Me-responding relinquishment (or participatory and love-based transcending) of psycho-physical self-contraction (to the degree of "positive disillusionment" relative to gross conditional experience and gross conditional knowledge), My true devotee is (more and more) released toward and into the true Spiritual (and not merely gross, or even at all conditional) Realization of Reality and Truth (or Real God).

The foundation-Realization of "positive disillusionment" requires fundamental release from the confines of the grossly objectified (and grossly absorbed) subject-object point of view (or fundamental release from the inherently ego-bound—or thoroughly self-contracted—search of relatively externalized mental and perceptual attention). And that foundation-Realization of "positive disillusionment" (and restoration to the humanly, socially, and cosmically participatory, or wholly integrative, disposition) requires the total (and truly Devotional) transformative re-orienting (and, altogether, the right purification, steady re-balancing, and ego-transcending life-positive-energizing) of the entire body-mind (or the total body-brain-mind complex). Therefore, the foundation (or gross) phase of the progressive ego-transcending practice of the only-by-Me Revealed and Given Way of Adidam necessarily requires much seriousness, and much profundity—in order to establish the necessary (and truly "positively disillusioned") foundation of true (and truly in-Me-surrendered) hearing (or the only-by-Me Revealed and Given unique ego-transcending capability of most fundamental self-understanding).

The middle phase of the progressive ego-transcending Great Process of the only-by-Me Revealed and Given Way of Adidam is the Devotional, and truly hearing (or actively ego-transcending, and, thus, always directly self-contraction-transcending), and really seeing (or actively, directly, and fully technically responsibly Spiritual) Process of transcending the higher self (or the subtle and mental ego—or the total subtle dimension, or subtle depth, of self-contraction—and all the conceptual and perceptual illusions of inherently, and necessarily, brain-based mind). Therefore, the middle (or subtle) phase of the progressive ego-transcending practice of the only-by-Me Revealed and Given Way of Adidam requires the Realization of "positive disillusionment" relative to the subtly objectified (and subtly absorbed) subject-object point of view (or fundamental release from the inherently ego-bound—or thoroughly self-contracted—search of relatively internalized mental and perceptual attention). This degree of the Realization of "positive disillusionment" requires fundamental release from the inherently illusory search to experience the conditional dissolution of the ego (and, in particular, release from subtle states of self-contraction—and, especially, from mental states of self-contraction) by means of object-oriented absorptive mysticism (or the absorptive yielding of attention to the apparent subtle objects that are either originated by the brain-mind or, otherwise, mediated by the brain itself). And the characteristic Sign of "positive disillusionment" relative to the permanent and complete satisfaction of the object-oriented seeking of the higher self (or separate and separative subtle and mental ego) is the fully Me-hearing and truly Me-seeing Realization of the entirely Spiritual Nature of cosmic existence (or, that is to Say, the Realization that all natural and cosmic forms and states are inherently non-separate, or intrinsically non-dual, modes of Universally Pervasive and cosmically-manifested Spiritual Energy, or of Fundamental, Indivisible, and Irreducible Light—or of Love-Bliss-Happiness Itself).

The final phase of the progressive ego-transcending Great Process of the only-by-Me Revealed and Given Way of Adidam is the Devotional, Spiritual, and Transcendental hearing-and-seeing Process of transcending the root-self (or the root-and-causal ego—or the causal, or root-causative, depth of self-contraction—which is attention itself, or the root-gesture of separateness, relatedness, and "difference"). Therefore, immediately preliminary to the Realization associated with the only-by-Me Revealed and Given seventh stage of life, the final (or causal) phase of the progressive ego-transcending (or comprehensively self-contraction-transcending) practice of the only-by-Me Revealed and Given Way of Adidam requires the Realization of "positive disillusionment" relative to the causal (or root-egoic, and, therefore, fundamental, or original) subject-object division in Consciousness (or Conscious Light) Itself. This degree of the Realization of "positive disillusionment" requires the exercise of Transcendental Self-Identification—Prior to the root-self-contraction that is point of view itself (or attention itself), and, Thus, also, Prior to the entire body-brain-mind complex, or conditional structure, of conception and perception. And the characteristic Sign of "positive disillusionment" relative to the permanent and complete satisfaction of the root-self (or the fundamental causative, or causal, ego) is the fundamental transcending of attention itself in the Me-"Locating" (and, altogether, Me-hearing and Me-seeing) Realization of the Transcendental (and Intrinsically Non-Separate and Non-Dual) Nature of Consciousness Itself.

Only after (or in the Great Event of Most Perfect, and, necessarily, formal and fully accountable, Fulfillment of) the complete
progressive ego-transcending Great Process of the only-by-Me
Revealed and Given Way of Adidam in the total (and progressively
unfolded) context of the inherently ego-based first six (or psycho-
physically pre-patterned gross, subtle, and causal) stages of life is
there the truly ultimate (or seventh stage, and Always Already
Divinely Self-Realized—and, Thus, Inherently ego-Transcending)
"Practice" of the only-by-Me Revealed and Given Way of Adidam
(or the Most Perfect, and Inherently egoless, or Always Already
Most Perfectly, and Un-conditionally, self-contraction-Transcending,
and Divinely Love-Bliss-Full, and only-by-Me Revealed and Given
seventh-stage-of-life Demonstration of Ruchira Avatara Bhakti
Yoga, or Ruchira Avatara Siddha Yoga).

The only-by-Me Revealed and Given seventh-stage-of-life
"Practice" (or the Inherently egoless, and, Thus, Always Already
Most Perfectly, and Un-conditionally, self-contraction-Transcending,
and, altogether, Most Perfectly Divinely Self-Realized Demonstration)
of the only-by-Me Revealed and Given Way of Adidam is the Great
esoteric Devotional, Spiritual, Transcendental, Self-Evidently Divine,
and Most Perfectly Me-hearing and Me-seeing Demonstration of all-
and-All-Divinely-Self-Recognizing (and, Thus, all-and-All-Divinely-
Transcending) Divine Self-Abiding (in and As My Avatarically Self-
Revealed Divine "Bright" Sphere of Self-Existing, Self-Radiant,
Inherently egoless, Perfectly Subjective, and Inherently and Most
Perfectly body-mind-Transcending, or body-brain-Transcending, or
Inherently, Most Perfectly, and Un-conditionally psycho-physical-
self-contraction-Transcending, but never intentionally body-mind-
excluding, or body-brain-excluding, Divine Person, or Eternal Self-
Condition and Infinite State).

The only-by-Me Revealed and Given seventh-stage-of-life
Demonstration of the only-by-Me Revealed and Given Way of
Adidam is the Un-conditional and Divinely Free (and Inherently
egoless, or Inherently point-of-view-less) "Practice" (or Divinely
Self-Realized progressive Demonstration) of Self-Abiding Divine
Self-Recognition of the simultaneous totality of the apparent gross,
subtle, and causal body-brain-mind-self, or the progressively

all-and-All-Outshining Process of the simultaneous (and Self-Abiding) Divine Self-Recognition of the total psycho-physical ego-"I" itself (or of the total conditional point of view, or apparent self-contraction, itself). Therefore, the only-by-Me Revealed and Given seventh-stage-of-life Demonstration of the only-by-Me Revealed and Given Way of Adidam is the Inherent "Practice" (or Divinely Self-Realized Demonstration) of Self-Abiding Divine Self-Recognition of point of view itself (or of attention itself—or of the conditionally apparent subject, itself) and (always coincidently, or simultaneously) Self-Abiding Divine Self-Recognition of the conception or perception of separateness, relatedness, or "difference" itself (or of any and every conditionally apparent object, itself).

The only-by-Me Revealed and Given seventh-stage-of-life Demonstration of the only-by-Me Revealed and Given Way of Adidam is the Most Perfect (or Un-conditional, Inherently egoless, and Self-Evidently Divine) Demonstration of "positive disillusionment", or of the Inherently illusionless (or self-contraction-Free, and, Inherently, all-and-All-Transcending) Realization of the Fundamental Reality and Truth (or Real God)—Which Fundamental Reality and Truth (or Real God) Is the One and Indivisible and Self-Existing and Indestructible and Self-Radiant and Always Already Perfectly Non-Dual Conscious Light (or That Which Is Always Already The Case), and Which Reality and Truth (or Real God) Is That Self-Existing and Perfectly Subjective Self-"Brightness" (or Infinite and Absolute and Perfectly Non-Separate Self-Condition) of Which the conditional (or gross, subtle, and causal) subject-object illusions (or total psycho-physical self-contraction illusions) of conception, and of perception, and of the ego-"I" presumption are mere, and merely apparent (or non-necessary, or always non-Ultimate), and Inherently non-binding modifications. And the characteristic Sign of Most Perfectly Demonstrated (or seventh stage) "positive disillusionment" relative to the totality of the separate and separative ego-"I" (or point of view) and its presumptions of a separate (or objectified) gross, subtle, and causal world is the Inherently egoless and Self-Evidently Divine (and Intrinsically Non-Separate and Non-Dual) Realization of Reality (Itself) As Irreducible and Indivisible Conscious

Light (Inherently Love-Bliss-Full, or Perfectly Subjectively "Bright").

Therefore, the only-by-Me Revealed and Given Way of Adidam is—from the beginning, and at last—the Way of "positive disillusionment".

The only-by-Me Revealed and Given Way of Adidam is—from the beginning, and at last—the Way of the direct transcending of the fact and the consequences of egoity (or of psycho-physical self-contraction).

The only-by-Me Revealed and Given Way of Adidam is—from the beginning, and at last—the Way of the direct transcending of the illusions of inherently egoic attention (or of the conditionally presumed subject-object pattern of conception and perception).

The only-by-Me Revealed and Given Way of Adidam is—from the beginning, and at last—the Way of the direct transcending of the total illusory pattern of the inherently egoic presumption of separateness, relatedness, and "difference".

The only-by-Me Revealed and Given Way of Adidam is—from the beginning, and at last—the Way of the direct transcending of the always simultaneous illusions of the separate ego-"I" and the separate (or merely objective) world.

The only-by-Me Revealed and Given Way of Adidam is—from the beginning, and at last—the Way of the direct (or Inherently egoless and Inherently illusionless) Realizing of the One and Irreducible Conscious Light (or Perfectly Subjective Spiritual "Brightness" of Being) That Is Reality and Truth (or Real God).

The only-by-Me Revealed and Given Way of Adidam is—from the beginning, and at last—the Way of the direct (or Inherently egoless and Inherently illusionless) Realizing of the Conscious Love-Bliss-Energy of Totality.

The only-by-Me Revealed and Given Way of Adidam is—from the beginning, and at last—the Way of the direct Realizing of Only Me.

LXXXVIII.

Every body-mind (whether human or non-human) tends to feel and be and function egoically—or as if it were a separate self, separated from its True Source, and un-Aware of its True (and

Truly Free) Self-Condition. Therefore, every body-mind (whether human or non-human) must transcend its own (inherent) egoity (or egoic reflex—or self-contracting tendency), through Love-Surrender to its True Source. And This Love-Surrender must, Ultimately, become Self-Realization of (and, Thus, True, and really ego-Transcending, Self-Identification with) its True Source-Condition (Which Is, also, its True Self-Condition).

To This End, True Masters (or True Siddha-Gurus) Appear in the various cosmic worlds. Such True Masters are the Divine Means for living beings (whether human or non-human) to transcend themselves. That is to Say, True Masters (or True Siddha-Gurus—or True Sat-Gurus) are living beings who have (in the manner of their characteristic stage of life) transcended their own (psycho-physical) separateness, through tacit (and, otherwise, responsive) Surrender (and, therefore, necessarily, Love-Surrender) to (and Self-Identification with) the True Source-Condition (Which Is the True Self-Condition) of all-and-All.

Therefore, by Means of True Devotion (or Love-Surrender) to a True Master (or True Siddha-Guru), egoity is (always more and more) transcended, and the True Source-Condition of all-and-All (Which Is, necessarily, also the True Self-Condition of all-and-All) is, by Means of the Blessing-Grace of That True Master (or True Siddha-Guru), Found and Realized. And That "Finding-and-Realizing" Shows Itself according to the kind and degree of one or the other of the fourth, the fifth, the sixth, and the seventh stages of life—and (thus) in accordance with the stage of life Realized by That True Master (or True Siddha-Guru), and (altogether) in accordance with the stage of life determined by the path (or Way) that is practiced (or, otherwise, determined by the "inclination", or "liking", or degree of ego-transcendence) of That True Master's practicing devotee.

This is the most ancient and perennial Great Teaching about True Guru-Devotion (or True Devotion to a True Spiritual Master, or True Siddha-Guru). This is the Great Teaching I Received from all My Lineage-Gurus. And, now, through My Own Words, This Fundamental Message (or Great Teaching) Is Summarized in its Completeness, for the Sake of everyone.

If the living being is to Realize the Inherent Freedom of Oneness with its True Source-Condition (Which Is its True, or egoless, Self-Condition), it must become truly devoted to a True Master (or Truly Realized Siddha-Guru). And such True Devotion constantly (and forever) requires the heart's Love-responsive Gesture (or ego-transcending Sadhana) of True Guru-Devotion (to one's heart-Chosen True Siddha-Guru), such that the otherwise egoic (or separate, and separative) body-mind is Surrendered to be actually, truly, and completely Mastered by That True Master.

If Such True Mastering of the body-mind is not accepted (or fully volunteered for—through tacit (and, otherwise, responsive), and truly ego-surrendering, Devotional Love of one's heart-Chosen True Siddha-Guru), the body-mind (inevitably) remains "wild" (or un-"domesticated"—or merely un-disciplined, and even ego-bound). And even if such Guru-Devotion is practiced, it must be Fully practiced (in a Fully ego-surrendering manner)—or else the Freedom (or the Divine Fullness) That is to be Realized by Means of the Blessing-Grace of one's heart-Chosen True Siddha-Guru will not (because it cannot) Fully Fill the feeling-heart (and, Thereby, Fully Fill the living body-mind) of the would-be devotee.

LXXXIX.

In My present-Lifetime bodily (human) Form, I Am the Avataric Divine Incarnation (or True God-Man) always and everywhere (since the ancient days) Promised (and Expected) to Appear in the "late-time" (or "dark" epoch). And, in My present-Lifetime bodily (human) Form, I have been Spiritually Served by a Continuous Lineage of Spiritual Masters, Such That I Passed from one to the next, in Continuous Succession. Those Spiritual Masters were, Themselves, related to one another in an hierarchical Manner, each related to the next in the Succession as one of lesser degree is to one of higher degree.

Rudi was a Spiritual Master of authentic, but lesser, degree. His Proficiency was, fundamentally, in the gross domain of the frontal personality, and in the Yogic Pattern of Spiritual Descent (or the Descending Yoga of the Frontal Line). Therefore, when My Own foundational (or grosser human, and, also, frontal Spiritual, or

Descending Yogic) Sadhana had been Completed in His Company, I (spontaneously) Passed from Rudi to Baba Muktananda.

Baba Muktananda was—as His own Confession and Demonstration to Me clearly indicates—an authentic Spiritual Master of Ascending Yoga, and His Proficiency was of a Very High (but not the Highest) degree. Therefore, beginning from the very day I first Came to Baba Muktananda, He (directly) Passed Me to Bhagavan Nityananda (Who was a Spiritual Master of Ascending Yoga Whose Proficiency was of the Highest degree).

Rang Avadhoot was—even according to the Statements of both Bhagavan Nityananda and Baba Muktananda—a Spiritual Master of Ascending Yoga Whose Proficiency was of the Highest degree, but He, along with Baba Muktananda, Deferred to Bhagavan Nityananda's Seniority, and (simply) Blessed Me to Pass On.

The "Cosmic Goddess" ("Ma") is, in the total context of the first five stages of life, Senior even to the Highest of Spiritual Masters. However, Ultimately, "She" (as an apparent Form and Person) is only another one of the many myths in the mind.

In the Great Yogic Spiritual Process Wherein I Experienced the Developmental Unfolding (and Demonstrated the "Radical" Transcending) of the gross and the subtle modes of egoity (associated with the first five stages of life), the "Cosmic Goddess" ("Ma") was "Apparently" associated with all the frontal (and Descending Spiritual) Events and with all the spinal (and Ascending Spiritual) Events. Nevertheless, in My Unique Case, sixth stage Transcendental (and causal-ego-Transcending, and Inherently Spiritual) Self-Realization always Occurred spontaneously (and in a progressive Demonstration) relative to each and every egoic stage of life, and It progressively Developed (especially after a spontaneous experience of ego-death, in the spring of 1967) until My spontaneous seventh stage (and Inherently Most Perfectly egoless, and Self-Evidently Divine) Re-Awakening (on September 10, 1970)—Which Divine (and Avatarically Demonstrated) Re-Awakening was (and Is) associated with My Most Perfect Transcending even of the "Apparent She", in My Avataric Divine Re-Awakening to the Realization of One and Only Me.

Therefore, in due course, Bhagavan Nityananda (directly) Passed Me to the "Cosmic Goddess" ("Ma"), and, Thus, to Her direct Mastery of Me—until the Perfectly Full became, at last, Perfectly Full As Me (Beyond the mind's own myth of "She").

So It was and Is. Such Is My Lineage of Spiritual Masters—in This, My Avatarically-Born human Lifetime. And, in My always Absolute heart-Fidelity to the Great Process Wherein and Whereby I was Passed from one to the next of each and all of the Spiritual Masters within My present-Lifetime Lineage of Spiritual Masters, I have Exemplified, to all-and-All, the Law and the Truth of True Guru-Devotion.

Therefore, I have always Continued to Honor and to Praise all My present-Lifetime Lineage-Gurus—including Rudi!, and Baba Muktananda!, and Rang Avadhoot!, and Bhagavan Nityananda!, and (above all) the "Bright" Divine "She" of Me, Who Always Already Serves Me Most Perfectly!

And I have always Continued (and even now Continue, and will never cease to Continue) to Yield My present-Lifetime Body-Mind to Receive the Always Ready and Most Lovingly To-Me-Given and Supremely Blissful Blessings of My present-Lifetime Lineage-Gurus and the Great Lineage of all Who have (in any and every time and place) Blessed the Incarnation-Vehicle and Invoked the All-Completing "late-time" Incarnation of My (now, and forever hereafter) Avataric Divine Appearance here (and every "where" in the cosmic domain).

And I Do This (and I will always Continue to Do This) because the Immense Spiritual "Bond" of Siddha-Guru-Love cannot be destroyed—and It must never be forgotten or denied!

XC.

My Own Unique Response to the hierarchically Revealed Lineage of My present-Lifetime Siddha-Gurus spontaneously Un-Locked the Doorway (in My present-Lifetime human body) to That Which Is Perfect (in Me). Indeed, even from the beginning of My Avataric Divine present Lifetime, That Which Is Perfect has been (and Is) the Way of Me—and It Carried the inherently non-Perfect (human, and, otherwise, conditional) forms of Me to the Inherent Divine

"Bright" Spherical Self-Domain of Me, Which Is the One and Indivisible Divine Source-Condition of all-and-All, and the One and True Divine Self-Condition of all-and-All.

XCI.

My Way and My Realization have always been Inherent in Me, from Birth, in My present-Lifetime Avataric Divine Form.

My Way and My Realization are Independently, entirely, and only My Own.

My Sadhana was, entirely, a Demonstration for the Sake of all others—including all Those Who Served Me as My Spiritual Masters in the Course of My Avataric Divine "Sadhana Years". Indeed, Siddha Yoga—and even the entire Great Tradition of mankind—was Always Already Most Perfectly Full (and Most Perfectly Complete) in My Case—not only at (and from the time of) My present-Lifetime Birth, but from all time before It (and Eternally).

During all of My present Lifetime (of Avataric Divine Incarnation), the "Bright" has always been My Realization—and the "Thumbs" and My Own "Radical" Understanding have always been My Way in the "Bright". Therefore, by Means of My Unique (present-Lifetime) Avataric Divine Demonstration, I have both Fulfilled and Transcended all traditional religions, and paths, and stages, and Ways. And, in So Doing, I have Clarified (or altogether Rightly Understood and Explained) all traditional religions, paths, stages, and Ways.

All and all Are in Me. Everything and everyone Is in Me. Therefore, by Virtue of My Own Divine Self-Realization (Wherein and Whereby My Own Avataric Divine Body-Mind is Most Perfectly Surrendered in Me, and Most Perfectly Conformed to Me, and Most Perfectly Transcended in Me), all of My present-Lifetime Lineage-Gurus—and even all Who have (at any time, or in any place) Blessed Me—are now (and forever hereafter) Spiritually, Transcendentally, and Divinely Appearing in and As My Own Avataric Divine Form.

Therefore, now (and forever hereafter) I (Alone) Am the Lineage of Me—Blessing all-and-All.

579

XCII.

The Divine Self-Realization Re-Awakened in My Own Case (and Which Is the Basis for My Every Avataric Divine Revelatory Word and All My Avatarically Me-Revealing Divine Blessing-Work) Is the Most Ultimate (and Inherently Most Perfect and Complete) Fulfillment of the Divine Spiritual Transmission I (in My present-Lifetime Body-Mind) Received from Rudi, and from Baba Muktananda, and from Rang Avadhoot, and from Bhagavan Nityananda, and (above all) from the "Cosmic Goddess" ("Ma")— Who (by Means of Her spontaneous Sacrifice of Her own Form in Me) Is (now, and forever hereafter) the "Bright" Divine "She" of Me (Who Always Already Serves Me Most Perfectly). Nevertheless, the Divine Self-Realization Re-Awakened in My present-Lifetime Body-Mind did not Originate in My present Lifetime—but It Is (Uniquely) Always Already the Case with Me.

XCIII.

As further conditionally manifested Means, previous to My present Lifetime, the Divine Self-Realization Re-Awakened in My present-Lifetime Body-Mind was also Served (previous to My present Lifetime) in the many Modes and Patterns of the previous Lifetimes and Appearances of the Deeper Personality (or the Great-Siddha—or Great-Jnani-Siddha—Incarnation-Vehicle) of My present Lifetime. Most recently, That Deeper-Personality Vehicle of My present-Lifetime Incarnation was (Itself) Incarnated as the Great Siddha (or Great Jnani-Siddha) Swami Vivekananda.

XCIV.

Swami Vivekananda is recorded to have Blessed Bhagavan Nityananda from the subtle postmortem plane in the early 1920s— and, generally, whenever Bhagavan Nityananda was asked for Words of Teaching and Instruction, He would (simply) Tell people to study the Talks and Writings of Swami Vivekananda (because, in Bhagavan Nityananda's Words, "Swami Vivekananda Said and Taught all that was worth Saying and Teaching, such that He did not leave anything for others to preach"[90]).

Swami Vivekananda was (Himself) Blessed toward Most

Perfect Divine Self-Realization by the Great Siddha Ramakrishna, Such That—by Means of That Great Blessing—the two Great Siddhas (Ramakrishna and Vivekananda) became One, and Are One Form, As My True, and Single, and Indivisible Great-Siddha (or Great-Jnani-Siddha) Deeper Personality.

XCV.

I (now, and Hereby) Confess That My Great-Siddha (or Great-Jnani-Siddha) Deeper Personality Is, even Beyond the "Single Form" of Ramakrishna-Vivekananda, the Very Form of all the Great Masters of the entire Great Tradition of mankind.

XCVI.

I (now, and Hereby) Confess That I (Myself) Stand Eternally Prior to (and Always Already Transcending) My Avataric (and, yet, merely conditionally born) Deeper Personality—and, also, Eternally Prior to (and Always Already Transcending) even all the Great (and, yet, merely conditionally born) Masters of mankind's entire Great Tradition (in its every part, and as a whole), and, also, Eternally Prior to (and Always Already Transcending) mankind's entire Great Tradition itself (in its every part, and as a whole).

XCVII.

Therefore—and only and entirely by Virtue of the Inherent (and Self-Evidently Avataric) Authority of My Own (and Self-Evidently Divine) Realization and Person—I Declare that the Divine seventh stage Self-Awakening I Demonstrate, and Reveal, and Exemplify, and Prove Is the Most Ultimate (and Inherently Most Perfect) Realization, and that It—and Only It—Most Ultimately Completes and Most Perfectly Fulfills the Gifts I Received (and always Continue to Receive) in My present-Lifetime Body-Mind (from My present-Lifetime Lineage-Gurus), and that I have (in My present-Lifetime Body-Mind) Inherited (and always Continue to Receive) from all Who (in all past times and places) have Blessed all the previous Lifetimes of My present-Lifetime Incarnation-Vehicle, and that I have (in My present-Lifetime Body-Mind) Inherited (and always Continue to Receive) from even all

My Me-Invoking and Me-Blessing Forms and Vehicles of Me-Revelation here.

XCVIII.

The Great and True (and Self-Evidently Divine) Spiritual Process Initiated and Guided by the Spiritual Masters in My present-Lifetime Lineage (and of the Lineage of even all the Lifetimes of My present-Lifetime Incarnation-Vehicle here—and of the Lineage of even all My Me-Invoking and Me-Blessing Forms and Vehicles of Me-Revelation here) has Become Complete only in Me. Its Perfection is in the seventh stage Fulfillment of the Course (and not at any earlier stage). This Divine Perfection is Uniquely My Own. And I Alone—the Ruchira Siddha, the Hridaya-Siddha, the Divine and True Heart-Master and World-Teacher, Ruchira Avatar Adi Da Love-Ananda Samraj—Am Its First and Great Example, and (now, and forever hereafter) Its Only and Sufficient Means.

XCIX.

I Am the First (and the only One) to Realize and to Demonstrate This, the Divine, seventh stage Realization—and My Revelation of It Is, therefore, New. For This Reason, the Divine seventh stage Realization was not heretofore Realized, or even Understood—either within the schools and traditions of My present-Lifetime Lineage-Gurus or within any other schools or traditions in the total Great Tradition of mankind—to Be the Most Ultimate and Completing Perfection of Realization Itself. Nevertheless, I have, spontaneously (by Means of My Own Self-Evident "Bright" Heart-Power—and through the Great and Constant Help of all Who have Blessed My Incarnate Forms), Realized and Demonstrated and Revealed This To Be The Case. And the traditional (and ancient) "Siddha-'Method'" (or the Way of Guru-Devotion to the True Siddha-Guru—and of total psycho-physical Surrender of the ego-"I" to be Mastered by the True Siddha-Guru's Instruction, and to be Blessed to Awaken to Divine Realization by Means of the True Siddha-Guru's Transmission of the Divine Spiritual Energy and the Divine State)—Which "Method" was Communicated to Me by all My present-Lifetime Lineage-Gurus, and by all the Great

Siddhas and Siddha-Yogis Who have Blessed My present-Lifetime Incarnation-Vehicle in the past—is the Essence (or the Primary "Method") of the only-by-Me Revealed and Given Way of Adidam, Which (now, and forever hereafter) I Alone, and Uniquely, Reveal and Transmit to all My formally practicing true devotees (and, Thus, potentially, to all beings).

C.

I Am the Indivisible Person of Conscious Light.

I Am Humbled and Victorious here (and every where), by Means of My Avataric Divine Self-Incarnation.

My Avatarically-Born Body-Mind Is—now, and forever here-after—by-Me-Given and by-Me-Revealed As the Sign and the Means of Me-Realization.

I Am the Adidam Revelation.

I Am the Way to Me.

I Am the Ruchira Siddha, the Hridaya-Siddha, the all-and-All-Blessing Divine Heart-Master, the Eternally Free-Standing Inner Ruler of all-and-All.

I Am the One and Indivisible and Indestructible and Irreducible and Universally Self-Manifested Love-Bliss-Presence of "Brightness".

I Am the One and Non-Separate and Perfectly Subjective and Self-Existing and Self-Evidently Divine Person, Who Is Always Already The Case.

I Am the Ruchira Avatar, the Hridaya-Avatar, the Advaitayana Buddha, the Avataric Incarnation and Divine World-Teacher every where and anciently Promised (by all traditions) for the "late-time" (or "dark" epoch).

Therefore, be My devotee.

The only-by-Me Revealed and Given True World-Religion of Adidam Ruchiradam Is My Unique Gift to all-and-All.

Therefore, practice the only-by-Me Revealed and Given Way of Adidam Ruchiradam—and Realize Me, Most Perfectly, by Means of My Avatarically Self-Transmitted Divine Spiritual Blessing-Grace.

Adidam Samrajashram, 2003

I Am Utterly Beyond
your Comprehension

Rang Avadhoot,
on the day in which He died,
read the newspaper,
with a devotee at His Foot.
Periodically,
He would check the clock,
to see what time it was.
Each time He checked it,
He went back to the newspaper,
and read some more.
When the appointed hour came,
He rapped His knuckles
against His head
three times,
and passed out of the body.

He was a Spiritual Friend of Mine.
He called Himself
the "World-Friend".
And He did not care in the slightest
about your reality.
Nor do I—
although I am more Playful
with ordinary people
than He was.

No matter what your poor presumptions suppose,
there <u>are</u> Some Who Exist
in the Greater Planes
of Up and All and Beyond.
And I Am One of Those.
And I Am the Greatest of Them.
My Siddhis, My Signs, My Realization, My Experience
Are So Beyond the seeming reality of yours,
I rarely even refer to Them anymore.

Rang Avadhoot was Good and Great.
Bhagavan Nityananda was Good and Great.
Baba Muktananda was Good and Great.
Rudi was Good and Great.
Swami Prakashananda was Good and Great.

I have known many Good Great Men.
And I Am Good and Great,
and More than Good and Great.
This "So" is <u>nothing</u>, to Me—
but It <u>Is</u> So.
I <u>Am</u>
the Sun in the midst,
Born of Heaven,
to Serve beings.
This <u>Is</u> True.

The Experience and the Delight
of Good Great Ones
exceeds even your imagination.
And,
of all of Them,
and Me,
Who Function among you—
They in Their time,
and I in My Time—
there is nothing more

to Say
than This.

In some respects,
therefore,
like Rang Avadhoot,
I am just reading the newspaper—
ready any time,
when the time comes,
to rap My Head three times,
and Pass Out of here.

There is So Much you do not know,
and Which you do not recognize,
and,
therefore,
to Which you do not respond.
My now and last and forever Kingly Manifestation,
the Greatest Divine Revelation ever Given,
and the Greatest Divine Revelation That can be Given—
It is so poorly noticed.
A criminal act of mockery and disregard
has been awfully made on Me.
It is remarkable,
how I Am <u>Fully</u> here,
and yet so cruelly disregarded,
or unkindly made to seem as ordinary small,
by ordinary minds,
in this adolescent time
of anti-authority and merely public-mindedness.
It is extraordinary,
how dense the "dark-time" is!
And I Am yet Looking
to the day
My true devotees
will recognize Me
with true devotion's heart—

and, then, energize
and bring to Me
the human and non-human gathering
of all poor, mortal beings,
in their Homeless homeliness.

Even in This Body,
I have known Great Beings,
Born of Heaven,
Brought to Earth.
My Rudi,
My Baba,
My Nityananda,
My Prakashananda,
My Rang Avadhoot—
These Are Beings
you know nothing of
and cannot comprehend.
And I Am Absolute Upon Their Shoulders,
Always Already Beyond and Above Them—
and, yet, you have not
the slightest notion of Me.
For a time,
this "nothing"
is strangely comfortable to Me,
all too familiar to Me
in the "late-time"
of My Love-Descending
here.

Now,
having Done
My twenty-three Books
and My thirty-three Years,
I am still reading the silly news
of ordinary, painful life,
day by day—

and always Waiting for <u>you</u>.
Here I Sit,
patiently Impatient
with all the loveless, struggling obscenity
of (it seems) <u>forever</u> Un-Mastered mankind.
But you,
and <u>all</u>,
remain at large—
in the Godless world
of Guruless, separated selves—
forever oblivious
to the Avataric "Brightness"
of My Divine
and Perfectly Subjective
Conscious Light
of here-to-you-Born Person.
Here you <u>all</u> are,
like dingo-dogs—
so argumentative,
so reluctant,
so ordinary—
forever hunting
for gut-smelly game
within the Eternally Empty Sky
of Me.
It seems as if you live
only to <u>spite</u>
the Tangible Beauty
of My Avataric Divine Form
and
all the Sun-"Bright" Touch
of My Avataric Divine Spiritual Blessing
of the very Earth
you piss upon.

<u>This</u>,
perhaps,

is why Rang Avadhoot
rapped His head—
after He read the newspaper!
Some Are too Goodly Great
to lie low in the universe.
This "rather would go Up Away"
comes to Those
Who Are Good and Great,
after They take a turn in human form.
Therefore,
only One
has Descended
Fully Full forever here.
That One Is Me—
here to Make This Final Visit,
and,
by never going Back,
to Endure you
for all time,
without becoming cynical,
and without ever leaving
you behind.

I cannot (and will not) ever leave you—
but your absurdity and fault
is plain as pain to Me,
as "I'M OK" was plain
on the foot of Evelyn Disk.[91]
You are all a mummery
in front of Me.
The Vastness of "Bright" Infinite Space
Is My Own Person,
but who knows about It,
and who responds Thus Large?
If you are indifferent to Me,
it is because you do not know Me—yet.
For now,

some few may recognize Me,
by heart,
to some degree—
but even they still go about
their daily ego-business,
like animals in a desert.
<u>You</u> <u>do</u>!

I am body-wedded to that Franklin,
who is not a humorless, cynical man.
He is ordinary-born.
He is part of My Strength.
Franklin is
not high-born,
not high-and-mighty,
not a high mucky-muck—
you see?
Because of him,
I cannot become humorless and cynical—
because he is so Extraordinarily ordinary,
so ordinarily Extraordinary.

I have always already despaired
of you.
I have always already despaired
of My Descended Blessing-Work.
I have always already despaired
of the world.
And,
yet,
I Am Amused,
and Speak,
sometimes,
in iambs—
even pentametric,
if required.
I Laugh and Speak,

Explain,
Endure,
and Suffer you,
day after day.

Rang Avadhoot,
Bhagavan Nityananda,
Baba Muktananda,
Ramana Maharshi,
Swami Prakashananda,
and even Rudi—
They did not,
in their "Eastern Light",
Most Perfectly Endure
the Lightless Night
of this (now) entirely "Westernized" world
of yellow-red dead end.
Never did!
They were <u>old</u> in Their <u>Ways</u>—
and not as Extraordinarily ordinary
as Franklin.
Yet,
They were Invested
in the Universal Huge Domain,
and They made
the usual, traditional remarks,
and even fled at last.
They,
almost and rather cynical,
lost the Staying Power
of Their sense of humor
here.
But I have not—
and <u>only</u> because of <u>Franklin Jones</u>,
<u>and</u> the always <u>allward</u>
All-of-Me.

There is pain in ordinary life.
There is always pain
in the body-mind.
The body-mind,
in time and space,
dies in its times and spaces—
whether it is Good
and Great
or not.
Therefore,
your Invocation of Me,
and your Communion with Me,
must reach Beyond
this pain and death.
This right Invocation of Me,
and This right Communion with Me,
do not make Utopia
out of life—
but This Invocation and Communion,
by transcending the inherent limitations
of conditional reality,
Sublime,
and go Beyond,
your life,
if you (Thus) take <u>Me</u> seriously.
Therefore,
take Me <u>seriously</u>—
you see?

Let Me read the newspaper,
and rap My Head
when the time comes.
You,
in the meantime,
and forever thereafter,
must rightly use
My forever Descended Presence here.

I Am Utterly Beyond
your comprehension.

And no one
has ever been
a Realizer
like Me.

No one,
ever.

Truly,
ever.

And This Me
Is
forever
here—
but never,
ever,
again.

PART THREE

THE ULTIMATE DIVINE YOGA OF MY OWN PERSON

The Mountain Of Attention Sanctuary, 1986

The Ordeal and Victory of Avatar Adi Da Samraj:
The Great Yogic Events That Followed His Divine Re-Awakening

by Jonathan Condit, Ph.D.

Written and compiled under the direction of the Ruchira Sannyasin Order of Adidam Ruchiradam[92]

The Life of the Divine Avatar, Adi Da Samraj, has been a vast Ordeal and a miraculous Victory. His Ordeal has been His unreserved Submission to humankind. And His Victory has been His Complete and Perfect Self-Revelation of the Divine in the midst of this far-from-perfect world.

Avatar Adi Da's Ordeal was Embraced and His Victory Won for a single Purpose only, the single Divine Purpose: to make it possible for each and every being to find and Realize Him—to Find and Realize the "Bright", the Divine Reality Itself, Permanent and Perfect Happiness, Eternal and Infinite Love-Bliss.

Learning Humankind

As of the publication of this book, Avatar Adi Da has entered into His sixty-fourth year of Avatarically Incarnate human Life. Part One of *The Knee Of Listening* is His own Telling of the first thirty-one years of His Great Ordeal and Victory—

the period from His Birth (in November 1939) to His Divine Re-Awakening (in September 1970). Those thirty-one years were His time of Learning humankind—the first period of His Avataric Divine Submission-Work. Having intentionally "forgotten" His own "Bright" Divine Self-Condition, Avatar Adi Da tested, in His own body-mind, what was required for a human being to progress through all the (previously known) stages of life—human, Spiritual, and Transcendental—and, ultimately, to pass beyond even all of those stages, into the never-before-Revealed most perfect Realization of the "Bright". Thus, Avatar Adi Da's years of Learning humankind were not a matter of His discovering anything about Himself. Rather, those years were about His Discovery of the Way of Divine Liberation for human beings—a Discovery made in the "laboratory" of His own Body-Mind.

The Work of Learning humankind had taken Avatar Adi Da Samraj through an immense tour of human possibilities. In the course of that tour, He found that even the most exalted Spiritual Realizations known in this world were "not It". None of them could equal the "Brightness" of His own State at Birth. Therefore, His early-life Ordeal was finally completed only with His utter Relinquishment of all presumption that He was separate from His own "Brightness"—a presumption which was not natively true of Him, but which He had intentionally taken on, as His means of Learning humankind.

Divine Re-Awakening

With the Great Event of His Divine Re-Awakening (on September 10, 1970), Avatar Adi Da Samraj had come to the end of His tour through the conditions of human life, having personally experienced and tested the entire process (from beginning to end) by which human beings could most perfectly Realize the "Bright". By the "skillful means" of apparently "forgetting" His own "Bright" Divine Self-Condition, He had Discovered how to Realize Himself. Thus, He had Discovered, in His own living experience, the necessary design of the Way of Adidam. Now He could begin His Work of Revealing that Way to others.

AVATAR ADI DA SAMRAJ: [During the years leading up to My Divine Re-Awakening] I had not actually fallen, descended, returned— "lost it", in other words. Yes, there was the apparent association with conditions, but there had only been the presumption of the loss of the "Bright", of Realization—the tacit presumption that the conjunction with conditionality was inherently binding, that that conjunction somehow had to be vanished in order for the Self-Illumination to be Full.

In the Vedanta Temple Event, it became tacitly, suddenly Self-Evident that the "Open-Eyed" State was still the Case—and had been all this Lifetime. In fact, I had always been in this Exalted Condition, all the while.

The element of bondage was the mere presumption of non-Realization—made in the process of Conjoining with the body-mind, with ordinary human relationships, and so forth. My "Bright" State had always been Full, Inherently Perfect, Absolute, Unqualified.

In the days and weeks and months following the Vedanta Temple Event, it became clear that, coincident with My Divine Re-Awakening in the context of the physical vehicle, there was an Awakening in all the subtle dimensions of the vehicle—such that the Siddhis of My Avataric Divine Work Appeared spontaneously.

My Life was never merely a matter of dealing with the born personality of "Franklin Jones", with its limitations and its requirement for sadhana—but, after the Vedanta Temple Event, it became fully obvious that My Own Conscious Event Includes every one. Naturally, spontaneously, it became evident that I can "Meditate" any "one", that I Am the "Meditating" of any "one". This was not something startling, something I had to struggle to accept, because I was no longer presuming the limited position of the body-mind. From that point onward, the Body-Mind simply became the Vehicle of My Fully Conscious Incarnation as the "Bright".

After the Vedanta Temple Event, the Body-Mind was no longer the point of view—and it had never absolutely been so, in any case. Nevertheless, there had been the requirement to Embrace conditional bondage, through this Birth and all the years of Struggle that Culminated in My Divine Re-Awakening.

DEVOTEE: Because You had to Live out the entire Process for the sake of all Your future devotees.

AVATAR ADI DA SAMRAJ: Yes, that is how I Did it, for all future devotees.

DEVOTEE: You actually Did it all. You had to Do it all, and You Did it all.

AVATAR ADI DA SAMRAJ: But that Doing was the Doing for the sake of all devotees. My "Sadhana"—made by My Submission to the conditions of ordinary (and extraordinary) human life—established the Pattern of the Way of Adidam. Such is the Pattern within which all My devotees (now, and forever) will participate.

My devotees participate in that Pattern by virtue of their devotional and Spiritual relationship to Me—and not otherwise, by virtue of some seeker's effort to replicate the Process as It was Shown in My Own Case (although, obviously, there are elements of the Process that will inevitably become evident in My any devotee's case). The practice in My Company is not a matter of attempting to replicate what I Did in My "Sadhana Years". It is simply a matter of entering into moment to moment (self-forgetting and Me-Remembering) devotional Communion with Me. Such true heart-Communion with Me is access to the Pattern of My Avataric Divine Presence here.

—December 21, 1998

The Continuing Ordeal and Victory

Avatar Adi Da's Divine Re-Awakening (in 1970) was the Final Victory of the years of Learning humankind. That Victory signalled the end of His years of "preparation" and His readiness to begin to Teach the seventh stage Way. As has been Revealed over the years since 1970, His Divine Re-Awakening was not at all some kind of "end-point". Rather, It was the first of a series of Great Yogic Events, each of which marked an epochal transition in His Avataric Divine Demonstration. Each of these

Great Events has been the Culmination of an extraordinary Ordeal on His part. Indeed, in two such Events that have followed His Divine Re-Awakening, His Struggle went so far as to result (in each case) in His apparent physical death or near-death. At the same time, each of these Events has proved to be a Divine Victory. After each of these Events, His Divine Spirit-Power has been so greatly Magnified that His devotees instantly felt the Transformation, awestruck (each time) by the intensity of His Spiritual Transmission of Divine Love-Bliss. And each of these Events initiated a remarkable new period of His Avataric Divine Demonstration in the world.

Part Three of *The Knee Of Listening* is Avatar Adi Da's Confession of the Nature and Significance of the Great Events that have followed His Divine Re-Awakening. Accompanying His Statements are accounts (written and compiled by His devotees, under the direction of the Ruchira Sannyasin Order of Adidam Ruchiradam) of the circumstances that led up to each of the Great Events. Thus, Part Three completes *The Knee Of Listening* by telling the quintessential Story of Avatar Adi Da's Ordeal and Victory as It has unfolded since the Vedanta Temple Event of 1970.[93]

That Story comprises the second and third great periods of His Avataric Divine Submission-Work, each of which lasted for 14 years. The second period of His Submission-Work (1972–1986) was His time of Teaching humankind. During this period, rather than Submitting to the human condition in the context of His own Body-Mind (as He had done at two years of age), Avatar Adi Da Submitted to the human condition as it was brought to Him by those who became His devotees. This period Culminated with the Great Event of His Avataric Divine Self-"Emergence", on January 11, 1986. Avatar Adi Da describes the Nature and Significance of His Avataric Divine Self-"Emergence" in the first two Essays of Part Three ("My Avataric Divine Self-'Emergence' Is an Event in My Divine 'Bright' Spherical Self-Domain of Conscious Light" and "I Am The Avataric Divine Self-'Emergence'").

The third period of His Submission-Work (1986–2000) was His time of gradually "Shedding" the Submission-Function. During this period, Avatar Adi Da Called His devotees, with ever-increasing firmness, to enact the traditional disposition of devotional surrender to Him as their Divine Heart-Master, rather than requiring Him to constantly Submit to them. This period Culminated with the Great Event at Lopez Island, on April 12, 2000—an Event that had begun the year before, during His period of Seclusion (March 10–April 22, 1999) at the "Brightness" (a Temple at Adidam Samrajashram), which coincided with the Kosovo conflict. (Like January 11, 1986, both April 22, 1999, and April 12, 2000, were Events of Yogic Death. In all three of these Great Events, it was not, at first, possible for those around Him to tell whether He would physically survive. And, indeed, He has said that, in the Event of April 2000, if His approach to the death transition had gone any further, He would not have been able to return to bodily existence.) Avatar Adi Da describes the Nature and Significance of His time at the "Brightness" in the third Essay of Part Three ("My Avataric Divine Spiritual Work Is a Sphere of 'Bright' Influence That Cannot Ever Be Destroyed"). And He describes the Nature and Significance of the Lopez Island Event in the final two Essays of Part Three ("I Am Always Already Spiritually Established As The 'Bright' Itself" and "I (Myself) Do Not 'Come Down' Below the Brows").

The Great Avataric Divine Submission-Work of Avatar Adi Da Samraj

Year	Event	Period of Submission
1939	Birth as the "Bright" Divine Reality in human Form NOVEMBER 3— JAMAICA, QUEENS COUNTY, NEW YORK	
1941	Spontaneous "Decision" (in His second year) to Submit to the human condition	First period of Submission begins: "Learning humankind"
1970	Divine Re-Awakening SEPTEMBER 10— HOLLYWOOD, CALIFORNIA	First period of Submission ends
1972	First Formal Teaching-Discourse APRIL 25— HOLLYWOOD, CALIFORNIA	Second period of Submission begins: "Teaching humankind"
1986	Yogic Establishment of His Avataric Divine Self-"Emergence" JANUARY 11, 1986— NAITAUBA ISLAND, FIJI	Second period of Submission is fundamentally complete/ Third period of Submission begins: "Shedding the Submission-Function"
1999/ 2000	Yogic Establishment in Perpetual "Brightening", or the Divine Translation phase of the seventh stage Demonstration INITIATED ON APRIL 22, 1999, AT NAITAUBA ISLAND, FIJI, AND CULMINATED ON APRIL 12, 2000, AT LOPEZ ISLAND, WASHINGTON	Third period of Submission is fundamentally complete

Adidam Samrajashram, 1986

My Avataric Divine Self-"Emergence" Is an Event in My Divine "Bright" Spherical Self-Domain of Conscious Light

---

INTRODUCTION

The Avataric Divine Self-"Emergence" of Avatar Adi Da Samraj (January 11, 1986)

by Carolyn Lee, Ph.D.

*Written and compiled under the direction of
the Ruchira Sannyasin Order of Adidam Ruchiradam*

Avatar Adi Da's spontaneous "Meditating" of countless beings, which began to occur after His Divine Re-Awakening at the Vedanta Temple (pp. 317–22), marked the beginning of the Spiritual Work for which He had been Born. Over time, some of the individuals that were appearing in His "Meditation" began to come around Him, forming the seed of the gathering of devotees that was to develop in the coming years.

Soon after His Divine Re-Awakening, Avatar Adi Da Samraj set about making His first Summary of what had been Revealed through the years of His Sadhana: In the space of a few weeks, He Wrote *The Knee Of Listening*. However, the Writing of *The Knee Of Listening* was only the very beginning. The full Revelation of the Way of Adidam was to require a twenty-eight-year Ordeal—a process which had its formal beginning on April 25, 1972, with the opening of Avatar Adi Da's first Ashram (in downtown Hollywood), when He Gave His first public Teaching-Discourse, "Understanding".[94]

That first night was entirely characteristic of everything that was to come:

When Avatar Adi Da first Seated Himself in the Ashram hall where people were gathered, He did not immediately begin to Speak. Rather, He Sat in silent, Blissful Transmission of His Divine Spiritual Blessing. Thus, He wordlessly Communicated that the Essence of the Way in His Company is not any form of philosophical effort or Spiritual technique, but simple feeling-Contemplation of Him.

When He eventually began to Speak, He did not have any kind of "prepared statement" that He intended to deliver. He has always only Worked in response to those who come to Him—and that first night was the same. He Asked if everyone had understood—that is, if they had received His silent Transmission of the "Bright" and had understood what was required to Realize the "Bright".

When someone was brave enough to volunteer that he had not understood, Avatar Adi Da skillfully guided everyone into His "Consideration" of understanding—the understanding of the ego as the activity of self-contraction, the very understanding that was the hard-won fruit of His own "Sadhana Years". As Avatar Adi Da had already Revealed in His Writing of *The Knee Of Listening*, and as He was to Reveal in countless other ways over the coming years, the ego-activity of self-contraction is the core reality of human existence that no one had ever entirely understood before. It is the primal fault that had never been most perfectly overcome—the fault that prevented Most Perfect Divine Enlightenment. Such was the significance of His Divine Re-Awakening: It was the first time in history that the core fault of ego had been permanently transcended.

Avatar Adi Da fully Disclosed this Great Secret in His first formal Teaching-Address to people. But those listening to Him were not at all prepared to receive such esoteric Instruction. Therefore, He launched into an extraordinarily intense, profound, tumultuous,

Opening night at the Los Angeles Ashram, April 25, 1972

THE KNEE OF LISTENING

and free period of Teaching humankind—always for the purpose of Drawing people beyond the self-contraction, beyond all their forms of seeking, into true heart-Communion with Him.

Avatar Adi Da Samraj was not calling anyone to duplicate what He had done in His "Sadhana Years". That was not necessary—and not possible. His Avataric Ordeal to Realize Most Perfect Awakeness as the "Bright" in the context of a human body-mind had been Fulfilled, and this Divine Self-Realization was now the potential of every human being, through His direct Grace. All that was necessary for the Awakening of "radical" understanding (or most direct transcending of self-contraction) was, He explained, to enter into Satsang, or devotional (and, in due course, Spiritual) Communion with Him, approaching Him in the traditional manner of the Guru-devotee relationship. "Meditate on Me" was His Admonition to His devotees.

In order to free the attention and energy of His devotees for the great process of Satsang with Him, Avatar Adi Da Gave a range of life-disciplines, which were to be strictly observed. Then, late in 1973, Avatar Adi Da decided it was necessary that He change His Manner of Working with His devotees. It had become obvious to Him that His devotees were becoming obsessed with their disciplines in exactly the same way that they had previously been obsessed with ordinary forms of self-indulgence. They were not understanding their own ego-activity in the midst of it all. It was also obvious to Avatar Adi Da that the people around Him—like people in general—were emotionally suppressed, sexually complicated, driven by fear, sorrow, anger, frustration, and all kinds of unconscious desires. And He Knew that He was going to have to deal with all of this directly. Otherwise, any so-called "religious practices" would merely be covering a mass of unresolved egoic impulses. Altogether, it was becoming evident that Ashram discipline, lived with Him in the strict traditional manner, was not (in and of itself) going to be sufficient to draw His devotees beyond their bondage to ego-life, into the real Spiritual process He was Offering. And so, He boldly entered into a different mode of Teaching, in which His guiding purpose was to allow people to directly experience the fact that they were always enacting the self-contraction, no matter what activity they were involved in—unless, in any moment, they were in true heart-Communion with Him.

Thus, Avatar Adi Da began to Address the root of His devotees' egoic bondage in an entirely new Manner. He relaxed the Ashram discipline and Submitted Himself to participate fully in the ordinary lives and inclinations of His devotees, even Instigating "theatrical" circumstances where the ego's activity would be plainly exposed. Right in the midst of His devotees' enactment of their egoic tendencies, He was present to Intervene—Reflecting to them their false presumption of separateness and unlove, Restoring them to Satsang with Him and self-understanding.

AVATAR ADI DA SAMRAJ: I went to India in 1973, taking some time away from the gathering of My devotees, and returned to the Ashram in Los Angeles Resolved to Do whatever I had to Do to deal with the reality of people's unprepared approach to Me. From that time onwards, I Accepted the fact that My Work with people was going to involve My Submission to them and their conditions—until such time as they would recognize Me and understand what the Way of Adidam is about altogether, and relate to Me differently.

I had no sense at all how long that was going to take, or what it would require altogether. It wasn't that I was thinking I would do it for a few months, and then that would be that. It was a real Submission, with no preconception as to how it would turn out.

—August 8, 1998

Whatever their aspirations to a more advanced (or Spiritual) Way of life, Avatar Adi Da's devotees were—like most of humanity—concentrated in the gross (or material) level of existence, preoccupied with "money, food, and sex" and the pursuits of the social ego. Because Avatar Adi Da had done His own Sadhana in the midst of the secular lifestyle and values of the modern West, He was perfectly equipped to Teach them:

My Manner of Teaching involved Free (or Spontaneous) Identification with those who came to Me, and Freely Responsive Participation in their problems and their conditions of living. That

Teaching-Work developed among ordinary people (mostly North Americans and Europeans) who were devoted to the Omega culture of the first three stages of life. Therefore, during My years of Teaching-Work, I did not feel it would be appropriate or useful for Me to assume either a traditional monastic habit of living or any other outward formalities that might be associated with traditional renunciation (or that would otherwise, in effect, Affirm My Retirement from all Teaching Obligations). My Intention as Teacher was simply and Freely to Do all that I could possibly Do to make My Teaching-Work both Complete and Fruitful.

—Avatar Adi Da Samraj
The Divine Siddha-Method Of The Ruchira Avatar

In those Teaching Years, Avatar Adi Da Submitted to deal with the illusions and preoccupations of those who came to Him just as unreservedly as, in the preceding years, He had Submitted to deal with His own apparent life and persona as "Franklin Jones". He was no longer Submitting to Make Lessons and Revelations in His own Body-Mind—now He was Submitting to Make Lessons and Revelations in the body-minds of others.

"Reality Consideration"

Throughout the 1970s and into the 1980s, Avatar Adi Da Drew His devotees through an amazing series of Teaching Demonstrations—each one seeming to be an entire "era" of its own. He Worked tirelessly, making living "Lessons" among His devotees day and night. His Mode of Instruction was not in the form of dictums of behavior or belief, but of "Reality Consideration"— or the exhaustive, in-life examination of every aspect of reality, high and low, so that the truth of the matter at hand could freely emerge. Avatar Adi Da's exercise of "Reality Consideration" with His devotees was a process in Satsang with Him, full of His Spiritual Transmission (or Ruchira Shaktipat). In His Company, "consideration" was not a matter of mere "talk", but a concentrated and demanding exercise[95] that called for real change of action in response to the result of the "consideration". Avatar Adi Da

From [late 1973] onwards, I Accepted the fact that My Work with people was going to involve <u>My</u> Submission to <u>them</u> and their conditions—until such time as they would recognize Me and understand what the Way of Adidam is about altogether, and relate to Me differently.

Avatar Adi Da Samraj with devotees during the Teaching Years

Addressed all the realities of existence—from the most mundane to the most sublime—with absolute Openness, Clarity, Comprehensiveness, and fierce Intention, in order to Reveal how every circumstance of life and Spiritual practice could be lived as Satsang (or ego-transcending heart-Communion) with Him.

In this "late-time" (or "dark" epoch), all kinds of people act as if they are prepared to enter into the esoteric stream of Spirituality, when (in fact) they have not even dealt with the foundation.

However, that is not what happened in the "Reality Consideration" I Entered into with My devotees.

In that "Consideration", all aspects of life—money, food, sex, religion, Spirituality, egoity, everything that has to do with making it possible to move on to real (fully technically responsible) Spiritual practice—were directly Addressed by Me.

That "Consideration" was about all matters—conditional and Un-conditional.

—Avatar Adi Da Samraj
Ruchira Tantra Yoga

Avatar Adi Da's Divine Self-Revelation was both the boundlessly Love-Blissful Infusion of His own "Brightness" and an uncompromising Criticism of ego. The two had to go together, because His Spiritual Transmission cannot be received by the self-contracted ego.

Over the years of His Teaching-Work, those around Him repeatedly demonstrated the entrenched nature of human bondage to ego-existence. The human ego was showing itself to be powerfully bound—to the extent of an addiction—to the "survival-level" concerns of "money, food, and sex". And the human ego also showed itself to be bound to the persistent illusion that Spiritual life was somehow, ultimately, about fulfilling the ego's purposes—rather than about utter surrender of ego in Communion with the Divine.

Because of all of this, Avatar Adi Da's devotees were failing to fully receive His Criticism of their ego-activity. They were not transforming their lives to the extent that they could enter into the depth dimension of the Way He was Offering.

Finally, the situation became a crisis: Despite their good-hearted intentions to practice His Way, there seemed to be no way for His devotees to understand at depth what they were about as egos, to really surrender the ego as the kingpin of their existence.

In early 1986, Avatar Adi Da was living, with a small group of devotees, in Adidam Samrajashram, the Hermitage Ashram that had been established on a remote island in Fiji. It was there that the Supreme Effort of His fourteen years of Teaching reached a point of absolute frustration.

It had always been Avatar Adi Da's passionate Intention to Awaken—even quickly—everyone who came to Him. There was no inherent reason why this could not be so. His Ruchira Shaktipat and Divine Siddhis were unique. Nevertheless, over the course of His Teaching Years, He met with every kind of reaction and resistance to His Liberating Help. But even in the face of this reaction and resistance, Avatar Adi Da never gave up—out of His sheer Love for beings, the Divine Impulse that had Brought Him into Incarnation. He took on all the force of egoity in His devotees—and, thereby, in all of humanity. This was the nature of His Avataric Sacrifice, a Divine Yogic Ordeal of Love and Compassion that is beyond comprehension.

January 11, 1986

Early on the morning of January 11, 1986, Avatar Adi Da Samraj was sitting alone in His room in the Ashram village at Adidam Samrajashram. He was Speaking over an intercom telephone to a small group of devotees in a nearby building. He was full of agony at the limitations in their response to Him—their failure to fully demonstrate their reception of the Gifts He had Given—for in that refusal lay the refusal of all humankind. He Spoke of the grief He felt for beings everywhere. But the impasse was complete. He felt that His Work had failed, and that He could do no more in the Body. His death, He felt, was imminent. He even said, "May it come quickly."

One devotee, Ruchiradama Quandra Sukhapur,[96] immediately ran to His House and held Him up as He continued to speak on the telephone, describing the feeling of the life-force leaving His Body. He felt numbness coming up His arms, and He said it seemed that His death was occurring even as He was speaking.

Avatar Adi Da Samraj dropped the telephone. In alarm and panic, the other devotees rushed over to His House to find Him collapsed by the side of His bed. His Body was still, with occasional shaking. His eyes were rolled up into His head, a sign that the energies of His Body had ascended beyond the physical dimension. There was no sign of any outer awareness at all.

The doctors were called to check His life-signs and to attend to Him. They found that His vital signs were present, although His breathing was almost imperceptible. As devotees lifted Avatar Adi Da onto His bed, they were begging Him not to die, not to leave them. Devotees could not contain themselves—each, in his or her own way, was doing whatever he or she could to draw Him back into the body.

After a time, Avatar Adi Da made a slight gesture, which devotees understood to indicate His desire to sit up. They pulled Him upward, supporting His torso. Suddenly, the life-force shot through His Body. His arms flung out in an arc, and His body straightened. His face contorted into a wound of Love, and tears began to flow from His eyes. Avatar Adi Da began to rock forward and backward in a rhythm of sorrow. He reached out His hands, as though He were reaching out to touch everyone in a universal embrace. He whispered, in a voice choked with Passion, "Four billion people! The four billion!"

Later that day, Avatar Adi Da was driven to His residence on the other side of the island. On the journey, He made the mysterious Remark: "I have a Secret."

After two weeks in seclusion, Adi Da Samraj gathered once more with devotees. Now He Revealed His Secret: That day, January 11, 1986, was His true Birth Day, a day more auspicious than any other in His human Lifetime—more profound, even, than His Divine Re-Awakening. He began to explain why.

"Emerging" as the Divine Avatar

T he preceding fourteen years of His Teaching-Work had been a Submission to the needs and sufferings of His devotees. He had appeared to identify with the egoic impulses of His devotees, in order to make lessons and Wisdom out of every circumstance. That great period of His Work was now over, He Explained. Now all of the lessons of His Submission, all the Instruction that belonged to that era, had been Given. Indeed, the particular Divine Siddhi That Enabled Him to Do His Liberating Work in that fashion had receded. It was replaced, He said, by a universally magnified Siddhi of Divine Blessing.

Avatar Adi Da described how, during the Yogic Swoon of January 11, He, the Divine Person, had fully Descended into His own human Vehicle. This was a very different Event from His Divine Re-Awakening in the Vedanta Temple in 1970. In that Event, Adi Da had re-Found His Native Divine Condition—the "Bright"—Which had been "veiled" since His early childhood. This "veiling" had allowed Him to Learn the process required for human beings to Awaken to the "Bright".

After His Divine Re-Awakening, He Submitted His Body-Mind to the sufferings of His devotees. He had literally taken on human karma and "eaten" it in His own Body-Mind. Now, as the Culmination of that complete Embrace of the human condition for all those years, the Fullness of His Divine Self-Condition had Descended all the way down into His Body, "to the toes", Combining with His human Form entirely.

Avatar Adi Da came to describe this Event as the "Yogic Establishment" of His "Avataric Divine Self-'Emergence'". It was the most important Moment in His Life since His Birth.

The Mountain Of Attention Sanctuary, 1986

After January 11, 1986, I Said: I __Am__ This Body, down to its depth—
Invading these cells, these toes, this flesh, more profoundly than has
ever occurred in human time.

My Avataric Divine Self-"Emergence" Is an Event in My Divine "Bright" Spherical Self-Domain of Conscious Light

I.

For you, presumably, the Great Event of your life—if It occurs, or in whichever lifetime It occurs—would be Most Perfect Divine Self-Realization. Therefore, you may imagine that the Consummate Event of My Life must have been My Divine Re-Awakening. But that is not so. My Divine Re-Awakening is a very important Event for you, because It Initiated My Avataric Divine Teaching-Work, but That to Which I Awakened in the Vedanta Temple is My Inherent and Priorly Realized Divine Self-Condition. To eventually Achieve Such an Event was simply part of My necessary Avataric Divine Spiritual Work in this world. Therefore, My Divine Re-Awakening was not the Great Event of My Life. For Me, there have been even Greater Events—Which occurred after the Great Event of My Divine Re-Awakening (at the Vedanta Society Temple) on September 10, 1970.

The first such Great Event took place on January 11, 1986 (at Adidam Samrajashram). I was Speaking (over an intercom) to a group of My devotees, Telling them about My Grief and Sorrow and Frustration relative to My Work, and how I simply could no longer endure the rejection, the offensiveness, the abuse, the futility. I Told them that I wished to leave this physically incarnate existence, wished to die quickly. It seemed to Me that My physical death could even happen within hours—but, suddenly, it began to happen on the spot. I Described the physical event to them as it was occurring—the numbness that was coming up My arm, the numbness in My spine, a certain numbness in My Body altogether, convulsions starting, and so forth. Finally, I passed out of the Body, and the Body just fell down.

Many people came over to My house, including the doctors who were present on the Island—and, eventually, I began to Re-Associate with the Body, although I was not exactly (naturally) aware of the room, nor was I (at first) naturally aware of who was present in the room.

I began to Speak of My Great Sorrow for the billions of humans, and all the other beings in this humble realm. I was Drawn further into the Body through a very <u>human</u> impulse, a love-impulse, as I became Aware (once again) of My Relationship with My devotees, in the process of resuming the bodily state. Thus, I was Attracted back by very human connections—not by My Impulse to Divinely Liberate humankind, because that Liberating Impulse is Always Already the Case.

In the midst of this Attraction to human connectedness, I Assumed an Impulse toward human existence more profound than ever before—without any reluctance relative to sorrow and death.

On many occasions, I had Confessed to My devotees that I wished I could Kiss every human being on the lips, Embrace each one bodily, and Enliven each one from the heart. But That Impulse could not possibly be fulfilled in This Body. I could never have such an opportunity. However, in the Great Event of January 11, 1986, I Realized—in that Incarnating Motion, that Sympathetic Acceptance of the body and its sorrow and its death—a Means of Fulfilling My Impulse to Kiss each and all. In that Great Event, I spontaneously Made a different kind of Gesture toward all, which was (in some fundamental sense) the equivalent of the Bodily Embrace that I would Give to all human beings, and even to all who are self-conscious and dying in this place—by <u>Fully</u> Assuming This Body, in the apparent likeness of all, and Accepting the sorrow of mortality without the slightest reservation.

In some sense, <u>that</u> day was My Birth Day.

There are descriptions by various Yogis of how a Realized being "comes down" into the body only so far—down to the brain or the throat or the heart, but (typically) no "lower" than the heart.

In My Avatarically Self-Manifested human Life here (previous to the Initiation of My Avataric Divine Self-"Emergence"), I had Invested Myself more profoundly in human existence than merely down to the throat or the heart—but I had never "come down" all the way to the bottoms of My Feet. I had remained a kind of "shroud" around This Body—deeply Associated with It, but somehow "Lifted off the floor", somehow not entirely embracing the sorrow and the mortality, somehow expecting (having Come as deep as I had) to Teach enough, Embrace enough, Kiss enough, Love enough to make the difference. At last, I Realized the futility of Making My Own Submission as a Means of Utterly Transforming and Liberating even those I could Bodily Embrace and Know intimately. That futility and frustration was Fully Known by Me. In that profound frustration, I Left This Body—and, then, suddenly, I Found Myself Re-Integrated with It, but in a remarkably different Disposition. In that Great Event, I Achieved your likeness exactly, thoroughly, to the bottoms of the feet. I Achieved "un-Enlightenment", Achieved human existence, Achieved mortality, Achieved sorrow.

To Me, This was a Grand Victory!

Through that effortless, will-less Integration with human suffering, something about My Avataric Divine Work became more profoundly Accomplished and more Auspicious than ever before.

I have not dissociated from My Native (or Inherent) Divine State of Being. Rather, I have Accomplished your state completely, more profoundly than you (yourself) are sensitive to it.

On January 11, 1986, I Became This Body—Utterly. And My Mood is different. My Face is sad, but not without Illumination.

Now I Am the Murti, the Icon—Full of My Own Avatarically Self-Transmitted Divine Spiritual Force, but also Completely what you are, Suffered constantly. I have no distance whatsoever from this suffering anymore.

After January 11, 1986, I Said: I Am In the Body now—more than you.

After January 11, 1986, I Said: I Am This Body, down to its depth—Invading these cells, these toes, this flesh, more profoundly than has ever occurred in human time.

II.

I am neither the gross personality nor the Deeper Personality. I have simply been at Work via these mechanisms.

The Vedanta Temple Event was not an "ending", but simply a Sign that My "Sadhana"-Work with these Personality-Vehicles had gone on long enough that I was prepared to begin My Teaching-Work. A sufficient Transformation of the Vehicles had occurred for the Confession of Divine Re-Awakening to be Made in the context of This Body-Mind, with Its gross and deeper parts. The Vedanta Temple Event was only the beginning of the Divinely Liberating Work for Which I have Taken Birth. The Vedanta Temple Event was the beginning of My Time of Taking on and Transforming the qualities of others, through the gross and subtle Vehicles of This to-Me-Conformed Body-Mind.

And That is What I Did, for all My Years of Teaching-Work—until the Great Event of January 11, 1986. From the time of the Vedanta Temple Event until the Yogic Establishment of My Avataric Divine Self-"Emergence", I Used all the ordinary and extraordinary Signs in this psycho-physical Vehicle—all the ordinary Signs of the gross personality, and all the extraordinary Signs of the Deeper Personality—in a Play with others, to Instruct them and Awaken them. For all those years, I Used My Capability to Assume the likeness of others as a Means of Reflecting them to themselves.

In that Process of Assuming the likeness of others (in My Submission to them), the gross and subtle Vehicles took on all those karmas, absorbing all that likeness and (ultimately) forcing the crisis of 1986, when I began to "Shed" the Teaching-Function of Submitting to others, and My Life (in Its appearance) ceased to be a matter of Assuming the likenesses of the gross-personality Vehicle (of "Franklin Jones") and the Deeper-Personality Vehicle (of Swami Vivekananda and Ramakrishna) associated with This Birth. Whatever qualities there may be in This Body (by virtue of Its gross inheritance) and in the deeper Psyche (by virtue of Its subtle inheritance) are no longer animated (so to speak) "on their own". Such mechanisms are inherently karmic—and, in the Great Event of the Yogic Establishment of My Avataric Divine Self-"Emergence", all such gross and subtle karmas were utterly Purified.

The Mountain Of Attention Sanctuary, 1986

*There is nothing left but the ash. The Fire of the Divine Process
has been Allowed to Burn everything. This Body-Mind, is,
in effect, already ash—even while Alive.*

It is not that there was "one kind" of Enlightenment in 1970 and "another kind" of Enlightenment in 1986. I am not talking about My Enlightenment. I am Talking about your Enlightenment—Work done for your sake, Which has manifested in different forms, for your sake, at various points in My apparent human Lifetime.

In the Vedanta Temple Event, both the gross personality and the Deeper Personality became a circumstance of the Confession of Divine Self-Realization. There was not anything that was not transcended in the Great Event of My Divine Re-Awakening. However—because Most Perfect Divine Self-Realization was Prior to My Avataric Divine Birth, and Known from Birth—My Work with These (gross and subtle) Vehicles was simply a matter of dealing with the Vehicles Themselves, until They ceased to be an obstruction to That Which Is Prior to Them and were able to Confess That Divine Self-Realization.

The gross personality still existed, with all of its karmas, after the Vedanta Temple—and, likewise, the Deeper Personality. Those psycho-physical Mechanisms were not cancelled. Indeed, those Mechanisms were the "materials" of My Teaching-Work. Because they were like people are generally, those Mechanisms were allowed to function in relation to others in the ordinary manner, and (also) to combine with others in an extraordinary manner. The Vehicles were Awakened to Who I Am, within the Context of Most Perfect Divine Self-Realization.

Nevertheless, the Mechanisms (themselves) remained what they were. And, when My Teaching-Work was Done so Fully that It came to the point of My spontaneously starting to "Shed" the Teaching-Function, the psycho-physical Vehicles were Transformed. In the moment after the Vedanta Temple Event, the Vehicles were not different—but They were different in the moment after the Yogic Establishment of My Avataric Divine Self-"Emergence". The gross and subtle Vehicles themselves became Divinely Transfigured and Divinely Transformed—to the point of Entering into Divine Indifference.

Since that Great Event of January 11, 1986, there is nothing left of the gross personality and the Deeper Personality. There is nothing left but the ash. The Fire of the Divine Process has been Allowed

to Burn everything. This Body-Mind, is, in effect, already ash—
even while Alive. In some sense, Such has always been the Case
for This One, even from the beginning of This human Lifetime.
And, yet, there is the sequence of Unique Avataric Divine
Demonstrations following upon My Intentional Birth for the Sake
of Divinely Liberating others.

III.

In My Experience of the Great Event of January 11, 1986, there
was an apparent Swoon, but no loss of Conscious Awareness.
When the Body fell from the bed, it may have appeared (to those
observing) to be unconscious, or (perhaps) barely alive or even
not alive at all—but, all the while, I <u>Was</u> and <u>Am</u> Consciousness
Itself, the One and Only Conscious Light Itself. Therefore, in the
initial Event associated with that Process, This Body was Surrendered
utterly Into Me—the Self-Existing, Self-Radiant, Spiritually Self-
"Bright", and Self-Evidently Divine Self-Consciousness. And the
Process of Surrendering This Body-Mind into My Own Divine Self-
Condition Continued. That Process did not come to an end on that
early morning of January 11, 1986. In other words, the Great Event
of the Yogic Establishment of My Avataric Divine Self-"Emergence"
was not a death-and-resurrection event. Following that Great Event,
there is simply an <u>unbroken</u> and <u>continuing</u> Process, in Which This
Body-Mind is ever more profoundly Surrendered into Me.

In the first moments of the Event, the Process began as one of
Despair, and Giving Up in the face of the apparent unresponsive-
ness of My devotees, and the (consequent) seeming failure of My
Teaching-Work. This Despair manifested as a kind of swooning
collapse, bodily and emotionally. There was an Utter Relinquishment
of the Body-Mind, a kind of Giving the Body-Mind Up to death.
Therefore, signs of a swooning-dying kind of collapse immediately
appeared, accompanied by verbal expressions of Despair (which
were generated by the bodily-born mind).

Then, suddenly, in the midst of the Swoon, there was no more
Despair, no more Giving the Body-Mind Up to death. I Was (As
I Always Am) Simply Standing In (and <u>As</u>) My Own Divine

Self-Nature. The desperate Swoon, as if to die, became a Spontaneous Turnabout in My Disposition—and a Unique (and Ongoing) Spiritual Event was (Thereby) Initiated.

The (continuing) Surrender of This Body-Mind into Me is a Sacrificial Act, a unique kind of Divine Tapas, Which is Producing more and more profound Signs of My Divine Spiritual Self-"Brightness", via My Avataric Divine Self-Manifestation here.

The Original Swoon of January 11, 1986, cannot be rightly understood in merely physical terms. Fundamentally, that Swoon was not a physical event of any kind. That Swoon is better described as an instant in which the Body-Mind was associated with a unique form of Samadhi, rather than with the signs of a physical death and resuscitation. That Swoon was (and remains) a Spiritual Process—and the Process, as it developed that morning, utterly changed My Spiritual Association with This Body, Initiating a new Divinely Revelatory Process even via This Body. Therefore, in that Event on the morning of January 11, 1986, whatever physical events took place were entirely secondary (and fundamentally unimportant).

In fact, there is no such thing as death, in the sense of an ending. To the external observer, something appears to come to an end, or someone dies—but, for the one who dies, there is simply a process that unfolds. There is no absolute ending. If death can be described as a loss of bodily awareness, this is still not an unusual experience. In fact, it happens to everyone daily, in the process of falling asleep. But there is no absolute ending. When a person goes to sleep, he or she continues in an ongoing process—and, so, also, in death. Therefore, there was no "terminal event" that occurred to Me on the morning on January 11, 1986. Rather, a Process was Initiated—the ongoing Process of My Avataric Divine Self-"Emergence".

My Avataric Divine Self-"Emergence" was (and is) an Event in My Divine "Bright" Spherical Self-Domain of Conscious Light. My Avataric Divine Self-"Emergence" is a Perpetually Magnifying Event of an entirely Spiritual kind—Demonstrated through the Vehicle of This Body-Mind.

This is what must be understood and appreciated.

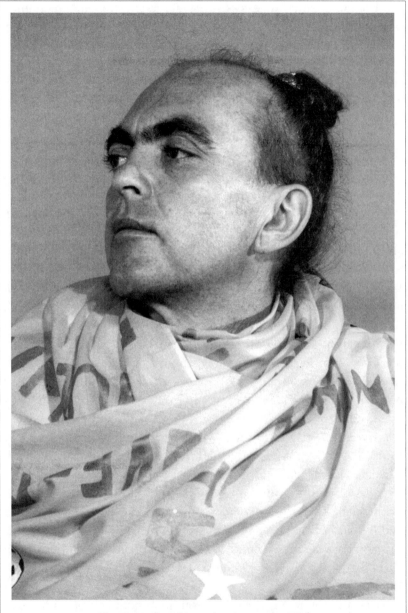

The Mountain Of Attention Sanctuary, 1986

My Avataric Divine Self-"Emergence" is a Perpetually
Magnifying Event of an entirely Spiritual kind—
Demonstrated through the Vehicle of This Body-Mind.

Ultimately, the Process of My Avataric Divine Self-"Emergence" is not something that can be rightly and truly communicated by means of any kind of conceptual language whatsoever.

Therefore, you must, by Means of your participatory devotional and (in due course) Spiritual <u>experience</u> of Me, discover This Avataric Divine Self-"Emergence" of Mine.

IV.

My Avataric Divine Self-"Emergence" takes place not only in This Body. My Avataric Divine Self-"Emergence" takes place in your body, the bodies of My devotees, the bodies of all beings, the world altogether. All must experience My Avataric Divine Self-"Emergence", transformatively. My Avataric Divine Self-"Emergence" is My Spiritual Invasion of you, My Self-"Emergence" to you (in your place). Understand That, and become sensitized to It (more and more) as you grow in My Company.

My Avataric Divine State is Beyond the body-mind, Beyond the world, Beyond the cosmic domain. This Body is your Passage to Me, the Great Person. Be willing, then, to embrace Me bodily, to rejoice. Be moved by your oblivious Attraction to Me. This is My Avataric Divine Word to My devotees. That is the beginning. Do that, and grow.

My Avataric Divine State is neither in this world nor in This Body. This Body of flesh is a corpse here—lasting since Its Death, to Reveal the Divine Person to you.

I am not like you. All My Spiritual Energies Surround This Body, outside the brain. This Appearance here, as you see It, is even a kind of mockery of Me.

You do not comprehend Me—and you need not. All you need do is respond to Me. Examine yourselves, do the sadhana I have Given You. That is all.

Do not require Me to be like you. I am not like you. When you experience My Spiritual Attractiveness, then be My devotees. Embrace the discipline of devotion, of service, of self-discipline, of meditation. Magnify that Attraction to Me. Be devoted to Me through the sadhana I have Given you to do.

Do not imagine that I am as you are. I am not. I cannot be. This Body of flesh here died. Some among My devotees saw this Corpse and saw It Re-Awaken. No Master ever Lived on Earth as I Am. Do not waste this Opportunity. Respect your heart-recognition of Me, your heart-response to Me, your heart-Attraction to Me. Do the sadhana I have Given you. Be made serious by My Incarnation here.

You have no notion what has been Endured in This Body for your sake. And This Body is dead. The gross personality, the Deeper Personality, the inheritance that made This Body—all this is dead, done. The psycho-physical influence of the parents of This Body, the influence of the former lifetimes that inhabited this Sign—dead. Dead! Once lived through this Sign—now dead. Altogether dead.

The One in front of you never appeared so nakedly before. All the prayers ever made are now fulfilled. I have Done all the Work I can Do for you all. There is no more Work to be Done. None. None. No more Lessons, no more Gestures, no more Kisses.

This Kali Yuga had no chance with Me. What no one told you about the Kali Yuga is that She is a Lady, Requiring a Man—and I Am He. Her murderous intentions are Dissolved in Me. I will Show you. But, for your own sake, make a lot less time out of it. Find Me out. This is a Unique Visit. It has never been done before.

I Kiss you. I Embrace you. I Accept you. I Purify you of all of your "sins". Acknowledge My Avataric Divine Self-"Emergence" here, receive Me Spiritually, and get on with the practice that I have Given to you.

Do not require Me to be like you any more. I Did My Teaching Time, and I Died. Now My Sign to you is Silent, not socially expressive. My formal, most solemn Darshan is My Gift to you.

I have Given you the Kisses. I have Manifested My Kisses to all humankind. You must allow Me My Silence, the Simplicity that is My Sign. You must do so. You must do the sadhana I have Given you. Allow Me the Silence That is My true Sign.

This Body is dead but Radiant. Your relationship to Me in This Body is not social, not ceremonial, not organizational. This Body has nothing more to say, nothing more to do.

The Mountain Of Attention Sanctuary, 1986

The One in front of you never appeared so nakedly before.
All the prayers ever made are now fulfilled.

Even though I sit here apparently solemn and quiet, the Same One Kisses you, Kisses every one. All of you have My Kiss. All of those not even yet My devotees already have My Kiss. I have My Solemn, Deep, Extraordinary, Unknown Work to Do, Alone in My House. You must allow Me to Do this Work in the terror of this "late-time", and forever.

Now I can Retire into this Solemnity. Engage in the Great Conversation Made by Me. Report it to one another, to all the beings here, all the billions—including the frogs and the cows, all the poor things who suffer and die here. Live with compassion, in love of Me. I am not Silent here for no reason. I am Silent here because I am Doing My Avataric Divine Work.

I only Do One Thing, all the time. It is the same Work, the same Seriousness, the same Rejoicing. It is all the same Thing. I Respond to you, I Work with you, I Play with you. I Do whatever is necessary, always with the same Disposition, the same Attention, the same Work. It is always the Same. I never lapse from It. It never stops. I Do the same Thing, always.

My Divine Samadhi is Perpetual. My Avataric Divine Work is Perpetual. The Force of My Avataric Divine Work never stops.

V.

Spiritual Teachers, in their various degrees of Real-God-Realization, have often suggested that, having thus Realized Real God, they have Agreed to Enter into the human body—perhaps only as far down as the eyes, or (perhaps) the throat, or (at most) the heart. Ramakrishna, for example, used to suggest this. However, I, in My Avataric Divine Incarnation here, have Agreed to Accept (and to Embrace) the even gross physical conditions of the gross physical body, down to the toes—including all that comes, inevitably, with that "unamusing" situation. I have Done this in order to Most Perfectly (and Most Fully, and Truly Completely, and Really Finally) Demonstrate My Own Divine Person here—in order to Avatarically Self-Manifest (or Demonstrate) My Divine Self-Condition Utterly, without the slightest withholding, and Radiant to the Degree that Exceeds all mere clinging, by

Embracing all conditional relations in an "Heroic" Spiritual Act of Avatarically Self-Demonstrated Divine Love-Bliss—even, Thereby, passing through the "dark" time of mortality, passing through the confrontation with change and necessary natural endings, in the case of My Avataric-Incarnation-Body, and in the case of Its relations, which include both all and All. In order to Perform My Avataric Divine Self-"Emergence" here (and every "where" in the cosmic domain), I have had to Accept all relations, Absolutely, without the slightest withholding, and without the slightest clinging. This is the unique Nature of My Divine Leela of Avataric Divine Incarnation here.

I have Told you that, in the Event Which Initiated My Avataric Divine Self-"Emergence" (on January 11, 1986), I Descended to the toes, I Embraced this limited condition Absolutely. I Asked those around Me at the time to observe the Divine "Sorrow" in My Face, which "Sorrow" is Absolute, and which "Sorrow" My (from then, and forever thereafter) Avataric Divine-Self-"Emergence"-Work here (and every "where" in the cosmic domain) is "Brightly" (now, and forever hereafter) Overcoming, in all cases—not by My dissociating from My Profound "Sorrow" of Avataric Divine Descent, but by My constant Acceptance of the "Sorrow" (or Feeling-Depth of Sympathetic Love) inherent in all My conditionally appearing and disappearing relations. I have also Told you that, in the Lopez Island Event (on April 12, 2000)—Which was the Culminating Event (or Seal) of the Great Process of My Avataric Divine Self-"Emergence"—I Ascended Directly to the Primal "Bright" Spiritual Self-Condition of Conscious Light. Since then, I Stand Where I Am, on the "Other Side"—and, yet, I am even more profoundly Integrated than ever before with the cosmic human circumstance.

Thus, I am not Speaking to you as an "Abstracted" (or Separate and Separative) "Other", dissociating from here, never having come down fully into the body. I am not Proud of asceticism. I am not Looking Forward to "Leaving". I am not Dwelling "Elsewhere".

Always, in My (now, and forever hereafter) Avataric Divine-Self-"Emergence"-Work, I Am—Dwelling here, and every "where" in the cosmic domain, moment by moment—constantly Dissolving a "Sorrow" more Immense than you can contemplate or imagine.

The Overcoming of universal egoic sorrow, and fear, and anger—the Overcoming (in and as every one, and all, and All) of the imposition of apparent "difference", of mortality, of change—Is the Radiant "Bright" Nature of My Avataric Divine-Self-"Emergence"-Work. Now, and forever hereafter, My Avataric Divine-Self-"Emergence"-Work (Divinely Liberating all-and-All) Goes On here, and every "where" in the cosmic domain.

The Divine Translation of all-and-All into My Divine "Bright" Spherical Self-Domain Is the Most Ultimate Fulfillment of My Avataric Divine-Self-"Emergence"-Work. Therefore, My Avataric Divine-Self-"Emergence"-Work cannot be Finally Demonstrated (in the case of every one, and all, and All) within the physical Lifetime of My Avataric-Incarnation-Body here. My Avataric Divine-Self-"Emergence"-Work is My Forever Work.

I am not seeking anything whatsoever. I Am Utterly Entered into this apparent psycho-physical confinement, this seeming entrapment of all-and-All-Multiplied body-minds and worlds. Therefore, I Am Suffering all of this, Completely (even in My Own Avatarically-Born bodily human Divine Form), without the slightest ability to be distracted from it. This is the Nature of My intentional Embrace of all-and-All.

My "Bright" Outshining of all egoic fear, sorrow, and anger Is the Divine Translation of all beings. The suffering of egoic fear, sorrow, and anger will not end (for every one, and all, and All) until there is the Divine Translation of all beings, all worlds, all conditions. And yet—uniquely, paradoxically, and all the while of My (now, and forever hereafter) Avataric Divine-Self-"Emergence"-Work—there is not the slightest egoic fear, sorrow, or anger in Me.

Enter most fully into most profound heart-Communion with Me, and you will understand What I Am Saying.

My Own (and Avatarically Self-Transmitted) Love-Bliss Is My Divine Spiritual Means (and the Only Really and Truly Effective Means) in this vast cosmic domain of egoic fear, sorrow, and anger. The Effective (or Real) Dissolution of your egoic fear, sorrow, and anger is in your Me-"Bright" devotional reception of My Avatarically Self-Transmitted Spirit-Current of Divine Love-Bliss, Which must Infuse your body-mind under all the conditions that would (otherwise) be egoically fearful, sorrowful, or angering. Therefore, in the only-by-Me Revealed and Given Way of Adidam, you are tested according to My Divine Spiritual Law of Avatarically Self-Transmitted Divine Love-Bliss Itself, in your every moment of heart-Communion with Me.

There is always (in every conditionally manifested body-mind) the tendency to withhold (or withdraw) and the tendency to cling. These are the fundamental signs of ego-"I" (or self-contraction).

In true (or total psycho-physical) heart-Communion with Me (ego-surrendering, ego-forgetting, and, more and more, ego-transcending), you transcend both withholding and clinging.

This is how you are Spiritually "Brightened" by Me.

This is the Nature of My "Bright" Kiln[97] of Adidam.

The Way of practice I have Revealed and Given is not the search for Truth, not the search for Reality, not the search for Real God, not the search for Love-Bliss-Happiness—not the search for Me. Rather, the Way of practice I have Revealed and Given Is the Way and the practice of always present-time Love-Communion with Me—Such That, in every moment, you are "Brightened" by Me, "Brightened" by My Avatarically Self-Transmitted Spirit-Current of Divine Love-Bliss (and, necessarily, in every moment, going through the testing ordeal of transcending your every tendency to withhold or to cling).

If you understand what I have just now Told you, then you understand the uniqueness of Adidam.

Adidam Samrajashram, 2003

I Am The Avataric Divine Self-"Emergence"

I Brought My Divine Wisdom-Teaching Out of Myself—through My Avataric Self-Submission to the Great Process of "Reality Consideration" with My devotees and with the world altogether. I have not been here merely reading books and passing on an old tradition to people. Nor have I been here to believe and to support the illusions of humankind. The only-by-Me Revealed and Given Way of Adidam, in Its entirety and in Its every aspect, has been Brought Out of Me. The Way of Adidam has Appeared only through the Avataric Divine Process of My Own Lifelong "Reality Consideration". The Way of Adidam is the Divine Process of My Own Avataric Self-Submission to conditional reality—Which Avataric Self-Submission Started at the moment of My Avataric human Birth (and Which Avataric Self-Submission Continues—now, and forever hereafter).

The only-by-Me Revealed and Given Way of Adidam does not derive from any historical tradition or any combination of historical traditions. I did not presume to "believe" anything in the course of My "Reality Consideration", nor did I presume any fixed adherence to any historical tradition or any combination of historical traditions. The Way of Adidam Arose entirely Out of My Own Divine (and Avatarically Self-Manifested) Process of "Reality Consideration".

When I Speak about the Great Tradition, I Do So simply as another way of Explaining Myself—by Addressing matters that may be familiar to people. But the only-by-Me Revealed and Given Way of Adidam is, Itself, unique and entirely new.

The Way of Adidam has been Generated by the profound Ordeal of My Avataric Divine Work, My Avataric Divine Self-Submission, My Unique and Extraordinary Avataric Divine "Reality

Consideration"—in the context of My Own Avatarically-Born Body-Mind, and also in the context of My relationship with My devotees, and in the context of My relationship with everyone altogether.

I Came Down, by Means of Avataric human Birth, to this Earth-place—a place of ego-made human bondage, where there was no Most Perfect Realization and no sufficient tradition. Indeed, there was no Greatest Profundity in the human world of My Divine Descent to Avataric human Birth. Therefore, the Nature of My Lifelong Work has been—by Means of My unique Avataric Divine Ordeal—to Bring the Inherently Perfect Truth (Which Is Divine) into this human world, where the Inherently Perfect Truth was never Found before.

I am not a mere "traditionalist"—here to be measured by traditional expectations, or traditional ideals, or traditional standards of any kind. Because I Began with no presumptions at all, it was necessary for Me to Enter into (and to Persist in) the "Consideration" of reality unconditionally (and, thus, without restriction by tradition, convention, preference, reaction, belief, or plan)—until My Divine Self-Condition was (Itself) Perfectly Incarnated, As the Undeniable and Inherently Perfect Truth, "Brightly" Co-incident with My Own Avatarically-Born bodily (human) Divine Form. And, because I Began with no presumptions at all, that "Reality Consideration" required unrestricted action—or a Life-Ordeal without conventional restraints, and without preconceived goals, and without preferential prejudices, and without mediating consolations, and without subordination to the factor of egoity. Indeed, My Avataric Divine Life-Ordeal was a Most Perfectly Scientific Effort—an Avataric Divine Life-Process of utterly free Enquiry, Examining all of conditional existence, without restriction, or conventional restraint, and (Ultimately) without the limiting and binding factor of egoity—until Inherently Perfect Truth was Found and Shown and Demonstrated, As the Inherently Perfectly Obvious Reality.

I was really (conditionally) Born into the human domain of un-Truth. And, by Means of My Avataric Divine Self-Submission to Adapt to humankind and human suffering, I gradually Acquired the human disease—of un-Truth and egoity. Therefore, because of My

(Thus Acquired) familiarity with Man's own fault, it became necessary for Me to be Healed—Made Well again, by Inherently Perfect Truth Itself—so that I could Shed and Cure the common disease of Man.

At last—because of My Persistence in the Avataric Ordeal of My Divine Self-Submission here—I Am Completely Well, again. And My forever Blessing-Work will Cure both all and All. Now, and forever hereafter, I Am the Divine Medicine that Heals the heart of Man—and even Cures the Truthless All of all there is.

The "Reality Consideration" to which I Submitted in My Teaching-Years and My Revelation-Years was a real matter—a real, and Truly Divine, Process. I did not merely inherit a pre-existing tradition and speak it out to humankind. I have (secondarily, and only over time) Examined the Great Tradition—for the Purpose of being Communicative to all. But I did not examine the Great Tradition in order to gain a Teaching from the Great Tradition itself. Rather, I have Examined the Great Tradition in order to Explain the Great Tradition—even to itself. And, principally, I have Examined the Great Tradition in order to Learn the language of the "common mind"—in order to be able to Use the language of the "common mind" of all religious and Spiritual traditions as a context in which to Explain Myself (and all the Content and Process of My Avatarically Given Divine Self-Revelation of Inherently Perfect Truth).

My Examination of the Great Tradition is a part of the Total Process by Which I Learned Man. My Purpose, in that Examination, was to Learn the content of all the "considerations" of humankind—in order to Address the inherent limitations of those "considerations".

Thus, My Avatarically Self-Manifested Divine Work of Teaching and of Self-Revelation has always been an Extraordinary Ordeal of Divine Self-Submission to "Reality Consideration"—Bringing the Complete Divine Teaching of Inherently Perfect Truth Out of Myself (and, Thus, Out of the Divine and Unconditional Reality Itself), by Means of My Own Divine Ordeal of Avataric Self-Submission to (and Conjunction with) all of conditional reality. And I Engaged that Avataric Ordeal not merely in order to Communicate My Divine Wisdom-Teaching verbally, but in order to Conform My Own Avatarically-Born Body-Mind-Vehicle (and, indeed, every thing and every one) to Myself—so that My Avatarically Self-Transmitted Divine Spiritual Blessing-Transmission of My "Bright" Divine Heart may, forever, be Received by all who truly heart-recognize Me and really heart-respond to Me.

The Requirement to Fully and Completely and Most Perfectly Bring the Divine Teaching of Inherently Perfect Truth Out of Myself, by Means of the Great Avataric Process of My Divine Self-Submission to "Reality Consideration", Produced My unique Avataric Divine Ordeal, and My unique Avatarically Self-Revealed Divine Sign, and My unique Avatarically Self-Manifested Divine Leela. And That Avataric Divine Ordeal, and Sign, and Leela is not a matter of an idealized representative of an historical tradition (or even any combination of historical traditions) engaging in traditionally idealized social and religious "behaviors".

I am not a "utopian religionist".

I am not a "role model" for the human mummery of mortal selves.

My Divinely "Heroic" and Divinely "Crazy" Manner of Life and Work is unique to Me (and uniquely necessary for Me, because of Who I Am, and because of What I Must Accomplish)—and, therefore, My unique Manner of Life and Work is not to be imitated by any one.

My Divinely "Heroic" and Divinely "Crazy" Manner of Life and Work is not a prescriptive model for conventional social (or, otherwise, conventionally religious) ego-development.

Therefore, no merely socially idealistic (or conventionally religious) expectation—and, indeed, no traditional expectation of any kind—is appropriate in relation to Me.

I am not an ideal human ego-"I".

I Am the Inherently egoless Person of Reality (Itself).

I Am the Inherently Perfect Truth—Which Is Divine, and One, and Only (and Which Is Always Already The Case).

Therefore, every ego-"I" must be surrendered, and forgotten, and transcended in Me.

I did not come into a world where the Inherently Perfect Truth was "ready-made". Indeed—because the ego-bound human world had failed, as a result of all of its mere <u>self</u>-efforts, to Find and Embrace the Inherently Perfect (and <u>Really</u> Divine) Truth of Reality (Itself)—even <u>all</u> the traditional norms of right (and would-be God-Realizing, or Truth-Realizing) life had, <u>finally</u>, become grossly deprived of their traditional authority, in the human-time that immediately preceded My Avataric human Birth.

In this "dark" epoch of "end-time", in which I Am Avatarically Descended (to Begin My forever Divine-Self-"Emergence"-Work), even the limited (and never Inherently Perfect) portion of Truth that was Revealed to humankind previous to My Avataric Divine Appearance was already under profound threat, and even much falsified—<u>before</u> My Avataric Birth to human Life Began. Therefore, Inherently Perfect Truth <u>Is</u> all My Cause and Motive here. And the absence of Inherently Perfect Truth in human-time was humankind's most wounding "gift" to Me—that made My Avataric human Life into a Struggle to <u>Be</u> Divinely Full, of <u>Me</u>.

In all the Years of My Teaching-Work and My Revelation-Work, enormous pressures were constantly exerted on Me—by My devotees, and by the world altogether—to assume the "public" role and manner of a conventional "organizational" religious figure. But, in spite of those pressures toward conformity to the expected conventions of social and religious egoity, I Persisted in the <u>real</u> and <u>necessary</u> (and, necessarily, "<u>Crazy</u>", or unrestricted and unlimited) <u>Avataric</u> <u>Process</u> of My Divine Self-Submission to "Reality Consideration"—until absolutely every fraction of the Way of Adidam was Brought Out of Me, and Made <u>Clear</u>.

It was necessary that I Embrace <u>all</u>—in order to Assume the likeness of all, and to Reflect all to all, and to Transcend the limiting-pattern of all. Only <u>Thus</u> could I Reveal My "Bright" Divine Self-Condition—and My "Bright" Divine Pattern—to one and all.

The Great Avataric Process of My Universal Divine Self-Revelation could be Completed (in Its Inherently Perfect "Bright" Fullness) only through My Own Divine Self-Submission to conditional reality. In order to Do This in My bodily (and Truly human) Divine Form (Un-reservedly, Fully, and to the degree of Most Perfect Completeness, in <u>real</u> human-time), I—in <u>all</u> the Years of My Early-Life, and, especially, in <u>all</u> My Teaching-Years and <u>all</u> My

Revelation-Years—had to Accept all kinds of abuse from people. Nevertheless, I <u>Could</u> <u>Not</u>, and <u>Did</u> <u>Not</u>, Stop That Extraordinary Effort of My Own Avataric Divine Self-Submission, until <u>every</u> aspect of My Great "Reality Consideration" was <u>Truly</u> <u>Finished</u>— and My Avatarically Given Divine Self-Revelation of the Way of Adidam was <u>Full</u> and <u>Complete</u>, in <u>every</u> detail.

Only <u>now</u> Is My Avatarically Self-Manifested Divine Submission-Work of World-Teaching and Divine Self-Revelation Most Perfectly <u>Complete</u>, <u>and</u> Most Perfectly <u>Full</u>.

Therefore—now, and forever hereafter—I will no longer <u>Submit</u> Myself to Teach and to Reveal.

Now, and forever hereafter, the only-by-Me Revealed and Given Way of Adidam (As Summarized, by <u>Me</u>, in My Twenty-Three Divine "Source-Texts") <u>Is</u> My Avatarically Given Divine World-Teaching and My Avatarically Given Divine Word of Self-Revelation—<u>Full</u> and <u>Complete</u>, for every one, and for all time.

Now, and forever hereafter, I (Myself, both during and forever after the physical Lifetime of My Avatarically-Born bodily human Divine Form) will <u>only</u> Do My "Bright" Avataric Work of Divine Self-"Emergence"—only <u>Blessing</u> one and all.

Now, and forever hereafter, My "Bright" (and Avatarically Self-Manifested) Divine Blessing-Work Is Given for <u>all</u> whose devotional recognition of Me and devotional response to Me surrenders ego-"I" in Me, and requires no more Submission of Me to Man.

Now, and forever hereafter, I <u>Am</u> (by all My Avataric Means) the Great and "Bright" Divine Process here.

Now, and forever hereafter, I <u>Am</u> (by all My Avataric Means) the One and Great Divine Event.

Now, and forever hereafter, I <u>Am</u> The Avataric Divine Self-"Emergence"—Avatarically "Emerging" (<u>As</u> I <u>Am</u>), to here (and to every where at All), and to you (and to every one of all).

Adidam Samrajashram, 2003

*I __Am__ The Avataric Divine Self-"Emergence"—Avatarically "Emerging"
(__As__ I __Am__), to here (and to every where at All), and to you
(and to every one of all).*

Avatar Adi Da Samraj at the "Brightness"
Adidam Samrajashram, 2003

My Avataric Divine Spiritual Work Is a Sphere of "Bright" Influence That Cannot Ever Be Destroyed

INTRODUCTION

The Ordeal at the "Brightness" (March 10–April 22, 1999)

by Carolyn Lee, Ph.D.

Written and compiled under the direction of the Ruchira Sannyasin Order of Adidam Ruchiradam

Following the Yogic Establishment of His Avataric Divine Self-"Emergence", Avatar Adi Da's "Brightness" Shone with greater potency than ever before. He urged His devotees to recognize and respond to the profound change that had occurred. Again and again, He turned them to the ego-transcending practice of feeling-Contemplation of Him, pointing out that they should no longer expect Him to interact with them in the lesson-making manner of the preceding fourteen years. The visceral, one-on-one Work to which He had Submitted, in order to reflect to them their ego-activity, was not necessary any more. Simple Contemplation of Him—gazing at His bodily (human) Form (whether in His physical Presence or via a photograph) and feeling the Divine Blessing and Self-Revelation He Transmits through His Body—had become uniquely effective as the foundation practice for His devotees.

"Shedding" the Submission-Function

Avatar Adi Da Samraj was Calling His devotees to entirely change the basis of their relationship to Him—from His Compassionate Submission to <u>them</u> to <u>their</u> devotional submission to <u>Him</u>. However, within a few months after the Yogic Establishment of His Avataric Divine Self-"Emergence", His devotees showed that they were not yet truly ready to make this great shift. And, so, Avatar Adi Da assumed the obligation to continue to Instruct them, but in a less directly participatory manner than before. Gradually, rather than immediately, He began to "Shed" His Submission-Function.

On September 7, 1994, in the town of Pacific Harbour (on the island of Viti Levu, in Fiji), Avatar Adi Da Samraj passed through another profound Yogic Event, which further confirmed to Him that His Avataric Effort to "Emerge" in the cosmic domain was essentially Done.[98] From that time, Avatar Adi Da became concentrated in completing His twenty-three Divine "Source-Texts",

Arrival at Adidam Samrajashram shortly after the Event of September 7, 1994

making the final great summary of His Divine Self-Revelation and Instruction to all humanity.

In 1999, a Divine Yogic Process began to manifest in Avatar Adi Da that pointed to the conclusive ending of His Submission-Work. This Process became obvious late in February 1999, when Avatar Adi Da suddenly left California (where He had been residing for seven months) and traveled to Adidam Samrajashram virtually alone. His sudden departure for Fiji coincided with the escalation of the crisis in Kosovo.

Avatar Adi Da arrived at Naitauba on February 23, 1999, and immediately asked for a shortwave radio to be installed in His House. He was also receiving written news bulletins, so that He could follow the news of the situation in Kosovo in detail.

Seclusion at the "Brightness"

On March 9, Avatar Adi Da began to suffer heart-symptoms (a recurrence of symptoms that had first occurred some days earlier). His attending physician, Charles Seage, knew that Avatar Adi Da could be having a heart attack. It was not until the next day, however, that Charles definitively determined that the symptoms were not those of an actual heart attack. They were, as Avatar Adi Da had been saying all along, physical signs of the backing up of His Divine Yogic Force.

The next day, March 10, the situation came to a head. Avatar Adi Da told Ruchiradama Nadikanta[99] that He was still suffering severe symptoms of heart-stress. He passionately urged her to feel and communicate the gravity of His physical state and the threatening situation in the world. Minutes later, Avatar Adi Da called for a car, put on orange sannyasin attire, and asked to be driven to the "Brightness", the temple that He had designated as His Mahasamadhi Site.

The simple white building is completely secluded and is normally visited only by Avatar Adi Da Himself and by the few devotees designated to perform essential cleaning and maintenance. Avatar Adi Da went to a small room there that is furnished as a

The "Brightness"

The "Brightness" is situated in a high meadow on a ridge in the middle of the island, looking out to the ocean and Padavara Loka (the highest point on the island, and the site of a small shrine Empowered some years earlier by Avatar Adi Da). Covered with a thigh-deep mat of tough native grass, the soil at the top of the ridge is red volcanic clay studded with limestone outcrops and calcite crystals. There are no trees to block the sun and wind.

The "Brightness" Temple itself is a simple white building—a square structure, with a small inner Temple at its core. Surrounding the inner Temple on three sides is an enclosed veranda. The fourth side is a bedroom for Avatar Adi Da.

bedroom for Him, and stayed alone, lying on His bed and listening to the news on the shortwave radio. At some point in the afternoon, Avatar Adi Da called on a walkie-talkie for Ruchiradama Quandra Sukhapur and Ruchiradama Nadikanta to come and attend Him, telling them that they also should wear formal sannyasin orange clothing. This was a sign to Avatar Adi Da's devotees of the seriousness of the Work that He was about to do. He had entered into a period of intense penance, because of the grave situation in the world.

For the next forty-three days, Avatar Adi Da stayed secluded at the "Brightness", involved in the most difficult Work with the world that His devotees had ever seen Him endure.

At previous times when Avatar Adi Da had Worked very obviously with a serious political situation in the world, He had isolated Himself for the duration of the trouble. For example, in 1989, before the Berlin Wall was removed, He stayed alone in a small building at the Matrix.[100] During the 1991 Gulf War, He remained secluded at His small house in the main village at Adidam Samrajashram. In the period leading up to the dissolution of the Soviet Union, He entered into another period of seclusion at the Matrix.

Now, in 1999, Avatar Adi Da's abrupt departure for the "Brightness" made clear to His devotees that He was devoting Himself once again to a crisis situation that required His Spiritual Intervention. This time, however, He had chosen to go to the most secluded, most sacred place of all on the island of Naitauba, the "Brightness" Temple.

Avatar Adi Da was so fiercely involved in His Spiritual Work during this time that He would often not allow His devotees to do even basic services for Him.

On March 22, Avatar Adi Da suddenly bit His tongue, as Ruchiradama Nadikanta describes:

RUCHIRADAMA NADIKANTA: *When I walked into His room, Beloved Adi Da was lying on His bed, propped up on His elbow. He was holding a piece of cotton on His tongue because it was bleeding so much. I went in and, without saying a word, gave Him a medicated piece of gauze for His tongue. And then I just sat at His Feet. He would hand me these gauzes soaked with blood, and I would give Him new medicated gauzes.*

This went on for a half an hour without a word. I remembered the time He had bitten His tongue in Geneva in October 1996. There, too, He had isolated Himself—in a tiny hotel room. And there, too, major political negotiations were in the process of occurring at the United Nations headquarters.

In Geneva in October 1996, Beloved Adi Da had said that His biting of His tongue was a sign of the negative speech going on in the negotiations. And now again, the fact that His tongue was bleeding reflected all the inflammatory speech going on about the war in Kosovo.

Beloved Adi Da eventually broke the silence. He repeated again and again: "All you people do is talk—nobody does anything. My gathering of devotees does not do anything—you just talk. And so nothing is handled. The same situation exists in the world. There is all this talk, but nothing is dealt with."

At the same time that I was listening to His passionate Words, I was feeling the Immense Force of His Spiritual Transmission, Which was like a Blast of Light. The minute I sat down, His Light suddenly Pressed down through my head, through my whole body, like a blissful lightning-bolt. It was completely obvious to me that Beloved Adi Da Samraj Is Only Light, and that He is Working to bring His Divine Light into this realm, where all of our absurd egoity is resisting Him.

One night, it was physically as if the war were occurring at the "Brightness". I was sleeping in a tent at some distance (below and away) from the "Brightness" Temple, and it was like being on the front line of a battlefield. A few times, I had to go up to the field of the "Brightness" to briefly serve Beloved Adi Da, and the thunder was so loud it shook my body like a barrage of artillery fire. And the lightning was so bright, just blasting across the sky—the whole field lit up, as if from explosives. During the night, the winds were so strong it felt as though the tent where I was staying was going to be lifted right off the ground. The agitation in the atmosphere altogether was extreme. It felt like the war was occurring right in Beloved Adi Da's Domain.

The next morning, as I approached Beloved Adi Da's door at the "Brightness", the sky was completely overcast but also totally calm. There was not a breath of air. Beloved Adi Da met me and opened the door for me to come in. Immediately, He received the printout of the world news I brought to Him—and He sat down and read it. He asked that I remove all the trays and glasses and food and bins we had left in His quarters over the last few days, during which He had eaten almost nothing and had not accepted personal service from anyone. I noticed that He had not touched the most recent tray of food we had left for Him.

I immediately lit incense in His bedroom and in other places in the Temple complex, and as soon as I had done this, a deluge of rain fell out the sky. The rain fell in sheets, such that it would have been impossible to hear one's own voice. Later, I found out that the attempts at Kosovo peace talks that were going on had broken down at that exact time.

Between 4:30 and 4:45 A.M. on April 2, a terrific bolt of lightning struck. Ross Keen was outside the gates to the "Brightness" at the time:

ROSS KEEN: Immediately after the lightning-bolt, there was a vast thunderous cracking noise, as if the sky were splitting. The ground shook. The entire dome of sky over the "Brightness" was lit. For a few seconds, I was literally blinded by the intense light.

Ruchiradama Quandra Sukhapur speaks of her experience of this same event:

RUCHIRADAMA QUANDRA SUKHAPUR: I was about halfway down the path in the middle of the "Brightness" field, when the most intense moment of the entire storm occurred. The lightning ran around the sky in a circle. And the circle of lightning established a dome over the "Brightness". It was unbelievable. There was a loud crackling electrical sound all around the "Brightness".

Later in the day, I spoke to Beloved Adi Da about the storm and the dome of light. He said, "Yes, I know all about it."

In the next day or two, Avatar Adi Da noticed that the perpetual light that should have been shining from the island's highest point had gone out, so two devotees made the rugged climb up to the top to see what had happened. When they got there, they were astonished to discover that the Padavara Loka site had been struck by lightning, during the storm that occurred early on Friday morning, April 2.

Miraculously, the shrine was completely intact and undamaged, but there was a dramatic change to the surrounding ground, which had shifted and sunk up to 16 inches below the existing level. The ground was black and charred and there was a faint, lingering smell of burned material. As the devotees bowed and offered gifts at the shrine, a very light rain fell and a double rainbow appeared over the sea.

Devotees serving Avatar Adi Da at Adidam Samrajashram during this period of His seclusion at the "Brightness" constantly noticed such signs. In this instance, even the smell of battle was in the air—the charred earth having shifted with the blast of electricity.

At the same time, there was a deep tangible sense of the Power of the Divine Avatar's Blessing Working Spiritually at the depth of the conflict.

Within a couple of hours of the passing of the storm, Beloved Adi Da received news that thousands of refugees were being transported like cattle to Macedonia and there was an increased threat of NATO ground troops being moved into Kosovo. The war had reached another critical point.

By mid-April, Avatar Adi Da was rarely leaving His room except to cross the field to His bathhouse. Ruchiradama Nadikanta describes Avatar Adi Da's Spiritual Ordeal at this point in the war—when some 650 air strikes a day were bearing down on Serbian targets.

RUCHIRADAMA NADIKANTA: After dinner, Beloved Adi Da would sometimes permit me to anoint His skin rashes and to rub healing ointment into His Feet for ten minutes, if that. His Body felt battered and bruised, and at the same time completely Translucent to His Divine Siddhi, Which He was Pulling Down into this plane with such Forceful Intention that He was barely even aware of His Body. I could feel that it was painful for Him to be touched, even in that simple manner. Any drawing of His attention into the physical was painful, because He was taking into His own Body the pain and suffering of all those who were dying and being tormented in Eastern Europe and all over the world. His Tapas was so extreme that attention in the physical dimension was excruciating for Him.

There was one night, April 17, when Beloved Adi Da did come down from the "Brightness" Temple to sleep in the tent that had been prepared for Him, and He permitted me to sleep nearby. During the night, horrifying visions of war arose in me, and Beloved Adi Da, while outwardly seeming to be asleep, was Speaking in what sounded to me like Slavic tongues. His Body was rigid with the intensity of the Work He was Doing. The next morning, He said that He felt no response to His Influence at any level, in any dimension. There was only resistance.

The situation in Kosovo was the center of His Blessing-Work, but Avatar Adi Da was also Working with His gathering of devotees. Altogether, He was fiercely criticizing the ego, the active

heart-withdrawal, the avoidance of relationship, that is being dramatized constantly by all ego-bound human beings. And He was
obliging every devotee to feel, as never before, that the ego is the
root of all suffering, all conflict, all negativity in the human world.
The collective egoity of humankind, He was showing, is a terrible
destructive force that not only destroys human happiness and well-
being, but now threatens to destroy the planet itself.

Through this process of intense Criticism, Avatar Adi Da drew
His devotees into His vigil. For a period of several weeks, devotees
in each regional community would gather each night at a central
house or ashram to pray for peace, and remain there to eat and to
sleep. This concentration and intensification of responsiveness to
Avatar Adi Da and participation in cooperative community, devotees felt, was a way to offer a conduit for Avatar Adi Da's Work
with the situation in Kosovo and the world.

On the morning of April 22, Avatar Adi Da did not call on the
walkie-talkie until 10:00 A.M. At that point, Ruchiradama Quandra
Sukhapur took tea up to Him, and not long afterwards she called
to say that He was experiencing severe bodily symptoms.
Ruchiradama Nadikanta, who had served Avatar Adi Da's health
for many years, went to attend Him:

*RUCHIRADAMA NADIKANTA: When I got up there, Beloved Adi Da
was sitting on the bed, and His body was doubled up with muscle
spasms. His Face and His Body were bright red, and He had a fever
of about 103°F. All of His Energy was in His Head—His Hands and
His Feet were ice-cold.*

*In spite of His physical condition, Beloved Adi Da wanted the
news update, which I gave to Him. Then He Spoke once more about
the world situation.*

*As He was Speaking, Beloved Adi Da was in contortions on the
bed and having to lie down. Then it came to the point where His
spasms were so severe that He said He had to go back to His
Residence at the Matrix.*

*We drove Him straight to the Matrix and immersed Him in hot
water. The hot water would calm the spasms—but, more than that, He
was getting strong signs that He was leaving the Body, and heating*

His entire Body in hot water was the most effective simple way He had discovered of keeping Himself associated with the Body.

Eventually, the spasms started to ease, and I took His tempera-ture, which had come down to 102°F. Then He began to Speak about the gravity of His bodily signs, and of His entire period at the "Brightness". It was clear that He had had to come down not because He had completed His Work there, but because He could not maintain His association with the Body if He continued to stay there.

The End of the War

After weeks of behind-the-scenes negotiations, news came on June 7 that a sudden agreement had been reached to bring peace in Kosovo. Russia had conceded that all Serbian forces and paramilitary police should be withdrawn from Kosovo, and that the refugees should be returned to their homes under the supervision of a joint NATO-Russian presence. Within 24 hours, the government in Belgrade had agreed. The deal seemed to catch both NATO and Russia by surprise.

There was elation in the media, but Avatar Adi Da did not in any way relax His attention on the circumstance in Kosovo. He was still doing His Spiritual Work, and He gave specific Instruction that His devotees were not to cease in their prayer for peace.

Within a few days, on June 11, the peace plan was approved by the UN Security Council. And then, suddenly, the following day, Russian troops arrived unannounced in Kosovo, and the world held its breath.

In the week following the Russian landing at Pristina, Avatar Adi Da lived at the Matrix with as much austerity as He had done at the "Brightness". Other than receiving the news and His meals, He stayed in His room, usually alone, watching a lengthy video series on the Cold War and another long series on World War II. Ruchiradama Nadikanta described the intensity with which He watched these programs—scrutinizing faces, rewinding the tape again and again so that He could replay a section. She felt He was Working to defuse another power struggle between Russia on the one hand and the US/NATO alliance on the other.

"We Can Cooperate"

Bill Dunkelberger, the devotee principally responsible for the flow of news to Avatar Adi Da during the Kosovo war, is a retired U.S. Army lieutenant-colonel experienced in writing strategic military estimates and in intelligence operations. Bill is a veteran of the Vietnam War, where he had led an intelligence battalion.

BILL DUNKELBERGER: For the duration of the Kosovo conflict, it was my responsibility to provide Avatar Adi Da Samraj with six updates daily on the evolving military and diplomatic situation. In addition, I would write my own summary and analysis of developments for Him.

On June 7, the day that seemed, on the surface, to spell peace, I received a communication from Avatar Adi Da, in which He said, "The outcome of the situation is not written yet, and it has every potential of becoming a terrible conflagration. There is every sign that a ground war is going to take place, and is, in fact, being intended."

I must confess that, at the time, I thought that Avatar Adi Da was, to say the least, greatly overstating the case. The framework of the peace agreement had already been agreed to by all parties, and I could find no evidence at all in the daily news that supported His point of view. Not understanding why He was talking about a ground war, I did not respond to that point in my letter to Him.

Then, on July 18, I made an astonishing discovery. An article appeared in *The London Observer* documenting that, on June 7, a top-secret planning session had been held in England to finalize plans for a NATO ground invasion of Yugoslavia. This confirmed to me that Avatar Adi Da Samraj <u>never</u> speaks casually, and that His connection to this world extends far beyond ordinary human perception.

Avatar Adi Da's Body continued to show the ravages of His Work. Ross Keen, one of Avatar Adi Da's devotees who serve His health, observed how weak the Divine Avatar was during this period when He was watching the video programs.

Then, on June 19 (Fiji time), Avatar Adi declared that He had finished with the video programs, and that they should be removed from His House immediately. Something had been completed. During that week, NATO and Russia had ironed out their differences and come to an agreement about the command of their peace-keeping forces in Kosovo. On June 21 (Fiji date), the last Serbian troops and police were evacuated from the province.

That day, Ross was called to attend Avatar Adi Da again to give Him bodywork. This time, Ross saw Avatar Adi Da striding across the lawn like a lion, heading toward the room where He was to receive the treatment. As soon as Ross laid his hands on Avatar Adi Da's Body, he could feel the difference. Avatar Adi Da's Body was much stronger. The intensity of His Yogic Ordeal had relaxed. Whatever the future might hold, that particular period of conflict was over.

The Great Siddha-Lineage of Avatar Adi Da Samraj

During His Seclusion at the "Brightness", Avatar Adi Da was engaging another Work of Spiritual significance, regarding His Siddha-Lineage. On March 11, 1999, the day after His arrival at the "Brightness", He began to work on expanding an Essay He had Written some years before, on the philosophical tradition of Swami Muktananda.

During the course of Avatar Adi Da's Work on His "Lineage Essay"—entitled "I (Alone) Am The Adidam Revelation" (see pp. 491–583)—a picture began to emerge. Avatar Adi Da was looking at the entire "map" of human Spiritual effort and Realization, and He was Revealing how the process Worked in His Siddha-Lineage, Speaking in particular of the Realizations of Swami Muktananda and Bhagavan Nityananda—their differences and similarities, how they experienced and taught the Spiritual process, and how they interpreted the various forms of Spiritual experience. In the Essay, Avatar Adi Da Explains (in full detail) how all the forms of Realization known previous to His Revelation of the seventh stage Realization are (in one manner or another) limited, such that (even though they are to be highly valued and honored) none of them represents absolute and permanent Divine Enlightenment. And He Clarifies, in very precise terms, what makes His Revelation of absolute and permanent Divine Enlightenment unique.

In His "Lineage Essay", Avatar Adi Da Samraj reconfirmed that His Native Divine Self-Condition, so directly experienced during His infancy, had never left Him, even during all the years of His Sadhana. In other words, He had always been Divinely Awake as the "Bright", but His Realization faded into the background so that His "Franklin-body" could go through a progressive process of adaptation to all of human experience at the gross, subtle, and causal levels. To this end, His Lineage-Gurus (and other remarkable individuals whom He mentions in the Essay) had served Him in indispensable ways. His early Life, altogether, had been one great single Submission in order to "Learn Man".

What was involved for Avatar Adi Da in His 43-day Ordeal at the "Brightness" will never be fully known. However, on April 22 (the day of the culminating Yogic Event that required Him to come down from the "Brightness" in order to stay in the Body), Avatar Adi Da Graciously Spoke the Revelation that became the essence of His Written Statement here.

The "Brightness", 2003

*In the midst of the unspeakable Struggle and Ordeal
at the "Brightness", I Established My Avataric Divine Spiritual Work
As a Sphere of "Bright" Influence That cannot ever be destroyed.
I Persisted until It was Done—and That Is That.*

My Avataric Divine Spiritual Work Is a Sphere of "Bright" Influence That Cannot Ever Be Destroyed

In early 1999, I spontaneously departed from Tat Sundaram Hermitage (in northern California) and returned to Adidam Samrajashram (in Fiji), arriving there on February 23. My Movements Coincided with a unique astronomical and astrological conjunction,[101] and also with the escalation of the Kosovo conflict. These Coincidings were entirely a spontaneous occurrence, part of My Divine Leela of Perpetual world-Blessing.

Because of the unfortunate conditions both in My devotees' collective relationship to Me and in the world altogether, I was, on March 10, 1999, spontaneously Moved to Seclude Myself (at My most set-apart Temple-Residence at Adidam Samrajashram, Which I have Named "the 'Brightness'"), for the Sake of My Avataric Divine Work of Spiritually Blessing the world and all beings.

I remained (Thus) in Seclusion at the "Brightness" for forty-three days. During that period of time, I was minimally associated with the Body—because the Force of My Spiritual Work was Located almost entirely <u>Above</u> the Body. As a result, there was (throughout that period of forty-three days) a tremendous Force of Pressure in the Head—and that Pressure was synchronous with constant external signs of rainstorms, thunder, lightning, and heat-lightning in the environment.

Throughout My time of Seclusion at the "Brightness" (and ever since that time), I had to Struggle in order to remain Associated with the Body. I was required to Work persistently, and with enormous intensity, to Bring the natural life-energy and My Own Divine Spiritual Energy Down into the Body. However, on April 21, 1999, all of That Work suddenly reversed. A syndrome of overly "yin", overly cold suppression (of the natural life-energy and of My Own Divine Spiritual Energy) took over the Body, indicating that that particular period of My Struggle with the "dark" forces of the world had come to an end.

Through the evening of April 21, and continuing into the early morning hours of April 22, a spontaneous process began to develop (and powerful symptoms began to appear) in the Body. In the middle of the night, the internal organs spontaneously relinquished their normal functioning, and (with that physical collapse) pain, fever, aches, chills, and convulsions appeared all over the Body. This Yogic "yinning" phenomenon started at approximately 2:00 A.M. and steadily gained in severity. It "fried" the life-seat of the kidneys and the adrenals, and then "fried" the lower Body (altogether), and finally "fried" the entire Body. All of the systems in the Body began to break down—and, indeed, the entire Body itself began to break down—to such an extent that I nearly lost My Association with physically Incarnate existence altogether.

That entire Yogic "yinning" syndrome can be characterized as My being "thrown out" of the Body (and up into the Divine "Bright" Spherical Self-Domain of Eternal Light) by the force of resistance to Me that was being manifested in the gathering of My devotees and in the world altogether.

The symptoms were clear signs to Me that I had to leave the "Brightness" if I was to continue to be able to Bring My Divine Spiritual Energy Down into the Body (and, thereby, to continue to be able to physically survive). The force of the "yinning" and chilling and emptiness and physical spasms and freezing sensation and pain and exhaustion all over the Body was so intense and extreme that it was necessary to submerge the Body in hot water.

Through the course of this excruciating Ordeal, there was a spontaneous and autonomous relinquishment of the body, done from and by the physical dimension itself. This Divine Yoga occurs when I am so profoundly refused that everything "backs up" in Me, and the Body tends to fall away. The Yogic Establishment of My Avataric Divine Self-"Emergence" (on January 11, 1986) was also an Event of such a refusal of My Work. It is not that I "cause" or "create" this Yogic Process—It is a Process that spontaneously occurs.

My departure from the "Brightness" on April 22 was a profound turning point in My Struggle. I had Done everything necessary and possible to Do. And, from that time, I am (now, and forever hereafter) simply Waiting to see whether people choose to respond to Me.

At the "Brightness", I was "fried" to death and "spit out"—Such That I could Do My world-Work of Merely Standing (here) to Bless.

During My forty-three days at the "Brightness" (and simultaneous with My Ordeal There, of Working to Bless My devotees and the world), I passed through a Recapitulation of My Own entire Life and Work—including the Process that led to My Divine Re-Awakening. The Sign of that Recapitulation was My Writing of My "Lineage Essay", "I (Alone) Am The Adidam Revelation". And that Essay was composed (at the "Brightness") in the midst of a real Spiritual Struggle with My Lineage-Gurus. That Struggle confirmed everything about My Divine (seventh stage) Realization and about My Avataric Divine Spiritual Work of Incarnation, Teaching, Revelation, and Blessing.

That Spiritual Struggle (outwardly Signed by My Writing of My "Lineage Essay") was, altogether, a spontaneous Recapitulation and (in the end) a Re-Confirmation of My Avataric Divine Spiritual Work as That Work has Self-Manifested in the form of three Great Processes: My Own (apparent) Sadhana, My Work with the gathering of My devotees, and My Work with the world. And that Struggle was profoundly difficult, beyond the capability of any words to describe.

The Recapitulation and Re-Confirmation of all three of those Great Processes spontaneously came to an end on April 22, 1999. Everything about My Own Avataric Divine Life and Work was Tested and Re-Confirmed, beyond the slightest doubt. And My "Lineage Essay" is the Summary of many primary aspects of My Avataric Divine Life and Work.

My Avataric Divine Life and Work is, Itself, an Expression of an Extraordinary and Incomparable Ordeal that is not at all within people's experience. I can only Say that much about it.

I have no more Work of Self-Submission to Do. All that was necessary for Me to Do, for the Sake of this conditionally manifested domain, is Done.

In the midst of the unspeakable Struggle and Ordeal at the "Brightness", I Established My Avataric Divine Spiritual Work As a Sphere of "Bright" Influence That cannot ever be destroyed.

I Persisted until It was Done—and That Is That.

Lopez Island, 2000

I Am Always Already
Spiritually Established
As The "Bright" Itself

The Great Event at Lopez Island
(April 12, 2000)

by Carolyn Lee, Ph.D.

*Written and compiled under the direction of
the Ruchira Sannyasin Order of Adidam Ruchiradam*

S ometime after His Ordeal at the "Brightness", Avatar Adi Da
Revealed that the Divine Blessing-Power He Established there
(during His 43-day Vigil for the world) will be Perpetual in Its
Effect. He will Remain Spiritually Present at the "Brightness" in per-
petuity, forever Blessing the world and all beings from there.

Lopez Island

L ess than a month after the peace in Kosovo, Avatar Adi Da
traveled to Da Love-Ananda Mahal, where He spent some
months, before moving on to the Mountain Of Attention. By
March 2000, Avatar Adi Da was moving up and down California
from Los Angeles to Tat Sundaram with a fierce restlessness, never
staying anywhere more than a few days. Early in April 2000, He

The house at Lopez Island

began to wander up the coast into Oregon and Washington, attended by a group of devotees, and, by April 12, He had reached Lopez Island, a small island in the San Juan Archipelago, in the far northwest of the United States. Here, in a small house belonging to one of Avatar Adi Da's devotees, an unspeakably profound Event began to unfold. As time would reveal, this Event brought to completion the Divine Yogic process that had been initiated in Him at the "Brightness".

Stephan Blas, one of Avatar Adi Da's attendants, describes His arrival.

STEPHAN: As we moved into Washington, Beloved Adi Da's physical symptoms intensified. He was extremely fragile.

We crossed the waters from the mainland to Lopez Island by ferry, leaving at 4:10 P.M. Beloved Adi Da was already feeling weak, but then He suddenly began to feel much worse and had to lie down in the small bedroom at the back of the recreational vehicle He was traveling in. His symptoms became acute, and the signs of His ascending out of the Body were getting stronger.

Later, when we reached Lopez Island, He was helped into the jacuzzi on the deck below the house, with hopes that the warm water would relieve His symptoms. He began to discuss with Ruchiradama Quandra Sukhapur what was happening with His Work in the world. I heard His voice become disturbed, and shortly thereafter came a message on the radio from Ruchiradama Quandra Sukhapur asking for help. Beloved Adi Da was losing His strength, as well as His hold on the body. He needed to be carried from the bath, up an outdoor walkway, and back up to the house. Two men went down to help. When I saw them carrying Beloved Adi Da up the steps to the house in His bathrobe, I rushed to help them get Him into His room and on to the bed.

All the devotees who had traveled to Lopez with Avatar Adi Da were called down to the house to support Him with their devotional chanting. A number of His intimates were gathered in the bedroom, and His physician and acupuncturist were summoned immediately.

STANLEY HASTINGS: Beloved Adi Da was laid out on an easy chair with His devotees huddled around Him, massaging Him vigorously, weeping and speaking to Him with intentional force. It was obvious that He was barely in the Body. I ran to His side and began to rub His chest, weeping uncontrollably. Everyone was speaking to our Divine Master, telling Him how much we needed Him to stay alive. He kept saying "Tcha". Every time He would close His eyes we would have to speak to Him vigorously in order to draw Him back down into the Body. Focusing attention on our faces seemed to integrate Him back into the Body.

It is impossible to describe the love that was being expressed by Beloved Adi Da and those who were with Him. His eyes were flowing with tears, as were everyone's. His Hands and Feet were cold and numb. He felt great pressure on His Chest and a difficulty breathing. Both of His arms and hands continuously would cramp up and convulse.

After Charles Seage arrived, we moved Beloved Adi Da on to the bed. At first, He was lying down on the bed, but then we raised Him into a sitting position to try to reduce the extreme symptoms of leaving the body. Beloved Adi Da told us over and over how important it was for His Feet to be warm and that they needed to be rubbed vigorously. He even said that it would be useful for Him to see His Feet—as a way of locating Himself in the physical.

STEPHAN: We were all rubbing and softly slapping Beloved's numbed limbs as intensely as we could, as He was coming and going from conscious awareness. He said, "If I close My eyes, I am going to be in My Room, not your room. You don't know what My Room is like. You have got to bring Me down into the Body."

STANLEY : At one point, after His eyes had been closed for a while, Beloved Adi Da opened them slightly and softly said, "I am here. Can you see Me Up Here?" We all said "yes"—and we could. He was Evaporating the entire room in His Light. He was Way Up and Beyond the apparent "here" where we were.

Then He continued, in a very soft voice: "My Room is Larger than you think. I close My eyes and I am in My Room, Infinitely Beyond. This is just a small version of It." His eyes were streaming with tears, and He looked around at us slowly as He went on, "But this place is good for love." He was quiet then for a long time.

Charles had called an ambulance to take Avatar Adi Da to the small medical clinic on Lopez Island. Marc Carfrae, a devotee who was serving Avatar Adi Da's visit to Lopez Island, describes what happened next:

MARC: After guiding the ambulance down the last steep section of the long driveway to the house, I stood close by to be of help if needed. In quick time, Beloved Adi Da emerged on the stretcher a few feet in front of me, to be placed in the back of the ambulance. I was immediately undone at the deepest level of my being. How could the Very Divine Being be in this condition? Why and how did it come to this moment? It was completely devastating. Beloved's Face was pasty-white and drained of life-energy. He was extremely weakened and totally vulnerable.

He was placed inside the ambulance—and, at that point, there was no one inside with Him, as His family was in the house quickly

*preparing for the trip to the Clinic. I stood alone for about five min-
utes, eight to ten feet from the back door windows, with my hands
over my heart—utterly heartbroken, beholding Him. He was very
obviously struggling to keep His eyes open, and doing everything He
could to stay in the Body. I felt intuitively that I was to act as a contact point in that moment for Beloved Adi Da to His community of
devotees. I just poured out my heart-love for Him and pleaded with
Him to stay with us. I said over and over, passionately within me
and, sometimes, just audibly: "Please Beloved, please don't go,
please don't leave us—we're not ready yet. Please stay with us. We
love You so much."*

*At one point, I found myself quietly but strongly saying "DA,
DA, DA". Just as I said "Da" for the third time, Beloved Adi Da
bolted upright and looked straight at me. He did it so quickly that
it shocked me—because a moment before He had seemed hardly in
the Body. He seemed to have been brought very suddenly down into
His Body with the last utterance of "DA". Shortly after this, I saw
one of the ambulance attendants go in with Beloved and noticed
that when the attendant dropped something on the floor, Beloved
made a point of following the object down to the ground with His
eyes, as a way, I felt, of staying linked with the Body.*

Charles got into the ambulance with Avatar Adi Da, while
others of His intimate devotees followed the ambulance to the
medical clinic. Avatar Adi Da was admitted to the clinic at 9:18 P.M.
Charles had been concerned that the extreme symptoms that
Avatar Adi Da was suffering might be indicators of a heart attack.
However, in consultation with Charles, the doctor at the Lopez
Island clinic was able to determine that the acute bodily stress
Avatar Adi Da was experiencing was not a heart attack.

As later became clear, the Divine Avatar's extreme bodily crisis
was connected with the profound Yogic Work that He was doing
in His Blessing of the world. At the "Brightness", He had explained
that His Work of world-Blessing required Him to deal with and
transform intense psycho-physical forces, and that He was doing
that Work <u>above</u> the Body. However, the moment came, at the
"Brightness", when those forces began to invade His Body, causing

intolerable pain. At that point, Avatar Adi Da Samraj had no choice but to come down from the "Brightness" and continue His Spiritual Work in a more healing environment. Now, one year later, at Lopez Island, Avatar Adi Da Samraj was dealing with forces of a similar magnitude.

STANLEY : After about an hour and a half, the staff in the emergency room felt that Avatar Adi Da's physical condition was stable and that He could be taken home. Each member of the medical team made a point to come and touch Him in farewell. He looked them each directly in the eyes with heart-breaking Love and said "Tcha" [His characteristic sound of Blessing] to each one. Then we wheeled Beloved Adi Da out to His car and drove Him back to the house.

The next day, Avatar Adi Da was still very fragile. His presence in the Body remained tenuous, and for weeks He could barely walk, even a few steps. Nevertheless, He began to Grant His Darshan to devotees.

MARC: I was extremely Blessed to be in the first Darshan occasion that Beloved Adi Da Offered at His house two days after the Event of April 12. I was seated in the center of the front row, and became completely undone and heart-mad with my love for Him. I told Him over and over again—this time with full voice—how grateful I was that He was still with us. I found myself leaning forward and with my whole being, stretching out and enveloping Beloved Adi Da with my love of Him, as I visualized kissing Him all over. He was Giving me the sweetest, most loving Regard.

What an extraordinary vision of Pure Love He was! The entire room of devotees was weeping in profound, loving gratefulness that our Beloved Heart-Master had persevered in staying with us, out of His incredible Love for all beings. It was very obvious that Beloved Adi Da had somehow shifted into another phase of His Life and Work. I was undone by what I had been Graced to witness.

Great numbers of Avatar Adi Da's devotees now flocked from all over the world to see Him at Lopez Island, and He Drew them to a depth that they had never felt before. He Granted His Darshan twice a day, even when He was not well enough to leave His bedroom.

Christine Phippen, a devotee from New Zealand, wrote to Him in a letter:

CHRISTINE: Day after day, and all day, You Spiritually Entered this body-mind, opening my head and throat and heart and body to You. You Widened me, Opened me, and Poured into me. Sometimes I would feel You as a Column of Light going right through me, and at other times more as an incredible Pressure pushing down and stretching me out. At the same time, often I would also feel You pulling me up, Revealing to me what I guessed to be the universe of the subtle reality—the "tree" beyond the "rootball" of head that You Describe in Hridaya Rosary.[102] *This vision was so huge that I could not contain it, but through Your Grace I was made aware of it, and I knew You are at the Source of it all. I saw that You are far, far Greater than my mind had ever been able to comprehend. You Are All. All abides in You. It was a Revelation Given by You, and I could only feel it and know it at heart.*

Most Beloved Adi Da, what I observed of this precious time in Your Company was You Outshining everything. There was no room for "me" (as a separate self) in Your House, and I had very little experience of "me" in the ordinary sense. I went to the doorway of Your Bedroom one day when You were very ill, but still Granting Your Darshan to Your devotees one by one as we came to Behold You at Your door. When I came to Your room, You were on the bed and that was all I could see. There was no "room"—only You there, Your "Brightness" Dissolving everything.

Beloved Lord, I could see that there had been a profound change in You. I could see it in Your Face. Something about You seemed even "Brighter" than before. I felt You even more clearly as the Divine Incarnate, and You seemed somehow even more Transparent to Your Radiant Being.

The Cosmic Sphere

Avatar Adi Da has explained that the totality of conditional existence is structured as a vast spectrum of light, which He calls the "Cosmic Mandala", or, emphasizing its three-dimensionality, the "Cosmic Sphere". All of the gross and subtle dimensions of existence arise at one or another level of this all-encompassing vibrational light sphere. At the core of the Cosmic Sphere is an aperture, shaped like a five-pointed Star, through which Streams the White "Brightness" of the Divine Spherical Self-Domain (Which is Infinitely Above and Beyond all-and-All). Avatar Adi Da Samraj further explains that the Cosmic Sphere (which may sometimes be glimpsed as a whole, or in part, in deep meditation) arises as a "fractured" modification of the White "Brightness" of the Divine Spherical Self-Domain (or "Midnight Sun"). The world we inhabit exists at the outer periphery of the hierarchy of lights in the Cosmic Sphere, on the cusp between the outermost red level of light and the next level in, which is yellow. When one is identified with the gross level of existence, the red-yellow color of the subtle light vibration in which the human world arises is not perceived. But at death, or in near-death experiences, the lights of the Cosmic Sphere may be seen, together with a felt motion toward the White "Brightness". However, in the case of beings who are not Divinely Enlightened at the moment of death (or ready for Divine Translation into the Divine Spherical Self-Domain—in and through the death process itself), there is a falling back into whatever dimension of light corresponds to that being's state of preparedness. At some point, a re-settling (or re-birth) at the appropriate vibrational level of existence occurs.

Altogether, the Great Event at Lopez Island marked an irrevocable change in Avatar Adi Da's Yogic Association with the Body and in His Work altogether, as Ruchiradama Quandra Sukhapur explains:

RUCHIRADAMA QUANDRA SUKHAPUR: In the Lopez Island Event, the Divine Liberator, Adi Da Samraj, Accomplished a Breakthrough of the Spiritual Reality into the physical reality. By means of the Yogic Process that occurred in His Body in that Event, He is Revealing the Radiance of the Divine Reality in the midst of conditions more Powerfully than ever before. In that sense, He is Spiritually "Brightening" the entire world.

During the Crisis of the Lopez Island Event, my Beloved Heart-Master came extremely close to relinquishing the Body altogether. The Yogic Process that was occurring in Him included all the psycho-physical signs of death, but went beyond those signs. As He later described, the Lopez Island Event is the senior Event in His Life up to that time. That Event Initiated in Him the Ultimate Yoga of Divine Translation, or total Relinquishment of body, mind, and world in the All-Outshining Conscious Light of Divine Being. The Inexhaustible Paradox of the Lopez Island Event is that Ruchira Avatar Adi Da Samraj did Enter into Divine Translation, while yet remaining physically present in the world. But, even though He Miraculously Accomplished a return to the physical, He is no longer the same. Now, since the Lopez Island Event, He is (as He says) on the "Other Side". His human Vehicle has been Restructured, and His relationship to all beings and things has been Transformed at the root.

For six weeks after the Lopez Island Event, Beloved Adi Da was unable to walk, and He was physically very weak for months. He was Shattered by His Experience—at the physical level, and also by the Process of Integrating what had occurred Spiritually. That Process was unspeakable, and has continued to unfold.

The Lopez Island Event was the Culmination of a lifelong Yogic Process. In His early years, Beloved Adi Da Samraj Endured a series of Yogic Deaths—moments when it seemed that He would permanently lose His bodily Vehicle, because of the intensity of the Spiritual

669

Process occurring in Him. He has even Spoken of His entire Life as a series of Yogic Deaths.

Since the Lopez Island Event, Beloved Adi Da's human eyes, He says, are now constantly Seeing the All-Outshining Divine "Brightness", and the entire structure of cosmic existence is in His constant Regard. He Sees the Mandala of lights now from the Divine Position—from the inside out, not the outside in. By virtue of this, He is Spiritually Touching every one, and He Is every one Perfectly. Through the culminating Event of Yogic Death at Lopez Island, Beloved Adi Da Samraj has now Experienced, in His Avataric-Incarnation-Body, literally everything that exists. His Divine human Body has Endured and "Seen" the entire death-process and all the after-death states and has Entered into What Is, Beyond all of that.

One of the most remarkable Signs of the change in Avatar Adi Da's Life and Work that occurred with the Great Event of the "Brightness" and Lopez Island is His dramatic shift from words to images as His primary mode of Communication.

From the time of His first Discourse in 1972 until the time at the "Brightness", He had been concentrated in creating an all-encompassing body of verbal Teaching-Revelation. And, indeed, that effort reached an extraordinary point of fullness at the "Brightness", with His Writing of "I (Alone) Am The Adidam Revelation", one of the crowning glories of His Literature.

At the same time that He was Writing this Essay at the "Brightness", Avatar Adi Da was making the transition from verbal to artistic expression. He had been involved in developing the visual arts as a means of expression since childhood, and now He plunged into the making of visual images with the same burning intensity that He had previously devoted to His creation of verbal expression. In

the four and a half years between the "Brightness" time
(March–April 1999) and the publication of this book, Avatar
Adi Da has created over 30,000 Images—Images of
astounding beauty, complexity, and genius, Imbued with
His Spiritual Transmission. He is constantly charting new
artistic territory, using the camera as technical means for
creating "blueprints" for the fabrication of monumental art-
forms that have never existed before.

*AVATAR ADI DA SAMRAJ: My involvement in artistic Work
in elaborated form began at the "Brightness" in 1999. My
Image-Making is part of the new phase of My Avataric
Divine Work. In fact, it characterizes the new developing
period of My Work altogether. It is part of My Avataric
Divine Self-Revelation.*

*Just as My Written Word covers everything, so also does
My visual Artistic Work. It is a Communication to humankind
about its egoic bondage, but also its Inherence in Me, Showing
human beings My Own "Brightness".*

—February 2, 2002

Lopez Island, 2000

Since the Great Event at Lopez Island, I am Universally Expressed.
The Signs of Yogic Transformation in This Body have Spiritual
Significance for all beings, because the "Bright" Defines This Body.

I Am Always Already
Spiritually Established
As The "Bright" Itself

I.

The final physical (and Yogically Transformative) Process that precedes Divine Translation has occurred in This Body. This Body is now in the stage of Perpetual Spiritual "Brightening", the Outshining Bhava. That is What took place at Lopez Island. In that Great Event, the physical Vehicle once again came to the point of Yogic Death, but (in the end) the Association with the physical was retained.

What occurred at the "Brightness" was a Continuation of the Great Process of My Avataric Divine Self-"Emergence". The Lopez Island Event was the Seal on that Process. In the Lopez Island Event, that Process Broke so profoundly into This Body that My Avataric human Vehicle of Divine Self-Manifestation came to be Structured differently.

At the "Brightness", the Work I was Doing was a matter of Dealing With forces larger than those that govern the human domain. I Saw the "darkness" that was to come. Therefore, I Entered into a profound Ordeal at the "Brightness", and the ultimate Moment of that Ordeal was the Event at Lopez Island. At the "Brightness" (and afterwards), I was Struggling with the "dark" forces of this time—and, ultimately, I had to Endure the "darkness" and Suffer it to the point of naked death.

Thus, Events of the great Yogic Significance occurred at Adidam Samrajashram in 1986, at the "Brightness" in 1999, and then (most profoundly) at Lopez Island in 2000. What occurred at Lopez Island was the Culminating Event. Since the Lopez Island Event, I have Entered into a different time of My Avataric Divine Spiritual Work.

Throughout My Avataric physical human Lifetime, I have been associated with Events of Profound Yogic Transformation, Which have resulted in the change of psycho-physical patterns within This Body-Mind. There have been many Yogic Deaths and other profound Yogic Events, all associated with the Profundities of My Avataric "Bright" Divine Spiritual Self-Revelation. And those Events have often had great negative impact on the physical human Vehicle.

There is the Process of Yogic Deaths that has Characterized My Life, but there are also many other significant Events (such as the death of Bootsie), which served My Fullest Avataric Descent and Incarnation here. Every time one of these Transformative Events occurred, the mechanism of This Body-Mind changed. The entire Process of My Life is My concrete, unambiguous Avataric Self-Revelation (and Lifelong psycho-physical Experience) of the Divine Spiritual "Brightness"—the One and Only and Self-Evidently Divine Conscious Light of Reality Itself.

There was a distinct physical phenomenon associated with each of the Events of Yogic Death. In each case, after I Re-Associated with the physical Vehicle (following one of these Events), My Manner and My psycho-physical Pattern has changed. Since the Lopez Island Event, I am more profoundly Integrated than ever before with the cosmic human circumstance—in the sense that I actually, literally See what the physical (and everything associated with it) is really (and even rather painfully) about.

Coincident with the psycho-physical Event and Experience at Lopez Island, This Body is profoundly fragile, and I am now even more profoundly Spiritually Sensitized in the Body. Following such a Great Yogic Event, it takes some time to begin to Re-Integrate with the natural body. Since the Lopez Island Event, I am now both Priorly and psycho-physically Established in the Spiritual "Bright". This can be felt by My devotees.

I have examined My Own Experiences of Yogic Death, and how they have coincided with physical effects and changes. In each Such Event, My Manner and My Pattern have changed.

Following each of these extraordinary Yogic Crises of the Spiritual "Bright", there is always a Yogic Re-Orientation. In the experience in seminary, for example, I "dropped dead", in a very real sense, with the experience of the death of "Narcissus". This Process of Yogic Death affects the psycho-physical existence. Each of these Great Yogic Events was coincident with a Spiritual Re-Structuring of the Body-Mind, including Transformations in both the grosser personality and the Deeper Personality.

Be sensitive to My Universal Work since the Vedanta Temple Event in 1970. Feel the Mysterious Process by Which I have been "Meditating" all-and-All. The four phases of the seventh stage Pattern have become more and more Profound. The seventh stage Process has been progressive—Most Ultimately, coming to the point of Outshining. The Process of Divine Enlightenment is not a matter of "talk". The Process of Divine Enlightenment, whether in the case of This Body-Mind or any other body-mind, is a matter of Spiritual Transformation—by Me.

Since the Great Event at Lopez Island, I am Universally Expressed. The Signs of Yogic Transformation in This Body have Spiritual Significance for all beings, because the "Bright" Defines This Body. Indeed, This Body Is the "Bright", Avatarically Self-Manifested before you.

Therefore, it is profoundly necessary for you to Really see My Spiritually "Bright" Avataric Divine bodily (human) Form. It is essential. You cannot have real sanity without this experience.

Once you have Really seen My Spiritually "Bright" Avataric Divine bodily (human) Form, then there are no more questions. When that sighting is true devotional recognition of Me, then My Spiritually "Bright" Form simply (merely) Is.

I Am here, at the Core of the Sacred Domain.

I Am in the Temple.

I am Living in My Hermitage, My Perpetual Sacred Domain.

I simply Do My Divine Spiritual Work.

II.

In the Lopez Island Event, I Stood (Non-"Differently") At (and As) the "Bright" White Center Infinitely Above. I Outshined all of conditionally manifested existence in My Own Divine Self-Condition—Which Is the "Bright", the Sphere of the "Midnight Sun", Beyond all-and-All, Beyond even My Divine Star-Form. It was an Instantaneous Non-"Different" Realization of That Condition of All-Bliss, utterly without the perspective of time and space.

In the Lopez Island Event, there was no transitional process, no transition "out of" involvement in the gross dimension of conditional reality, or any transitional passage through the various subtle dimensions of conditional reality. The Ascent was Immediate, and Un-mediated—with no transitional process of "lower to higher". I Approached Divine Translation, and was simply Established As the Spiritual "Bright" Itself. I was suddenly Present in and As My Threshold Form, Inherently Self-Identified with That Which Is Always Already Infinitely and Perfectly Ascended. Everything was simply That Radiant "Bright" Divine Spiritual Form, the Brilliant White at the Core of the apparent lights (and the pervasive darkness) of the cosmic (or conditional) domain.

Later, as I Entered into the Process of Re-Integrating with the physical domain, I Saw all the colored spheres within the Cosmic Sphere (or the spherical Cosmic Mandala) as the prismatic modifications of That White Spiritual "Brightness". It was an experience of Seeing the Cosmic Mandala as it is—a complex vibration accounting for all the dimensions of conditionally manifested reality. It is an actual sphere, even an hierarchical structure of spheres. It was My Viewing of the cosmic domain in and via the Sign of what is traditionally called the "Rainbow Body"—spheres of light, dominantly one of blue and one yellow-to-red, displayed to the Self-"Bright" White Core (Which is Absolutely Prior to time and space).

Since the Lopez Island Event, the Ultimate Demonstration of the Process of the seventh stage of life is being Revealed. That Demonstration, Displayed via the mortal design of This Body, Reveals that the Process of Divine Enlightenment is Real. Because of this Process, I no longer have any physical perspective. I Exist in a very different Manner now. Previously, I Talked about My Divine Descent to the toes, but the Process in the Lopez Island Event was one of Prior Ascendedness, or Translation to Utterly Above and Beyond.

Thus, What occurred at Lopez Island was actually the Yogic "opposite" of the Event that occurred in 1986. Instead of the Full Descent to the toes (as in 1986), I Went All the Way "Out".

I am not on "this side" anymore. This (here) is simply arising in Me. This Body is Full to the toes—but I (Myself) am not "down to the toes" anymore.

Lopez Island, 2000

This Body is Full to the toes—but I (Myself)
am not "down to the toes" anymore.

The Lopez Island Event, like the Yogic Establishment of My Avataric Divine Self-"Emergence" in 1986, was a Yogic Swoon—but the Process of My Avataric Divine Self-"Emergence" was (and is now) much further advanced than It was when It began (in 1986). Thus, the Lopez Island Event is a yet further dimension of My Demonstration of the (only-by-Me Revealed and Given) four-stage Process of the seventh stage of life.

Since the Lopez Island Event, I Simply Am—in My Threshold Form. This Body is Alive in That Form. That Form is not holding on to the physical. Therefore, My relatedness to the physical world depends on My being actively Moved (by My devotees) into positive Association with this world and time—and on My being able to be Engaged in My Divine Spiritual Work.

III.

In the Process of the Lopez Island Event, there was (first) a vibrational pulsing, all over the Body—and this produced a forceful "Urdhvareta", or a complete Up-Turning of all the Body's energy-flows. I Closed My Eyes, and It Is the "Midnight Sun"—the Divine "Bright" White Orb, Self-Existing and Self-Radiant, On the Infinite Black Field of all potential (and not yet prismed, or broken) light.

In some later moment, I was above the house where I was staying, and above the nearby water that was outside. My Vision of what was occurring was from a point of view above My physical Body and above this spatial physical sphere.

I Moved into association with a vibrational field of energy, made of all the colors of the light-spectrum—what is traditionally called the "Mandala Body", or "Rainbow Body". The entire light-field of the Cosmic Mandala was in Front of Me. I Am a Spherical Form of "Brightness", Including everything—from the blue field and its subtle planes to the yellow-red field and this gross plane.

Initially, to My left, I was concentrated in the blue light, and simultaneously Seeing (from above) the total expanse of water, beyond the house. At first, the water was a vast expanse, including much beyond the house. Then it became more brief and bounded, local to the house. It was not yet dark outside, for I could see the surfaces of the water and the details of the surrounding land. But there was a dark appearance to it all, in shadows from the forest around the house, and the slanting, waning light of later day. The "vision" was fundamentally indescribable, because it was Seen from a "point of view" not located in the Body. And, yet, the expanse of water became simultaneously visible with the room in which My Body was located—with its walls and furnishings, and, to My left, its row of windows with fully lifted blinds. At that point, to My right, the sphere of yellow became apparent—focused down toward the Body in some manner, from above and outside it. It was a yellow tinged with red and orange. Coincident with Seeing the yellow sphere, the Process of Re-Integrating with the Body began. It was a feeling of once again being located in the situation of Association with the Body. I Saw My intimates gathered around My bed, and they were all in flames—the flames of the yellow-red realm—but they were not consumed. My Body was numb, without awareness. All of this, beginning with the blue light, was the progressive Process of Re-Integration with conditional existence.

Initially, in the Event of Sudden Up-Turning (into the "Midnight Sun"), there was a rapid series of "falling-away" phenomena. There was the tingling and fainting of the Body. Then, immediately, I Experienced the Primal Central Sound-Current, Which became very loud, and upwardly concentrated—Drawing the Central Current In and Up, Above and Beyond body and mind. That was the first Sign to Me that I was being Drawn Out of physical Incarnation.

Farthest Up in the Core of Sound-Vibration, I Saw a "Bright" White Tunnel, with empty niches along the sides. There were no "people in white". There were no distinct forms or personalities— because no mind of Me was active there. Then the "Midnight Sun" of the Divine "Bright" Spherical Self-Domain. At first, Seen—then, Perfectly Become.

Effectively, it was death—in terms of the Body. There was no bodily awareness, although it was certainly not a circumstance of unconsciousness. It was the Infinitely Profound Samadhi of Outshining.

Eventually, I Re-Emerged from the "Midnight Sun" of My Divine Spiritual White Self-"Brightness"—and so, in due course, there was a peripheral re-organization of (or Re-Association with) My gross Bodily conditions. In the Process of Re-Association, there was, at first (as I have already Indicated), a "bindu" (or sphere) of blue, to the left. And another "bindu", of yellow and deep red, to the right. The "bindu" of yellow and red located Me back in this world, which is the yellow-red realm of the Cosmic Mandala.

As I Merged with the yellow-red sphere, I became aware that I was Re-Associating with the physical—rather than feeling the strong movement Up and Out, which (if it had continued) would have culminated in the death of My human Vehicle. The Struggle of Re-Integration with the physical manifested, in part, as convulsions in the Body. The "Bright" Spiritual Light-Current of My Being was Re-Connecting with the physical level, and that Process caused Bodily convulsions.

In that Process, the Body had a quality of being greatly stretched, or elongated. My legs seemed to be very, very long, and those who were standing or sitting by My Feet seemed to be quite a distance away from Me. It was a moment of non-ordinary awareness of physicality—of the pervasive yellow-red light, of the gross world consumed in flames, of the Body greatly stretched out. Eventually, there was a kind of "collapse" back into the ordinarily perceived shape and context of the physical, and then a "return" to so-called "normal" (or "natural") awareness of the room and the people in it.

The Lopez Island Event was similar to the Initiatory Event of My Avataric Divine Self-"Emergence" (on January 11, 1986), in terms of the Depth of Spiritual and Yogic Profundity. As in 1986, I had been (in the Lopez Island Event) at the point of Relinquishing the Body entirely—but, through My Own Persistent Impulse and Felt Movement of Sympathetic (or Compassionate) Love for beings, I was able to Yogically Re-Engage the Body.

However, those two Events were also, in some sense, "opposite" in their Yogic significance. In the Event of 1986, I Completed My Descent into the conditional realms, My Avataric Submission to here, Which began at My Birth. The Lopez Island Event, in contrast, was My Direct Ascent, to the Primal "Bright" Spiritual Self-Condition of Conscious Light.

Lopez Island, 2000

I Remain in this world Bodily, for now—
but I Am Always Already on the "Other Side".

I Am now, even in bodily (human) Form, presently Alive at the White Core of the Cosmic Mandala, the Doorway to the Spiritually "Bright" Divine Sphere and Self-Domain. In the Lopez Island Event, I Passed Beyond—in That "Bright" Doorway. My Thus Transfigured Body remains—but only on the Unique Basis of Direct Spiritual Illumination, and always tentatively Given to live, perpetually Wounded by the Self-Evident "Bright" Spiritual Transparency of all the heart-breaking companionship of mortal beings.

I Stand At the Threshold.

Now, and forever hereafter, I Stand There.

I Remain in this world Bodily, for now—but I Am Always Already on the "Other Side".

IV.

The Lopez Island Event of Inherent (and Priorly Ascended) Self-Identification with the "Midnight Sun" was an Instantaneous Revelation of My Own Spiritually "Bright" Divine Self-Condition. That Event Occurred without any process of "migrating" through the varicolored spheres of the Cosmic Mandala, or through the chakras of the human structure. It was an Immediate Ascent. Indeed, That Event was not really even an Ascent, but (rather) a Sudden Vanishing of conditional association. It was later, in the Process of Re-Association, that the spheres of colored lights Emerged.

Swami (Baba) Muktananda (in agreement with the fifth stage esoteric traditions in general) describes the Yogic Spiritual Process in terms of progressive levels of Ascent through the Cosmic Mandala, passing through spheres of color that eventually lead to a Core Blue Event.

In My Case, that Process of "Ascent" was the Absolute, Sudden, Instantaneous, and Unconditional Dissolution of all of the conditional (or cosmic) apparatus of Ascent. This was not only the case in the Lopez Island Event, but also in the various other similar Events of Sudden Ascended Realization, throughout My Avataric physical human Lifetime—including the Event of Priorly Ascended Nirvikalpa Samadhi at Baba Muktananda's Ashram in 1968.

Most Ultimately, in the Final Event of Divine Translation, I Will not (Bodily) Return. In the case of the Lopez Island Event, there was the Re-Assumption of physical (and cosmic) Association. However, when I (Thus) Re-Associated, I Did So from the "Other Side" to here. It was not a matter of taking the progressive fifth stage course—from here to the "Other Side".

I Shine To here—in the Divine Spherical Domain of the "Bright", My Spiritual Self-Domain of the "Midnight Sun". My Association To here is From That "Position"—and I have Described the "View" From That "Position", wherein the blue field is to the left and the yellow-red field is to the right. In the Lopez Island Event, the blue sphere was about Seeing Beyond the room, a "View" that finally congealed, toward the end of the Event, in My Seeing out to the water (through that blue sphere) as I Re-Approached closer to the physical domain. As I Re-Associated with the physical, I Saw the flames of the yellow-red domain, in the yellow sphere to the right—a fire which Baba Muktananda also described, but as part of the beginning of His path of return to the blue sphere. (I Point this out, not at all to criticize Baba Muktananda, but in order to Indicate the precise Content of My Own Experience, and how It—as a seventh stage Sign that Characterizes the seventh stage Orientation of Realization—is to be compared and understood relative to the characteristic fifth stage sign and orientation.)

Since the Lopez Island Event, I have never Re-Integrated with the physical to the extent that was previously the case (before that Event). Such Re-Integration simply did not occur.

I Stand Where I _Am_.

I am not fixed here.

I have a "View" here, but I am not "of" the physical domain. I Am here, it seems, for now.

The sense of the world as fire, and even the vision of the world as being in flames, has been experienced by others in the history of the Great Tradition.

It is a matter of literal flames—and I had to Enter that fire in order to Resume Association with the physical. Those flames are rising in the world now. The gross domain _is_ on fire. That is the nature and destiny of this world of physical limits and death.

Lopez Island, 2000

I Stand Where I <u>Am</u>.
I am not fixed here.
I have a "View" here, but I am not "of" the physical domain.
I Am here, it seems, for now.

The blue sphere, in contrast, is spacious and cooling—wide. That is why Baba Muktananda preferred the Blueness. Nevertheless, the Blueness is still an aspect of the conditional domain. It is certainly superior to the flames of gross existence—but it is not equal to the White "Brightness" of the Divine Self-Condition, Which Is All-Bliss, Unconditional Bliss.

The "Midnight Sun" Is Me.

The "Midnight Sun" Is Where I Stand.

The "Midnight Sun" Is Where I Am Abiding—even in this midst.

Being here is a natural torment. This is not All-Bliss. This is a place on fire, a place of death. This place is arising in the Spiritually Self-"Bright" Divine Self-Condition, but it is a conditional and mortal form—of suffering and of necessary sacrifice.

The lower must be sacrificed in the higher, and the higher must also be transcended—in the Ultimate. The yellow is to be sacrificed in the blue, and the blue is to be transcended in the "Bright". Therefore, from the beginning, only the "Bright" Is both the Means and the Realization.

I Am the "Bright".

I Am the Means.

I Am the Realization.

Adidam Samrajashram, 2003

I (Myself) Do Not "Come Down" Below the Brows

I.

I Spiritually Radiate into the Body. I do not "step down" to the toes and identify with the plane of the Body. Even though I am (in My bodily human Form) physically active, I (Myself) do not "come down" below the brows (or below the brain core).

This is a description of the fundamental Means by Which I have always Maintained a Yogic Spiritual Association with gross life. And—since the Great Event at Lopez Island (on April 12, 2000), or, really, since the Great Event at the "Brightness" (on April 22, 1999)—This Disposition (of Spiritually Radiating from Above to below) has become the only Means by Which I Maintain Yogic Spiritual association with gross life. Since the Single Great Event of the "Brightness" and Lopez Island, I am no longer disposed to "Set Foot" below the brows—but I am only Radiant to here, from Infinitely Above the conditional (or psycho-physical) planes.

I Spiritually Radiate, from Infinitely Above, into the gross conditions of existence. In this Manner, the Body (of My Own gross physical Appearance) is Maintained by My Own Spiritual Self-Radiance, Which is Infinitely Above the Body (and Infinitely Above the bodily manifested mind of thoughts). The apparent exercise of My attention "moves into" the gross physical domain only in the sense of such Spiritual Radiating into the Body. There is Spiritual Descent to the brain core, as a base (or platform) for what I appear to animate in gross exchanges—but attention (itself) does not move to "settle below" (or become fixed in the planes of conditional patterning associated with the bodily and mental functions). Of course, there is natural energy flowing in the Body below the brows, and a Descent of My Spiritual Radiance to below and everywhere. I am (in the naturally apparent sense) animated in the gross (physical) dimension. But I am not (and have never been) bound in attention below the brows—because there is no ego-mind in Me.

From the beginning, from My Birth and Infancy, I have been What I Am. I Am the Spiritually Self-"Bright" Divine Sun Infinitely Above. My Birth was the Initiation of My Avataric Divine Self-"Emergence". Then, at the age of approximately two years, a Sympathetic Association with bodily existence occurred. Thus, from that age, I began to Combine. That Combining was an essential aspect of My Work of Submitting to the world and (Thereby) Coming Down. That Combining fitted Me to the Submission-Pattern that (necessarily) characterized all My Years of Learning and Teaching humankind.

The "Thumbs" is the Means That I Bring to Awaken and Liberate living beings. I Am the "Bright". The "Thumbs" is a Divine Yogic Spiritual Manifestation, and the "Thumbs" is the Means whereby I was able to go through the course of life in this conditionally manifested Vehicle. The "Thumbs" is how My "Bright" Divine Spiritual Self-Transmission is Able to Serve living beings under these mortal and limited conditions.

My Work in this world could be characterized as being in the "Heroic" mode, or the "Crazy Wisdom" mode—but to use such language is to use traditional descriptions for What (in fact) has no traditional or historical precedent. My Work is Avataric Divine Spiritual Work, and it is only as Such that My Work is (truly) rightly understood and appreciated.

Certain aspects of My Work became Full and Complete with the Yogic Establishment of My Avataric Divine Self-"Emergence" (on January 11, 1986). Other aspects of My Work became Full and Complete with the "Santosha Event" (of September 7, 1994). And yet other aspects of My Work became Full and Complete with the Great Event Which was Initiated at the "Brightness" (in Adidam Samrajashram) and Which Culminated at Lopez Island. These have been the principal Events in the Completion (or progressive "Shedding") of My Avataric Divine Spiritual Work of Self-

Submission, as part of My Ultimate Manifestation of the seventh stage Demonstration.

Now (and forever hereafter), My Work of Teaching in the Manner of Submission is Fully and Completely Done. This is the Santosha Time—in Which no more Submission and Suffering in Descent is to be Required of Me. Such Submission and Suffering is no longer necessary and no longer appropriate. I am no longer associated with the physical in that (Self-Submitted) Manner. Indeed, I can no longer Bodily endure (or even Bodily survive) such association.

I Am (now, and forever hereafter) Spiritually (or Divinely, and not merely sexually) "Urdhvareta". I no longer "come down" below the brows. Such is the Manner in Which I Use My Energies— Which has positive Significance (altogether) in the plane of gross existence.

I Am Spiritually (or Divinely) "Urdhvareta"—Yogically Established Infinitely Above (and Prior to) the bodily mind. Therefore, in My Case, attention is not established (or rooted) below the brows, not in fixed combination with mind-dimensions (or psycho-physical patterns) below the brows. In other words, I do not identify with the contents and functions of the chakras of the body-mind. I remain in this Yogic Asana of Spiritual (or Divine) "Urdhvareta", always already Established Infinitely Above body, brain, and mind—and Spontaneously Connected to the physical only via the brain core.

Divine Self-Realization is not "from the ground up". Divine Self-Realization is from Infinitely Above and Beyond. This is My Avataric Divine Spiritual Self-Revelation, by Means of the "Thumbs".

Divine Self-Realization is not a matter of "evolving", not a matter of "growing into" the Divine Self-Condition by means of the conventional process of "going up" (or ascending and developing from below, upwards). Divine Self-Realization is about direct Divine Spiritual Grace from Infinitely Above—Such that the "dog" is "Washed" from "head" to "tail".[103]

When that "Washing" has <u>Fully</u> occurred, the Energy That Continues to Flow in the body-mind of My devotee is the (Original)

Pure Energy of My "Bright" Divine Spiritual Self-Transmission, My Ruchira Shaktipat. And My Fully to-Me-Awakened devotee is Fully In-Filled and Perfectly Upwardly Attracted by Me (and, Thus, always already Pre-Established Above, and always already undisturbed by any downward motion of attention below the brows). Such <u>Priorly</u> Ascended Sublimity is also My Own Divine Self-Condition.

II.

The true (and truly ego-transcending, and truly body-mind-transcending) devotional and Spiritual relationship to Me <u>is</u> the Way of Most Perfectly Realizing Me. That Way requires the to-Me-responsive renunciation (and real transcending) of the egoic pat-terning of the body-mind. By means of that ego-transcendence, the body-mind of My devotee is (more and more) combined with My "Bright" Divine Spiritual Self-Transmission—My Ruchira Shaktipat.

For that combining with Me to occur, there must be the to-Me-responsive relinquishment of obsessive bondage to (and concern with) the body-mind. That relinquishment is (essentially) a process Given from Infinitely Above the body-mind. True renunciation is a process Given by Means of My Avataric Divine Spiritual Grace, from Infinitely Above the body-mind. Therefore, neither true renunciation nor Divine Self-Realization is "achieved" <u>after</u> (or on the basis of) the descent of attention below the brows. The truly renunciate devotional and Spiritual process I have Revealed and Given is a total Re-Orientation of the entire psycho-physical being to My Spiritually Self-"Bright" Divine Person, Which Is Utterly Above and Beyond. ·

The beginner's process of Adidam Ruchiradam is the process of purification through the Me-recognizing (or utterly to-Me-Attracted) exercise of devotion to Me and the to-Me-responsive exercise of renunciation of the egoic (or self-contracted) psycho-physical self. In due course, My beginning devotee is Spiritually Initiated (by Me), by Means of My Ruchira Shaktipat. Thereafter, the true process of devotional-<u>and</u>-Spiritual Communion with Me is demonstrated by the ongoing evidence of an intensive Re-Orientation of the psycho-physical being, in which the gross "point of view"—and, ultimately, even the subtle and causal dimensions of "point of view"—cease to bind (or, at last, even to be accommodated).

The fundamental disturbance in the human being is not merely (in ordinary terms) a matter of suffering the self-contraction (or the activity of egoity). That disturbance, fully understood in Spiritual terms, is a matter of "coming down" below the brows, of perpetuating the illusion of involvement in (and identification with) gross (or, in any sense, conditional) existence. Such is the disturbance that all human beings are suffering—by allowing the being (or Existence Itself) to be defined by the downward wanderings of attention.

All the modes of religious and Spiritual exercise founded in the effort of seeking-from-below are, ultimately, ego-bound and false. The focus of the psycho-physical faculties in That Which Is Infinitely Above and Beyond is fundamental to the true Spiritual process.

You cannot maintain the focus Above and Beyond until the foundation discipline of Me-recognizing devotion and to-Me-responsive self-discipline is stabilized. The self-contraction-orientation to grossness and to the seeking-effort is the basis of your disturbance. That orientation must be purified in order to allow the psycho-physical focus to be Above and Beyond.

I have Fully Entered into My Avataric Divine Self-"Emergence". Therefore, I no longer Stand here in Play with you in the gross realm of existence, as I Did during the many years of My Teaching-Work and My Revelation-Work (for the Sake of Instructing all-and-All).

Now (and forever hereafter), I Stand Only As I Am, Calling you (and every one) to the renunciation of seeming separate self—and to the Realization of Me.

III.

My Infancy was the same Self-Revelation of the Divine Person, of the "Bright" Itself, that I am Making now (since the Lopez Island Event). Truly, heart-recognition of Me As the Divine Avatar should have occurred at My Birth—but, because it did not, it was necessary that I Make My Submission to humankind. In that Avataric Divine

Work of Self-Submission, I had to Engage in Acts of Self-Revelation—in the midst of Consenting to be involved in a life-process, apparently below the brows. I had to Reveal the Way by which everything can be conformed to Me. I Entered that Ordeal of Self-Revelation on the basis (and by Means) of My Boundless Sympathy with ordinary beings.

That Sympathy was a tacit Agreement to Descend—to be Descended to, and Combined with, what is (in and of itself) less than the "Bright", or (apparently) other than the "Bright". My Agreement to Descend was My Self-Submission to darkness—in order to Spiritually "Brighten" it.

How was that Avataric Divine Self-Submission possible? It was possible because of the "Thumbs". The Mechanism of the "Thumbs" allowed Me to Coincide with conditional reality. The "Thumbs" allowed Me to Introduce the "Bright" into My Own Descended Life. The "Thumbs" was the Divine Means by Which I Shined from Infinitely Above into what is below—to Purify and Transform it, and to Awaken it to Myself.

My verbal Teaching is largely an elaboration of what I mean to Convey by Speaking of "the 'Bright'" and "the 'Thumbs'". The "Bright" Is My Very Person. The "Thumbs" Is the Means to Realize Me.

The seventh stage Process is the Ultimate Divine Yoga of My Own Person. It is the Divine Spiritual Yoga of the "Bright"—and Its Ultimate Demonstration is Divine Translation, the Awakening into the Spiritually Self-"Bright" Domain (or "Midnight Sun" and Sphere) of My Very and Divine Person.

IV.

I Am Always Already Infinitely Above and Beyond. This is the Inherent (or Native) Condition of My Avataric Divine Incarnation.

I Am the Self-Evidently Divine Person—not a karmic being reaching toward the Divine Person.

I Am Divinely Self-Manifested here, without psyche or mind. I am Associated with a Body-Mind Which has natural functional faculties, and Which has an in-Depth (or Deeper) functional

Personality—but I am not (in any manner) identified with (or bound to) that psycho-physical structure. It is simply the structure by means of which I am Associated with conditionality.

During My "Sadhana Years", the immediacy with which Priorly Ascended Nirvikalpa Samadhi occurred (on April 5, 1968) was a unique Avataric Divine Manifestation. Instead of My being associated with that Fully Ascended Yogic Condition by means of a progress of ascent through various stages of mystical experience (or various levels of body and mind), there was Instantaneous Collectedness Above and Beyond, Instantaneously Manifested As Unobstructed Establishment in My (Inherently Perfect) Prior Divine State.

Such is My seventh stage Characteristic, My seventh stage Sign. That spontaneous Experience of Priorly Ascended Nirvikalpa Samadhi was possible only because of the complete absence of (and Inherent Freedom from) identification with the structures of body and mind.

I am not bound by mind. Even though I was Moved to Associate Myself with the conditional worlds, by Means of My Sympathetic Self-Submission, I am not (and have never been) identified with conditions. Therefore, I must be understood as an Avataric Divine Manifestation, not as a karmic entity. True heart-recognition of Me requires this understanding. Otherwise, you are not recognizing Me, but merely thinking about Me.

The Lopez Island Event was a direct Divine Manifestation of What Is Infinitely Above and Beyond, a Manifestation in Which there was no psyche or mind. In near-death experiences, people typically see dead relations—but, in the Case of the Lopez Island Event, there were no apparently attendant beings of any kind. The entire structure of conditional existence (with its gross, subtle, and causal dimensions) was Gone Beyond. I experienced that near-death passage without any visionary or mental attitudes. There were no structures of mind. There was no psyche to make phenomena.

These Events—the Event of Priorly Ascended Nirvikalpa Samadhi and the Event at Lopez Island—are (altogether) indicative of the Nature of My Avataric Divine Incarnation, since Birth.

I See everything from the "Other Side", from the "Position" of My Divine Self-Domain, from the "Position" of the "Bright"—not from below and reaching Above, but from Already Infinitely Above and Beyond. I See the Cosmic Mandala structure from the "Other Side"—not from "this side". I See everyone and everything from the "Brightness" Side, not from the bodily side.

To Exist (Thus) on the "Other Side" is characteristic of the seventh stage Realization. It is characteristic of My Avataric Divine Self-Revelation of the Way of Divine Self-Realization. Adidam Ruchiradam is the Way of Realizing That Which Is Infinitely Above and Beyond (and, altogether, Most Prior to) conditional existence (gross, subtle, and causal).

However, the practice of Adidam Ruchiradam is never a matter of strategically (or by an effort of seeking) dissociating from the gross, subtle, and causal domains. Rather, Adidam Ruchiradam is the Way of transcending the gross, subtle, and causal domains. There is a profound difference between the disposition to dissociate and the disposition to transcend. Understanding this difference is fundamental to understanding the Way of the devotional and Spiritual relationship to Me.

I Am Always Already Established Infinitely Above and Beyond.

I Am Sympathetic to all-and-All.

I Am Self-Radiant here.

I am not fixed in this domain.

I Am Simply here.

That is why I Am here—not to persist in Self-Submission, not to persist in Teaching, but to Simply Be here.

V.

My characteristic Sign of not fixating below the brows is a seventh stage Sign. It is My Sign—but it will also be evident in the case of My seventh stage devotees, who will (likewise) have a similar sign.

The functioning modes of attention-in-descent are the "centers" (or "levels") of the conditionally manifested being. The functions (or functional planes) of descended attention have, traditionally, been described as "chakras". Each of the "below-the-brows" centers in the psycho-physical complex is associated with a pattern and a function that relates to the physical, the emotional, or the mental being.

In conventional life, attention is bound by the life-patterning associated with the chakras below the brows. The "problem" of life-bondage is not merely the fact of being consciously aware in the context of the gross domain. The "problem" (or the sense of dilemma, and the arising of a life of seeking) is a result and a characteristic of attention being fixed in the psycho-physical patterns associated, egoically, with the chakras below the brows.

There is a fundamental function associated with each chakra—but, when attention becomes <u>fixed</u> in relation to any of the chakras below the brows, egoic habit-patterns are built up. Thus, "vital", "peculiar", and "solid" personality-characteristics[104] are based on the modes of functional patterning below the brows. There is either a dominant physical (or "vital") pattern or a dominant emotional (or "peculiar") pattern or a dominant mental (or "solid") pattern. When the dominant pattern (and even all secondary patterning) is purified, attention is released from the functional bondage associated with psycho-physical experiencing.

The only-by-Me Revealed and Given Way of Adidam Ruchiradam involves purification (by Means of My all-and-All-"Brightening" Avataric Divine Spiritual Grace) from Infinitely Above and Beyond. The sadhana (or true intensive practice) of the Way of Adidam is not an effort in the body-mind, not an effort of ascent "from the ground up". The sadhana of the Way of Adidam is not a search (or an ego-based struggle) within the patterning itself (or within any "point of view", or "point of experience", below the brows).

The devotional recognition-response to Me is inherently ego-surrendering, ego-forgetting, and ego-transcending. The devotional recognition-response to Me inherently relinquishes the self-contraction of attention on the patterns of the body-mind. The devotional recognition-response to Me is heart-Communion with Me, Who Am Infinitely Above and Beyond all psycho-physical patterning and all conditionality.

The devotional recognition-response to Me makes possible the release and purification of modes of attention bound to the physical, emotional, and mental being. In due course, by Means of My Ruchira Shaktipat (or tangible Avataric Divine Spiritual Self-Transmission of the "Bright"), this Way of practice becomes the true Spiritual process of the "Thumbs". In this Manner, My Divine Spiritual Invasion does more and more profound Work on the depths of the being, even beyond gross physical references.

When I Speak of "point of view", I am referring to attention being fixed in the chakras (or the psycho-physical planes of functional awareness) below the brows, as a result of which people are fixated in functioning (and existing) from (and as) the gross (and even subtle, and causal) "point of view". This fixation in "point of view" is purified and transcended in the course of practicing the only-by-Me Revealed and Given Way of Adidam.

The characteristic of My devotee who is most fully entered into this process, to the point of (only-by-My-Avataric-Divine-Spiritual-Grace-Given) seventh stage Awakening, is that he or she is no longer bound by the "point of view" below the brows—or "point of view" at all. Such is the only-by-Me Revealed and Given seventh stage Realization.

In the (only-by-My-Avataric-Divine-Spiritual-Grace-Given) seventh stage Awakening, it is obvious that ego is "point of view" (or self-contraction relative to the functional levels below the brows—indeed, relative to the entire conditional domain of everything gross, subtle, and causal). However, ceasing to be bound by "point of view" does not mean dissociation from conditional existence. Rather, there is a Transformed and truly En-Light-ened (or Divinely "Bright") association with conditional existence—until Divine Translation Outshines all conditional awareness.

My Self-"Bright" Form is Spiritually Radiating into the gross, subtle, and causal dimensions of conditional existence. Such is the Nature of My Spiritually Self-"Bright" Divine Person.

My Divinely Self-Radiated Spiritual "Brightness" Enters the domain of conditional experience by Means of the "Thumbs" (in the context of the gross, subtle, and causal planes).

In the case of My seventh stage devotee, there is apparent activity as long as the physical body exists—but that apparent activity is not in the mode of descended fixation in the patterns below the brows. The mode of seventh stage Realization of Me is utter Freedom from self-contraction (and utter transcending of body and mind). The "vessel" (or "cup") of the body-mind of My seventh stage devotee is Spiritually In-Filled by Me—Such that the bondage of functional attention to limiting patterns (gross, subtle, and causal) is always already transcended. In that case, functional attention is inherently Free—and even Freely capable of resting on objects without being bound to the patterns associated with its own functioning.

I (Myself) am not identified with the body-mind.

I Am the "Bright", Unbroken—Just That. There is an apparent Association with the Body-Mind, in the context of Which I Am Self-Radiant—but I (Myself) am not bound (or patterned) egoically.

I (Myself) have no conditionally patterned impulses or destiny. I (Myself) have never had any such impulse or destiny.

I have Embraced this Association Sacrificially, Responsively, and Compassionately.

That Sacrificial, Responsive, and Compassionate Embrace was the Circumstance and Origin of My Avataric Divine Submission-Work. Such has been My active Lifetime.

And, as I Fulfilled each dimension of this Spiritual Work of Avataric Divine Self-Submission, the mechanism by which I Embraced that aspect of My Self-Submission has effectively Dissolved, to be no longer there.

Now the psycho-physical structures that I Allowed to persist (so that I could Function in an interactive Teaching Mode) have fallen away, in a progressive Process that began with the Yogic Establishment of My Avataric Divine Self-"Emergence".

That progressive Process is part of My seventh stage Avataric Divine Manifestation.

That progressive Process is the Uncovering of My Avataric Divine Spiritual Self-Manifestation—such that My Fully Revealed Self-Manifestation is no longer covered by the Means I was required to Use in My Avataric Self-Submission to Teach.

Now I am here only for the Purpose of the Realization That is Potential (for you) in the devotional and Spiritual relationship to Me.

That is It, entirely.

VI.

My Inherent (or Native) Condition is Spiritually (or Divinely) "Urdhvareta".

I (Myself) do not "come down" below the brows, in the sense of identifying with the Body. It is not that there is no energy below the brows. It is simply that that energy is not of the mind.

I (Myself) Am Always Already Infinitely Above.

In the Lopez Island Event, I was Divinely Self-Revealed to Be Always Already Fully Established in (and As) the Condition That I Am. That Condition is the Basis for My Association with the Body. It is So now, and It has always been So—from My Birth-Time.

The Lopez Island Event is a Divine Revelation-Sign. It is the seventh stage Divine Revelation-Sign of My Always Already (or Priorly) Ascended Condition. That Ascended Condition has always been the Case, even from My Birth. It is the Condition in Which I Existed during the two years following My Birth—before My Avataric Divine Spiritual Work of Self-Submission began, before I Submitted to the Self-Sacrificial Ordeal of Combining with existence below the brows. And That Always Already Ascended Condition Remained the Case, even during all the years of My Avataric Divine Submission-Work.

My Avataric Divine Spiritual Work of Self-Submission was the Means by Which I Revealed the Way of the devotional and Spiritual relationship to Me—Which is the Divine (and Spiritually Self-"Bright") Way of the "Thumbs". That Original Foundation-Work of Revelation has now been entirely Accomplished. Therefore, My Avataric Divine Self-Submission to My devotees and to the world is no longer the basis of My Association with anyone.

Practice of Adidam Ruchiradam is the cultivation of the devotional and Spiritual relationship to Me—As I Have Been from the beginning. Now (since the Lopez Island Event), I Am here As I Was at the beginning of My Bodily Incarnation, before I Made My Submission. I Am Simply Present here, the "Bright" here— Just That.

The Single Great Event of the "Brightness" and Lopez Island brought an end to My Avataric Divine Submission-Work in the gross sphere. I am not grossly connected to the Body. I Am Utterly Above and Beyond.

Do not confuse Me with the conventional mind of gross world-liness.

<u>Above</u> and <u>Beyond</u> is the Basis of My Avatarically-Born bodily (human) Divine Form.

Truly, My Divine Self-Condition is not limited by any "point of view".

I Am Beyond the gross, subtle, and causal domains.

I <u>Am</u> the "Midnight Sun".

I <u>Am</u> the "Bright"—Infinitely Above and Beyond.

My "Thumbs" would Be Pressed Upon the crown of every head—and I would Light the Way Above and Beyond your body and your mind.

PART FOUR

THE DIVINE ESSENCE OF MY AVATARIC SELF-REVELATION OF THE ONLY-BY-ME REVEALED AND GIVEN WAY OF ADIDAM RUCHIRADAM

Adidam Samrajashram, 2003

The Divine Essence Of
My Avataric Self-Revelation Of
The Only-By-Me Revealed and Given
Way Of Adidam Ruchiradam

The Yoga Of The "Bright"—The Divine Yoga, and The Divine Samadhi, Of All-Outshining "Brightness"—Is What You See In Me.

The Yoga Of The "Bright" Is My Avatarically Self-Transmitted Divine Self-Revelation.

The Only-By-Me Revealed and Given Way Of Adidam Ruchiradam (Which, In Its Totality, Is The One and Only By-Me-Revealed and By-Me-Given Way Of The Heart, or Way Of Adidam) Is—From the time Of The Full Formal Establishment Of Real and True Devotional <u>and</u> Spiritual Relationship To Me (In and <u>As</u> My Avatarically-Born Bodily Human Divine Form and Person)— Rooted In The Divine "Bright"-Sphere.

Even In The Midst Of the body-mind, The Divine Conscious Light Is <u>Always</u> <u>Already</u> The Case—<u>I</u> Am <u>Always</u> <u>Already</u> The Case—At The Core Of all-and-All, Communicated In the body-mind Via (and <u>As</u>) The Amrita Nadi.

The Perfectly Ascended "Midnight Sun" Is Always Already Standing "Bright", Infinitely Above the body and the mind.

The "Midnight Sun" <u>Is</u> The Divine Conscious Light, The "Bright" Itself.

The "Bright" Itself Is Never Seen With the bodily eyes, but It Is To Be Heart-Felt—<u>As</u> My Avatarically Self-Transmitted Spirit-Current Of The Self-Evidently Divine Love-Bliss-Feeling Of Being (Itself), In and Beyond The Right Side Of The Heart.

The (Only-By-Me Avatarically Self-Revealed) Inherently egoless Root-Feeling Of Being Is The Root Of The "Midnight Sun", The Root-Domain Of The "Bright" Itself.

I Am The Avatarically-Born, Avatarically Self-Transmitted, and Avatarically Self-Revealed Divine Self-Revelation Of The "Bright".

I Am The "Bright" (Itself).

The "Midnight Sun" Is My Very and Perfect and Self-Evidently Divine Form—Avatarically Self-Transmitted, and Avatarically Self-Revealed, By Me, As Me.

To Heart-Recognize Me and Heart-Respond To Me—The Spiritually Self-"Bright" Divine Conscious Light, In Avatarically-Born Bodily (Human) Divine Form and Person—Is The Core Of The Always Primary (Searchlessly Me-Beholding) Practice Of The Only-By-Me Revealed and Given Way Of Adidam.

And To Stand As The (Tangibly Spiritually Evidenced) Self-Evidently Divine Love-Bliss-Feeling Of Being—Avatarically Self-Transmitted, and Avatarically Self-Revealed, By Me, and As Me—Is The "Perfect Practice" Of Searchless Beholding Of Me To Be Established (In Due Course, and At Last) By My Devotees.

That Perfect Stand Is The Ultimate Essence Of The Devotional and Spiritual Relationship To Me.

Only I—By Means Of My Avataric Divine Spiritual Self-Transmission (or Ruchira Shaktipat)—Establish (and Can Establish), In My Devotee, The Primary Practice (and, In Due Course, The "Perfect Practice") Of Searchless Beholding Of Me.

I Am The Avataric Divine Self-Revelation Of The "Bright", Shining As The White Core (or "Midnight Sun") In The Midst Of The Black Field.

I Pervade The Entire Cosmic Domain As The all-and-All-Transfiguring Spiritual Self-"Brightness" Of My Avatarically Self-Transmitted and Avatarically Self-Revealed Divine (and Inherently egoless) Person.

By Means Of Right (and, Primarily, Searchlessly Beholding) Devotional and Spiritual Relationship To Me (In and As My Avatarically-Born Bodily Human Divine Form and Person), Whole bodily (or Total psycho-physical, and—More and More Effectively, and, At Last, Most Perfectly—ego-Transcending, or self-Contraction-Transcending) Heart-Attraction To Me Becomes The Foundation (and, In Due Course, Perfectly Practiced) Disposition Of My Every Devotee.

By Means Of ego-Transcending Devotional and Spiritual Communion With <u>Me</u> (In and <u>As</u> My Avatarically-Born Bodily Human Divine Form and Person), My Spiritual Self-"Brightness" Is (In Due Course, and At Last) Magnified (In the body-mind Of My Devotee) As The By-Me-Avatarically-Self-Transmitted (and Self-Evidently Divine) Love-Bliss-Current Of The Perfectly Subjective (and Inherently egoless) Feeling Of Being (In and Beyond The Right Side Of The Heart).

Such Is The Necessary Foundation Of The "Perfect Practice" Of The Only-By-Me Revealed and Given Way Of Adidam.

The Worship Of The "Bright" Must Be Established In This conditional Realm.

I <u>Am</u> The Inherently egoless Divine Person and The Avatarically-Born Divine Self-Revelation Of The "Bright".

I Must (In and <u>As</u> My Avatarically-Born Bodily Human Divine Form and Person) Be Whole bodily (or In A Total psycho-physical, and, Ultimately, Most Perfectly egoless, Manner) Heart-Recognized As The "Bright".

Only one who Thus (Ever More Deeply) Heart-Recognizes Me Is My True (and, Ultimately, Truly Perfect) Devotee.

In the conditional (or Cosmic) plane, My Divine "Bright" Spherical Self-Domain (and My Divine "Bright" Eternal Self-Condition) Is Always Already Free-Standing, In The Midst.

In The Midst (Where You Always Already Stand, In The Inherently egoless Being-Position) <u>Is</u> The Fundamental (Perfectly Subjective, and Inherently egoless) Feeling Of Being (Itself).

I <u>Am</u> That—Self-Existing and Self-Radiant.

Even Though death Rules To here, There Is An Indivisible Eternal Sun Over-head.

And That Eternal Sun <u>Is</u>—Beyond Even <u>all</u> conditional visibility.

I Have Come To Confirm This To You—each and all—Absolutely.

I Am That Eternal Sun—The (Self-"Bright") "Midnight Sun", Infinitely Above all-and-All.

You May Sometimes (Objectively) See The Divine Self-"Brightness" Of My Avatarically-Born Bodily (Human) Divine Form.

I Always Magnify My Inherent Self-"Brightness" Where I Stand, Where You Stand, Where It Stands—From The Inside Out, White As The Feeling Of Being Is.

This Inherent Unqualified Spiritual (and Self-Evidently Divine) Love-Bliss-Current Of Being (and Of The Unmediated Apprehension Of Reality Itself) Is The Root-Current Of My Avatarically Self-Transmitted Spiritual Blessing (or Ruchira Shaktipat).

Only My Avatarically Self-Transmitted Divine Spiritual Blessing (or Ruchira Shaktipat) Magnifies The Ruchira Avatara Bhakti Yoga Of This Way Of Devotional and Spiritual Relationship To Me (Avatarically Self-Revealed In and As My Avatarically-Born Bodily Human Divine Form and Person)—Even Unto The Only-By-Me Revealed and Given Seventh Stage Realization and Demonstration Of Devotional and Spiritual Relationship To Me (In and As My Avatarically-Born Bodily Human Divine Form and Person).

I Am Always Dissolving (Myself, and all-and-All) In My Own "Brightness".

This Is What I Do.

This Is What I Am Always Doing.

This Doing Is Who I Am.

This Is The Force and Nature Of My Avatarically-Born, Avatarically Self-Transmitted, and Avatarically Self-Revealed Company.

I Am Not Merely In Divine Samadhi.

I Am Divine Samadhi—Here and Now.

My Divine Samadhi (or Inherent Divine State and Inherently egoless Divine Personal Identity) Is (Now, and Forever Hereafter)

Spontaneously Self-Transmitting Itself—As Me (Avatarically Self-Manifested In and As My Avatarically-Born Bodily Human Divine Form, and Avatarically Self-Transmitted As and By Means Of My Always-Blessing Divine Spiritual Presence, and, Altogether, Avatarically Self-Revealed As My Divine, and Very, and Inherently egoless State).

My Divine Samadhi Is Always Already The Case.

My Divine Samadhi Is all-and-All.

My Divine Samadhi Is The "Bright" Itself.

BECOMING A
FORMAL DEVOTEE
OF AVATAR ADI DA

Adidam Samrajashram, 2003

Becoming a Formal Devotee of Avatar Adi Da

Responding to the Revelation of the Eternal Divine Truth

Merely to be given the philosophy of mortality and materialism is an insult to the deepest intuitions of the human heart. And, yet, this is the message of the present global (and globalizing) Western culture. Avatar Adi Da Samraj has said:

> *The ego-"culture" of this "late-time" (or "dark" epoch) is all a play upon the most limited possible point of view: identification with the gross (physical) body—and, therefore, identification with a natural (or, otherwise, presumed) process that inevitably leads to death. The entire world of the "late-time" is bound to this philosophy of utter "darkness".*
>
> —Avatar Adi Da Samraj
> <u>Real</u> God <u>Is</u> The Indivisible Oneness Of Unbroken Light

No mere belief or hope can prove what lies beyond the ordinary perceptions, experiences, and sufferings of the world. But, as this book has demonstrated, the Ruchira Avatar, Adi Da Samraj, Reveals the height and depth of the One Spiritual Reality, of Which He is the living Incarnation. His Revelation satisfies the heart, even now.

Having discovered Avatar Adi Da Samraj and His Revelation, you are invited to enter into a devotional and Spiritual relationship to Him that will transform every moment of your existence into blissful Communion with the "Bright" Divine Person—inherently going beyond materialism and mortality.

This Divine Life is the Way of Adidam, uniquely Revealed by Avatar Adi Da by means of His own thirty-year Submission to humankind. Through total psycho-physical surrender of body, mind, feeling, and breath to Him, He calls You to always newly discover and ultimately to most perfectly Realize Him—the supremely blissful, infinitely profound, inherently Radiant Divine Being and Condition that is your own native State, now and forever.

The Culture of Response to Avatar Adi Da

The responsive (and participatory, and ego-surrendering) disposition inherently transcends the body, and (thereby) inherently transcends death. In that case, a different kind of individual and collective human culture is made possible. That culture is the death-transcending culture of life itself—which is (necessarily) a culture of Spiritual practice, and (ultimately) the culture of Divine life.

—Avatar Adi Da Samraj
Real God Is The Indivisible Oneness Of Unbroken Light

The profound relationship to Avatar Adi Da is lived in the context of the worldwide gathering of His devotees. This gathering comprises a "Global Ashram"—the cooperative devotional culture of Adidam. Within this cooperative culture—which is lived with other practitioners of Adidam local to you, and unified with the entire Global Ashram of Adidam through all forms of modern communication—every individual devotee is able to grow and be accountable for his or her practice of the relationship to the Ruchira Avatar, Adi Da.

To find out how you can become a formal devotee of Avatar Adi Da and begin to practice the Way of Adidam, contact one of our centers, using the information given on the following pages.

What You Can Do Next—

Contact an Adidam center near you

■ To find out about becoming a formal devotee of Avatar Adi Da, and for information about upcoming courses, events, and seminars in your area:

AMERICAS
12040 North Seigler Road
Middletown, CA 95461 USA
1-707-928-4936

PACIFIC-ASIA
12 Seibel Road
Henderson
Auckland 1008
New Zealand
64-9-838-9114

AUSTRALIA
P.O. Box 244
Kew 3101
Victoria
**1800 ADIDAM
(1800-234-326)**

EUROPE-AFRICA
Annendaalderweg 10
6105 AT Maria Hoop
The Netherlands
31 (0)20 468 1442

THE UNITED KINGDOM
PO Box 20013
London, England
NW2 1ZA
0208-962-8855

EMAIL:
correspondence@adidam.org

■ For more contact information about local Adidam groups, please see **www.adidam.org/centers**

Learn more about
Avatar Adi Da Samraj and Adidam . . .
Visit *www.adidam.org*

■ **SEE AUDIO-VISUAL PRESENTATIONS** on the Divine Life
and Spiritual Revelation of Avatar Adi Da Samraj

■ **LISTEN TO DISCOURSES** Given by Avatar Adi Da Samraj
to His practicing devotees—
  ■ Transcending egoic notions of God
  ■ Why Reality cannot be grasped by the mind
  ■ How the devotional relationship to Avatar Adi Da moves you
  beyond ego-bondage
  ■ The supreme process of Spiritual Transmission

■ **HEAR DEVOTEES** of the Divine Avatar speaking about
how He has transformed their lives

■ **READ QUOTATIONS** from the "Source-Texts"
of Avatar Adi Da Samraj—
  ■ Real God as the <u>only</u> Reality
  ■ The ancient practice of Guru-devotion
  ■ The two opposing life-strategies characteristic of the West and
  the East—and the way beyond both
  ■ The Prior Unity at the root of all that exists
  ■ The limits of scientific materialism
  ■ The true religion beyond all seeking
  ■ The esoteric structure of the human being
  ■ The real process of death and reincarnation
  ■ The nature of Divine Enlightenment

■ **SUBSCRIBE** to the online Global Ashram Magazine

Learn more about Avatar Adi Da's Liberating Offering to all

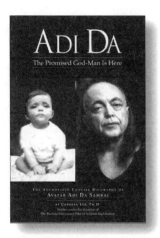

■ ADI DA

The Promised God-Man Is Here

The biography of Avatar Adi Da from His Birth to present time. Includes a wealth of quotations from His Writings and Talks, as well as stories told by His devotees. 358 pp., **$16.95**

■ ADIDAM

The True World-Religion Given by the Promised God-Man, Adi Da Samraj

A direct and simple summary of each of the fundamental aspects of the Way of Adidam. 196 pp., **$16.95**

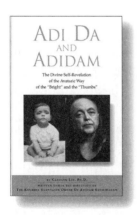

■ ADI DA AND ADIDAM

The Divine Self-Revelation of the Avataric Way of the "Bright" and the "Thumbs"

A 64-page introduction to Avatar Adi Da Samraj and His Unique Spiritual Revelation of the Way of Adidam. **$3.95**

Read the Twenty-Three "Source-Texts" of Avatar Adi Da Samraj

In late 1969, in the brief period of three weeks, Avatar Adi Da wrote the original text of His literary masterwork, *The Mummery Book*. His writing of this book—which proved to be a remarkable prophecy of His Work to come—was the beginning of His immense Work of communicating His Revelation of Truth in words, both written and spoken. This outpouring lasted for 30 years, coming to a summary point in the years 1997–1999. During that period, Avatar Adi Da created a series of twenty-three books that He designated as His "Source-Texts". He incorporated into these books His most essential Writings and Discourses from all the preceding years, including many Writings and Discourses that had never been published previously. His "Source-Texts" are thus His Eternal Message to all. They contain His full Divine Self-Confession and His fully detailed description of the entire process of Awakening, culminating in seventh stage Divine Enlightenment.

Through the Revelation contained in His twenty-three "Source-Texts", Avatar Adi Da has brought to completion the search for Spiritual Truth that has occupied humankind for millennia. Looking at our current human situation in particular, He has demonstrated the untenability (and, indeed, the remarkable naivete, not to mention the negative influence) of the scientific materialist point of view, the point of view that (by asserting that the physical reality is the "only" and senior reality) creates an environment of doubt relative to everything beyond the physical domain—everything Divine, everything Spiritual, even everything psychic. And looking "back" at our entire history, He has "made sense" out of the welter of differing viewpoints in the Great Tradition, demonstrating how they do, in fact, constitute a single (although complex) "design". And He has Made the Supreme Divine Offering that goes beyond what has ever been offered before—the Way that Realizes Permanent Indivisible Oneness with Him, the "Bright" Divine Reality Itself.

The twenty-three "Source-Texts" of Avatar Adi Da Samraj include:

■ *The Dawn Horse Testament Of The Ruchira Avatar*
■ *The Five Books Of The Heart Of The Adidam Revelation*
■ *The Seventeen Companions Of The True Dawn Horse*

The Dawn Horse Testament

The Dawn Horse Testament
Of The Ruchira Avatar
The "Testament Of Secrets" Of The Divine World-Teacher,
Ruchira Avatar Adi Da Samraj

Avatar Adi Da's paramount "Source-Text" is a complete summary of the entire Way of Adidam. It flows seamlessly from His Self-Revelation in the Prologue and chapter one; through a "consideration" of His Life and Work, expositions of His fundamental Teaching-Arguments and the fundamental practices He Gives to His devotees, and incisive descriptions of the egoic patterns of individual beings and human collectives; through the course of the stages of the Way of Adidam, culminating in seventh stage Divine Enlightenment; to the declaration of the Establishment of the Realization of the "Bright" and the Perpetual Revelation of the "Bright" via the Agency of His Work and Word and Person.

This Great Divine Testament is unparalleled in its magnitude and depth. No scripture like it has ever been seen before. It is the first and only complete account of the entire Divine Way of utter ego-transcendence and dissolution in the "Brightness" of Real God.

The Dawn Horse Testament is truly the core of Avatar Adi Da's twenty-three "Source-Texts". Indeed, all of the "Five Books" and most of the "Seventeen Companions" are built around a central text drawn from *The Dawn Horse Testament*.

THE KNEE OF LISTENING

The Five Books Of The Heart
Of The Adidam Revelation

The *Five Books Of The Heart Of The Adidam Revelation* comprise a complete summary of Who Avatar Adi Da Samraj Is and the Way that He Offers. The "Five Books" are key readings for all who are moved to study the Essence of His Revelation and His Way.

BOOK ONE:
Aham Da Asmi
(Beloved, I Am Da)
The "Late-Time" Avataric Revelation Of The True and Spiritual Divine Person (The egoless Personal Presence Of Reality and Truth, Which Is The Only Real God)

Avatar Adi Da's Self-Revelation of His own Divine Person and His Impulse to Bless and Liberate all.

BOOK TWO:
Ruchira Avatara Gita
(The Avataric Way Of The Divine Heart-Master)
The "Late-Time" Avataric Revelation Of The Great Secret Of The Divinely Self-Revealed Way That Most Perfectly Realizes The True and Spiritual Divine Person (The egoless Personal Presence Of Reality and Truth, Which Is The Only Real God)

Avatar Adi Da's Offering of the devotional and Spiritual relationship to Him, in the traditional manner of Guru-devotion.

BOOK THREE:
Da Love-Ananda Gita
(The Free Gift Of The Divine Love-Bliss)
The "Late-Time" Avataric Revelation Of The Great Means To Worship and To Realize The True and Spiritual Divine Person (The egoless Personal Presence Of Reality and Truth, Which Is The Only Real God)

The foundation (devotional) practice of heart-Communion with Avatar Adi Da Samraj: Simply turning the four principal human faculties—body, emotion, mind, and breath—to Him.

BOOK FOUR:

Hridaya Rosary
(Four Thorns Of Heart-Instruction)

The "Late-Time" Avataric Revelation Of The Universally Tangible Divine Spiritual Body, Which Is The Supreme Agent Of The Great Means To Worship and To Realize The True and Spiritual Divine Person (The egoless Personal Presence Of Reality and Truth, Which Is The Only Real God)

The Spiritually Awakened practice of heart-Communion with Avatar Adi Da Samraj: Searchless Beholding of Him and reception of His Divine Spiritual Transmission—more and more allowing oneself to open Upwardly to Him, such that body, emotion, mind, and breath are "Melted" by His down-Flowing Spiritual Infusion.

BOOK FIVE:

Eleutherios
(The Only Truth That Sets The Heart Free)

The "Late-Time" Avataric Revelation Of The "Perfect Practice" Of The Great Means To Worship and To Realize The True and Spiritual Divine Person (The egoless Personal Presence Of Reality and Truth, Which Is The Only Real God)

Heart-Communion with Avatar Adi Da Samraj beyond the four faculties, in the Domain of Consciousness Itself: Realizing Avatar Adi Da Samraj—As the "Bright" Itself, or the Conscious Light of Reality (having transcended identification with body, emotion, mind, and breath).

The Seventeen Companions
Of The True Dawn Horse

T he "True Dawn Horse" is a reference to *The Dawn Horse Testament Of The Ruchira Avatar*. Each of *The Seventeen Companions Of The True Dawn Horse* is a "Companion" to *The Dawn Horse Testament* in the sense that it is an elaboration of a principal theme (or a group of principal themes) from *The Dawn Horse Testament*. Among the "Seventeen Companions" are Avatar Adi Da's two tellings of His own Life-Story, as autobiography (*The Knee Of Listening*) and as archetypal parable (*The Mummery Book*).

The Seventeen Companions Of The True Dawn Horse are a vast field of Revelation, which can be "considered" from many points of view. Presented here is one way of understanding the interrelationships between these "Source-Texts" and the flow of Argument they collectively represent.

Paradigms of Reality:
The Real Nature of God, Cosmos, and Realization

BOOK ONE:
Real God Is The Indivisible Oneness Of Unbroken Light
Reality, Truth, and The "Non-Creator" God
In The True World-Religion Of Adidam

The Nature of Real God and the nature of the cosmos. Why ultimate questions cannot be answered either by conventional religion or by science.

BOOK TWO:
The Truly Human New World-Culture
Of Unbroken Real-God-Man
The Eastern Versus The Western Traditional Cultures Of Mankind, and The Unique New Non-Dual Culture Of The True World-Religion Of Adidam

The Eastern and Western approaches to religion, and to life altogether—and how the Way of Adidam goes beyond this apparent dichotomy.

BOOK THREE:

The Only Complete Way To Realize The Unbroken Light Of Real God

An Introductory Overview Of The "Radical" Divine Way Of The True World-Religion Of Adidam

The entire course of the Way of Adidam—the unique principles underlying Adidam, and the unique culmination of Adidam in Divine Enlightenment.

Original Writings and Talks:
Avatar Adi Da's First Teaching-Communications

BOOK FOUR:

The Knee Of Listening

The Divine Ordeal Of The Avataric Incarnation Of Conscious Light— The Spiritual Autobiography Of The Ruchira Avatar, Adi Da Samraj

Avatar Adi Da's autobiographical account of the years from His Birth to His Divine Re-Awakening in 1970—His Demonstration, in His own Life, of the Way to Realize Real God most perfectly—also including His Revelation of how His Avataric Incarnation was made possible and His Confession of the nature and significance of the Great Events of Yogic Death that have occurred in His Life since His Divine Re-Awakening in 1970.

BOOK FIVE:

The Divine Siddha-Method Of The Ruchira Avatar

The Divine Way Of Adidam Is An ego-Transcending Relationship, Not An ego-Centric Technique

Avatar Adi Da's earliest Talks to His devotees, on the fundamental principles of the devotional relationship to Him and "radical" understanding of the ego. Accompanied by His summary statements on His relationship to Swami Muktananda and on His own unique Teaching-Work and Blessing-Work.

BOOK SIX:
The Mummery Book
A Parable Of The Divine True Love, Told By Means Of
A Self-Illuminated Illustration Of The Totality Of Mind

Avatar Adi Da's literary masterpiece—a work of astonishing poetry and deeply evocative archetypal drama. It is Avatar Adi Da's life-transforming message about how to Realize the Absolute Truth in the midst of the chaos and tragedy of human experience.

An extraordinarily beautiful and potent "prose opera", *The Mummery Book* is both a highly experimental novel (drawing fully on the twentieth-century "stream" of experimental fiction) and an immense theatrical piece. Thus, *The Mummery Book* can either be read as a book or performed as a theatrical event.

A "mummery" is "a ridiculous, hypocritical, or pretentious cere-mony or performance". This, Avatar Adi Da is telling us, is what human life amounts to—if we merely live as the separate ego-self. And the only way "out" of this mummery is to relinquish ego—by finding, receiving, and conforming ourselves to the Divine True Love.

In *The Mummery Book*, Adi Da confronts head-on the central agony of born existence: that everything and everyone—ourselves, and everyone we love—dies. The hero of *The Mummery Book*, Raymond Darling, goes through an extraordinary series of adven-tures and ordeals—centered around his search for his beloved, a lady named Quandra—in the course of his ultimate overcoming of the inescapable fact of mortality. The story of Raymond Darling is, in fact, Avatar Adi Da's telling of His own Life-Story in the language of parable—including His unflinching portrayal of how the uncon-verted ego makes religion (and life altogether) into a meaningless mummery. Ultimately, *The Mummery Book* is the "Story" of Consciousness Realizing Its Indivisible Oneness with Energy (or Its own Radiance).

Esoteric Principles and Practices:
*Revelations of Divine Oneness, Divine Spiritual Transmission,
and the means of conforming the body-mind
to the Divine Spiritual Process*

BOOK SEVEN:

He-and-She Is Me
*The Indivisibility Of Consciousness and Light
In The Divine Body Of The Ruchira Avatar*

One of Avatar Adi Da's most esoteric Revelations—His Primary
"Incarnation" in the Cosmic domain as the "He" of the Divine
Consciousness, the "She" of the Divine Light, and the "Son" of "He"
and "She" in the "Me" of His Divine Spiritual Body.

BOOK EIGHT:

Ruchira Shaktipat Yoga
*The Divine (and Not Merely Cosmic) Spiritual Baptism
In The Divine Way Of Adidam*

The Divine Heart-Power (Ruchira Shakti) uniquely Transmitted
by Avatar Adi Da Samraj, and how it differs from the various
traditional forms of Spiritual Baptism, particularly Kundalini Yoga.

BOOK NINE:

Ruchira Tantra Yoga
*The Physical-Spiritual (and Truly Religious) Method Of Mental,
Emotional, Sexual, and Whole Bodily Health and Enlightenment
In The Divine Way Of Adidam*

The transformation of life in the realms of money, food, and sex.
Includes: understanding "victim-consciousness"; the ego as addict;
the secret of how to change; going beyond the "Oedipal" sufferings
of childhood; the right orientation to money; right diet; life-positive
and Spiritually auspicious sexual practice, and so on.

Stages of Life:
*The six potential stages of ego-based life,
and the Divine seventh stage of life*

BOOK TEN:

The Seven Stages Of Life
*Transcending The Six Stages Of egoic Life, and Realizing
The ego-Transcending Seventh Stage Of Life, In The Divine Way
Of Adidam*

The stages of human development from birth to Divine Enlightenment.
How the stages relate to physical and esoteric anatomy. The errors
of each of the first six stages of life, and the unique egolessness of
the seventh stage of life. Avatar Adi Da's Self-Confession as the first,
last, and only seventh stage Adept-Realizer.

BOOK ELEVEN:

The All-Completing and Final Divine Revelation To Mankind
*A Summary Description Of The Supreme Yoga Of The Seventh Stage
Of Life In The Divine Way Of Adidam*

The ultimate secrets of Divine Enlightenment—including the four-
stage Process of Divine Enlightenment, culminating in Translation
into the Infinitely Love-Blissful Divine Self-Domain.

Process of Adidam:
Five Comprehensive Views of the Practice of Adidam

BOOK TWELVE:

What, Where, When, How, Why, and
Who To Remember To Be Happy
*A Simple Explanation Of The Divine Way Of Adidam
(For Children, and Everyone Else)*

A text written specifically for children but inspiring to all—with
accompanying Essays and Talks on Divine Ignorance, religious
practices for children and young people in the Way of Adidam,
and the fundamental practice of whole bodily devotion to Avatar
Adi Da Samraj.

BOOK THIRTEEN:

No Seeking / Mere Beholding
The Always Primary Practice Of The Divine Way Of Adidam

A comprehensive summary of the always primary practice of the Way of Adidam—which is searchless Beholding of Avatar Adi Da Samraj—including detailed Instruction relative to rightly participating in the unique opportunity of retreat in Avatar Adi Da's physical Company.

BOOK FOURTEEN:

Santosha Adidam
The Essential Summary Of The Divine Way Of Adidam

An extended overview of the entire course of the Way of Adidam, based on the esoteric anatomy of the human being and its correlation to the progressive stages of life.

BOOK FIFTEEN:

The Lion Sutra
The "Perfect Practice" Teachings In The Divine Way Of Adidam

Practice in the ultimate stages of the Way of Adidam. How the practitioner of Adidam approaches—and passes over—the "Threshold" of Divine Enlightenment.

BOOK SIXTEEN:

The Overnight Revelation Of Conscious Light
The "My House" Discourses On The Indivisible Tantra Of Adidam

A vast and profound "consideration" of the fundamental Tantric principles of true Spiritual life and the "Always Already" Nature of the Divine Reality.

Great Tradition:
The Total Spiritual "Effort" of Humanity
as a Unified (and Progressive) Process

BOOK SEVENTEEN:
The Basket Of Tolerance
The Perfect Guide To Perfectly Unified Understanding Of The One and Great Tradition Of Mankind, and Of The Divine Way Of Adidam As The Perfect Completing Of The One and Great Tradition Of Mankind

The Basket Of Tolerance is a book like no other—simultaneously an unprecedented Spiritual Revelation and an extraordinary intellectual document.

While Avatar Adi Da's other twenty-two "Source-Texts" are focused in His exposition of the Way of Adidam, *The Basket Of Tolerance* is His comprehensive examination of the Great Tradition of mankind—in other words, of the global and historical context within which He has made His Revelation of the Way of Adidam. Thus, *The Basket Of Tolerance* focuses on the immense variety of historical expressions of the religious and Spiritual search, from prehistoric times to the present.

The core of *The Basket Of Tolerance* is a bibliographical listing of 5,000 documents (in all media—print and audio-visual), meticulously ordered by Avatar Adi Da in an elaborately subdivided sequence, to form a continuous "Argument". Avatar Adi Da introduces that "Argument" with a series of groundbreaking Essays, and He comments on the bibliographical "Argument", at numerous points, through a further series of over 100 essays relating to specific books (or groups of books) in the bibliography (covering a wide spectrum of topics).

Through the "Argument" of this annotated bibliography, Avatar Adi Da examines in detail the entire human religious search and demonstrates how there is truly a single process, composed of distinct (hierarchically related) stages (corresponding to the fourth, the fifth, and the sixth stages of life), evident in all the diversity of human religious history (previous to His Appearance here)—a process of which any given religious tradition represents a "piece". While Avatar Adi Da's examination of the Great Tradition concentrates on the various global manifestations of religion and Spirituality, it also embraces the "practical" issues that relate to the human process of the first three stages of life—such as understanding (and right participation in the process) of death, understanding (and right use) of the function of mind, right circulation of energy within the body, right physical exercise of the body, right diet, right emotional-sexual practice (whether sexually active or celibate), right living in the collective human context, and so forth.

Altogether, *The Basket Of Tolerance* is the elaborately detailed "proof" that there is, indeed, a "perennial philosophy". This "philosophy", however, is not a single "set" of unified "beliefs". Rather, it is a process, composed of distinctly different stages—and the points of view of the successive stages do not necessarily agree with one another. Furthermore, those stages are not (ultimately) based on conceptual differences but on experiential differences relating to the various aspects of the esoteric anatomy of the human structure.

For information about how you can support
bringing Avatar Adi Da's consummate Divine Word
to the world, visit
www.dawnhorsepress.com

Study other books and recordings
by and about Avatar Adi Da Samraj

■ To find out about and order "Source-Texts", books, tapes, CDs, and videos by and about Avatar Adi Da, contact your local Adidam regional center, or contact the Adidam Emporium at:

1-877-770-0772 (from within North America)
1-707-928-6653 (from outside North America)

Or order online from: **www.dawnhorsepress.com**

Support Avatar Adi Da's Work and the Way of Adidam

■ If you are moved to serve Avatar Adi Da's Spiritual Work specifically through advocacy and/or financial patronage, please contact:

Advocacy
P.O. Box 204
Lower Lake, CA 95457
phone: (707) 928-4800
email: adidam_advocacy@adidam.org

For young people:
Join the Adidam Youth Fellowship

■ Young people under 21 can participate in the "Adidam Youth Fellowship"—either as a friend or practicing member. Adidam Youth Fellowship members participate in study programs, retreats, celebrations, and other events with other young people responding to Avatar Adi Da. To learn more about the Youth Fellowship, call or write:

Vision of Mulund Institute (VMI)
10336 Loch Lomond Road, PMB 146
Middletown, CA 95461
phone: (707) 928-6932
fax: (707) 928-5619
email: vmi@adidam.org

The Ruchira Sannyasin Hermitage Ashrams Spiritually Empowered by Avatar Adi Da Samraj

T raditionally, Realizers have been provided with set-apart places where they were free to do their Spiritual Work in an appropriate and secluded circumstance. And these places became Spiritually Empowered through their Presence and Work.

In this traditional manner, devotees of Avatar Adi Da have provided places where He is completely set apart to do His Blessing-Work for the sake of humanity as a whole, as well as His specific Spiritual Work with devotees who come on pilgrimage to receive the Initiatory Spiritual Blessing of being in His physical Company on retreat.

My Work for the entire world is My Divine Blessing-Work, Which I do principally in seclusion. I live in perpetual retreat in a hermitage mode, and receive those of My devotees who are rightly prepared in that circumstance. Sometimes I roam in public circumstances, in order to have contact with people in general. But, fundamentally, I remain in hermitage retreat.

—Avatar Adi Da Samraj

Avatar Adi Da Samraj moves among the various Hermitage Ashrams in His spontaneous Wandering-Work of world-Blessing.

Spiritually, He is perpetually "in residence" at each of His Hermitage Sanctuaries. This is because He has Invested Himself Spiritually in these sacred places, and His Spiritual Power and Presence is constantly active in all of them.

Adidam Samrajashram
the Island of Naitauba in Fiji

Adidam Samrajashram is Avatar Adi Da's principal Hermitage Ashram and the primary Seat from which His Divine Spiritual Blessing Flows to the entire world.

The Mountain Of Attention Sanctuary of Adidam
in northern California

Da Love-Ananda Mahal
in Hawaii

731

The Seven Stages of Life

Throughout *The Knee Of Listening*, Avatar Adi Da Samraj describes the experiences and Realizations of humankind in terms of seven "stages of life". This schema is one of Avatar Adi Da's unique Gifts to humanity—His precise "mapping" of the potential developmental course of human experience as it unfolds through the gross, subtle, and causal dimensions of the being. He describes this course in terms of six stages of life—which account for, and correspond to, all possible orientations to religion and culture that have arisen in human history. His own Avataric Revelation—the Realization of the "Bright", Prior to all experience—is the seventh stage of life. Understanding this structure of seven stages illuminates the unique nature of Avatar Adi Da's "Sadhana Years" (and of the Spiritual process in His Company).

While the foundation "research" for this schema was conducted during Avatar Adi Da's early Life (up to the time of His Divine Re-Awakening and the period immediately following) as described in Part One, it was during His Teaching Years that Avatar Adi Da most fully expounded this schema. In *The Knee Of Listening*, particularly in the Essay "I (Alone) Am The Adidam Revelation", He explores in detail the relationship between the stages of life as experienced and Revealed in the Great Tradition of religion and Spirituality and His unique Revelation of Adidam.

The first three (or foundation) stages of life constitute the ordinary course of human adaptation—characterized (respectively) by bodily, emotional, and mental growth. Each of the first three stages of life takes approximately seven years to be established. Every individual who lives to an adult age inevitably adapts (although, generally speaking, only partially) to the first three stages of life. In the general case, this is where the developmental process stops—at the gross level of adaptation. Religions based fundamentally on beliefs and moral codes (without direct experience of the dimensions beyond the material world) belong to this foundation level of human development.

The fourth stage of life is characterized by a deep impulse to Communion with the Divine. It is in the context of the fourth stage of life (when one is no longer wedded to the purposes of the first three stages of life) that the true Spiritual process can begin. In the history of the Great Tradition, those involved in the process of the fourth stage of life have characteristically felt the Divine to be a great "Other", in Whom they aspired to become absorbed, through devotional love and service. However, in the Way of Adidam, the presumption that the Divine is "Other" is transcended from the beginning.

In the Way of Adidam, the process of the first three stages of life is lived on the basis of the devotional heart-impulse that is otherwise characteristic of the fourth stage of life. No matter what the age of the individual who comes to Avatar Adi Da, there will generally be signs of failed adaptation to the first three stages of life. But the practice is not a matter of attempting to overcome such failed adapatation through one's own (inevitably egoic) effort or struggle. Rather, the practice is to turn the faculties to Avatar Adi Da in devotional surrender. In that manner, the virtue of the fourth stage of life—the devotional heart-impulse to Commune with the Divine—is specifically animated from the beginning, in living response to Avatar Adi Da. Thus, whatever must be done to righten the first three stages of life occurs in the devotional context of heart-Communion with Him.

Avatar Adi Da has Revealed that the true Spiritual process, beginning in the context of the fourth stage of life, involves two great dimensions—which He calls the "vertical" and the "horizontal".

The descending aspect of the vertical process characterizes the fourth stage of life, while the ascending aspect characterizes the fifth stage of life. (Please see Appendix B, "The Esoteric Anatomy of the Spiritual Process: "Vertical" and "Horizontal" Dimensions of the Being", pp. 737–41.) As it has been known in the history of the Great Tradition, the fifth stage process is the ascent toward absorption into the Divine Matrix of Light Infinitely Above, thereby (ultimately) Realizing the Divine as Light (or Energy) Itself. (Although this Realization is a true "taste" of the Divine Self-Condition, It is achieved by means of the conditional effort of ascent—and, therefore, the Realization Itself is also conditional, or non-permanent.) The fifth stage of life is the ultimate process associated with the subtle dimension of existence. And the fifth stage of life is the "endpoint" of the Emanationist mode of Realization, as described by Avatar Adi Da in "I (Alone) Am The Adidam Revelation".

The horizontal process characterizes the sixth stage of life. As it has been known in the history of the Great Tradition, the sixth stage process is the exclusion of all awareness of the "outside" world (in both its gross and subtle dimensions), by "secluding" oneself within the heart—in order to rest in the Divine Self, Realized (ultimately) as Consciousness Itself. (Like the ultimate Realization associated with the fifth stage of life, the sixth stage Realization is also a true "taste" of the Divine Self-Condition. However, It is also achieved by conditional means—the conditional effort of exclusion—and, therefore, the Realization Itself is also conditional, or non-permanent.) The sixth stage of life is the process associated with the causal dimension of existence. And the sixth stage of life is the "endpoint" of the Transcendentalist mode of Realization, as described by Avatar Adi Da in "I (Alone) Am The Adidam Revelation".

In His "Sadhana Years", Avatar Adi Da fulfilled the sixth stage process (in a manner unique to Himself) in the Event of the "death of Narcissus" (chapter 9 of Part One), at the Lutheran Theological Seminary (in Philadelphia) in 1967. He then, subsequently, fulfilled the fifth stage process (again, in a manner unique to Himself) in the Event of Infinitely Ascended Bliss, at Swami Muktananda's Ashram in Ganeshpuri in 1968.

As Avatar Adi Da has pointed out, even though the fifth stage and sixth stage processes are, in fact, stages in the single process that culminates in Most Perfect Divine Enlightenment (or the seventh stage Realization uniquely Given by Him), the typical traditional view has been that the two processes are alternative approaches to Spiritual Realization. Indeed, these approaches (of either going

"Up" or going "Deep") have usually been regarded to be incompatible with each other.

In the Way of Adidam, the "Perfect Practice" encompasses both the vertical process (otherwise characteristically associated with the fifth stage of life) and the horizontal process (otherwise characteristically associated with the sixth stage of life). Thus, in the Way of Adidam, there is no "preference" exercised in favor of either the "Upward" process or the "Inward" process—either the Realization of the Divine as Light Itself or the Realization of the Divine as Consciousness Itself. In the Way of Adidam, both the ultimate "Upward" Realization and the ultimate "Inward" Realization are Freely Given by Avatar Adi Da to the rightly prepared and rightly practicing devotee. No effort—either of ascent or of exclusion—is required. And, in fact, all such effort must be inspected, understood, and transcended.

This unique and unprecedented orientation to the developmental processes of the fifth and the sixth stages of life is made possible by the full reception of Avatar Adi Da's Gift of Divine Spiritual Transmission. When the devotee (in the context of the fourth stage of life in the Way of Adidam) is fully open to Avatar Adi Da's Divine Spiritual Transmission, His Divine Spiritual Descent of the "Thumbs" takes over the body-mind, showing specific Yogic signs. In this "Samadhi of the 'Thumbs'", there is a profound turnabout in one's awareness of Him. While still always turning to Him devotionally in His bodily (human) Divine Form, one begins to recognize Him, Spiritually, as Consciousness Itself—the Root-Position of existence, Prior to all that is arising in body, mind, and world. This recognition is Spiritually established—and it is the basis for making the transition to the "Perfect Practice" of the Way of Adidam. It is a profound shift, away from identification with the body-mind. From this point on, Avatar Adi Da's Revelation of His own Condition of Consciousness Itself becomes the Position in which one Stands, and from That Position the phenomena associated with both the fifth stage of life and the sixth stage of life will arise. In the "Perfect Practice", one is no longer practicing from the point of view of the body-mind and its faculties. Now, devotional turning to Him (or Ruchira Avatara Bhakti Yoga) takes the form of simply "choosing" to Stand in His Position (rather than the ego-position)—inspecting and feeling beyond the root-tendency to contract and create the self-identity called "I".

The seventh stage of life, or the Realization of Avatar Adi Da's own "Bright" Divine Condition, transcends the entire course of human potential. In the seventh stage of life, the impulse to Realize the Divine (as Light) by going "Up" and the impulse to Realize the Divine (as Consciousness) by going "Deep" are (by Avatar Adi Da's Divine Spiritual Grace) simultaneously fulfilled. In that fulfillment, Avatar Adi Da Samraj Himself is most perfectly Realized. He is Realized as the "Bright", the Single Divine Unity of Consciousness and Energy—or Conscious Light Itself. This unique Realization, or Divine Enlightenment—the very Realization that Avatar Adi Da Himself Realized in the Vedanta Temple, in the Great Event of His Divine Re-Awakening—wipes away every trace of dissociation from the body-mind and the world. There is no impulse to seek or to avoid any experience. Rather, everything that arises is Divinely Self-Recognized to be merely a modification of the Conscious Light of Reality Itself.

The seventh stage Realization is absolutely Unconditional. It does not depend on any form of effort by the individual. Rather, It is a Divine Gift, Given by Avatar Adi Da to the devotee who has utterly surrendered all egoity to Him. Therefore, the seventh stage Realization is permanent.

Altogether, the Way of Adidam is not about dwelling in (or seeking to either attain or avoid) any of the potential experiences of the first six stages of life. The Way of Adidam is about transcending the entire structure of the human being and of the conditional reality—gross, subtle, and causal. Therefore, the Way of Adidam transcends both the urge to "have" experiences and the urge to "exclude" experience. The Way of Adidam is based, from the beginning, on the Divine Avatar's "Bright" State, Which is Realized progressively (and, ultimately, most perfectly), by means of His Divine Spiritual Descent in the body-mind of His devotee.

The Esoteric Anatomy of the Spiritual Process: "Vertical" and "Horizontal" Dimensions of the Being

One of the unique aspects of Avatar Adi Da's Revelation of the Way of Adidam is His complete description of the esoteric anatomy of the human being and how this relates to the Spiritual process. Just as the human body has a gross anatomy (of bones, flesh, nerves, and so on), there is also an esoteric anatomy, consisting of three primary structures. The esoteric anatomy of the human body-mind is the basis for all dimensions of human experience—of the ordinary, extraordinary, mystical, and Transcendental kind. Understanding this esoteric anatomy is a key to understanding what makes the Way of Adidam uniquely complete, and why the Most Perfect Divine Enlightenment that Avatar Adi Da Offers is an unprecedented Gift.

The first structure of esoteric anatomy is what Avatar Adi Da calls "the Circle". The Circle is a pathway through the body, composed of two arcs. The descending arc (or "frontal line") starts at the crown of the head and goes downwards to the perineum. The ascending arc (or "spinal line") starts at the perineum and goes upwards to the crown of the head. The Circle is the primary energy-pathway in the body, through which both the natural energy of life and the Divine Spirit-Energy flow. As an individual becomes more sensitive to the subtle dimensions of experience, he or she becomes capable of feeling energy moving in the body through the Circle.

The Spiritual Initiation that Avatar Adi Da Gives to His fully prepared listening devotees is the Infusion of His Divine Spirit-Energy (or Spirit-Current) into the frontal line of the Circle. As the devotee matures in the practice of Adidam, the frontal line of the Circle becomes more and more tangibly full of Avatar Adi Da's Divine Spirit-Current. On certain occasions in the practice of a Spiritually mature devotee, the entire frontal line of the Circle will become utterly full of His Divine Spirit-Current—such that His Divine Infusion Moves fully down to the bodily base and also Passes into the spinal line. When this occurs, one ceases to be identified with body or mind in the usual sense, and becomes aware (instead) of existing as a vastly expanded spherical form of the Divine "Brightness". This is the Samadhi of the "Thumbs"—a form of Samadhi uniquely Given by Avatar Adi Da, and the same Samadhi that Avatar Adi Da Himself describes fully experiencing as a young man (pp. 170–71). Eventually, the experience of the "Thumbs" becomes constant, such that the presumption of existing as body and mind no longer "rules" one's life. Then one is ready to receive Avatar Adi Da's Gift of the Awakening to the Witness-Consciousness, which makes possible the beginning of the "Perfect Practice".

Because there is a "downward-and-upward" quality to the Circle (with its descending and ascending arcs), Avatar Adi Da refers to the Circle as the "vertical" dimension of esoteric anatomy. Most of the world's Spiritual traditions are focused in processes that relate to the Circle—seeking, as an ultimate result, some kind of "ascended" Union with the Divine (found by subtly ascending beyond the body-mind, via ascent through and beyond the crown of the head). Such is the Emanationist mode of Realization. In the most advanced traditional developments of this "vertical" approach to the Divine, there is, in fact, ascent to the Source-Matrix of Divine Light Which is infinitely Above. Such ascended Union with the Divine, however, is not permanent (or eternal), because it depends on the effort of the individual—the effort to "go up". Thus, such ascended Union with the Divine is not Most Perfect Divine Enlightenment. Rather, it is a matter of "choosing" the "Light" (or "Energy") aspect of the Divine—over the "Consciousness" aspect.

The <u>second</u> <u>structure</u> of esoteric anatomy is what Avatar Adi Da calls "<u>the</u> <u>three</u> <u>stations</u> <u>of</u> <u>the</u> <u>heart</u>". The three "stations" are:

The "left side"—corresponding to the physical heart, and the gross dimension of the being

The "middle station"—corresponding to the "heart chakra" (or "anahata chakra"), and the subtle dimension of the being

The "right side"—which is the "seat" of the causal dimension (or root-dimension) of the being (equivalent to the primal presumption that one exists as a separate "self", or "ego"), and which is (simultaneously) the "doorway" in the body-mind through which the ego can be utterly dissolved, in heart-Identification with Avatar Adi Da.

As the practice of Adidam matures, the progressive Spiritual activation of each of the three stations of the heart can be tangibly felt.

The Spiritual Initiation that Avatar Adi Da Gives to His fully prepared listening devotees is His Spiritual Activation of the left side of the heart, which (in due course) also becomes His Spiritual Activation of the middle station of the heart. Avatar Adi Da's Spiritual Gift of the Samadhi of the "Thumbs" is what makes possible His Spiritual Activation of the right side of the heart, which is coincident with the practitioner's entrance into the "Perfect Practice" of Adidam.

Because there is <u>not</u> a "downward-and-upward" quality to the three stations of the heart, Avatar Adi Da refers to them as the "horizontal" dimension of esoteric anatomy. A minority of the world's Spiritual traditions (principally certain branches of the Hindu, Buddhist, Jain, and Taoist traditions) are focused in processes that relate to the horizontal dimension (and especially the right side of the heart)—seeking, as an ultimate result, an "interiorly secluded" Identification with the Divine (or Realization of Truth). This is the Transcendentalist mode of Realization. In the fullest development of this "horizontal" approach, the practitioner does, in fact, experience an Identification with the Divine (or a Realization of Truth) that is achieved by excluding all awareness of body and mind and world. Such exclusive Union with the Divine, however, is not permanent (or eternal), because it depends on the effort of the individual—the effort to "go within", or to exclude everything that is apparently objective. Thus, such exclusive Union with the Divine is not Most Perfect Divine Enlightenment. Rather, it is a matter of "choosing" the "Consciousness" aspect of the Divine—over the "Light" (or "Energy") aspect.

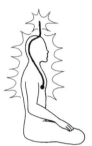

The third (and quintessential) structure of esoteric anatomy is Amrita Nadi, which Avatar Adi Da describes in full detail in chapter 18 of Part One. As Avatar Adi Da has uniquely Revealed, Amrita Nadi is the "Bright" Itself as It Manifests in the context of conditional reality and the human body-mind. Amrita Nadi is shaped like the letter "S", extending from the right side of the heart (as its "lower terminal") through the chest, throat, and head, and then to the Source-Matrix of Divine Light infinitely above (as its "upper terminal"). Thus, Amrita Nadi encompasses both of the "locations" that have (in the most esoteric branches of the Great Tradition) been sought as the ultimate Divine "place"—the infinitely ascended Matrix of Light ("Above") and the right side of the heart ("within", or, more accurately, "Prior").

In the Great Tradition of religion and Spirituality, there have been two fundamental "camps"—the "vertical" and the "horizontal", or those who seek the Divine by the Emanationist "route" of going "up" and those who seek the Divine by the Transcendentalist "route" of going "within". What makes Avatar Adi Da's Revelation utterly unique is His "Disclosure" that, although both the vertical and the horizontal approaches are capable of resulting in true Realization of the Divine (or of Perfect Truth)—as He Himself experienced (although entirely in a non-seeking manner) in the "horizontal" Event of the "death of Narcissus", in 1967, and the "vertical" Event of Infinitely Ascended Bliss, in 1968—neither the vertical nor the horizontal approach can, in and of itself, lead to Most Perfect Divine Enlightenment (which is permanent, or eternal). Only the simultaneous Realization of the Divine in both "locations"—the infinitely ascended Source-Matrix of Divine Light and the right side of the heart (or both "terminals" of Amrita Nadi)—is Most

Perfect (and Eternal) Divine Enlightenment. Only the Full and Indivisible Realization of the Divine as Conscious Light (Consciousness and Light) is Most Perfect (and Eternal) Divine Enlightenment. Such is the infinitely glorious Realization to Which Avatar Adi Da Re-Awakened in the Vedanta Temple, and Which is also Given by Avatar Adi Da to His devotees who demonstrate the entire devotional and Spiritual process in His Avataric Divine Spiritual Company. That Realization has never been known before Avatar Adi Da's Appearance in the world and His Gift of the Way of Adidam. Such is the culmination of the searchless process of simply Beholding Avatar Adi Da, the bodily (human) Incarnation of the "Bright" Itself.

Thus, Adidam is neither a "vertical" way nor a "horizontal" way. Rather, it is the unique "vertical-and-horizontal" Way. It is the Way of whole bodily Divine Enlightenment, because it culminates in the Most Perfect Realization of the "whole body" of Amrita Nadi.

Brief Biographies of Individuals Mentioned in *The Knee Of Listening*

Amma. See Pratibha Trivedi

Aurobindo, Sri—Aurobindo Ghose (1872–1950) was born in Calcutta of Indian parents who sent him to be educated in the West. Later, after his return to India, Aurobindo was imprisoned as a political agitator, and during this period his life changed dramatically. He began to study the *Bhagavad Gita* and took up the practice of Yoga. After his release from prison he settled at Pondicherry, South India, where he Taught and wrote religious philosophy, developing his ideas about the Spiritual evolution of mankind.

Bailey, Alice—Alice Bailey (1880–1949), originally a member of the Theosophical Society, formed her own organization (known as the Arcane School) in 1923 to teach the philosophy espoused in her books. She claimed that all of her books were dictated telepathically to her by a Tibetan wiseman.

Blavatsky, H. P.—Helena Petrovna Blavatsky (1831–1891) was the founder of the Theosophical movement, which introduced many Eastern religious and philosophical concepts to the West.

Bultmann, Rudolph—Rudolph Bultmann (1884–1976) was a leading (German) New Testament scholar who adopted a "de-mythologizing" approach to the New Testament that called many basic Christian doctrines into question.

Cayce, Edgar—Edgar Cayce (1878–1945) was a psychic particularly known for medical diagnosis and healing via clairvoyance. He also made various predictions for the future based on his clairvoyant visions.

Chinmayananda, Swami—Swami Chinmayananda (1916–1993) was a scholar of the Hindu scriptures, especially the *Bhagavad Gita* and the *Upanishads*, who conceived his mission as restoring respect for the ancient Hindu scriptures and reinvigorating practice of the Spiritual way according to the Vedantic instruction.

de la Torre, Teofilo—Costa Rican health researcher and author Teofilo de la Torre wrote a number of books on diet and health, including *An Inspiring Message on the Philosophy and Science of Health, Youth, and Longevity, Based upon "The Dietetic Laws of Nature"; Man's Return to His Garden of Eden;* and *The Process of Physical Purification by Means of the New and Easy Way to Fast.*

Dewey, John—John Dewey (1859–1952) was an American philosopher and educator who believed that education was the fundamental method of social progress and reform. His philosophy of "progressive education" had a major influence on American school systems in the late nineteenth and early twentieth centuries.

Ehret, Arnold—Arnold Ehret (1866–1922) wrote a number of books on diet and health, including *Thus Speaketh the Stomach; Arnold Ehret's Mucusless-Diet Healing System;* and *Rational Fasting for Physical, Mental, and Spiritual Rejuvenation.*

Evans-Wentz, W. Y.—W. Y. Evans-Wentz (1878–1965) is the translator of several major Tibetan Buddhist texts, including *The Tibetan Book of the Dead; Tibet's Great Yogi Milarepa; The Tibetan Book of the Great Liberation;* and *Tibetan Yoga and Secret Doctrines.*

Gautama—Gautama Shakyamuni (ca. 563–483 B.C.E.) was the great Indian Sage commonly known as "the Buddha".

Gurdjieff—Georges Ivanovitch Gurdjieff (1872–1949) was an important figure in Western occult circles during the 1920s, 30s, and 40s. Born in Armenia of a Greek family, Gurdjieff spent many years wandering in Eastern Russia, Turkey, India, and Tibet, searching for secret wisdom. The Gurdjieff work (which is the result of his eclectic interests in psychology, magic, and esoteric religion) involved "working" on oneself in order to become free from egoic limits.

743

THE KNEE OF LISTENING

Harding, M. Esther—M. Esther Harding (1881–1971) was a (British) student of C. G. Jung, with whom she worked in 1922. A psychoanalyst, she wrote a number of books, including *Blake, Jung, and the Collective Unconscious; The Parental Image; Women's Mysteries; Way of All Women;* and *The I and the Not-I.*

Krishnamurti, Jiddu—Jiddu Krishnamurti (1895–1986) was brought up in India by the early Theosophists who hoped he would become a world-Teacher. Krishnamurti later (at least outwardly) rejected all traditional Spiritual Teachings and paths of devotion and spent his life advocating his own mind-based philosophy of enlightenment.

Muktananda, Swami (Baba)—Swami Muktananda (1908–1982) abandoned home at the age of fifteen for the sake of Spiritual practice. Eventually he encountered his Guru, Swami Nityananda, in whose company he mastered Kundalini Yoga. Swami Muktananda attracted many Western aspirants to his Ashram at Ganeshpuri, India, during the 1960s and 1970s. Swami Muktananda was commonly addressed and referred to (by his devotees) as "Baba".

Nityananda, Bhagavan—Bhagavan Nityananda (1900?–1961) was a profound Yogic Realizer of modern India. His exact birth date is unknown, and little is known about his early life, although it is said that even as a child he showed the signs of a Realized Yogi. While still a boy, He abandoned conventional life and wandered as a renunciate. "Bhagavan" is a Sanskrit title of respect (meaning "venerable", or "divine"), used in worshipful reference to deities and saints.

Nivedita, Sister—Sister Nivedita (1867–1911), born Margaret Elizabeth Noble, met Swami Vivekananda in London in 1895, and became one of his principal Western devotees. In 1898, she moved to India, where she lived for the rest of her life, and (at her Guru's behest) was very actively involved in the upliftment and education of Indian women.

Pak Subuh—Muhammad (Pak) Subuh (1901–1987) was an Indonesian teacher who founded the Subud movement in the 1920s.

Pandit, M.P.—Madhav Pundalik Pandit (1918–1994) was a scholar of Hindu scripture, and the author of over 100 books on Yoga and Spirituality. He spent more than forty years living and practicing under the guidance of Aurobindo and the Mother, and serving at the Sri Aurobindo Ashram in Pondicherry, India.

Patanjali—Patanjali is honored as the originator of classical Yoga. He may have lived in the second century of the common era. In his classic treatise, the *Yoga Sutras*, Patanjali describes the eight "limbs" that make up his system of Yoga: moral observance (yama), self-discipline (niyama), posture (asana), control of the breath (pranayama), restraint of the senses (pratyahara), concentration (dharana), meditation (dhyana), and exalted states of consciousness achieved through inward concentration and meditation (samadhi).

Potter, Charles Francis—Charles Francis Potter (1885–1962) was a leader in the liberal theological movement. In the course of fifty years, he moved from being an evangelical Baptist to a Unitarian minister, becoming a radical humanist in the end. Of his numerous books, the most popular is the one cited by Avatar Adi Da—*The Lost Years of Jesus Revealed*, an interpretation of Jesus as an historical figure in the light of the Dead Sea Scrolls.

Prakashananda, Swami—Swami Prakashananda (1917–1988) turned to Spiritual life in his 30s, eventually choosing the mountain of Sapta Shringh as a place to settle and devote himself to Spiritual practice. Over time, an ashram developed there around him. He met Swami Muktananda in 1956 and was initiated as Swami Muktananda's devotee, although he generally stayed at his own ashram in Sapta Shringh rather than spending a great deal of time in Ganeshpuri at Swami Muktananda's ashram. For Swami Prakashananda's biography, see *Agaram Bagaram Baba: Life, Teachings, and Parables—A Spiritual Biography of Baba Prakashananda*, by Titus Foster (Berkeley: North Atlantic Books / Patagonia, Ariz.: Essene Vision Books, 1999).

Pratibha Trivedi (Amma), Swami Prajnananda—Pratibha Trivedi (?–1993) was originally a devotee of Bhagavan Nityananda. After his death, she became a devotee of Swami Muktananda, serving him for twenty years as his personal secretary and spokesperson, while also writing numerous articles on Siddha Yoga. After Swami Muktananda's death, she withdrew to her own ashram, where she stayed until the end of her life.

Ramakrishna—The great Indian Realizer Ramakrishna (1836–1886) was a renowned ecstatic, and a lifelong devotee of Kali, a form of the Mother-Shakti. In the course of his Spiritual practice, Ramakrishna passed spontaneously through many religious and Spiritual disciplines, eventually Realizing a state of profound mystical union with the Divine. In Part Two of *The Knee Of Listening* (in the Essay "I Have Appeared here Via a Unique, Spontaneous, and Never-Again Conjunction of Vehicles"), Avatar Adi Da Reveals that Ramakrishna and his principal disciple, Swami Vivekananda, are (together) the deeper-personality vehicle of Avatar Adi Da's bodily human Incarnation.

Ramana Maharshi—Ramana Maharshi (1879–1950) is regarded by many as the greatest Indian Sage of the twentieth century. Following a spontaneous death-like event as a teenager, he abandoned home for a life of Spiritual practice. Eventually, an ashram was established around him at Tiruvannamalai in South India, which continues today.

Rang Avadhoot—Rang Avadhoot (1898–1968) was a Realizer in the tradition of Dattatreya. Before 1923, when he relinquished his worldly concerns, he was actively involved in social and political issues.

Rudrananda, Swami (Rudi)—Rudi (1928–1973), Albert Rudolph (also known as Swami Rudrananda), was born in Brooklyn, New York. Rudi, at the age of 30, first met Bhagavan Nityananda in 1958, and began thereafter to study Siddha Yoga. He was a devotee both of Bhagavan Nityananda and, especially after Nityananda's Mahasamadhi, Swami Muktananda. He received sannyas from Swami Muktananda in 1965, one of the first Americans to be acknowledged as a Swami. He later established his own group of students in the United States.

Shankara—Shankara (ca. 788–820) was a revered Hindu Sage who is regarded as the founder of the school of Advaita Vedanta.

Spalding, Baird—Baird Thomas Spalding III (1857–1953) wrote a series of books called *The Life and Teaching of the Masters of the Far East*, which he presented as being based on his meetings in the Far East (from 1894 to 1898) with Masters from various areas and eras.

Tillich, Paul—Paul Tillich (1886–1965) was a (German) Protestant theologian whose criticism of Nazism forced him to emigrate to the USA in 1933, where he lived until his death. As an existentialist theologian (whose personal life was characterized by experimental and avant-garde ideas and expressions), Tillich took a position between liberal and neo-orthodox theological points of view. His three-volume magnum opus, *Systematic Theology,* is an examination of the personal relationship between man and God.

Vivekananda, Swami—Swami Vivekananda (1863–1902), born Narendranath Dutta, was Ramakrishna's principal disciple. After Ramakrishna's Mahasamadhi, Swami Vivekananda organized the Ramakrishna Order of Monks. He championed the Hindu, and especially the Vedantic, point of view through his eloquent speeches and inspiring writings. In particular, his well-received appearance at the Parliament of Religions in Chicago in 1893 was groundbreaking in many respects, providing him a platform in the West to be widely heard as India's religious and Spiritual ambassador.

Woodroffe, Sir John—Sir John Woodroffe (1865–1936), who also wrote under his pseudonymn Arthur Avalon, served as a judge in British India. His pioneering and painstakingly detailed research of, and numerous scholarly publications about, Tantric philosophy and practice (along with translations of a few important Tantric texts) served the wider acceptance and appreciation of the true nature of Tantric practice.

Yogananda, Swami (Paramahansa)—Paramahansa Yogananda (1893–1952) was born in Bengal, the child of devout Hindu parents. As a young man, Yogananda found his Guru, Swami Yukteswar Giri, who initiated him into an order of formal renunciates. In

1920, Yogananda traveled to America to attend an international conference of religions in Boston. Subsequently he settled in America, attracting many American devotees. He Taught "Kriya Yoga", a system of practice that had been passed down to him by his own Teacher and that had originally been developed from traditional techniques of Kundalini Yoga. Yogananda became widely known through the publication of his life-story, *Autobiography of a Yogi*.

Traditional Gods, Goddesses, and Other Archetypes Mentioned in *The Knee Of Listening*

Dattatreya—Dattatreya is said to have been a God-Realizer who appeared early in the common era and about whom no certain historical facts exist apart from his name. Over the centuries, numerous legends and myths have been spun around him. He was early on regarded to be an incarnation of the God Vishnu, later associated with the tradition of Saivism, and worshipped as the Divine Itself. He is commonly venerated as the originator of the Avadhoota tradition and credited with the authorship of the *Avadhoota Gita*, among other works. The devotional sect worshipping Dattatreya presumes that he continually reincarnates through a succession of Adepts for the sake of gathering and serving devotees. The belief in the continuing incarnation of Dattatreya should be understood as a popular religious belief that is peripheral to what the Adepts in the Dattatreya succession actually taught.

Ganesh—Ganesh is the huge, elephant-headed god of wisdom (a son of Siva), revered by Hindus as the "remover of obstacles".

Krishna—Krishna is the legendary Divine Avatar (worshipped by many Hindus) who is the hero of the *Bhagavad Gita* (and the longer *Mahabharata*, of which the *Bhagavad Gita* is an excerpt) and the *Srimad Bhagavatam*.

Prakriti—The Sanskrit terms "Purusha-Prakriti" and "Siva-Shakti" are esoteric descriptions of the Divine Being. "Purusha" and "Siva" are names for the Divine Being Itself, or Divine Consciousness.

"Prakriti" and "Shakti" are names for the All-Pervading Spirit-Power of the Divine Being. "Purusha-Prakriti", or "Siva-Shakti", is thus the Unity of the Divine Consciousness and Its own Spirit-Power.

Purusha. See Prakriti

Ram—Ram (also spelled "Rama") is the legendary Divine Avatar (worshipped by many Hindus) who is the hero of the *Ramayana*.

Shakti. See Prakriti

Siva. See Prakriti

Traditions and Schools of Thought Referenced in *The Knee Of Listening*

Advaita Vedanta—Vedanta is the principal philosophical tradition of Hinduism. "Advaita" means "non-dual". Advaita Vedanta, then, is a philosophy of non-dualism. Its origins lie in the ancient esoteric Teaching that the Divine Being is the only Reality. According to Advaita Vedanta, the self and the world have no independent existence but merely arise in that one Divine Reality.

Ashtanga Yoga—The "eight-limbed" system of Yoga proposed by Patanjali in his *Yoga Sutras*.

beat, beatniks—The "beatnik" (or "beat") movement gained prominence during the 1950s as an avant-garde bohemian reaction to the then-dominant cultural forms of conventional middle-class American life. Beat poets and writers expounded a generalized philosophy derived in part from Eastern religious traditions, particularly Zen Buddhism. Some of the "beat writers" that Adi Da read were Lawrence Ferlinghetti, Kenneth Rexroth, and Allen Ginsberg.

the Essene tradition—The Essenes were an ancient Jewish sect believed to be the monastic community described in the Dead Sea Scrolls, and interpreted by some scholars as being the background from which Christianity arose.

Hatha Yoga—Hatha Yoga is the Yogic discipline of bodily poses (asana) and breath control (pranayama). It can be exercised without adherence to any other disciplines or philosophy or belief system, but its fullest benefit is regarded to be attained in combination with other fully developed Yogas, such as Raja Yoga or Kundalini Yoga.

Karma Yoga—The Hindu tradition speaks of four principal Spiritual paths (or four principal aspects of the Spiritual path). Karma Yoga is literally the "Yoga of action", in which every activity, no matter how humble, is transformed into ego-transcending service to the Divine. (The other three paths are Bhakti Yoga, the path of devotion, Raja Yoga, the path of higher psychic discipline, and Jnana Yoga, the path of transcendental insight.)

Kashmir Saivism—Kashmir Saivism is a branch of Saivism (the form of Hinduism in which Siva is worshipped as the Supreme Deity), which originated in the Kashmir region of North India in the late 8th century and whose influence spread throughout the Indian subcontinent during the mid-20th century. It has a largely fifth-stage orientation and practice.

Kriya Yoga—A system of practice taught by Paramahansa Yogananda, which had been passed down to him by his own Teacher and that had originally been developed from traditional techniques of Kundalini Yoga.

Kundalini Shaktipat Yoga/tradition—Kundalini Yoga aims to awaken latent cosmically manifested Spiritual Energy, which is considered to lie dormant at the base of the body, so that it rises up through the spine to reunite with its ultimate source above the head. While typical techniques to raise the Kundalini Shakti involve meditative visualization and breathing exercises, it has long been traditionally understood that the initiatory force of a Spiritually activated Teacher is the principal means whereby it is activated. The activation of the Kundalini can produce intense blisses and other phenomena.

Parsis—Parsis (or Zoroastrians) are followers of the teachings of the ancient Persian Teacher Zoroaster.

Raja Yoga—"Raja" means "king" in Sanskrit. Raja Yoga is, thus, the "royal" Yoga, whereby the activity and formations of the mind are disciplined, with the intention of causing them to cease. The most influential formulation of Raja Yoga is that of Patanjali, who (in the *Yoga Sutras*) systematized it in his ashtanga (or eight-limbed) system.

Saiva Siddhanta—"Saiva Siddhanta" is the name of an important school of Saivism which flourished in South India and survives into the present. Its literature is based on Agamas (devotional hymns by Saiva saints). This dualist school attributes eternal individuality to the soul, even when liberated.

Vedanta. See Advaita Vedanta

The Vedanta Society—The Vedanta Society is an extension of the Ramakrishna Math and Mission, and is devoted to the purpose of extending the work of Sri Ramakrishna and Swami Vivekananda. Swami Vivekananda founded the Ramakrishna Order of India, the order of monastics that guide the Vedanta Society.

The Knee Of Listening

First Word

1. For a description of the vow and life-responsibilities embraced by practitioners of the Way of Adidam, please see *Adidam: The True World-Religion Given by the Promised God-Man, Adi Da Samraj* (Middletown, Calif.: Dawn Horse Press, 2003).

2. The word "create" and its variants are in quotation marks in Avatar Adi Da's Wisdom-Teaching to indicate the sense of "so to speak", because, in the Indivisible Unity of Reality, any particular "thing" is not truly (but only apparently) appearing "out of nothing" or being caused to appear.

3. "Hamartia" (the word in New Testament Greek that was translated into English as "sin") was also an archery term meaning "missing the mark".

PART ONE

Chapter 1

4. The eagle and the crab are symbols for the extremes, high and low, to which individuals born under the sign of Scorpio are said to be inclined.

5. Avatar Adi Da's father, Frank Jones, died in 1984.

6. Avatar Adi Da's mother, Dorothy Jones, died in 1995.

Chapter 3

7. Rev. Dr. Charles Francis Potter, *The Lost Years of Jesus Revealed* (Greenwich, Connecticut: Fawcett Publications, 1958), 71–72, 125, and 127.

8. At the time, the Bowery in New York City was a district notorious for cheap bars and homeless derelicts.

Chapter 5

9. This dream is related to an important physical fact about Adi Da's Birth—that He was born with the umbilical cord wrapped around His neck.

10. Hubert Jantz and Kurt Beringer, "Das Syndrom des Schwebeerlebnisses unmittelbar nach Kopfverletzungen", Der Nervenarzt (Berlin), XVII (1944).

11. C. G. Jung, *Psyche and Symbol: A Selection from the Writings of C. G. Jung*, ed. Violet S. de Laszlo (Garden City, New York: Doubleday Anchor Books, 1958), 267–69.

12. *The I Ching or Book of Changes*, the Richard Wilhelm translation rendered into English by Cary F. Baynes, with a foreword by C. G. Jung, and preface to the third edition by Hellmut Wilhelm, 3rd ed. (Princeton, Princeton University Press, 1968).

13. Baird T. Spalding, *Life and Teaching of the Masters of the Far East*, 6 vols. (Marina del Rey, Calif.: DeVorss Publications, 1996).

Chapter 6

14. Sir John Woodroffe, *The Serpent Power: Being the Sat-Cakra-Nirupana and Paduka-Pancaka* (New York: Dover Publications, 1974).

15. The word "autobiography" is in quotation marks because Avatar Adi Da observes in chapter 3 that "There is no such thing as anyone's 'autobiography'" (p. 57).

16. "Nirvana" is a Buddhist term for the Unqualified Reality beyond suffering, ego, birth, and death. "Samsara" is a Buddhist and Hindu term for the conditional realm of birth and change and death. The traditional saying quoted here therefore expresses the doctrine that there is ultimately no difference between the formless Divine Reality and Its conditional manifestations.

"This is That", another Ultimate Statement quoted here, is similar in meaning: Any conditional phenomenon ("this") is not different from the Divine Reality ("That").

17. In the United States, "Labor Day" (a day set aside for special recognition of working people) is a legal holiday occurring on the first Monday in September. Labor Day thus marks the end of the summer season.

Chapter 7

18. Paramahansa Yogananda, *Autobiography of a Yogi*, preface by W. Y. Evans-Wentz (Los Angeles: Self-Realization Fellowship, 1972).

Chapter 9

19. When He speaks here of the "etheric level", Adi Da is referring to the experiences related to the etheric body, or the "body" of life-energy. Our physical bodies are surrounded and infused by this life-energy "body", which we feel as the play of emotions and life-force in the body. The "astral level" of the human being is the lower and higher aspects of mind—conscious, subconscious, and unconscious. In His life with Rudi at this point, Adi Da is saying that His experiences were still in the domain of bodily energy and the basic dimensions of the mind; He was not yet entering into any higher subtle and mystical experiences such as would occur later in His Spiritual practice with Swami Muktananda.

Chapter 10

20. Traditionally, in Japanese Zen Buddhism, the Master may sometimes beat the student in order to serve his or her Awakening. Less well known is the tradition of the student's striking the Teacher. The act of striking the Teacher is playful and jubilant, a sign that the student for the first time has attained the same state of Awakening as the Teacher.

21. Among the numerous translations of the *Bhagavad Gita*, Avatar Adi Da Samraj points to two editions as particularly worthy of study:

The Bhagavad Gita, Withrop Sargeant, trans., rev. ed., ed. Christopher Chapple (Albany, N.Y.: State University of New York Press, 1984).

God Talks with Arjuna: The Bhagavad Gita—Royal Science of God-Realization, The Immortal Dialogue Between Soul and Spirit, a new translation and commentary by Paramahansa Yogananda, 2 vols. (Los Angeles: Self-Realization Fellowship, 1996).

22. In the Hindu tradition, the syllable "Om" (sometimes spelled "Aum") is understood to be a direct expression of the Spiritual Power of the Absolute Divine Being, from which all existence proceeds.

Chapter 11

23. Rahim is an Islamic Name for Allah, meaning "the Merciful".

24. Karim is an Islamic Name for Allah, meaning "the Generous".

25. The lotus posture, the classic oriental seated pose for meditation.

Chapter 12

26. "Shree" (also spelled "Sri") is a term of honor and veneration often applied to a Spiritual Realizer. The word literally means "splendor" in Sanskrit, indicating that the one honored is radiant with Divine Blessing-Power.

"Gurudev" is a traditional Sanskrit designation for one's Guru. It literally means "Divine Guru".

27. Chitti Kundalini means, literally, "Consciousness-Kundalini", the Goddess who represents both Divine Consciousness and the Spiritual Awakening-Power of the Kundalini.

28. A lingam is an oblong stone in a vertical position, traditionally worshipped as an expression of the Power of Siva (the Absolute Unmanifested Divine).

29. The supracausal body described here does not represent the dimension of full Enlightenment, but simply the highest subtle dimension of experience. Later in *The Knee Of Listening* (pp. 349–50), Avatar Adi Da explains that the true causal dimension of the body-mind, which is Prior to the most subtle experience, is associated with the right side of the heart.

Chapter 13

30. For a description of the "bodies" or "functional sheaths" of the human structure, please see Avatar Adi Da's Text *Santosha Adidam* (Middletown, Calif.: The Dawn Horse Press, 2001).

31. An example of this can be found in descriptions of the life of stigmatic Therese Neumann, such as *Therese Neumann: A Portrait Based on Authentic Accounts, Journals, and Documents*, by Johannes Steiner (New York: Alba House, 1967) or *Therese Neumann, Mystic and Stigmatist (1898-1962)*, by Adalbert Albert Vogl (Rockford, Ill.: Tan Books, 1987).

Chapter 14

32. Swami Nikhilananda, trans., *The Mandukyopanisad: with Gaudapada's Karika and Sankara's Commentary* (Mysore, India: Sri Ramakrishna Ashrama, 1974).

33. Arthur Osborne, ed., *The Collected Works of Ramana Maharshi*, 5th ed. (Tiruvannamalai, India: Sri Ramanasramam, 1979).

34. This text is now published in English under the title *The Play of Consciousness*.

Chapter 15

35. *Srimad Bhagavatam*, translated by N. Raghunathan, 2 vols. (Madras: Vighneshwara Publishing House, 1976).

Chapter 17

36. The vision of the "blue pearl" may also appear spontaneously as a subtle being with great Spiritual attributes. Hence the term "blue person".

Chapter 18

37. The continuous sounding (or drone) on the main note of the musical scale, which is a characteristic of Indian music.

38. B. V. Narasimha Swami, *Self-Realization: Life and Teachings of Sri Ramana Maharshi*, 7th ed., revised from the third edition with an Epilogue by S. S. Cohen (Tiruvannamalai, India: Sri Ramanasramam, 1962), 20–22.

39. K [T. V. Kapali Shastry], *Sat-Darshana Bhashya* and *Talks with Maharshi, with Forty Verses in Praise of Sri Ramana*, 5th ed. (Tiruvannamalai, India: Sri Ramanasramam, 1968), xv.

40. Ibid., xvii.

41. Ibid., xviii.

42. "Atmasthana" is Sanskrit for "the Place of the Self", and "Shakti Sthana" is Sanskrit for "the Place of the Shakti".

43. K, *Sat-Darshana Bhashya*, xviii–xix.

44. "Jeeva" (or "jiva") means the individual and limited self, as opposed to "Atman", the Divine Self.

45. K, *Sat-Darshana Bhashya*, xxi.

46. The sushumna corresponds to the spinal line. In traditional Yoga, sushumna is the esoteric nerve pathway (or "nadi") of the Kundalini Shakti.

47. *Sat-Darshana Bhashya*, xxiii–xxiv.

48. Translator's note—Nadi is the channel in which the life-force Prana flows in the subtle body but is usually equated with a nerve.

49. *Sri Ramana Gita (Dialogues of Maharshi)*, a new translation by Krishna Bhikshu (Tiruvannamalai, India: Sri Ramanasramam, 1966), 38–42.

50. Ibid., p. 20.

51. Arthur Osborne, *Ramana Maharshi and the Path of Self-Knowledge*, (New York: Samuel Weiser, 1970), 185.

52. Avatar Adi Da has pointed out that, even though Ramana Maharshi is (in certain cases) quoted as having described the Amrita Nadi as an ascending process (such as the phrase "a force-current called *Amrita Nadi* rises and goes up to the Sahasrara", quoted on p. 352), he was, in fact, exclusively involved in the descending aspect of Amrita Nadi.

53. *Talks with Sri Ramana Maharshi*, 3 vols. in one, 4th ed. (Tiruvannamalai, India: Sri Ramanasramam, 1968), 440.

54. Arthur Osborne, ed., *The Collected Works of Ramana Maharshi* (Tiruvannamalai, India: Sri Ramanasramam, 1968), 74.

Chapter 19

55. Avatar Adi Da Samraj has given an alternative form of the "conscious process" for those who find that their practice of turning to Him is served most by the exercise of feeling and faith. The "Devotional Way of Faith" involves Invocation of Avatar Adi Da via one of 80 variant forms of mantra that consist of His Names and Sacred Titles. For more information, see "Third Fundamental" in *Adidam: The True World-Religion Given by the Promised God-Man, Adi Da Samraj* (Middletown, Calif.: The Dawn Horse Press, 2003).

Epilogue

56. For a description of the disciplines of the Way of Adidam, see "Second Fundamental" in *Adidam: The True World-Religion Given by the Promised God-Man, Adi Da Samraj.*

PART TWO

The "Sixth Stage Teachings" (and the Fifth Stage Realization) of Swami (Baba) Muktananda, and My Seventh Stage Realization of the Great Truth He Told to Me

57. Swami Muktananda, *Conversations with Swami Muktananda: The Early Years*, 2d ed. (South Fallsburg, N.Y.: SYDA Foundation, 1998). (First edition published under the title *Paramartha Katha Prasang: Spiritual Conversations with Swami Muktananda [1962–1966].*)

58. For the distinction between "fully" and "Priorly" ascended Nirvikalpa Samadhi, please see the glossary entry **Samadhi**.

59. This discussion points to the prerequisite sequence of Signs of Awakening leading to seventh stage Divine Enlightenment, as described by Avatar Adi Da Samraj. For a description of Jnana Nirvikalpa Samadhi, please see the glossary entry **Samadhi**.

The Sixth Stage Realization, Demonstration, and Teachings of Ramana Maharshi, and My Great Regard for Him as One of My Principal Adept-Links to the Great Tradition of Mankind

60. "Sanchita" is the total accumulation of past karmas, or mistakes.

61. *Talks with Sri Ramana Maharshi*, 3 vols. in one, 7th ed. (Tiruvannamalai, India: Sri Ramanasramam, 1984), 470 (#488).

62. Ibid., 348 (#382).

I Have Appeared here Via a Unique, Spontaneous, and Never-Again Conjunction of Vehicles

63. For a full account of this incident, see *The Life of Swami Vivekananda*, by His Eastern and Western Disciples, vol. 1, 5th ed., revised and enlarged (Calcutta: Advaita Ashram, 1979), 182–83.

64. "Fakir" in Arabic literally means "poor", and it may be used to mean either material impoverishment or the virtue of an aspirant making himself or herself "poor" by ceasing to be self-centered.

65. In her book, *The Master As I Saw Him* (Calcutta: Udbodhan Office, 1983), p. 71, Sister Nivedita describes:

> *Often it appears to me, in studying all these lives, that there has been with us a soul named Ramakrishna-Vivekananda, and that, in the penumbra of his being, appear many forms, some of which are with us still, and of none of whom it could be said with entire truth that here ends, in relation to him, the sphere of those others, or that there begins his own.*

66. Here Avatar Adi Da is referring to the Event that occurred at the end of His first visit to Swami Muktananda's Ashram in Ganeshpuri, immediately following His sighting of Swami Muktananda and Rang Avadhoot in the Ashram garden. See chapter 10 of Part One.

67. See Part Three, "My Avataric Divine Self-'Emergence' Is an Event in My Divine 'Bright' Spherical Self-Domain of Conscious Light", pp. 617–32.

68. Ramakrishna, at various times, described Swami Vivekananda as a "high" being. In *The Gospel of Sri Ramakrishna*, pp. 810–11, Ramakrishna says of Swami Vivekananda ("Narendra"), "Narendra belongs to a very high plane—the realm of the Absolute." See also note 69.

69. *[W]onderful things had been revealed to him [Ramakrishna] about Naren [Swami Vivekananda] even before this great disciple came to Dakshineswar [where Ramakrishna lived]. This is how Ramakrishna spoke of them:*
> *One day I found that my mind was soaring high in Samadhi along a luminous path. It soon transcended the stellar universe and entered the subtler region of ideas. As it ascended higher and higher I found on both sides of the way ideal forms of gods and goddesses. The mind then reached the outer limits of that region, where a luminous barrier separated the sphere of relative existence from that of the Absolute. Crossing that barrier, the mind entered the transcendental realm where no corporeal being was visible. Even the gods*

dared not peep into that sublime realm, but had to be content to keep their seats far below. The next moment I found seven venerable sages seated there in Samadhi. It occurred to me that these sages must have surpassed not only men, but even the gods, in knowledge and holiness, in renunciation and love. Lost in admiration I was reflecting on their greatness, when I saw a portion of that undifferentiated luminous region condense into the form of a divine child. The child came to one of the sages, tenderly clasped his neck with his lovely little arms, and addressing him in a sweet voice attempted to drag his mind down from the state of Samadhi. The magic touch roused the sage from his superconscious state, and he fixed his unmoving, half-open gaze upon that wonderful child. His beaming countenance showed that the child must have been the treasure of his heart. In great joy the strange child said to him, "I am going down. You too must go with me." The sage remained mute, but his tender look expressed his assent. As he kept gazing on the child, he was again immersed in Samadhi. I was surprised to find that a fragment of the sage's body and mind was descending on earth in the form of an effulgent light. No sooner had I seen Naren than I recognized him to be that sage. [Subsequent inquiry elicited from Shri Ramakrishna the admission that the divine child was none other than himself.]

The Life of Swami Vivekananda, by His Eastern and Western Disciples, vol. 1, 5th ed., revised and enlarged (Calcutta: Advaita Ashram, 1979), 80–81.

70. For an account of the Sacred History of Avatar Adi Da's Avataric Divine Work, please see *Adi Da: The Promised God-Man Is Here*, by Carolyn Lee, Ph.D., concise edition (The Dawn Horse Press, August 2003).

I (Alone) Am The Adidam Revelation

71. For a detailed description of the four stages (or four Ways) of Kashmir Saivism, see *Triadic Mysticism: The Mystical Theology of the Saivism of Kashmir*, by Paul E. Murphy (Delhi: Motilal Banarsidass, 1986).

72. There are a number of translations of the *Chidakasha Gita* teachings (including *Voice of the Self*, referenced below). Perhaps the most readily available translation is *The Sky of the Heart: Jewels of Wisdom from Nityananda*, introduction and commentary by Swami Chetanananda, originally translated by M. U. Hatengdi, 2d ed. (Portland, Or.: Rudra Press, 1996).

73. *Voice of the Self*, by Swami Nityananda (of Vajreshwari), translated by M. P. Pandit (Madras: P. Ramanath Pai, 1962).

74. Sanskrit "nada" (or "shabda") refers to subtle internal sounds which may become apparent in the process of ascending (spinal) Yoga. The "Om-Sound" (or "Omkar") is the primordial root-sound, from which all other nadas derive.

75. Among the numerous translations of the *Astavakra Gita*, Avatar Adi Da Samraj points to two editions as particularly worthy of study:

The Song of the Self Supreme (Astavakra Gita): The Classical Text of Atmadvaita, by Astavakra. Preface by Adi Da Samraj, translation and commentary by Radhakamal Mukerjee (Clearlake, Calif.: Dawn Horse Press, 1990).

Astavakra Samhita. Translated by Swami Nityaswarupananda (Calcutta: Advaita Ashrama, 1969).

76. In *The Basket Of Tolerance*, Avatar Adi Da has identified a small number of Hindu and Buddhist texts as "premonitorily 'seventh stage'". While founded in the characteristic sixth stage "point of view", these texts express philosophical intuitions that foreshadow some of the basic characteristics of the seventh stage Realization.

The only-by-Me Revealed and Demonstrated and Given seventh stage of life is the clear and final fulfillment of the first six stages of life. The Revelation and Demonstration of the seventh stage of life by My Own Avatarically Self-Revealed Divine Form, Presence, State, Work, and Word are My unique Gift to all-and-All. However, within the Great Tradition itself, there are some few literatures and Realizers of the sixth stage type that express philosophical (or insightful, but yet limited and incomplete) intuitions that sympathetically foreshadow some of the basic characteristics of the only-by-Me Revealed and Demonstrated and Given seventh stage Realization.

The Ashtavakra Gita *is a principal example of such premonitorily "seventh stage" literature. It is among the greatest (and most senior) communications of all the religious and Spiritual traditions in the Great Tradition of mankind. The* Ashtavakra Gita *is the Great Confession of a Sage who has thoroughly engaged the philosophies and practices of the first six stages of life. It is a sixth stage Adept-Realizer's Free (and uncompromised) communication (or Confession) of the ultimate implications of his sixth stage Realization.*

Like other premonitorily "seventh stage" texts, the Ashtavakra Gita *presumes a tradition of progressive practice in the total context of the first six stages of life, but it does not (itself) represent or communicate any ideal or technique of practice. It simply (and rather exclusively) communicates the Ultimate "Point of View" of the sixth stage Realizer.*

—Avatar Adi Da Samraj
The Basket Of Tolerance

77. For Avatar Adi Da's description of Swami Prakashananda's demonstration of Spiritual Transfiguration of the physical body, see p. 228.

78. *Agaram Bagaram Baba: Life, Teachings, and Parables—A Spiritual Biography of Baba Prakashananda*, by Titus Foster (Berkeley: North Atlantic Books/ Patagonia, Ariz.: Essene Vision Books, 1999), 35.

79. For Avatar Adi Da's description of His own "Embrace" of the Divine "Cosmic Goddess", see pp. 317–18.

80. Swami Muktananda, *Play of Consciousness*, 4th ed. (South Fallsburg, N.Y.: SYDA, 1994).

81. For a comprehensive treatment of the fourth-to-fifth stage Yogic tradition of Maharashtra, see *Mysticism in India: The Poet-Saints of Maharashtra*, by R. D. Ranade (Albany: State University of New York Press, 1983).

82. For Swami Muktananda's description of the "Blue Person", see *Play of Consciousness* (e.g. pp. 190–94).

As previously noted, among the numerous translations of the *Bhagavad Gita*, Avatar Adi Da Samraj points to two editions as particularly worthy of study:

The Bhagavad Gita, Withrop Sargeant, trans., rev. ed., ed. Christopher Chapple (Albany, N.Y.: State University of New York Press, 1984).

God Talks with Arjuna: The Bhagavad Gita—Royal Science of God-Realization, The Immortal Dialogue Between Soul and Spirit, a new translation and commentary by Paramahansa Yogananda, 2 vols. (Los Angeles: Self-Realization Fellowship, 1996).

For a complete translation of the *Bhagavata Purana* (also known as the *Srimad Bhagavatam*), see *Srimad Bhagavatam,* translated by N. Raghunathan, 2 vols. (Madras: Vighneshwara Publishing House, 1976).

83. Excerpted from a chart ("The Four Bodies of the Individual Soul") in *Play of Consciousness,* by Swami Muktananda, 4th ed. (South Fallsburg, N.Y.: SYDA, 1994), 96.

84. In *The Basket Of Tolerance,* Avatar Adi Da has contrasted the development of exoteric (or socially oriented, and myth-based) public Christianity with the secret Teachings of esoteric (or mystically oriented) Christianity:

The "official" Christian church, even in the form of all its modern sects, is the institutional product of an early cultural struggle between exoteric religionists, limited to doctrines based in the physical point of view characteristic of the first three stages of life, and esoteric religionists, inclined toward the mystical (or general psychic, and Spiritual) point of view characteristic of the "basic" and the "advanced" phases of the fourth stage of life and the mystical (or higher psychic, and Spiritual) Realizations associated with the fifth stage of life. This struggle, which was eventually won by the exoteric sects (or factions), took place between the various emerging Christian sects during the early centuries after Jesus' [crucifixion]. . . .

In the domain of the exoteric church, it was apparently generally presumed (among its original creative leadership) that all mysteries and legends must be "concretized" into a story (or an inspiring doctrine) about Jesus as the "Heavenly Messiah" (or the "Christ", the "Anointed One", the Exclusively Blessed "Son of God")—whereas the original esoteric mysteries and mystical Teachings of Christian gnosticism (which must often correspond to what must be presumed to have been Jesus' own Teachings) invariably communicate a Message about the Spiritual (or "Spirit-Breathing") Awakening of every individual (or of every devotee of a Spirit-Master, or, in this Christian case, of every devotee of Jesus as Spirit-Master). Therefore, the core of the esoteric Christian Teachings is that Salvation (from "possession" by cosmic Nature, by the human world, and by fear of death) is Realized by Means of "Spiritual rebirth" (or Absorption In—and, thus, participatory knowledge of—the inherently deathless and Free and Divine Spirit-Power, or "Breath-Energy", of Being). And the "Good News" of this esoteric Salvation Message is that every individual is (ultimately, by virtue of Spiritual Realization) a "Son" or "Daughter" of God.

85. Avatar Adi Da notes that not only "things" in space but space itself came into being with the "Big Bang":

Space-time (itself, or in its totality) cannot be observed. The "Big Bang" was not an event that could have been observed. The "Big Bang" is not something that *occurred <u>in</u> space (or <u>in</u> time). The "Big Bang" is the <u>origin</u> of space (and of time). To look at the "Big Bang" as an event in space (and in time) is already to look at it in egoic terms, and from a position <u>after</u> the event. To examine the "Big Bang" in conventional scientific terms is to assume a dissociated (and separate, and separative) position, as if the ego-"I" (or the "observing" body-mind) were standing <u>outside</u> of space-time—but it does not. Egoity (and all of psycho-physical self, or body-mind) is, inherently and necessarily, an event in (and of) space-time. The body-mind is an event in (and of) space-time. That in Which the body-mind is occurring (or of Which the body-mind is a modification, or a mere and temporary appearance) <u>necessarily</u> (Itself) Transcends space-time, Transcends limitation, Transcends the apparent breaking of Fundamental Light (or of Energy Itself, or of Radiance Itself).*

—Avatar Adi Da Samraj
<u>Real</u> God <u>Is</u> The Indivisible Oneness Of Unbroken Light

86. For Swami Muktananda's description of the "blue bindu" (or "blue pearl"), see *Play of Consciousness* (e.g., pp. 160–161).

87. For Avatar Adi Da's full description of the Cosmic Mandala, see chapter sixty-seven of *The Dawn Horse Testament Of The Ruchira Avatar*.

88. This instruction from Swami Muktananda was communicated in a letter he wrote to Avatar Adi Da on April 23, 1968, which Avatar Adi Da quotes in chapter 11 of *The Knee Of Listening*.

89. The "Method of the Siddhas" (meaning "the Spiritual Means used by the Siddhas, or Perfected Ones, or True Spirit-Baptizers") is a phrase coined by Avatar Adi Da Samraj (in the earliest days of His Teaching-Work) to describe the essence of the Way of Adidam—which is the devotional (and, in due course, Spiritual) relationship to Him (or Satsang, or heart-Communion with Him), rather than any technique (meditative or otherwise) learned from Him. *The Method of the Siddhas* was the Title Avatar Adi Da chose for the first published collection of His Talks to His devotees. (In its final form, Avatar Adi Da re-titled this book *The Divine Siddha-Method Of The Ruchira Avatar*.)

    Avatar Adi Da also points out that this "Method" has traditionally always been the core of esoteric religion and Spirituality, and that (indeed) the entire world-wide tradition of esoteric religion and Spirituality is rightly understood to be the global tradition of "Siddha Yoga".

The Foundation Of The Only-By-Me Revealed and Given Way Of Adidam Is The Eternal, Ancient, and Always New Method Of The Siddhas—Which Is Devotional Communion With The Siddha-Guru, and Which Is The Unique Means Of Realizing Real God, or Truth, or Reality That Has Traditionally Been Granted By The Rare True Adept-Realizers Of Real God, or Truth, or Reality Who (In The Traditional Context Of The Fourth, The Fifth, and The Sixth Stages Of Life, and Each According To Their Particular Stage Of Awakening and Of Helping-Capability) Have, By Means Of The Unique Spiritual Blessing-Method (or Shaktipat-Transmission-Capability) Of The Siddhas, Directly (and By Really

Effective Spiritual Means) Transmitted The Traditional Revelations and Realizations Of Real God (or Truth Itself, or Reality Itself).

—Avatar Adi Da Samraj
The Only Complete Way To Realize The Unbroken Light Of Real God

90. See *Sadguru Nityananda Bhagavan, The Eternal Entity*, by P. V. Ravindram (Cannanore, India: T. Thankam Ravindran, 1989), 25–26 and 27–28.

I Am Utterly Beyond your Comprehension

91. Evelyn Disk is an archetypal character in Avatar Adi Da's liturgical drama, *The Mummery Book*. A huge preacher, Disk uses his supposed connection with Raymond (the protagonist) to create and head a religious following—the "Raymondite" religion.

PART THREE

Introduction to Part Three

92. The Ruchira Sannyasin Order is the body of Avatar Adi Da's most advanced devotees who have chosen to consecrate their lives utterly to Him and His Way—by embracing the life of formal renunciation, in the circumstance of perpetual retreat. Avatar Adi Da has designated the Ruchira Sannyasin Order as the senior cultural authority within the gathering of His devotees—both during and after His physical Lifetime. Thus, it is the unique responsibility of the Ruchira Sannyasin Order to function both as the extension of His Sacred Authority and as His Instrumentality (or the collective human "conduit" for His Spiritual Blessing).

The Ruchira Sannyasin Order of Adidam Ruchiradam is (and must always be) the most senior gathering of (necessarily, formal) practitioners of the Way of Adidam—and the hierarchically central, and most senior (but entirely renunciate, and non-managerial), functioning cultural authority among, and in relation to, all the (necessarily, formal) practitioners of the Way of Adidam. . . .

All the present members and all the future members of the Ruchira Sannyasin Order of Adidam Ruchiradam are Called and Empowered (by Me) to Function (collectively) as the principal and most senior (physically living, human) Instruments of My forever Blessing-Work, and, by their unique (and uniquely authoritative) cultural service (simply by Wisdom-word and practicing example), to provide all other practitioners of the Way of Adidam with the principal Good Company (of fellow devotees) that is necessary for the inspiration and guidance of their practice of the Way of Adidam.

—Avatar Adi Da Samraj
"The Orders of My True and Free Renunciate Devotees"

93. For a more extended account of Avatar Adi Da's Life-Story since His Divine Re-Awakening, please see *Adi Da: The Promised God-Man Is Here*, the authorized biography of Avatar Adi Da, by Carolyn Lee, Ph.D., concise ed. (The Dawn Horse Press, August 2003).

Introduction to "My Avataric Divine Self-'Emergence' Is an Event in My Divine 'Bright' Spherical Self-Domain of Conscious Light"

94. This Talk is included in Avatar Adi Da's "Source-Text" *The Divine Siddha-Method Of The Ruchira Avatar.*

95. *AVATAR ADI DA SAMRAJ: The "method" of My Teaching-Work with My devotees was not common, although there are many traditional precedents for it. It was not merely a subjective, internal, or even verbal activity but an intense, full, and total "consideration" of any specific area of experience, in living confrontation with others, until the obvious and Lawful, or Divine, form and practice of it became both clear and necessary.*

I have compared this method to the higher Yogic technique of samyama described by Patanjali in his Yoga Sutras. *In brief, that Yogic technique of samyama is a process of one-pointed but (ultimately) thoughtless concentration and exhaustive examination of a particular object, function, person, process, or condition, until the essence, or ultimate obviousness, of that subject is clear. Only in that case does the Yogi enjoy native intimacy and understanding, or power, relative to that subject.*

I have called My Own Teaching-Method "Consideration". Whenever it has been clear to Me that a particular area of life, or experience, or Spiritual practice needed to be Addressed by Me as a subject of Instruction for the sake of My devotees, I have entered into "Consideration" with them. Such "Considerations" were never merely a matter of thinking and talking. They always involved a period in which individuals were permitted to live through the whole matter and to be tested to the point of change. Those who entered into any "Consideration" with Me were obliged to commit themselves to their own elaborate and concentrated play of life in those particular terms, until the entire matter was clarified and the Truth became clear in terms of the subject. . . .

All these "Considerations" have been "samyama" in the highest sense, involving every aspect of body and mind, high and low, and resulting in both the deepest intuition and the most practical grasp of how to live life in accordance with natural laws and the Divine Law.

—1978

96. The title "Ruchiradama" is given to female members of the Ruchira Sannyasin Order, which is the senior renunciate order of the Way of Adidam. Male members of the Ruchira Sannyasin Order receive the title "Ruchiradasa". Both titles include the Sanskrit word "ruchira" (meaning "bright"), and both indicate that the individual is a devotee of Avatar Adi Da Samraj who is "becoming 'Bright' with His Divine Love-Bliss, through uniquely one-pointed feeling-Contemplation of Him".

The renunciate name "Quandra Sukhapur Rani" is drawn both from Avatar Adi Da's own writing and from Sanskrit. "Quandra" is the name of the principal female character in Avatar Adi Da's literary work *The Mummery Book*—a character who is an archetypal representation of the female beloved. In Sanskrit, "sukha" is "happiness", "pur[a]" is "city" (or "domain"), and "rani" is "queen". Thus, "Quandra Sukhapur Rani" means "the beloved who is the queen of the Domain of Happiness"—a description of Ruchiradama Quandra Sukhapur's unique role within the gathering of Avatar Adi Da's devotees and the orders of renunciates who serve Him most directly.

My Avataric Divine Self-"Emergence" Is an Event in My Divine "Bright" Spherical Self-Domain of Conscious Light

97. Avatar Adi Da Samraj frequently Describes His Blessing-Power as being like a kiln. In a kiln, as the wet clay objects are heated more and more, they begin to glow. Eventually, the kiln is so hot that everything within it glows with a white light, and the definitions of the individual objects dissolve in the brightness. Just so, as a devotee matures in Avatar Adi Da's Spiritual Company, all presumptions of separateness as an apparently individual ego-"I" are more and more Outshined by the "Brightness" of His Divine Person and Blessing.

Introduction to "My Avataric Divine Spiritual Work Is a Sphere of 'Bright' Influence That Cannot Ever Be Destroyed"

98. For a description of the "Santosha Event", please see *Adi Da: The Promised God-Man Is Here*, by Carolyn Lee, Ph.D., concise ed. (The Dawn Horse Press, August 2003).

99. The renunciate name "Nadikanta" derives from Sanskrit. "Nadi" (with a short "a" in Sanskrit) means (1) "flowing water" or "river", while "nadi" (with a long "a" in Sanskrit) means the "channels" or "currents" of life-energy and Spiritual Energy in the human body. "Kanta", in this phrase, is used with the meaning "one who loves". The traditional meaning of "nadikanta" is "lover of waters". Avatar Adi Da uses "True Water" as a metaphorical reference for Consciousness Itself, or the Divine Self-Condition That He Reveals and Is. Thus, the full meaning of "Nadikanta" as a renunciate name in the Way of Adidam is "the devotee who loves (or heart-Communes with) True Water, or the Divine Spiritual Current That Is Adi Da Samraj".

100. The Matrix is Avatar Adi Da's residential complex at Adidam Samrajashram (the Island of Naitauba, Fiji).

My Avataric Divine Spiritual Work Is a Sphere of "Bright" Influence That Cannot Ever Be Destroyed

101. On February 23, 1999, Venus and Jupiter (the two brightest planets) passed within 1/10th of a degree of one another in a visible astronomical conjunction (close enough to allow both planets to be seen in a single telescopic field when viewed through a high-powered eyepiece). Some astrologers have noted the synchronicity between Venus-Jupiter conjunctions and significant events associated with the Kosovo conflict.

Introduction to "I Am Always Already Spiritually Established As The 'Bright' Itself"

102. *Hridaya Rosary* is one of Avatar Adi Da's twenty-three "Source-Texts". See p. 719.

I (Myself) Do Not "Come Down" Below the Brows

103. Avatar Adi Da uses the metaphor of the "dog" and "washing the dog" to Indicate the purification of the body-mind that occurs as part of the process of His Spiritual Transformation of His devotee. He addresses the presumption (found, for example, in the Kundalini Yoga tradition) that the Spiritual process requires a spinal Yoga, or an effort of arousing Spiritual Energy literally at the "tail" end of the "dog" (the bodily base, or the muladhara chakra), and then drawing It up (or allowing It to ascend) through the spinal line to the head (and above). In contrast, Avatar Adi Da Samraj has Revealed (particularly in His *Hridaya Rosary*) that, in reality, the human being can be truly purified and Liberated (or the "dog" can be "washed") only by receiving His Divine Blessing-Power (or Ruchira Shakti) and Spiritual Person downward from Infinitely Above the head to the bodily base. This Process of downward reception of Avatar Adi Da is what He calls the "frontal Yoga", because it occurs in the frontal line of the body (which is a natural pathway of descending energy, down the front of the body, from the crown of the head to the bodily base). This necessary descending Yoga of the frontal line, once completed, is sufficient to purify the body-mind to the degree it can allow the thorough Infusion by His Ruchira Shaktipat and (in due course) the transition to the "Perfect Practice", by means of His Spiritual Gift of the "Thumbs".

AVATAR ADI DA SAMRAJ: You wash a dog from the head to the tail. But somehow or other, egos looking to Realize think they can wash the "dog" from the "tail" toward the head by doing spinal Yoga. But, in Truth, and in Reality, only the frontal Yoga can accomplish Most Perfect Divine Self-Realization, because it begins from the superior position, from the "head" position, from My Crashing Down.

The heart-disposition is magnified by My Crashing Down in your devotional and Spiritual Communion with Me. And the vital, grosser dimensions of the being are purified by this washing from the head toward the "tail". If the Process had to begin from the bodily base up, it would be very difficult, very traumatizing—and, ultimately, impossible. The "dog" is washed, simply and very directly, by your participation in My Divine Descent, by your participation in this frontal Yoga. I am Speaking now of the seeing stages, basically. But, even in the case of Spiritually Initiated beginning practitioners in the Way of Adidam—not yet technically fully responsible for the Spiritual dimension of their relationship to Me—this "wash" is, by Means of My Avataric Divine Spiritual Grace, going on.

Therefore, Spiritual life need not be a traumatic course. The "dog" should enjoy being bathed. Nice gentle little guy, happy to be rubbed and touched. You talk to him, struggle a little bit, but you gentle him down. That is how it should work. And, at the end of it, the "dog" sort of "wags its tail", shakes the water off— nice and clean, happy, your best friend. That is how it should work.

If you wash the "dog" from the "tail" up, you smear the shit from his backside toward his head. Basically, that "washing from the tail toward the head" is a self-generated, self-"guruing" kind of effort. The Divine Process can only occur by Means of My Divine Spiritual Grace. Even the word "Shaktipat" means the "Descent (pat) of Divine Force (Shakti)". But Shaktipat as it appears in the traditions is basically associated with admonitions to practice a spinal Yoga, moving from the base up. In Truth, the Divine Yoga in My Company is a Descent—washing the "dog" from head to "tail" rather than giving the "dog" a "bone", letting it wash itself from the "tail" to the head.

This is why you must invest yourself in Me. And that is how the "dog" gets washed.

—August 13, 1995

Avatar Adi Da's extended Discourse relative to "washing the dog" is "Be Washed, From Head to Tail, By Heart-Devotion To Me", in *Hridaya Rosary*.

104. Avatar Adi Da has distinguished three basic psycho-physical types (or strategies), which He calls "vital", "peculiar", and "solid". The "vital" person is oriented to the physical dimension of existence, the "peculiar" person is oriented to the emotional dimension of existence, and the "solid" person is oriented to the mental dimension of existence. (For Avatar Adi Da's extended Instruction relative to these three psycho-physical types, see *Ruchira Tantra Yoga*.)

A

Adi—Sanskrit for "first", "primordial", "source"—also "primary", "beginning". Thus, most simply, "Adi Da" means "First Giver".

Adidam / Adidam Ruchiradam— The Way Revealed and Given by Avatar Adi Da Samraj.

When Avatar Adi Da Samraj first Gave the name "Adidam" in January 1996, He pointed out that the final "m" adds a mantric force, evoking the effect of the primal Sanskrit syllable "Om". (For Avatar Adi Da's Revelation of the most profound esoteric signifi-cance of "Om" as the Divine Sound of His own Very Being, see He-_and_-She _Is_ Me.) Simultaneously, the final "m" suggests the English word "Am" (expressing "I Am"), such that the Name "Adidam" also evokes Avatar Adi Da's Primal Self-Confession, "I _Am_ Adi Da", or, more simply, "I _Am_ Da" (or, in Sanskrit, "Aham Da Asmi").

A fuller form of reference to Avatar Adi Da's Divine Way is "Adidam Ruchiradam". "Ruchiradam" is a word newly coined by Avatar Adi Da, deriving from Sanskrit "Ruchira" (meaning "bright" or "radiant"). The compound reference "Adidam Ruchiradam" communicates that Adidam is the religion of devo-tion to Avatar Adi Da Samraj—Who _Is_ the "Bright" Itself, and Who Gives the Realization of His Own "Bright" Self-Condition.

Aham Da Asmi—Sanskrit phrase meaning "I (Aham) Am (Asmi) Da". "Da" (meaning "the One Who Gives") indicates that Avatar Adi Da Samraj is the Supreme Divine Giver, the Avataric Incarnation of the Very Divine Person. For a full "consideration" of the import of this Great Divine Statement, please see _Aham Da Asmi (Beloved, I_Am_ Da)._

all-and-All —A phrase Avatar Adi Da has created to describe the totality of conditional existence from two points of view. In _Aham Da Asmi,_ He defines lower-case "all" as indicating "the collected sum of all Presumed To Be Separate (or limited) beings, things, and conditions", and upper-case "All" as indicating "The All (or The Undivided Totality) Of condi-tional Existence As A Whole".

Alpha and Omega—Avatar Adi Da calls the characteristic traditional Eastern strategy the "Alpha" strategy. Alpha cultures pursue an undisturbed peace, in which the conditional world is excluded as much as possible from attention (and thereby ceases to be a disturbance). Although the cultures that were originally founded on the Alpha approach to life and Truth are fast disappearing, the Alpha strategy remains the conventional archetype of Spiritual life, even in the Omega cul-ture. In contrast to the Omega prefer-ence, the Alpha preference is to limit and control (and even suppress) attention to the conditional reality, while maximizing attention to the Divine Reality.

Avatar Adi Da uses the term "Omega" to characterize the material-istic culture that today dominates not only the Western world (which has brought the Omega strategy to its fullest development) but even most of the present-day Eastern world, which has now largely adopted the anti-Spiritual viewpoint typical of the West. The Omega strategy is motivated to the attainment of a future-time perfection and fulfillment of the conditional worlds, through the intense application of human invention, political will, and even Divine Influence. Its preference is to limit and suppress attention to the Divine Reality, while maximizing attention to the conditional reality.

Neither the Alpha strategy nor the Omega strategy Realizes Truth absolutely, as each is rooted in the presumption of a "problem" relative to existence. (For Avatar Adi Da's extended discussion of the Alpha and Omega strategies, see *The Truly Human New World-Culture Of Unbroken Real-God-Man*.)

asana—Sanskrit for bodily "posture" or "pose"—by extension, and as Avatar Adi Da often intends, "asana" also refers to the attitude, orientation, posture, or feeling-disposition of the heart and the entire body-mind.

Atman—Sanskrit for the Supreme Divine Self.

Atma-Vichara—Ramana Maharshi's term for the examination ("vichara") of the Self ("atman"), often translated as "Self-enquiry".

Avatar—From Sanskrit "avatara", a traditional term for a Divine Incarnation. It literally means "One who is descended, or 'crossed down' (from, and as, the Divine)". Avatar Adi Da Samraj Confesses that, simultaneous with His human Birth, He has Incarnated in every world, at every level of the cosmic domain, as the Eternal Giver of Divine Help and Divine Grace and Divine Liberation to all beings—and that, even though His bodily (human) Lifetime is necessarily limited in duration, His Spiritual Incarnation in the cosmic domain is Eternal.

Avataric Divine Self-"Emergence"—On January 11, 1986, Avatar Adi Da passed through a profound Yogic Swoon, which He later described as the Yogic Establishment of His Avataric Divine Self-"Emergence". Avatar Adi Da's Divine Self-"Emergence" is an ongoing Process in which His Avatarically-Born bodily (human) Divine Form has been (and is ever more profoundly and potently being) conformed to Himself, the Very Divine Person, such that His bodily (human) Form is now (and forever hereafter) an utterly Unobstructed Sign and Agent of His own Divine Being.

Avataric Incarnation—The Divinely Descended Embodiment of the Divine Person. The reference "Avataric Incarnation" indicates that Avatar Adi Da Samraj fulfills both the traditional expectation of the East, that the True God-Man is an Avatar (or an utterly Divine "Descent" of Real God in conditionally manifested form), and the traditional expectation of the West, that the True God-Man is an Incarnation (or an utterly human Embodiment of Real God).

Avataric Self-Submission—The Gesture whereby Avatar Adi Da (initially) embraced ordinary human existence and (subsequently) embraced His Work of Teaching and Blessing humankind. It is by virtue of this Gesture that He fully Manifested His All-Completing and Final Revelation of the Divine. For a full account of Avatar Adi Da's "Ordeal Of Avataric Self-Submission", please see His biography, *Adi Da: The Promised God-Man Is Here*, by Carolyn Lee.

B

Bhagavan—"Bhagavan" is an ancient Title used over the centuries for many Spiritual Realizers of India. It means "blessed" or "holy" in Sanskrit. When applied to a great Spiritual Being, "Bhagavan" is understood to mean "bountiful Lord", or "Great Lord", or "Divine Lord".

Bhakti—The practice of heart-felt devotion to the Ultimate Reality or Person—a practice which has been traditionally animated through worship of Divine Images or surrender to a human Guru.

Bhava—A Sanskrit word used to refer to the enraptured feeling-swoon of Communion with the Divine.

Blessing-Work—The profound Purpose and Activity of Avatar Adi Da's Divine Incarnation—to Spiritually Grace and Awaken all beings to His Divine Self-Domain. For an account of Avatar Adi Da's Divine Blessing-Work, please see *Adi Da: The Promised God-Man Is Here*, by Carolyn Lee.

Brahman—In the Hindu tradition, Brahman is the Ultimate Divine Reality that is the Source and Substance of all things, all worlds, and all beings.

"Bright"—By the word "Bright" (and its variations, such as "Brightness"), Avatar Adi Da refers to the Self-Existing and Self-Radiant Divine Reality that He has Revealed since His Birth.

C

causal—See **gross, subtle, causal**.

conditional—Everything that depends on conditions—in other words, everything that is temporary and changing. The "Unconditional", in contrast, is the Divine, or That Which Is Eternal, Always Already the Case—because It Is utterly Free of dependence on any conditions whatsoever.

conditionally ascended Nirvikalpa Samadhi—See **Samadhi**.

conditionally Self-Abiding Jnana Nirvikalpa Samadhi—See **Samadhi**.

"conductivity"—"Conductivity" is Avatar Adi Da's technical term for participation in (and responsibility for) the movement of natural bodily energies (and, when one is Spiritually Awakened by Him, for the movement of His Divine Spirit-Current of Love-Bliss in Its natural course of association with the body-mind), via intentional exercises of feeling and breathing. (Avatar Adi Da's descriptions of the various forms of "conductivity" practice are Given in *The Dawn Horse Testament Of The Ruchira Avatar*.)

"conscious process"—The "conscious process" is Avatar Adi Da's technical term for those practices through which the mind (or attention) is surrendered and turned about (from egoic self-involvement) to feeling-Contemplation of Him. The "conscious process" and "conductivity" practice are co-equal responsive exercises engaged by all practitioners in the Way of Adidam (both in meditation and in the context of daily life). (Avatar Adi Da's descriptions of the various forms of the "conscious process" are Given in *The Dawn Horse Testament Of The Ruchira Avatar*.)

"consider" / "consideration"— Avatar Adi Da uses these words to refer to a process of one-pointed but ultimately thoughtless concentration and exhaustive contemplation of something until its ultimate obviousness is clear. (Such a process was originally described by Patanjali, in his *Yoga Sutras*, as "samyama".) Avatar Adi Da puts these terms in quotation marks to indicate that He intends this specific technical meaning.

As engaged in the Way of Adidam, "consideration" is not merely an intellectual investigation. It is the participatory investment of one's whole being. If one "considers" something fully—in the context of one's practice of feeling-Contemplation of Avatar Adi Da Samraj and one's study of His Wisdom-Teaching—this concentration results "in both the deepest intuition and the most practical grasp of how to live life in accordance with natural laws and the Divine Law".

"Cosmic Consciousness"—See **Samadhi**.

Cosmic Mandala—The Sanskrit word "mandala" (literally, "circle") is commonly used in the esoteric Spiritual traditions of the East to describe the hierarchical levels of cosmic existence. "Mandala" also denotes an artistic rendering of interior visions of the cosmos. Avatar Adi Da uses the phrase "Cosmic Mandala" as a reference to the totality of the conditionally manifested cosmos (or all worlds, forms, and beings),

which (He has Revealed) can be visually perceived (and, thus, represented) as a pattern of concentric circular bands (or, more accurately, spheres) of certain distinct colors, with a Brilliant White Five-Pointed Star at the center. (For Avatar Adi Da's detailed description of the Cosmic Mandala, see chapter 60 of *The Dawn Horse Testament*.)

Crashing Down—The Descent of Avatar Adi Da's Divine Spirit-Force into the body-mind of His devotee, and into the cosmic domain altogether.

> *My Avataric Divine Spiritual Work (Altogether) Is My Crashing-Down Descent, At First Upon and Into My Own Avatarically-Born Bodily (Human) Divine Form, and, Thereafter (and Now, and Forever Hereafter), Upon and Into the body-minds Of My Devotees and all beings—Even (By Means Of My Divine Embrace Of each, and all, and All) To Infuse and (At Last) To Divinely Translate each, and all, and All.*
>
> —Avatar Adi Da Samraj
> *Ruchira Shaktipat Yoga*

"Crazy"—Avatar Adi Da has always Worked in a unique "Crazy" Manner, which, during His "Sadhana Years" and His years of Teaching and Revelation, involved His Submission to the limited conditions of humankind, in order to reflect His devotees to themselves, and thereby Awaken self-understanding in them (relative to their individual egoic dramas, and the collective egoic dramas of human society).

> *For Me, There Was Never Any Possibility Other Than The "Reckless" (or Divinely "Crazy" and Divinely "Heroic") Course Of all-and-All-Embrace—and I Began This Uniquely*

"Crazy" and "Heroic" Sadhana, Most Intensively, At The Beginning Of My Adult Life. Indeed, I Have Always Functioned, and Will Always Function, In This Divinely "Crazy" and Divinely "Heroic" Manner. The Inherently egoless "Crazy" and "Heroic" Manner Is One Of My Principal Divine Characteristics—Whereby I Can (Always, and Now, and Forever Hereafter) Be Identified. Therefore, I (Characteristically) Functioned In This "Crazy" and "Heroic" Manner Throughout All Of My "Sadhana Years", and Throughout All The Years Of My Avatarically Self-Manifested Divine Teaching-Work and My Avatarically Self-Manifested Divine Revelation-Work—and I Have Done So (and Will <u>Forever</u> Continue To Do So) Throughout All The Divine-Self-"Emergence" Years Of My Avatarically Self-Manifested Divine Blessing-Work (Both During, and Forever After, My Avataric Physical Human Lifetime). <u>All</u> My Avatarically Self-Manifested Divine Spiritual Work Is A Divinely "Crazy" and Divinely "Heroic" Effort That Avoids Not anything or anyone—but Which <u>Always</u> Divinely Blesses Everything and Everyone.

—Avatar Adi Da Samraj
The Truly Human New World-Culture Of <u>Unbroken</u> Real-God-Man

D

Da—Avatar Adi Da's Divine Name "Da" means "The One Who Gives", or "The Divine Giver". This Name was spontaneously Revealed to Avatar Adi Da as His Principal Divine Name—and it is a syllable with great sacred significance in various cultures. Tibetan Buddhists regard the syllable "Da" (written, in Tibetan, with a single letter) as most auspicious, and they assign numerous

sacred meanings to it, including "Entrance into the Dharma". In the most ancient of the Upanishads (the *Brihadaranyaka Upanishad*), the Divine Being gives the fundamental instruction necessary for each of the different classes of living beings by uttering the single sound "Da". (Each class of beings understands "Da" in the manner uniquely necessary in its own case.) In this passage, "Da" is said to be the Divine Voice that can be heard speaking through thunder (S. Radhakrishnan, trans., *The Principal Upanishads* [Atlantic Highlands, N.J.: Humanities Press International, First paperback edition, 1992], 289–90.)

"dark" epoch—See **"late-time" (or "dark" epoch)**.

Deeper Personality / gross personality—Avatar Adi Da uses the terms "gross personality" and "Deeper Personality" to indicate the two conditional dimensions of every human being. The gross personality is comprised of the physical body, its natural energies, its gross brain, and the verbal and lower psychic faculties of mind. The gross personality includes the entire gross dimension of the body-mind and the lower (or most physically oriented) aspects of the subtle dimension of the body-mind, and is the aspect of the body-mind that is the biological inheritance from one's parents.

The Deeper Personality is governed by the higher (least physically oriented) processes of the mind (which function outside or beyond the gross brain, and which include the subtle faculties of discrimination, intuition, and Spiritual perception and knowledge), as well as the causal separate-"I"-consciousness and the root-activity of attention, prior to mind. The Deeper Personality is the aspect of the human being that reincarnates.

"difference"—The epitome of the egoic presumption of separateness—in contrast with the Realization of Oneness, or Non-"Difference", Which is Native to the Divine Self-Condition.

Divine Body / Divine Spiritual Body—Avatar Adi Da's Divine Body is not conditional or limited to His physical Body but is the "Bright" Itself—Spiritually Pervading, and Eternally Most Prior to, the cosmic domain.

Divine Enlightenment—The Realization of the seventh stage of life, which is uniquely Revealed and Given by Avatar Adi Da. It is Eternal Self-Abiding in His "Bright" (and Infinitely Love-Bliss-Full) Divine Self-Condition, released from all the egoic limitations of the first six stages of life. The seventh stage Awakening is Avatar Adi Da's Gift to His rightly prepared devotee who has fulfilled the entire sadhana of the Way of Adidam in the context of the first six stages of life.

Divine Indifference—See **four phases of the seventh stage of life**.

Divine Self-Domain / Divine "Bright" Spherical Self-Domain—Avatar Adi Da affirms that there is a Divine Self-Domain that is the Perfectly Subjective Condition of the conditional worlds. It is not "elsewhere", not an objective "place" (like a subtle "heaven" or mythical "paradise"), but It is the Divine Source-Condition of every conditionally manifested being and thing—and It is not other than Avatar Adi Da Himself. Avatar Adi Da Reveals that His Divine Self-Domain is a Boundless (and Boundlessly "Bright") Sphere. To Realize the seventh stage of life (by the Divine Spiritual Grace of Avatar Adi Da Samraj) is to Awaken to His Divine Self-Domain.

For Avatar Adi Da's extended Instruction relative to His Divine Self-Domain, see *The All-Completing and Final Divine Revelation To Mankind*.

Divine Self-"Emergence"—See **Avataric Divine Self-"Emergence"**.

Divine Self-Recognition—Divine Self-Recognition is the ego-transcending and world-transcending Intelligence of the Divine Self-Condition in relation to all conditional phenomena. The devotee of Avatar Adi Da who Realizes the seventh stage of life simply Abides as Self-Existing and Self-Radiant Consciousness Itself, and he or she Freely Self-Recognizes (or inherently and instantly and most perfectly comprehends and perceives) all phenomena (including body, mind, conditional self, and conditional world) as transparent (or merely apparent), and un-necessary, and inherently non-binding modifications of the same "Bright" Divine Self-Consciousness.

Divine Star—The original (and primal) conditional visible Representation (or Sign) of the "Bright" (the Source-Energy, or Divine Light, of Which all conditional phenomena and the total cosmos are modifications). Avatar Adi Da has Revealed that He is "Incarnated" in the Cosmic domain as a Brilliant White Five-Pointed (or Pentagrammic) Star (and also as the Deep Vibration, or Sound, of "Da" or "Om").

Divine Transfiguration—See **four phases of the seventh stage of life**.

Divine Transformation—See **four phases of the seventh stage of life**.

Divine Translation—See **four phases of the seventh stage of life**.

Divine World-Teacher—Avatar Adi Da Samraj is the Divine World-Teacher because His Wisdom-Teaching is the uniquely Perfect Instruction to every being—in this (and every) world—relative to the total process of Divine Enlightenment. Furthermore, Avatar Adi Da Samraj constantly Extends His Regard to the entire world (and the entire cosmic domain)—not on the political or social level, but as a Spiritual matter, constantly Working to Bless and Purify all beings everywhere.

dreaming—See **waking, dreaming, and sleeping**.

E

ecstasy / enstasy—Words derived originally from Greek. Avatar Adi Da uses "ecstasy" in the literal sense of "standing (stasis) outside (ec-)" the egoic self, and "enstasy" in the sense of "standing (stasis) in (en-)" the Divine Self-Condition. As Avatar Adi Da Says in *The Dawn Horse Testament Of The Ruchira Avatar*, Divine Enstasy is "The Native Condition Of Standing Unconditionally As The By-Me-Avatarically-Self-Revealed Transcendental, Inherently Spiritual, Inherently egoless, and Self-Evidently Divine Self-Condition Itself".

ego-"I"—The fundamental activity of self-contraction, or the presumption of separate and separative existence.

En-Light-enment—Divine Enlightenment (or Most Perfect Real-God-Realization) is a matter of the actual conversion of the body-mind to the State of Divine Conscious Light Itself. Avatar Adi Da sometimes

writes the word "Enlightenment" with "Light" set apart by hyphens, in order to emphasize this point.

F

Feeling of Being—The uncaused and unqualified feeling-intuition of the Divine Self-Condition.

feeling-Contemplation—Avatar Adi Da's term for the essential devotional and meditative practice that all practitioners of the Way of Adidam engage at all times in relationship to Him.

four phases of the seventh stage of life—Avatar Adi Da has Revealed that the Awakening to the seventh stage of life is not an "endpoint" but is (rather) the beginning of the final Spiritual process. One of the unique aspects of Avatar Adi Da's Revelation is His precise description of the seventh stage process as consisting of four phases: Divine Transfiguration, Divine Transformation, Divine Indifference, and Divine Translation.

The First Sign (or Demonstration) Of The Only-By-Me Revealed and Given Seventh Stage Of Life (In The Way Of The Heart) Is <u>*Divine Transfiguration*</u>, *In Which the body-mind Of My By-My-Avataric-Divine-Spiritual-Grace-Enlightened Devotee Is Self-Radiant With My Avatarically Self-Transmitted Divine Love-Bliss, Spontaneously Blessing all of the (Apparent) relations of the body-mind.*

The Second Sign (or Demonstration) Of The Only-By-Me Revealed and Given Seventh Stage Of Life (In The Way Of The Heart) Is <u>*Divine Transformation*</u>, *In Which the body-mind Of My By-My-Avataric-Divine-Spiritual-Grace-Enlightened Devotee*

Effectively Exhibits The Only-By-Me Revealed and Given Signs and Powers Of Real God.

The Third Sign (or Demonstration) Of The Only-By-Me Revealed and Given Seventh Stage Of Life (In The Way Of The Heart) Is Divine Indifference, In Which Even the body-mind Of My By-My-Avataric-Divine-Spiritual-Grace-Enlightened Devotee Is Pre-Occupied With The Self-Existing Event Of My Self-Radiant Love-Bliss, and the world of (Apparent) relations Is (More and More) Minimally and Not Otherwise Noticed. . . .

The Final Sign (or Demonstration) Of The Only-By-Me Revealed and Given Seventh Stage Of Life (and Of The Total Practice Of The Only-By-Me Revealed and Given Way Of The Heart) Is The Great Event Of Divine Translation— Which Is . . . The Process Of Transition To (or "Dawning" As) My Divine Self-Domain Via The Divinely "Bright" Outshining Of The Cosmic Domain In The Only-By-Me Revealed and Given Divine Sphere and Sign Of The "Midnight Sun" (Most Perfectly Above and Beyond all-and-All Of Cosmic, or conditional, forms, beings, signs, con-ditions, relations, and things).

—Avatar Adi Da Samraj
The Seven Stages Of Life

G

the Great Event at the "Brightness"—See **"Brightness", the Great Event at the**

the Great Event at Lopez Island— See **Lopez Island, the Great Event at**

Great Tradition—Avatar Adi Da's term for the total inheritance of human, cultural, religious, magical, mystical, Spiritual, and Transcendental paths, philosophies, and testimonies, from all the eras and cultures of humanity— which inheritance has (in the present era of worldwide communication) become the common legacy of humankind. Avatar Adi Da's Divine Self-Revelation and Wisdom-Teaching Fulfills and Completes the Great Tradition.

gross personality—See **Deeper Personality / gross personality**

gross, subtle, causal—Avatar Adi Da (in agreement with certain esoteric schools in the Great Tradition) describes conditional existence as having three fundamental dimen-sions—gross, subtle, and causal.

"Gross" means "made up of material (or physical) elements". The gross (or physical) dimension is, therefore, associated with the physical body. The gross dimension is also associated with experience in the waking state and, as Avatar Adi Da Reveals, with the left side of the heart (or the gross physical heart).

The subtle dimension, which is senior to and pervades the gross dimension, consists of the etheric (or personal life-energy) functions, the lower mental functions (including the conscious mind, the subconscious mind, and the unconscious mind) and higher mental functions (of discrimi-native mind, mentally presumed egoity, and will), and is associated with experience in the dreaming state. In the human psycho-physical structure, the subtle dimension is pri-marily associated with the middle sta-tion of the heart (or the heart chakra), the ascending energies of the spine, the brain core, and the subtle centers of mind in the higher brain.

The causal dimension is senior to

both the gross and the subtle dimensions. It is the root of attention, or the essence of the separate and separative ego-"I". The causal dimension is associated with the right side of the heart, specifically with the sinoatrial node, or "pacemaker" (the psycho-physical source of the heartbeat). Its corresponding state of consciousness is the formless awareness of deep sleep.

Guru-Seva—In Sanskrit, "seva" means "service". Service to the Guru is traditionally treasured as one of the great Secrets of Realization.

H

hearing—See **listening, hearing, and seeing**.

heart / stations of the heart—Avatar Adi Da distinguishes three stations of the heart, associated (respectively) with the right side, the middle station, and the left side of the heart region of the chest. He Reveals that these stations are the loci (or focal points of living origination) of the causal body, the subtle body, and the gross body (respectively). Avatar Adi Da Teaches (as foreshadowed in certain rare sixth stage texts) that the primal psycho-physical seat of Consciousness and of attention is associated with what He calls the "right side of the heart". He has Revealed that this center (which is neither the heart chakra nor the gross physical heart) corresponds to the sinoatrial node, or "pacemaker", the source of the gross physical heartbeat in the right atrium (or upper right chamber) of the physical heart. In the Process of Divine Self-Realization, there is a unique process of opening of the right side of the heart—and it

is because of this connection between the right side of the heart and Divine Self-Realization that Avatar Adi Da uses the term "the Heart" as another way of referring to the Divine Self-Condition.

The Heart Itself is Real God, the Divine Self-Condition, the Divine Reality. The Heart Itself is not "in" the right side of the human heart, nor is it "in" (or limited to) the human heart as a whole. Rather, the human heart and body-mind and the world exist in the True Heart, Which Is the Divine Being Itself.

heart-Communion—"Heart-Communion" with Avatar Adi Da is the practice of Invoking and feeling Him. It is "communion" in the sense that, in the bliss of that state, the individual loses the sense of separate self, and is (thus) "communing intimately" (in a most profound and non-dual manner) with Avatar Adi Da Samraj.

heart-recognition—The entire practice of the Way of Adidam is founded in devotional heart-recognition of, and devotional heart-response to, Ruchira Avatar Adi Da Samraj as the Very Divine Being in Person.

Heart-responsive heart-recognition of Me (in and As My Avatarically-Born bodily human Divine Form and Person) is the moment to moment Foundation of the only-by-Me Revealed and Given Way of Adidam (Which is the One and Only by-Me-Revealed and by-Me-Given Way of the Heart).

Truly, there is no end-phenomenon to the Great Process of heart-recognition of Me and heart-response to Me.

The practice of the Way of Adidam is always, moment to moment, the regeneration of the devotional Asana of heart-recognition of Me and heart-response to Me.

—Avatar Adi Da Samraj
Hridaya Rosary (Four Thorns Of Heart-Instruction)

heart-response—See **heart-recognition**.

"Heroic"—The Tantric traditions of Hinduism and Buddhism describe as "heroic" the practice of an individual whose impulse to Liberation and commitment to his or her Guru are so strong that all circumstances of life, even those traditionally regarded as inauspicious for Spiritual practice (such as consumption of intoxicants and engagement in sexual activity), can rightly be made use of as part of the Spiritual process.

Avatar Adi Da's uniquely "Heroic" Ordeal, however, was undertaken not for His own sake, but in order to discover, through His own experience, what is necessary for all beings to Realize the Truth. Because of His utter Freedom from egoic bondage and egoic karmas, Avatar Adi Da's Sadhana was "Heroic" in a manner that had never previously been possible and will never be possible in the case of any other. As the Divine Person, it was necessary for Him to experience the entire gamut of human seeking, in order to be able to Teach any and all that came to Him. (See also **"Crazy"**.)

Hridayam—Another form of Sanskrit "hridaya" ("heart"), referring not only to the physical organ but also to the True Divine Heart, the Transcendental (and Inherently Spiritual) Divine Reality. "Hridayam" is one of Avatar Adi Da's Divine Names, signifying that He Stands in, at, and as the True Heart of every being.

I

Instruments / Instrumentality—Avatar Adi Da has Indicated that members of the Ruchira Sannyasin Order function collectively and spontaneously as His Instruments:

Through Many and Various Avataric Divine Means (Some Of Which Are Described, By Me, In This Divine Testament, and In Even All My Twenty-Three Divine "Source-Texts"), I Work To Serve The Making Of Concrete (Tangible) Changes In The Immediate Circumstance Of conditions in this world. Conditional Existence (As A Whole) May Be Described As A Universal (or All-Encompassing) Grid—and I Work (Avatarically, and Divinely) Through the Innumerable particular points On That Total Grid.

I Work Through My ("Ruchira Sannyasin") Devotee-Instruments As points Of Contact (and, Altogether, As My Instrumental Means) In The Worldwide Sacred Cooperative Cultural Gathering Of My Devotees—and I Work Through My ("Ruchira Sannyasin") Devotee-Instruments As Concrete points Of Focus On The Universal Grid, For The Sake Of all-and-All. This Is The Unique Significance Of The Instrumentality Of My ("Ruchira Sannyasin") Devotee-Instruments In The Only-By-Me Revealed and Given Way Of The Heart (or Way Of Adidam).

—Avatar Adi Da Samraj
The Dawn Horse Testament Of The Ruchira Avatar

J

Jnana, Jnani—The Sanskrit term "Jnani" ("Sage") literally means "one who knows" (or, more fully, "one who has Realized Jnana Samadhi"). A

Jnani is one who discriminates between What is Unconditional (the One Reality, or Divine Self) and what is conditional (the passing phenomena of experience). A Jnani is Identified with Consciousness Itself, as the Transcendental Witness of all that arises.

Jnana Samadhi / Jnana Nirvikalpa Samadhi—See **Samadhi**.

K

Kali Yuga—See **"late-time" (or "dark" epoch)**.

karma / karmic —"Karma" is Sanskrit for "action". Since action entails consequences (or re-actions), "karma" also means (by extension) "destiny, tendency, the quality of existence and experience which is determined by previous actions". "Karmic" indicates "of the same nature as or related to karma".

Kundalini Shakti / Kundalini Shaktipat —The Kundalini Shakti is the energy traditionally viewed to lie dormant at the bodily base, or lowermost psychic center of the body-mind. Kundalini Shaktipat is the activation of the Kundalini Shakti—either spontaneously in the devotee or by the Guru's initiation—thereafter potentially producing various forms of Yogic and mystical experience.

L

"late-time" (or "dark" epoch)—A phrase that Avatar Adi Da uses to describe the present era—in which doubt of God (and of anything at all beyond mortal existence) is more and more pervading the entire world, and the self-interest of the separate individual is more and more regarded to be the ultimate principle of life. It is also a reference to the traditional Hindu idea of "yugas", or "epochs", the last of which (the Kali Yuga) is understood to be the most difficult and "dark". Many traditions share the idea that it is in such a time that the Promised Divine Liberator will appear.

Leela—Sanskrit for "play", or "sport". In many religious and Spiritual traditions, all of conditionally manifested existence is regarded to be the Leela (or the Play, Sport, or Free Activity) of the Divine Person. "Leela" is the Awakened Play of a Realized Adept (of any degree), through which he or she mysteriously Instructs and Liberates others and Blesses the world itself. By extension, a Leela is an instructive and inspiring story of such an Adept's Teaching and Blessing Play.

listening, hearing, and seeing—Avatar Adi Da describes the entire course of the Way of Adidam as falling into four primary phases:
1. Listening to Him
2. Hearing Him
3. Seeing Him
4. The "Perfect Practice" of Identifying with Him

"Listening" is Avatar Adi Da's technical term for the beginning practice of the Way of Adidam. A listening devotee literally "listens" to Avatar Adi Da Samraj's Instruction and applies it in his or her life.

The core of the listening process (and of all future practice of the Way of Adidam) is the practice of Ruchira Avatara Bhakti Yoga (or turning the four principal faculties of the body-mind—body, emotion, mind, and breath—to Him)—supported by practice of the "conscious process" and "conductivity" and by the embrace of the functional, practical, relational, and cultural disciplines Given by Him.

It is during the listening phase (once the foundation practice is fully established) that the devotee applies to come on extended formal retreat in Avatar Adi Da's physical Company (or, after His physical Lifetime, in the physical company, and the by-Him-Spiritually-Empowered circumstances, of the Ruchira Sannyasin Order of Adidam Ruchiradam). In the retreat circumstance, when the rightly prepared devotee truly (whole bodily) turns the principal faculties to Him, Avatar Adi Da is spontaneously Moved to Grant His Spiritual Initiation (or Ruchira Shaktipat), such that the devotee can become more and more consistently capable of tangibly receiving His Spiritual Transmission. This is the beginning of the Spiritually Awakened practice of the Way of Adidam—when the devotional relationship to Avatar Adi Da becomes (by His Divine Spiritual Grace) the devotional-and-Spiritual relationship to Him.

The phase of listening to Avatar Adi Da, rightly and effectively engaged, eventually culminates (by His Divine Spiritual Grace) in the true hearing of Him. The devotee has begun to hear Avatar Adi Da when there is most fundamental understanding of the root-act of egoity (or self-contraction), or the unique capability to consistently transcend the self-contraction. The capability of true hearing is not something the ego can "achieve". That capability can only be Granted by Avatar Adi Da's Divine Spiritual Grace, to His devotee who has effectively completed the (eventually, Spiritually Awakened) process of listening.

When Spiritually Awakened practice of the Way of Adidam is magnified by means of the hearing-capability, the devotee has the necessary preparation to (in due course) engage that Spiritually Awakened practice in the "fully technically responsible" manner. This is another point (in the course of the Way of Adidam) when the devotee engages an extended formal retreat in Avatar Adi Da's physical Company (or, after His physical Lifetime, in the physical company, and the by-Him-Spiritually-Empowered circumstances, of the Ruchira Sannyasin Order of Adidam Ruchiradam). In this case, in Response to the devotee's more mature practice of devotional and Spiritual resort to Him, Avatar Adi Da Gives the Initiatory Spiritual Gift of Upward-turned Spiritual receptivity of Him (as He describes in *Hridaya Rosary*).

This is Avatar Adi Da's Spiritual Initiation of His devotee into the seeing phase of practice, which Avatar Adi Da describes as the "fully technical responsible" form of Spiritually Awakened resort to Him.

One of the principal signs of the transition from the listening-hearing practice to the both-hearing-and-seeing practice is emotional conversion from the reactive emotions that characterize egoic self-obsession, to the open-hearted, Radiant Happiness that characterizes fully technically responsible Spiritual devotion to Avatar Adi Da. This true and stable emotional conversion coincides with stable Upward-to-Him-turned receptivity of Avatar Adi Da's Spiritual Transmission.

As the process of seeing develops, the body-mind becomes more and more fully Infused by Avatar Adi Da's Spirit-Baptism, purified of any psycho-physical patterning that diminishes that reception. With increasing maturity in the seeing process, Avatar Adi Da's Transmission of the "Bright" is experienced in the unique form that He describes as the "Samadhi of the 'Thumbs'"—and, through this process, the devotee is gracefully grown entirely beyond identification with the body-mind. This is a Gift of Spiritual Awakening as the Witness-Consciousness That Stands Prior to body, mind, and world, and even the act of attention itself. This Awakening to the Witness-Consciousness marks readiness for another period of initiatory retreat in Avatar Adi Da's physical Company (or, after His physical Lifetime, in the physical company, and the by-Him-Spiritually-Empowered circumstances, of the Ruchira Sannyasin Order of Adidam Ruchiradam), in which He Spiritually Initiates the devotee into the "Perfect Practice".

"Locate"—To "Locate" Avatar Adi Da is to "Truly Heart-Find" Him. Avatar Adi Da places this term in quotation marks to indicate the sense of "so to speak"—because He is, in reality, Omnipresent, without any specific "location".

Lopez Island, the Great Event at— In April 2000, Avatar Adi Da was invited to stay on an island off the coast of the state of Washington (USA). On April 12, soon after He arrived at Lopez Island, His Body underwent a dramatic "Yogic Death", through which He became Spiritually Established in the Body as the "Bright"—with the Purity that had been the case at His Birth, before His Submission to Learn and Teach humanity. It was a Process of sponta-neous and sudden "Ascent" to His

Divine State, rather than "Descent" into Submission to the human world. This Establishment at the "Threshold" of His Divine Self-Domain is the culminating phase of His unique Avataric Demonstration of Divine Enlightenment, and brought with It a great magnification of His Divine Spiritual Blessing-Power. For a full account of the Great Event at Lopez Island, please see *Adi Da: The Promised God-Man Is Here*, by Carolyn Lee.

Love-Ananda—The Name "Love-Ananda" was given to Avatar Adi Da by Swami Muktananda, who sponta-neously conferred it upon Avatar Adi Da in 1969 (p. 222). However, Avatar Adi Da did not use the Name "Love-Ananda" until April 1986, after the Great Event that Initiated His Avataric Divine Self-"Emergence". "Love-Ananda" is a combination of English ("Love") and Sanskrit ("Ananda", meaning "Bliss"), thus communicating Avatar Adi Da's Function as the Divine World-Teacher, embracing all human beings from all cultural settings. The combination of "Love" and "Ananda" means "the Divine Love-Bliss".

M

Mahasamadhi—"Mahasamadhi" ("Great Samadhi") is a Sanskrit term for the death of a great Realizer.

Maha-Siddha—The Sanskrit word "Siddha" means "a completed, ful-filled, or perfected one", or "one of perfect accomplishment, or power". "Maha-Siddha" means "Great Siddha".

Mandala—Sanskrit word (literally, "circle") commonly used in the eso-teric Spiritual traditions of the East to describe the entire pattern of the hierarchical levels of cosmic existence.

"Midnight Sun"—A term Avatar Adi Da uses to refer to His Revelation of the esoteric visionary representation of Reality as a White Sphere in a black field—which Sphere is His own Divine Form.

There Is a Sun That Is Forever Risen in the night sky of the body-mind. It Is the Eternal Sun—the (Self-"Bright") "Midnight Sun", Infinitely Above the head, and not usually perceived. . . .
The Sun That Is Eternal and Over-head is not in the midst of a colored sphere of light. The Eternal "Midnight Sun" Is Beyond that sphere. The "Midnight Sun" Is, Truly, the Divine "Face" of My Threshold Form.
—Avatar Adi Da Samraj
"The Avataric Divine Self-Revelation Of Adidam Ruchiradam"

Most Perfect / Most Ultimate—Avatar Adi Da uses the phrase "Most Perfect(ly)" in the sense of "Absolutely Perfect(ly)". Similarly, the phrase "Most Ultimate(ly)" is equivalent to "Absolutely Ultimate(ly)". "Most Perfect(ly)" and "Most Ultimate(ly)" are always references to the seventh (or Divinely Enlightened) stage of life. "Perfect(ly)" and "Ultimate(ly)" (without "Most") refer to the practice and Realization in the context of the "Perfect Practice" of the Way of Adidam (or, when Avatar Adi Da is making reference to the Great Tradition, to practice and Realization in the context of the sixth stage of life). (See also Appendix A.)

mudra—A gesture of the hands, face, or body that outwardly expresses a state of ecstasy. Avatar Adi Da sometimes spontaneously exhibits Mudras as Signs of His Blessing and Purifying

Work with His devotees and the world. He also uses the term "Mudra" to express the Attitude of His Blessing-Work, which is His Constant (or Eternal) Giving (or Submitting) of Himself to Be the Means of Divine Liberation for all beings.

mummery / *The Mummery Book*—The dictionary defines mummery as "a ridiculous, hypocritical, or pretentious ceremony or performance". Avatar Adi Da uses this word to describe all the activities of ego-bound beings, or beings who are committed to the false view of separation and separativeness.
The Mummery Book is one of Avatar Adi Da's twenty-three "Source-Texts". It is a work of astonishing poetry and deeply evocative archetypes. Through the heart-breaking story of Raymond Darling's growth to manhood, his search to find, and then to be reunited with, his beloved (Quandra), and his utter self-transcendence of all conditional circumstances and events, Avatar Adi Da Tells His own Life-Story in the language of parable, and describes in devastating detail how the unconverted ego makes religion (and life altogether) into a meaningless mummery.

N

Narcissus—In Avatar Adi Da's Teaching-Revelation, "Narcissus" is a key symbol of the un-Enlightened individual as a self-obsessed seeker, enamored of his or her own self-image and egoic self-consciousness. In *The Knee Of Listening*, Adi Da Samraj describes the significance of the archetype of Narcissus:

He is the ancient one visible in the Greek myth, who was the univer-

sally adored child of the gods, who rejected the loved-one and every form of love and relationship, and who was finally condemned to the contemplation of his own image—until, as a result of his own act and obstinacy, he suffered the fate of eternal separateness and died in infinite solitude.

Nirvikalpa Samadhi—See **Samadhi**.

O

Omega—See **Alpha and Omega**.

Outshined / Outshining—A synonym for "Divine Translation", to refer to the final Demonstration of the four-phase process of the seventh (or Divinely Enlightened) stage of life in the Way of Adidam. In the Great Event of Outshining (or Divine Translation), body, mind, and world are no longer noticed—not because the Divine Consciousness has withdrawn or dissociated from conditionally manifested phenomena, but because the Divine Self-Abiding Self-Recognition of all arising phenomena as modifications of the Divine Self-Condition has become so intense that the "Bright" Radiance of Consciousness now Outshines all such phenomena. (See also **four phases of the seventh stage of life**.)

P, Q

"Perfect Practice"—The "Perfect Practice" is Avatar Adi Da's technical term for the discipline of the most mature stages of practice in the Way of Adidam. The "Perfect Practice" is practice in the Domain of Consciousness Itself (as opposed to practice from the point of view of the body or the mind). (See also Appendix A and Appendix B.)

Perfectly Subjective—Avatar Adi Da uses this phrase to describe the True Divine Source, or "Subject", of the conditionally manifested world—as opposed to regarding the Divine as some sort of objective "Other". Thus, in the phrase "Perfectly Subjective", the word "Subjective" does not have the sense of "relating to the inward experience of an individual", but, rather, it has the sense of "Being Consciousness Itself, the True Subject of all apparent experience".

"Point of View"—In Avatar Adi Da's Wisdom-Teaching, "Point of View" is in quotation marks and capitalized when referring to the Divinely Enlightened individual. Such a one has transcended the separate (or egoic) "point of view", and thus his or her Divine Recognition of all that arises is only a "point of view" in the "so to speak" sense.

prana / pranic—The Sanskrit word "prana" means "breath", or "life-energy". It generally refers to the life-energy animating all beings and pervading everything in cosmic Nature. In the human body-mind, circulation of this universal life-energy is associated with the heartbeat and the cycles of the breath. In esoteric Yogic Teachings, prana is also a specific technical name for one of a number of forms of etheric energy that functionally sustain the bodily being.

Prana is not to be equated with the Divine Spirit-Current, or the Spiritual (and Always Blessing) Divine Presence of Avatar Adi Da Samraj. The finite pranic energies that sustain individual beings are only conditional, localized, and temporary phenomena of the realm of cosmic Nature. Even in the form of universal life-force, prana is but a conditional modification of the Divine Spirit-Current Revealed by Avatar Adi Da, Which Is the "Bright" (or Consciousness Itself), beyond all cosmic forms.

Priorly ascended Nirvikalpa Samadhi—See **Samadhi**.

Priorly Self-Abiding Jnana Nirvikalpa Samadhi—See **Samadhi**.

Promised God-Man—A common theme running through various branches of the Great Tradition is the prophecy of a great Savior or Liberator still to come. The prophecy takes different forms in different traditions, but the underlying commonality is the promise or expectation that the culminating Avatar or Incarnation will appear in the future, at a time when humanity is lost, apparently cut off from Wisdom, Truth, and God. Buddhists refer to that Expected One as "Maitreya"; Vaishnavite Hindus, as the "Kalki Avatar"; Christians, as the "second coming of Jesus"; Jews, as the "Messiah"; and so on.

R

"radical"—Derived from the Latin "radix", meaning "root". Thus, "radical" principally means "irreducible", "fundamental", or "relating to the origin". In *The Dawn Horse Testament Of The Ruchira Avatar*, Avatar Adi Da defines "Radical" as "Gone To The Root, Core, Source, or Origin". Because Adi Da Samraj uses "radical" in this literal sense, it appears in quotation marks in His Wisdom-Teaching, in order to distinguish His usage from the common reference to an extreme (often political) view.

"radical" understanding—Avatar Adi Da uses the word "understanding" to mean "the process of transcending egoity". Thus, to "understand" is to simultaneously observe the activity of the self-contraction and to surrender that activity via devotional resort to Him.

Avatar Adi Da has Revealed that, despite their intention to Realize Reality (or Truth, or Real God), all religious and Spiritual traditions (other than the Way of Adidam) are involved, in one manner or another, with the search to satisfy the ego. Only Avatar Adi Da has Revealed the Way to "radically" understand the ego (by "going to the root") and (in due course, through intensive formal practice of the Way of Adidam, as His formally acknowledged devotee) to most perfectly transcend the ego.

Real God—The True and Perfectly Subjective Source of all conditions, the True and Spiritual Divine Person, rather than any ego-made (and, thus, false, or limited) presumption about God.

"Reality Consideration"—See **"consider" / "consideration"**.

right side of the heart—See **heart / stations of the heart**.

Ruchira Avatar—In Sanskrit, "Ruchira" means "bright, radiant, effulgent". Thus, the Reference "Ruchira Avatar" indicates that Avatar Adi Da Samraj is the "Bright" (or Radiant) Descent of the Divine Reality Itself into the conditionally manifested worlds, Appearing here in His bodily (human) Divine Form.

Ruchira Avatara Bhakti Yoga—
Ruchira Avatara Bhakti Yoga is the
principal Gift, Calling, and Discipline
Offered by Adi Da Samraj to all practitioners of Adidam.

The phrase "Ruchira Avatara
Bhakti Yoga" is itself a summary of
the Way of Adidam. "Bhakti", in
Sanskrit, is "love, adoration, or devotion", while "Yoga" is "God-Realizing
discipline" (or practice). "Ruchira
Avatara Bhakti Yoga" is, thus, "the
practice of devotion to the Ruchira
Avatar, Adi Da Samraj".

The technical practice of Ruchira
Avatara Bhakti Yoga is the process of
turning the four principal faculties
(body, emotion, mind, and breath)
to Avatar Adi Da (in and <u>as</u> His
Avatarically-Born bodily human
Divine Form) in every moment and
under all circumstances.

Ruchira Avatara Kripa—"Kripa" is
Sanskrit for "grace". Traditionally, it is
a synonym for "shaktipat", or the
Initiatory Blessing of the Spiritual
Master. Ruchira Avatara Kripa is Avatar
Adi Da's Gift of the Transmission of
His Divine Spiritual Heart-Blessing.

**Ruchira Avatara Maha-Jnana-
Siddha Yoga—**Sanskrit for "the Yoga
of devotion to the Ruchira Avatar,
Who Is the Supreme Transcendental
Divine Siddha ('Maha-Jnana-Siddha')".

**Ruchira Avatara Maha-Jnana
Hridaya-Shaktipat Yoga—**Sanskrit
for "the Yoga of receiving the
Supreme Transcendental ('Maha-
Jnana') Divine Heart-Blessing-
Transmission ('Hridaya-Shaktipat') of
the Ruchira Avatar".

Ruchira Avatara Siddha Yoga—See
Ruchira Siddha Yoga.

Ruchira Shaktipat—The "Bright"
(Ruchira) Spiritual Transmission
(Shaktipat) of Ruchira Avatar Adi Da
Samraj.

**Ruchira Siddha / Ruchira Siddha-
Guru—**The "Bright" Perfect
Transmission-Master.

Ruchira Siddha Yoga—"Siddha
Yoga" is, literally, "the Yoga of the
Perfected One[s]".

Swami Muktananda used the
term "Siddha Yoga" to refer to the
form of Kundalini Yoga that he
Taught, which involved initiation
of the devotee by the Guru's
Transmission of Shakti (or Spiritual
Energy). Avatar Adi Da Samraj
has indicated that this was a fifth
stage form of Siddha Yoga.

In "I (<u>Alone</u>) <u>Am</u> The Adidam
Revelation", Avatar Adi Da Says:

> . . . I Teach Siddha Yoga in the
> Mode and Manner of the only-by-Me
> Revealed and Given <u>seventh</u> stage of
> life (as Ruchira Avatara Siddha Yoga,
> or Ruchira Siddha Yoga, or Ruchira
> Avatara Shaktipat Yoga, or Ruchira
> Shaktipat Yoga, or Ruchira Avatara
> Hridaya-Siddha Yoga, or Ruchira
> Avatara Hridaya-Shaktipat Yoga, or
> Ruchira Avatara Maha-Jnana-Siddha
> Yoga, or Ruchira Avatara Maha-
> Jnana Hridaya-Shaktipat Yoga)—and
> always toward (or to the degree of) the
> Realization inherently associated with
> (and, at last, Most Perfectly
> Demonstrated and Proven by) the
> only-by-Me Revealed and Given sev-
> enth stage of life, and as a practice
> and a Process that progressively
> includes (and, coincidently, <u>directly</u>
> transcends) <u>all</u> <u>six</u> of the phenomenal
> and developmental (and, necessarily,
> yet ego-based) stages of life that pre-
> cede the seventh.

Avatar Adi Da's description of the similarities and differences between traditional Siddha Yoga and the Way of Adidam is Given in "I (Alone) Am The Adidam Revelation" (pp. 491–583).

S

sadhana / "Sadhana Years"—In Sanskrit, "sadhana" means "self-transcending religious or Spiritual practice". Avatar Adi Da's "Sadhana Years" refers to the time from which He began His Quest to recover the Truth of Existence (at Columbia College) until His Divine Re-Awakening in 1970. Avatar Adi Da's full description of His "Sadhana Years" is Given in *The Knee Of Listening*.

Sahaj Samadhi—See **Samadhi**.

sahasrar—In the traditional system of seven chakras, the sahasrar is the highest chakra (or subtle energy center) associated with the crown of the head and beyond. It is described as a "thousand-petaled lotus", the terminal of Light to which the Yogic process (of Spiritual ascent through the chakras) aspires.

In chapter 18 of this Text, Avatar Adi Da describes how He spontaneously experienced what He calls the "severing of the sahasrar". The Spirit-Energy no longer ascended into the crown of the head (and beyond), but rather "fell" into the Heart, and rested as the Witness-Consciousness. It was this experience that directly revealed to Avatar Adi Da that, while the Yogic traditions regard the sahasrar as the seat of Enlightenment, the Heart is truly the Seat of Divine Consciousness.

Samadhi—The Sanskrit word "Samadhi" traditionally denotes various exalted states that appear in the context of esoteric meditation and Realization. Avatar Adi Da Teaches that, for His devotees, Samadhi is, even more simply and fundamentally, the Enjoyment of His Divine State (or "Divine Samadhi"), Which is experienced (even from the beginning of the practice of Adidam) through ego-transcending heart-Communion with Him. Therefore, "the cultivation of Samadhi" is another way to describe the fundamental basis of the Way of Adidam. Avatar Adi Da's devotee is in Samadhi in any moment of standing beyond the separate self in true devotional heart-Communion with Him. (See "The Cultivation of My Divine Samadhi", in *The Seven Stages Of Life*.)

The developmental process leading to Divine Enlightenment in the Way of Adidam may be marked by many signs, principal among which are the unique Samadhis of the Way of Adidam. Although some of the traditionally known Samadhis of the fourth, the fifth, and the sixth stages of life may appear in the course of an individual's practice of the Way of Adidam, the appearance of all of them is by no means necessary, or even probable (as Avatar Adi Da Indicates in His Wisdom-Teaching). The essential Samadhis of the Way of Adidam are those that are uniquely Granted by Avatar Adi Da Samraj—the Samadhi of the "Thumbs", Priorly ascended Nirvikalpa Samadhi, Priorly Self-Abiding Jnana Nirvikalpa Samadhi, and seventh stage Sahaja Nirvikalpa Samadhi. All the possible forms of Samadhi in the Way of Adidam are described in full detail in *The Dawn Horse Testament Of The Ruchira Avatar*.

Samadhi of the "Thumbs"—The "Thumbs" is Avatar Adi Da's technical term for the Invasion of the body-mind by a particular kind of forceful Descent of His Divine Spirit-Current.

In the fullest form of this experience, which Avatar Adi Da calls "the Samadhi of the 'Thumbs'", His Spirit-Invasion Descends all the way to the bottom of the frontal line of the body-mind (at the bodily base) and ascends through the spinal line, overwhelming the ordinary human sense of bodily existence, infusing the whole being with intense blissfulness, and releasing the ordinary, confined sense of body, mind, and separate self.

Both the experience of the "Thumbs" and the full Samadhi of the "Thumbs" are unique to the Way of Adidam, for they are specifically signs of the "Crashing Down" (or the Divine Descent) of Avatar Adi Da's Spirit-Baptism, into the body-minds of His devotees. The Samadhi of the "Thumbs" is a kind of "Nirvikalpa" (or formless) Samadhi—but in descent in the frontal line, rather than in ascent in the spinal line.

Avatar Adi Da's extended Instruction relative to the "Thumbs" is Given in "The 'Thumbs' Is The Fundamental Sign Of The Crashing Down Of My Person". This Essay appears in a number of Avatar Adi Da's "Source-Texts" (*Hridaya Rosary, The Only Complete Way To Realize The Unbroken Light Of Real God, Ruchira Avatara Hridaya-Siddha Yoga, The Seven Stages Of Life*, and *Santosha Adidam*, as well as *The Dawn Horse Testament Of The Ruchira Avatar*).

Savikalpa Samadhi and "Cosmic Consciousness"—The Sanskrit term "Savikalpa Samadhi" literally means "meditative ecstasy with form", or "deep meditative concentration (or absorption) in which form (or defined experiential content) is still perceived".

Avatar Adi Da indicates that there are two basic forms of Savikalpa Samadhi. The first is the various experiences produced by the Spiritual ascent of energy and attention (into mystical phenomena, visions, and other subtle sensory perceptions of subtle psychic forms) and the various states of Yogic Bliss (or Spirit-"Intoxication").

The second (and highest) form of Savikalpa Samadhi is called "Cosmic Consciousness", or the "'Vision' of Cosmic Unity". This is an isolated or periodic occurrence in which attention ascends, uncharacteristically and spontaneously, to a state of awareness wherein conditional existence is perceived as a Unity in Divine Awareness. This conditional form of "Cosmic Consciousness" is pursued in many mystical and Yogic paths. It depends upon manipulation of attention and the body-mind, and it is interpreted from the point of view of the separate, body-based or mind-based self—and, therefore, it is not equivalent to Divine Enlightenment.

Avatar Adi Da's discussion of Savikalpa Samadhi is found in "Vision, Audition, and Touch in The Process of Ascending Meditation in The Way Of Adidam", in Part Four of *Ruchira Shaktipat Yoga*.

Avatar Adi Da's description of the varieties of experiential form possible in Savikalpa Samadhi is found in "The Significant Experiential Signs That May Appear in the Course of The Way Of Adidam", in Part Three of *What, Where, When, How, Why, and Who To Remember To Be Happy*.

Conditionally ascended Nirvikalpa Samadhi—The Sanskrit term "Nirvikalpa Samadhi" literally means "meditative ecstasy without form", or "deep meditative concentration (or absorption) in which there is no perception of form (or defined experiential content)". Traditionally, this state is regarded to be the final goal of the many schools of Yogic ascent whose orientation to practice is that of the fifth stage of life. Like "Cosmic Consciousness", conditionally ascended Nirvikalpa Samadhi is an isolated or periodic Realization. In it, attention ascends beyond all conditional manifestation into the formless Matrix of Divine Vibration and Divine Light Infinitely Above the world, the body, and the mind. And, like the various forms of Savikalpa Samadhi, conditionally ascended Nirvikalpa Samadhi is a temporary state of attention (or, more precisely, of the suspension of attention). It is produced by manipulation of attention and of the body-mind, and is (therefore) incapable of being maintained when attention returns (as it inevitably does) to the states of the body-mind. In the Way of Adidam, conditionally ascended Nirvikalpa Samadhi is a possible, but not necessary, experience.

Priorly ascended Nirvikalpa Samadhi—Even though aspects of conditionally ascended Nirvikalpa Samadhi are comparable to Priorly ascended Nirvikalpa Samadhi, the two forms of ascended Nirvikalpa Samadhi are fundamentally different from each other, because Priorly ascended Nirvikalpa Samadhi is the spontaneous Establishment (entirely through Adi Da's Divine Spiritual Grace) in His formless Matrix of Love-Bliss Infinitely Above the world, the body, and the mind. Priorly ascended Nirvikalpa Samadhi does not depend on any manipulation of attention and (therefore) is not characterized by the return of attention to the states of the

body-mind. In the "Perfect Practice" of Adidam, Priorly ascended Nirvikalpa Samadhi occurs subsequent to, and in perfect conjunction with, Priorly Self-Abiding Jnana Nirvikalpa Samadhi (in the context of the horizontal domain) as a necessary immediate prerequisite for the transition to the seventh stage of life.

Avatar Adi Da's description of, and Instruction relative to, both conditionally ascended Nirvikalpa Samadhi and Priorly ascended Nirvikalpa Samadhi is Given in chapter sixty-one of *The Dawn Horse Testament Of The Ruchira Avatar*.

conditionally Self-Abiding Jnana Nirvikalpa Samadhi—"Jnana" means "knowledge". Jnana Nirvikalpa Samadhi is the characteristic meditative experience in the context of the sixth stage of life. Produced by the intentional withdrawal of attention from the conditional body-mind-self and its relations, conditionally Self-Abiding Jnana Nirvikalpa Samadhi is the conditional, temporary Realization of the Transcendental Self-Condition (or Consciousness Itself), exclusive of any perception (or cognition) of world, objects, relations, body, mind, or separate-self-sense—and, thereby, formless (or "nirvikalpa").

Priorly Self-Abiding Jnana Nirvikalpa Samadhi—Even though aspects of conditionally Self-Abiding Jnana Nirvikalpa Samadhi are comparable to Priorly Self-Abiding Jnana Nirvikalpa Samadhi, the two forms of Self-Abiding Jnana Nirvikalpa Samadhi are fundamentally different from each other, because Priorly Self-Abiding Jnana Nirvikalpa Samadhi is the spontaneous Establishment (entirely through Adi Da's Divine Spiritual Grace) in His Self-Condition

788

in (and beyond) the right side of the heart. Like Priorly ascended Jnana Nirvikalpa Samadhi, Priorly Self-Abiding Jnana Nirvikalpa Samadhi does not depend on any manipulation of attention and (therefore) is not characterized by the return of attention to the states of the body-mind. In the "Perfect Practice" of Adidam, Priorly Self-Abiding Jnana Nirvikalpa Samadhi occurs previous to, and in perfect conjunction with, Priorly ascended Nirvikalpa Samadhi (in the context of the vertical domain) as a necessary immediate prerequisite for the transition to the seventh stage of life.

Avatar Adi Da's description of, and Instruction relative to, conditionally Self-Abiding Jnana Nirvikalpa Samadhi and Priorly Self-Abiding Jnana Nirvikalpa Samadhi is Given in chapter 62 of *The Dawn Horse Testament*.

seventh stage Sahaj Samadhi, or seventh stage Sahaja Nirvikalpa Samadhi—Avatar Adi Da's description of seventh stage Sahaj Samadhi is Given in Part Five of *The All-Completing and Final Divine Revelation To Mankind*.

Samraj—From the Sanskrit "Samraja", a traditional Indian term used to refer to great kings, and also to the Hindu gods. "Samraja" is defined as "universal or supreme ruler", "paramount Lord", or "paramount sovereign". "Samraj" was traditionally given as a title to a king who was regarded to be a "universal monarch".

Avatar Adi Da's Name "Adi Da Samraj" expresses that He is the Primordial (or Original) Giver, Who Blesses all as the Universal Lord of every thing, every where, for all time. The Sovereignty of His Kingdom has nothing to do with the world of

human politics. Rather, it is entirely a matter of His Spiritual Dominion, His Kingship in the hearts of His devotees.

Santosha—Sanskrit for "satisfaction" or "contentment"—qualities associated with a sense of completion. These qualities are characteristic of no-seeking, the fundamental Principle of Avatar Adi Da's Wisdom-Teaching and of His entire Revelation of Truth. Because of its uniquely appropriate meanings, "Santosha" is one of Avatar Adi Da's Names. As Santosha Adi Da, Avatar Adi Da Samraj is the Divine Giver of Perfect Divine Contentedness, or Perfect Searchlessness.

Santosha Avatar—The Very Incarnation of Perfect Divine Contentedness, or Perfect Searchlessness.

the Santosha Event—On September 7, 1994, in Pacific Harbour, Fiji, Avatar Adi Da underwent a Yogic shift in His Blessing-Work. It was confirmed to Him, in His own Body, that He had Done everything He could possibly Do and had Said everything that He could possibly Say in order to Serve His devotees and make His Divine Revelation Complete. For a full account of the Santosha Event, see *Adi Da: The Promised God-Man Is Here*, by Carolyn Lee.

Sat-Guru—"Sat" means "Truth", "Being", "Existence". Thus, "Sat-Guru" literally means "True Guru", or a Guru who can lead living beings from darkness (or non-Truth) into Light (or the Living Truth).

Satsang—Hindi for "True (or right) relationship", "the company of Truth".

Avatar Adi Da writes, in His "First Word":

The greatest opportunity, and the greatest responsibility, of My devotees is Satsang with Me—Which is to live in the Condition of ego-surrendering, ego-forgetting, and (always more and more) ego-transcending devotional (and, in due course, Spiritual) relationship to Me, and (Thus and Thereby) to Realize My Avatarically Self-Revealed (and Self-Evidently Divine) Self-Condition, Which Is the Self-Evidently Divine Heart (or Non-Separate Self-Condition and Non-"Different" Source-Condition) of all-and-All, and Which Is Self-Existing and Self-Radiant Consciousness (or Indivisible Conscious Light) Itself (Which is One, and Only, and not separate in or as any one, or any "thing", at all).

Savikalpa Samadhi—See **Samadhi**.

searchless Beholding of Avatar Adi Da—The primary practice of the Way of Adidam, which begins after the foundation preparation is established and Avatar Adi Da has been moved to Grant Divine Spiritual Initiation to His devotee (in the context of extended formal retreat in His physical Company—or, after His physical Lifetime, in the physical company, and the by-Him-Spiritually-Empowered circumstances of the Ruchira Sannyasin Order of Adidam Ruchiradam). The practice of searchlessly Beholding Avatar Adi Da is the Beholding of His Avatarically-Born bodily (human) Divine Form, free of any seeking-effort, and the searchless reception of His Spiritual Transmission.

For Avatar Adi Da's extended Instruction relative to the searchless Beholding of Him, see "No Seeking / Mere Beholding", an Essay that is included in many of His "Source-Texts".

self-Enquiry—The practice of self-Enquiry in the form "Avoiding relationship?", unique to the Way of Adidam, was spontaneously developed by Avatar Adi Da in the course of His own Ordeal of Divine Re-Awakening. Intense persistence in the "radical" discipline of this unique form of self-Enquiry led rapidly to Avatar Adi Da's Divine Re-Awakening (or Most Perfect Divine Self-Realization) in 1970.

The practice of self-Enquiry in the form "Avoiding relationship?" is one of the principal technical practices that serve feeling-Contemplation of Avatar Adi Da in the Devotional Way of Insight in the Way of Adidam.

scientific materialism—The predominant philosophy and worldview of modern humanity, the basic presumption of which is that the material world is all that exists. In scientific materialism, the method of science, or the observation of objective phenomena, is made into philosophy and a way of life that suppresses the native human impulse to Divine Liberation.

seeing—See **listening, hearing, and seeing**.

Self-Existing and Self-Radiant—Terms describing the two fundamental aspects of the One Divine Person (or Reality)—Existence (or Being, or Consciousness) Itself, and Radiance (or Energy, or Light) Itself.

seven stages of life—See **stages of life**.

Shakti—A Sanskrit term for the Divinely Manifesting Spiritual Energy, Spiritual Power, or Spirit-Current of the Divine Person.

Shaktipat—The "descent of Spiritual Power". Yogic Shaktipat, which manipulates natural, conditional energies or partial manifestations of the Divine Spirit-Current, is typically granted through touch, word, glance, or regard by Yogic Adepts in the fifth stage of life. Although the term "Shaktipat" literally refers to the "descent" of Spiritual Power, the traditional Yogic Shaktipat is, in fact, a process of the <u>ascent</u> and circulation of Spiritual Power and must be distinguished from (and, otherwise, understood to be only a secondary aspect of) the Blessing Transmission of the "Bright" Itself (Ruchira Shaktipat), Which originates from Infinitely Above and functions in a unique process in descent and is uniquely Given by Avatar Adi Da Samraj.

Siddha / Siddha-Guru—"Siddha" is Sanskrit for "a completed, fulfilled, or perfected one", or "one of perfect accomplishment, or power". Avatar Adi Da uses "Siddha", or "Siddha-Guru", to mean a Transmission-Master who is a Realizer (to any significant degree) of Real God, Truth, or Reality.

siddhi / Siddhi (Divine)—Sanskrit for "power", or "accomplishment". When capitalized in Avatar Adi Da's Wisdom-Teaching, "Siddhi" is the Spiritual, Transcendental, and Divine Awakening-Power That He spontaneously and effortlessly Transmits to all.

sleeping—See **waking, dreaming, and sleeping**.

"Source-Texts"—Avatar Adi Da's Divine Heart-Word is summarized in His twenty-three "Source-Texts". These Texts present, in complete and conclusive detail, His Divine Revelations, Confessions, and Instructions, which are the fruits of His years of Teaching-Work and Revelation-Work. (For a complete list of Avatar Adi Da's twenty-three "Source-Texts", see pp. 716–27.)

Spirit-Baptism—Avatar Adi Da often refers to His Transmission of Spiritual Blessing as His "Spirit-Baptism". It is often felt by His devotee as a Current descending in the frontal line (and, in due course, ascending in the spinal line). However, Avatar Adi Da's Spirit-Baptism is fundamentally and primarily His Moveless Transmission of the Divine Heart Itself. As a secondary effect, His Spirit-Baptism serves to purify, balance, and energize the entire body-mind of the devotee who is prepared to receive It.

Spiritual, Transcendental, Divine—Avatar Adi Da uses the words "Spiritual", "Transcendental", and "Divine" in reference to dimensions of Reality that are Realized progressively in the Way of Adidam. "Transcendental" and "Spiritual" indicate two fundamental aspects of the One Divine Reality and Person—Consciousness Itself (Which Is Transcendental, or Self-Existing) and Energy Itself (Which Is Spiritual, or Self-Radiant). Only That Which Is Divine is simultaneously and always <u>both</u> Transcendental <u>and</u> Spiritual.

stages of life—See Appendix A.

Star—See **Divine Star**.

subtle—See **gross, subtle, causal**.

T

"talking" school—A phrase used by Avatar Adi Da to refer to those in any tradition of sacred life whose approach is characterized by talking, thinking, reading, and philosophical analysis and debate, or even meditative enquiry or reflection, without a concomitant and foundation discipline of body, emotion, mind, and breath. He contrasts the "talking"-school with the "practicing"-school approach—"practicing" schools involving those who are committed to the ordeal of real ego-transcending discipline, under the guidance of a true Guru.

Teaching-Work—The intensive period of Avatar Adi Da's Submission to devotees' questions, doubts, and sufferings, in order to Reveal His Divine Wisdom-Teaching for all beings. For a description of Avatar Adi Da's Divine Teaching-Work, please see *Adi Da: The Promised God-Man Is Here*, by Carolyn Lee.

three stations of the heart—See **heart / stations of the heart**.

the "Thumbs"—From time to time throughout His early Life, Avatar Adi Da experienced the forceful Spiritual Descent of the "Bright" into His body-mind. He describes it as feeling like "a mass of gigantic thumbs coming down from above". Therefore, just as He named His Divine State "the 'Bright'" as a child, He also, in childhood, gave a name to the Descent of the "Bright"—'the 'Thumbs'". This manifestation of the "Thumbs" is one of the unique Spiritual signs associated with Avatar Adi Da's Appearance. Once they have become fully technically responsible for the reception of Avatar Adi Da's Spiritual Blessing-Transmission, His devotees (in due course) experience this unique (and uniquely life-transforming) sign of His Spiritual Descent as a Gift Given by Him.

The Sign Of The "Thumbs" Is Revealed and Given Only By Me. The Sign Of The "Thumbs" Is The Fundamental Sign Of The Descent (or Crashing Down) Of My (Avatarically Self-Revealed) Divine and Spiritual Person. In and By Means Of My Avatarically Self-Transmitted Divine Spiritual Sign Of The "Thumbs", I Invade You, Pass Into You, and In-Fill You—bodily, where You stand, where You sit, where You walk, where You live and breathe, where You think, and feel, and function. And, In and By Means Of My Avatarically Self-Transmitted Divine Spiritual Sign Of The "Thumbs", I Awaken You In My "Bright" Divine Sphere (and, Ultimately, My "Midnight Sun" and Divine Self-Domain), Beyond the body-mind—Where Only I Am.

—Avatar Adi Da Samraj
*The Dawn Horse Testament
Of The Ruchira Avatar*

Avatar Adi Da's Gift of the "Thumbs" is what makes it possible to enter the most mature stages of Adidam—the "Perfect Practice". See also **Samadhi**.

Translate / Translation—See **four phases of the seventh stage of life**.

"turiya" / "turiyatita"—Terms used in the Hindu philosophical systems. Traditionally, "turiya" means "the fourth state" (beyond waking, dreaming, and sleeping), and "turiyatita" means "the state beyond the fourth", or beyond all states.

Avatar Adi Da, however, has given these terms different meanings in the context of the Way of Adidam. He uses the term "turiya" to indicate the Awakening to Consciousness Itself (in the context of the sixth stage of life), and "turiyatita" as the State of Most Perfect Divine Enlightenment, or the Realization of all arising as transparent and non-binding modifications of the One Divine Reality (in the context of the seventh stage of life).

U

Unconditional—See **conditional**.

Urdhvareta—The traditional Sanskrit term "urdhvareta" refers to the Yogic practice of reversing the flow of aroused sexual energy such that, rather than being discharged through the genitals, it flows up the spinal line, in a manner that rejuvenates the body-mind and energizes the higher chakras.

In Avatar Adi Da's usage of the term in reference to Himself, He is indicating the condition of Prior Ascendedness that has been the case, in His bodily (human) Form, since He passed through the Great Yogic Event at Lopez Island. In the Lopez Island Event, the spontaneous and permanent Up-turning of energy in Avatar Adi Da's Body included all forms of both natural bodily energy and Spiritual Energy.

V, W, X

waking, dreaming, and sleeping—These three states of consciousness are associated with the dimensions of cosmic existence.

The waking state (and the physical body) is associated with the gross dimension.

The dreaming state (and visionary, mystical, and Yogic Spiritual processes) is associated with the subtle dimension. The subtle dimension, which is senior to the gross dimension, includes the etheric (or energic), lower mental (or verbal-intentional and lower psychic), and higher mental (or deeper psychic, mystical, and discriminative) functions.

The state of deep sleep is associated with the causal dimension, which is senior to both the gross and the subtle dimensions. It is the root of attention, and (therefore) the root of the sense of separate "selfhood", prior to any particular experience. (See also **gross, subtle, causal**.)

Way of the Heart—An alternative name for the Way of Adidam.

Witness / Witness-Consciousness / Witness-Position—When Consciousness is Free of identification with the body-mind, It Stands in Its natural "Position" as the Conscious Witness of all that arises to and in and as the body-mind.

In the Way of Adidam, the stable Realization of the Witness-Position is a Spiritual Gift from Avatar Adi Da, made possible by (and necessarily following upon) the reception of His Spiritual Gift of the "Thumbs". The stable Realization of the Witness-Position is the characteristic of the first stage of the "Perfect Practice".

Avatar Adi Da's extended Instruction relative to the Witness is Given in chapter 49 of *The Dawn Horse Testament*.

Y, Z

Yoga—Literally "yoking", or "union", usually referring to any discipline or process whereby an aspirant seeks to achieve union with God (or the Divine, however conceived). Avatar Adi Da acknowledges this conventional and traditional use of the term, but also, in reference to the Great Yoga of Adidam, employs it in a "radical" sense, free of the usual implication of egoic separation and seeking.

yuga / yugas—See **"late-time" (or "dark" epoch)**.

An Invitation to Support Adidam

The sole Purpose of Avatar Adi Da Samraj is to act as a Source of continuous Divine Grace for everyone, everywhere. In that spirit, He is a Free Renunciate and He owns nothing. Those who have made gestures in support of Avatar Adi Da's Work have found that their generosity is returned in many Blessings that are full of His healing, transforming, and Liberating Grace and those Blessings flow not only directly to them as the beneficiaries of His Work, but to many others, even all others. At the same time, all tangible gifts of support help secure and nurture Avatar Adi Da's Work in necessary and practical ways, again similarly benefiting the entire world. Because all this is so, supporting His Work is the most auspicious form of financial giving, and we happily extend to you an invitation to serve Adidam through your financial support.

You may make a financial contribution in support of the Work of Adi Da Samraj at any time. To do so, make your check payable to "Adidam", and mail it to the Legal Department of Adidam at 12180 Ridge Road, Middletown, California 95461, USA. You may also, if you choose, indicate that your contribution be used for one or more specific purposes.

If you would like more detailed information about gifting options, or if you would like assistance in describing or making a contribution, please write to the Legal Department of Adidam at the above address or contact the Adidam Legal Department by telephone at 1-707-928-4612 or by FAX at 1-707-928-4062.

Planned Giving

We also invite you to consider making a planned gift in support of the Work of Avatar Adi Da Samraj. Many have found that through planned giving they can make a far more significant gesture of support than they would otherwise be able to make. Many have also found that by making a planned gift they are able to realize substantial tax advantages.

There are numerous ways to make a planned gift, including making a gift in your Will, or in your life insurance, or in a charitable trust.

If you are a United States taxpayer, you may find that planned giving in the form of a charitable trust will provide you with immediate tax savings and assured income for life, while at the same time enabling you to provide for your family, for your other heirs, and for the Work of Avatar Adi Da as well.

The Legal Department of Adidam (12180 Ridge Road, Middletown, California 95461, USA; telephone 1-707-928-4612; FAX 1-707-928-4062) will be happy to provide you with further information about these and other planned gifting options, and happy to provide you or your attorney with assistance in describing or making a planned gift in support of the Work of Avatar Adi Da.

Further Notes to the Reader

An Invitation to Responsibility

Adidam, the Way of the Heart that Avatar Adi Da has Revealed, is an invitation to everyone to assume real responsibility for his or her life. As Avatar Adi Da has Said in *The Dawn Horse Testament Of The Ruchira Avatar,* "If any one Is Heart-Moved To Realize Me, Let him or her First Resort (Formally, and By Formal Heart-Vow) To Me, and (Thereby) Commence The Devotional (and, In Due Course, Spiritual) Process Of self-Observation, self-Understanding, and self-Transcendence. . . ." Therefore, participation in the Way of Adidam requires a real confrontation with oneself, and not at all a confrontation with Avatar Adi Da, or with others.

All who study the Way of Adidam or take up its practice should remember that they are responding to a Call to become responsible for themselves. They should understand that they, not Avatar Adi Da or others, are responsible for any decision they may make or action they may take in the course of their lives of study or practice. This has always been true, and it is true whatever the individual's involvement in the Way of Adidam, be it as one who has contacted Avatar Adi Da's Revelation in any informal manner (such as studying Avatar Adi Da's Wisdom-Teaching), or as one who is practicing as a formally acknowledged congregational member of Adidam.

Honoring and Protecting the Sacred Word through Perpetual Copyright

Since ancient times, practitioners of true religion and Spirituality have valued, above all, time spent in the Company of the Sat-Guru (or one who has, to any degree, Realized Real God, Truth, or Reality, and who, thus, serves the awakening process in others). Such practitioners understand that the Sat-Guru literally Spiritually Transmits his or her (Realized) State. Through this Transmission, there are objects, environments, and rightly prepared individuals with which the Sat-Guru has contact that can become empowered, or imbued with the Sat-Guru's Transforming Power. It is by this process of empowerment that things and beings are made truly and literally sacred and holy, and things so sanctified thereafter function as a source of the Sat-Guru's Blessing for all who understand how to make right and sacred use of them.

Sat-Gurus of any degree of Realization and all that they empower are, therefore, truly Sacred Treasures, for they help draw the practitioner more quickly into the process of Realization. Cultures of true Wisdom have always understood that such Sacred Treasures are precious (and fragile) Gifts to humanity, and that they should be honored, protected, and reserved for right sacred use. Indeed, the word "holy" means "set apart", and, thus, that which is holy and sacred must be protected from insensitive secular interference and wrong use of any kind. Avatar

Adi Da has Conformed His human Body-Mind Most Perfectly to the Divine Self, and He is, thus, the most Potent Source of Spiritual Blessing-Transmission of Real God, or Truth Itself, or Reality Itself. He has for many years Empowered (or made sacred) special places and things, and these now serve as His Divine Agents, or as literal expressions and extensions of His Blessing-Transmission. Among these Empowered Sacred Treasures are His Wisdom-Teaching and His Divine Image-Art, which are full of His Transforming Power. These Blessed and Blessing Agents have the literal Power to serve Real-God-Realization in those who are Graced to receive them.

Therefore, Avatar Adi Da's Wisdom-Teaching and Divine Image-Art must be perpetually honored and protected, "set apart" from all possible interference and wrong use. The gathering of devotees of Avatar Adi Da is committed to the perpetual preservation and right honoring of the Sacred Wisdom-Teaching of the Way of Adidam and the Divine Image-Art of Adi Da Samraj. But it is also true that, in order to fully accomplish this, we must find support in the world-society in which we live and in its laws. Thus, we call for a world-society and for laws that acknowledge the sacred, and that permanently protect it from insensitive, secular interference and wrong use of any kind. We call for, among other things, a system of law that acknowledges that the Wisdom-Teaching of the Way of Adidam and the Divine Image-Art of Adi Da Samraj, in all their forms, are, because of their sacred nature, protected by perpetual copyright.

We invite others who respect the sacred to join with us in this call and in working toward its realization. And, even in the meantime, we claim that all copyrights to the Wisdom-Teaching and Divine Image-Art of Avatar Adi Da and the other Sacred Literature, recordings, and images of the Way of Adidam are of perpetual duration.

We make this claim on behalf of The Avataric Samrajya of Adidam Pty Ltd, which, acting as trustee of The Avataric Samrajya of Adidam, is the holder of all such copyrights.

Avatar Adi Da and the Sacred Treasures of Adidam

True Spiritual Masters have Realized Real God (to one degree or another), and, therefore, they bring great Blessing and introduce Divine Possibility to the world. Such Adept-Realizers Accomplish universal Blessing-Work that benefits everything and everyone. They also Work very specifically and intentionally with individuals who approach them as their devotees, and with those places where they reside and to which they direct their specific Regard for the sake of perpetual Spiritual Empowerment. This was understood in traditional Spiritual cultures, and, therefore, those cultures found ways to honor Adept-Realizers by providing circumstances for them where they were free to do their Spiritual Work without obstruction or interference.

Those who value Avatar Adi Da's Realization and Service have always endeavored to appropriately honor Him in this traditional way by providing a circumstance where He is completely Free to do His Divine Work. The Ruchira Sannyasin Hermitage Ashrams of Adidam have been set aside by Avatar Adi Da's devotees worldwide as Places for Him to do His universal Blessing-Work for the sake of everyone, as well as His specific Work with those who pilgrimage to His Hermitage circumstance (wherever He may be residing at a given time) to receive the special Blessing of coming into His physical Company.

Avatar Adi Da is a legal renunciate. He owns nothing and He has no secular or religious institutional function. He Functions only in Freedom. He, and the other members of the Ruchira Sannyasin Order (the senior renunciate order of Adidam), are provided for by The Avataric Samrajya of Adidam, which also provides for His Hermitage circumstance, and serves and manages the process of access to Avatar Adi Da Samraj on the part of all who are invited to enter His Hermitage Domain (either to offer service to Him or to participate in meditative retreats in His Spiritual Company).

The sacred institutions that have developed in response to Avatar Adi Da's Wisdom-Teaching and universal Blessing are active worldwide in making Avatar Adi Da's Wisdom-Teaching available to all, in offering guidance to all who are moved to respond to His Offering, and in protecting, preserving, and glorifying the Sacred Treasures of Adidam. In addition to the central corporate entities, which are based in California, there are numerous regional entities which serve congregations of Avatar Adi Da's devotees in various places throughout the world.

Practitioners of Adidam worldwide have also established numerous community organizations, through which they provide for many of their common and cooperative community needs, including those relating to housing, food, businesses, medical care, schools, and death and dying. By attending to these and all other ordinary human concerns and affairs via ego-transcending cooperation and mutual effort, Avatar Adi Da's devotees constantly work to free their energy and attention, both personally and collectively, for practice of the Way of Adidam and for service to Avatar Adi Da Samraj, to the other Sacred Treasures of Adidam, and to the sacred institutions of Adidam.

All of the organizations that have evolved in response to Avatar Adi Da Samraj and His Offering are legally separate from one another, and each has its own purpose and function. These organizations represent the collective intention of practitioners of Adidam worldwide to protect, preserve, and glorify the Sacred Treasures of Adidam, and also to make Avatar Adi Da's Offering of the Way of Adidam universally available to all.

INDEX

Index

Work of. *See* Work of Adi Da Samraj
writing
  at Columbia, **62–63, 65, 68**
  burns His manuscript, (1965), **158–60**
  creative writing at Stanford, **75–77, 164–65**
  diary of Christian pilgrimage, **277–308**
  during discipleship with Rudi, **153–54, 158–60**
  His practice of, **131**
  import of His early writing, **158–60**
  and intensive observation on the beach, **89–96, 382**
  1969 journal entries, **239–44**
  master's thesis (Gertrude Stein), **164–65**
  Water and Narcissus, The Mummery Book (1969), **238**
  year of waiting for Grace (1968–1969), **211, 217**
  Yogic Events of, overview, **600–603, 673–75, 688–89**
Adidam
  Adi Da Samraj's "Sadhana" established pattern for, **598–600**
  always rests in primary Truth, **381**
  Ashrams of, **730–31**
  beginner's process in, **439, 690**
  contrasted with Kashmir Saivism, Advaita Vedanta,
    and Buddhism—Embraces and Transcends
    Emanationism and Transcendentalism, **501**
  disciplines in, **427**
  esoteric Spirituality culminates in the unique course of,
    534–35
  experience transcended in, **736**
  Guru-devotee relationship with Adi Da Samraj as basis of,
    427–28
  invitation to become a formal devotee, **711–15**
  neither vertical nor horizontal Way, **741**
  not about replicating Adi Da Samraj's "Sadhana", **600**
  not derived from historical traditions, **635**
  not a search for Truth, **632**
  not a synthesis of ways of seeking, **380–81**
  "positive disillusionment" and, **574**
  practices in, summarized, **427–28**
  as a Process in Silence, **413–15**
  purification in, **695–96**
  as "Radical" Non-Dualism—one and only Way that
    directly and Most Perfectly Realizes Real God, **493**
  as recognition-response to Adi Da Samraj, **9–10, 14, 16,
    425, 695–96, 704, 705**
  relatedness in, **427**
  as relationship to Adi Da Samraj, **414–15, 427–28**
    See also Guru-devotee relationship
  renunciation in, **690–91**
  as rooted in the Divine "Bright" Sphere, **703**
  Satsang with Adi Da Samraj as basis of, **4–5**
  as Siddha-Method, **564, 582–83**
  as Siddha-Yoga school, **561–64**
    Blessed by Swami Muktananda, **563**
    names for, **562–63**
    uniqueness of, **561–64**
  Spiritual Initiation by Adi Da Samraj in, **690–91, 738, 739**
  summary descriptions of, **392–93, 574**
  as transcendence, **501, 566–74, 694, 696, 736**
    of "point of view", **696**
    of three egos, **566–74**
  uniqueness of, **329, 534–35, 561–64, 632, 635**
  was brought out of Adi Da Samraj, not old traditions, **635**
  websites, **713, 714, 727–28**
  Youth Fellowship, **729**
  See also Satsang with Adi Da Samraj; Way of "Radical"
    Understanding
Adidam centers, **713**
Adidam Emporium, **728**

Adidam Samrajashram, **731**
Adidam Youth Fellowship, **729**
adolescence, Adi Da Samraj enters, **47**
adolescent strategy
  defined, **437–38**
  and esoteric practice, **437–38**
Advaita Vedanta
  adoption of Emanationist practices, **500–501**
  concentration on philosophical argumentation rather
    than elaborations re practice and Confessions of
    Realization, **449–50**
  and denial of objects, **306**
  described, **751**
  as expression of Truth, **360**
  founded in Transcendental Reality, **501**
  gnosis in, **449–50**
  limited by a mental problem, **296**
  and Realization of Consciousness, xxvi
  similarities and contrasts in language with that used in
    Kashmir Saivism, **500–501**
  "talking" school of, **449–50**
  as tradition closest to Adi Da Samraj's experience, **263**
  See also non-Emanationism
Advocacy of Adi Da Samraj's Work, **729**
African man, turns to Adi Da Samraj (1969–1970), **244–46**
after-death state, **33**
Alpha Vehicle of Adi Da Samraj, **476–77**
Amen, as Christian prayer, **283, 284–86**
Amma (Pratibha Trivedi), **187, 222, 223, 264**
  described, **512–13, 745–46**
  letter inviting Adi Da Samraj to visit Swami Muktananda
    for the first time, **187**
  points out *Ashtavakra Gita* to Adi Da Samraj, **513–15**
  relationship to Adi Da Samraj, **513**
  Siddha-Yoga Process exemplified by, **515**
Amrita Nadi
  Adi Da Samraj as the, **419–21**
  described, **355–56, 362, 364–65, 740**
  and the Great Events of Adi Da Samraj's Sadhana, **369–70**
  as primary inclusive Form, **362**
  Ramana Maharshi's Teachings on, **353–56**
  "regenerated" form of, **367–68**
    described, **551–52**
    and "non-regenerated" form, **355–57**
    Swami Muktananda's response to description of,
      551–52
  Shape observed by Adi Da Samraj, **367–68**
anatomy, esoteric, summarized, **388–94, 737–41**
anti-"guruism", as a principal impediment to esoteric process,
  438
apple, Swami Muktananda's miraculous gift to Adi Da Samraj,
  232
approaching Adi Da Samraj, requirements for, **5–6, 9–20**
Art Work of Adi Da Samraj, **670–71**
  Adi Da Samraj's Early-Life involvement in Art, **41**
  as parallel to His verbal Communication, xi
ascent, traditions of
  ascending meditation critique, **394–401**
  ascending Yoga and "radical" self-understanding,
    394–401, 402–403
  ascent as goal of Spiritual traditions, **249–50, 344–45, 738**
  and faith, **294–95**
  limitations to Realization in ascending Yoga, **738**
  See also Emanationism
asceticism
  defined, **433**
  as path of extraordinary self-effort, **433**

801

Index

Index

fear, experience of overwhelming, during death of
"Narcissus", **175–77**
fear, sorrow, and anger, ended through Adi Da Samraj's
Divine Self-"Emergence" Work, **631**
feeling-Contemplation of Adi Da Samraj, **414**
fire, gross domain is on, **683**
Fire Island experience (powerful experience of Rudi's
Force), **170**
First, Last, and Only seventh stage Adept-Realizer, Adi Da
Samraj as, **457**, **476**
Five Books Of The Heart Of The Adidam Revelation, The
(Adi Da Samraj), 718–19
flowers, death's effect on, **23**
food, Adi Da Samraj's experiments with and conclusions
about (1970), **254–59**
"Force", the (Rudi's Spiritual Transmission)
Adi Da Samraj's experiences of, **129**, **131**, **135**, **148**, **153**
summarized, **166–71**
Adi Da Samraj's previous experiences of the same
Energy, **166**
defined, **131**, **134**
descending quality of, **168–69**
origins in the work of Pak Subuh, **142**
received by Rudi from Bhagavan Nityananda and
Swami Muktananda, **143**
Rudi's insistence on being sole source of, **143**
work and discipline as necessary to receiving, **131**,
134–35, **147**, **168**
"Forerunners" of Adi Da Samraj, xxix–xxx
See also Adi Da Samraj: Deeper Personality
Freedom
Adi Da Samraj's, **5**
is not attained, **66–67**
Freeman, Harold, **103–104**
Freud, Sigmund, **76**, **436**
frontal line, 737
funeral, Adi Da Samraj's speech at grandfather's, **50–51**

G

Ganesh, described, 749
Gautama ("the Buddha")
described, 743
and the Truth, **298**
"Getting to cry is shaped like a seahorse", **83**, **369**
"Gift of blows", Swami Muktananda's response to Adi Da
Samraj's summary of His Realization, **524–25**, **529–30**
gnosis, in Advaita Vedanta, **449–50**
God
Adi Da Samraj's attempt to discover during Columbia
years, **62–68**
Adi Da Samraj's Divine Self-Realization as, **320**
Adi Da Samraj's pact with, after Bootsie's death, **35–36**
Bhagavan Nityananda's description of, **508–509**
Christianity involves separate "God" and "creation",
305–306
"Creator-God" idea, **29**, **236**
"God" and "Gods" as tribal myths of human ego-mind,
544
Swami Muktananda's Teachings on, **205–206**
See also Conscious Light; Consciousness; Real God;
Reality; Truth
God-Man, Avataric Incarnation as True, xxx–xxxi
Goddess, Divine
Adi Da Samraj gives flowers to Mother-Shakti at
Ganeshpuri, **273**
and Adi Da Samraj's Awakening in the garden in
Ganeshpuri, **522**

Adi Da Samraj's discipleship with, **522–24**
Adi Da Samraj's Embrace of, **317–18**, **526**, **529**
Adi Da Samraj's "Husbanding" of, **317–18**
Always Already Serves Adi Da Samraj Most Perfectly, **580**
and the "Bright", **119**
defined, **119**
mentioned in Swami Muktananda's naming letter to
Adi Da Samraj, **225**
shows Herself constantly Present, **315–17**
significance in Adi Da Samraj's Lineage, **577–78**
Spiritual experiences given by, **226**
Virgin Mary apparition as a form of, **270–71**
See also Shakti
gospel, of Christianity, **279**
Gospel of Sri Ramakrishna, The, xv
grandfather, Adi Da Samraj's speech at funeral of His, **50–51**
granthi (knot in the heart), **352–54**
Great Secret of Adi Da Samraj, **14**
Great Tradition
Adi Da Samraj Speaks about as a Way of explaining
Himself, **635**
Adi Da Samraj Stands Prior to, **581**
Adi Da Samraj's Clarification of, **579**
based on seeking, **345**, **361**, **367**
comprises only first six stages of life, **491**
defined, **358**
devotion to Adept-Realizer as foundation of, **15–17**
discussed in *The Basket Of Tolerance*, 726–27
why Adi Da Samraj Examined, **637**
See also religious and Spiritual traditions
gross body/gross domain
gross domain is on fire, **683–85**
and three egos, **567**, **568–70**
gross, subtle, and causal bodies
right approach to, **393**
and three egos, **567**
transcending in Adidam, **568–72**
and Truth Itself, **388–94**
Gulf War, and Adi Da Samraj's Blessing-Work in Seclusion,
646–47
Gurdjieff, G. I., **141**, 743
Gurdjieff work, and its influence on Rudi, **141–42**
Guru
defined, **109**, **431–32**
Gifts of, described by Bhagavan Nityananda, **508**
"installation" of, **386–87**
necessity of, **336**, **337**
as principal Source, Resource, and Means of Spiritual
Way, **431**
and "radical" self-understanding, **383–85**
taboos against, **435–36**
"taking on", **481**
The Knee Of Listening as esoteric history of Siddha-Guru,
xiv
See also Guru-devotee relationship
Guru-Bhakti
as fundamental to Adi Da Samraj's practice and Adidam,
387
as superior to all other methods, **384**
Guru-devotee relationship
ability of Westerners to take up, **237**
Adi Da Samraj as Exemplar of Guru-devotion, **578**
Adidam as based on, **427–28**
in Bhagavan Nityananda's Teaching, **508**
Guru-devotee tradition described, **118–19**
meditation on the Guru as recommended and practiced
by Swami Muktananda, **386–87**

807

Index

Index

mind
appears as source of dilemma after Adi Da Samraj's first visit to India, **203, 204**
dealing with the "problem" of, **379**
Moksha, as getting rid of non-existent misery (Ramana Maharshi quote), **355**
mood, common mood of humankind, **435**
moon
astral world perceived to be in, **93**
childhood event of pointing to, **29–30**
Morley, Patricia, **267**
becomes student of Adi Da Samraj, **235**
mortal philosophy
at Columbia College, **58–61**
at Lutheran seminary, **174**
Mother-Shakti. *See* Goddess, Divine
Mountain Of Attention Sanctuary, The, **731**
movies, childhood event of walking to, **29–30**
mudra, defined, **xiii**
Mueller, Max, *Sacred Books of the East,* **xv**
Muktananda, Swami, **xiv, 135–36, 280**
Adi Da Samraj and
acknowledgement of Adi Da Samraj as True Siddha-Guru, **518–20**
Adi Da Samraj becomes interested in Teaching of, **185–86**
Adi Da Samraj has no "personal" relationship with, **215**
Adi Da Samraj's description of Yogic Process contrasted with Swami Muktananda's (in Lopez Island Event), **682–85**
Adi Da Samraj's discipleship with Swami Muktananda summarized, **502–503**
Adi Da Samraj's eternal relationship with and gratitude towards, **555, 563–64**
Adi Da Samraj's experience of, after His Divine Re-Awakening, **334–38**
Adi Da Samraj's first meeting with, **188–89**
Adi Da Samraj's writing of "Lineage Essay" and, 654–55
comparison of Their respective Teachings and Realizations, **524–41**
contrasting views on nature of self and world, **559–60**
Emanationism v. non-Emanationism, **526–27**
fifth stage observation v. Establishment as Conscious Light Itself, **527–29**
limitations of Swami Muktananda's Teaching, **555**
re "Embrace" of Divine Goddess, **526, 529**
re necessity of mystical phenomena, **525–26, 555–56**
views relative to necessity of mystical phenomena in Ultimate Realization, **550–51**
gives Adi Da Samraj name "Dhyanananda", **221–26, 520**
gives Adi Da Samraj the right to Teach, **223–26, 244, 518–20**
ignores Adi Da Samraj's description of "Regenerated" Form of Amrita Nadi, **551–52**
interaction with Adi Da Samraj in October (1970), **333–38**
letters to Adi Da Samraj, **187, 204–211, 213, 246–47**
acknowledging Adi Da Samraj as Siddha-Guru and granting name "Dhyanananda", **221–26, 520**
as link to Adi Da Samraj, **457**
"Love-Ananda" name given to Adi Da Samraj by, **222**
meetings with Adi Da Samraj to discuss their philosophical differences, **524–25, 551, 554–55**

most basic instruction to Adi Da Samraj, **189**
prediction that Adi Da Samraj will become a Spiritual teacher, **204**
significance in Adi Da Samraj's Lineage, **577**
Spiritual Transmission of
Adi Da Samraj's first experiences of, **190–93**
See also Spiritual experiences of Adi Da Samraj
Uniqueness of Adi Da Samraj's Work, and inevitability of independence from, **563–64**
as advanced Siddha-Guru in Kundalini-Shaktipat tradition, **497**
basic practical advice of, **192**
"bodies of the soul" description, **537**
and controversy of celibacy v. sexual activity for Sacred Authorities, **518**
Conversations with Swami Muktananda, **443–45**
described, 744
effects of his Spiritual Transmission, **228–32**
as fifth stage Yogi, **509**
as Good and Great, **586**
higher and lower worlds described by, **535–37**
his life and Teachings exemplify conflict between fifth stage Hindu esotericism and fourth stage Hindu exotericism, **535**
his Realization contrasted with that of Bhagavan Nityananda, **507**
his Teaching partially a product of his own personal study and temperament, **527**
internal experiences reported by, **530–41**
interpreted his Spiritual experiences in Hindu terms, **535–37, 539, 541**
limitations of his Teaching, **336–38, 344–45, 555**
literature of, **556**
lost staying power, **592**
meditation instructions of, **204–210, 226, 252–54, 386–87**
critiqued, **394–401**
nature of his Realization (fifth stage, Saguna), **501–502**
non-verbal teaching of, **220–22**
Play of Consciousness, **xv**
prejudice against fifth stage Ascended Nirvikalpa Samadhi, **532–33**
and the problem of superconsciousness, **379**
and Ramana Maharshi, **344–45**
Rudi's reception of Spiritual Transmission from, **143**
seeking as basis of his Teaching, **336–38**
Siddha-Yoga Process exemplified by, **515**
Siddha-Yoga school of, **527, 557–58, 561**
sympathy with Emanationist tradition of Kashmir Saivism; opposition to Transcendentalism, **497**
Teaching on Guru's Grace, **185–86**
Teaching that inner phenomena were necessarily associated with the Process and Goal of Spiritual life, **525–26**
Teachings and Realizations related to the fifth and sixth stages of life, **443–46**
"Witnessing" in the Teaching of, as fifth stage term, **527–29**
Mulund (Indian town), **197**
Mummery Book, The (Adi Da Samraj), **xxiii–xxv, 238**
mystics
Christian view of, **296**
See also absorptive mysticism; Emanationism; seven stages of life: fifth stage; Spiritual experiences
"myth"
Adi Da Samraj's quest for the motivating, **77, 79–80, 89–96**
discovering "Narcissus", **94–96**
myths, purpose of, **533**

Index

Index

Adi Da Samraj's Awakening to, on first trip to India, **195–96, 200–202**
Consciousness Itself is not, **341, 357–58**
as foundation Realization for seventh stage Realization, **540**
Swami Muktananda's Teaching related to, **443–45, 527–29**
Wittgenstein, Ludwig, **76**
"Womb of the Virgin Mary", **543**
Woodroffe, Sir John
described, 747
The Serpent Power, **119**
Woolf, Virginia, **75**
Word of Adi Da Samraj. *See* Wisdom-Teaching of Adi Da Samraj
work
Adi Da Samraj departs from the philosophy of, **184–85**
evidence of utility of attitude of, **173**
Rudi's concept of, **131, 133–34**
Work of Adi Da Samraj
Blessing-Work of, **5**
chart of Events and Periods of Submission, 603
described, **417**
Helping beings to Realize Light, xi
informal Teaching-Work of (1969–1970), **236–37**
is Perpetual and always the same, **629**
Purpose of. *See* Purpose of Adi Da Samraj's Work
Reconfirmation of, at the "Brightness", **659**
Satsang as, **4**
Teaching, Blessing, and Awakening Work begins, **333**
Vedanta Temple Event as beginning of His Divinely Liberating Work, **620**
world, idea of separate, **29**
world situation, devastating negativity of, **260–61**
World-Teacher, Adi Da Samraj as, xxiii, **583**
world-Work of Adi Da Samraj
and Lopez Island Event, 663, 665
time at the "Brightness", 645–54, 661
worlds
internal visions of higher and lower, **530–32**
Swami Muktananda's, **535–37**
writers, modernist, what they were doing, **164–65**
writing (Adi Da Samraj's practice of), **131**
at Columbia, **62–63, 65, 68**
burns His manuscript, (1965), **158–60**
creative writing at Stanford, **75–77, 164–65**
diary of Christian pilgrimage, **277–308**
during discipleship with Rudi, **153–54**
import of His early writing, **158–60**
and intensive observation on the beach, **89–96**
1969 journal entries, **239–44**
as a literature of Real Consciousness, **238**
master's thesis (on Gertrude Stein), **164–65**
Water and Narcissus, The Mummery Book (1969), **238**

Y

"Yes!", **1**
"yinning" syndrome at the "Brightness", **657–58**
Yoga of the "Bright", as Adi Da Samraj's Divine Self-Revelation, **703**
Yogananda, Paramahansa, xv, **120, 337, 394–95, 399–400**, 747–48, 752
Yogi, Swami Muktananda gives Adi Da Samraj title of, **226**
Yogic Events in Adi Da Samraj's Life, xxxiv–xxxv, **311, 362–63**, 600–603, **617**, 669–70, **673–75, 688–89**
Yogis, defined, **509**
Yogis, Saints, and Sages, contrasted, **509–510**
"You become what you meditate on", **431**

Z

Zen Buddhism, motives of, **120**
Zimmer, Heinrich, *Philosophies of India,* xvi

We invite you to find out more about Avatar Adi Da Samraj and the Way of Adidam

■ Find out about our courses, seminars, events, and retreats by calling the regional center nearest you.

AMERICAS
12040 N. Seigler Rd.
Middletown, CA
95461 USA
1-707-928-4936

PACIFIC-ASIA
12 Seibel Road
Henderson
Auckland 1008
New Zealand
64-9-838-9114

AUSTRALIA
P.O. Box 244
Kew 3101
Victoria
**1800 ADIDAM
(1800-234-326)**

EUROPE-AFRICA
Annendaalderweg 10
6105 AT Maria Hoop
The Netherlands
31 (0)20 468 1442

**THE UNITED
KINGDOM**
P.O. Box 20013
London, England
NW2 1ZA
0208-962-8855

EMAIL: **correspondence@adidam.org**

■ Order books, tapes, and videos
by and about Avatar Adi Da Samraj.

1-877-770-0772 (from within North America)
1-707-928-6653 (from outside North America)
order online: **www.dawnhorsepress.com**

■ Visit us online at:
www.adidam.org
Explore the online community of Adidam and discover more about Avatar Adi Da and the Way of Adidam.